NATURAL HISTORY *of the* PACIFIC NORTHWEST MOUNTAINS

PLANTS · ANIMALS · FUNGI · GEOLOGY · CLIMATE

Daniel Mathews

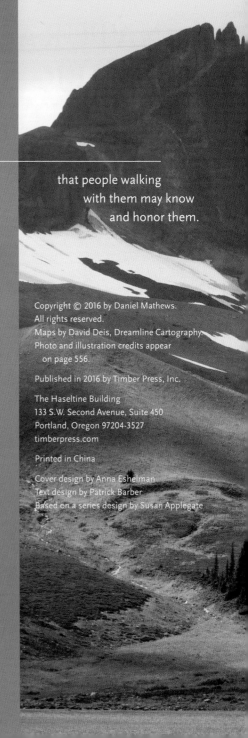

This book is for
the fourlegged people
the standing people
the crawling people
the swimming people
the sitting people
and the flying people

---

that people walking
with them may know
and honor them.

Library of Congress Cataloging-in-Publication Data

Names: Mathews, Daniel, 1948– , author. | Mathews, Daniel, 1948– Cascade–Olympic natural history.
Title: Natural history of the Pacific Northwest mountains: plants, animals, fungi, geology, climate / Daniel Mathews.
Description: Portland, Oregon: Timber Press, Inc., 2017. | Series: Timber Press field guide | "Expanded and updated third edition of Cascade–Olympic natural history"—Preface. | Includes bibliographical references and index.
Identifiers: LCCN 2016017918 (print) | LCCN 2016039649 (ebook) | ISBN 9781604696356 (flexibind) | ISBN 9781604697841 (e-book)
Subjects: LCSH: Mountains—Northwest, Pacific. | Animals—Northwest, Pacific—Identification. | Plants—Northwest, Pacific—Identification. | Fungi—Northwest, Pacific—Identification. | Geology—Northwest, Pacific.
Classification: LCC QH104.5.N6 M38 2017 (print) | LCC QH104.5.N6 (ebook) | DDC 508.795—dc23
LC record available at https://lccn.loc.gov/2016017918

A catalog record for this book is also available from the British Library.

Maps by David Deis, Dreamline Cartography.
Photo and illustration credits appear on page 556.

Published in 2016 by Timber Press, Inc.

The Haseltine Building
133 S.W. Second Avenue, Suite 450
Portland, Oregon 97204-3527
timberpress.com

Printed in China

Cover design by Anna Eshelman
Text design by Patrick Barber
Based on a series design by Susan Applegate

CONTENTS

PREFACE

This book is a field guide to everything Northwest and montane: it wraps together all of the usual field guide categories under the sun. The key is in the wrapping together, as nature's parts are infinitely intertwined. So I'm going with "Natural History" in the title to highlight that grand symbiosis, as well as to give a nod to my forebears, the science writers of earlier centuries.

This is essentially an expanded and updated third edition of *Cascade-Olympic Natural History*. I enlarged the geographic range to include the mountains of southwestern British Columbia and coastal Oregon—mountain ranges with different geologic stories, but absolutely part of the same region as defined by what lives there.

I expanded the coverage with 132 species that I could no longer bear to leave out. (How did I ever think I could skip dragonflies?) More than 100 scientific names have been updated.

I haven't stopped traipsing around in the mountains, noticing new details, and coming up with new questions I have to find answers to. So revisions are salted throughout the book. And I read scientific literature as it comes out, and go to scientific conferences, gleaning countless fresh bits of information to add or adjust.

In the years since the second edition, hikers have seen wolves and wolverines in the Cascades. You could be the first to spot a fisher, following their reintroduction here, or a grizzly bear. The exceedingly rare Cascades red fox, on the other hand, is seen up close by all too many National Park visitors, since a few foxes have become habituated to food handouts.

That makes five charismatic carnivores with upticks in visibility. Yet threats outweigh the good news for biodiversity overall. Bees, bats, and amphibians, for example, are huge, numerous, ecologically invaluable groups of animals that are seeing dramatic declines.

Salmon populations have put up exciting numbers in some years: Fraser River sockeye in 2010 and Columbia River chinook in 2015 each had their best year in almost a century. These ups and downs remain mysterious. The 2014 Fraser run, after predictions that it would rival 2010, did not. Then "the blob," a huge pool of abnormally warm water in the northeast Pacific that lasted for most of 2015, took a severe toll on that year's Fraser run. Indirectly, the blob helped make 2015 Washington's worst wildfire year since the days when fires ran unimpeded by humans.

Fire is an element in the one subtle but pervasive increased emphasis in this edition: how plants, animals, fungi, rivers, fires, and glaciers are responding to climate change, and what changes scientists predict during our lifetimes. The changes seen here, both in recent decades and in the few decades to come, are milder than those in many parts of the world. But the predictions are sobering. I hope that by spreading awareness of warming's ramifications I can help spur action to progress beyond the massive release of greenhouse gases.

ACKNOWLEDGMENTS

My profound gratitude goes out to Gary Braasch, photographer and reporter; friend and inspiration; steadfast optimist; uncanny eye for the image; and advocate for diverse populations of the natural world, who never let his activism spill over into antagonism to the human populations. He died in 2016 while snorkeling on the Great Barrier Reef in the course of documenting climate change. We are bereft.

And it goes also to the scientists who generously gave of their time to help me understand the Pacific Northwest. Blair Csuti, Kathie Dello, Eric Eaton, Jim Jackson, Aaron Liston, Bruce Newhouse, and Steve Trudell each reviewed a chapter and suggested improvements. Others talked or wrote to me about particular issues: Steve Acker, Keith Aubry, Scott Babcock, Ken Chambers, Gary Chastagner, Janet Coles, Steve Engel, Dan Gavin, Jerry Franklin, Keala Hagmann, Patti Happe, Mark Harmon, Mark Huff, Tim Hiller, Andrew Larson, Chris Marshall, Cliff Mass, Garrett Meigs, David Metzler, Steve Meyers, Lars Norgren, Dave Peterson, Dave Wagner, and Rick Westcott. I also owe much to countless scientists who don't know me from Adam—simply for doing and publishing their work. (But if I somehow still managed to get something or other wrong, that's on me.)

To the photographers and artists who generously gave of their gorgeous images. Their names are credited on page 556, but right here I want to proclaim the names Nick Dean, Ginny Skilton, Richard Droker, Walt Siegmund, and the late Doug Waylett and Jeanne Janish for their copious contributions. David Deis of Dreamline Cartography created the gorgeous maps, and was patient with me when I said, more than once, "No, actually, can you change it to this. . . ."

To the team at Timber Press who whipped my sprawling manuscript and spreadsheets into the elegant artifact you hold in your hands: Mike Dempsey, Patrick Barber, Sarah Milhollin, Anna Eshelman, Susan Applegate, and Andrew Beckman.

To Sabrina, without whose companionship and steadfast support my writing work could not proceed. And to Gabriel and Margot, who hold me up emotionally with their encouragement and, for that matter, with their very existence.

ORGANIZATION

Each species account begins with common and scientific names. The word "Also," when present, lists other names you may see for the same species. An identifying description follows, concluding with notes on likely location, habitat, and sometimes season.

Where descriptions start with just a genus name, like *Anemone* spp. ("spp." means species plural) two or more species are then named and described in two or more paragraphs below. The first paragraph (beginning with "*Anemone* spp.") lists descriptive characters that all of the following species of *Anemone* share, and then their separate paragraphs list characters that help you tell them apart. Sometimes the differences are subtle or variable, unfortunately.

To help you find the chapters quickly, their top edges are color-coded. Within these color bars, you'll find narrower categories written out. In the second half of the book, these categories are taxonomic groups like Carnivores, Songbirds, or Dragonflies, many of them familiar enough that you likely know which one you're looking for.

In the first half of the book—the plants and the fungi—the marginal "tabs" collectively form a nested key using conspicuous characteristics: evergreen leaves vs. deciduous, alternate leaves vs. opposite, regular flowers vs. irregular (bilaterally symmetrical), flower petals in threes vs. fours vs. fives, and so on. If any of these characters are new concepts to you, they should be easy to learn. Grouping plants by these characters keeps similar plants together, making it easy for you to compare similar things. Since that's roughly the same idea that got taxonomy started, you'll often find members of a taxonomic family clustered together.

Up-to-date taxonomy contributes to the sequence in this book, but does not rule: I made a few shifts from the current official sequence of orders (which is based on the sequence in which scientists think they evolved) in order to put similar-seeming orders next to each other—like hawks next to falcons.

Starting with the conifers chapter, here are all the nested key characters in sequence, with page numbers.

NAMING

For over a century we writers of field guides preached that you readers should learn Latin names because, in contrast to common names, they are used consistently from one region, or nation, or book, or decade, to another.

We lied!

Sorry. Or maybe it was true up until a few decades ago.

For example, the common names red elderberry and blue elderberry have been solidly established for a century or two, but you find three different scientific names for the blue and five for the red, and that's just in recent, respected floras.

Scientific names are in turmoil. One reason is decentralization. Taxonomic judgments used to be made by a few senior taxonomists at a few major institutions examining animal skeletons or pressed, dried herbarium specimens. Today's taxonomists have more time and more specimens, and often have seen the live organism in its native habitat, where differences may be more visible. And they have DNA sequencing.

There's also a divergence between two main functions of scientific names. Carl Linnaeus's intent was to standardize the naming of organisms so that scientists could communicate about them without confusion. He also sorted organisms into ranked, nested categories based on their degree of similarity.

Linnaeus's system had served Western science for a century by the time Darwin published *On the Origin of Species.* At that point, taxonomists began to say that Linnaeus's ranked, branching categories might also represent a family tree of evolutionary descent. That became the second function of scientific names. It was a marriage of convenience, and like others it often proves inconvenient. Molecular biology offers a level of accuracy in drawing the family tree that Darwin never dreamed of, and taxonomists have leapt at the opportunity. They virtually all agree that scientific names should reflect evolutionary descent, but also that the Linnaean-ranked branches are a terrible fit for the real tree of life. Many have dropped the notion of rank having any absolute meaning; that is, calling something a genus does not mean it is in any way equivalent to other genera in breadth or value, it just means that it groups some species below it, and is grouped within the family above it. (So don't worry: demoting Animalia from being one of the two kingdoms to being one of several kingdoms within one of three domains does not mean that animals are now less important than Archaea, which are a domain.) But few taxonomists are ready for a divorce from ranked branches.

From the other side of the marriage—field biologists and field guide writers and users—the problem is that the initial purpose of Linnaean names is ill-served: names are well on their way to being too unstable to facilitate communication. Thanks to internet speed, authorities today tend to adopt name changes soon after they are published. In several cases (*Stipa, Tamias*), authorities drop a long-established name and then readopt it ten or fifteen years later, after a new study comes out.

Recent taxonomic revisions split a species (or a genus) far more commonly than they lump two of them together. In the age-old war between "splitters" and "lumpers," splitters are ascendant. A definition of species that many favor is "the smallest population or group of populations within which there is a parental pattern of ancestry and descent and which is diagnosable by unique combinations of character states." If the species is the *smallest* useful taxon, there's little use for subspecies or varieties. Many newly described species are cryptic, meaning that they are identifiable only by genetic analysis—not by anything visible, not even under a microscope, nor by simple chemical tests.

(Some revisions are based solely on molecular analysis of genes, but many others evaluate a wide range of clues to evolution. Looking at plants, for example, they may consider insects that coevolved with plants as pollinators, fungal partners as well, and unusual chemical compounds the plant produces. They take a broader view than Linnaeus did when he classified plants by their flower structure. But analyses based solely on genes may take over in the future, which would make sense and simplify the process, if genes are the last word on evolutionary descent anyway.)

Taxonomists are aware of their customers' discomfort. Some try to reassure us: "This is a necessary but temporary phenomenon that is needed to correct our unnatural classifications." When exactly will this phenomenon be done? From others I hear that the pace of revision will only accelerate as technology improves. Some see our pleas for stability as a threat to the advancement of knowledge—"folk taxonomy weakening 21st-century science. . . . 'Stable taxonomy' obscures attempts to reconstruct Earth history" and "weakens the ability to map biodiversity."

(Not all scientists studying evolutionary descent are so embattled over naming: some see naming as a distraction, and prefer to publish relationship trees without concerning themselves with scientific names.)

Conservation politics are a hidden hand tipping the scales in favor of splitting. When you name more species, you're seeing more biodiversity, they say. That sounds like semantic quibbling. More concretely, if you name newly diagnosed taxa at the level of species rather than subspecies, then there are more endangered species, and stronger legal grounds for protecting them. Some splitters accuse their critics of shilling for anti-conservationist powers. Those critics, on the other hand, worry that rapid proliferation of endangered species (by splitting) will overwhelm species-protection programs (and budgets) and undermine public trust.

As a field guide writer, I think that my readers are interested in the natural history of things we can see out there. It will be hard to care about (cryptic) species whose own authors can't identify them in the field.

But let's step back and remember that in the real world, Nature has never heard of "species." The web of life does not break down into discreet species. That's bound to be the case; just think about it. If species A and B are related, that means they have a common ancestor. Was the common ancestor species A, or B, or some other species X? At what moment did it transform from X to A and B? Necessarily, there was a time when species X had two or more populations that were on the cusp of becoming A and B. Some such transitions were relatively brief, but some undoubtedly stretched out over thousands of years.

Our present day is just a moment—actually an exceptionally fast-changing moment—in the history of evolution. A portion of today's organisms are in the throes of speciating, to some degree. While some pairs of related species are just what we want species to be—discreet and non-interbreeding—many others appear to be discreet in some locales, but where they meet up they act like they're one species: they interbreed more or less freely, and their characteristics intergrade. Some large and diverse genera, like lupines, hold dozens of species, almost any two of which would probably hybridize where they get the chance. Yet other species pairs are the reverse: they appear to be identical, but do not interbreed. Those are cryptic species.

"Family trees" of relationship are also something of an imaginary construct. Fairly often, evolution is reticulate—a net rather than a tree, because lines of descent can converge as well as diverge. Or the two species in a genus may be "parent and child," a relationship misrepresented by tree branches.

If plant and vertebrate animal species are a fairly amorphous concept, fungal and one-celled species are even more so. Their breeding is more often asexual, and even when it is sexual it often works differently from how that works in plants and animals. The question of what is an individual gets difficult as well.

Be that as it may, the scientific project of delineating the course of evolution is progressing at a thrilling pace, thanks to technological advances. For better or worse, the inconvenient marriage between that project and Linnaeus's project of standardizing the names people use for living things will stumble along for the foreseeable future.

Common names may become more useful to us than scientific names. But that would be vernacular common names, not the common names from nomenclature committees as long as the latter are committed to matching all their common names one-to-one with scientific names. We would have to declare the independence of "folk taxonomy" from systematics: our common names could represent groups of similar species, as the species concept moves into realms where field biology cannot follow. Mushroom pickers will continue to pick black morels, white morels, and fuzzy-foot morels as they always have; they gain nothing by inventing seven different common names for black morels, to keep up with molecular taxonomy. There's no way they're going to send their pickings in for chromosomal analysis anyway, and that's the only way to identify them to species.

But we aren't all the way there, yet. I still like Latin names. At least they're more international than common names. The code regulating them anchors them to particular specimens—something common names can never offer. Biologists continue to use them.

Note that in this book I use the word "Also" (short for "also known as") to present some of the other names you're likely to run across for this organism—either common or scientific names. The other names are not always synonyms in the strict sense. For example, in many cases the "also" taxon and our taxon were formerly combined and are now separated, with the "also" taxon living outside our range; so the two are not synonymous, but the valid name for a species outside our range is a name you'll see in older books for the species in our range.

Common Names

I also like real common names—the ones that came up on their own, through the vernacular. I hate to see common names coined purely for the sake of avoiding italics. If you invented the name, how "common" can it be?

In this book I put a common name on every species. I do not coin any new ones. In a few cases I perpetuate a name that charms me, even if I only heard it from neighbors or saw it in one faded book.

For birds, reptiles, amphibians, and fishes, I follow standard committee-revised checklists of common names that are broadly accepted, at least in the United States and Canada. (Exception: I choose consistent style over two checklist idiosyncrasies—capitalizing bird and herp names within sentences, and compounding snake names like gophersnake.) The checklists and online floras that I follow are listed on page 549.

Compared to the situation with animals, plant names are the Wild West, and fungus names are in outer space. The US Department of Agriculture nobly took on the task of standardizing both scientific and common names of plants. However, their determinations don't seem to carry a lot of weight when botanists compile a regional flora. The USDA also makes up long, compounded "common" names based on a logic that escapes me. My chief references for plant common names are regional: the Washington and British Columbia online floras, certain wildflower books, and my own taste. I hate calling a plant a "false" something, especially when there's no way my readers are going to see the plant as a ringer for the one it is said to falsify. But I do use a name starting with "false" if it is the only name in wide circulation.

I have no objection to vernacular names that originated long ago as taxonomic falsehoods. For example, hemlock, the tree, was named for hemlock, the poisonous parsley, just because both have "lacy" foliage. But what else are you going to call this tree, if you ban misnomers? And if you can call a tree a hemlock, why would you stop calling a flower a brodiaea just because taxonomists decided that, though related, it no longer belongs in genus *Brodiaea*?

Back to that "outer space" comment, taxonomy of fungi is especially unstable. Fungus family names are so fluid that I decided not to use them in this book. Fungal morphology is turning out, in the light of DNA study, to be a stunningly poor predictor of lineage: fungi that don't look related at all may be the same species in two different life phases, or taking two forms for reasons we can only guess at. Concepts of the species (and of the individual) that work tolerably well for higher animals and plants don't fit fungi very well. Some mycologists estimate there are 1.5 million species of fungi in the world, of which 5 percent have been named. But doing so may be ill-advised. In a dead-serious article titled "Against the Naming of Fungi," a well-published mycology professor wrote, "It may be more fruitful to abandon the notion of fungal species pending further basic research."

Few lichens have common names in vernacular use. However, the excellent tome *Lichens of North America* picked sensible names for 805 lichen species, and I have generally followed its lead, replacing some common names I used in the past. A quirkier set of lichen names is found on E-Flora BC; many of these I list under "Also." Unanimous common names for lichens would be a fine thing, as the outlook for their scientific names is dim. The scientific name is that of one fungal partner, not the whole lichen. With different partners, the same primary fungal species can produce very different lichens.

Pronouncing Scientific Latin

Pronunciations of genus and species names are provided in this guide simply to make Latin names more approachable. I devised no airtight phonetic system; my intent is simply to break each name into units that would be hard to misread. If you want to pronounce them some other way, feel free. Biologists are far from uniform in their pronunciations. There is an American style and a Continental style. *Colorado Flora* argues that Americans should adopt the Continental style so that taxonomic Latin can be more of an international language. Unfortunately, the two styles are different enough that Americans who adopt Continental pronunciation will find themselves misunderstood during the 99 percent of their discussions that are with other Americans.

That said, I wistfully admire the Continental style's consistency: the five vowels are always "ah, eh (or ay), ee, oh, oo," the *ae* diphthong is "eye," *c* is always "k," and *t* has a crisp sound even in *-atius* (AH-tee-oos).

In contrast, American style Americanizes vowel sounds, both long and short, but sticks to Greek or Latin rules on most consonants and syllable stressing. An initial consonant *x* is pronounced "z," final *es* is "eez," *ch* is "k," *j* is "y," and *th* is always soft as in "thin," never hard as in "then."

Syllable stressing causes difficulty and variation within the American style. The Latin rule says the second-to-last syllable is stressed if its vowel is long, is a diphthong (vowel pair), or is followed by two consonants or by *x* or *y* before the next vowel. Otherwise the third-to-last syllable gets the stress. Thus *-ophila* is AH-fill-a, but *-ophylla*, thanks to the double *l*, is o-FILL-a. When unsure whether the vowel is long, I consult Webster's *Third New International Dictionary*, Gray's *New Manual of Botany* (1908), Jepson's *Manual of the Flowering Plants of California* (1925), or Robbins's *Birds of North America* (1966).

I depart from Latin rules for a few names that have entered the English language: we stress the third-to-last syllables in *Anemone* and *Penstemon*. Native Latin speakers would have stressed the second-to-last.

In the many cases of proper names with Latin endings tacked on, I try, up to a point, to respect the way the person whose name it was would have pronounced it. For example, *jeffreyi* obviously starts with a "j" sound rather than the "y" sound of the Latin *j*. Limiting this principle requires a judgment call based partly on what will roll easily off the tongue. Sometimes the honoree's pronunciation is just too counterintuitive for us. Menzies is "ming-iss" in Scotland, and Douglas is "DOO-glus," but the scientific names based on them are pronounced American-style on these shores. (When I heard a Scot say *menziesii*, he eschewed Scots pronunciation in favor of Continental style: "men-zee-AY-see-ee.")

Where I omit the pronunciation and translation of a genus or species, it's either the same genus as the preceding entry or obviously similar to its English translation, like *densa* or *americanus*.

For the *-oides* ending I hear "-oy-deez" today, rather than the "oh-eye-deez" I once learned in Leo Hitchcock's class. I still usually hear "ee-eye" for the *-ii* ending, which could nicely be elided into just "-ee." Plant families end in *-aceae* with the "a" stressed, and here again most of us streamline, calling the Pinaceae "pie-NAY-see"; Dr. Hitchcock said "pie-NAY-seh-ee." Animal families end in *-idae*, with the third-to-last syllable stressed: Felidae is "FEE-lid-ee." Bird orders end in *-formes*, "FOR-meez." Insect orders end in *-ptera*, with the *p* pronounced and stressed, as in "DIP-ter-a."

LANDSCAPE

This book's range comprises eight physiographic provinces based on landform styles that you could almost pick out intuitively on a good relief map. Geologically they are so distinct that some have hardly any rock formations in common with their neighbors, and yet, while rocks and landforms vary, the living things unite them all. Though the wet west-sides contrast dramatically with the dry east-sides, north-to-south changes are fairly gradual all the way from Alaska to the far tip of the Sierra Nevada.

The greatest exception—the sharpest vegetational shift within that north-south spectrum—comes between central and southern Oregon, so I draw a southern limit to our range there, at the Willamette-Umpqua divide. That means omitting, for the sake of ecological cohesion, a quarter of the Cascade volcanic chain. On the north end, I draw the line just past the last undisputed Cascades volcano, Mt. Meager, at the 51st parallel of latitude. (Roughly the same south and north boundaries delimit the new *Flora of the Pacific Northwest.*)

An eastern boundary for our range is easy: where the montane forests end dramatically east of the Cascades and Coast Mountains, giving way to open country classed as steppe. At the western edges, I leave out the salt-tinged seashore habitats, and also the agricultural and urban lowlands where the human influence dominates. (The book is still 98 percent applicable in "natural areas" within those lowlands.) Only by excluding steppe, salt, and the southern Cascades was I able to hold the book to a reasonable size.

The name "Cascade Range" originated at the Cascades of the Columbia back when they were a high-risk hurdle on overland voyages to and from the Pacific Northwest. (Later they were drowned by Bonneville Dam.) Early Euro-American visitors, either portaging around the cascades or running them, had an awareness of a mountain range forced upon them there, but it stuck in their memories almost like mere parentheses around their scary passage. The botanist David Douglas seems to have been first to put "Cascade Range" in writing, in 1825. An Oregon town was named Cascadia in 1898. In 1954, Burlington Northern Railway named a passenger train The Cascadian. In 1970 a sociology professor described a huge region he called Cascadia. Concurrently, earth science was being turned upside down by the concepts of plate tectonics; by 1977 geologists were writing about the Cascadia Subduction Zone—the chief scientific use of "Cascadia." Cascadia subduction built these mountains—the range of this book, which I may lapse into calling Cascadia or simply "here."

The Olympic Mountains

The Olympics are an anomaly: a nearly round mountain range, with drainage patterns radiating out from the center. That pattern seems to result from the domal uplift rather than predating it.

With help from a geologic map (p. 508) and your imagination, you can see the deeper geologic pattern of northwest-to-southeast arcs, bowed out to the northeast. The biggest arc is the Olympic Basaltic

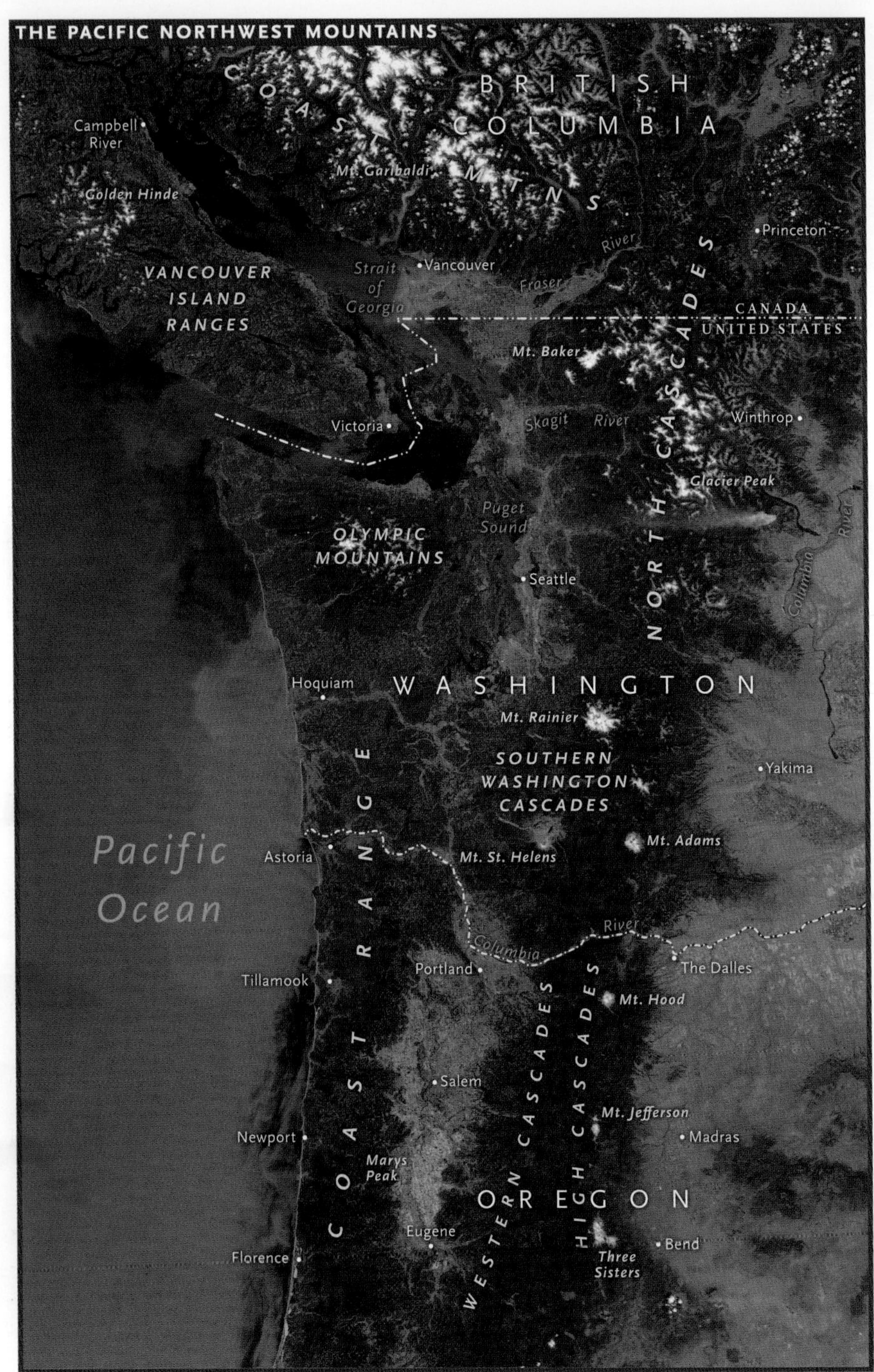
THE PACIFIC NORTHWEST MOUNTAINS
COAST MTNS
BRITISH COLUMBIA
Campbell River
Golden Hinde
Mt. Garibaldi
Princeton
VANCOUVER ISLAND RANGES
Strait of Georgia
Vancouver
Fraser River
CANADA
UNITED STATES
Mt. Baker
NORTH CASCADES
Victoria
Skagit River
Winthrop
Glacier Peak
Puget Sound
OLYMPIC MOUNTAINS
Seattle
Columbia River
Hoquiam
WASHINGTON
Mt. Rainier
SOUTHERN WASHINGTON CASCADES
Yakima
COAST RANGE
Pacific Ocean
Astoria
Mt. St. Helens
Mt. Adams
Columbia River
The Dalles
Portland
Tillamook
Mt. Hood
WESTERN CASCADES
HIGH CASCADES
Salem
Mt. Jefferson
Madras
Newport
Marys Peak
OREGON
Eugene
Bend
Florence
Three Sisters

Horseshoe, a belt along the southeast, east, and north flanks of the range and running WNW out to Cape Flattery. Just inside it lie narrower belts—ridges, valleys, faults, additional slices of basalt. Each belt includes prominent peaks, evidence that this basalt resists erosion better than the marine sedimentary rocks that make up the rest of the range.

During the last Ice Age, major ice sheet tongues grinding west through the present-day Strait of Juan de Fuca and south through Hood Canal shaved the abrupt north and east flanks of the Olympics. These mega-glaciers brought huge loads of rock from Canada, leaving individual boulders as "erratics" at elevations up to 4500 feet on Olympic slopes—proof of the enormous thickness of ice. Interior valleys have since been recarved by smaller alpine glaciers, of which today's glaciers are the uppermost remnants. The glaciers left the broad valley floors lined with outwash gravels and cobbles, and later terraced by "Little Ice Age" glacial advances and retreats of the last 600 years.

The same processes worked on many Cascade valleys, but here in the western Olympics some poorly understood combination including ocean fog, heavy selective browsing by elk, and cobbly soils frequently overhauled by the rivers, has produced a unique style of forest. These Olympic Rainforests are famous for huge conifers, both standing and down, and an abundance of tree-draping mosses, lichens, and ferns unequaled outside the subtropics. Compared to other west-side Northwest old-growth these forests are more parklike and open—to sunlight, and to people on foot.

Timberline—the transition from closed forest to meadow vegetation—begins below 4000 feet in the western Olympics, yet some trees grow on 6000-foot crags nearby. The broad elevational belt in between includes extraordinarily luxuriant subalpine meadows. This differs from other regions where alpine timberlines mark the point above which it's too cold for trees. A timberline based only on cold would lie above 6000 feet in the Olympics. Our low but diffuse timberlines are caused instead by the the sheer quantity of snow, leading to a short growing season. Annual precipitation, mostly snow, likely exceeds 240 inches—the highest in the lower 48 states—somewhere high on Mt. Olympus.

Precipitation decreases sharply northeastward in a rain shadow effect. The northeast corner of the Olympics has dramatically different forests—younger, because of more frequent fires, and with Douglas-fir and grand fir dominating at lower elevations.

Vancouver Island

Most of Vancouver Island is one continuous mountain area, with ruggedness to spare. At least 17 small individual ranges have names. The island's mountains in toto bear two official names, both obscure perhaps because they are dull: the Ranges of Vancouver Island, or the Insular Mountains. The Insulars include a long stretch of undersea ridges northward, then reemerge on Haida Gwaii (the Queen Charlotte Islands).

Several glaciers survive in the central part around the 7201-foot highest peak, Golden Hinde (named after Sir Francis Drake's ship). In today's warming climate, glaciers are shrinking faster on the island and in the Olympics than in the higher ranges to the east.

The island is ecologically more distinct from mainland British Columbia than modest intervening brine can explain. That's because a mere 16,000 years ago it was separated from the mainland by broad lobes of the Cordilleran Ice Sheet. The island's ice-free refugia were slim and frigid. More than half of the mammal species now on the adjacent mainland failed to regain the island, including chipmunks, grizzly bears, coyotes, red foxes, porcupines, mountain goats, and moose. The island has its own species of marmot, whose numbers are small and precarious.

The contrast from rainy west- to dry east-side is extreme. Henderson Lake, in a valley, is the wettest weather station in North America, claiming 260 inches a year. The rain shadow of the Insulars gets 40 inches. Victoria, the island's driest point, is in a different rain shadow, the one behind the Olympics.

Rainforests of the coastal side have seen few fires ever, aside from occasional patch burns on south-facing slopes. Fire was, however, the chief disturbance on the island's rain-shadowed east-side, and also at subalpine elevations, which used to burn often enough to maintain large areas of parkland. With fires suppressed, trees now encroach on meadows and heather.

Hikers accustomed to our other wet ranges may notice a shortage of creeks—or a plethora of broad rocky creek beds with only desultory water in them by late summer. The island has extensive limestone, a rock that slowly dissolves in water. Where water flows underground, it tends to eat away at limestone, enlarging underground conduits that then steal a much of the runoff. (The limestone areas are too small to show on the geologic map, p. 508, but are scattered within the "ocean basalt and sedimentary rocks.")

A glance at the map suggests that Vancouver Island and the Olympic Mountains might be one mountain range neatly sawed in two. They are not. Though the topography, climate, and ecology are similar, the bedrock has little in common. The island has limestone and marble, very little shale or sandstone, a lot of granitic and metamorphic rock, and especially a lot of basalt. Though the southwest shoreline bears a slice of 52-million-year-old Crescent basalt (shared with the Olympics), most island basalt represents a flood basalt province 225 million years old, a signature component of an exotic terrane named Wrangellia (p. 514).

The island's Pacific shore was a wealthy population center in pre–British times. In the 1780s, the Nuu-chah-nulth (Nootka) people here were briefly the leading exporters of "soft gold," or sea otter furs, making the island the hottest property in all of western North America. Britain and Spain almost went to war over it in 1790.

In the recent century the gold was all green: forests, now heavily logged. The logging got serious later here than in Washington and Oregon, leaving the island with a lion's share of champion trees today: the largest Douglas-fir, the second largest Sitka spruce, and the (arguably) first or second largest western redcedar. Those three species are the next largest trees after California's redwoods and sequoias. Protected rainforests on the island include the impressive Carmanah Valley.

The Coast Range

Coast Range forests are among the most biologically productive on earth. Great volumes of sawtimber have left them. They don't have very much protected wilderness, but even second-growth forests here can be huge and deep. Plant communities are similar to those at low to low-mid-elevations in the Cascades; milder winters allow a few additional species. Higher elevations get snow, but the snowpack is typically intermittent and thin. Though lightning without rain is infrequent, evidence of past fires is widespread, and trees older than 400 years are rare. The rain shadow effect east of the range is significant but not extreme, dropping from a maximum possibly exceeding 160 inches just west of the divide to less than 40 inches in the Willamette Valley.

The Coast Range does not rival our other landscape provinces in elevation or ruggedness. Glaciers never reached it. Marys Peak in west-central Oregon is the highest in our part of the Coast Range, at 4087 feet. Saddle Mountain, in northwest Oregon, juts out from its surroundings at 3283 feet. Those and a few other high ridges support grass balds with several disjunct or endemic species. Washington's part of this province, the Willapa Hills (WILL-a-PAH), is lower, and belongs mostly to timber companies.

Coast Range climate and terrain were relatively hospitable to native peoples, who managed vegetation with fire, and maintained networks of trails both along ridges in in valleys. They used the valleys heavily, year-round in some places.

The geologic core of the Coast Range is a massive oceanic basalt formation thought to have arrived here around 50 million years ago as an exotic terrane called Siletzia. (The same basalt comprises the Olympic Horseshoe.) Equally extensive at the present-day surface are beds of sediments eroded from nearby mountains onto the old basalt while it was still submerged; then all were pushed up, presumably by the slab subducting under them. Where sedimentary rocks lie thick upon the surface, the mountain slopes are a mosaic of landslides. Siletzia basalts are somewhat more erosion-resistant; still more so are two younger igneous rock formations, which hold up the highest peaks: Columbia River basalt at Saddle Mountain, and small sills and dikes of gabbro at Marys Peak.

The High Cascades

The Oregon Cascades are subtly divided into two parallel ranges, the Western and High Cascades. From certain viewpoints, or on a relief map, you can see a difference in the shapes of the mountains, and see stretches where they are divided by north-south valleys of the otherwise west-flowing Clackamas, North Santiam, and McKenzie Rivers. The High Cascades are a long, fairly gentle plateau, generally at 5500–6500 feet in elevation, studded with cones that look more or less like volcanoes. Which of course they are.

Oregon's famous snowcapped volcanoes are here, with elevations of 7500–11,235 feet. Some are still active, and will erupt again. All but the youngest (South Sister and Bachelor) are markedly eroded by glaciers. Most have had sides of their craters breached (Hood, Jefferson, North Sister). Several are stripped down to mere cores of their former selves (Three-Fingered Jack, Washington), their "necks" remaining after their more fragmental flanks have eroded away. These prominent stratovolcanoes date from the last 750,000 years; the conspicuous lava flows and small cinder cones are generally younger than 20,000 years. The intervening plateau includes low-profile shield volcanoes and the eroded remains of older volcanoes of the past 3 million years.

Also in this province lies the dry side of the Oregon Cascades, with some of our best stands of ponderosa pine at the lowest forested elevations. Grand fir and Douglas-fir stands—or lodgepole pine on substrates of pumice or other volcanic gravels—dominate the mid-elevation belt.

The drainage divide separating east-side and west-side climates poses a mountain barrier more than 500 miles long, broken by just one river valley close to sea level.

That valley, the Columbia River Gorge, funnels air and weather from one side of the mountains to the other. The gorge is not only a windy place (great for wind surfing) but also a place where plant and animal species meet that do not meet elsewhere, or that reach low elevations though they are strictly montane elsewhere. During the Ice Ages, the gorge provided an outlet to the sea for staggeringly great glacial outburst floods (p. 30), which scoured its slopes to create 4000-foot cliffs misted with waterfalls.

The Western Cascades

These mountains are a mostly forested jumble of ridges left standing between river valleys cut out of a great mass of volcanic material that began erupting 46 million years ago. (By 4 million years ago, the volcanic arc shifted 20–40 miles east in Oregon, and the High Cascades began.) The Ancestral Cascade volcanoes were every bit as high and as active as the High Cascades, producing a far greater volume of rock over their longer span of activity. Today though, where you see a mountain it is generally not "a volcano" but an erosional form carved out of volcanic rock; the original vents are no longer the high points. A few exceptions, like Battle Ax, are young (High Cascades) outliers.

Western Cascade ridges top out at 4000–5600 feet. They bear no glaciers, and lie entirely below true timberline, though grass balds and hanging meadows persist with the help of fires on exposed, thin-soiled sites. These are not true subalpine meadows, but can rival them visually, and feature some flowers that are alpine elsewhere. From the Clackamas River southward, climate is warm enough to add such trees as sugar pine and incense-cedar, along with greater numbers and sizes of golden chinquapin and madrona.

Less spectacular than the High Cascades and with far greater timber value, they have received scant and belated protection as wilderness. Magnificent old-growth forest remains in some valleys here and there. On their lovely, riffled rivers, fishery and recreation values have often lost out to hydro power.

The Southern Washington Cascades

The High Cascades and the Ancestral Cascades continue northward in Washington, but overlapping rather than aligned east and west. Our youngest and most active High stratovolcano—Mt. St. Helens, less than 40,000 years old—lies way over near the western edge. Ancestral lavas extend well east of Mt. Rainier, and of the drainage crest. The crest wanders east and west, respectively, of our two highest peaks, Rainier and Adams, which were built over the last half-million years. It runs right through the Goat Rocks, a major High Cascade stratovolcano about five times as old, now eroded beyond semblance to a cone. The one other High Cascade volcanic center here, Indian Heaven, is a cluster of basaltic shields rather than a dramatic peak.

Rising two vertical miles from valley floors at its feet in four different directions, Mt. Rainier ranks first of all mountains in the lower 48 states in spire measure, a computation of vertical relief and steepness in all directions. It has been called America's most dangerous mountain because of the number of people living in striking distance of a mudflow from its slopes (p. 513).

The remainder of this landscape comprises erosional forms carved out of 40- to 5-million year-old igneous rocks of the Ancestral Cascades. Especially around Mt. Rainier, these include magma that did not erupt as lava, but cooled into intrusive rocks, such as granite. Similar intrusive rock bodies exist under the whole volcanic chain, but northward they are more widely exposed at the surface, thanks to bigger Ice Age glaciers and greater uplift of the entire chain.

This province has few species that don't occur elsewhere in our region, perhaps because it is centrally located. Noble fir achieves its best growth here, and sets a regional standard for biomass per acre.

The North Cascades

At its north end the High Cascade volcanic arc turns abruptly northwest. The five northernmost volcanic centers are superimposed upon—and humbled among—expanses of stupendous nonvolcanic mountains. These are split between the North Cascades (mostly in the United States) and the Coast Mountains (entirely in Canada).

If you reach a high central viewpoint on a clear day, you can't miss the resemblance of North Cascade topography to waves on a stormy sea—wild array, whitecaps, vastness, and generally equal height. The similar peak heights are attributed to a glacial erosion "buzzsaw": the higher peaks rise about 2000 feet above cirque floors, whose elevation is determined by glacial equilibrium during the last Ice Age. Filling the stream valleys nearly brimful with ice, Ice Age glaciers deepened them and reshaped them from V to U cross-sections. Heads of major valleys in the heart of the range were eroded to within 3000 feet of sea level, leaving such a low gradient (slope of descent) out to sea that current stream cutting is relatively slow. With the ridgetops eroding as fast or faster than the valley bottoms, relief is about as high as it can get (unless uplift speeds up or the glaciers grow again). Today, the majority of active glaciers in the lower 48 states are here; most of the rest are on Cascade volcanoes or Olympic peaks.

Major peaks near the Cascade Crest from Canada to just southeast of Glacier Peak tend to be 8000–9000 feet high. To the north, south, and west of that backbone, elevations of peaks and valleys decrease together, so that local relief is scarcely less; 6000-foot peaks like Index and Baring near the western front are as impressive in their vertical relief as 8500-foot peaks on the crest.

Eastward the ruggedness decreases (the Stuart Range excepted) even though many of the peaks are just as high. The rain shadow effect makes alpine glaciers scarce east of the crest, and slower erosion actually leads to slower tectonic uplift (p. 511). Ice Age glaciation had a gentling rather than a sharpening effect on some east-side topography when the Okanogan Lobe of the Cordilleran Ice Sheet ground across the area east of Ross Lake for a few centuries, just before its abrupt retreat 17,000 years ago.

Following a dramatic drainage reversal (p. 25), the Skagit cuts across the inherent North Cascades crest, which runs up the center of the National Park through the Picket Range. That ancient crest persists as the main climatic divide, with typical east-slope vegetation common in the Ross Lake drainage.

Geologically, the North Cascades are a bewildering variety of rock formations of widely differing ages, thought to be a cluster of exotic terranes that have been part of North America for only around 50 million years (p. 514). The rocks in them are mostly much older than that. Major North Cascade peaks are made of gneiss, schist, hornfels, or granitic rocks, all rarities in the volcanic Cascades. Conversely, lavas are only a small fraction of North Cascade rocks—two High Cascade–age volcanoes

(Mt. Baker and Glacier Peak) and a few small patches of Ancestral Cascade lavas. Ancestral volcanoes did erupt here, but subsequent uplift was so great that they eroded off of the top of the range. About half of the granitic rocks are the roots of those missing volcanoes. The other half are older products of volcanism on some Pacific island that later became a terrane here.

The Coast Mountains

British Columbia's Coast Mountains present a world of superlatives. They make up the deepest, soggiest, wildest, ruggedest range of mountains in the Pacific Northwest, carved out of the world's biggest granitic batholith, rising straight from a seashore of fjords up to 70 miles long, and capped not with mere glaciers but with icefields larger even than those in the Canadian Rockies. Their highest peak, 13,177-foot Mt. Waddington, is slightly higher than any in the Canadian Rockies, and second only to Mt. Rainier within our range.

Above all, they are least touched by the hand of man—and hardest to get to. Only a few valleys have roads open to the public, and most of the coastal side of the range (even where it has roads) can only be reached by boat. I expect relatively few users of this guide to be in those remote recesses. Hiking trails concentrate at the southern end of the mountains. Backpackers throng in Garibaldi Provincial Park, which (atypically for the Coast Mountains) has extensive volcanic rocks from a Cascade volcano, Mt. Garibaldi.

Northwest of Garibaldi, two more High Cascades volcanoes poke through the granite: Mt. Cayley and Mt. Meager. The latter erupted explosively just 2360 years ago. The east edge of the mountains has a few older (Ancestral Cascades) volcanic centers.

The roster of plant and animal species is shorter here, in accord with the general rule that those rosters shrink toward the poles. Both black and grizzly bears are here. Near the coast just north of our range lives an unusual white race of the black bear, which has been named the Spirit Bear and proclaimed the official Provincial Mammal.

Timberlines get lower northward. Alpine rock and ice and the occasional brave outpost of alpine vegetation dominate this high region. Forests of the west-side lowlands have seen few if any forest fires because they are too wet, even through the summer. Western redcedar and Sitka spruce predominate at lowest elevations. An area called the Great Bear Rainforest was substantially protected from logging by a 2006 agreement. It lies entirely north of Knight Inlet (and of the range of this book), so we may see logging and possibly mining on the more southerly mainland, though the rugged topography may inhibit development to some degree.

The eastern slope is drier, and fire-prone. Whistler, in the center of a long crosswise valley at just 2215 feet, actually straddles the main Coast Mountains divide and shows the beginnings of a rain-shadow effect—Engelmann spruce and interior-type Douglas-fir, but no ponderosa pines or western larches until you cross a farther divide. The Lillooet River valley, in between, can be considered east-side, but is much less dry than the hardcore east-side, the slopes that drain directly to the Fraser River.

Granitic rocks of the Coast Plutonic Complex underlie most of the range and stretch northward to Alaska. The complex is a mosaic of intrusions of varying compositions and ages. The plutonic magmas, 170 million to 45 million years old, are the exposed plumbing of one or more subduction-zone volcanic arcs. (Within that same time span, arcs south along the continental edge were emplacing the Idaho and Sierra Nevada Batholiths.) The plutonic magmas buried the boundary between two exotic terranes, Wrangellia in the west and Stikinia in the east (p. 514).

Ice Age Mountains

If you love dramatic high-relief scenery, count yourself lucky to have been born in the aftermath of an ice age. Mountain erosion without ice typically produces relatively tame, monotonous slopes.

Alpine glaciers give us spire-shaped mountains, U-shaped valleys, bowl-shaped cirques, and countless alpine lakes. They even make the peaks rise higher in the more glaciated part of a range (see p. 511). The glaciers we see today continue to carve, but most of their work was done during the Pleistocene Ice Ages between perhaps 3 million and 11,700 years ago. That interval saw many cycles between glacial stages averaging 100,000 years each and interglacial stages averaging 20,000 years.

During a typical glacial stage, about half of North America lay under two huge ice sheets similar to those blanketing Greenland and Antarctica today. The western one covered much of Alaska, the Yukon and British Columbia, and a little of Washington briefly at its most recent maximum, 14,000 years ago. At that point it shoved up against the Olympics, extended a Puget Lobe to just past Olympia, and ground across eastern North Cascade ridges. Southwest British Columbia and the North Cascades must have resembled southeast Alaska's mountains of today—great banded river-like glaciers with branching tributaries filling the valleys, and marginal peaks protruding as nunataks. Wherever you see a U-shaped valley cross-section today, picture an alpine glacier flowing for 1000 years or longer.

In several North Cascades valleys, tongues of the Cordilleran Ice Sheet dammed north-flowing rivers to create lakes that rose until they spilled over a more southerly pass. Some of these overflow streams were temporary, and the main signs they left of their passage were sharp gorges that had to have been cut by fiercer streams than the ones in them today (e.g., Canyon Creek.) Others cut deeper, creating a new southerly outlet lower than the old northerly one, so that when the ice sheet melted away, the river kept its new course.

The Skagit offers a grand example of such a drainage reversal. Before the Pleistocene, its Ross Lake reach flowed north to join the Fraser at Hope, British Columbia. One of the glacial stages reversed its drainage as described above, breaching a former divide near today's Diablo Dam. This explains why the Skagit crosses the North Cascades, and why its gorge below Diablo is narrow and V-shaped, while its valley both above and below there is glacially U-shaped; the Puget ice lobe sent a distributary tongue up the Skagit Valley, U-shaping it as far as Rockport.

The old north-flowing Skagit emptied into a Fraser River that also reversed its direction, either before or after the Skagit reversal. Many British Columbia geologists have identified signs of past northward flow through the Fraser Canyon—without deigning to tell us where that water went. Candidates would be the Skeena, Peace, and Columbia River systems.

One effect of great ice sheets was to lower sea level as much as 400 feet by retaining ice that would otherwise be seawater. This turned a wide area of shallow sea between Siberia and Alaska into habitable dry land, allowing many new mammals, including humans, to migrate to the New World.

As the ice sheets melted, sea level rose

Cirques, Tarns, and Horns

These characteristic glacial landforms are shaped by small alpine glaciers, more than by continental ice sheets. Small, high glaciers scoop out the mountainside under them. After melting, they leave half-bowl-shaped valley heads called cirques (The word means both "circle" and "circus" in French, and derives from Greco-Roman amphitheaters.) At the lip of a glacial cirque, just above a dropoff, look for bedrock that the glacier rounded off and scratched with parallel striations (p. 30). The dropoff may be long—especially if this is a hanging side valley above a deep main valley—or slight. Some valleys have a series of cirque-lip dropoffs, each marking a pause in the glacier's retreat.

A cirque.

A cirque may hold a small, usually shallow cirque lake or tarn. Tarns tend to fill with sediment until they turn into marshes, or perhaps gravel flats laced with braided streams, and eventually into meadows.

Where the glaciers of two back-to-back cirque glaciers continue scooping until they almost touch, they leave a saw-edged ridge, an arête. Where cirque glaciers on three

worldwide. However, Vancouver Island has wave terraces indicating late–Ice Age shorelines higher than the present one. How can that be? Continental ice sheets literally weighed continental crust down wherever it was under or even near an ice sheet. When that weight melted away and refilled the ocean basins, the depressed crust rebounded upward; but the rebound lagged centuries behind the rise in sea level, because rock flows very slowly compared to water. The ocean reached present levels and even a bit higher while Vancouver Island was still depressed.

Clearly, ice sheets, and even glaciers, are heavyweights—they're geology, not weather! They have some ability to suppress both earthquakes and volcanism. Several High Cascade volcanoes display interactions between lava and ice. Near Mt. Garibaldi, The Table—whose shape resembles Devil's Tower—erupted up through thick ice, forming cliffs on all sides where lava cooled against ice. Mt. Garibaldi itself pushed enough lava up through thick ice that some lava solidified on the ice, then collapsed as the ice melted.

Ripsaw Ridge, an arête above a cirque.

Boston Peak, a horn.

or four sides of a peak keep scooping long enough, they carve a spire-like horn, as in Matterhorn.

With remarkable consistency, cirque floors are found at the glacier equilibrium line—the elevation where snow adds to the glacier's thickness as fast as melting diminishes it—not today's equilibrium, but the average over the past two million years (the Ice Ages and interglacial stages together). Just as consistently, the elevations of higher peaks are about 2000 feet higher. This "glacial buzzsaw" effect explains why all the peaks in a panorama look pretty similar in height.

Thin alpine glaciers also shape lava flows. When hot lava meets ice, some ice melts of course, but at the same time some lava freezes, forming a skin that directs the continuing lava flow away from the glacier. Lava flows end up perched on ridges between glaciers.

The timing of the last few ice age cycles suggests that we should be headed back into one by now. During the interglacial stages, atmospheric carbon dioxide tended to begin dropping early on, and to keep dropping, setting the stage for ice to return. Humankind's emissions of greenhouse gases have apparently thwarted that pattern and postponed the next ice age, for tens of thousands of years at a minimum. A controversial but tenacious hypothesis argues that by means of deforestation, rice paddies, and cattle herds, our ancestors first tipped the climate scales toward warming several thousand years ago.

Glaciers

Wherever an average year brings more new snow than can melt, snow accumulates and slowly compacts into ice. Eventually, the ice gets so thick and heavy that it flows slowly downhill until it reaches an elevation warm enough to melt it as fast as it arrives. This flowing ice is a glacier, a mechanism that balances the snow's mass budget.

The Coast Mountains have not only a lot of snowfall but rather blocky topography, with broad areas at high elevation. Those circumstances create icefields—plateaus of thick ice that barely moves except near the edges, where outlet glaciers extend their tongues down into the valleys.

When the rate of flow is equal to both the snow accumulation in the upper part of the glacier and the melting in the lower part, you have a balanced mass budget, and an ideal glacier that neither advances nor retreats. Few glaciers are so stable. Instead, the elevation where the glacier terminates in a melting snout advances and retreats in response to climate. (Retreating glaciers don't turn around and flow back uphill, of course; they merely melt away at the bottom faster than they arrive there.) For more than a century now, climatic warming has caused widespread glacial retreat. In our region this intensified in the warm, dry 1930s and 1940s, paused or reversed in the 1950s and 1960s, then resumed and is now accelerating, turning many smaller glaciers into mere snowfields. A glacier stagnates when it no longer has enough mass and slope to flow.

If you could find an advancing glacier, it would have a high, cliff-like front where ice blocks come crashing down. Retreating glacier snouts are thin, even concave, and dirty with surface debris concentrated over recent decades; it may be hard to tell where the glacier leaves off and the rock rubble or till ensues.

Where glaciers bend or where their flow accelerates, the ice stretches. The stretch marks are deep cracks, or crevasses. They may be bridged by masses of recent snow that may or may not be solid enough to walk across. Don't try to cross glaciers unless you are trained and prepared for crevasses.

Paralleling either the sides of a glacier or the arc of its snout, you often find low ridgelines of rubble. These are recessional moraines deposited where the retreating glacier advanced or held a line for a time, before receding again. Many formed during the last 200 years' retreat. Older ones obscured by vegetation reveal to the practiced eye a map of the end of the latest Ice Age, 14 to 11 thousand years ago. Terminal moraines are found below the present terminus, crossing the mountain slope. Picture the glacier not as a bulldozer but as a conveyor belt delivering rock rubble. Lateral moraines form along a glacier's sides; they run parallel to a glacier's course, regardless of whether you find them alongside modern glaciers or at elevations far below.

Small glaciers in pockets on steep faces appear to be nearly vertical. Gnarly blue wrinkles show that they are glaciers. Often they terminate over bands of vertical rock. Ice blocks that break off and avalanche down the rock band may recoalesce into a lower glacier, if the basin where they collect is high and shaded enough for them to stay frozen. Some basin glaciers are supplied more by avalanches than by direct snowfall.

No matter whether it formed from fresh snow, avalanches, or blocks of old ice, glacial ice has a consistency utterly unlike a snowbank. Under a firn of last year's snow, what was once snow is now recrystallized into coarse, nubbly granules with hardly any air space. Eventually even the granular texture will grade into massive blue ice with a texture (visible only under a microscope) more granular than that of frozen lake ice.

Our temperate-zone glaciers are "warm"

Rock Flour

A milky white color in streams betrays water that recently melted from glaciers, and carries fine particles pulverized by the glacier, now held in suspension. They aren't mud-colored because until very recently the cold preserved them from altering into clay, and they haven't had time to alter since.

In lakes, the same rock flour conjures an insanely intense blue-green opacity. It works best where only the very finest particles are still suspended. Uniform in size and distribution, they bounce a narrow blue-green spectrum of wavelengths around, and eventually back at us, while the other wavelengths drown in the depths. Garibaldi Lake is a jaw-dropping example. In Diablo Lake, the color intensifies over the course of summer, as glacier melt takes over from rain and snowpack as the main source of runoff. Ross Lake, just upstream from Diablo, can't compare, as glaciers are sparse in its drainage basin. Diablo Lake gets its rock flour from the Thunder Creek drainage, with big glaciers on Mts. Logan, Boston, and Eldorado. In the Olympics, most rock flour is in the Hoh, the Queets, and Silt Creek. The Elwha snowfinger was described as a glacier in the early 1900s, and its output is still a bit milky.

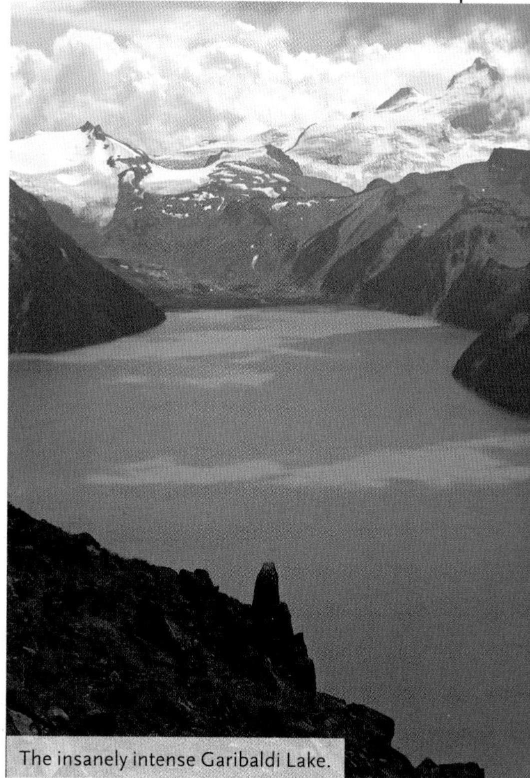

The insanely intense Garibaldi Lake.

Some writers find milky meltwater unpalatable, but I like it just fine—unfiltered, since I don't want to clog the filter. I figure it comes with a mineral supplement and a negligible risk of giardia (p. 503). Filtering it will shorten your filter's lifespan.

Glacial striations.

glaciers at close to 32°F throughout, in contrast with "cold" arctic glaciers. Warm glaciers, like ice skaters, glide on a film of pressure-melted water. They pour around bedrock outcrops by melting under pressure against the upstream side of the knob and refreezing against the downstream side (repaying the heat debt incurred by the first change of state). They erode rock ferociously, not because either the water layer or the ice itself is abrasive, but because sand, pebbles, and boulders are gripped and ground along over the substrate. It's the rock sediment load that does the grinding in both glacier and river erosion; glaciers work like belt-sanders, whereas river rocks chip away more like sandblasting. The glacier's grit leaves parallel grooves or striations across bedrock. In the area east of Ross Lake, striations even cross high divides—proof that the Cordilleran Ice Sheet crossed here, since alpine glaciers necessarily operate below the high ridges.

British Columbia has more glacier-covered area than any other Canadian province, easily outdoing Washington, which has most of the glacier cover in the lower 48 states.

The Missoula Floods

Steep cliffs laced with waterfalls commonly owe their steepness to scouring by glacier ice. Those of the Columbia Gorge, in contrast, were scoured by water that came in torrents only Ice Age glaciers could release—floods 400–1000 feet deep. Yes, the Columbia ran 1000 feet deep at The Dalles where it backed up against the Cascades, tapering to 700 feet at Crown Point and 350 feet deep over Portland. And not just deep, but fast, like towering flash floods. The flow rate of the biggest one was 200 times that of the biggest historic Columbia River flood, 46 times that of the biggest weather-caused river flood anywhere. There were perhaps 80 of these Missoula Floods between 21,000 to 13,000 years ago, plus several series of them earlier in the Pleistocene Ice Ages.

Given that early Americans occupied a

cave in southern Oregon 14,300 years ago, I imagine that some of them witnessed the last floods.

The flood source, Lake Missoula, was an ice-dammed lake in western Montana with about half the volume of modern Lake Michigan. It formed each time the Cordilleran Ice Sheet in Canada extended a big lobe south into Idaho, damming the Clark Fork river. The ice dam either floated or burst each time the lake rose high enough, at intervals of a few decades, and the entire lake drained within a few days. Sudden floods due to ice-dam failure are called jökulhlaups by anyone who can actually pronounce that. Such people typically live in Iceland, where small jökulhlaups occur to this day. Alaska sees them, too.

The floodwaters ripped eastern Washington, showing about as much respect as a sneaker wave shows to a sand castle. It cut the Washington features called Dry Falls, Coulees, Potholes, and Channeled Scablands, and left current ripples 35 feet high in Montana. In between floods, winds picked up the silt they left behind and deposited it as the Palouse Loess, the soil that enables dry farming of wheat in Washington and Oregon.

Boulders ended up sprinkled across the Willamette Valley. Glacial erratics are rocks transported by a glacier and dropped typically 10 to 100 miles from their bedrock source. The Willamette erratics were a mystery, found where no glaciers ever were, 500 miles from the closest similar rocks in Montana or British Columbia. They rode the floods in icebergs that drifted out to the margins of a backwater lake filling the Willamette Valley, beached there, and melted. The valley was buried in silt 100 feet deep. Credit the floods with *both* of the economically outstanding soils in the Northwest states: Palouse Loess and Willamette Silt.

They were initially named Bretz Floods. Geologist J Harlan Bretz spent from 1922 to 1952 overcoming the withering skepticism of the geologic community as he presented evidence after evidence of these biblical-scale floods. (One reason the geologic community was so resistant to the idea was that it had spent the previous two centuries fighting the idea that biblical floods ever happened.) Eventually, truth won out. Before long, geologists began seeing signs of the same type of Ice Age megaflood elsewhere. One in central Asia came close to the Missoula Floods in size. British Columbia had glacial lakes and catastrophic floods from them, but detailed evidence of their size and possible cyclic repetition has yet to be described.

CLIMATE

Weather and climate strongly influence the landforms and life forms you see in these mountains. First off, as you doubtless know, it rains a lot here.

- **It rains a lot in winter**, almost as much in fall and spring, and relatively little in June through September.
- **It rains a lot west** of each of our mountain range crests, but far less on the east slopes, approaching desert conditions at the foot of the Cascades.
- **It rains and snows a lot** at higher elevations. The resulting snowpack is slow to melt due to its sheer mass rather than to really cold weather; it commonly persists into July at higher elevations, or sometimes longer, and produces more glaciers and permanent snowfields, than snow in some nearby mountains with colder winters, such as the US Rockies.

When It Falls

Our summer drought is without equal among rainy climates. Most climates with strong wet seasons and dry seasons are tropical, and lack summers and winters. Most of the Temperate Zone, on the other hand, gets precipitation year-round, or more in summer. Our climate is a midpoint between California's Mediterranean type (long dry summers, moderately wet winters, subtropical temperatures) and southeast Alaska's West-Coast Marine type (copious rain, slightly reduced in the summer, and cool temperatures year-round). Our closest analogs are parts of southern Chile, western Scotland, the northern Honshu coast on the Sea of Japan, and Norway's fjord country. Each of those wet West-Coast Marine climates produces 1½ times as much rain and snow in its wettest winter month as in its driest summer month. That's nothing; here, the wetter weather stations record between 6 and 20 times as much precipitation in November as in July. (The ratio increases from north to south.)

Causes for our unique weather lie in the border tension between the cold polar air mass and the warmer subtropical air mass. The front between those masses runs around the world between roughly 40 and 60 degrees N latitude; rather than running due east it wanders in giant lobes directly beneath the polar jet stream, a lofty belt of high-velocity west wind circling the globe.

The jet stream wanders, but it has a typical annual cycle. Nearly every autumn brings a southward migration; the polar jet crosses Anchorage in September on average, Ketchikan in October, Bella Coola in early November, Forks in late November, and Eureka in January. In those months, each of those locales is in line for rainy storms. The air in the storms, originally quite cold, travels for days across relatively warm ocean to reach our shores modestly warmed and immodestly moistened. For much of the winter we get alternating warm fronts—low overcast and steady rain—and cold fronts—mostly cloudy, showery weather.

At times during the wet season, the Aleutian low expands southward in the Pacific, and the jet stream hits us from far to the southwest. This brings an atmospheric river, a long, narrow band full of tropical moisture. Known locally as the Pineapple Express, atmospheric rivers bring Cascadia's rainiest spells and nearly all of our floods. Being warm as well as wet, they often melt a lot of mountain snow, so that during some storms the runoff into mountain rivers is even greater than the precipitation.

Atmospheric rivers commonly align just to the south of the jet stream, and are far below it. (They're in the lowest two miles of the atmosphere, whereas the jet is around five miles up.) They are at work somewhere on earth at any given moment, accomplishing about 90 percent of all transport of atmospheric moisture out of the tropics.

Rarely in winter, the jet stream arches far northward, dragging warm, sunny California weather into our area for days or weeks—commonly warmer and sunnier at mid-elevations than in the Puget-Willamette lowlands, which can get a temperature inversion and smog or haze.

As summer approaches, the jet stream snakes its way back north, taking the frontal systems with it. Our dominant summer air consists of Northwest breezes spiraling clockwise out from the center of the North Pacific High. These travel across ocean colder than themselves and evaporate little moisture from it. They are chilled by contact with the water, often creating vast ocean fog banks, but on hitting the warmer land surface they warm, and the fog soon dissipates. Sometimes during high pressure, the moist marine push gets strong enough to blanket west-side valleys and much of the Georgia-Puget-Willamette Trough with low clouds and even drizzle, while peaks and slopes above 3000 feet remain crystal clear.

All this means that it's certifiably possible to enjoy fine summer weather anywhere in our range, despite rumors to the contrary. It does not mean that you can safely go unprepared for bad weather. Some Julys have brought heavy snow as low as 4000 feet in the North Cascades.

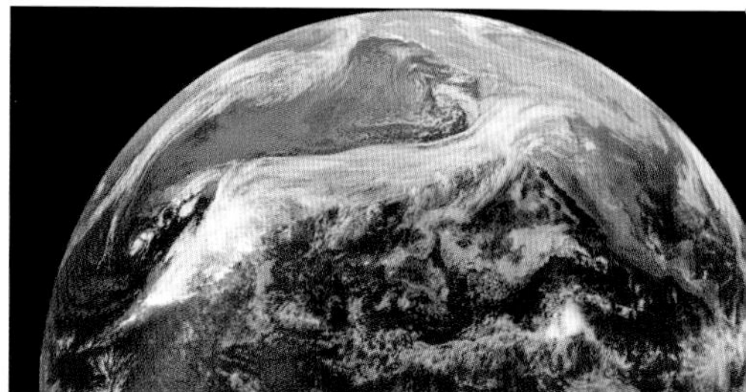
The Pineapple Express of December 2012 broke many local rainfall records.

A marine push fills the Skagit Valley.

Where It Falls

In contrast to our precipitation's unique summer–winter split, its west–east imbalance is common in mountain regions, typifying mountains as rainmaking devices and as barriers between moist marine air and drier continental air.

When air crosses mountains, it must rise. In rising, it gets thinner—because it has less air above it weighing on it—and cooler. (Other factors being equal, clear air cools 5.5°F with each 1000 feet of altitude. Other factors are rarely equal, and the actual lapse rate is usually less; not infrequently it's negative, in a temperature inversion, when cooler air stagnates in valleys and warmer air sits on it and blesses the mountains.)

Warmer air can hold more moisture than cooler air. Put that law of physics together with the one about rising air chilling, and you get mountains writing clouds and precipitation—orographic precipitation, from the Greek for "mountains" and "writing." Moving air meets mountains and is forced to rise, therefore cooling, eventually to the point where it cannot hold the water vapor it held easily before it rose. The water molecules suspended invisibly in the air must coalesce into liquid droplets or ice crystals, in either case forming visible clouds. With further cooling, the droplets or crystals coalesce further, becoming so heavy that they fall. In our mountains, ice crystals are typical, and they form snowflakes, but as they fall they may enter warmer air and melt into rain.

Where the air descends after crossing mountains, the effect is reversed: it warms and the clouds change back into gaseous water. Drizzling clouds on the windward slope may abruptly vanish as they cross the crest; heavier weather on the windward slope may turn to scattered showers and sun breaks on the downwind side.

Sometimes the condensation and then reevaporation of moist air flowing over a mountain becomes a graphic image in the sky—a lenticular (lentil-shaped) cloud (p. 38). These pure white slivers or crescents hang motionless over high peaks. They may stack up two or three deep, or more, and they may stand downwind instead of—or in addition to—directly over the peak. A lenticular cloud is that portion of a uniform layer of air that, as it flows over the mountain, is cooled enough to condense some of its water vapor into cloud droplets. After descending abruptly, the layer may bounce upward once or twice, in waves, to form downwind lenticular clouds.

Since the prevailing wind here is from the WSW in winter and the SW during spring and fall wet weather, and the Olympics are a more or less round mountain range, their downwind side, the rain shadow, is on the NE. The Elwha and North Fork Skokomish drainages are rain-shadowed, receiving less than a third as much precipitation as the Hoh and Quinault; the Dungeness and Dosewallips drainages are drier still. You don't have go to the far edge of a range to see a rain shadow effect: it's unmistakable at the Elwha in the Olympics, at Whistler and the Lillooet River in the Coast Mountains, and at Ross Lake and Mt. Adams in the Cascades.

The Georgia-Puget-Willamette Trough is moderately rain-shadowed by the coastal ranges. The occasional ponderosa pines and abundant grand firs in the Willamette Valley are indicators of that. Though urbanites of Seattle and Portland may think they see a lot of rain, their actual recorded precipitation of 33–42 inches per year is run-of-the-mill, as North American cities go. Vancouver has a wider internal range, with 35 inches in some neighborhoods and 85 inches in others. The number of gray and rainy days per year is high in Northwest cities, but the actual heavy precipitation—60 to 250 inches—falls on the mountain flanks. A legendary rain gauge placed in the 1920s at Henderson Lake on Vancouver Island measured 79.45 inches in a single December, and 16.61 inches in 24 hours of an atmospheric river. That gauge was subject to sharp local effects at the foot of a mountainside; more cautiously placed modern gauges don't come close.

Paradise on Mt. Rainier is the snowiest year-round US weather station, averaging

680 inches a year. The single-season record snowfall, 1141 inches (or 95 feet), hit Mt. Baker Ski Area in 1998–1999. Maury Pelto calculates that that season's snowfall high on the nearby Easton Glacier was at least 187 feet! Snowpack still covered many Washington trails when 1999's first autumn snow fell. It's possible that some glacier on Vancouver Island gets even deeper snow.

If the day for your trip arrives gray and showery, consider an east-side destination. You might not find clear skies, but you will likely get less wet than on the west-side. Similarly, the eastern edges of the North Cascades, Olympics, and Coast Mountains accumulate thinner snowpacks, which melt off weeks earlier each summer. Use that information to pick a hike with less (or more) snow in early summer.

Mesoclimate

Just as the sun is hotter at noon than in morning and evening, hotter at the equator than here in the mid-latitudes, and hotter in summer than in winter, it heats south-facing slopes more than other slope aspects. South slopes have hotter, drier plant community types than north slopes. That isn't just because of the difference in sunlight angle: windward and leeward sides of a ridge get different precipitation. Though the orographic mechanism (and also fog drip, p. 36, where forested) produces the most precipitation directly above the ridgeline or a bit upwind, the raindrops blow downwind as they fall, so the greatest rain falls just downwind of the ridge. Compounding that effect, snow blows over the ridge crest and settles in the wind lull, often building a cornice that may last and continue to release water well into the summer. Where the prevailing wind is from the WSW, the sun angle and precipitation effects both make the northeast side of a mountain wetter. In our mountains you'll notice that glaciers, cirques, and the steepest faces all favor the northeast side of peaks.

The lowest slopes on the leeward side get the least precipitation, but have moist soils, partly because they receive subsurface drainage from higher lee slopes, which get the most rainfall but have soils too coarse to hold on to it. Over time, cool moist soils are self-reinforcing: they grow shadier vegetation, and often suppress fire better, so they retain more organic content, which does a better job of holding on to water.

Bottoms of steep-sided valleys also get reduced hours of sunlight, and may receive cold air drainage as well, because cold air sinks. The effect is strongest in valleys that run east to west, and weakest in south-draining valleys where midday sun hits the bottom head-on. Cold air settles in valleys and slight depressions protected from wind. Caves collect cold air drainage so effectively that some hold ice year-round. On high nonforested peaks and ridges, at the other extreme, the thin air can't hold the heat that the surfaces absorb, and tends to be chilly.

The warmest level in mountains is a mid-elevation thermal belt subject to neither cold air drainage nor thin air heat loss. If you want to sleep warmer, you may gain as much as 15°F by leaving a stream bottom and camping on a slightly higher bench.

Microclimate

Climatic subjects that you can chart on a regional map are macroclimatic; aspect and cold air drainage operate on a mesoclimatic scale. Of equal concern to hikers and other creatures is the microclimate, or narrow climate near the ground.

A microclimate may be much warmer or cooler than its surroundings for several reasons:

- **Ground and lakes heat up** in the sun, even on cloudy days, and heat the air next to them. Dark surfaces heat much more than pale ones, south-facing slopes much more than north-facing ones. High peaks are subject to especially intense solar radiation, including heat, by way of reradiation from clouds, snow, or ice. Dark, dry humus soil on one high south-facing slope was found to reach 175°F while the surrounding air was only 86°F. For a seedling or a crawling invertebrate, 175°F summer afternoons may be a fact of life—or death.
- **Vegetation insulates.** The tree canopy, the shrub, herb, and moss layers, and the snowpack are all blankets, keeping everything under them warmer in cold weather, and vice versa. The combination of ground heat retention and snowpack insulation create a winter-long 30–32°F environment utilized by many rodents that neither hibernate nor migrate downslope. Deer and elk take thermal cover in deep forests during cold spells of winter. On summer days, on the other hand, the forest is cooler than clearings.
- **Vegetation and rough topography impede wind.** This allows cold air collected by sinking (and air heated by warm ground) to stay put longer than they otherwise would.

A forest canopy can make its understory either drier or moister. You may notice that throughfall (drippage from a forest canopy) starts and ends later than individual showers in nearby clearings, and falls in bigger drops. Measured during a rain shower, it amounts to less rainfall; much water is absorbed by the canopy and the epiphytic plants on the trees, eventually evaporating again without ever reaching the ground. Light drizzle around here may fail to wet the forest floor at all.

On the other hand, when fog sweeps the forest canopy, moisture condenses on foliage, and some drips to the ground as throughfall even without any rain. Since low vegetation can catch only a fraction of the the fog that a tall forest can, clearcutting a high watershed on the west side of a divide is estimated to immediately reduce its total precipitation by about half.

Rain, fog throughfall, wind, and sun all hit different parts of a tree differently, so that each tree offers several microclimates for small plants that would grow on it (p. 328).

The canopy's effects on evaporation are also mixed. Trees shade the forest floor from the drying sun, but they also suck great volumes of soil moisture up through their roots and transpire it into the air. Given how little rain falls in the summer here, that leaves many understories in our mountains parched, especially on gravelly, underdeveloped post–Ice Age soils. Small plants in competition with overstory trees may be handicapped even more in terms of water than light; many of our sparsest understory communities are found under somewhat open canopies. Nongreen plants (p. 184) deal with this by borrowing water back from the tree roots, through fungal lifelines.

Snowpack depth is reduced under forest cover. Though most snow that settles in the canopy does reach the forest floor, some of it melts first, and most of it, falling in big clumps, is much compacted on impact. Winter melting is greater in the forest, as the dark canopy absorbs solar radiation and reradiates some heat downward into the insulated forest microclimate.

In clearings, the bright snow reflects nearly all solar radiation that hits it, and doesn't heat up as much, at least in winter. But when warmer air masses arrive in spring, the canopy insulates the forest floor from this warmth, and many clearings melt out faster. Within meadows, individual trees hasten snowmelt because their heat-absorbing dark body effect trumps their insulating effect.

Mountain Winds

Our mountains lie within a very broad zone (the north temperate latitudes) of prevailing westerly winds: the average direction of high-altitude winds, clouds, and weather systems is from the WSW. Sometimes we experience some of this wind down as low as the mountaintops, which do tend be windier than lowlands. But a lot of the time, especially in summer, our high ridges are calm for hours or days on end.

Most of the winds we feel are driven instead by pressure gradients; they flow gravitationally from high-pressure to low-pressure areas within the lower atmosphere. They get especially interesting where they have to cross a massive barrier, such as the long axis of the Cascade and Coast Mountains. When the opposite sides of the range develop a strong pressure difference, air pours across the mountains from high pressure to low. In summer, the dry basins east of the mountains develop low pressure over the course of the day because, with their clear, dry air, they heat up faster in the sun than the west-side does, and heated air thins and rises, creating low pressure. So as the day warms, west winds develop across the range—but they don't cross everywhere, they seek out passes and gaps. Salient peaks like Mt. Hood may remain calm. Snoqualmie and Stevens Passes are windy gaps, but the two huge, windiest gaps are the Fraser and Columbia Gorges. Gorge winds draw the wind-surfers to Hood River.

In the fall and winter, we get the reverse: high pressure often settles over a large area to our east, and spills over as cold east winds coming down those same gaps and gorges. This is not an afternoon event but a days-long event, so these east winds blow all day and night. Sometimes they slide in under arriving warm fronts to produce ice storms in the gorges and the cities at their lower ends—Chilliwack, even Bellingham, and Portland. British Columbia's coastal fjords experience similar ferocious cold outflow winds, called Squamishes, coming down from the Coast Mountains in winter. Both Gorge east winds and Gorge west winds are strongest at the downwind end of the constricted stretch, where the air escapes the constriction and can spread out and speed up. (Put another way, the air's pressure collapses there to create the strongest pressure gradient.) On the Columbia, that would be Crown Point for the east winds and Rowena for the west winds.

Moist air that crosses mountains the hard way—up one slope and down the other—under certain conditions gets rapidly warmer, drier, and gustier during the downslope leg. These warm, dry foehn winds have many local names around the world. In the Rockies they are called Chinooks. In coastal Cascadia, where the word originated, Chinooks are warm, wet spells blowing in from the ocean. That same onshore flow may end up as a warm, dry Chinook after it has crossed mountains and had the moisture wrung out of it. Still, dry downslope winds can be a significant factor here—even at Sequim or Forks at the foot of the Olympics, when the wind is right, but

Storm Warnings

It takes years of familiarity with the weather patterns of a particular mountain area to develop a really good eye for weather signs. Whether you think you have such an eye or not, always go to the high country with enough insulation, shelter and food to keep you alive, and enough navigation aids and skills to get you out again, should the weather happen to turn bad.

Mare's-tails These are cirrus clouds—the very high, thin, wispy family—arrayed in parallel, all or most of them upturned at one end like sled runners. If blowing northward, they may presage a weather front by 12 to 24 hours. Broad sheets of cirrus whiteness, if northbound or thickening and lowering, may have the same meaning. However, scattered shreds of cirrus resembling pulled-out cotton puffs are common in good weather.

Mare's-tails

Cloudcaps Lenticular (smooth, lens-shaped) clouds above or downwind of high peaks reveal an increase in wind speed or moisture of the air. These sometimes come and go without producing heavy weather, but more often they foretell rainier weather. Small puffy clouds sitting all day around the heads of outstanding peaks aren't ominous unless they thicken steadily for hours. Ominous or not, they are already bad weather ahead if the peak they cap is your goal. Reconsider: the view will be erased, the wind strong and cold.

Cloudcaps

Cumulus clouds

Cumulus clouds—the white, rounded puffy kind—increasing in the afternoon are usually a stable fair weather pattern, not a bad omen. Along a mountain range they may by evening build and darken into cumulonimbus, perhaps generating thunderstorms. Even if this pattern repeats for days, it may be followed by either better or worse weather. Morning cloudiness filling west-side valleys is no disaster either, even if it brings droplets or if it rises rapidly and engulfs the ridges, pouring over them and then dissipating.

Cumulonimbus clouds are tall, and may have a top layer that spreads out in an anvil shape. But when they are overhead we don't see any of that; we know them instead by the sound and the fury.

Layers within thunderclouds build up positive and negative electrical charges for reasons that remain unresolved. The huge sparks we call lightning serve to neutralize opposing charges. Cloud-to-ground lightning begins as a descending negative leader, exploring more or less randomly for a splinter of a second; when it gets close to a salient point on the ground, like a peak or a big tree, a positive streamer shoots up to meet it. They connect, and one or more return strokes, often branching, jet up into the cloud at about one-third the speed of light. Those make the big streaks of light. Air in their path heats instantly to around 30,000°F in an explosive expansion that we experience as loud noise. If you're fairly close, you hear the full spectrum, KER-RACKKKK! Farther away, the high pitches fall off and you get a boom or a rumble, up to 15–25 miles away. Farther than that, we hear nothing and call it heat lightning. Every five seconds elapsing between the flash and the boom, or crack, indicate a mile of distance. At 20 seconds or less, start considering your safety.

Both the electricity and the chill are hazards. (Getting struck by lightning is one wilderness hazard that is not less likely than getting struck by lightning.) You are reasonably safe in a forest, but if you're at timberline, with just a few tree clumps, stay away from them if lightning is striking nearby. Also avoid cliffs. Squat in a low spot that isn't collecting runoff. Spread your party out. Give immediate mouth-to-mouth resuscitation to lightning strike victims; it can save a life.

more typically around Ellensburg, Entiat, or Osoyoos.

Slope winds are another type of mountain wind you are sure to experience. The air contained in valleys expands in the daytime heat and contracts again at night. A main trunk valley wind develops along the creek or river of the valley, while thinner sheets of wind blow up or down the valley flanks. Up in the day and down at night is the rule. The valley wind, being larger, lags behind the side-slope wind. For example, in early morning the upslope wind begins while the night's down-valley wind continues in the valley's center. When upslope winds on opposite sides of a ridge join at the top and continue straight up, they can form convective clouds. Typically these are cumulus clouds that just sit there even as air blows through them; sometimes they build into cumulonimbus clouds, and thunderstorms. Occasionally just after sunset, when downslope and downvalley winds join forces, the wind buffets in fierce pulses lasting a few seconds each.

East-slope towns like Yakima commonly experience summer days that are ruled by eastward downslope winds in the early morning and westward upslope winds in the afternoon—until those are overpowered in the late afternoon by eastward pressure-gradient flow spilling over the Cascades.

Climate Oscillations

El Niños have brought us some anomalously warm, dry winters. (Their effects are different elsewhere.) El Niño and it's opposite number, La Niña, constitute the El Niño Southern Oscillation (ENSO), the best-known of several oscillating patterns that affect our weather. Our La Niña winters are often wet. El Niño Southern Oscillation is southern in that the defining phenomenon involves South Pacific ocean temperature, and the strongest effects are felt in South America and Southeast Asia. The Pacific Decadal Oscillation (PDO) is a slower cycle centered in the North Pacific, with perhaps greater effects on us. Its alternating cool and warm regimes commonly last a decade or two, in contrast to a year or two for an El Niño. Recent warm regimes were 1925–1947, 1977–1997, and 2002–2007, and probably resuming in 2014. Warm regimes tend to correlate with:

- **warm and dry winters** in the Pacific Northwest;
- **El Niño** phases stronger;
- **few salmon** here, but sometimes bumper crops in Alaska;
- **few hurricanes** in the Atlantic;
- **drought** in sub-Saharan Africa.

The cycles seem connected to shifts between strong and weak thermohaline circulation in the ocean. *Thermo* refers to temperature, *haline* to salt. Off Greenland and Antarctica, relatively cold, unsalty seawater accumulates and then sinks because it is heavier than warmer, saltier water. It flows away across the sea floor, and warmer, saltier water flows as a surface current to replace it where it sank. These cold deep currents together with some of the surface currents make up the Conveyor, a global loop involving all five oceans.

Future Climate

Here's a capsule sketch of current estimations of what our climate may look like in our lifetimes.

It will continue to warm, but by fewer degrees than in most parts of the world. That hemisphere-sized ocean we have on our upwind side ameliorates temperature changes not only daily and seasonally but also over

What Needs to Change

Elsewhere in this book I describe effects of the warming climate—both current and predicted—on many of our living things. I hope that this information will move readers to strongly support a transformation of the world's energy practices to bring anthropogenic greenhouse warming to a halt. We have to leave most of the world's remaining fossil fuels in the ground; we need to develop technologies for other forms of energy; and once we've done that I suspect we will find we need to use a lot less energy. We also need to aggressively develop technology for long-term carbon sequestration. Regionally, we need forest management that optimizes our forests' benefits to the global carbon budget.

the decades. The greatest warming is foreseen in continental interiors, and especially in the far north.

Projections for our mean annual precipitation lean toward a slight increase during the winters, countered by a somewhat longer dry season. (We'll edge toward a truly Mediterranean climate.) The big change will be in the amount that falls as snow. Since most of our precipitation comes between October and May, and since more falls in the mountains than in the lowlands, much of our region's precipitation over the past century has fallen as snow. Just 4°F of warming is enough to make a lot of that snow fall instead as rain, and enough to make the snow that does fall at middle elevations melt away at times during the winter. Climate models suggest that most snow may fall during occasional extreme events when heavy precipitation coincides with cold spells.

The winter of 2014–2015 in Washington and southwest British Columbia was a preview. At a typical snow-measuring station in a subalpine meadow in the northeast Olympics, precipitation for the winter was normal, temperature was a record 4.5°F above normal, and on 15 April the snowpack held about one-eighth of the normal amount of water. It had melted away to zero snowpack for a week and a half in February. In mid-May, a time when plants and animals are accustomed to several feet of snow on the ground, the meadow was nearly bare. Toward mid-July, when in a past normal year the snow would finish melting and the flowers would bloom in well-soaked soil, the soil was dry and the plants crisp around the edges. This is a challenge that some plants will meet better than others. By July's end, wildfires started—mostly on the Cascade east slope and the Okanogan Highlands. There was even one in a rainforest valley in Olympic National Park that started in mid-May.

Subalpine meadow as we know it is likely to shrink. The drier ones may shift toward grassland-steppe, and others may shift to forest as timberline moves up (see p. 64).

Ice Age warming cycles demonstrated that many plants can survive warming and respond to it by migrating. But many will lose out.

Weeds are winners: the ability to migrate rapidly and to exploit habitats novel to them is most of what put them into our "weed" category in the first place. They also benefit from two trends besides warming: global trade and travel, and nitrogen pollution.

Glaciers are losing out already. Their decline began 150 years ago, as the Little Ice Age relented. The Coast Mountains, with their combination of high elevation, heavy snow, cool marine air, and exceptionally massive ice today, should retain big glaciers through our lifetimes. For the other Cascadia ranges, possibly not. Every decade, some glaciers disappear. On our volcano slopes, thawing and glacier retreat expose old frozen ash to erosion, exacerbating outburst floods.

Fire will be a winner, air quality a loser. The "preview summer," 2015, saw far more forest acres burn in Washington than any year in the historical record.

Atmospheric rivers on the West Coast are projected to increase in strength and number, so there will likely be more floods and more landslides. Springtime marine air with fog and low clouds is also projected to increase. Streams and rivers will run a little higher in the winter and considerably lower in the summer, because up until now the runoff has been much delayed by the heavy mountain snowpack lasting into June or July. The higher winter flow will increase the flood risk, while the low summer flow will warm in the sun, excluding cold-loving trout from many streams.

If annual precipitation stays as high as the models say, water supply for humans should be a relatively modest challenge in the Northwest, requiring some conservation and some changes in reservoir management. (The biggest challenge related to water supply may be the number of people moving here because we still have enough water.)

South of here lies a region with a climate several degrees warmer than ours, with longer dry summers but with plenty of fog near the coast. That's the Klamath region of Oregon and California. Madrona grows there better than anywhere, as well as redwoods, the world's (currently) tallest trees and highest-aboveground-biomass forests. It isn't a bad climate at all. I just hope the world stops warming before the Pacific Northwest overshoots that climate. But seriously, for the plants, animals, fungi, and all of their symbioses to migrate or adapt to even that big a climate shift will be . . . interesting.

Plants in general may be able to grow faster and to use water more efficiently, thus consuming CO_2 faster and helping to counter our greenhouse gas emissions. That's probably happening now, but clearly not to a degree that saves us, since one of the things we are most certain of is that atmospheric CO_2 has risen relentlessly for decades.

All animal and fungal life owes its existence to oxygen and hydrocarbons produced by photosynthesis. Bacteria were the original fount of free oxygen; the first plants apparently evolved after animals and fungi. Plants then took the baton and ran with it in grand style, though with much ongoing support from bacteria, especially via nitrogen fixation.

In any year, plants consume 20 times as much carbon dioxide as fossil fuels release. They soon release half of that CO_2 through respiration, leaving the other half tied up in biomass. The biomass half will also be released if and when the biomass burns or decomposes, so it's almost a zero-sum game in the long run. Its benign aspect is equal to the amount of carbon tied up in biomass at any given time, plus (especially) the amount tied up long term, in deep sediments and rocks.

Northwest and northern California forests may tie up carbon in biomass better than any other plant communities on earth. In full old-growth flower they contain the greatest amounts of standing biomass per acre. Even richer in carbon is the belowground biomass—the roots, down wood, fungi, and humus in the soil. Cool soil temperatures slow down decomposing bacteria and fungi, so that wood in our soils takes centuries to decompose, in dramatic contrast to tropical rainforest, where it takes a year or two.

Longer-term carbon sequestration typically starts with settling to the anaerobic bottom of the sea, or of swamps. Some of it ends up as fossil fuels, which only release their carbon in meaningful amounts when an organism evolves the ability to dig them up and burn them in mass quantities.

CONIFERS

If when you think of hiking here in the Pacific Northwest, you think of cool, dark, mysterious forests of huge conifers, you've got the right picture. The area made rainy by the mountains of the Pacific Northwest is the Conifer Capitol of the World, the only large temperate-zone area where conifers utterly overwhelm their broadleaf competitors. It grows conifers bigger than anywhere else, and the resulting tonnage of biomass and square footage of leaf area, per acre, is the world's highest, even greater than in tropical rain forests.

Combined living and dead biomass translates directly to stored carbon, which can help to minimize climate change. Vegetation and the ocean are the two biggest carbon sinks (they absorb more carbon then they release), and the vegetation of Northwest and California coastal conifer forests does this best of all. If we are to get serious about offsetting carbon emissions, we should manage forests to maximize carbon storage.

Our conifers don't just win growth contests against other trees when each grows in its native habitat, they also outgrow natives of similar climates when they're planted in each other's habitats. The superiority must be more in the trees' genes than in our climate and soil. (Indeed, they seem to grow a little faster in New Zealand than here, and are becoming aggressively weedy there.) Sitka spruce, noble fir, and Douglas-fir have been heavily planted in Europe, New Zealand, and Chile for almost two centuries, whereas the Northwest's tree farmers have had no reason to try nonnatives. One possible explanation is that European conifer genes were sabotaged by ten to twenty centuries of "high-grading"—logging the best trees and leaving the rest to perpetuate the forest. (High-grading ruled here, too, but only for only a century or so.) Also, our climate may have nurtured the cream of the crop by selecting trees that handle both huge snow loads in winter and, actually, drought in summer.

It's *when* the rain falls that makes our region unique. Generally, wet temperate climates on this planet either supply rainfall throughout the year or concentrate it in the warmer months. Here, summer brings low humidity and frequent drought, so severe for weeks at a time that conifers and broadleaf trees alike close their leaf pores, shutting down photosynthesis to reduce water loss through open pores. For a deciduous broadleaf tree, whose activity is confined to the half-year when it has leaves, this is a great handicap. Our evergreen conifers, in contrast, get more than half their photosynthesis done during spring, fall, and even winter, when sunlight and temperature are limiting but moisture is not.

Nutrient uptake during the cooler seasons is similarly crucial, since summer drought shuts down the decay activities that liberate nutrients. Evergreen conifers, though slower than flowering trees in acquiring nutrients, acquire them all year long. They also deploy them efficiently, retaining their needles rather than jettisoning them each growing season.

Sheer size is an advantage here, providing ample storage space for water through summer. In many other regions, typhoons and hurricanes blow through often enough to make the genes for great height and longevity just about pointless. (Even here, the Columbus Day Storm of 1962 killed more trees than any one fire in historical time.)

Lots of popular trails here visit stands whose older trees are older than 400 years. We call them "ancient forest," yet as a forest community type they are barely out of diapers; they are not the product of millions of years of genetic refinement coevolving *in situ*. The best estimates say that forests just like our ancient forests have only existed for 3000 to 6000 years. Before the last Ice Age ended 14,000 years ago, our region was too cold for today's giant conifers; it had forests resembling those in the northern Rockies today. Then for 5000 years it may have been too warm for them; much of the west-side saw frequent fires and supported relatively sparse forests with a lot of alder and even oak. The Georgia-Puget-Willamette Trough held great oak savannas.

Development of the forest community hinged on twists of climate. Ancient forests south of the Olympics largely originated from the ashes of fires between 1448 and 1625. We speculate that that period had dry summers with prolonged strong east winds, to allow so much fire spread. Coastal ancient forests of British Columbia look similar but have much less Douglas-fir, because of the infrequency of fire. These stands developed during a cooler time, the Little Ace Age.

Conifer is a common name for a group of related trees and shrubs, many (but not all) of which bear needlelike leaves and woody cones. (They were formerly treated as a phylum, but botanical systematists today are inclined to either demote the broadest taxa or just call them "clades" without ranking them.) The largest family of conifers, the pine family (Pinaceae, p. 54–77, 79–89) bears both needles and cones. The yew family (p. 78) has needles but carries its seeds singly, in juicy berrylike orbs. The cypress family (Cupressaceae, p. 90–99) has small cones ranging to dry, mealy berries, and has sprays of short, crowded, usually scalelike leaves. Outside of the Northwest there are additional conifer families.

Conifers produce resin, or pitch, a viscous blend of aromatic volatiles (terpenes) evolved as a defense against herbivores and pathogenic fungi. Sticky pitch oozes into holes made by insect larvae, to clog them and trap the larvae, or into the wood near wounds in the bark, to resist fungal attack. Resins provide the aromas of conifer needles and bark. Don't confuse pitch with sap, the water-based, often sugary liquid that serves the circulatory systems of all kinds of plants. Broadleaf trees rarely have pitch; conifers have both. The pine family is pitchier than the cypress family, which evolved an additional class of volatiles that do an even better job of resisting insects and fungi (p. 92).

All conifers are woody, that is, they are trees or shrubs. They produce true seeds by sexual fertilization, but they lack true flowers. The young cones are the female flower counterparts, receiving airborne pollen from small male staminate cones. Seed plants other than conifers are flowering plants or angiosperms.

Confusion abounds in the many terms for conifers and flowering plants. Flowering trees and shrubs are called broadleaf, even though a few, like heather, have needle-thin leaves while some conifers, like the bunya-bunya, have rather broad ones. To a forester or a lumberman, conifers are softwoods—even those few that are very hard, like yew. Evergreen and its opposite, deciduous, refer to whether the foliage remains alive through more than one growing season; people tend to think of them as synonymous with conifer and broadleaf, but in fact there are several deciduous conifers, like larch, and a great many broadleaf evergreens, like madrona.

Forests and Fire

Forest fire is the prevalent disturbance type that hits forests from the Cascade Crest eastward all across the Rocky Mountains, and in California. That generalization fits pretty well west of the crests as well, but less so northward, becoming untrue in most of coastal British Columbia. That transition into nearly fire-free forests raises interesting questions, especially because it will likely be in play as climate warms.

For a background on fire, look first at our east-side and the Rockies, a fire-ruled ecosystem. Each tree species has a fire strategy. Pines and larches have remarkable and varied strategies, from the fireproof bark of larch and ponderosa monarchs to the uncanny reseeding methods of lodgepole and whitebark pines. Western larch and ponderosa pine are adapted to frequent, low-intensity fires confined mostly to the understory. Individual trees may survive for three to seven centuries, their lower trunks bearing many scars that record a fire history we can read in the tree rings.

In contrast, when fire strikes stands of lodgepole pine, subalpine fir, grand fir, or Engelmann spruce, most are killed right through their thin bark, or when fire climbs into the branches and torches the trees. These are stand-replacing or high-severity fires. In typical forests of those species, all of the trees are roughly the same age, dating from a few years after the last fire. So those low-severity, low-density stands of ponderosa are actually outnumbered (even east of the crests) by denser forests prone to high-severity fire—and more so today than 150 years ago, when parklike ponderosa stands were more extensive (p. 80).

It's really the forest, more than the climate or the site, that determines fire severity. (Fire severity is a measure of the percentage of overstory trees killed; intensity is a measure of fire heat and height.) A particular site might happen to get seeded with lodgepole pines and soon be prone to high-severity fire, or it might get densely stocked with ponderosa pines, with the same result. That's right: ponderosa pines aren't fire-resistant until they mature, and they also need to be spaced apart from each other and from other small trees that can carry flame into the canopy. Achieving that condition takes more than a century, plus a lot of luck. Once reached, it may sustain itself indefinitely, but not perfectly.

If you look at them on a broad enough scale, most fires are mixed-severity because fires are patchy. Ferocious fires skip over some unburned patches; and at the other extreme the tamest ground fires torch or kill a clump of trees here and there. (The strongest determinants of fire type and fire patches—even more than what kind of trees grow there—are weather and the quantity and moisture content of the fuels.)

When you walk through a recent burn, look at the needles to see the patches. In some patches, the needles are still green, on the tree, while the low vegetation may have burned or may have been skipped over. In others, brown needles carpet the ground: that's a somewhat hotter ground fire. It burned hot enough to kill the trees but not high enough to consume the needles, which fell after things cooled down. Sometimes the dead trees' bark is barely even scorched, as it

Six years after a fire in the Olympics.

doesn't take much heat to kill our fire-sensitive species. In other patches—after a crown fire (one that spreads from treetop to treetop)—needles have vanished, along with fine twigs on the branches. And in some patches the trees are reduced to black snags. That was a very intense crown fire. Living tree trunks have too much water in them to burn up, but if intense fire returns years later it may consume the snags.

At its most intense, the Biscuit Fire in southwest Oregon created firestorms that left patches of ground looking like a gravel parking lot. Not only was the organic matter near the soil surface vaporized, but the fine mineral soil near the surface was sucked out, vacuumed sky-high, and carried off. It's hard to see that level of intensity as anything but destructive. Some burns have failed to regenerate forest vegetation even after many decades. Where a site favorable for forest growth turns, in the course of climate change, into one more suited for chaparral or grassland, that regime shift is likely to wait for a fire to trigger it.

Up until now, though, the great majority of fires were ecologically beneficial. The 1988 Yellowstone fires certainly were.

Shortly after fire the ground looks barren, but within a few years the area may be much brighter green than before the fire. If you come the summer after a fire, check whether the green coming up consists of herbs that seeded in or of shrubs or perennial herbs whose underground parts survived. Seeds themselves can be adapted to travel into the burn on wind or fur or feces, or to wait in the soil for decades without spoiling, and then germinate after they've felt the high heat of a fire.

The pioneer plants' shade and transpiration make new microclimates; their roots, in symbiosis with fungi and bacteria, improve the soil physically and chemically; fast-growing annuals donate their corpses to the humus fund; perennials and shrubs contribute leaves; and forest succession is underway.

Over the past half-century, fire seems to have touched easily half of the forest acreage on the east slope of the Cascades. The west-side is a different story: hiking in the moist west-side forests, we don't see many recent burns. (By "moist" I mean to exclude the somewhat drier west-side forests south of the Mackenzie River and in eastern parts of coastal ranges.) This large area stayed 99 percent green while much of the West went up in smoke. These forests are moist enough that fires can usually be put out before they get big.

Enormous fires did burn on the west-side between 1849 and 1951. Most were human-caused, and several hit areas made more flammable by recent clearcutting. Long before that, there were extensive fires between 1448 and 1625, followed by two centuries with less fire (allowing the post-fire generations to grow into old-growth forests). Whereas post-1850 fires were described in writing at the time, the older ones have to be teased out from tree rings and bits of charcoal, leaving us less sure of what they were like. Until recently they were thought to be vast stand-replacing fires like the post-1850 ones. Closer study finds instead that there were countless smaller fires and patchy fires that left many canopy trees green.

The oldest Douglas-fir cohort in a typical old forest embraces a 30- to 100-year age range, suggesting either that regrowth was broken up by more fires in close succession, or that broadleaf trees partially held firs at bay for many decades—or both.

Another question about fires before 1850 is whether they were caused by lightning or Native Americans. Scientists argue over this, and timber politics seem to cloud some of the thinking. It was probably both. The northern Coast Range is one of the least lightning-prone regions in the lower 48, but lightning does spark a fire there occasionally. The region's Indians, on the other hand, set countless fires to manage vegetation. Specific purposes here included promoting growth of plant species for human consumption (huckleberries); enhancing the yield of the desired plant parts (beargrass) or the ease of collecting them; promoting deer and elk forage; and simply maintaining prairie because they liked it. They preferred to set fires in spring or early summer, when fires were less likely to grow huge.

Farther north, the rainy Olympic Peninsula had at least some fires: Indians maintained prairies, and a long-term fire study in the lower mountains found fine charcoal deposited fairly regularly for the past 13,700 years. But within the rainforest valleys, fires—including the only recent ones, Paradise in 2015 and Hoh in 1978—occur mainly on the south-facing slopes. (The Paradise Fire persisted for months, most of the time in the form of mosses and lichens smoldering and flaring. Few conifers caught fire, but many did die. Initial observations suggest they were killed where fire in the duff layer burned their roots, or fire in the canopy epiphytes cooked their needles.) The deep east-west valleys hold fog in and keep sun out, and the valley floors may not have burned for a thousand years. Vancouver Island's wet side and the British Columbia fjord lands extend that pattern: low sun, steep topography, fog, and heavy precipitation whose summer component increases northward, all resulting in forests whose main disturbances are wind and rot, and fire only on some south-facing slopes.

Since 1950, the trend among forest ecologists has been to view fire as our friend, and to learn to use it as a management tool. They agree broadly that the dry forests need some fire for their health. Programs reintroducing fire to the dry forests have been underway for years.

Though west-side forests are shaped by fire historically, we cannot prescribe fire there and expect desirable results. The argument that suppressing fire now will lead to worse fires later has a sound basis in many dry lands, but less so near our coast. (The sound basis involves increases in tree density, but on the west-side the forests are dense anyway.) And they grade northward into forests that lack much fire but are fairly similar. Granted, without fire there are fewer Douglas-firs. But it takes many hundreds of years for Douglas-fir to die out via succession without fire. Given climate change on the one hand and the number of planted Douglas-firs on the other, I don't see lack of fire as a threat to Douglas-fir numbers.

The high value of west-side forests as a carbon sink is another reason to prefer that they not burn. They mitigate climate change better with less fire. That said, fire may help maintain healthy heterogeneity, and help forests adapt to climate change by making way for species and genetic strains suited to a warmer climate.

In sum, fire science supports a view that west-side forests should be managed to leave unlogged old-growth completely alone, and on previously logged land to employ logging systems ("variable retention") that mimic the patchiness of historic fires by leaving sizable clumps uncut, leaving snags and down trees in place, and encouraging mixed or patchy regrowth of both deciduous trees and conifers. Carefully planned patterns of different ages and tree types—including deciduous trees—could potentially interrupt the spread of fires, helping to limit the area burned and to perpetuate patchy diversity.

A warmer world will be effectively drier. There will be fire.

Trees in a Changing Climate

Climate change is affecting our forests in ways that will likely accelerate in our lifetimes.

Looking at climate effects very broadly, we can say that species will adapt by shifting northward and upslope. During the Ice Ages there were cycles of sudden warming that may have been at least as fast; Greenland is thought to have warmed 29°F in 50 years—more than once! No doubt it went a little slower down at latitudes that had trees. Species migrated northward then. It was a chaotic process, taking a thousand years or more to recombine species into long-lasting communities.

Scientists have published many climate envelope studies that look at the exact climate each tree is found in today and plot where that climate would exist at various future dates under various climate models and scenarios. I wouldn't bet the farm on those predictions. There are too many variables—too many climate variables to make precise climate predictions, and then on top of that you must add uncountable interactions of different organisms responding to climate. How fast does this tree migrate relative to its competitors, including potential new invasive species? Relative to its symbiotic partners? Its herbivores and pests? For long-lived species, will individuals that already tower over the competition be able to live a normal lifespan after their climate envelope shifts away from them? The climate envelope tells you where the species currently competes successfully; but cultivated trees demonstrate good growth in diverse climates. A species' chances will improve where its competitors fare poorly. In sum, future plant communities, like present ones, will be novel combinations that result from unpredictable coincidences in the trajectories of climate and of other species.

(Climate envelope studies do offer guidance on where to plant species northward. Redwood, say, or western larch, can be planted in all the areas predicted for them. Many plantings may fail; some may succeed, multiply, and replenish the earth.)

Aside from the trees invading subalpine meadows, the predicted range shifts within our range aren't clearly happening yet. Elsewhere in the West, warming-related regional die-offs have hit two of our trees—aspen and Alaska cedar are declining dramatically due to warming.

There is a little more certainty regarding broader climate-related trends:

- faster growth with CO_2 enrichment
- pests extending their ranges
- slower growth or higher mortality with longer dry seasons
- faster growth with longer snow-free seasons
- more fire

Since carbon dioxide (CO_2) is the basic feedstock of photosynthesis, higher concentrations of it in the air can enable plants to photosynthesize more efficiently, using less water, and thereby to grow faster. This is the biggest known negative feedback from rising CO_2 levels (*negative* means it's a good thing: it keeps CO_2 from increasing even faster). While many studies confirm gains in efficiency at the leaf level, results are mixed as to whether they produce a net gain in growth. Studies in our area are among the more positive. Apparently either drought or limited availability of nitrogen block the potential gains in a great many areas. Some soils may take care of the nitrogen limitation, up to a point, as plant roots and symbiotic partners in the soil respond to revved-up photosynthesis by revving up nitrogen cycling.

Insect pests have sweeping effects on tree populations. Some are likely to increase with climate change. For example, the worst pest of Douglas-fir and grand fir, the western spruce budworm, mounts outbreaks that tend to follow droughts. The overall worst recent insect epidemic—mountain pine beetles since 2000—swept into areas that had until now been too cold for this pest to mount epidemics, including higher elevations and much of British Columbia (p. 474).

There's little doubt that tree mortality from diseases, pests, and fire is on the increase. But what about less visible background mortality? Even in a healthy forest, some trees die most years. Over a recent 30-year period, the percentage of trees dying per year on a set of 47 study plots in the Pacific Northwest shot up from around 0.4 to 1.3 percent. These were protected old-growth forests not hit by fires or pestilences. The authors of this bombshell study ruled out simple forest succession and all other possible causes but one: they speculated that drought stress in the warming climate must be to blame. Less water supports fewer trees. (I hesitate to present that study as established fact until corroborating studies appear; there have been some partially countervailing studies on smaller geographic or time scales.)

Drought stress increases when temperatures rise. As far as a plant is concerned, our region is getting drier even if annual precipitation is going up. And yes, the climate models generally lean toward increased total precipitation for us, at least in winter and spring. But with warmer temperatures, more of that precipitation will be rain, less will be mountain snow. Our "traditional" mountain snowpack doles out water and keeps the streams full well into July. When winter rains alternate with (and tend to melt) winter snow, the winter precipitation will run off much earlier in the year, and will be unavailable for a large part of the growing season. Hotter air also evaporates water faster from soil, creeks, and plant leaves—another reason warmer means dryer, to a plant.

Depending on where you are in our mountains, limits on the plant growing season may include freezing temperatures, burial in snow, or drought. Where it's snow, most plants should be happy with warming, and trees should grow a little faster. Due to competition, this benign effect makes losers as well as winners. For example, Alaska cedar grows slowly and succeeds mainly on sites too snowy and wet for most trees; even if it grows a bit faster than before it will be outpaced by new competitors in a less snowy world.

On the other side of our range, the dry side, many plants tend to shut down in late summer when it gets really dry. With climate change, that will happen earlier, probably more than offsetting earlier growth in spring. The growing season will be shorter on these sites, tree growth will slow, and drought-stressed trees will be more vulnerable to pests and fire.

CONIFERS: SINGLE NEEDLES

Douglas-Fir

Pseudotsuga menziesii (soo-doe-TSOO-ga: false hemlock; men-ZEE-see-eye: for Archibald Menzies, p. 136). Needles ½–1½ in., varying from nearly flat-lying to almost uniformly radiating around the twig, generally with white stomatal stripes on the underside only, blunt-pointed (neither sharp to the touch nor notch-tipped nor broadly rounded); cones 2½–4 in. × 1½ in., with a paper-thin 3-pointed bract sticking out beneath each woody scale; soft young cones sometimes crimson or yellow briefly in spring; young bark gray, thin, smooth with resin blisters; mature bark dark brown, deeply grooved (up to 12 in. thick with grooves 8 in. deep), made up of alternating tan and reddish brown layers visible in cross-section slice; winter buds ¼ in. long, pointed, not sticky; trunk tapering little, commonly 6 ft. dbh × 250 ft.; biggest living tree, on VI, is 13 ft. 10 in. dbh; tallest today is 326 ft. Almost ubiquitous up to at least 4000 ft. Pinaceae.

This is far and away our most abundant and widespread tree, and one of our biggest. It's the mainstay of the Northwest timber industry, leading in both volume and high value per board foot. It would be a good candidate for World's strongest, straightest, fastest-growing tree.

I'll go out on a limb and claim that it's also the tallest. The tallest tree standing is a 379-foot coast redwood, but the redwood's claim is an artifact of early logging, which wiped out the finest Douglas-fir stands. Two felled firs measured by professional foresters were 400 and 393 feet tall; another with fairly reliable stats was said to stand 415 feet. The 400-footer was 13 feet 8 inches thick, rivaling redwoods in bulk as well as height. Logging may have claimed taller redwoods, but no such measurement has come to light. A Doug-fir planted in New Zealand in 1859 is 229 feet tall, probably the world record for a cultivated conifer.

The tree is named for David Douglas, sometimes ridiculously called "the Discoverer of Douglas-fir." There were many people around these firs for 10,000 years before him. Even to Western science, this species was described by another Scot, Archibald Menzies, botanist on Captain Vancouver's ships in 1791. The tree didn't escape Lewis and Clark's notice either, in 1806. All that was left for Douglas to do in 1825 was to ship its seeds to England, where it was an immediate hit in gardens, and later in plantations. You can say he popularized it.

Douglas called it a pine; later taxonomists tried "yew-leafed-fir," "spruce," and finally "false-hemlock," while sticking with fir for the common name. It is none of these. Like our hemlocks and cedars (two more botched European names), it is in a genus with species in Japan and China.

For a century, while timber extraction ruled Northwest economics, Doug-fir was the top timber species and Washington and Oregon were the top timber states. A century of overcutting finally caught up with us in the 1990s, and fewer board feet of Doug-fir are logged in the United States today than of pines from southeastern plantations. British Columbia is still a huge timber producer, but Douglas-fir's share of British Columbia's timber stock and production has generally been around 10 percent.

In earlier decades, clearcuts in Oregon and Washington were replanted in nothing but Doug-fir, seen as the fastest way to regrow lumber, but current advice steers planters away from Doug-fir in locales that have either of two fungal diseases. The first, Swiss needle cast, infests Oregon's coastal slopes, stunting the growth of Doug-firs so much that hemlocks outpace them. The second, laminated root rot, spreads death slowly and inexorably in patches throughout our region. Both diseases are native; the Swiss described needle cast first, but it got there from here. Swiss needle cast is increasing, perhaps due to warmer winters and wetter springs. Or possibly it wasn't severe in natural forests simply because Douglas-fir was mixed with greater numbers of spruce, hemlock, and cedar. It's a threat in the coastal fog belt, the range of Sitka spruce, not apparently in the Cascades.

Even more than disease, climate change makes mixed planting smarter than monocultures. Some landowners already plant coast redwood in the Coast Range. Since we don't know which species will do best fifty years from now, we should increase diversity, not only of species but of the geographic sources of each species, favoring diverse sources from farther south and from lower elevations.

Douglas-fir abounds over a wider elevational range than our other trees, and equally so on both sides of the Cascade Crest. On the east slope it is considered shade-tolerant because it is more so than pines and larches, which are most of the competition. East-side canopies are sparser and don't produce deep shade. On the west, it is seral, meaning it may yield to more shade-tolerant trees in the course of forest succession. It's seedlings can't grow in the shade of a closed forest canopy. But canopies don't stay closed long enough to sweep Doug-fir off the board in Oregon and Washington; there are too many fires and other gap-forming agents, and Doug-firs live too long. Researchers who watched the rate of species change in a 400-year-old west-side forest for 20 years calculated that Douglas-fir would take an additional 755 years to disappear.

Considering how much Douglas-fir there is, it's remarkable that no insect has evolved to eat it in damaging quantities, let alone kill it in epidemics—at least on the westside. East of the crest, epidemics of western spruce budworm (a moth larva) defoliate firs and their neighbor trees in great swathes. Trees usually survive a defoliation, but spruce budworm gets lethal when it defoliates a tree two or three years in a row, weakening it to where it dies of other causes. Let's hope that a drying climate doesn't bring

Douglas-fir

Douglas-fir

David Douglas

If I were Pope I would canonize David Douglas, giving Northwest backpackers a patron saint. Time and again he set off into the wilderness, usually with Indian guides or Hudson's Bay Company trappers, but also often alone. He packed a cast-iron kettle, a wool blanket, lots of tea and sugar, trade items such as tobacco and vermilion dye, his rifle and ammunition, and pen, ink, and reams of paper for wrapping plants, seeds, and skins—no shelter usually, no dry change of clothes, no waterproofing but oilcloth for the papers and tins for the tea and gunpowder. Often without food in his pack, he might eat duck, venison, woodrat, salmon, or wapato roots; other days he consoled himself with tea, and berries if he was lucky. Once while boiling "partridge" for dinner, he fell asleep exhausted and, waking at dawn to a burnt-through kettle, counted himself clever to boil up a cup of tea in his tinderbox lid.

He approached each Indian as a potential friend, accepting his dependence on them for food, information, or portage while also knowing some of them would rather kill him or steal from him than barter for his goods: "They think there are good and bad spirits, and that I belong to the latter class, in consequence of drinking boiling water and lighting my tobacco-pipe with my lens and the sun." Perhaps they didn't intend to kill Man of Grass quite as many times as he thought.

Douglas was first to put the name Cascades Range in writing.

He figured he walked and canoed 6037 miles of Washington and Oregon in 1825–26. In 1827 he crossed the Canadian Rockies to Hudson's Bay to catch a ship back to England. For all that, the Royal Horticultural Society paid him their standard collector's salary of £100 a year, plus £66 for expenses. His mission was to ship them seeds or cuttings to grow lucrative exotics for English gentlemen's gardens. He enjoyed minor celebrity in London

budworm epidemics to the west-side.

Douglas-fir moved into the Northwest fast 14,000 years ago, at the end of the last ice age. We don't know where it moved in from. Some areas near the Oregon-California line were probably warm enough for it, but its pollen does not predominate in any ice age pollen study. The warm era between 9000 and 5000 years ago established it in the west-side foothills and lower mountains. Frequent fires apparently kept those forests relatively open, preventing shade-tolerant hemlocks and true firs from becoming abundant. Mature Doug-fir bark, thick and corky, is as fireproof as any in our region.

The seedlings are a winter staple for deer and hares, and the seeds are eaten by small birds and rodents. Bears strip the bark to eat its succulent inner layer (photo on p. 380). This wounds the tree, sometimes fatally, by

briefly, but soon ran into the proverbial difficulty keeping his head above water in high society.

He undertook a still more ambitious plan to trek from northwest Mexico to Sitka, Alaska, catch a ship to Kamchatka, and hike back the length of Siberia and Russia. He did cover central California, the Columbia region again, and British Columbia to north of Prince George—capsizing on the upper Fraser and losing all his notes, journals, and instruments—before sailing to Hawaii where, at the age of 34, he came to a gruesome end. Out walking alone with Billy, his faithful Scotty dog, he was gored and trampled in a pit trap for feral bulls. Did he fall, or was he pushed? Rumors that he was pushed persist to this day.

As a boy in Scotland, Douglas was too rebellious (hyperactive?) for school. His stonemason father pulled him out at age 11 to apprentice in gardening. As his interest grew, he gleaned a botanical education wherever he could, eventually auditing lectures by William Jackson Hooker, who then took young Douglas on field trips in the Highlands, was impressed with his fanatical drive and enthusiasm, and sent him off to London and fame. Before sailing for northwest America he was briefed by Archibald Menzies (p. 136), who had been there (and described Douglas-fir) in 1792. Despite his spotty education, Douglas wrote eloquently in his journals. In contrast with botanist Thomas Drummond, whose laconic response to the Canadian Rockies was that they "gratified him extremely," Douglas wrote of

> mountains towering above each other, rugged beyond all description; the dazzling reflection from the snow, the heavenly arena of the solid glacier, and the rainbow-like tints of its shattered fragments . . . the majestic but terrible avalanche hurtling down from the southerly exposed rocks producing a crash, and groans through the distant valleys, only equalled by an earthquake. Such gives us a sense of the stupendous and wondrous works of the Almighty.

making an opening for insects or rot; but some trees survive for many decades.

Douglas-fir's commercial reputation was built upon our legacy of old-growth fir trees. That kind of wood, sold today as CVG (clear vertical-grain) fir, is pricey, since most remaining old growth is now protected from logging. Fir from rapidly grown second-growth trees is softer, lighter, paler, knottier, and weaker—but still stronger than many competing softwoods. A hundred years ago, CVG was nothing special, and was used for beams in any and every building. Beams salvaged from old buildings are now the richest lode of CVG fir.

The most surprising commercial use of Douglas-fir is in fine alcoholic spirits—an *eau de vie* infused with young Douglas-fir branch tips. Distiller Steve McCarthy "struggled with getting the intense spring conifer aroma of the Douglas Fir, the citrus flavor, and the emerald green/chartreuse color of the buds to reveal themselves in the same batch." After 15 years of trials, he got it. A hint of sweetness in it recalls the legendary "Douglas-fir sugar," a treat exuded by Douglas-fir needles under rare weather conditions in northeastern Washington.

Other Indian uses of the tree were also minor: sap could be chewed, thick bark gathered for fuel, and the trident-bristling cones, either tossed into the fire or gently warmed next to it, fortified people's hopes for a break in the weather. Douglas-fir wood was economically unimportant until white men came with steel tools; redcedar was much preferred, both for aesthetics and for ease of working. Only in Hawaii were the war canoes made from Doug-fir. That's right: Doug-fir drift logs washed up on Hawaii shores.

In a Christmas tree lot, the fragrant trees are true firs, not Douglas-firs. But in the early summer midday sun on a Cascade slope, their foliage emits a heavenly balsam with a hint of strawberries.

Western Hemlock

Tsuga heterophylla (TSOO-ga: hemlock in Japanese; hetero-FILL-a: varied leaves). Needles of mixed lengths, ¼–¾ in., round-tipped, flat, slightly grooved on top, with white stomatal stripes underneath only, spreading in flat sprays; most cones just ¾–1 in. long, thin-scaled, pendent from branch tips; mature bark up to 1 in. thick, platy, checked (almost as much horizontal as vertical texture); inner bark streaked dark red-purple; branch tips and treetop leader drooping; commonly 42 in. dbh × 200 ft.; champion tree is 9 ft. 1 in. dbh, in OlyM; tallest is 259 ft. in nw CA; greatest ring count was 1238, but such longevity is rare. Pinaceae.

My image of western hemlock is of a sapling's limbs, their lissome curves stippled a soft green made incandescent, in the understory dimness, by a stray swath of sunlight. Western hemlock is far and away our commonest understory sapling, owing to its efficiency at utilizing those scant filtered rays—its shade tolerance. Coastal British Columbia has more of it than any other tree species, and it is the state tree of Washington.

Western hemlock does not grow as large (nor live as long) as the largest Douglas-firs, Sitka spruces, or coast redwoods. Nevertheless, hemlocks tend to replace those behemoths in forest succession. Size and longevity may impress humans, but as competitive strategies they are useful mainly to trees that need a major disturbance in order to establish seedlings, and hence need old seed trees to hold out until the next such opportunity. Hemlock does not.

Notice the profusion of little hemlock cones on the forest floor, or on the tree, lending it a purplish cast. Cones are produced copiously every year—unlike most other conifers that drastically vary their seed production in order to limit the numbers of seed-eating creatures. Each year, a mature hemlock drops more than one viable seed per square inch under it. Precious few of them will grow into trees, especially if they land on the ground. More than any other species, western hemlock reproduction is confined to rotting logs, snags, and rootwads (p. 76).

On the Oregon coast, very young pure hemlock stands produce biomass at the fastest rate yet measured in the world. On into maturity, hemlock stands do well with density, and often hold a greater volume of wood than a like-aged stand of larger but necessarily sparser Douglas-firs. Hemlocks achieve their efficiency partly by sheer leafiness—a 6-inch trunk can support over 10,000 square feet of leaf surface area, almost twice as much as Douglas-firs. While the greater leaf area catches more light, it also loses more moisture; shade tolerance tends to be a tradeoff against drought tolerance.

A moth caterpillar called the hemlock looper is western hemlock's only serious

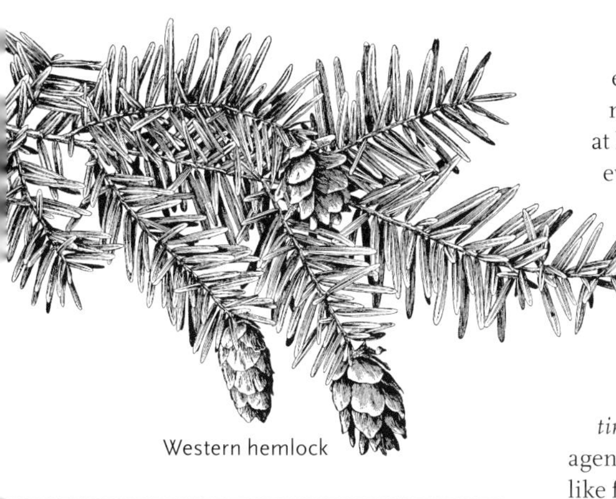
Western hemlock

Competitive advantages surely must exist to make western hemlocks much more numerous than Pacific silver firs at lower elevations, and vice versa. However, each can thrive at the other's elevation. Most of the biggest and oldest western hemlocks are up in the silver fir zone, apparently because cold inhibits the rot fungi, allowing the hemlocks to survive much longer.

Indian Paint fungus, *Echinodontium tinctorium*, is hemlock's chief heart rot agent. It produces huge hard conks (shelf-like fruiting bodies) that were traded throughout the West as the first-choice pigment for red face paint. They were ground to powder and mixed with animal fat. Northwest tribes smeared hemlock pitch on their faces as a dark sticky base for face paint, or to prevent chapping. They used tannin-rich hemlock bark to tan skins; to dye and preserve wood (sometimes mashed with salmon eggs for a yellower dye); to shrink spruce-root baskets for watertightness; to make nets invisible to fish; and on their own skins to stop bleeding.

Under the bark lies a soft layer that some tribes ate to tide them over the lean times of late winter, after the dried salmon was all eaten or putrid. Countless hemlocks (and some Sitka spruces and other trees) died, their bark stripped to keep the Indians from starving. Though edible fresh, the "slimy cambium" was preferred steamed in pits over heated rocks laden with skunk-cabbage leaves, then pressed with berries and dried in cakes for later consumption with the universal condiment, eulachon oil.

The English word *hemlock* traces back to the year 700 as applied to deadly parsleys known for their role in Socrates's execution. The English somehow saw parsley in the lacy foliage of a New England conifer, which they called hemlock spruce—later shortened to hemlock.

Western hemlock

pest. Historically, outbreaks were infrequent but locally severe. They tend to correlate with consecutive warm summers that stretch out into dry Septembers, the season when the moth flies and lays eggs. These conditions are becoming more frequent.

With thin bark and shallow roots, hemlocks are vulnerable to fire, wind, and heart rot. A high proportion develop heart rot by age 200, and become hollow. A hollow tree eventually snaps and falls in a big piece, instantly creating a canopy gap that lets sun in, enabling understory plants to grow.

Succession vs. Chance

In the forest you can see a succession of slow changes—different kinds of conifers increasing or decreasing in number, stature, and health or vigor. It might look like this: deep forest; canopy foliage way up out of view; the biggest trunks mostly groove-barked Douglas-fir; a few fibrous-barked redcedar and checkery-barked western hemlock; ground profusely littered with cones conspicuously including Douglas-fir cones with their three-pointed bracts; but the saplings are hemlock—not one Douglas-fir! If it all could age several centuries without other forces coming into play, the Doug-firs would die and hemlocks, along with silver firs in higher forests, would replace them in succession.

This would happen because hemlocks tolerate understory conditions (primarily shade) but intolerant young Doug-firs do not survive the deep shade of west-side forests. Western hemlock and Pacific silver fir are the most tolerant tall trees here and possibly anywhere in the Temperate Zone. Old-growth forests containing a lot of them are considered late-successional.

Succession used to be thought of as a predictable series with a stable end-state called a climax community; the series would reach climax if it wasn't interrupted by a disturbance such as a forest fire, flood, blowdown, landslide, avalanche, or logging. Ecologists have learned that it's not that simple. Disturbances come in infinite shapes and sizes, they're prevalent, and even without them the path of succession has countless random elements and feedback loops. For example:

Plants alter the soil to stabilize their own positions. Though hard to see and insufficiently studied, the changes are profound. They involve soil texture; acidity; beneficial mites and protozoans; beneficial fungi; antagonistic fungi; and allelopathic chemicals produced by one plant species and toxic to others.

Browsers, grazers, and predators alter vegetation. Human actions thus pervade wilderness, as when elk hunting and wolf eradication outside Olympic National Park caused elk to concentrate in park valleys, affecting seemingly pristine rain forests.

Mycorrhizal fungi can transfer carbohydrates from big trees that produce them to little seedlings that need them. This subsidy helps determine which seedlings survive long enough to take advantage of a canopy gap and become independent.

Gaps are key. Even a hemlock or silver fir will slow to negligible growth for many decades in deep shade, and will reach canopy stature only if a gap opens for it to grow into. Wind can create gaps, though most windthrown trees here are already victims of rot fungi.

Fungal (rot) diseases create gaps by killing some dominant trees. One root rot species lives and expands for well over 1000 years, slowly killing several kinds of conifers within its perimeter. The resulting patches have more diversity of both animals and plants, including more broadleaf trees.

The classic parklike ponderosa pine forest results from frequent low-intensity fires (p. 80). That can be a steady state for a very long time, but since fire is a disturbance, what's the climax community there?

Fungal diseases, insect infestations, and fires (or lack of them) all interact.

Certain understory plants (for example, peat mosses, salmonberry, and manzanita) can take over and prevent tree growth indefinitely. Chance variables determine when and where this happens. Many boreal forests tend to be replaced by treeless muskeg, but this is forestalled where enough trees are windthrown, their roots raising mineral soil for tree seedlings to grow on.

Plants alter climate. In our mountains, old lichen-draped trees can double local precipitation by intercepting cloud droplets; young forests are less effective at this, so precipitation can shrink a lot locally following logging or a fire. In the Amazon basin overall, the rainforest doubles rainfall by recycling it through transpiration.

Climate is always changing. It can oscillate from year to year (El Niño and La Niña); it can slide over a 50-year period or flipflop drastically in the space of a decade; changes can be regional or global, natural or human-caused. The old-growth forests we know developed during the Little Ice Age; forests originating over the past (warmer) century cannot exactly duplicate them.

Feedback loops tend to involve at least three species, often from three kingdoms. Trying to study a relationship between just two species often produces an incomplete or distorted picture. Understanding ecology requires understanding whole systems.

Mountain hemlock

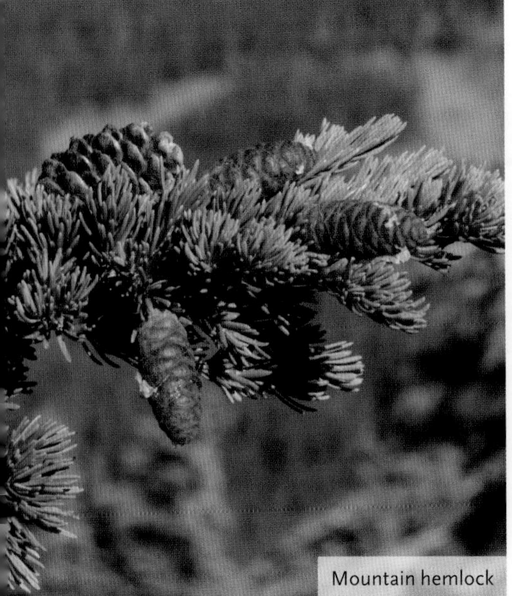
Mountain hemlock

Mountain Hemlock

Tsuga mertensiana (mer-ten-see-AY-na: for Karl H. Mertens, p. 147). Also black hemlock. Needles ½–¾ in., bluish green with white stomatal stripes on both top and bottom, somewhat ridged and thus 3- or 4-sided, radiating from all sides of twig, or upward- and forward-crowding on exposed timberline sites; cones 1–2½ in., light (but coarser than spruce cones), often purplish, borne on upper branch tips; bark much furrowed and cracked; mature crown rather broad; also grows as prostrate shrub at highest elevs; commonly 36 ft. dbh × 110 ft. (average much smaller); biggest tree of our subspecies is 4 ft. 2 in. dbh × 194 ft.; the CA subspecies has stouter specimens, but not taller ones; oldest about 1400 years. Subalpine; abundant near and w of both crests. Pinaceae.

The compact, gnarled shoulders of mountain hemlocks shrug off the heaviest snow loads in the world, from the Sierra Nevada to southeast Alaska's coastal mountains. At every age, this species' form is brutally determined by snow. The seedlings and saplings are gently buried by the fall snows, then flattened when the snowpack, accumulating weight, begins to creep downslope. When tramping across the subalpine snowpack on a hot June afternoon, you can almost hear the tension underfoot of all those young trees straining to free themselves and begin their brief growing season. The stress of your foot on the surface may trip some unseen equilibrium, snapping a hemlock top a few feet into the air. After the trees grow big enough to take a vertical stance year-round, they may keep a sharp bend at the base ("pistol-butt") as a mark of their seasons of prostration. Even in maturity they may get tilted again, on sites so steep and unstable that even the soil creeps downslope. Their crowns grow ragged from limbs breaking.

Some limbs, after being encased in snow the better part of the year, spend the remainder matted with snow mold, a weird black fungus, *Herpotrichia nigra* (which translates to "creeping black hair," but the really hair-like black stuff is horsehair lichen, p. 334). Fortunately, snow mold isn't as deadly as it looks.

Mountain hemlock is the predominant timberline tree of the wetter half of our subalpine zone. Eastward, it mixes with increasing numbers of subalpine firs, which predominate still farther east and may mix with whitebark pines or alpine larches. A little lower are the closed subalpine forests where it shares dominance with Pacific silver fir except in areas hit by laminated root rot (p. 314), which is deadlier to hemlocks than to true firs. Mountain and western hemlocks seldom grow in the same place; where they do, they may hybridize.

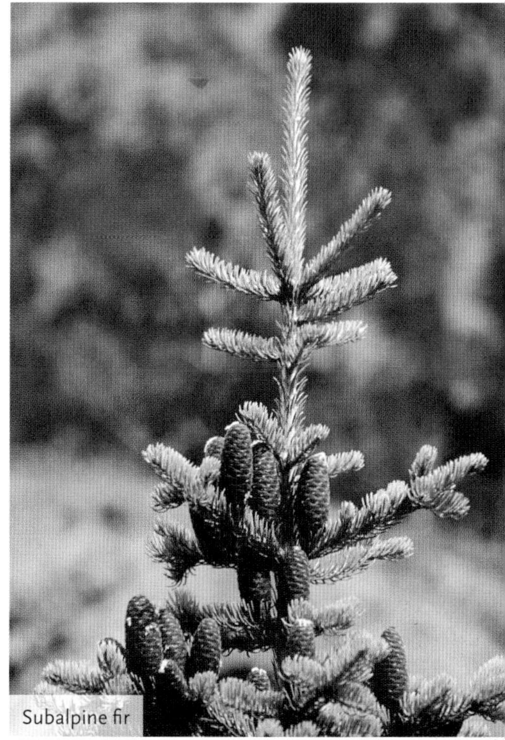
Subalpine fir

Subalpine Fir

Abies lasiocarpa (AY-beez: Roman for fir; lazy-o-CAR-pa: shaggy fruit). Also *A. bifolia.* Needles ¾–1½ in., bluish green with one broad white stomatal stripe above and two fine stripes beneath, usually curving to densely crowd the upper side of the twig, tips variable; cones purplish gray to black, barrel- to cigar-shaped, 2½–4 in. × 1¼ in., borne erect on upper branches, dropping their seeds and scales singly while the core remains on the branch; bark thin, gray, smooth except in great age, without superficial resin blisters; upper branches short, horizontal, lower branches at ground level, long; commonly 2 ft. dbh × 100 ft., or shrubby, prostrate; biggest tree is 6 ft. 8 in.; tallest is 171 ft.—both in WA. Abundant at timberline, more so eastward; rarely down to low elevs. Pinaceae.

Subalpine fir

The peculiar narrow spires of subalpine firs, ubiquitous at timberline here and in the northern Rockies, stay in my mind's eye as the archetype of a subalpine tree. The upper limbs are short and stubby because, being true fir limbs, they're stiffly horizontal and brittle; if they were long, they wouldn't hold up to the snow and wind in the subalpine zone. The long lower limbs escape those

Timberlines

Timberline is really an elevation belt encompassing three lines, each rather irregular:

Forest line is the upper boundary of continuous closed forest growth. Meadows enclosed by forest may also occur below forest line at any elevation, usually due to patch fires or to soil peculiarities. (Lower timberline is the similar boundary on the Cascades' east slope below which forest gives way to steppe.)

Tree line is the upper boundary of erect tree growth.

Scrub line is the upper boundary of conifer species growing in the prostrate, shrubby form called krummholz ("crookedwood").

Everything above tree line is alpine. Everything between forest line and tree line—a mosaic or parkland of meadows, heather, tree clumps, and sometimes rocks—is subalpine. It's deceptively broad: we think we're at tree line until we look a thousand feet up the slope and see trees in crevices on the crags. The term "subalpine forest" combines the parkland tree clumps with the highest elevational belt of closed forests, defined mainly by the dominance of subalpine trees species like mountain hemlock, subalpine fir, and Alaska yellow cedar.

Not cold itself, but length of the snow-free season determines our upper timberlines. Needles need enough time to grow and then harden to protect themselves against freezing. Once hardened, they can easily handle winter temperatures here. Ecologists distinguish our timberlines from the "cold timberlines" in many parts of the world. Thanks to the prodigious amounts of snow here, we get a lower tree line and thus a wider subalpine parkland belt.

Though a little bit of lasting snow may be a conifer's friend up on windswept alpine ridges, deep long-lasting snow is the biggest hindrance to tree establishment in subalpine parkland. (Another is downslope snow creep, which scours seedlings away.)

Once seedlings are several feet tall they can start photosynthesizing long before the snow is gone, but making it past the seedling stage in the open requires a run of longer than average snow-free seasons. Such a run between 1920 and 1945 started a generation of trees scattered across subalpine meadows. Region-wide tree invasion of subalpine meadows has resumed in recent decades.

Such invasions contrast with the normal mode of slow tree-clump expansion. It's easier for seedlings to get their start next to a tree, for two reasons. First, most subalpine trees are adept at layering, or growing a new stem where branches in contact with earth take root; the parent limb feeds the new shoot intravenously, a big advantage over growing from seed. Second, during spring thaw tree foliage, being dark, absorbs more of the sun's heat than open snow does, and melts itself a little well in the last few feet of snow. The well is a microsite with a growing season several weeks longer than the surrounding meadow—just what seedlings need. Hence trees in subalpine parkland typically grow in tight, slowly expanding clumps, often elongated downslope into a teardrop shape. Look for a sort of successional sequence from the edge of a tree clump inward, such as red heather to black huckleberry to white rhododendron to subalpine fir to mountain hemlock to silver fir. Sometimes the pioneer trees in the center die and nothing but shrubs manages to grow there, leaving a hollow tree clump or timber atoll.

Subalpine fir krummholz that has erected a tree.

Timberline is a visible dynamic equilibrium. It responds to slight changes in climate—but so slowly that timberline soils and communities today are still recovering from the Ice Age.

Charcoal in meadow soil profiles reveals that most meadow areas below tree line have grown trees at least once since the Ice Age. With warming climate, trees will take over subalpine meadows, but this probably won't happen soon everywhere. Subalpine fires are likely to increase, and high meadows can persevere for decades after each fire, as we see from the grass balds common on mountaintops of our lower ranges.

Subalpine meadow plants should be able to take over some present-day alpine tundra, but will be held back from doing so by a lack of developed soils. Even without the soil problem, we'd be looking at a shrinking land base for our subalpine zone, since it is already near our mountaintops. Subalpine meadows are likely to be among the biggest losers from climate change.

stresses by spending the winter buried in the snow; their way of hugging the ground puts them where they need to be for layering, or reproducing by sprouting new roots, and then stems, from branches in contact with soil.

At highest elevations—the scrub line—subalpine fir grows as a low, twisty shrub thicket called krummholz, and spreads almost exclusively by layering. Occasionally it becomes a tree-shrub chimera—a little tree with voluminous krummholz skirts. Krummholz is confined to the outline of the winter snowpack, because any foliage above the snowpack was killed by a combination of wind desiccation, frost rupturing, and abrasion by driven snow. This is the krummholz way of life. The tree with skirts may occur after a couple of winters with deeper snow, providing growing room for half a dozen little vertical shoots. The next time a normal-snowfall winter came, one of the shoots managed to survive with some needles on its downwind side—the side relatively protected from desiccation and abrasion. Years later, the little tree is likely flagged, its surviving limbs positioned downwind and above the snow abrasion zone (the first 8–12 inches above the snow or krummholz level).

Subalpine firs acquired a serious enemy here in 1957, when the balsam woolly adelgid reached our area. Mortality reaches 80 percent in a few mid-elevation stands, but it doesn't seem to reach the species-threatening level seen in the Appalachians with the closely related hemlock woolly adelgid. It may get worse in the near future, as the aphid seems to prefer the warmer years here. You can recognize this European aphid's victims (in any of our true fir species) by their extremely swollen branch tips. The weakened victims often fall prey to the western balsam bark beetle, a native insect that is more of a chronic low-level killer than its pine beetle cousins (p. 473).

In subalpine forests of northeast Washington and much of the Rockies, subalpine fir and Engelmann spruce are late-successional codominants. In our range, subalpine fir in forests can be replaced by the more shade-tolerant hemlocks, silver and grand firs. It reaches elevations as low as 3000 feet or even 2000 feet in cold air pockets and scant-soil sites like lava flows and talus.

Pacific Silver Fir

Abies amabilis (a-MA-bil-iss: lovely). Also lovely fir. Needles of two sizes: some 3/4–1 1/4 in., flat-spreading, others 1/4–3/4 in., pointing forward and upward along the twig and hiding it; dark glossy green on top, with two white stripes beneath; notch-tipped except on cone-bearing branches; cones dense, heavy, barrel-shaped, 3–5 in. × 1 1/2–2 in., green maturing to brown, borne erect on upper branches, dropping their seeds and scales singly while the cores remain on the branch a year or more; bark resin-blistered, gray or white-lichen-coated and smooth except in great age; commonly 40 in. dbh × 165 ft.; biggest tree was 7 ft. 9 in. dbh; tallest is 236 ft.; both on Olympic Peninsula; oldest is 725 years. Dense mature forests, mainly 3000–5000 ft. on w-side and near crests on e-side. Pinaceae.

The handsome dark needles of silver fir lie mostly in a flat plane; an additional series of shorter ones presses forward in a herringbone-like pattern that neatly hides the twig from directly above. This unique arrangement is the first clue both to which species this is and to what it's up to—shade tolerance. Hiding the twig from above means not letting any sunlight go to waste on a nonphotosynthesizing surface. The dark surface also maximizes light absorption.

The first appearance of these forest-green saplings can bolster your sense of progress during slow hours of switchbacking up from valley floor to high basins. Vistas unfold, even while you can't see out of the forest. The shrub layer is thinning, showing off charming montane herbs like bunchberry, bead lily, false-Solomon's-seal, coralroot and wintergreens. It can be incredibly quiet, with only faint fricative sounds sifting

Pacific silver fir

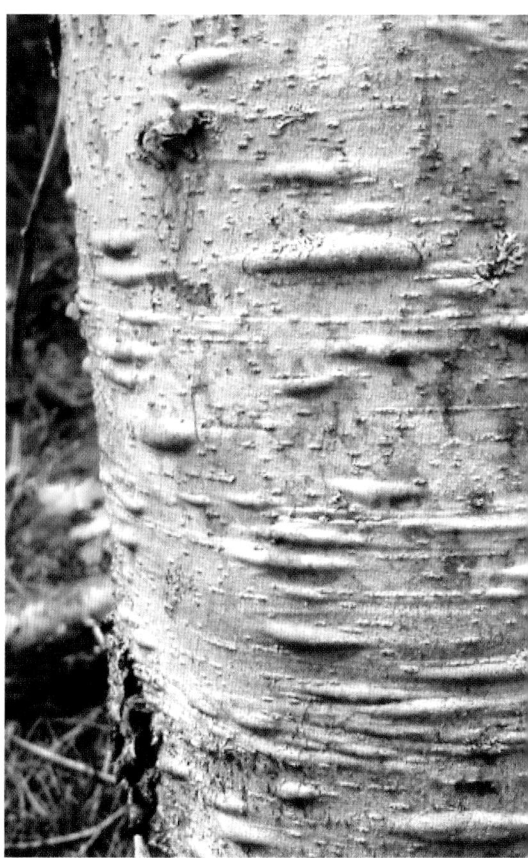
Young silver firs have resin blisters and silvery crust lichens.

up from some torrent far below. A grouse flushing under your nose can set your heart pounding. Don't be alarmed if an unseen assailant high in the trees bombards you in September; it's only a Douglas squirrel harvesting big thudding silver fir cones for winter stores.

Expect silver fir to be a late-successional dominant everywhere you see it's saplings, since it's our most shade-tolerant tree. Mainly that's in a mid-elevation belt that gets lower northward, reaching sea level in southeast Alaska. Silver fir occurs sporadically in lowlands here, and actually grew a world's-biggest specimen on low-elevation state forestry land near Forks, Washington (this tree was "saved" from the chainsaw when it was identified as a champion; after the logging operation took down all its neighbors, it inevitably blew down a few years later). Silver fir can reach tree line in the company of other trees, but does less well in the open, being prone to windthrow and excessive transpiration.

Along with deep shade, late-lying deep snow is a second challenge silver fir confronts. The dry season is often well under way before the snowpack melts from silver fir habitats; within a few weeks the meltwater is gone and the needle duff seedbed may

Saplings Released from Bondage

Forest fires tend to kill all the little understory trees but leave some of the big trees, which then seed the next forest. Some other disturbance types—wind storms, insect epidemics, and gap-forming diseases—tend to target tall trees and leave saplings unscathed, giving them a big head start toward forming the next forest.

Foresters call these saplings advance regeneration. One example would be the subalpine firs that are taking over some lodgepole pine stands killed by bark beetles. Even more dramatically, a pure stand of young Pacific silver firs is growing from saplings that survived Mt. St. Helens' blast because they were buried in snow while the canopy trees over them snapped.

The typical examples in our region are shade-tolerant saplings surviving for decades while so starved for sunlight that they barely grow at all. Though suppressed, they endure, ready to burst into growth if a canopy tree near them dies, increasing the supply of sunlight. Each of our most shade-tolerant tree species has that ability, which is really the only way to be part of the forest in locations where forest fires are rare (there are many such in British Columbia, a few in northwest Washington).

At 4 feet tall and an inch in diameter, a hemlock or silver fir can be older than 100 years. These saplings typically look top-heavy, their longest limbs very near the top. Alaska cedar is a bit different: its seedlings rarely live longer than 15 years in deep shade, but the trees can layer, or grow new stems and roots where low branches or bent-over tops are touching the ground. That kind of sapling receives some energy stores from the parent tree, and can survive as advance regeneration.

be bone dry. Silver fir seeds germinate the moment they see the light of day after the winter chill—even though this means all too many of them germinate on snow and die. Luckier ones survive by putting more of their energy into growing down than up—raising their shoots an inch or so while their root descends a few feet to tap into summer-long moisture.

Amabilis is one of several names we have from the pen of David Douglas. Travelers of his day found that, of all boughs, silver fir made the loveliest bedding.

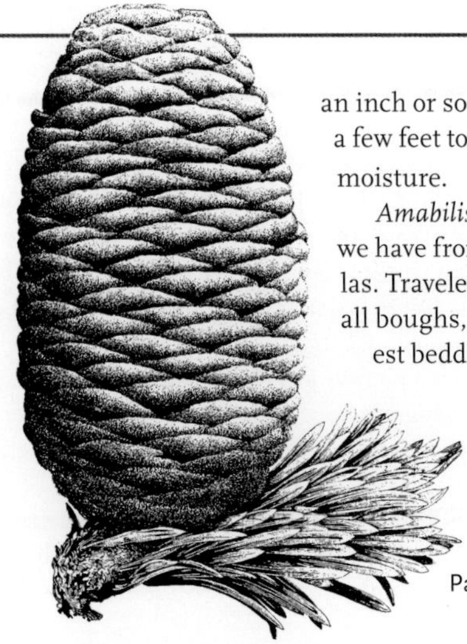

Pacific silver fir

Grand Fir

Abies grandis (GRAN-dis: big). Needles 3/4–2 in., quite broad and thin, spreading in a flat plane from the twig, notch-tipped to rounded, dark green above, two white stomatal stripes beneath (but needles of topmost branches often neither flat-spreading nor dark); cones dense, heavy, cylindrical, 2½–4 in. × 1½ in., greenish, borne erect on upper branches, dropping their seeds and scales singly while the core remains; bark gray to light brown, resin-blistered, becoming ridged and flaky with age; commonly 44 in. dbh × 200 ft.; largest is 7.3 ft. dbh; historical record heights near 300 ft.; relatively short-lived. Common e of CasCr, 3200–5000 ft.; scattered on w-side. Pinaceae.

Grand fir

The foliage on a grand fir sapling catches your eye, the tidy flat array of long, broad needles showing off the glossy green color. Flat leaf arrays imply shade tolerance. Grand firs are only slightly less tolerant than western hemlocks and silver firs, and prefer less rainfall—30–45 inches per year, especially where summer drought is ameliorated by streamside groundwater or by mountain coolness.

That "either/or" preference makes the species ecologically two-faced, with two ecotypes sometimes treated as varieties. "Typical" grand fir is most common below 1500 feet west of the Cascade Crest, mostly in mildly rain-shadowed areas like the northeast Olympics and the Willamette Valley. "Montane" grand fir grows at mid-elevations in the Cascades and eastward, typically mixed with Douglas-fir, locally with ponderosa pine and other trees. Given a natural regime of frequent low-intensity fires, the pines and Douglas-firs would predominate—the thin-barked, shade-tolerant grand fir has been the beneficiary of Smokey's firefighting campaigns. This has turned it into an ecological bad boy: the notoriously "sick" and fire-prone stands of the Blue Mountains are typically overly dense grand fir stands that filled in where ponderosa pines were logged out.

Grand fir's close relative white fir, *Abies concolor,* plays similar roles in California. In southern Oregon the two species intergrade, or hybridize in proportions that vary along a continuum. (Many authorities show white fir in parts of Oregon, but *Flora of Oregon* disagrees, treating those Oregon trees as white-grand hybrids.) The ways that montane grand fir differs from typical grand fir—longer needles, more stomata in the upper groove, more upward curve, less notch at the tip—suggest that it may be part of that hybrid spectrum. Variable needles and lots of intergrading make our true firs notoriously hard to tell apart.

Grand fir

Why Deep-Forest Leaves Lie Flat

Flat leaf arrays, an adaptation to deep forest habitats, are conspicuous on both herbs (vanillaleaf, bunchberry, twisted-stalk) and conifers (western hemlock, silver and grand firs). They make the most of weak sunlight filtering from straight above.

Knowing this helps us connect the descriptive traits of trees with their habitats. Unfortunately for us when we try to identify trees, those flat leaf arrays usually grow only in the shady low levels of the forest. When a western hemlock grows in the open—not uncommon along east-side streams—it adopts a round bottlebrush leaf array much like that of mountain hemlock. Luckily, we can check for the top-and-bottom stomatal bloom of mountain hemlock's needles or, better, for its much larger cones on the ground.

True firs (*Abies* species) are harder; we may have to see cones, since both leaf array and stomatal bloom (our handy ID characters) vary not only from site to site, but from branch to branch on the same tree. Topmost branches in the forest canopy are always in full sun, and don't develop the flat leaf arrays and bottom-only stomata that typify the shade-tolerant silver and grand firs. The shaded low branches in a mature forest are too high to see, and the branchlets we do see are the atypical topmost ones that turn up on the forest floor, either snapped by the wind or as bycatch from a squirrel harvesting cones. We can only hope to identify a cone before the squirrel caches it.

Noble Fir

Abies procera (PROSS-er-a: noble). Needles ¾–1¼ in., bluish silvery green, usually with a central groove on top and white stomata on both top and bottom, typically in 4 distinct stripes, not notch-tipped, thick, more or less 4-sided, crowding and curving upward from the twig, many with a sharp "hockey-stick" curve at the base; cones dense, heavy, nearly cylindrical, 4–7 in. × 1¼–2½ in., green maturing dark red-brown, scales almost entirely covered by papery green to straw-colored bracts with slender upcurved points; cones erect on upper branches, dropping their seeds and scales singly while the core remains; young bark gray, smooth, resin-blistered; mature bark red-brown, thin, flaking, cracked rectangularly; branches horizontal; commonly 50 in. dbh × 210 ft.; a champion 9 ft. 5 in. dbh, died in 2009; oldest is a mere 321 years. W-side OR and WA CasR, OR CoastR, mainly at 3000–5500 ft. Pinaceae.

Noble fir

David Douglas and friends gave the West's true firs scientific names meaning grand, lovely, magnificent, and noble. His choice *nobilis* was replaced in 1940 by *procera*, meaning tall, which fits at least as well, for this is the tallest

Noble fir

Noble fir

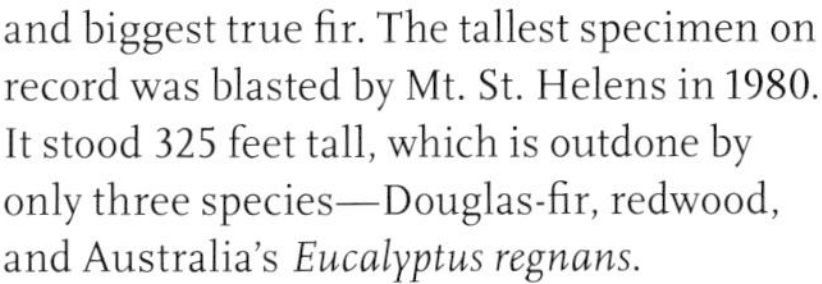

and biggest true fir. The tallest specimen on record was blasted by Mt. St. Helens in 1980. It stood 325 feet tall, which is outdone by only three species—Douglas-fir, redwood, and Australia's *Eucalyptus regnans*.

The evenly spaced annual tiers of stiffly horizontal limbs can be seen even from a quarter-mile away as a fine horizontal lined texture. Clean geometric form and balsam fragrance make this the top Northwest species for Christmas trees and wreaths. They cost more than similar-sized Douglas-firs because noble firs don't grow as fast in their youth. Growth rate picks up impressively after the second decade, ranking among the best. Hundred-year and older noble firs are typically larger than like-aged Douglas-firs they grow with, and one noble fir stand has the highest measured biomass per acre outside of California.

Noble firs pioneer after fire, often mixed with Douglas-firs. Lovely stands result, with massive straight trunks supporting a dense canopy way up somewhere above 100 feet. As much as three-quarters of the total height may be limb-free, since their shade-intolerant foliage doesn't photosynthesize enough to earn its keep after losing its place in the sun.

The wood is stronger than other true firs, and for a time it was sold as "larch" to avoid tarring it with the same brush as the soft, lightweight true firs. That effort lapsed once the supply was too small to bother; today it's mostly sold as "hem-fir" or "whitewood." The trees are planted in many foreign lands, both for lumber and for Christmas. They are less plagued by pests and diseases than some Northwest trees, and should be planted more, especially northward, to increase diversity and resilience.

Noble firs' northern limit is Stevens Pass, Washington, though when planted farther north they thrive. Fossil pollen shows that they once grew far to the north, but have yet to reclaim either Canada or the Olympics following the retreat of ice age glaciers. Blame their slow migration on heavy seeds (poor wind-carrying distance) and shade intolerance; each time the northernmost noble firs are replaced by climax silver firs, the migration is pushed back until fire clears a path again.

Toward their southern limit, starting near the Mackenzie River, Oregon, they hybridize and intergrade with Shasta red fir, *Abies magnifica* var. *shastensis*, whose needles are not grooved on top.

Canopies and Their Gaps

Mature trees in a Northwest coastal forest live on a level that's hidden from us, out of sight way up over our heads. We look up and see the lowest branches maybe 60 feet up; the forest canopy goes on up for another 100 or 200 feet.

Up there, trees breathe and photosynthesize, and many of the forest's species live—insects and other invertebrates, lichens, a majority of the birds, and several mammals. (At least as much life goes on on another, even harder-to-study level: the root zone.)

The canopy realm was obscure even to forest scientists until the 1970s, when some of them decided they just had to go up and start looking around. Research is done with climbing ropes, often placed with the help of a bow and arrow. Key findings in the canopy include countless animal species that were barely or not at all known before; huge masses of epiphytes that contribute much to the ecosystem (p. 327); and great diversity in the structure of canopies and trees, reflecting complex histories.

Some forests develop via an overcrowded early stage (this is common in postlogging forests, but only happened in a fraction of today's ancient forests when they were young). Only the top of a crowded canopy gets much sunlight, so shade-intolerant trees self-prune their lower limbs, which can't photosynthesize efficiently enough to earn their keep. After several decades the canopy only amounts to about the top third of the trees' height. But that will change.

Many of the shorter trees die during that stage. However, a few western hemlocks or silver firs that fall far behind survive as "advance regeneration," barely growing at all (p. 68).

Somewhere around 413 feet (the height of the tallest recorded Douglas-fir) trees may reach an absolute height limit based on the force needed to lift water from the roots up into their highest leaves. Each pore in a leaf surface is the top opening in a sap-filled tube running all the way from a root

Sitka Spruce

Picea sitchensis (PIS-ia: Roman name, from "pitch," for some conifer; sit-KEN-sis: of Sitka, Alaska). Needles stiff and very sharp, 3-sided (flat on top), ½–1 in. long, equally on all sides of the twig, light green with 2 stomatal stripes on top only; young twigs smooth, old defoliated twigs rough and scratchy with the peg-like bases of the fallen needles; cones 2–3½ in., light, scales thin and finely, irregularly toothed; bark scaly, thin (less than ¾ in., even on huge trees); mature trunks very straight, round, and untapering, though often buttressed; commonly 7 ft. 6 in. dbh × 235 ft.; biggest tree (biggest of any species of spruce) on the Queets River, WA, is 15 ft. dbh; there are old photos of a 24-footer in Gods Valley, OR; tallest is 317 ft., in ne CA; not remark-

tip. Transpiration of water out through the pore into the air creates suction, drawing sap all the way up the 400-foot tube. Imagine the amount of force that takes! At some point gravity and friction overcome the capillary suction force, bubbles form, the water column breaks, the tree can grow no taller.

By age 400, tall Doug-firs and Sitka spruces approach their maximum height; on most sites that's less than 300 feet. Typically they have some rot in them by then, and rot, perhaps assisted by bark beetles, will be the eventual cause of death. But some live many centuries with rot, even continuing to grow rapidly in girth and in some big limbs. If no fire comes along to send it back to square one, the forest goes into an extended maturity to which the chief disturbances are gap-forming ones.

Gaps in the canopy occur when individual trees or small groups fall due to rot, wind, pests, or lightning. One falling giant takes several younger trees down with it. When a canopy tree gets a new gap next to it, light begins to hit its trunk down where the original branches were all self-pruned. The tree responds with new epicormic branches that grow from dormant buds in the inner bark. When you see small, irregular branches with green needles, like bushes on the trunk below the still-living long, regular branches, those are epicormic. Larger epicormic branches are the ones that shoot off at tangents, often clustered or fanning out from one point.

A rotten top will break off in the wind. A hormone produced in the topmost branch (leader) normally tells all the other branches to grow horizontally—in other words, not to try to be leaders. After the top breaks off, that hormone is gone, and one or more branches turn vertical, becoming reiterated trunks. Reiterations often grow faster than typical branches because they're getting more light. Thanks to reiterations and epicormic branching, the simple, shallow canopy of the young-adult forest grows into a deep, complex canopy spread out over perhaps two-thirds of the forest height.

ably long-lived. W-side lowlands; abundant near Pacific, infrequent in WA CasR; not in OR CasR. Pinaceae.

Sitka spruce occupies a 2100-mile coastal strip bounded by the reach of ocean fog. While it thrives almost anywhere in the fog belt, it reaches its true glory on floodplains, especially on the western rivers of the Olympic Peninsula and Vancouver Island.

These rivers are extravagantly dynamic, with peak flow in winter 100 times greater than their summer minimum flow. Meandering across their floodplains, they topple groves of forest and lay down bare cobble beds for new ones. Willows and alders pioneer on the new river bars; a few Sitka spruce seedlings may also grow on sites with silt and protection. Leaf litter from

A rainforest spruce towers over red alders.

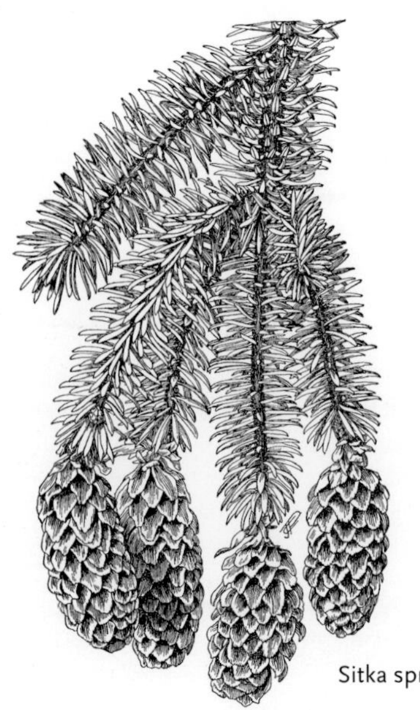

Sitka spruce

the alders rapidly produces fertile soil, and most spruces and cottonwoods get started a few decades later, as the alders start to die off. This pathway produces a rather open-crowned forest—and ideal conditions for Sitka spruces. They grow very fast, often reaching 8 feet in diameter within 225 years. Few of the enormous spruces of the Queets, Quinault, or Carmanah valleys are more than 300 years old. In the estimation of champion-tree archdruid Bob Van Pelt, the champion Queets Spruce is 400 years old, whereas the similar-sized champion Queets Douglas-fir is 1000.

At first, Sitka spruce is the only conifer growing on this former river bar—the only one that can tolerate the frequent winter floods. The bar gradually "rises" out of the flood zone as erosion lowers the riverbed; soils also get deeper, and in the second century western hemlocks and maples get going. Hemlocks tolerate shade better than spruces, and theoretically may take over eventually, but we don't often see these spruce canopies closing up enough to completely shade out spruce seedlings. Elk may help: they congregate in Olympic valleys every winter, browsing some hemlock seedlings, avoiding prickly spruce, and especially browsing broadleaf shrubs, which helps to keep the forest open. Enormous and relatively short-lived, the spruces eventually begin to fall and create big canopy gaps and nurse logs for a next generation.

As you might expect with fast growth, the wood is lightweight, but it is strong—probably the strongest of all woods in proportion to weight, hence ideal for aircraft. It got pounced on to provide airplane frames for the Allies in World War I. Sitka spruce logging in the United States peaked then at more than twice the volume of any time since—except for World War II, when airplanes again used a lot of spruce.

Today the arts claim the highest-grade spruce. It has the best resonance for piano sounding-boards and guitar tops, especially the big clear, straight-grained sections from big old trees. Sitka spruce is easily the most-planted timber species in Europe. A naturally occurring hybrid with the more northerly white spruce, *P. glauca*, has potential for commercial planting on the Northwest Coast, as it seems to resist the white pine weevil, which can stunt and deform young Sitka spruces.

The long, tough, sinewy small roots of Sitka spruce were vital to Northwest Coast culture. They supplied most of the exquisite and highly functional basketry, and also twine and rope, including whaling lines. A spruce twig stuck in the hair was a charm for whaling, while the harpoon tips were protected, and the canoes caulked, with spruce pitch. The Makah and Quinault were fond of chewing spruce pitch; it's fragrant and spicy-sweet, turning bitterish as you chew it. Try some.

Engelmann spruce

Engelmann spruce

Engelmann Spruce

Picea engelmannii (eng-gell-MAH-nee-eye: for Georg Engelmann). Also *P. glauca* subsp. *engelmannii*. Needles 3/4–1 1/4 in., sharp, 4-sided, bad-smelling when crushed, crowding upward and forward from the twig or evenly around it, deep blue-green with stomatal stripes on all sides; young twigs minutely fuzzy (through 10× lens); cones 1 1/2–2 1/2 in., light, much like mountain hemlock cones but scales are thinner, closer, with wavy-toothed edges; often with cone-like galls from branch tips; bark thin, scaly; crown dense, narrow, with pendent branchlets; commonly 40 in. dbh × 160 ft.; or prostrate, shrubby; biggest living tree is 223 ft. tall (n CasR); greatest dbh 7 ft. 3 in.; oldest is 911 years. 3000–8000 ft. e of CasCr, often in n- to e-draining ravines; rare in ne OlyM. Pinaceae.

Spruce foliage looks denser, drapier, darker, and slightly bluer than our other conifers. Spruces are the second most northerly conifer genus, after larches. In the Rockies, Engelmann spruce and subalpine fir dominate the higher forests. Here, this spruce specializes in cold, wet east-side sites, ranking about average in shade tolerance. Though it is large and distinctive among subalpine trees, its three stands in the Olympics, including two champion-sized Engelmann spruces, went undiscovered until 1968. Take that as a challenge to your tree-spotting skills.

Grouse like dense spruce crowns for relatively warm, dry roosts. These crowns often reach to the ground, and catch fire easily. Engelmann spruces can grow slowly but steadily for several centuries, but rarely achieve that potential because they are so susceptible to fire. Wet locations may protect some of them. They like aerated moisture—streamsides, not marshes.

In addition to their cones, many spruces bear curious cone-like appendages—galls,

Nurse Logs

The best seedbed for a Northwest hemlock or spruce is the rotting trunk, stump, or upended rootwad of a fallen tree. In some stands these nurse logs support hundreds of seedlings and saplings while the ground in between has none. Redcedars and some other plants may grow on nurse logs, but are less dependent on them than hemlock and spruce. Evidence of past nurse logs, in the form of buttresses, prop roots, and colonnades, remains long after the nursing wood itself is gone.

By age 10 or sooner, a seedling extends fine rootlets down a nurse log's sides to mineral soil, even from perches 20 feet up on snag tops. Over the decades, the rootlets grow into sturdy root "stilts" while the nurse log slowly rots out from underneath. At some point the support relationship may reverse, a few chunks of rotting nurse now dangling from tree stilts. Over two to six centuries, the nurse log disappears and the stilt roots fill in, remaining as buttresses on the lower trunk of a huge spruce, hemlock, or Douglas-fir (redcedars develop flaring buttresses without stilt root origins). Where adjacent trees' buttresses head straight toward each other, more or less meshing, they were once stilt roots on the same nurse log. Under a row or colonnade of trees with aligned buttress roots, you may infer a bygone nurse log.

A nurse log plainly offers advantages to a seedling. Several hypotheses may explain why:

Competition for light Mark Harmon, who has studied our nurse logs more than anyone, prefers this explanation. In one study area, soil was cloaked in mats of moss too thick for seedlings to grow through to reach light in their first year. Nearby nurse logs had different moss species only an inch deep, and first-year shoots could get through that.

Surface soil drought Mountain and river-terrace soils are often stony and raw, holding water poorly. In some forests, canopy trees suck up most water near the surface, while dim light slows growth of a seedling's root as it races to catch up with receding soil moisture in late summer. Even in the Olympic rainforest valleys, growth of a Sitka spruce is limited by its soil's water-holding capacity. Soggy rotten logs offer moisture all summer long.

Fungal associates Several possible angles here: Decay fungi and bacteria convert nitrogen in the log into forms available to plants. Mycorrhizal fungi, which seedlings need to meet up and link with, are available in soil, but plausibly the kinds found in nurse logs may make better partners for hemlock and spruce seedlings. And in one study back east, hemlock seedlings in soil were killed by pathogenic fungi that were kept out of nearby nurse logs by thriving populations of decay fungi. Termites also help make the nurse log an easy substrate to root in.

Saturated soil Nurse logs are the rule in cedar swamps, where seedlings would drown during winter without a log to perch on.

Litter In high-elevation forests, hemlock seedlings in one study were flattened by mats of tree litter that coalesced within the snowpack as it melted. Litter sloughed harmlessly off of the nurse logs.

When you're in shady forests, pay attention to the conifer seedlings, saplings, and young trees. Are the seedlings almost all on rotting wood? Do the older conifers show the stilts, buttresses, and alignments that indicate they were once nursed by logs? Then look at the ground. Is there a thick moss mat, or a crowd of small flowering plants—enough to shade out a conifer seedling?

Competition with small plants may be the main factor in some forests, but I've often seen nurse log forests where the first six inches above the ground don't sport enough verdure to smother anything. The competition often looks fiercer up on the nurse logs.

A spruce propped over the space where its nurse log was.

or "houses" for aphid larvae (p. 471). Gall tissue is secreted by a plant in response apparently to chemical stimulation, usually by a female insect laying eggs. A spruce gall terminates and envelopes new growth at a branch tip, but rarely harms the tree. The dead needles turn a tan color along with the gall; together they look much like a 1- to 2-inch cone with needle-tipped, melted-together "scales" hooding openings into a larval chamber. The gall may hang from the branch long after the larvae mature and move on. Other insects may move in.

After decades at the low end of the value scale, Engelmann spruce lumber at last found a market that appreciates it in Japan. Very white, it reminds of certain Japanese woods that are scarce now. It's logged mainly east of our range, being rather scarce and inaccessible here.

Spruce pitch is chewable, fragrant, and sweetish, but sure sticks to your teeth. In the British Columbia Interior it was once a valued trade commodity.

Western Yew

Taxus brevifolia (TAX-us: Greek name; brev-if-OH-lia: short leaf). Also Pacific yew. Needles ½–¾ in., grass-green on top, paler and concave beneath, spreading flat from the twig, broad and thin, drawing abruptly to a fine point but too soft to feel prickly; new twigs green; ♂ and ♀ "cones" on separate plants; seeds single within juicy red ¼-in. cup-shaped fruits; bark thin, peeling in large purple-brown scales to reveal red to purple new bark; upper branches angled up, often much longer than the leader; commonly 16 in. dbh × 35 ft.; or sometimes a sprawling shrub; champion is 4 ft. 9 in. dbh; trees 80 ft. tall have been reported. Scattered below 4500 ft. Taxaceae.

Our yew is a conifer, with evergreen needles—but without cones. Instead it bears its seeds singly (on female trees) cupped within succulent red seed coats loosely termed "berries," but technically arils. These are treacherously pleasant-tasting; the seeds of many yew species contain alkaloids capable of inducing cardiac arrest. Attractive but poisonous fruits are few in our area; smooth bright red berries are the ones to keep your kids away from (see baneberry, p. 270). Birds love yew berries, passing the toxic seeds undigested.

Woodworkers class all conifers as softwoods, but yew is among the hardest of woods. It can be worked with power tools, or even carved to make extraordinarily durable and beautiful utensils, with cream-colored sapwood and orange to rose heartwood. Yet few have worked it.

The Indians knew better. They made it into spoons, bowls, hair combs, drum frames, fishnet frames, canoe paddles, clam shovels, digging sticks, splitting wedges, war clubs, sea lion clubs, deer trap springs, arrows, and bows. (Yew species were the wood of choice for bows worldwide. The Greek name for yew, *taxos*, spawned both "toxin" and *toxon*, meaning "bow.") Young Swinomish men rubbed yew limbs on their own in the belief that the yew's strength, elasticity, and hardness would rub off on them. They also sometimes added yew needles to their smoking mixtures, perhaps more for "toxins" than flavor.

The beautiful, smooth underbark can be almost cherry red.

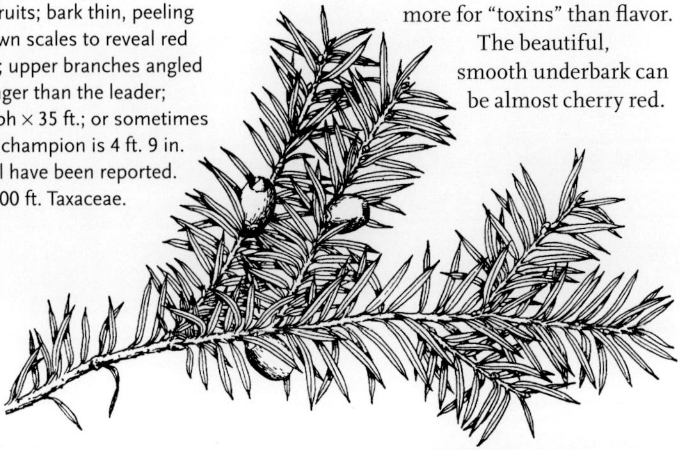

Western yew

In 1987, Western science suddenly wanted yew bark. An order was filled for 60,000 pounds of bark from which to extract a tiny amount of taxol (paclitaxel), the cancer chemotherapy drug sensation of the 1990s. For a few years we feared that bark stripping might wipe the species out in its native habitat. (Those years and the matsutake bubble were the most lucrative recent years for Northwest brushpickers.) Fortunately for yew, the industry stopped buying bark after finding they could more economically synthesize the drug from cultivated European yew needles. Taxol also shows promise for reducing spinal cord injury, and stands as a sterling example of lifesaving drugs discovered growing under our noses.

Taxol in nature appears to be a coproduction of yews themselves and fungal endophytes living symbiotically in their needles. It may have evolved as a defense against pathogenic fungi and *Phytophthora*, a mysterious genus that includes the notorious killers sudden oak death and Port Orford cedar root rot. Western yew is the only species known to carry both of those pathogens, yet it has not been decimated by them anywhere—perhaps thanks to taxol.

Paradoxes about western yew go on and on. The largest of all yews, the smallest of our forest conifers. More tree than shrub in form, but its stature places it in the tall shrub layer. Like vine maple, it will root and start a new tree where its long limbs get pinned to the ground by branches fallen from above. Described anecdotally as a moist-site tree, in research plots it proved indifferent to climatic variation within westside forests. Often called "scarce" or "little known," it ranked 13th among all plant species in total cover in a big survey of westside old growth. It is also common along east-side streams below 4000 feet. It is never a canopy tree here, but seems able to take over from taller trees in Montana's Bitterroot Mountains—thanks to fire suppression, since even low fires kill it. A shade plant, it turns orange all over when shade is removed, but it can survive. I've seen orange yew shrubs on steep, burningly exposed southwest slopes where it appeared they had never enjoyed any shade at all.

Western yew

CONIFERS: BUNCHED NEEDLES

The needles are bunched differently in these two genera: Pines of every species bear long evergreen needles in fascicles (bundles) bound together at the base by tiny membranous bracts. The number of needles per bundle (5, 3, 2, or 1) is the easiest way to identify pines; check a few bundles, since individual trees may be inconsistent. Five-needle pines (p. 84) are a subgenus loosely termed "white pines"; three-needle pines (p. 80) are sometimes called "yellow" or "red" pines. The Southwest has pinyon pines with bracted fascicles of just one needle.

Larches (p. 88–89) bear soft deciduous needles, mostly in fat false whorls of 15 to 40 needles at the tips of peg-like spur twigs about ¼ inch long and wide. However, on this year's twigs the needles are single, and spirally arranged. Technically, the pegs and their whorls are also twigs—very short ones, with compressed spirals of single needles—hence "false whorls." To the naked eye they are bunches.

Ponderosa Pine

Pinus ponderosa (PIE-nus: the Roman name; ponder-OH-sa: massive). Also western yellow pine. Needles in bundles of 3, 4–10 in., yellowish green, clustered near branch tips; cones 3–6 in. × 2–3 in., closed and reddish until late in their second year, scales tipped with stout recurved barbs; young bark very dark brown, soon furrowing, maturing yellowish to light reddish brown and very thick, breaking up into plates and scales shaped like jigsaw puzzle pieces, and fragrant when warm; commonly 44 in. dbh × 175 ft.; two tallest trees are 268 ft. (sw OR); oldest is 929 years. Dry low elevs e-side and in c OR w CasR; a few in e OlyM. Pinaceae.

> Our drive of the forenoon of [September 8th, 1853] was still among the pine openings. The atmosphere was loaded with balm.
>
> —Harvey Kimball Hines

> I can almost say I never saw anything more beautiful . . . the forests so different from anything I have seen before. The country all through is burnt over, so often there is not the least underbrush, but the grass grows thick and beautiful. It is now ripe and yellow and in the spaces betweeen the groves (which are large and many) looks like fields of grain ripened, ready for the harvest.
>
> —Rebecca Ketcham

Oregon Trail emigrants like Harvey Kimball Hines and Rebecca Ketcham loved the ponderosa pine forests of eastern Oregon, and not just because they were easy to haul a covered wagon through. They're gorgeous, and ineffably aromatic in the summer sun—like warm butterscotch, vanilla, or caramel, but with an edge. A little less saccharine, a little more toast. (The Jepson Manual, however, uses *lack* of a vanilla fragrance in bark crevices as an ID character for ponderosa. I guess people vary in their sense of smell, or in their vocabularies for smells.)

That classic parklike ponderosa stand is a product of frequent ground fires. Old ponderosas typically have fire scars showing that fires came through at 3- to 20-year intervals. Picture these as grass and brush fires, neither tall nor particularly hot. They weeded out most conifer saplings and some of the bigger trees, especially those with thinner bark. Here and there the flames leapt up and torched an old pine, too, but enough survived to provide all the "yellowbellies" the pioneers saw. Mature ponderosas are the most fire-resistant trees in their range, thanks to thick bark and high crowns, but young ones are vulnerable. The sapling that stands the best chance of surviving fires to reach full size is the one growing away from others, because the two fuels that would bring ground fire to it are other saplings and the needle litter under big trees.

Ponderosa pines don't just tolerate

Ponderosa pine

Ponderosa pine

low-severity fires; they foment them. In contrast to puny needles that quickly decompose as duff, long pine needles dry out and persist as quick-flaring fine fuel, either on the ground or as "needledrape" on shrub twigs. Falling needles drape because they fall as three needles bundled together at the base.

Those classic open stands are uncommon today, because that fire regime ended with white settlement. First came sheep that overgrazed, eliminating grass fires. Later came "high-grading"—logging that picked the valuable biggest and most fire-resistant pines first. Then intentional fire suppression. The stands filled in with grand firs and Douglas-firs. Crowded trees are more vulnerable to several kinds of lethal pests, and they also carry flame to the ponderosa pine crowns. Today, forest fires in the range of ponderosa tend to be high-severity, stand-replacing fires. Foresters have figured all this out and begun programs to restore ponderosa pine forests, using thinning followed by prescribed fire. This shows much promise, though there are kinks to work out and budgets are grossly inadequate to treat all the federal lands that need it.

All too often, logging companies have taken advantage of restoration thinning projects to log more big trees than restoration calls for. A vocal minority of ecologists think that restoration is often just an excuse to log, and is overall a cure that's worse than the disease. To back that up, they pose an alternative view of ponderosa pine ecology in which crowded, mixed stands like today's were the presettlement norm, and ponderosa parks and low-severity fires were not the norm. This scenario has a hard time accounting for the verifiable numbers of big, old ponderosa pines. I can only conclude that it is politically inspired. (I'm happy, though, to hear them debunk the media nonsense of calling every severe fire "catastrophic," or saying that a fire "destroyed" X number of acres of forest.)

Ponderosa pine has lower rainfall requirements than any other big tree in our range. As a result, lower timberlines on the east slope are ponderosa groves (joined locally by scrubbier junipers or white oaks). Soil texture becomes a factor. Central Oregon's Lost Forest is an isolated stand of ponderosas and junipers neatly filling a patch of sandy soil, surrounded by 40 miles of sagebrush steppe on clayey soil. It lives on 8.7 inches of precipitation a year, the least rainfall supporting a forest anywhere in the American West. Kansas and Nebraska have more—so who knows why the ponderosas in the Black Hills haven't spread across the Great Plains?

Ponderosa pine: New needles emerging surrounded by pollen cones.

Ponderosas less than a century old are called "black pine," because they have dark gray bark, not warm-colored puzzle pieces. They don't compare with mature ponderosas in fire resistance or in timber value. Old ponderosas fetched top dollar, but the relatively small number left today are an irreplaceable natural resource, and should be left alone.

Soft new inner bark, or cambium, of ponderosa was an important spring food resource for interior tribes. While most "pine nuts" in commerce come from pinyon and European stone pines, the seeds of all pines are delicious, fatty, and prized by birds and rodents, who bury countless seeds in small caches. They intend to come back for them some day but inevitably overlook some caches, a few of which germinate.

Ponderosas evolved spines on their cones to discourage seed eating, but pines also benefit from it: critters plant seeds where wind might never carry them, and plant them deeper, in mineral soil often in litter-free spots, sparing the seedlings from drought and the eventual saplings from ground fire. When you see a clump of several pine seedlings within a square inch, it's a forgotten cache.

Lodgepole Pine

Pinus contorta Needles in twos, semicircular in cross-section, 1½–2½ in. long, yellow-green; cones 1½–2 in. long, egg-shaped, point of attachment usually quite off-center, scales sharp-tipped; cones abundant, borne even on very young trees (5–20 years), often persistent on the branch for many years either closed or open; bark thin (less than 1 in.), reddish brown to gray, scaly; commonly 20 in. dbh × 100 ft. tall; biggest is 43 in. × 135 ft. Common above 3500 ft. in e OlyM and CasR volcanic soils; scattered elsewhere. Pinaceae.

Lodgepole pines are tricksters on the ecological playing field. They don't bother to compete with our other conifers in size, longevity, shade tolerance, or fire resistance. They excel instead at rapid growth early in life, copiously produced and cleverly designed cones, and tolerance of any kind of soil. Prolific to a fault, they produce both pollen and seeds prodigiously year after year (a rarity among conifers). Their pollen drifts like an amber fog over midsummer's meadows.

(Their signature punch, related to fire, is a trait prevalent in Rocky Mountain lodgepoles but rather uncommon here: cones sealed shut by a resin with a melting point of 113°F. The seeds inside, viable for decades, are protected through the fire by the closed cone. The fire kills the pines but melts their cone-sealing resin; the cone scales slowly open, shedding seeds upon a wide-open field. Seeds in these serotinous cones are a steady year-round food for the few animals, such as crossbills, capable of opening them. They do get a little easier to open as they weather, and have been seen opening prematurely during summer heat waves.)

As in rabbits, prolificacy leads to overpopulation—a dog-hair stand stunted by intraspecies competition. In this all-too-common circumstance, the speed demon slows to a near halt, like the rabbit that lost the race with the tortoise. It looks dismal to both foresters and hikers, but isn't so bad in terms of species survival. In nature, the stagnant stand might well persist until fire comes and resets the stage, favoring lodgepole all over again.

Lodgepole pines abound in the Rockies from Colorado north; in our region they are widespread but somewhat fewer, and they

Lodgepole pine

Lodgepole pine

Corkscrew Trees

After old dead trees lose their bark, you may notice many of them display sharply spiraled wood grain. In any one species, most individuals lack this spiral, but the twisted ones all twist in the same direction—to the right. Spiral grain happens mainly in harsh mountain environments, and it happens only as trees get old: trees have it only in the outer portion of their wood, which grew in advanced age.

The one scientific paper devoted to explaining corkscrew trees concludes that asymmetrical tree crowns twist in the direction the prevailing wind pushes them in. Our broad prevailing wind direction is WSW, and our trees tend to grow a little more foliage on their south sides, where the sun hits them. The opposite would apply in the Southern Hemisphere's temperate zone, and sure enough, most conifers there twist to the left. However, so does one Rocky Mountain pine species. Perhaps the key is simply the broader point that spiraling makes the trunk stronger, an advantage in windy places.

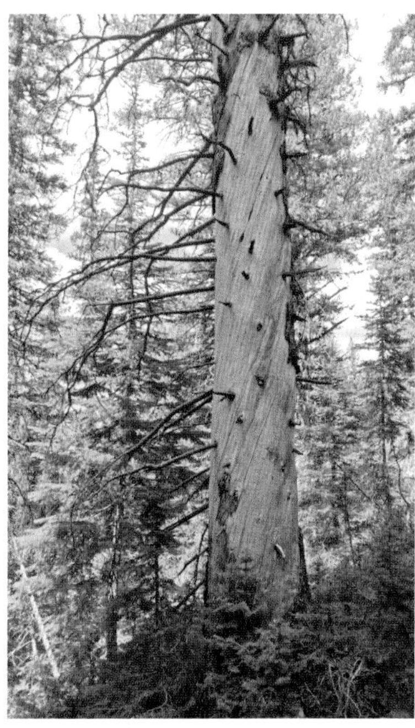

Another hypothesis holds that spiral grain distributes sap (water and nutrients) from each root to all the branches, rather than only to the branches directly above that root. This would become more of an advantage after age and environmental hard knocks have damaged the vessels on one or more sides of the tree trunk.

usually bear cones that open without waiting for a fire. Instead they dominate their sites by tolerating difficult microclimates and substrates, like lava flows, mudflows, and pumice deposits from Cascade volcanoes—especially the 100-mile stretch of Oregon's Cascade Crest and east-side mantled with pumice from the great Mt. Mazama eruption 7700 years ago. Frost pockets with extreme temperature fluctuations are another specialty. A third is soils derived from serpentine rock, whose chemistry many plants can't handle (p. 532). Whatcom County's Twin Sisters, a rare large block of the serpentine rock dunite, support lodgepole pine in krummholz form at timberline. This is our only tree species that grows both at timberline and sea level. Yes, "shore pines" in the salt spray zone at the coast are a form of lodgepole. The species name *contorta* describes that twisty, small type, whereas "lodgepole" describes the straight skinny interior type that Plains tribes used in tee-pees. (Taxonomically, some authorities don't think the two forms warrant recognition, some treat them as two varieties, and some authorities recognize three of four varieties or subspecies.)

Where the Puget Ice Lobe melted away 14,000 years ago, lodgepole pines colonized and dominated the deglaciated land (with its raw soils) for several thousand years.

The epidemic of mountain pine beetles (p. 473) between 2000 and 2013 may have killed half of the full-grown lodgepole pines over much of the species' range. Central Oregon had a severe beetle epidemic in the 1980s, and somewhat lower mortality this time around. Lodgepole pines dominated much of central British Columbia, where winters had formerly been too cold for bark beetles. By 2009 it was an area of dead trees the size of Wisconsin. Lodgepole pines had been the preferred trees for industrial lands there, but the textbooks are being rewritten now.

Whitebark Pine

Pinus albicaulis (al-bic-AW-lis: white bark). Needles in bundles of 5, 1½–3 in. long, yellow-green, in tufts at branch tips; cones 1½–3 in. long, egg-shaped, purplish, dense, long persistent on the tree while remaining closed; bark thin, scaly, superficially whitish or grayish; pollen cones carmine red; mature trees have several massive limbs, not just one straight trunk; commonly 20 in. dbh × 65 ft. tall; tallest is 90 ft. (ne OR); greatest dbh is 9 ft. 2 in. Alp/subalpine near and e of the crests; not on VI, infrequent in OlyM.

With their broad crowns and tufted, paler foliage, whitebark pines are easy to pick out from the other high-country conifers. They're especially easy to identify when dead. If you see a subalpine ghost forest with whitened, forked, and crooked dead tree trunks towering over young spruces and firs, that was once a fine whitebark pine grove. The ghost trees may stand for many decades, giving an exaggerated sense of recent death, yet it's true that we're in the midst of a catastrophic decline of whitebark pines. The culprits are pine beetles (p. 473) and the introduced white pine blister rust disease (p. 87), abetted by fire suppression and climate change.

The pines are pioneers that establish after fire and then (without subsequent fires) gradually yield to faster-growing, more shade-tolerant fir and spruce. Cold limits both pine beetles and blister rust, so warming expands their range. Beetles ravaged whitebark pines in a warm phase around 1930, then were killed off in whitebark habitat by the cold winter of 1933. The recent warm phase, in contrast, shows no sign of letting up.

While studying whitebark mortality in Idaho, ecologist Dana Perkins found some magnificent survivors. One is 1267 years old—placing whitebark pine eleventh on the longest-lived tree species list.

Growth form varies with elevation. As krummholz (dense prostrate shrubs) whitebark pines reach the highest elevations of all our conifers—8200 feet in Washington's Stuart Range. At their lowest (5000 feet) they grow straight, resembling lodgepole pines. Their main range is subalpine parkland, where they are usually contorted and multistemmed, but nevertheless erect up to 7000 feet. Blue grouse find their dense crowns cozy in winter.

Whitebark pine nuts travel on adopted wings. Their own undersized wings remain stuck to the cone scales while the cones remain stuck to the branch. Fat, heavy, and wingless, the seeds wouldn't go far in the wind even if the cone did open, but they fly as far as 20 miles in the beaks of Clark's nutcrackers, who then cache them to retrieve later. Nearly all whitebark seedlings originate from the tiny fraction that are cached in suitable soil, and then forgotten. This enables whitebarks to rapidly recolonize large burns where wind-disseminated trees can only crawl back, generation by generation, from the green periphery.

Nutcrackers cache as many as 15 pine nuts together. Several may germinate and grow as a clump. Ecologist Diana Tomback investigated whether the multistemmed form typical of whitebarks is genetic or a result of clumped seedlings fusing as they grow up. The answer: both, with fusers in the majority. You can't tell fusers from clones visually.

Nutcrackers came to North America from Asia only two million years ago, likely bringing whitebark pine's ancestors with them. While whitebarks were coevolving with nutcrackers, their closest European relatives coevolved as Swiss stone pines and spotted nutcrackers. Key elements to both mutualisms are big, oily seeds, cones that don't open until forced, beaks and muscles to force them open, and food-caching behavior. Whitebarks and stone pines have traits with no clear adaptive value other than to accommodate birds. Cones grow on vertical branches near the top of the tree, making them easy for birds to see and work on.

The birds may possibly help save the pines from blister rust (p. 87). This deadly fungus kills trees from the top down, eliminating cone and seed production early. In infected stands, nutcrackers are thus forced to find the whitebarks with rust-resistant genes. Our region very likely suffered over 50 percent whitebark mortality by 1950, but there seems to be resistance in many populations today, both in the old survivors and the younger generation. A strong new cohort of whitebark seedlings established in 2007 thanks to heavy cone crops, and many of those seedlings that survive 20 years from now will presumably be rust-resistant.

But we can't count on the birds, which are not as dependent on whitebarks as vice

Whitebark pine

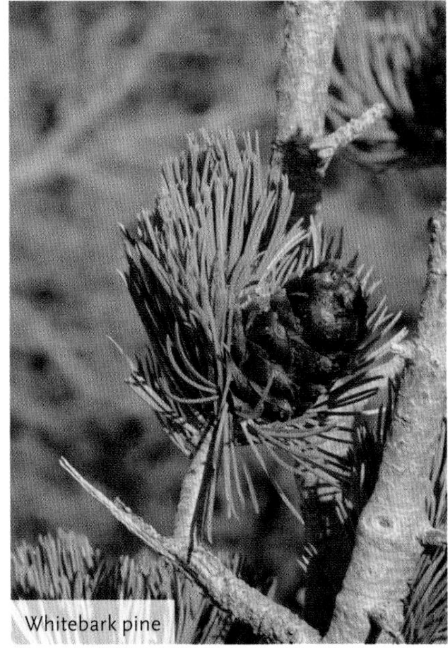
Whitebark pine

versa. When whitebark nuts are too scarce, nutcrackers migrate elsewhere; they like ponderosa pine nuts, too. Humans need to lend a hand in the replanting effort.

The mountain pine beetle, which has been killing whitebark pines in catastrophic numbers in the Rockies, has not yet reached some westernmost fringes of whitebark's range. Still, the pines' future looks bleak based on mapping the climate where they live now and where that climate will exist in 2080. They would need assistance to move fast enough to the new area such maps show for them, in northern British Columbia. Reality may not be that simple, though; they could benefit in their current range if increased fire and drought hold their competitors in check.

Sugar Pine

Pinus lambertiana (lam-ber-tee-AY-na: for Aylmer Lambert). Needles in bundles of 5, 2–4 in. long, blue-green with white bloom on all surfaces, sharp; cones 10–18 in. × 3–6 in. (the largest of all conifer cones) hanging from upper branch tips by stout 1½- to 3-in. stalks; seeds with wings 1–1½ in.; dark gray bark maturing reddish brown, deep-furrowed and scaly; commonly 4 ft. dbh × 180 ft.; the first sugar pine ever measured (by David Douglas in 1826, a fallen tree) remains the largest recorded diameter, 18 ft. 4 in.; a 274 ft. tallest grows in Yosemite NP. Low to mid elevs in c OR. Pinaceae.

The biggest pine of all is this California tree, fairly common also in southern Oregon and petering out midstate, with a northernmost occurrence on the upper Clackamas River. Western white pine, our common five-needled, big-coned pine, overlaps sugar pine's range, so don't think you're looking at a really big cone unless it's a foot long. If it's only 8–10 inches, it's probably western white. Sugar pine is limited to hot dry sites on the west-side, mostly below 3000 feet, and (less commonly) well-watered sites on the east-side. Like other five-needle or "white" pines, it is vulnerable to white pine blister rust. (p. 87). The tasty, nutritious seeds from these giant cones are good-sized, but no larger than commercial pine nuts from small pines.

David Douglas counted the sugar pine as his greatest Northwest discovery. He trekked south from Fort Vancouver specifically to find it after being shown some seeds and told of the cones by Indians. When he found it he was alone in country almost totally unexplored by whites, somewhere near the Umpqua Divide. He retrieved cones by shooting them down with his rifle, leading forthwith to what he felt was his closest brush with death at the hands of Indians. He managed to divert them and run off with his precious specimens. The fallen sugar pine he measured that day remains the largest pine ever measured. The biggest sugar pines were all logged, with the sorry result that the largest pines living today are ponderosa pines. Sugar pine lumber fetches the best prices of any western pine.

Explaining the tree's name, John Muir wrote that its sugar "is to my taste the best of sweets—better than maple sugar. It exudes from the heartwood, where wounds have been made, either by forest fires, or the ax, in the shape of irregular, crisp, candy-like kernels."

Sugar pine

Sugar pine

Western White Pine

Pinus monticola (mon-TIC-a-la: mtn dweller). Needles in bundles of 5, 2–4 in. long, blue-green with white bloom on inner surfaces only, blunt-tipped; cones 6–10 in. × 2–4 in., thin-scaled and flimsy for their size, often curved, borne by a short stalk from upper branch tips; young bark greenish gray, maturing to gray with a cinnamon interior, cracking in squares; commonly 3 ft. dbh × 120 ft.; biggest living tree is 6 ft. 9 in. dbh; tallest is 232 ft. Widely scattered at mid-elevs. Pinaceae.

Its Latin name notwithstanding, western white pine grows in coastal bogs as well as low-subalpine forests. The Idaho state tree, it once dominated vast forests (and the lumber trade) in northern Idaho, where diameters up to 8 feet 5 inches were recorded. Ironically, the hottest demand in the decades of peak western white pine production was for matchsticks.

In our mountains, white pines were a small minority a hundred years ago, and they're even fewer today. You might walk by without noticing them, if it weren't for their outsized cones on the ground among smaller cones from larger trees. Most you see today are young. The big, old ones were nearly all killed by an introduced fungus, white pine blister rust, *Cronartium ribicola*. This fungus may originally have been Asian, as it first gained notoriety as an invasive scourge of white pines (the eastern North American species) planted in Europe. Foresters were all watching in alarm, but couldn't do much to stop it, as it spread first to eastern North America and then by 1923 to British Columbia, from where it spread throughout the West, attacking all of the five-needle or "white" species of pine.

Since the rust fungus requires an alternate host and the known hosts at the time were currants, programs to exterminate currants went on for decades. They proved futile. The disease killed off western white pines almost as inexorably as European chestnut blight killed American chestnuts.

A portion of white pines today grow big enough to produce seeds, sustaining a small, scattered population. Natural selection should increase the number of rust-resistant trees, and foresters assist that process through breeding. But blister rust can develop its own counter-resistance, and natural selection may spread that, too. In nature, species and their enemies coevolve over long periods, with selection ultimately eliminating genetic strains that fail to develop mutual survivability. The main reason we have so many catastrophic pests

Western white pine

Western white pine

(and weeds) in modern times is that all our trade and travel continually make new bad matches between pests and hosts. When it comes to living organisms, free trade is a terrible thing.

Western Larch

Larix occidentalis (LAIR-ix: the Roman name; ox-i-den-TAY-lis: western). Also tamarack. Needles deciduous, soft, pale green, 1–1¾ in., 15–30 in apparent whorls on short peg-like spurs (but on this year's twigs, needles are single and spirally arranged); cones 1–1½ in., often persistent, reddish until dry, bristling with pointy bracts longer than the scales; young bark thin and gray, maturing 3–10 in. thick, often resembling either mature Douglas-fir (furrowed, brown) or ponderosa pine (colorful jigsaw flakes); commonly 52 in. dbh × 170 ft.; biggest living tree is 7 ft. 3 in., in Montana; tallest is 192 ft., in OR. 2500–5000 ft. e or very slightly w of the CasCr; barely in n CasR and not in CoastM, though abundant in ne WA and se BC. Pinaceae.

A larch is something many people mistakenly think of as a contradiction—a deciduous conifer. The deciduous needles always set it off visually, even from a distance: intensely chartreuse in spring, then a subtler but still distinctive grass-green through summer, smashingly yellow for a few weeks in October, and conspicuous by their absence for a five- or six-month winter. You can tell a larch in winter from a maple or cottonwood by its coniferous form (single, straight trunk, and symmetrical branching) and from a dead evergreen by its warty texture (pegs on its twigs). The trunks tend to be skinnier than nearby conifers of similar height.

(The other deciduous conifers you might see—not native, but planted in Pacific Northwest cities—are dawn redwoods and bald-cypresses; they're unrelated to larches but closely related to each other, in family Cupressaceae.)

Relative to other east-slope conifers, larch is fast-growing, long-lived, shade-intolerant, fire-resistant, and water-demanding. Since evergreen competitors photosynthesize through much of winter, a larch has to make up for lost time with high photosynthetic efficiency. This requires full sunlight and ample groundwater through the dry months. Deciduousness helps larches recover from defoliating insects or fires; a larch is going to produce a whole new crop

Western larch

Western larch

of needles every year anyway. It can afford to have a few grouse munching on its irresistibly tender needles.

Western larch wood is beautifully reddish, strong, and among the most valuable in the Northwest. The tree has few lethal pests or diseases, resists fires, and grows fast once it gets past the first few decades. It looks like an excellent candidate for planting both in and north of its present range.

Subalpine larch

Subalpine Larch

Larix lyallii (lye-AH-lee-eye: for David Lyall, p. 171). Also alpine larch, woolly larch. Needles deciduous, soft, pale green, 1–1½ in., 30–40 in apparent whorls on short peg-like spurs (but on this year's twigs, needles are single and spirally arranged, and on lowest branches of saplings they are usually evergreen); cones 1½–1¾ in., bristling with pointy bracts much longer than the scales; this year's twigs densely, minutely woolly; bark gray, rarely more than 1 in. thick; tree broad-crowned, heavily branched or multistemmed; commonly 32 in. dbh × 70 ft. tall; rarely a low shrub; biggest is 7 ft. 1 in. dbh; tallest is 126 ft.—near each other in WA; oldest record 1011 years. 5800–7500 ft., e-side in CasR from Wenatchee Mtns, WA, n to Manning Park, BC. Pinaceae.

Though evergreen conifers inhabit colder climates than broadleaf trees, on average, the most cold-loving of all trees are deciduous conifers, the larches. They are the most northerly and the most alpine genus of trees all around the Northern Hemisphere.

Where it is so cold that plants go for months without liquid water for their roots, the winter wind sucks all the moisture (even frozen) out of needles, killing them. Any foliage caught showing above the snow in midwinter gets nipped, so the outlines of evergreen krummholz show summer hikers the depth and shape of the winter snowpack. But in some places we find big subalpine larches growing amid krummholz, their bare branches relatively safe in winter from both cold desiccation and storm breakage.

Sometimes an early frost "freezes" the needles in place through the winter; they drop when they thaw in spring, and are soon replaced.

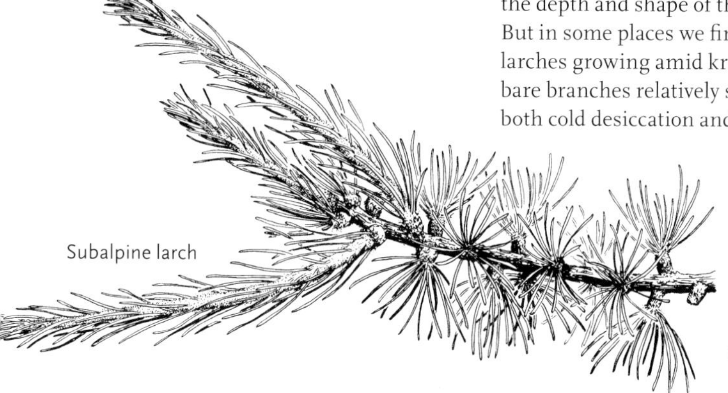
Subalpine larch

While the tree's base is still deep in snow, its upper branches leaf out, providing spring's first greens—a treat for grouse that survived winter on a diet of tough old fir needles. Larch needles taste like tender young grass, with an initial spicy resinous burst. They're a visual treat, too, contrasting dramatically with other needles twice a year—bright grass-green in June, yellow in late September or October.

On congenial sites, subalpine larches reach impressive sizes, and on tough sites they can live a thousand years. Outcrops of bedrock or talus are typical, since this larch needs to be snow-free by July; that's on the early side for the Cascades, especially near the crest, which forms the tree's western limit. Subalpine larches on Luna Peak in Washington are among the botanical signs that the climatic Cascade Crest runs through the Picket Range, not the Skagit-Pasayten divide.

CONIFERS: TINY SCALELIKE LEAVES

This group consists of the cypress family, Cupressaceae. Though the foliage is typically compressed and scalelike at maturity, most family members also have a juvenile phase of sharp, spinelike needles up to 3/4 inch long, closely packed along the stem. These differ from other conifer needles in being arranged (like the mature scales) in opposite pairs or in whorls of three. In the three genera we call cedars, juvenile foliage grows only for the seedlings' first year or two, but in many junipers it continues for years—through sapling size and even into maturity on lower branches. Common juniper is included here to keep the family together; its leaves are all of the "juvenile" spinelike type, never scalelike.

Western Redcedar

Thuja plicata (THOO-ya: a Greek name for some tree; plic-AY-ta: pleated). Leaves tiny, yellowish green, in opposite pairs, tightly encasing the twig, strongly flattened, the twig or leaf 4–8 times wider than thick; foliage dies after 3–4 years, turning orange-brown but persisting several months before falling; cones about 1/2 in. long, consisting of 3 opposite pairs of seed-bearing scales, plus a narrow sterile pair at the tip and 0–2 tiny sterile pairs at the base; bark reddish, thin (1 in. or less), peeling in fibrous vertical strips; leader drooping; trunk very tapered, its base fluting and buttressing with age; commonly 7 ft. dbh × 200 ft.; a champion with 19 ft. 8 in. dbh blew down in 2014; greatest ring count 1460 years (older cedars doubtless exist with rotten hearts, which can't be ring-counted). Moist or wet sites below 4200 ft. Cupressaceae.

Cedars are manifestly a breed apart, easily recognized (as a family) by their droopy sprays of foliage and vertical-fibrous bark. The bark is relatively clean, being too acidic to encourage lichens, fungi, or moss. Though slow-growing, our cedars resist windthrow, rot, and insect attack, and commonly live over 1000 years. Western redcedars can develop buttressed waistlines 30 to 60 feet around.

Pure stands of redcedar can occur on ground too wet for other big trees, or they can develop very slowly where moist forests go more than 1000 years without fire. That is the case over much of the Olympic Peninsula's coastal plain, and in many coastal forests of British Columbia, where redcedar is the provincial tree. The Olympic populations are decimated and the British Columbia ones are heading the same way: cedar is being logged disproportionately, and it does not reseed itself effectively.

Western redcedar

Scattered individuals are fairly widespread region-wide. Once established, they are too tolerant to shade out, and they also tend to make the soil more alkaline, which favors redcedar seedlings over hemlocks. East of the crests, their soil moisture requirement—about 12 percent through August—limits them to year-round seeps, typically in ravines. As long as their roots are wet, they can venture into drier climates than hemlocks or silver firs. Western redcedar branches and fallen trunks in contact with earth can produce roots and stems that grow into new trees.

Redcedar stood at the crux of Northwest Coast culture. Easy to work with stone tools and fire, the wood made up in durability and aesthetics what it lacked in strength. Cedar canoes up to 60 feet long by 8 feet wide enabled trade, war, and whaling to flourish along the coast. They took a long time to make. Chisels and fire were used for felling, fire and adzes for hollowing, then the hollow was filled with water and heated with hot rocks until the canoe was flexible enough to widen by inserting thwarts. Cedars were rarely felled, though. For houses, planks up to 33 feet long were split out from standing live cedars, using wedges of yew wood or antler. Thin planks were steamed and bent into boxes—a stellar art medium along with baskets woven from cedar and spruce roots. Cedar branches were softened in water until they could be twined into ropes strong enough to tow dead whales. Cedar bark was stripped, shredded with deer bone, and put to more uses than any other part of the tree: roofing, warm clothing, soft cradle lining, menstrual pads, floor mats, blankets, hats, dishes, among others.

Buds, twigs, seeds, leaves, and bark had medicinal uses. Cedar charms sanctified or warded off spirits of the recently deceased. Cedar bough switches were skin scrubbers for both routine and ceremonial bathing. A Lummi boy preparing for his spirit quest would rub himself with cedar switches, then tie them to the top of a cedar tree.

Western redcedar

Western redcedar

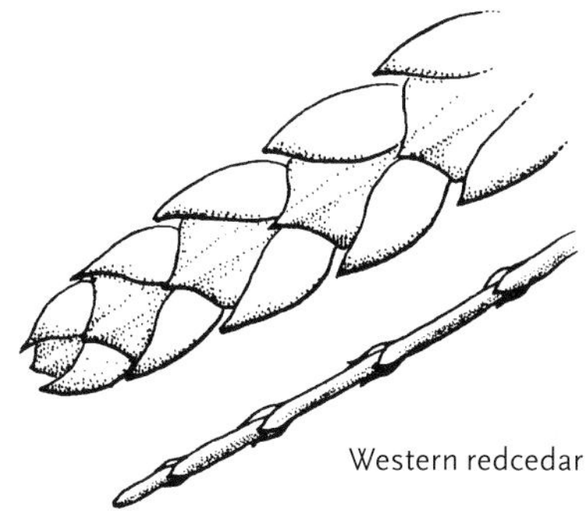
Western redcedar

Aromas of Cedar

Western redcedar aroma beautifies cedar cabins and saunas. I poke my fire with split cedar and leave it smoldering like incense. You may know the fragrance of eastern redcedar, *Juniperus virginianus*, from cedar chests and other moth-repellent products. Port Orford cedar wood is so fragrant I would buy it as a perfume.

Alaska cedar, on the other hand, invokes descriptors like "musty," "raw potato," "old damp menthol cigarette butts in dirt," and "old bong water." Coastal tribes avoided it when building lodges or making fires; some held that it made people crazy. Millworkers subjected to its sawdust suffer everything from headaches and laxative effects to kidney problems. The fragrant cedars also cause asthma in many millworkers, and I do not recommend cedar shavings as beds for pets. But wait, there's an up side: recent studies find that Alaska cedar oils are powerful, long-lasting mosquito repellents and insecticides. The most promising one, nootkatone, is also found in grapefruit and is in commercial use as a grapefruit-essence flavoring. Human trials of it as a repellent have begun. For it to pan out, the cost of producing it would have to drop precipitously, and it would have to prove safe when left on the skin day after day, not just when eaten in minute amounts in grapefruit.

The pine family evolved resins as a defense against insect pests. The cypress family (our "cedars") is far less resinous, but instead evolved these aromatic tropolones that combat both rot and insects. This has worked well for them, as you can tell from the number of oldest, biggest, and tallest tree species that are in this family. (The family was recently enlarged to include redwood and giant sequoia, formerly in the bald-cypress family.)

Hyphens have long been used in common names that are not true cedars, true firs, and so on; those hyphens have fallen out of favor, except in Douglas-fir. The true cedars, genus *Cedrus* in the pine family, are native to the Himalayas and the Mediterranean, and are much planted in Pacific Northwest cities. There was no good reason for naming our cedars after them, as they have little in common except beauty.

Each of our cypress family genera, aside from *Juniperus,* has other members in the Americas or East Asia, but none in Europe. *Tsuga* and *Pseudotsuga* are also shared only with East Asia, whereas pines, spruces, larches, and true firs circle the globe.

Surprisingly, Northwest cultures have put redcedar to all these uses for only about 3500 years. Pollen in buried sediments shows that redcedar was uncommon here before a small climatic cooling around 5500 years ago. It took another 2000 years for big specimens to become common, and for people to learn how to reduce them to usable pieces. That transformative advance together with another one they made at around the same time—preserving salmon—set them on the path to becoming one of the richest and most artistic cultures north of Mexico.

Cedar heartwood is warm red, weathering to silver-gray; it smells wonderful, resists rot, and splits very straight if it comes from an old, slow-grown tree. Shakes of split cedar made superlative roofs in pioneer days. Flammability makes them a poor choice today, considering all the alternatives and the overexploitation of the old cedar resource.

Alaska cedar

Alaska Cedar

Callitropsis nootkatensis (cali-TROP-sis: resembling genus *Callitris*; nootka-TEN-sis: of Nootka, BC). Also yellow-cedar; *Chamaecyparis nootkatensis, Xanthocyparis nootkatensis, Cupressus nootkatensis.* Leaves tiny, bluish green, encasing twig but diverging from it at the sharp tips, prickly feeling, the twig or leaf up to twice as wide as it is thick; foliage turns brown after 2 years but persists another year before falling; cones round, less than ½ in., like hard green bumpy berries their first year, brown and woody the second year and opening into 4–8 scales like tiny shields with a central prickle; bark thin, silvery gray, red-brown inside and on saplings, flaking in thin strips; leader and branch tips very droopy; mature bases fluted; trees commonly 4 ft. dbh × 130 ft., or alpine krummholz. A biggest tree 13 ft. 8 in. dbh × 200 ft. fell in 2010; greatest ring count is 1834. Moist subalpine forest, wet n aspects, avalanche tracks. Cupressaceae.

The name "weeping cedar" suggests itself for this lovely tree whose willowy branches slough snow. Flexibility minimizes snow breakage, whether from accumulation on the limbs, snow creep on a slope, or avalanches. Alaska cedar fills the upper parts of many avalanche tracks, while lower down it is likely outnumbered by faster-growing Sitka alders. Soggy, steep north slopes with devil's club and sword ferns typify Alaska cedar habitat, but it is also found on dry, rocky, exposed ridgetops. Apparently it selects not wet sites but poor ones, as it grows too slowly to thrive with vigorous competition.

A spell of sunny weather while the soil is frozen may kill upper parts of the tree, bleaching them to white "spike-tops." The wood resists rot and insects so well that wood in snags dead for 80 years is just as strong as it ever was.

Alaska cedar is probably the longest-lived plant

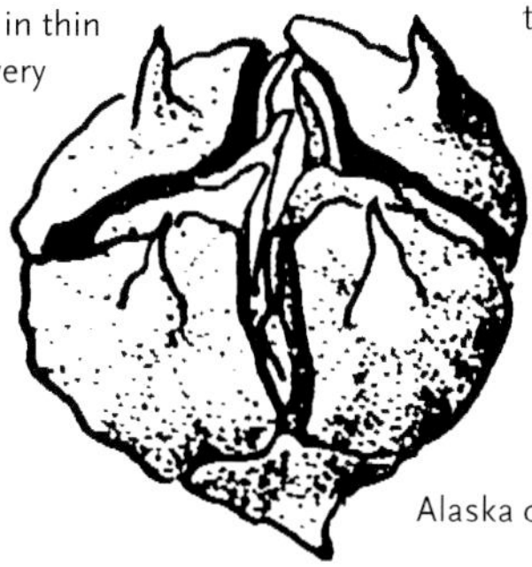

Alaska cedar cone

in the Pacific Northwest. Proof of that may never arrive, as the oldest cedars have heart rot, which prevents complete ring counts. It was not given a place among the world's giants until 1989, when the first of several huge specimens was found on Vancouver Island. Measured by volume, only seven conifer species (and only three in Canada) can best the champion Alaska cedar.

Alaska cedar wood is much harder and heavier than western redcedar, and clear pale yellow with faint annual rings. Its durability when soaked led Alaskans to use it for fishing boats, the US Navy for small craft during World War II, the Japanese for temples, Oregonians for hot tubs, and the Haida, Tlingit, and Tsimshian for canoes, paddles, and mortuary ("totem") poles. Indians found the inner bark even softer and finer than western redcedar's; they stripped, soaked, and pounded it for weaving and plaiting into clothing, bedding, or rope. Little Alaska cedar is logged in Oregon or Washington, but much is logged in coastal British Columbia and Alaska and shipped to Japan because of its close resemblance to the revered *hinoki* (*Chamaecyparis obtusa*).

In the lower part of its elevational range in coastal Alaska and into British Columbia, Alaska cedar has been gradually dying off and failing to regenerate. Researchers blame this on a warming climate, but not on anthropogenic warming, since it began around 1880, the end of the Little Ice Age. Paradoxically, the trees are dying of cold because of warmer winters. In wet soils, a cold snap can damage the tree's shallow roots when they lack a good winter blanket of snow. Either of two conditions can protect the cedars: well-drained soil or a snowpack deep enough to outlast the cold weather each spring. In our range the species fortunately grows mainly in well-drained soil.

You can find four different genus names for this species even in very recent publications. Its first scientific name, in 1824, treated it as a cypress, *Cupressus nootkatensis*. Over most of the next two centuries it was placed instead with Port Orford cedar, in *Chamaecyparis*. The current brouhaha erupted after a new species was discovered deep in the jungles of Vietnam. Its discoverers coined a new genus name, *Xanthocyparis*, for it together with Alaska cedar. That event landed in the midst of debates over what are the closest relationships among those two, Port Orford cedar, *Juniperus*, and Eurasian and California cypresses. The name *Callitropsis* turned up in a musty, little-read nineteenth-century publication, and has priority if Alaska cedar warrants a genus to itself, and potentially also if it is combined with California cypresses.

Alaska cedar

Alaska cedar

Incense Cedar

Calocedrus decurrens (cal-o-SEE-drus: beautiful cedar; de-CUR-enz: running down). Also *Libocedrus decurrens*. Leaves small, average 1/4 in. but up to 3/4 in. on large twigs, yellowish green, tightly encasing the twig, flattened, the twig or leaf 3–6 times wider than thick, in opposite pairs that combine as

Incense cedar

whorls of 4; cones about 1 in., of apparently only 3 scales; seeds with 2 unequal wings; bark red-brown weathering grayish, fibrous but smooth, furrowed, up to 4 in. thick; leader erect; crown typically dense and neatly conical; commonly 40 in. dbh × 140 ft. Record trees are in sw OR: one 15 ft. dbh; one 229 ft. tall; one possibly 933 years old. Sunny slopes below 4000 ft.; OR CasR and on Marys Peak. Cupressaceae.

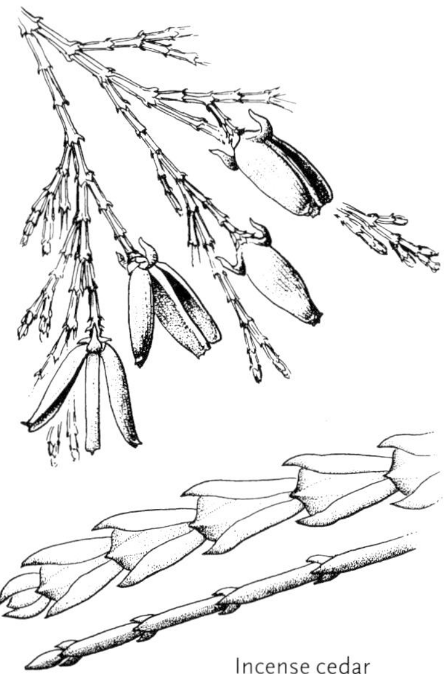
Incense cedar

Incense cedar's aroma takes some of us back to school days when we first sharpened pencils. Ticonderoga pencils are still made from incense cedar. The lumber often has fine parallel, linear holes left in it by a shelf fungus, *Tyromyces amarus*. Fashions in some decades found that defect attractive.

Outliers of a primarily Californian range, our incense cedars grow on hot dry sites in Oregon. Not quite as fire-resistant as Douglas-fir and ponderosa pine, they may increase in between fires.

A year-old incense cedar seedling displays several juvenile leaf styles. First come the two cotyledons, or "seed leaves," about 1 inch by 1/8 inch. Above these grow needles half as large, in whorls of four. As soon as the seedling branches, it graduates to scalelike, close-packed foliage.

Western Juniper

Juniperus occidentalis (ju-NIP-er-us: the Roman name; ox-i-den-TAY-lis: western). Mature leaves tiny, scalelike, yellowish green, tightly encasing the twig in whorls of 3, each whorl rotated 60 degrees; juvenile leaves (on seedlings, saplings, lowest limbs of young trees) needlelike, average 1/4 in., prickly; cones berrylike, blue to blue-black, rather dry, resinous, 1- to 3-seeded, 1/4 in.; bark red-brown, fibrous, shreddy; dense small pyramidal trees commonly 18 in. dbh × 30 ft., with limbs nearly to the ground; or shrubs. Dry low e-side, OR; Klickitat and possibly Chelan Counties, WA. Cupressaceae.

These are dry-country trees with no defense against fire; their strategy is to grow where fire can't reach them—where there's too little vegetation to spread it. After reaching large size, a juniper tree can survive some low fires because its own shade and litter create a small grass-free firebreak.

In central Oregon, this species has spread dramatically over the past 130 years, with sweeping effects on hydrology, erosion, and ecology. The spread is often attributed to fire suppression, but another theory blames livestock grazing for reducing the cover

Western juniper

Western juniper

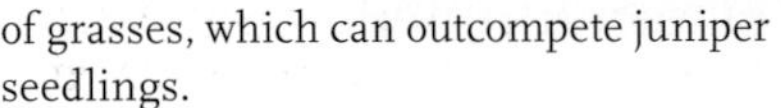

of grasses, which can outcompete juniper seedlings.

A tree with a diameter of 12 feet 9 inches and a height of 86 feet, in the Sierra Nevada, is widely listed as the biggest western juniper; another one there died at 2675 years of age, which puts the species in fourth place among longest-lived tree species. However, a top juniper expert reclassified those Sierra Nevada junipers as a new species, *J. grandis*. Western junipers by the new narrower definition are not so big, but still do get on in years. One in Oregon's Ochoco Mountains is about 1600 years old.

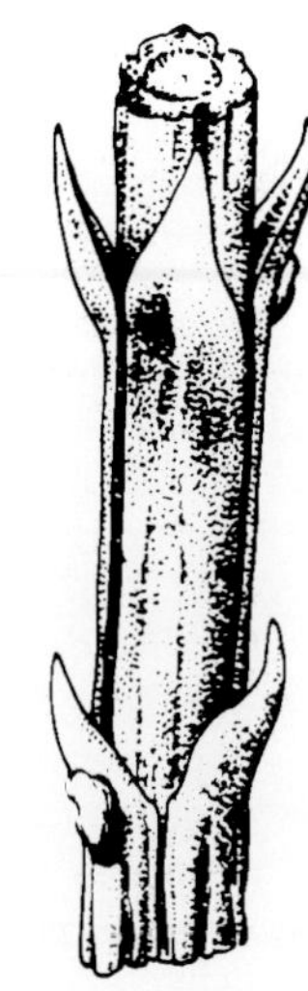
Western juniper

Junipers are richly aromatic with insect-repellent and disinfectant chemistry. Native Americans boiled juniper leaves to steam sickness out of a house, or to bathe a sick person in juniper leaf tea.

Similar Rocky Mountain juniper, *J. scopulorum*, with 4-angled stems, occurs in a few spots near Ross Lake and the dry sides of the Olympics and Vancouver Island.

Common Juniper

Juniperus communis (com-YOU-nis: common). Leaves all 1/4–3/4 in., sharp, curved upward, closely packed along the twig in whorls of 3, from a distinct joint at each leaf base (unlike juvenile *J. occidentalis*, whose 3-whorled needles bend sharply, with no joint, to run down the twig); cones berrylike, blue-black with bloom, round and quite fleshy, 1/4–3/8 in., 1–3-seeded, resinous but sweet; bark red-brown, thin, shreddy; our variety a prostrate, mat-forming shrub. Mainly alpine here. Cupressaceae.

One of the world's most widespread conifer species, common juniper is humble, but well suited to cold windswept ridges and slopes where even tall conifer species grow as low creeping krummholz.

Junipers are anomalous among conifers in enclosing their seeds in fleshy, edible fruits. (Yews cup—but do not enclose their poisonous seeds in "berries"). Properly speaking, a berry is a fruit and a fruit is

Common juniper

Common juniper

a thickened ovary wall, so neither junipers nor yews have true berries; juniper berries are technically cones of very few, fleshy, fused scales. They have a sweetish resiny flavor of suspiciously medicinal intensity. Used with restraint, they're a delicious seasoning in teas, stuffings, gin (a word derived from the French *ginevre*, for juniper), or your water bottle, if your water is getting stale. Those with inquisitive palates will try them straight off the bush. Look for the year-old ones: under the glaucous coating, they ripen blackish. They're too strong to feature significantly in human diets, but birds love them, and disseminate the indigestible seeds.

FLOWERING TREES AND SHRUBS

The distinction between trees and shrubs is descriptive, not absolute nor taxonomically meaningful. Many species in this chapter grow as either trees or shrubs depending on their environment. You would be safe to call anything a tree if it has a single, woody, upright, main stem at least 4 inches thick or 26 feet tall at maturity. Think of 6 feet as the minimum height for Tall Shrubs. Non-self-supporting shrubs (canes or vines) arein the Medium Shrubs category (p. 116).

TREES AND TALL SHRUBS: DECIDUOUS OPPOSITE LEAVES

Bigleaf Maple

Acer macrophyllum (AY-sir: the Roman name; macro-FILL-um: big leaf). Leaves deeply 5-lobed, 5–12 in. wide and long, on equally long leafstalks, turning rich yellow in fall; flowers small, yellow-green, 10- to 50-in. long pendent clusters when leaves are just emerging; 1½- to 2-in. winged seeds in acute-angled Siamese-twin pairs; bark gray-brown and smooth in youth, later furrowed and often mossy; trunk and limbs often moss-laden, knobby and crooked; 30 in. dbh × 75 ft.; champion is 14 ft. × 103 ft. W-side below 2000 ft.; less common higher, and in e-side Canyons. Sapindaceae.

The largest of all maples is the broadleaf tree that makes the greatest inroads into the coniferous coastal forests. Not confined, like cottonwood and red alder, to streamsides and disturbed sites, bigleaf maple is nevertheless confined to sites where conifers have failed to create deep shade.

Prime examples can be found in the Olympic rainforests. Bigleaf maples grow there on old rockslides fanned out across river terraces. Rocky soil may help answer the mystery of why these valley bottoms, which obviously grow conifers to perfection, don't grow them to maximum density. "Halls of Mosses" there are named for their extravagant raiment of epiphytic plants: lichens, club-mosses, some ferns, and higher plants, as well as mosses proper. Epiphytes are photosynthetically active in late fall and early spring, and take advantage of the brighter light under deciduous trees when their leaves are gone. They also like the alkalinity and porosity of maple bark, even though they rarely draw nutrients out of their tree hosts (drawing *no* nutrients was the doctrine on epiphytic lichens until 1988, when two research papers unmasked an abundant lichen as a partial parasite on oaks).

Epiphytes do compete with their host trees for nutrients that come trickling down the tree trunk. To nab a share of these

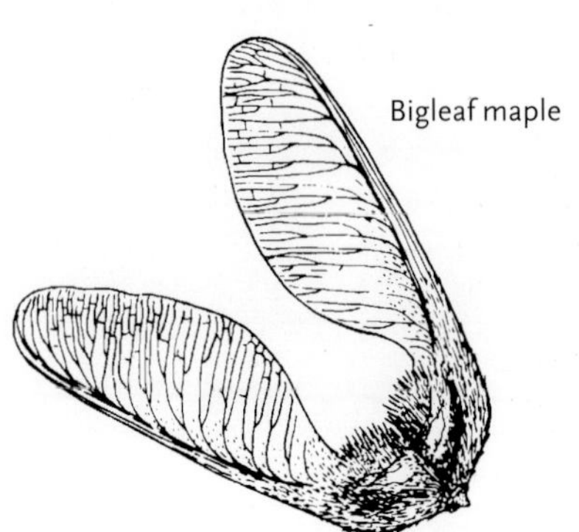

Bigleaf maple

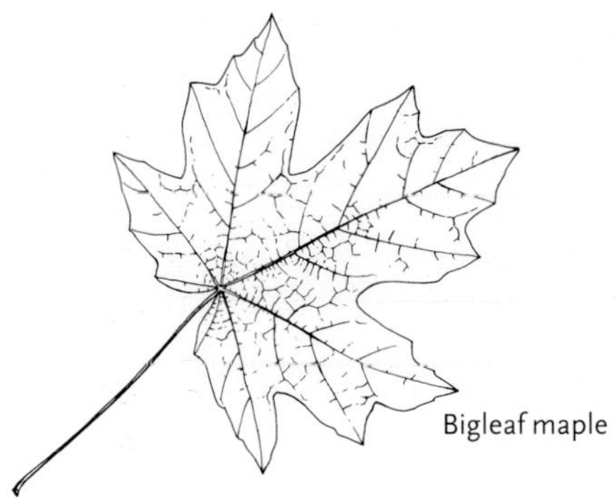

Bigleaf maple

Bigleaf maple

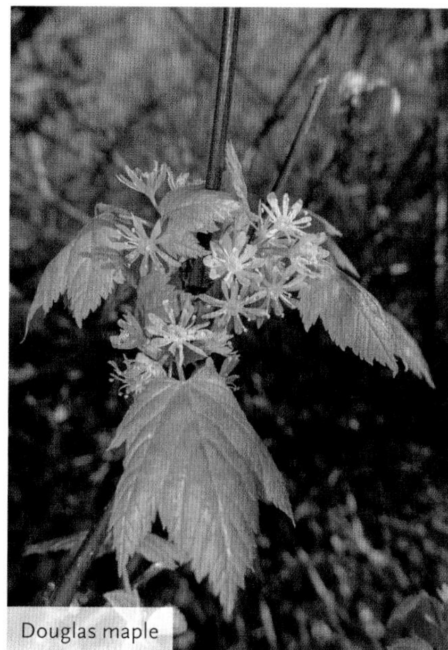
Douglas maple

nutrients, maples and other trees extend small roots among the epiphytes on their own bark. Tree dripwater originates as pure rain and fog; nutrients are contributed by nitrogen-fixing lichens and by insects and mites that graze in the tree canopy.

Deer and elk relish maple leaves when they can reach them. People relish maple syrup, which is maple sap with 98 percent of its water and volatiles boiled away. It is possible to make bigleaf maple syrup—sugar content and flavor are adequate by most accounts, and plenty of sap flows, though without the strong spring burst (following an icy winter) exploited in New England's sugar maples.

Maple wood is very hard, and makes good flooring. It's most valuable (for furniture, guitar tops, or art woodworking) when the grain is curly, birdseye, or tiger. This figured maple develops where the wood is under compression, such as on the downhill side of a lean. Some tree farmers induce figured grain by tying a young maple in a bent-over position for a season, then letting it grow straight. Recent years have seen a rash of thefts of bigleaf maple trees from national forests, because of the lucrative market for figured maple for guitars.

Difficult to cut and carve without metal tools, maple wood was used in Northwest Indian culture for utensils, tools, and ornaments. The inner bark was plaited into straps or woven into baskets, and the leaves were used to line berry baskets and baking pits, or as rags for cleaning fish.

Douglas Maple

Acer glabrum* var. *douglasii (GLAB-rum: smooth; da-GLASS-ee-eye: for David Douglas, p. 56). Also Rocky Mountain maple. Leaves 3-(or 5-)lobed, toothed, red-orange in fall, 2¼–5 in., on equally long, often reddish leafstalks; twigs reddish; flowers small, green, in small clusters; winged seeds rarely over 1 in. long, straight-backed, in pairs at right angles; bark gray to purplish; tall shrubs or trees up to 40 ft. Shrub thickets and moderately dry open forests. Sapindaceae.

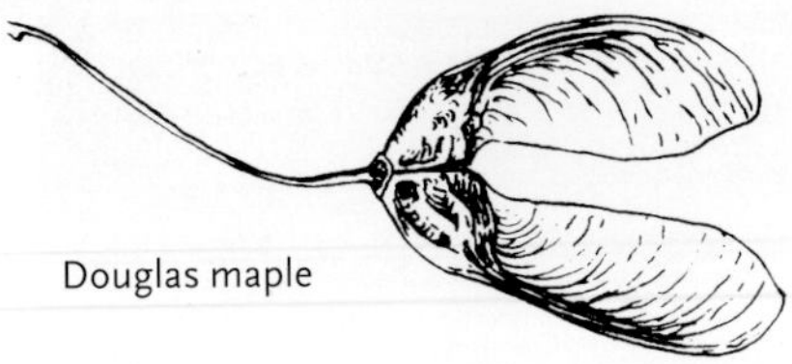

Douglas maple

The common maple of eastern Washington and Oregon, Douglas maple is vital winter browse there for deer, elk, and sheep, who eat the twigs. Brilliant red blotches on the leaves may be induced by either fungal infection or eriophyd mites. The redness occurs the same way as in fall color: vessels carrying sap are blocked, and trapped sugars from photosynthesis convert into red anthocyanin pigments. But when it's actually fall, this maple's leaves usually turn yellow.

The hard, strong wood bends well after soaking and heating, making it a favorite for snowshoe frames, fishnet handles, drum hoops, spoons, and arrows.

Vine Maple

Acer circinatum (sir-sin-AY-tum: round, referring to the leaf outline). Leaves 3–5 in., circular overall, with fine teeth on 7 or 9 shallow, pointed lobes, coloring intensely in fall or late summer, on short (1- to 3-in.) reddish leafstalks; new twigs often deep red in sunny places; flowers small with red sepals, in small loose clusters; seeds in obtuse-angled (to 180 degrees) pairs, each seed with a 1¼- to 2-in. wing; sprawling multistemmed shrubs to 20 ft., or small trees to 30 ft. Forest, mainly w-side. Sapindaceae.

The vine maple is Mr. Hyde to loggers, and Dr. Jekyll to landscapers and nursery workers. Loggers call it "vining maple," implying some devilish animism in its tendency to ensnare passing feet and lash at passing heads. Sunday drivers love it as our one abundant lowland source of rich fall color. Landscapers appreciate that being native here, it is hardier and faster-growing than Japanese maples, while rivaling them in the delicate incisions of its leaves, the contortions of its branches, and the intensity of its seasonal red. Hikers bushwhacking just have to learn to thread the thickets. Deer and elk browse it enthusiastically. The Quinault called it "basket tree," and wove long shoots of it into heavy baskets for firewood or shellfish. They swung babies' cradles from its saplings.

Vine maple limbs often sag into contact with the ground and sprout new roots there as soon as they're buried in rotting leaves.

Maples have a lovely helicopter-like way of extending their seeds' range in a breeze.

Vine maple

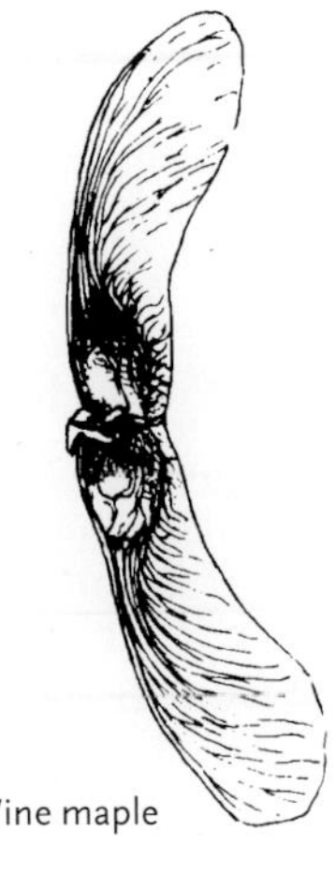

Vine maple

Vine maple

Vine maple

Their fruits (called samaras, or winged achenes) provide each seed with a long wing, sending it into a fast spiral for a slow fall.

Vine maples are the most ubiquitous tall shrubs in our mountains south of Squamish, British Columbia. They flourish at all forested elevations, but avoid dry, well-drained ridges and slopes. Elk browsing holds them back in the Olympic valleys, and unknown factors keep them infrequent on Vancouver Island.

Pacific Dogwood

Cornus nuttallii (COR-nus: Roman name, from "horn" due to toughness; nut-ALL-ee-eye: for Thomas Nuttall, p. 102). Leaves 3–5 in., bright green, elliptic, pointed, wavy-edged, with veins curving around to merge along the leaf margin; flowers tiny, greenish white, in a tight head surrounded by 4–7 large (1- to 2½-in.) white bracts; berries bright orange-red, mealy, dry, bitter, tightly crammed; trees commonly 8 in. dbh × 30 ft. tall, or tall shrubs; champion is 48 in. dbh × 61 ft. Scattered in lower forests, mainly w-side. Cornaceae.

Pacific dogwood is the official floral emblem of British Columbia, despite growing only in the province's southwest corner.

The function of showy petals is to offer a target for nearsighted insects as they buzz around gathering nectar and inadvertently strewing pollen. This function can be performed just as well by, say, leaves close to the flower, and that's what evolution came up with in this instance: those showy white parts are specialized leaves, or bracts. (Other strategies common among tiny flowers involve fragrances to attract insects without rewarding them, or more often skipping the insects and relying on wind pollination.)

Dogwoods put on a second show in the

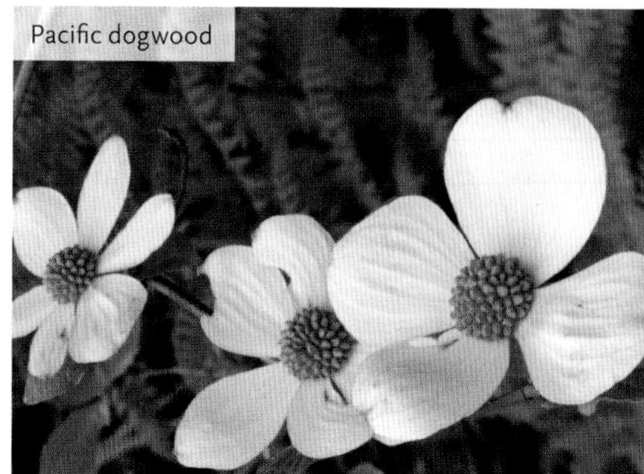
Pacific dogwood

Thomas Nuttall

Thomas Nuttall probably collected and named more new species from west of the Mississippi than anyone else. He came along at the ideal time: crossing the Rockies was easier and safer for him than for Meriwether Lewis or David Douglas, but plenty of conspicuous species remained to be described. Following early work on Great Plains flora, he wrote his magnum opus, *The Genera of North American Plants*, in 1818. In 1834, the visionary settler and entrepreneur Nathaniel Wyeth persuaded Nuttall to quit his prestigious chair at Harvard and join an expedition to the Oregon Territory. Nuttall collected all along the way, then sailed to Hawaii, California, and home via Cape Horn. Having exhausted his savings on the trip, he retired to an inherited estate in his native England.

His enthusiasm inspired praise from botanists, and sometimes a little derision from others: "When the boat touches the shore, he leaps out, and no sooner is his attention arrested by a plant or flower, than everything else is forgotten. The inquiry is made, *ou est le fou?* where is the fool? . . . he is gathering roots."

fall, a fine painterly smear of plum, bronze, russet, and magenta on their leaves. A modest second flowering may appear then as well, alongside red-orange berries from the spring flowering. Pacific dogwood can grow up to 60 feet tall, but is more often suppressed by shade, joining vine maple, yew, or chinquapin in a tall shrub layer.

The tough wood was used here for bows and salmon spears. Europeans used their species for mallet heads, tool handles, and weaver's shuttles.

Pacific dogwood

Red-Osier Dogwood

Cornus sericea (ser-ɪss-ia: silky). Also creek dogwood. Leaves 2–5 in., elliptic, pointed, wavy-edged, with veins curving around to merge along the leaf margin, coloring richly but inconsistently in fall; petals 4, white, 1/8 in., stamens 4, as long as petals, sepals 4, minute, flowers in flat-topped clusters; berries dull pale bluish or greenish, 1/4 in., single-seeded, unpalatable; new twigs deep red or purplish; shrubs 6–16 ft. Widespread in wet places. Cornaceae.

This dogwood's flowers lack the big white bracts we think of as dogwood flowers. You can see a resemblance, though, in the tiny true flowers, as well as the outline, venation, and fall coloring of the leaves. As the leaves get ready to fall, the young stems (osiers) turn color, to a dark red. They fade to gray-green again in spring.

Osier is an old French word meaning a long new shoot, originally of willow, suitable for wicker. *Dogwood* derives from the Scandinavian *dag*, for "skewer." The Shuswap

Red-osier dogwood

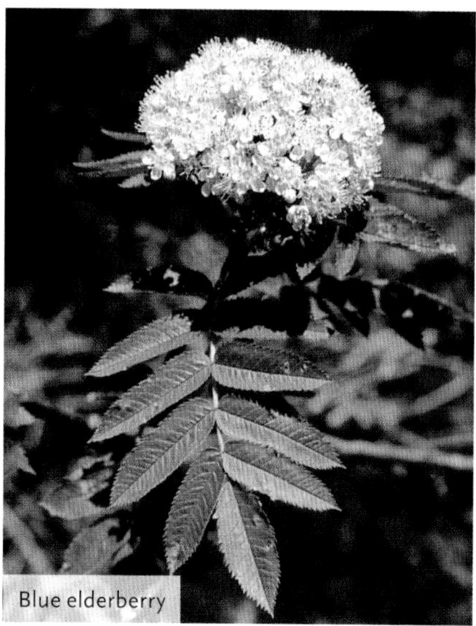
Blue elderberry

and Okanagan also liked this species for skewers, and for racks for roasting and drying salmon, for the nice salty flavor it infused. Dogwood smoke flavor was relished in dried berries and smoked fish. Bark was dried for smoking, as Prince Maximilian of Wied noted presciently, while exploring for adventure in 1833: "Like all the Indians, he inhaled the smoke, a custom which is, doubtless, the cause of many lung diseases. The mixture the Indians of this part of the country smoke, is called kini-kenick, and consists of the inner green bark of the red willow, dried, and powdered, and mixed with the tobacco of the traders."

The dry, mealy berries are not tasty. Berries exist to be eaten by wildlife, in an adaptive strategy for getting the seeds carried farther from the parent plant. What, you may ask, would attract an animal to berries like these with little sugar, fat, or protein? Lots of wild berries are like that. The attraction is that they are also unattractive to bacteria. Being slow to rot, they outlast sweet juicy berries on the bush, becoming a crucial food resource in winter. In the case of red-osier dogwood, the stems are also a top winter food for moose and elk.

This very cold-tolerant shrub is common in arctic tundra, surviving winter by forcing so much water out of its cells that freezing can't damage them.

Elderberry

***Sambucus* spp.** (sam-BEW-cus: the Greek name). Also elders. Leaves pinnately compound, 5–12 in. long; leaflets narrowly elliptic, pointed, fine-toothed, asymmetrical at base; flowers creamy white, tiny, in dense clusters, flower parts in 5s; berries ¼ in. round, 3- to 5-seeded; stems pith-filled; shrubs or shrubby trees 3–20 ft. Roadsides, streamsides, clearings, thickets. Adoxaceae.

Blue elderberry, *S. nigra* subsp. *caerulea* (NIGH-gra: black; see-RUE-lia: blue). Also *S. mexicana*, *S cerulea*. Leaflets usually 7, 9, or 11; leaf undersides and twigs whitened; flowers and (later) berries in flat-topped clusters without a single central stem; berries blue (black with a blue bloom). Common e-side, less so W.

Red elderberry, *S. racemosa* var. *arborescens* (ras-em-OH-sa: bearing racemes; arbor-ES-enz: treelike). Leaflets usually 5

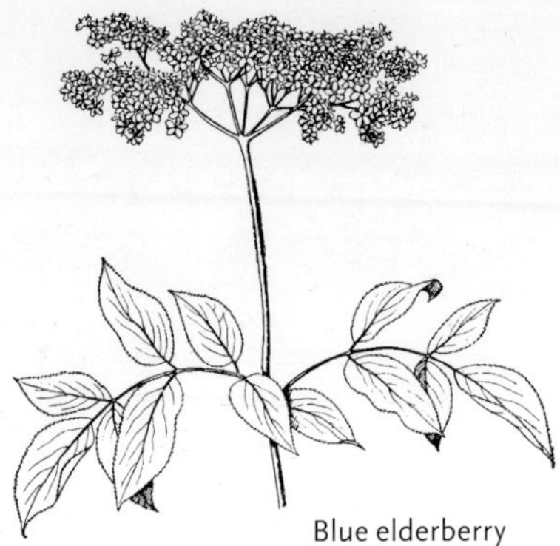
Blue elderberry

Red elderberry

or 7, not whitened; flowers or berries in conical clusters with a main central stem; berries bright red, bitter. Common w-side, less so E.

Black elderberry, *S. racemosa* var. *melanocarpa* (melon-o-CAR-pa: black fruit). Like red elderberry, but berries blackish dark red; shrubs mostly 3–6 ft. E edge of CasR.

Where they grow together, red elderberry blooms, sets fruit, and ripens a good month ahead of blue elderberry. Our blue elderberry is now considered a subspecies of *S. nigra*, the Old World black elderberry, source of legendary wines. (This transfer unfortunately invites confusion with our black elderberries, which are in our other species.)

The blue berries are more popular for jelly, wine, or eating fresh than our red or black ones. Northwest tribes ate berries of both species, fresh or more often steamed or stored until lean times. The Okanagan devised a unique way to refrigerate them. They waited to harvest blue elderberries just before the first snows of winter, then spread the bunches on a thick layer of ponderosa pine needles and laid another layer of needles on top, to be covered in turn by snow. The berries stayed moist and just above freezing. They were easy to locate, since a bit of berry juice would surface as a pink-tinged blue stain.

Elder flowers, bark, leaves, twigs, roots—and also berries—have long been seen as toxic or medicinal. Foliage and bark contain cyanide, a defense against browsing. Nevertheless, in the Olympic rainforest valleys, elk browse red elderberries so heavily that the plants are barely able to produce fruit. Northwest tribes used the bark to induce perspiration, lactation, or vomiting, or alternatively to reduce swelling, infection, or diarrhea—an odd mix of prescriptions. They hollowed the soft pith out of elder stems to make pea shooters for children, pipestems, whistles to lure elk, and drinking straws for girls subject to ritual restrictions during puberty. Rich in antioxidants, the berries have health benefits confirmed in many studies. They can be mildly toxic when underripe, and are safer to eat after cooking.

Red elderberry

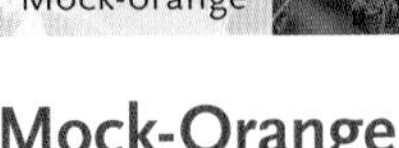
Mock-orange

Squashberry

Mock-Orange

Philadelphus lewisii (fil-a-DEL-fus: honoring Ptolemy Philadelphus, King of Egypt; lew-ISS-ee-eye: for Meriwether Lewis, p. 262). Also syringa; *P. trichothecus*, *P. confusus*. Leaves oval to lanceolate, 1–3 in. long, with 3 main veins from the base; flowers 1–2 in. across, fabulously fragrant (rarely inodorous), in showy clusters; 4 white petals, 4 sepals, many yellow-tipped stamens; 3–10 ft. tall. Scattered rocky, sunny spots. Hydrangeaceae.

As if a mock-orange exuding perfume in the July sun weren't heavenly enough already, you're likely to find it aflutter with swallowtails. This native mock-orange is a good choice for Northwest gardens; unfortunately, most nurseries sell a European mock-orange.

Squashberry

Viburnum edule (vie-BURN-um: Roman name; ED-you-lee: edible). Also high-bush-cranberry, moosewood. Leaves 1–4 in. long and about the same width, sharply toothed, usually 3-lobed, turning crimson in fall; flowers white, 1/4 in. across, in small clusters; 5 petals, 5 calyx lobes, 5 short stamens; berries red to orange, juicy, tart, aromatic, with 1 flat seed; 2–10 ft. Low to mid-elev moist or boggy forest, from Santiam Pass, OR, n. Adoxaceae.

These sour berries, which can often be picked and eaten in the frozen state in winter, were popular with all tribes. Not only the berries but also the bark and twigs soothed sore throats. Similar common viburnum, *V. ellipticum*, with conspicuous stamens and unlobed leaves, grows from Seattle south.

TREES AND TALL SHRUBS: DECIDUOUS ALTERNATE LEAVES, CATKINS

Catkins are wind-pollinated flowers that lack showy petals for attracting insects. In our species, male and female catkins are dissimilar.

Red Alder

Alnus rubra (AL-nus: the Roman name; ROO-bra: red). Leaves 2–8 in., oval, pointed, flat green above, pale gray with fine hair beneath, margins with small teeth upon large teeth, wavy and/or rolled under; catkins, ♂ and ♀ on the same tree, first appear in summer and mature in late winter before leaves appear; ♀ catkins ½–1 in. long, woody, like miniature spruce cones; ♂ catkins 2½–6 in., dangling in clusters; bark smooth, pale lichen-coated; commonly 24 in. dbh × 110 ft.; biggest tree (in CA, alas) is 7 ft. 8 in. dbh. Abundant w-side on streamsides, logged land, and burns. Betulaceae.

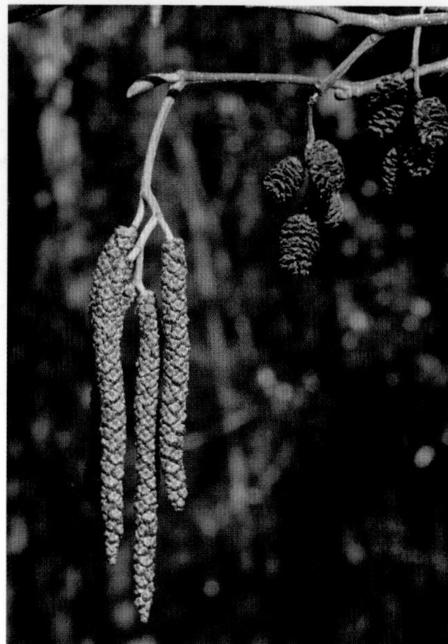

This year's male and last year's red alder female flowers.

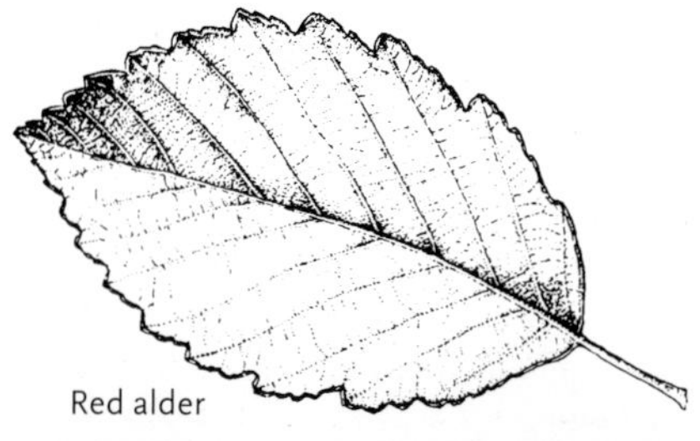

Red alder

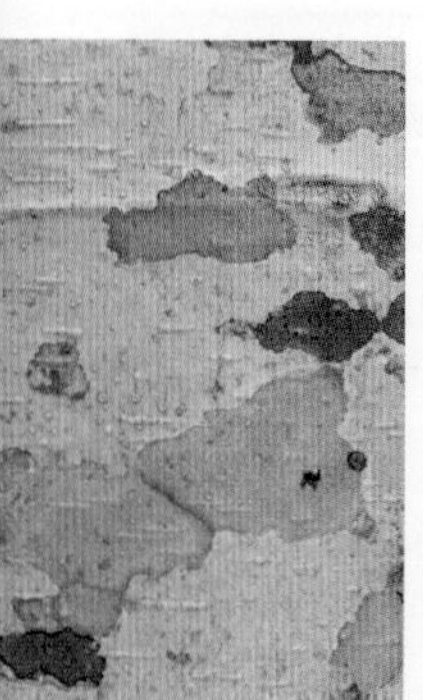

LEFT: Typical lichen-crusted red alder bark. RIGHT: Urban lichen-suppressed bark.

The splotchy whiteness of red alder bark, ranging from paper birch white through various pearl grays, is really a crust of lichens that the bark reliably hosts as long as the air is reasonably clean (urban red alders have greenish gray bark, without the lichens). The red in "red alder" could be the gorgeous antique rose cast lent to hillsides in early spring by millions of alder catkins and buds. Or it could be the deep stain that appears on freshly cut alder bark or green wood. Indians boiled, chewed, or urinated on cut bark and wood in various techniques to make dye; one use for the dye was to make nets invisible to fish. Alder's easily carved, flavor-free wood was good for spoons and dishes, and its rich, oily smoke for smoking salmon.

Northwest alders serve an invaluable role in nature, pioneering on wet gravel exposed by retreating glaciers and by shifting rivers. Fresh or still mobile river bars, with little or no sand between their cobbles, support mainly willows and annuals; slightly older bars become alder flats. Alder seedlings don't need soil nitrogen. They host bacteria in nodules on their roots that convert atmospheric nitrogen for plant use, fixing some in the soil and some directly into the plant. They grow fast, and rapidly improve soil structure and fertility with their fast-decomposing, nitrogen-rich leaf litter. Their leaves are still green when they fall—still full of chlorophyll—because alders, unlike most trees, don't need to scavenge and store the nitrogen from their chlorophyll for reuse the following year.

Fresh deglaciated terrain is above red alder's elevation range here, but often grows

Sitka alder. Alders were abundant on deglaciated lowlands for several thousand years after the last ice age, likely leaving a significant long-term legacy of fertility for our rainforests.

Alder growth may be accelerating as the atmosphere gets richer in carbon dioxide. Most plants have some chance of benefiting from CO_2 enrichment (p. 52), but the benefit is thwarted where either nitrogen or water are limiting. Nitrogen is not an issue for red alder, and water rarely is.

In nature, red alders in our region grew mainly along lowland streams and in swamps. After white settlement, red alder became an invader of cleared land, especially in the coastal ranges. The better the land for tree farming, the more likely it was to be taken over by alder. Nitrogen fixation—long appreciated in legumes—went undiscovered in alders. As long as there was plenty of stronger wood, alder was used for little but firewood. For decades, Northwest tree farmers looked for ways to massacre young alders without harming Douglas-firs.

The ugly duckling of forestry, however, matured into a swan. Planting alders mixed with Douglas-firs is an economical way of feeding firs nitrogen. Alder is also planted in disease centers of laminated root rot, to which red alder is toxic. Alder lumber is finding success as furniture and in engineered lumber products. More broadly, our broadleaf trees are the pillars of the early successional stage, a beneficial step along the way to a healthy old-growth forest (p. 60).

Every ten years or so an outbreak of tent caterpillars (p. 482) makes the region's alder stands look wretched, consuming billions of leaves down to the midvein and tenting the remains under cobwebby shelters. This stunts the alders' growth for the year, but most recover.

Sitka Alder

Alnus viridis* subsp. *sinuata (VEER-id-iss: green; sin-you-AY-ta: bent). Also slide alder; *A. crispa*, *A. sinuata*. ♂ and ♀ catkins on the same plant; ♀ catkins appear in spring, simultaneous with leaves, on stalks often longer than the catkins, becoming woody, like miniature spruce cones ½–1 in. long; leaf undersides often sticky, rarely whitish, leaves 1½–4 in., oval, pointed, with small teeth upon large teeth, more or less wavy-edged; bark more or less smooth, gray or reddish; sprawling shrubs 5–16 ft. tall. Higher-elevation streamsides, seepy slopes, avalanche basins and tracks; locally dominant in Mt. St. Helens blast zone. Betulaceae.

A Sitka alder has the genetic information for growing upright, as a tree, but it also knows how to flex and bow and sprawl where its environment demands. We know it best where it's at its worst—the downhill-sprawling "slide alder" of avalanche tracks. What the roaring avalanche finds accommodating, the sweating bushwhacker finds maddeningly intransigent, a tangle of springy, unstable stems always slipping us downslope like flies in the hairy throat of a pitcher-plant. Too often, what we slip onto is a neighboring devil's club. If, like the avalanche, we could stick to downhill travel, we'd have little problem with slide alders. To this yielding nature it owes its dominant position in avalanche tracks and basins of our mountains. A typical North Cascades track has a superficial avalanche trimming the top of the plant community every few years, or every year in some places. Full-depth avalanches come at 6- to 20-year intervals, snapping some of the larger Alaska cedars, mussing up the Sitka alders a bit, and demolishing nearly every other woody plant in their paths.

Sitka alder

Sitka alder

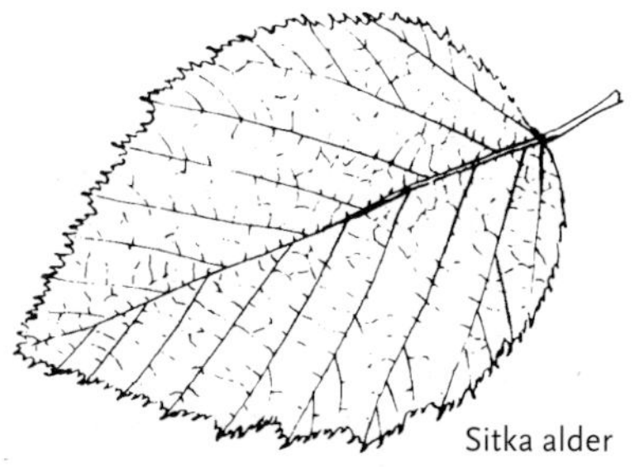
Sitka alder

Paper birch

Almost every tribe that lived near these alders used their inner bark for red and orange dyes—one application being on fishing nets, to make them invisible underwater. Catkin tea was said to improve children's appetites. Alder seeds, buds, and catkins provide critical winter staples for siskins and chickadees.

Paper Birch

Betula papyrifera (BET-you-la: Roman name; pap-er-IF-er-a: paper-bearing) Leaves pointed-oval, 1½–4 in., with teeth of two sizes, turn yellow in fall; ♀ catkins erect, 1–2 in.; their cores remain after dropping bracts and seeds; ♂ catkins on same plant, pendent; twigs usually downy, not sticky; bark lustrous bronze on young trees, becoming more or less chalky white, peeling in papery sheets; bark has raised horizontal dark streaks ("lenticels"); tree up to 3 ft. dbh × 100 ft.; champion specimens are back east. Moist, open forest at low to mid-elevs in sw BC and nc WA.

Paper birch bark was made into canoes and beautiful baskets by British Columbia Interior tribes; the Carrier people even made watertight foldable birchbark canoes. By carefully peeling only the outer layer, they could harvest it without killing the tree (don't try it; it's above your skill set). Some tribes thought birch bark could be brewed into an effective contraceptive or abortifacient.

Hazel

Corylus cornuta* var. *californica (COR-il-us: Roman name; cor-NEW-ta: horned). Also filbert. Leaves 2–5 in., broadly oval, doubly toothed, velvety on both sides; ♀ flowers tiny buds with red stigmas, appearing very early in spring along with the ♂ catkins; nuts much smaller than cultivated filberts, in heavy shells about ½ in., within hairy long-necked husks; tall shrubs 4–18 ft., rarely treelike in our mtns. Relatively warm, dry forest or thickets at low to mid-elevs. Betulaceae.

A tiny female hazel catkin.

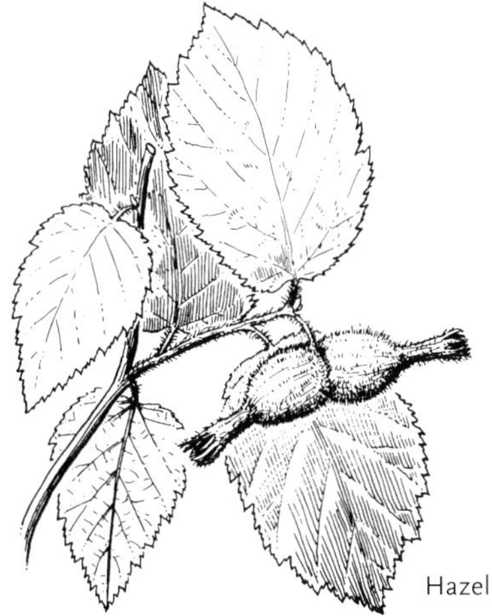

Hazel

Hazelnuts grow in back-to-back pairs, each nutshell encased in a fuzzy leaf shaped like a fringe-topped, long-necked vase. Jays, squirrels, and chipmunks harvest them avidly, which may be why I rarely see a ripe one. The Kalapuya roasted the whole nuts on coals, both for flavor and to help remove husks and shells. Accustomed to orchard nuts, we find our native nutmeats puny, but Lewis and Clark were more than grateful for the ones they bought from the Indians.

The European hazelnut, *C. avellana*, escapes cultivation and grows wild in Northwest lowlands. It blooms earlier, and has larger catkins, nuts, and stature.

Black Cottonwood

Populus trichocarpa (POP-you-lus: the Roman name; try-ko-CAR-pa: hairy fruit). Also *P. balsamifera* subsp. *trichocarpa*. Leaves 3–6 in., long-pointed, round-based or heart-shaped (but longer and diamond-shaped on saplings); glossy dark green above, dull light gray beneath, bright yellow in fall; leaf buds (and their fallen scales in spring) sticky and richly sweet-scented; round seedpods, in long strings, split three ways to release many tiny seeds with cottony fluff; ♀ and ♂ catkins on separate trees; bark gray, grooved; tall single-stemmed trees with V-shaped crowns, commonly 40 in. dbh × 150 ft.; biggest is 9 ft. 3 in. dbh × 155 ft. Low to mid-elev streamsides. Salicaceae.

Cottonwoods rarely grow far from water. With stout crotches at 80 feet up or higher, they provide choice nest sites for river-fishing ospreys, bald eagles, and herons. In spring they ravish with their honey-like scent, which you can get all over your fingers if you pick up the sticky bud scales littering the ground.

On west-side river flats, cottonwoods join Sitka spruces and maples in replacing red alders. The spruces will outlive them

Black cottonwood

Black cottonwood

and eventually hemlocks will replace them. Alders, willows, and cottonwoods share an ability to colonize fresh gravel bars, a nitrogen-poor substrate. Alders can do that because they fix nitrogen. The mystery of willows' and cottonwoods' similar success may have been solved recently. Microbiologist Sharon Doty finds that willow and cottonwood also fix nitrogen, in a new way. It was long thought that plants can only host nitrogen-fixing bacteria in root nodules, which are found in only a tiny fraction of all plant species. Then, in the 1990s, sugarcane was identified as a nonnodulated nitrogen-fixer. Doty's work greatly expands the field. What's more, she has successfully fertilized crop plants by inoculating them with bacteria from cottonwood.

Like other nitrogen-fixing shrubs, young cottonwoods are choice browse for elk and deer, especially in winter, when their protein content is highest. They are severely reduced in places like Olympic valleys where elk populations are swollen in the absence of both predators and hunting. The park has cougars to prey on its deer, but might benefit from reintroducing wolves.

Black cottonwoods are easily our largest broadleaf trees and our fastest-growing trees of any kind, reaching full size at age 60 in Oregon (later northward). Bulk and speed seem to recommend them for planting, and 19th-century plantations did produce some cottonwood lumber, but it failed in the marketplace.

A century later, the idea came back, this time to produce either pulp for paper, chips for fiberboard, biomass for fuel, or organic compounds to replace petrochemicals. A modern plantation of hybrid poplars is all one clone, with all the stems eerily similar in vast grids, thanks to identical genes and mechanized irrigation. Hybrid poplars, a staple of plantation forestry worldwide, involve any of several species; on Northwest plantations, black cottonwood is usually one parent. Some can reach 60 feet by age six. Scientists are splicing genes to make them grow even faster; or to resist the herbicide Roundup; or to produce less lignin, making it more economical for either paper or biofuel. In China, plantings are of clones genetically modified to produce an insecticide.

Poplar species hybridize easily. Because of widespread hybrids, some taxonomists demote black cottonwood to a subspecies of the balsam poplar, *P. balsamifera*, a runty tree or tall shrub of eastern North America. I was relieved when *Flora of North America* kept black cottonwood as a species, finding that it and balsam poplar are not each other's closest relatives.

Quaking Aspen

Populus tremuloides (trem-you-LOY-deez: trembling-like). Also trembling aspen. Leaves 1–2½ in., broadly heart-shaped to round, point-tipped, bumpy-edged to fine-toothed, on leafstalks 1–2½ in. long and flattened sideways; ¼-in. conical seedpods, in long strings, split in two to release minute seeds; ♀ and ♂ catkins on separate trees; bark greenish white, smooth, or dark and rough on old trees only; commonly 10 in. dbh × 40 ft. E-side streamsides and avalanche tracks. Salicaceae.

Ranging from Alaska to New England and down the Rocky Mountains and Sierra

Madre to Guanajuato, quaking aspen is the widest-ranging American tree. In the Rockies it provides the bulk of the fall color: yellow. In the Okanogan Highlands it fills avalanche tracks, like Sitka alder. But our range, atypical as it is of North American forests, offers quaking aspen only a small role along east-side streams. Wildlife, from elk and beaver to grouse and pika, make the most of it, since aspen leaves and shoots are choice browse.

Aspen leaves quake or flutter in the lightest of breezes because their flat leafstalks are limp in the lateral direction only (try rolling one between your fingers). This fluttering suggested the name *tremula* for the European aspen, and thence *tremuloides* for its American cousin.

Most aspen trunks grow from root suckers, a type of asexual reproduction. Whole groves are clones or genetic individuals, all of one sex, with a single huge root system. A clone's extent is dramatically visible in autumn, since the timing and hue of fall color are identical throughout, while varying from one clone to the next. Aspen clones can be vast, and live for a very long time. Russian botanist Nikolai Lashchinsky told me that the *P. tremula* clones in his study area "never die." Aspen roots there—after 300 years of complete invisibility—sent up abundant suckers when cattle were taken away. A clone in Utah had 47,000 stems at its peak, covered 106 acres, was around 80,000 years old from the day it's original seed germinated, and weighed about 6600 tons—arguably the world's largest living thing (p. 305).

That clone, along with many others in the Rockies and Alberta, is suffering from "sudden aspen decline" (SAD). This new type of dieback since 2000 appears to show aspen range shrinking at its drier edges due to climate change. Overall, though, aspens' prognosis is not SAD. While they lose range at warm, dry low elevations, they appear to be gaining ground at their upper limit, while growing 50 percent faster than

Quaking aspen

Quaking aspen

before—fertilized by increased CO_2 in the air—in core ranges where rain increases; they also take advantage of openings created by fire and beetles.

The previous half-century fostered a different worry over aspen's future: that new aspen stem cohorts had trouble growing tall enough to escape browsing. Blame was placed on lack of fires, and on lack of wolves leading to high deer and elk numbers. How were conditions different in past decades

John Scouler

At 19, John Scouler signed on as surgeon to HMS *William and Ann* for the same 1824 sailing that brought David Douglas here. By chance the two had been school pals in Glasgow. Scouler spent only seven months in the Northwest, taking a few walks with Douglas, and botanizing on his own when the ship visited the San Juan and Queen Charlotte Islands. The same ship and all aboard were lost entering the Columbia River a few years later, but Scouler was safely back in England, where he completed his MD and lived a long life without further exploration.

when new aspen cohorts thrived? Were they aided by natives setting fires and hunting elk? At Yellowstone, studies so far disagree with whether the reintroduced wolves are solving the browsing problem.

Scouler Willow

Salix scouleriana (SAY-lix: the Roman name; scoo-ler-ee-AY-na: for John Scouler, above). Also fire willow. Catkins appear in early spring before leaves unfurl, even before snowmelt; ♂ and ♀ catkins on separate plants, rather stout, borne stalkless along branches; leaves 2–4 in., blunt-tipped, typically broadest past the midpoint, sparsely whitish- or reddish-velvety underneath, with prominent netted veins; young twigs velvety; bark often skunky-smelling when crushed; shrubs or small trees 3–26 ft. tall; champion is 66 ft. tall × 4 ft. thick. Burns, open to forested slopes at mid-elevs, streambanks. Salicaceae.

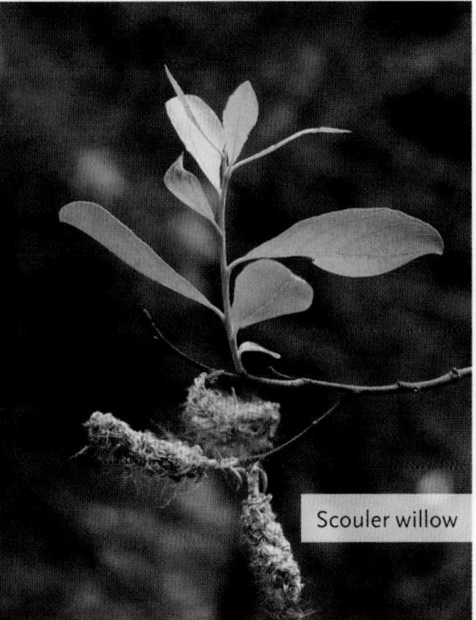
Scouler willow

Scouler willow pioneers in two utterly different settings. On gravel bars and banks of braided mountain rivers where little soil has accumulated, it is often the only shrub able to grow, and rarely exceeds 4 feet in height. In clearings (such as recent burns) on the dry east slope of the Cascades, it invades along with snowbrush. Unlike most willows, it can grow in partial shade or on slopes far from water. After severe fires, it can either resprout from deep roots or seed itself with wind-carried seeds. Stump sprouts become multistemmed shrubs, whereas seeds typically grow into small trees.

Willow shoots are choice browse, the staple food of moose. Beavers also eat willows, and they greatly increase the number of willows because they expand wetlands. Even the cut stems they use in dams often take root and produce new willows.

Umpteen species and hybrids of *Salix* line streams throughout our range; they are notoriously hard to identify. Most have narrower, pointier leaves than Scouler willow.

Northwest tribes twisted willow bark into twine for many vital uses—fishnets, baskets, tumplines (forehead straps for loads carried on the back), even harpoon lines for sea lions. Willow poles supported fishing platforms; they would often take root where implanted in the riverbed. The bark and roots were used in many ways to relieve pain and inflammation, stop bleeding (even menstruation) or reduce fever. European herbalists discovered similar uses, leading to the synthesis in 1875 of acetylsalicylic acid, or aspirin. Aspirin's greatest future value may be as a blood anticoagulant to help prevent strokes and heart attacks. Paradoxically, another willow bark component, salicin, is an astringent used topically to staunch blood flow.

Oregon white oak

Oregon White Oak

Quercus garryana (QUER-cus: the Roman name; gary-AY-na: for Nicholas Garry). Also Garry oak. Leaves 3–6 in., deeply pinnately blunt-lobed; ♂ catkins on same tree with ♀, which are single or paired in leaf axils, each consisting of a 3-styled pistil in a cup-shaped involucre that later hardens into the cap of the acorn; acorns ¾–1½ in. long; bark gray, furrowed; limbs gnarly; commonly 36 in. dbh × 80 ft. Dry rocky spots near the Columbia River. Fagaceae.

When Euro-Americans first saw the Willamette Valley, it was a savanna of grasses and scattered, huge white oaks, thanks to centuries of prairie-burning by the natives. White settlers cleared the flats for farming, leaving the hills that dot and line the valley to be taken over, in the absence of fire, by closed forests of relatively puny white oak. A few scattered old giants remain. The oaks are long-lived (300 years or so) but intolerant of shade, so they are being replaced by grand fir and Douglas-fir saplings. The Puget-Willamette Trough has a much drier climate than the mountains on either side of it; residents may have a hard time believing that, but oaks show it by their presence. In our mountains, oaks grow only on the dry margins of east-slope pine forests from Ellensburg, Washington, to Pine Grove, Oregon; on rocky slopes of the Columbia Gorge; and scattered in Oregon's western Cascades. During the warmer, drier period of 9000 to 5000 years ago, oaks were fairly common in the Coast Range, and oak savannas were vast around Puget Sound and the southern Georgia Strait; small vestiges of those savannas remain today.

Most tribes of Oregon white oak country ate the acorns after processing them to reduce the tannins, which make acorns bitter and somewhat toxic. Boiling was a favored leaching method in California, where acorns were a dietary staple. Here, the preferred methods involved roasting and then burying

Oregon white oak

them in mud, often for several months.

Oak galls—hard, hollow round structures on oak twigs—show that oaks are favored hosts of gall wasp larvae. Oaks of the eastern Columbia Gorge have been hard hit since 2009 by a European oak pit scale, a sap-feeding insect. The pest is more deadly to oaks during drought conditions.

TREES AND TALL SHRUBS: DECIDUOUS ALTERNATE LEAVES, TINY FLOWERS

Cascara

Frangula purshiana (FRAN-gue-la: fragile, referring to the wood; pur-she-AY-na: for Friedrich Pursh, p. 119). Also cascara buckthorn; *Rhamnus purshiana*. Leaves 2–6 in., oval, with recessed, strikingly parallel veins, dark glossy green above and sometimes rather leathery but deciduous (or persistent on saplings); flowers tiny, greenish, with 4–5 calyx lobes and minute petals, clustered in leaf axils; berries up to ½ in., 1-seeded, yellow or red ripening to black; bark thin and smooth, or scaly on mature trees only, numbingly bitter; trees commonly 12 in. dbh × 35 ft., or shrubs. Scattered, w-side below 2500 ft. Rhamnaceae.

Settlers in the Northwest learned from the natives that this tree's bark, after curing for many months, is a potent laxative. The medicine leapt to commercial success in the 1890s under the strangely religious name Cascara Sagrada—"Holy Bark" in Spanish, in sharp contrast with the scatological American "chittambark." It is still collected in the Pacific Northwest and sold worldwide. Though a felled cascara regenerates luxuriantly from stump sprouts, a bark-peeled tree dies. Cascara is far from abundant, and mature specimens are rare. United Plant Savers has it on their "To Watch" list.

Cascara prefers south aspects with conifers, or swampy lowland clearings with alder and vine maple. It tolerates shade, unlike most broadleaf trees here. The berries are edible, nutritive, and nonlaxative, yet unliked by humans.

Cascara

TREES AND TALL SHRUBS: DECIDUOUS ALTERNATE LEAVES, MANY STAMENS

Bitter Cherry

Prunus emarginata (ee-margin-AY-ta: notch-tipped). Leaves 1–3 in., elliptic, round-tipped or occasionally pointed, fine-toothed; flowers ½ in., white with 20–30 yellow stamens, in loose clusters of 2–4, with several clusters grouped together; cherries ¼ in., bitter, bright translucent red, drying dark; bark has raised horizontal dark pores; shrubs or trees up to 18 in. dbh × 80 ft. Moist lowland woods. Rosaceae.

These cherries are astringent and bitter, but somehow tasty to birds and rodents. The lustrous bark peels in horizontal strips almost like birch bark. Sometimes reaching a

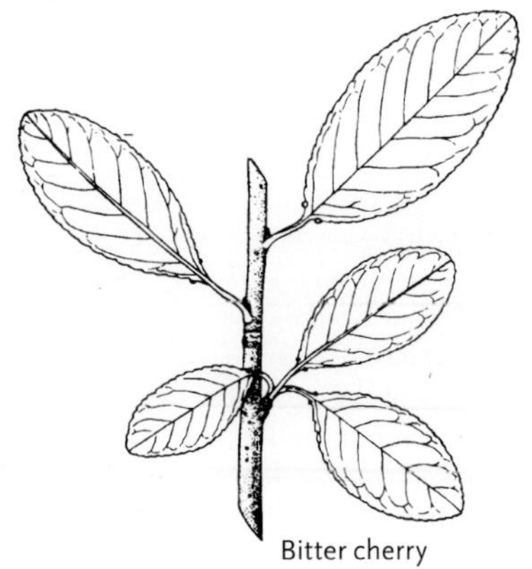
Bitter cherry

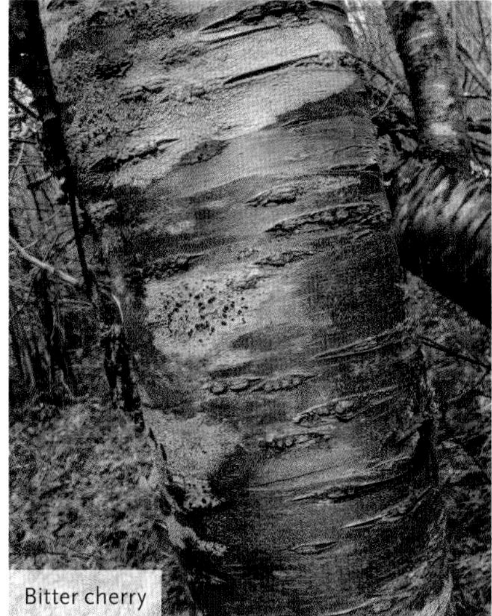
Bitter cherry

Chokecherry

bronzed maroon color, it played a key decorative role in spruce-root basketry patterns, and was used medicinally. The wood is dark, lovely, and aromatic when split, or while burning.

Several cultivated cherries (especially *P. avium*, sweet cherry) have escaped and naturalized to varying extents in our mountains. They sometimes hybridize with bitter cherry.

Chokecherry

Prunus virginiana (PRUNE-us: the Roman name). Leaves 2–4 in., oval, pointed, fine-toothed; flowers 3/8 in., white, with 20–30 bright yellow stamens, very showy, in long dense racemes; cherries oval, 1/4 in., sweetish but astringent, crimson to black; shrubs or (rarely) small trees up to 20 ft. In sun, e-side lowlands; also (var. *demissa*) in w-side lowlands. Rosaceae.

The genus *Prunus* includes all cherries, prunes, and plums. Chokecherries are named for powerfully puckering the mouth and throat. Fortunately, their sweetness preserves better than their astringency; plains tribes pounded them into pemmican, settlers boiled them into jelly. Though pemmican contained quantities of pounded chokecherry pits, some modern texts advise scrupulous avoidance of all cherry, peach, and apricot pits, since they contain amygdalin, which can break down into cyanide. Chokecherry leaves, though choice browse among deer and elk, in large quantities have killed cattle.

Infusions of chokecherry leaves, twigs, or bark were popular medicines in times past. Both Anglo- and Native Americans prescribed them for diarrhea, intestinal worms, and other stomach ills. The Okanagan considered them so beneficial to stomachs that they could prevent postpartum stretch marks. The Blackfoot and others soothed sore throats and coughs with cherry juice, either fresh or reconstituted from dried cherries—the original cherry cough syrup. Meriwether Lewis, camped on the upper Missouri in 1805, cured his own case of severe stomach cramps with two pints of "a strong black decoction of an astringent bitter taste," brewed from chokecherry twigs. As an East Coast plant (named for Virginia), it was well known to him already. Later, crossing the Bitterroots, the party held starvation at bay with chokecherries.

Oregon crabapple

Oregon Crabapple

Malus fusca (MAY-lus: the Roman name; FUS-ca: dusky). Also *Pyrus fusca*. Leaves 1½–3 in., oval, pointed, fine-toothed, often with a small lobe on one or both sides; flowers white to pink, ½–1 in. across, broad-clustered; apples ½ in., egg-shaped, greenish yellow to red; twigs armed with stout thorn-like spur twigs; tall shrubs, or trees to 40 ft. Infrequent; low w-side. Rosaceae.

Our crabapples are hard and sour, but after several months' storage most tribes found them sufficiently softened and sweetened to eat very happily; maybe that really works, as it does with Anjou pears, or maybe it's just that several months on winter rations could make anything taste sweeter. In any case, pioneer women found it more effective to cook them with lots of sugar. Crabapple bark tea was used for all kinds of stomach troubles among the Indians, and the hard, tough wood made seal harpoon points and other tools.

MEDIUM SHRUBS: DECIDUOUS ALTERNATE LEAVES, MANY STAMENS

Think of 2–15 feet as the Medium size family. Those with many stamens are in the rose family. Two herbs that almost pass for small shrubs are goatsbeard (p. 246) and baneberry (p. 270).

Indian-plum

Indian-Plum

Oemleria cerasiformis (ohm-LAIR-ia: for August Oemler; ser-ass-if-OR-mis: cherry shaped). Also osoberry; *Osmaronia cerasiformis*. Leaves 2–5 in., elliptic, smooth-edged, pointed; flowers white, bell-shaped, borne very early in pendent racemes below the new leaves, stamens 15 or none, since ♂ and ♀ flowers are on separate trees; berries ⅜ in., 1-seeded, bitter, peach-colored ripening to blue-black; shrubs or rarely small trees 5–15 ft. Low w-side elevs. Rosaceae.

Indian-plum's tassels of blooms below upraised sheaves of new leaves would be welcome any time of year, but are all the more so in February and early March. Legend has it the Indians used to know where the sweet ones grow. Maybe we just never taste ripe ones because birds eat them first.

Serviceberry

Amelanchier alnifolia (am-el-AN-she-er: archaic French term for a related shrub;

al-nif-OH-lia: alder leaf). Also saskatoon. Leaves 1–2 in., broadly oval, toothed at the tip but not at the base; petals white, ½–1 in. long, narrow, often so widely spaced and twisted that the inflorescence of 3–15 flowers is a jumble of petals; berries ½ in., several-seeded, red ripening to purplish black, with bloom; typically a 4- to 8-ft. shrub here, sometimes a small tree. Mainly on sunny e-side slopes. Rosaceae.

Serviceberry

Meriwether Lewis said "sarvisberry," as many Easterners still do. The word derives not from "serving" but from *Sorbus,* Latin for mountain-ash. Serviceberry leaves look somewhat like mountain-ash and wildrose leaflets. Just remember that a compound leaf (on a rose or mountain-ash) terminates in a leaflet, while a stem of simple leaves (like serviceberry's) terminates in a bud, flower(s), or a growing shoot. Despite that difference, serviceberry and mountain-ash are related closely enough to have produced natural hybrids.

Our serviceberry is another edible fruit no longer much eaten. Don't be picky eaters, though, they're good for you (rich in anthocyanin). Birds and bears eat them, all the Northwest tribes ate them, Lewis and Clark ate them, and traditionalists on the Plains and in the Appalachians eat them still. That said, I haven't had any in our mountains as sweet and plentiful as the ones from the same species in Montana.

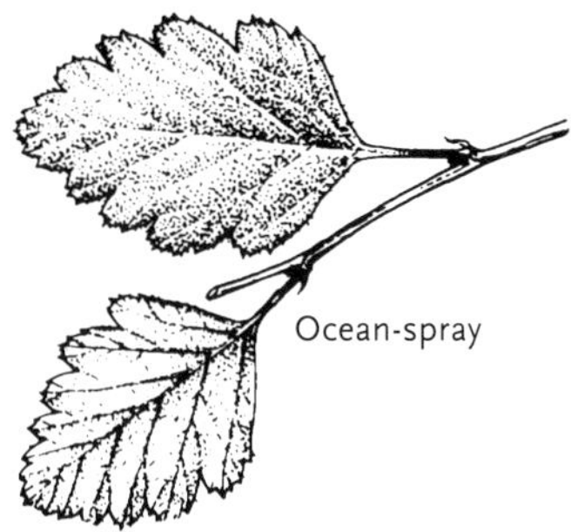
Ocean-spray

Ocean-Spray

Holodiscus discolor (ho-lo-DIS-cus: entire disk; DIS-color: variegated). Also ironwood, arrowwood, creambush, rock-spiraea. Leaves instantly recognizable once you know them: 1–2½ in., roughly oval, with coarse teeth and often fine teeth upon those; flowers tiny, whitish, profuse in 4- to 7-in. conical clusters; seeds single in tiny dry pods, the clusters of pods persisting in place through winter; shrubs 4–12 ft. Dry, exposed sites up to mid-elevs. Rosaceae.

Ocean-spray

Blooming with masses of tiny cream-white flowers in parallel sprays, ocean-spray

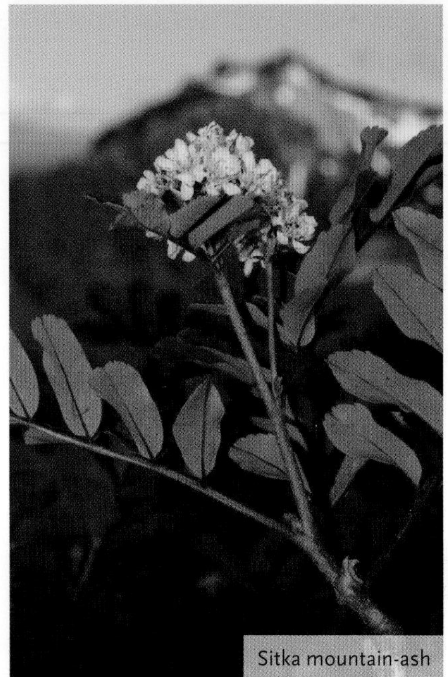
Sitka mountain-ash

Rocky Mountain mountain-ash

resembles an ocean wave breaking. "Ironwood" and "arrowwood" tell of uses Indians found for the straight branches after hardening in fire—arrows, fishing spears, digging sticks for clams and roots, roasting tongs, drum hoops, and baby's cradle hoops.

Mountain-Ash

***Sorbus* spp.** (SOR-bus: the Roman name). Leaves pinnately compound, leaflets 7–13, 1¼–2½ in., oblong to elliptic, fine-toothed at the tip but not at the base (note similarly placed teeth on serviceberry, p. 116, and wildroses, p. 122); flowers white, ½ in. across, in dense, flat-topped clusters 1¼–4 in. across, fragrant; berries red to orange, ⅜ in., several-seeded, mealy, bitter; leaves color brightly, mostly yellow, in fall, and berries may turn purplish; dwarfed to tall shrubs or rarely small trees. Mainly subalpine, with at least some sun. Rosaceae.

Sitka mountain-ash, *S. sitchensis* (sit-KEN-sis: of Sitka, Alaska). Leaf tips toothed, round in outline.

Rocky Mountain mountain-ash, *S. scopulina* (scop-you-LIE-na: of the Rocky Mountains). Also Greene's, Cascades, and so on. Leaf tips toothed, pointed. Mainly CasR and CoastM.

Mountain-ash berries are important forage for birds and subalpine small mammals, especially since they stay on through winter. Judging by reports of birds flying under the influence, they have enough sugar to ferment on the bush. If so, it hides behind an acrid taste and a mealy texture. When Northwest tribes ate them at all, they usually boiled them; one report says the berries added flavor to marmot meat. Wine is sometimes made from the sweeter berries of the European mountain-ash or rowan tree, *S. aucuparia*.

Bitterbrush

Purshia tridentata (PUR-shia: for F. Pursh, opposite; try-den-TAY-ta: 3-toothed).

Friedrich Pursh

German botanist Friedrich Pursh spent several years in the eastern United States where he fell into the opportunity to describe and publish his era's prize set of unpublished plant specimens: those from the Lewis and Clark Expedition (p. 262). Lewis was supposed to describe the plants himself, but was either too busy or too depressed, and paid Pursh $70 to do the job. Before it was done, Lewis died and Pursh, falling out with his American employers, returned to Europe with one quarter of the collection. In 1814 he published his *Flora Americae Septentrionale*, the first-ever attempt at a coast-to-coast American flora. The specimens eventually found their way back to these shores, but Pursh remained—unfairly, perhaps—an object of intense resentment among American botanists. At least he did a creditable job of naming and describing. He devoted twelve years to an intended second magnum opus, a flora of Canada, only to see it lost in a fire.

Also antelopebrush. Petals yellow, flat-spreading, 3/8 in.; calyx funnel-shaped, fuzzy, 5-lobed; 25 orange stamens; capsules 1-seeded, long-pointed; leaves aromatic, narrow, 3-pointed, grayish, white-woolly underneath, edges rolled under, 3/4 in.; stiff bushy shrubs 3–6 ft.+; leaves persist through some winters. Ponderosa pine forest and steppe e of CasCr. Rosaceae.

Bitterbrush thrives on sites marginal for forest growth, such as the lower timberlines east of the Cascades. It enjoys an advantage over most shrubs in being able to fix nitrogen, fertilizing itself and its successors. Technically, plants don't fix nitrogen, but bacteria living symbiotically with them do so. The same roots also host mycorrhizal fungi that support the nitrogen-fixing effort.

Though bitter to us, bitterbrush is rated just about tops by browsing animals. Protein content is a major concern to browsers, and a good nitrogen supply helps plants be protein-rich. Game managers have succeeded in greatly increasing deer populations by disseminating bitterbrush. Years of heavy browsing often "hedge" bitterbrush into a low, neatly mounded shape.

Bitterbrush shares with big sagebrush the name *tridentata* and the three-toothed fuzzy gray leaves that it describes. They aren't related, though; it must be convergent evolution on similar habitat (sagebrush leaves, p. 131, do not roll under at the edges, and are equally woolly on top and bottom surfaces).

Bitterbrush

Salmonberry

Salmonberry

Salmonberry and Thimbleberry

***Rubus* spp.** (ROO-bus: the Roman name). Rosaceae.

Salmonberry, *R. spectabilis* (spec-TAB-il-is: showy). Leaves ternate; leaflets 1–3 in., pointed or oval, fine-toothed, often lobed; petals red or hot pink; fruits like large juicy raspberries in form, in mixed shades of yellow to scarlet irrespective of ripeness; stems erect, 4–10 ft., somewhat woody but weak, sparsely thorny or occasionally thornless. Abundant on wet slopes and bottoms, w-side.

Thimbleberry, *R. parviflorus* (par-vif-LOR-us: small-flowered, a misleading name). Leaves 3–8 in., at least as broad as long, palmately 5-lobed (maple-like), fine-toothed, soft and fuzzy; petals white, ½–1 in., nearly round, crinkly; berries red, like thin fine-grained raspberries; stems erect, 4–7 ft., somewhat woody but weak, thornless. Very widespread.

Thimbleberry

Rooted in the collective subconscious is a controversy concerning the palatability of salmonberries and thimbleberries. Authors praise one or the other, but never both. I belong to the thimbleberry cult. I often try a salmonberry just to attune myself with the bears, or to see once again if the yellow ones are really any different from the red ones, or maybe because their vapidity challenges my powers of gastronomic recall. But thimbleberries! How anyone could call the thimbleberry "insipid" defies comprehension. Perhaps it's a colorblindness of the palate. I grant that thimbleberries are a bit gritty, not the juiciest, almost exceedingly tart, and exasperatingly sparse on the bush, and yet I find in a good thimbleberry the most exquisite berry flavor on earth.

Indians ate both salmonberries and thimbleberries, of course. Young salmonberry shoots, peeled, were a major food. Their astringent flavor cut the greasiness and fishiness of all those salmon dinners. That may be how salmonberries got their name.

Both shrubs colonize roadsides, clear-cuts, and burns west of the Cascades. In the mountains, low lobes of subalpine meadow are often full of thimbleberry and bracken dense enough to exclude conifer seedlings indefinitely. Salmonberry, which prefers soggy streambanks and marshy flats, can also present an obstacle to trees. It grows tangles of rhizomes just beneath the soil surface, with buds ready to sprout new plants after a fire or a landslide. Salmonberry thickets under red alders abound on Coast Range streamsides. By sending up copious new canes every year, salmonberry crowds out seedlings of anything else, and may take over as the alders die out. (Salmonberry might even outlast a Douglas-fir overstory in the same way, but that would take centuries.) Laws require loggers to leave streamside buffer strips. The riparian virtues that the buffer law was meant to preserve—plant diversity for rich animal habitat, tree shade to keep the water cool for fish, and trees to fall into the stream and slow its flow—are diminished if salmonberries take over. Salmonberry-choked riparian zones are common even in never-logged watersheds, so they may well have been the presettlement norm here.

Trailing blackberry

Trailing blackberry

Trailing Blackberry

Rubus ursinus (ur-SIGH-nus: of bears, specifically Ursa Major and Minor, i.e., northern). Also Pacific dewberry. Leaves compound, often persistent but not thick nor truly evergreen; 3 (sometimes 5) leaflets elliptic, pointed, toothed; flowers white, usually with either stamens or pistils stunted, the functional ♂ and ♀ on separate plants; flowering stalks up to 16 in. tall, from long trailing stems with many slender thorns. Widespread in clearings and sunny forest. Rosaceae.

The Northwest is famous for growing mouthwatering blackberries like weeds. They *are* weeds. The most eaten ones are exotic backyard nuisances, archetypal briarpatch—but mouthwatering. They sometimes sweeten dreary approaches over logging roads.

This "wild" blackberry, our only native blackberry, is not the sweetest but the most elegant, distinctively firm-textured, long, and fine-grained. Though dwarfed and outnumbered by exotic blackberries in the towns and farms, it is the abundant species of lower mountain-slope forests.

The invasive weed blackberries differ in having bisexual flowers, robust high-climbing canes, and heavy, flattened thorns. Himalayan blackberry, *R. bifrons,* was refined and named as a garden variety by botanist Luther Burbank in 1885. The Northwest's most familiar blackberry, it combines great flavor with sleeve-shredding prolificacy. The tall (20–30 feet, given something tall to clamber on) arching canes bear compound leaves of usually five fine-toothed oval leaflets that often persist through mild winters. This ability to photosynthesize in winter characterizes the Northwest's most successful shrubby weeds—Scotch broom, English ivy, gorse, and these blackberries. Evergreen blackberry, *R. laciniatus,* often grows near the Himalayan. Its five dark green leaflets are deeply incised.

The blackcap, *R. leucodermis,* is a bland black low-elevation raspberry. Fruits of genus *Rubus* can be divided into raspberry and blackberry types. A raspberry, when picked, is cupshaped, pulling cleanly from its receptacle, or core. A blackberry pulls its core with it. Both salmonberries and thimbleberries are raspberries by this definition, but don't taste at all like a garden raspberry.

Pacific ninebark

Pacific Ninebark

Physocarpus capitatus (fie-zo-CAR-pus: bladder fruit; cap-it-AY-tus: headed). Also sevenbark. Flowers small, white (stamens often pink), in dense hemispheric heads 1¼–2 in. across; 5 petals; 3–5 pistils, 3–5 seedpods; leaves 1–3 in., palmately veined and 3-(rarely 5-)lobed, coarsely toothed; bark flaking away, reddish or yellowish brown; shrubs 6–13 ft. Wet thickets, forest, lower w-side. Rosaceae.

On ninebark, the bark of large stems shreds and peels in layers—but rarely, if ever, so many as nine, or even seven.

Wildrose

***Rosa* spp.** Leaves pinnately compound; leaflets 5 to 11, oval to elliptic, 1–2½ in. long, toothed except at the base; flowers pink, ¾–3½ in.; fruit orange, turning red or purple, many-seeded, dry and sour; more or less prickly shrubs 1½–8 ft. tall. Low to mid-elev clearings to semi-open forest. Rosaceae.

Baldhip rose, *R. gymnocarpa* (gym-no-CAR-pa: naked fruit). Flowers ¾–1 in., single; fruits ⅜ in., unique among our roses in not retaining the crown of 5 sepals—hence "bald"; plants 1½–4 ft., bristling all over with fine prickles. Widespread, mainly w-side.

Pacific ninebark

Baldhip rose

Nootka rose, *R. nutkana* (noot-KAY-na: of Nootka, Vancouver Island). Flowers (2¼–3½ in.) and fruits large, single; prickles variable, typically in stout pairs at leaf nodes. Lower elevs.

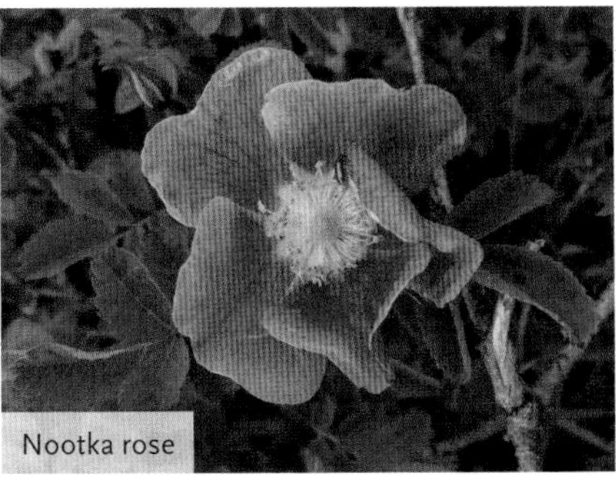
Nootka rose

Woods rose, *R. woodsii* (WOODS-ee-eye: for Joseph Woods). Flowers 1–2 in., in small clusters; fruit ¼–½ in.; prickles usually few; the paired prickles below each leaf axil are heaviest; central leaflet widest past midlength. E-side.

Woods rose

One wonders if unassuming five-petaled blooms like these could ever have carried the mythic and symbolic weight of "The Rose" of which the troubadours sang. Had horticultural wizards been at work multiplying rose petals and colors even before the Middle Ages? Yes, they had. "Hundred-petaled" roses were bred by the year 400 BCE. Our wildroses' fruit, the rose "hip" or "apple," has lots of vitamin C, and a breath-freshening flavor after a few frosts have broken it down. Wildrose hips, leaves, and stems are collected for herbal medicines.

Spiraea

***Spiraea* spp.** (spy-REE-a: the Roman name). Leaves 1–3 in., oval, toothed on outer half only; flowers tiny, in dense fuzzy heads, the 25–50 stamens protruding; seedpods tiny, 2- to several-seeded; commonly reproducing by shoots from rhizomes. Rosaceae.

Douglas spiraea, *S. douglasii* (da-GLASS-ee-eye: for David Douglas, p. 56). Also hardhack, steeplebush. Flowers pink, in conical to spikelike heads often over 3 in. tall; leggy shrubs 2–7 ft. tall. Streamsides, marshy thickets.

Subalpine spiraea, *S. splendens* Also rose meadowsweet; *S. densiflora*. Flowers rich pink, in slightly convex-topped heads 2 in. across; leaves downy underneath; prostrate to low shrubs, up to 3 ft. Moist thickets and meadows, typically 3000–5500 ft. w of CasCr.

Douglas spiraea

Subalpine spiraea

Birchleaf spiraea

Shrubby cinquefoil

Birchleaf spiraea, *S. betulifolia* (bet-you-lif-OH-lia: birch leaf). Also white or shinyleaf spiraea; *S. lucida*. Flowers white to pinkish-tinged, in slightly convex-topped heads 2 in. across; leaves hairless underneath; up to 3 ft. Low to timberline on both E- and W-side.

Shrubby Cinquefoil

Dasiphora fruticosa (day-sif-OR-a: hair-bearing; fruit-ic-OH-sa: shrubby). Also *Potentilla fruticosa, Pentaphylloides floribunda*. Petals yellow, ½ in. long; sepals apparently 10 (5 smaller bracts alternating with 5 true sepals); compound leaves of 3, 5, or 7 leaflets, hairy, not toothed; seedpods long-haired; dense, rounded to matted shrubs 6–24 in. tall. Rocky alp/subalpine sites. Rosaceae.

Shrubby cinquefoil

Though shrubby cinquefoil or "yellow rose" is an alpine specialist in our area, it also grows on rocky hills all across the country and in Eurasia, and is cultivated in cities. It increases on overgrazed sites since grazers aren't fond of it. Under the name *Potentilla fruticosa,* it was until recently the only shrub in a genus of dozens of herbs, the cinquefoils (p. 249).

MEDIUM SHRUBS: DECIDUOUS ALTERNATE LEAVES, 5 STAMENS

Currant and Gooseberry

***Ribes* spp.** (RYE-beez: Arabic term for rhubarb, applied to currants by mistake). Flowers more or less tubular, the 5 sepals united about half their length; 5 petals smaller and less colorful than sepals, attached just inside calyx mouth alternately with the 5 stamens; leaves palmately lobed; weak-stemmed shrubs 2–12 ft. Grossulariaceae.

Red-flowering currant, *R. sanguineum* (sang-GWIN-ee-um: bloody). Flowers ¾ in. long, red to pink, 10–30 in dense pendent clusters; berries black with a heavy white

Red-flowering currant

Maple-leaf currant

Wax currant

bloom; leaves 1½–4 in, spicy-fragrant when crushed. Lowland woods.

Maple-leaf currant, *R. acerifolium* (ay-sir-if-OH-lium: maple leaf). Also *R. howellii.* Sepal lobes flat-spreading, dull red; berries black; leaves 2–3 in. Mid-elevs to subalpine, common in streamside thickets.

Wax currant, *R. cereum* (SEE-ree-um: wax). Flowers yellowish white, tubular, ¾ in. long, ending in short spreading calyx lobes; berries red; leaves grayish, nearly round in outline, ½–1¼ in., blunt-toothed, gummy, muskily aromatic when crushed. Sunny slopes e of CasCr.

Swamp gooseberry, *R. lacustre* (la-CUS-tree: of lakes). Also prickly currant. Flowers saucer-shaped, dull pinkish, 10–15 in pendent clusters; berries hairy, dark purple; leaves ½–2½ in.; stems covered with tiny prickles, larger spines whorled at stem nodes; straggly or sprawling shrubs. Forested wet spots.

Stink currant, *R. bracteosum* (brac-tee-OH-sum: with bracts). Flowers saucer-shaped, greenish to nearly white, 20–50 in sparse erect racemes, with 2 small bracts on each flower stalk; berries black to pale blue with bloom; leaves, young stems, berries, and flower bases downy and sticky; leaves

Wax currant

Swamp gooseberry

Swamp gooseberry

Stink currant

Sticky currant

rank-smelling, up to 5 in. wide, with 5 or 7 maple-like lobes; no prickles. Wet forest, thickets, and avalanche tracks at low to mid-elevs.

Sticky currant, *R. viscosissimum* (vis-co-SEE-sim-um: stickiest). Flowers bell-shaped, greenish or pinkish white, 5–12 in loose clusters; berries blue-black; leaves, young stems, berries, and flower bases downy and sticky; leaves musky, 1¼–3 in. wide, with 3 (or 5) shallow rounded palmate lobes; no prickles. Open forest at mid- to high elevs in CasR and OlyM.

The gooseberry has nothing to do with geese; the word derives rather carelessly from a French name for them, *groseille*. Gooseberry plants are distinguished from currants by having prickles. All Northwest *Ribes* fruits are edible and nutritious, and most were widely eaten both fresh and dried by the Indians, but today they are sought only by phytonutrient fanatics. (These species have not been analyzed, but European black currants score very high.) Various authors suggest that certain species are worth eating, but don't agree as to which ones. Some will take your mouth to the movies, running sweet moments tightly sandwiched between sour and bitter episodes; others are only insipidly bitter. Many thickets offer side-by-side currant tastings.

Our showiest currant, the red-flowering, blooms deep pink profusely in early spring. It is an esteemed ornamental outside of the Northwest; David Douglas's original exportation of this species alone is said to have paid off his sponsors' investment in his two-year expedition.

Gooseberry thorns inflict painful allergic reactions in some people. Nonetheless, some tribes used big ones for tattooing or for removing splinters, or as fishhooks or needles.

White pine blister rust, an introduced fungus that devastates five-needle pines, lives on *Ribes* species as alternate hosts without harming them. Hoping to help pines, foresters waged a "War on *Ribes*." Unhappily for *Ribes*, the time was the Great Depression when the US government was looking to employ as many people as possible. Soon, 13,000 men were on WPA and CCC payrolls killing shrubs. When those men went off to fight World War II, the war on *Ribes* conscripted delinquent teens and POWs; later it turned to the herbicides 2,4-D and 2,4,5-T. Some million currant and gooseberry plants died between 1930 and 1946.

The currants won. They far outnumbered us.

Recently, scientists learned that currants aren't required as alternate hosts after all; widespread species of paintbrush and lousewort serve just as well. Another pointless ecotragedy brought to you by Hubris Productions.

Redstem ceanothus

Redstem Ceanothus

Ceanothus sanguineus (see-an-OATH-us: thistle, a puzzling name; san-GWIN-ius: blood-colored). Also buckbrush. Flowers tiny, white, in dense fluffy 2- to 5-in. clusters; 5 spoon-shaped petals, 5 calyx lobes, 5 stamens; seedpods of three 1-seeded cells; leaves 1½–5 in., oval, fine-toothed, often sticky above, hairy along the veins beneath, with 2 veins from base prominent and long but not reaching the tip; stems purplish; 3–10 ft. Open forest or sunny slopes at low to mid-elevs. Rhamnaceae.

Though redstem was once called Oregon-tea, any tea made from its leaves would be ersatz ersatz. The reference is to New Jersey–tea, an eastern *Ceanothus* brewed by patriotic colonists wanting to declare their independence from the tea taxed under the Stamp Act. Like its evergreen cousin snowbrush (p. 141), redstem nourishes both four-legged browsers and nearby plants, since it fixes nitrogen. It is a post-fire pioneer, sprouting either from root sprouts or more often from seeds that germinate in spring following "scarification" by fire heat the previous summer.

Orange honeysuckle

Orange Honeysuckle

Lonicera ciliosa (lo-NISS-er-a: for Adam Lonitzer; silly-OH-sa: fringed). Petals orange to almost red, 1–1½ in., fused (tubular) over three-quarters of their length, one petal lobe drooping apart from the upper 4, hairy inside tube; calyx insignificant; flowers and red ½-in. berries in terminal clusters nestled in a perfoliate leaf; leaves opposite, oval, 1½–3 in., finely hairy-margined; perennial vines climbing 5–20 ft. Low-elev openings. Caprifoliaceae.

This honeysuckle attracts its pollinators (hummingbirds) visually, whereas sweet-scented honeysuckles attract night-flying moths. Its flowers, long and narrow like a hummer's bill, are crammed together to make a bright orange bullseye in the center of a target comprised of the uppermost pair of opposite leaves modified into a single fused leaf—often shaped like a full pair of lips—with the stem passing through the center.

Northwest tribes saw honeysuckle as women's medicine, using tea or steam from the leaves to encourage lactation, discourage conception, ease cramps, or add luster to little girls' hair. The vine occasionally clasps its host tightly enough to kill it by allowing no room for growth.

Black Twinberry

Lonicera involucrata (in-vo-lu-CRAY-ta: with involucres). Also bush honeysuckle, inkberry. Petals pale yellow, ½–¾ in., fused (tubular) over half their length, stamens just appearing at tube mouth, calyx tiny and scarcely lobed, flowers paired, as are the glossy black ¼-in. berries; leaves opposite, elliptic, pointed, 1½–5 in., hairy especially at margins and under veins; 3–8 ft. Seeps, streamsides. Caprifoliaceae.

Black twinberry

Black twinberry

Coast tribes called black twinberries "crow food," Crow being the only spirit crazy and black enough to relish such bitter black fruit. Interior tribes call them "grizzly berries," and think that bears relish them. "Inkberry" juice provided face paint for dolls or dye for graying hair.

Black twinberry plants carry twinning (oppositeness) to an extreme: opposite leaf axils bear opposite stalks, each bearing a pair of flowers between two pairs of hairy bracts, two of them two-lobed. The bracts typically turn deep magenta and reflex downward over time to better offset the paired, purplish black berries that replace the pale flowers. This display typically hides in a damp thicket.

Purple-flowered bush honeysuckle, *L. conjugialis*, grows less abundantly, in the Oregon and southern Washington Cascades. Its flower pairs are "conjugally" fused at the base, and produce just one two-tipped berry from their fused ovaries.

Snowberry

***Symphoricarpos* spp.** (sim-for-i-CAR-pus: gathered fruit). Also waxberries. Flowers pinkish to white, bell-shaped, less than ¼ in., petals fused over half their length; berries pure white, tightly clustered, pulpy, 2-seeded; leaves and twigs opposite; fast-growing young plants sport highly variable leaves up to 6 in. long with odd lobes, symmetrical or not; mature plants have oval leaves 1 in. long. Both species tend to avoid the wettest parts of our range. Caprifoliaceae.

Common snowberry, *S. albus* (AL-bus: white). Berries ½ in.; shrubs 3–7 ft. tall. Abundant in thickets and dryish forests.

Trailing snowberry, *S. mollis* (MOL-iss: soft). Also *S. hesperius*. Berries ¼ in.;

trailing shrubs with erect stems less than 20 in. Lowlands.

These berries, as light as popcorn, are unlikable as food; Indians said they are "good for the kids to throw at each other." Might kids at play be the disseminators they evolved for? In truth, many kinds of berries avert rot by skimping on sugars, fats, and moisture. They get themselves eaten and disseminated about as effectively as the yummier berries do—in winter, when the richer fruits are long gone.

Common snowberry

Trailing snowberry

Devil's Club

Oplopanax horridus (op-lo-PAN-ux: heavily armed cure-all; HOR-id-us: horrid). Leaves 6–24 in. across, palmately 7- to 9-lobed, fine-toothed, lying flat, all near top of stem; leafstalks and main leaf veins spiny; flowers 1/4 in., whitish, in a single spike up to 10 in. tall; berries bright red, 2- to 3-seeded, 1/4 in.; stems 3–14 ft. tall, 1/2–1 1/2 in. thick, punky, crooked, usually unbranched, entirely covered with yellowish tan prickles. Seeps and small creeks. Araliaceae.

Devil's club prefers cold, shaded, sopping, "gloomy" spots. A devil's club thicket is thorniness in the extreme, borne on knobby, twisted, tangled, untapering stalks rising out of wet black earth. In summer these hide devilishly under an attractive umbrella of huge leaves. Worse, the spines inject a mild irritant. The scarlet berries, eventual centerpiece to the broad table of leaves, aren't recommended either. Stunningly, it is now becoming a garden ornamental. Handle with care.

The plant does have a beneficent side, which the oxymoron *Oplopanax* hints at. *Oplo* implies weaponry; *panax* is a cure, as in *panacea*. The cure half of the name refers to a relative, ginseng (genus *Panax*), perhaps

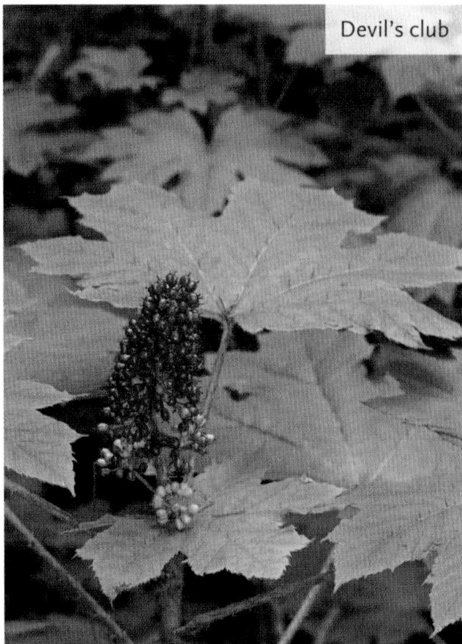

Devil's club

the most cross-culturally recognized of all herbal panaceas.

Under devil's club's thorns lies a thin bark, which has claims as a panacea on its own merits. Northwest tribes used it to alleviate colds, arthritis, bronchitis, diabetes, tuberculosis, body odor (a concern of hunters when near game), excessive milk, amenorrhea, and more. The Cheyenne and Crow smoked devil's club roots (obtained through trade, along with the tobacco they mixed with it) to cure headaches. The Tlingit make it into an antibiotic salve today, which my informant swears by, and an infusion that some believe cures cancer.

Poison-Oak

Toxicodendron diversilobum (toxic-oh-DEN-dron: poison tree; diverse-il-OH-bum: varied lobes). Also *Rhus diversiloba*. Leaves compound, leaflets 3 (rarely 5), 2–4 in., with variable coarse, round-tipped lobes; foliage red and glossy when new; some leaves scarlet again by late summer; flowers 1/4 in., greenish white; berries in drooping strings, white, 1/4 in., striped lengthwise; straggly shrubs 2–6 ft. or sometimes vines climbing up to 40 ft. on trees. Low in CGorge, up to mid-elevs in w CasR. Anacardiaceae.

Leaflets in threes almost always.

Some leaflets crimson by midsummer; others merely yellowing just before dropping in fall.

New foliage reddish and glossy in spring; later, foliage is not often strikingly glossy in our region.

Translucent white berries (for mnemonic aid, think of blisters) in bunches, present by late summer and into winter, long after the leaves; many plants may fail to fruit.

Often on or near white oak, its leaflets seeming to mimic nearby oak leaves in shape, sheen, and shade.

Unlike nettle stingers—an elaborate and effective defense against browsing—poison-oak (and -ivy or -sumac) poison has little survival value to the plant. Call it an accident of biochemistry, or one of the commonest allergies in *Homo sapiens*. Other animals are rarely affected; some even gather the nectar, eat the berries, or browse the leaves.

In humans, susceptibility can be acquired but rarely shed. People sure of their immunity have tried to show it off, only

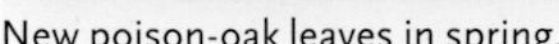

New poison-oak leaves in spring.

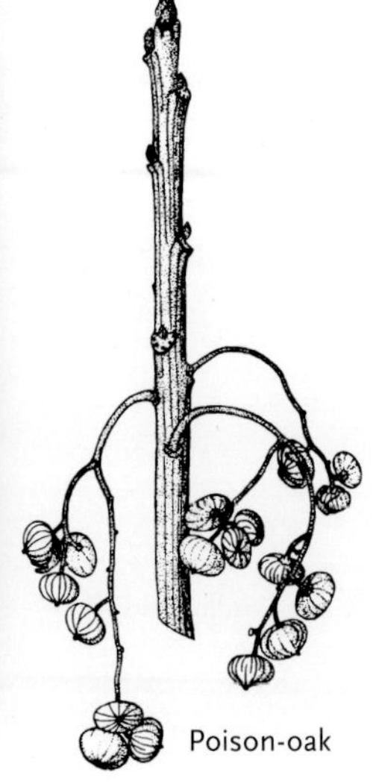

Poison-oak

to get a rude shock a couple of days later. Apparently this never happened to C. Leo Hitchcock, senior author of *Flora of the Pacific Northwest,* who liked to show off by casually picking specimens with his bare hands on class field trips. Lore has it that immunity can be cultivated by eating tiny leaves over the period of their development in spring. Don't try it.

Symptoms usually appear, if at all, between 12 and 72 hours after contact. We may start itching within minutes of laying eyes on poison-oak, but that's due to other irritants—like anxiety. If you wash your exposed parts within ten minutes with soap and hot water (or, in the field, with a skin cleanser like Tecnu) and quarantine your exposed clothes (and dogs) until laundry, your chances of escaping are excellent. The allergen, urushiol, may be anywhere on the plant, definitely including bare twigs in winter. A few people are alarmingly sensitive. There have been fatalities following poison-ivy smoke inhalation—drownings, technically, in a sea of blister fluid in the lungs. (The toxin is destroyed by complete burning, but smoke may carry unburned particles.)

For most of us, the only defense needed is to know when we are going into areas where poison-oak or -ivy grows, and then to spot the plants without fail, and circumvent them. If you want to be extra cautious, try IvyBlock, a barrier cream that you spread on your skin. All in all, our mountains are almost as good a place for staying away from poison-oak and -ivy as from poisonous snakes.

Western poison-ivy, *T. rydbergii,* with pointier leaves, barely enters our range at lowest elevations east of the Cascades.

LOW TO MEDIUM SHRUBS: DECIDUOUS ALTERNATE LEAVES, STAMENS NOT COUNTABLE

Big Sagebrush

Artemisia tridentata (ar-tem-EE-zhia: the Greek name, honoring either a goddess or a queen; try-den-TAY-ta: 3-toothed). Composite flower heads drab yellowish, tiny, in loose spikes; leaves spicy-aromatic, grayish-woolly, wedge-shaped, 3-lobed at the tip (average ½ in. wide), tapering gradually from there to base; bark shreddy; average 2–6 ft. tall where growing abundantly at lower timberline (and eastward *ad nauseam*); or dwarfed to 1–1½ ft. on subalpine ridges. Asteraceae.

Big sagebrush

Vast sagebrush-dotted steppes lie east of the forested Cascades; this legendary bush could have been left out of this book but for its role in subalpine communities on ridges east of the crest in Washington. The form growing there is a dwarfed, isolated ecotype sometimes regarded as a distinct species. Sagebrush is closely related not to culinary sage (*Salvia,* in the mint family) but to culinary tarragon and wormwood (p. 199).

Dwarf Willow

***Salix* spp.** (SAY-lix: Roman for willow). ♀ and ♂ catkins on separate plants; twigs yellowish to purplish; mat-forming shrubs usually less than 4 in. tall. Alp/subalpine in BC and WA. Salicaceae.

Snow willow, *S. nivalis* (niv-AY-lis: of snow). Also *S. reticulata.* Catkins maturing before

Snow willow

Arctic willow

Cascade willow

leaves, 4- to 17-flowered, 1⁄4–5⁄8 in. long; leaves oval, round-tipped, 3⁄8–11⁄2 in., green above, grayish but hairless beneath, conspicuously net-veined, leathery.

Cascade willow, *S. cascadensis* Catkins maturing after leaves, 15- to 35-flowered, 3⁄8–1 in. long; leaves elliptic, point-tipped, 1⁄4–1⁄2 in., about equally green above and below, leathery.

Arctic willow, *S. arctica* Catkins maturing after leaves, 30- to 60-flowered, 3⁄4–11⁄4 in. long; leaves 1⁄2–3 in. long, 1⁄4–2 in. wide, round or point-tipped, green above, grayish beneath.

True willows reduced to carpet stature abound in alpine tundra, as they do in the Arctic. Some of these species grow taller elsewhere. An arctic willow in Greenland had 236 annual rings.

LOW TO MEDIUM SHRUBS: DECIDUOUS ALTERNATE LEAVES, 8 OR 10 STAMENS

Huckleberry or Blueberry

***Vaccinium* spp.** (vac-SIN-ium: the Roman name). Leaves elliptic; flowers pinkish, small, globular, with 5 (rarely 4) very short, bent-back corolla lobes, and similar calyx lobes on the tip of the berry. Ericaceae.

This diverse and well-distributed genus has always been of great interest to bears, birds, Indians, and hikers. Toward summer's end, bear scats are often little more than barely cemented heaps of huckleberry leaves; the cement is first to decompose, so you may wonder, a week or two later, how these heaps of dry leaves came to be so neatly molded. Bears urgently need to fatten up at that time of year, and don't waste much time separating berries from leaves before eating.

Northwest tribes used carefully timed fire to maintain extensive berry patches. That legacy dwindled under Smokey's anti-fire administration, before the Forest Service rediscovered the beauties of a low blaze; one USFS report assigned twice as high a cash value per acre per year to berries as to the trees likely to replace them on subalpine sites. A bear as spokesman for the anti-fire campaign is ironic at best, since bears undoubtedly prefer management that maximizes berry crops.

"Huckleberry" vs. "blueberry" is a murky issue. In the East a related genus (*Gaylussacia*) with seedy black berries has first claim to the name huckleberry. Some authors use the old English names "whortleberry" and "bilberry," but I have trouble saying those with a straight face. Another calls them all blueberries, even the "red blueberries." Following western vernacular use, I call the wild ones huckleberries unless they're low and quite blue. Only easterners will be confused.

The Northwest has twelve species of huckleberry. The six included here, taken in order of descending elevation, are each important in one or more montane community types.

Cascades blueberry, *V. deliciosum* Berries bright blue due to a heavy bloom; flowers spherical; leaves slightly toothed; plants 2–18 in. tall. Alp/subalpine.

Cascades blueberries provide about 90 percent of the gorgeous scarlet fall color of subalpine slopes, and can also be credited for a lot of excitement in the animal kingdom at that time of year. *Deliciosum*, indeed. And good for us, too. Their blue pigments are flavonoids that work in our bodies as antioxidants. Rats fed a rat equivalent of one cup of blueberries a day were able to reverse the effects of aging on memory: older rats' memories kept improving until they could beat

Blueberries ablaze.

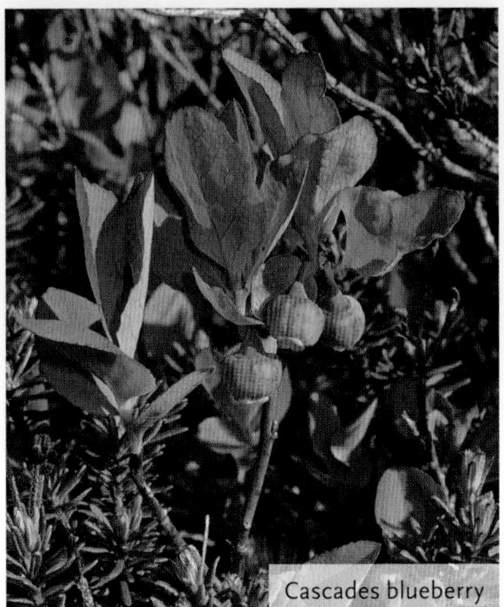
Cascades blueberry

Dwarf blueberry

Grouseberry

young rats on memory tests. Potential beneficial effects on glucose metabolism, heart disease, and cancer have been seen *in vitro*, but not conclusively in clinical studies.

On moist alpine sites, they often grow on a 2- to 3-inch scale that makes the berries look hugely rotund. Both there and in the subalpine zone, where they average a foot in stature, they often grow with red, yellow, or white mountain heathers. This low heath community is highly characteristic of our range. Typical sites are next to subalpine trees or on rocky subalpine convexities, in either case getting a longer snow-free season than nearby herbaceous meadows.

Dwarf blueberry, *V. cespitosum* (see-spit-OH-sum: growing in clumps). Berries light blue with heavy bloom, ¼–⅜ in.; flowers much longer than wide; twigs usually minutely hairy, reddish brown to yellow-green; 2–14 in. tall. Mainly alp/subalpine; a few low records.

The narrow flowers easily separate this from the more abundant Cascades blueberry, but when in fruit it's easy to conflate the two.

Grouseberry, *V. scoparium* (sco-PAIR-ium: broom—). Berries bright red, tiny (⅛ in.); leaves ¼–½ in.; twigs green, with angled edges, numerous, making a broomy shrub 4–14 in. tall. Near and e of CasCr; a few VI records, and Saddle Mtn, OR.

Grouseberry is locally abundant on dry habitats, often on gravelly volcanic soil. The fruit is good but hard to gather in quantity.

Black huckleberry, *V. membranaceum* (mem-bra-NAY-see-um: thin). Also thinleaf huckleberry. Berries black to dark red; flowers much longer than broad; leaves 1–2½ in., thin, pointed, minutely toothed; 2–6 ft. tall. Clearings and forests not far from timberline.

The top huckleberry for combined availability, flavor, and texture, black huckleberry is the main attraction of the

Grouseberry

Black huckleberry

Oval-leaf huckleberry

huge wild huckleberry fields southwest of Mt. Adams. Though it grows and bears fruit most lavishly in burns and other clearings, it also dominates the shrub layer of many midmontane forests. It mingles there with the following two species, or with Cascades blueberry around timberline.

Oval-leaf huckleberry, *V. ovalifolium* (o-val-if-OH-lium: oval leaf). Also *V. alaskaense*. Berries blue with bloom or purplish black without bloom; leaves 3/4–2½ in., smooth edged; 1½–5 ft. Abundant in mid-elev w-side forests.

Typically a straggly understory shrub, oval-leaved huckleberry is prepared to burst forth after fire or clearcut.

Red huckleberry, *V. parvifolium* (par-vif-OH-lium: small leaf). Berries bright red; flowers at least as broad as long; leaves ¼–1 in., smooth-edged; twigs squarish, angled; 3–12 ft. W-side.

Red huckleberry is widely scattered in lower west-side forest spots that have some warmth. Its berries are sparse, juicy, and

Red huckleberry

sour; if only they were easier to gather in quantity, the legendary red huckleberry pie would be better known.

White Rhododendron

Rhododendron albiflorum (roe-doe-DEN-dron: rose tree, a doubly misleading name; al-bif-LOR-um: white flower). Also Cascades azalea. Flowers white, 3/4 in. across, broadly bell-shaped, petals fused no more than half their length, 1–4 in clusters just below

White rhododendron
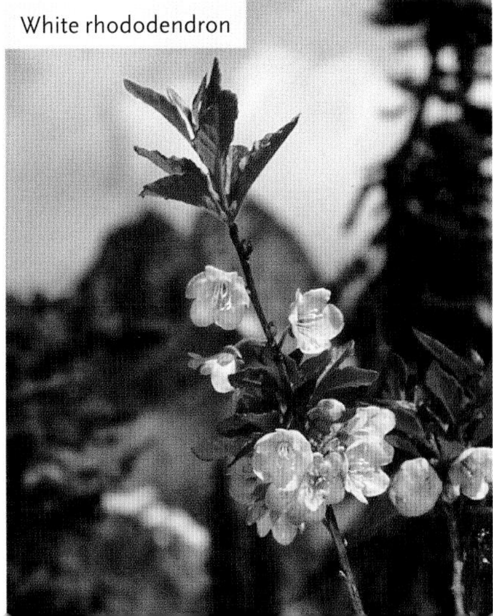

Archibald Menzies

Archibald Menzies was the first European scientist in the Northwest south of Alaska. On the strength of a brief and relatively inconsequential first visit to Vancouver Island, in 1787, he was appointed surgeon-naturalist on HMS *Discovery* under Captain George Vancouver. Menzies's journal records the *Discovery*'s 1792 landing at Discovery Bay, Washington, and the naming of many land and water features after officers on the ship (Puget, Whidbey, Baker, Vancouver) and Englishmen the captain admired (Rainier, St. Helens, Hood). The ship's mission allowed Menzies little time for botanizing ashore, and his live collections all died on board, but his plant descriptions and dried specimens that did reach England aroused intense interest in the Northwest, eventually leading to voyages by David Douglas and others. Menzies was an old man in 1824 when young Douglas visited him for a briefing on Northwest plants.

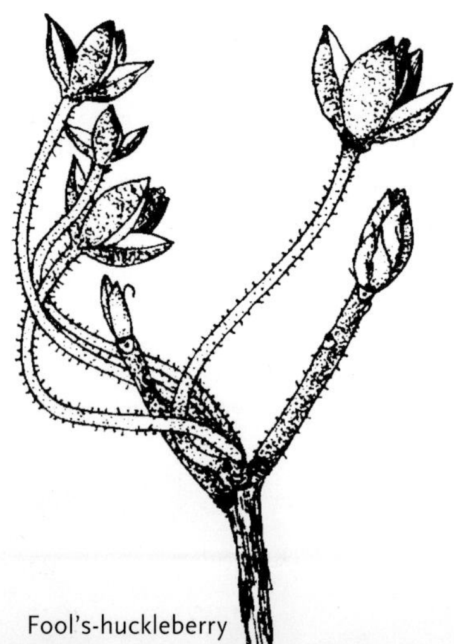

Fool's-huckleberry

Fool's-huckleberry

the whorl-like leaf clusters at branch tips; leaves elliptic, 2–3½ in., glossy, bumpy, slightly reddish-hairy; capsules 5-celled; bark shredding; leggy shrubs 3–6 ft. Openings and thickets not far from timberline, or sometimes lower. Ericaceae.

It's hard to see these blossoms—modest by garden "rhodie" standards—as rhododendrons, but few who reach their habitat by trail would slight their beauty.

Fool's-Huckleberry

Menziesia ferruginea (men-ZEE-zia: for Archibald Menzies, above; fair-u-JIN-ia: rust-red). Also false-azalea, rusty-leaf. Flowers pale rusty orange, jar-shaped, pendent on sticky-hairy pedicels, ¼ in., calyx and corolla shallowly 4-lobed, stamens 8; capsules 4-celled; leaves 1½–2½ in., elliptic, seemingly whorled near branch tips, often hairy, coloring deeply in fall; bark shreddy; leggy shrubs 3–6 ft. Cold moist sites, mid-elevs to subalpine. Ericaceae.

Producing no berries to tempt anyone, this is at best a fool's fool's-huckleberry. True, its summer foliage might be carelessly mistaken for black huckleberry, or for white rhododendron, both of which it often grows with. In coastal British Columbia it is more abundant in valleys that lack salmon, which enrich soils with nitrogen and phosphorus. Thanks to symbiotic fungi, fool's-huckleberry competes more effectively in relatively infertile soils.

Menziesia's flower parts in fours are unusual in the heath family.

Copperbush

Cladothamnus pyrolaeflorus (clad-a-THAM-nus: sprouting bush; pie-roll-ee-FLOR-us: flowers like *Pyrola*). Also *Elliottia pyroliflora.* Flowers salmon-orange, mostly single, up to 1 in. across; 5 narrow, spreading petals, 5 narrow calyx lobes, 10 stamens, 1 up-curved or hooked style; fruit a 5-celled round capsule; leaves pale underneath, entire, oblanceolate, drawing to a pointed tip, alternate but sometimes appearing almost whorled; bark coppery, exfoliating; 2–10 ft. tall. Often in wet places, but not always; mid-elevs to subalpine in BC, nw WA; CoastR s to Saddle Mtn. Ericaceae.

The Tsimshian brewed copperbush tea as an apéritif.

Copperbush

TREES AND SHRUBS: BROADLEAF EVERGREEN, MEDIUM TO TALL

Broadleaf evergreens are primarily a tropical and subtropical life form: where the growing season is year-round, it makes no sense for leaves to go away for half the year. Though our region has winters, it offers advantages to evergreen plants that can continue their life functions, even at sharply reduced rates, through the cool seasons (p. 46). Our type of broadleaf evergreens, called sclerophylls ("hardened leaves"), have adapted with heavy, rigid leaves that dry out partially in summer, reducing transpiration and conserving water, without danger of wilt damage. Most of temperate North America's sclerophylls are found in Pacific coastal forests—many here in our range, but far more in southwestern Oregon and northern California. Down there, wet mild marine winters like ours alternate with summers longer, dryer, and hotter than ours. That sounds just like the climate that the models predict for up here. Sclerophylls of the Klamath region may do well here in the near future.

This section begins with our two tree-form sclerophylls, and moves on down in size, yielding to the Low category at around 2 feet of stature. The heath family (Ericaceae) dominates this section; members typically have elliptic leaves and small, often white to pink, jar-shaped flowers.

Madrona

Arbutus menziesii (ar-BEW-tus or AR-but-us: Roman name; men-ZEE-zee-eye: for Archibald Menzies, opposite). Also arbutus, madrone, madroño. Flowers small, white, jar-shaped, 5-lobed, berries bright orange, pebbly skinned, many-seeded, ¼–½ in. in large clusters; leaves heavy, glossy dark green above, silvery beneath, oblong, 2½–6 in.; bark flaking in thin sheets, very smooth and pale green when young, turning through bronze to deep red, finally becoming rough dark gray-brown near base; irregularly branched trees commonly 24 in. dbh × 60 ft. Sunny, rocky slopes at low

Madrona

elevs as far n as Desolation Sound, BC; up to mid-elevs in w CasR, OR. Ericaceae.

I can't stop gazing at madrona bark, can't resist touching it, only barely resist stripping it—such elegant voluptuous limbs, so smooth and richly colored. Similar limbs on a smaller scale grow on manzanitas, similar leaves on rhododendron; but of all the heath family, only *Arbutus* grows as a tree. It is by far the most northerly broadleaf evergreen tree on the continent, growing along the coast from mountains near San Diego to rocky shorelines up on the Georgia Strait. To cover that stretch it has to be indifferent to precipitation (18–166 inches a year) and temperature, requiring only that its own spot be well drained and sunny. It is most abundant in the Klamath region, where its ability to resprout from roots that survive a fire is a great boon to the forest. The thriving madrona sprouts sustain populations of mycorrhizal fungi that would otherwise die out after the fire; the fungi enable conifer seedlings to thrive around the madrona nurse trees.

Since 2011, madronas have been afflicted by a leaf blight that turns the leaves brown and crisp, leaving many trees looking almost dead by late spring. Then the new leaves come out. Little is known yet about this blight's long-term effects.

Around the Mediterranean grows a shrubby tree, *A. unedo,* called *arbutus* by the Romans, *madro* by the Spanish, and "strawberry tree" by the English. Spaniards in early California recognized its relative, calling it "big madro," madroño, later corrupted by Anglos into madrone or madrona. The sweetish berries of the strawberry-tree flavor a liqueur, *crème d'arbouse,* but madrona berries are bitter and slightly narcotic. The wood is heavy, hard, strong, and beautiful, but tends to split during drying. Indians made spoons and ladles from it.

Golden Chinquapin

Chrysolepis chrysophylla (cris-a-LEP-iss: gold scale; cris-a-FILL-a: gold leaf). Also *Castanopsis chrysophylla.* Catkins clustered erect at branchtips, each bearing a series of ♂ fuzzballs, with fewer ♀ flowers near the base of the catkin; nuts ¼–½ in., in very spiny ¾-in. hulls; leaves 3–6 in., narrow, tapering, dark glossy green above, with a rough yellow-brown ("golden") coating beneath; new twigs yellow-coated; bark white-splotched in youth, eventually thick

Golden chinquapin

Golden chinquapin

and furrowed; shrubs or trees up to 40 ft. Drier forests and thickets, mainly OR w-side. Fagaceae.

In its best range—southwestern Oregon and northwestern California—the golden chinquapin is a big tree, up to 150 feet by 6 feet diameter, which would top any of our broadleaf trees except cottonwood. In our range, however, it's more often a tall shrub. It is easy to spot in much of Oregon's Cascades as the only big shrub with such long, narrow, evergreen leaves. In Washington it grows only in a few stands—near the Columbia Gorge; the southeast corner of the Olympics; and near the King-Snohomish county line—that are relict from the warm era of 9000 to 5000 years ago, when chinquapin was widespread in Washington.

Chinquapins are in a family with oak, beech, and chestnut trees. The word *chinquapin*, for chestnut trees (genus *Castanea*), is originally Algonquinian. Chinquapin nuts and chestnuts alike are edible, and borne one to three in a bristly hull. The wood is easily worked, and takes on a beautiful hue. Pioneers made it into implements.

Chinquapins grow swellings called burls right at the soil surface. Burls send up new sprouts after the higher parts of the plant die in fires.

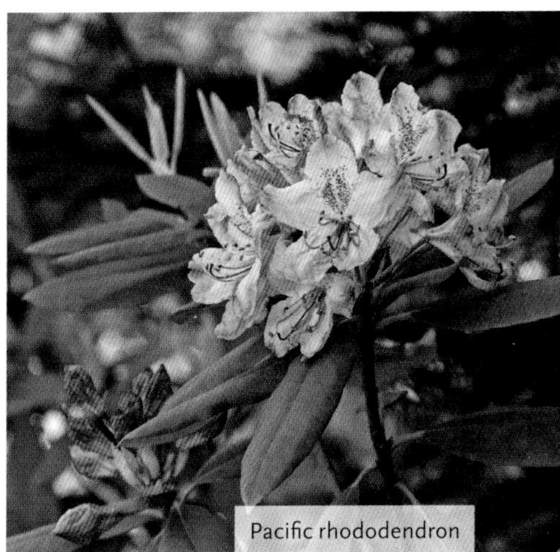
Pacific rhododendron

Pacific Rhododendron

Rhododendron macrophyllum (roe-doe-DEN-dron: rose tree, two misleading words for this genus; macro-FILL-um: big leaf). Flowers pink, 1–2 in., broadly bell-shaped, in large dense clusters, petals and sepals 5, fused at the base, 1 upper petal usually spotted; capsules woody, 5-celled, ½–¾ in.; leaves heavy, deep glossy green, 3–8 in. long, with smooth rolled-under edges; often straggly shrubs 3–15 ft. Abundant in some drier mid-elev forest, OR and s WA CasR and e OlyM. Ericaceae.

The 600-odd species of genus *Rhododendron*—mostly Asian—have been recombined into thousands of garden "rhodies" and azaleas of all colors. They make overwhelming displays. Our native rhododendron is plain pink, spends most of its time in the shade, and runs to legginess. Still, when the woods are in bloom with them, like fat pink mirages on a gray day, or like randomly bursting fireworks in the shifting sunbeams of a sunny day, they have power to enchant. Washington named them its state flower, perhaps to make up for having fewer of them than Oregon.

Trapper's tea

Labrador tea

Salal

Trapper's Tea and Labrador Tea

***Rhododendron* spp.** Flowers white, 1/2 in. across, in showy rounded clusters; 5 petals, around 10 stamens; leaves oval, thick, resinous; twigs sticky-hairy; 1½–5 ft. Ericaceae.

Trapper's tea, *R. neoglandulosum* (neo-gland-you-LO-sum: North American, with sticky glands). Also *R. columbianum*, *Ledum glandulosum*. Leaves nearly flat, whitish or green underneath and rough with dense glands, ¾–1½ in. Mid-elev boggy forest to subalpine meadow; e CasR from Mt. Rainier n.

Labrador tea, *R. groenlandicum* (green-LAND-ic-um: of Greenland). Also *Ledum groenlandicum*. Leaves covered with rusty wool underneath, ¾–2½ in., edges usually strongly rolled under, making the leaf look narrow. Swamps, boggy forest at low to mid-elevs; BC, w-side in WA.

All across the continent, leaves of this genus were popular as a stimulant tea. Tribes of our region may have learned this use from whites, as suggested by the traditional names trapper's tea and Hudson's Bay tea. The toxic and stimulant alkaloids are much stronger in trapper's than in Labrador tea, which enjoyed far more use as tea. I don't recommend either, but especially not trapper's.

Salal

Gaultheria shallon (galth-EE-ria: for Jean-Francois Gaultier; SHALL-on: NW tribal term). Corolla pinkish to white, bell-shaped to spherical, sepals red; flowers 6–15, pendent along a horizontal stalk; berries purple-black; flowers, berries, and their stalks minutely hairy and sticky; leaves glossy, leathery, broadly oval, pointed, 2–3½ in.; branches zigzagging at leaf nodes; shrubs 1–8 ft. W-side low to mid-elevs. Ericaceae.

April 1825. Saturday the 9th in company with Mr. Scouler I went ashore on Cape Disappointment as the ship could not proceed up the river in consequence of heavy rains and thick fogs. On stepping on the shore *Gaultheria shallon* was the first plant I took in my hands. So pleased was I that I could scarcely see anything but it. Mr. Menzies correctly observes that it . . . would make a valuable addition to our gardens. . . .

> (1826) Called by the natives "salal," not "shallon" as stated by Pursh. . . . Bears abundantly, fruit good, indeed by far the best in the country.
>
> —David Douglas

Surely David Douglas would not have logged this appraisal if he weren't new here—if he had been in the mountains in huckleberry season. Regardless, salal berries deserve a better reputation than they now enjoy. They almost rival huckleberries in flavor—less acid, with spicy resinous overtones—but their skins and seeds are heavy, so they are most popular strained for jelly. Formerly, salal was the sweetest and most available berry for coastal tribes. Northwest tribes dried huge quantities of them in big cakes or loaves, stored them wrapped in skunk-cabbage leaves, and ate them all winter long dipped in seal or candlefish oil. According to Kwakiutl protocol (some of the most elaborate and stringent protocol ever known) pure salal cakes were exclusive fare for chiefs at feasts; the *hoi polloi* were allowed only cakes of salal berries stretched with fruit, such as red elderberries, that are barely edible by themselves.

As for becoming "a valuable addition to English gardens," it looked true enough for a century or more, but the English are starting to regard salal as weedy. Don't waste your pity on them. Several of our worst invasives—Scotch broom, gorse, English ivy, holly, and stinky Bob—came here from the British Isles.

The leaves, which live about four years, are important winter browse for deer. Salal branches are the Northwest's volume leader in the florist greens trade. Cropped plants respond by becoming bushier. Salal picking rights are lucrative enough that one brush-picker murdered another over them in a tragedy that echoed several murders among matsutake mushroom pickers in the 1990s.

At higher elevations, two dwarf shrubs called wintergreen (p. 148) are recognizable as salal's baby brothers.

Salal

Salal spreads by sprouting from rhizomes. Big clonal thickets often grow in areas of poor soil. (Like others in its family, salal has a rich partnership with mycorrhizal fungi that procure ample nitrogen and phosphorus from soils deficient in same; adding fertilizer actually stunts salal's growth.) Typically, salal grows under gappy canopies. When a canopy gap closes up over salal plants, they respond by growing bigger, thinner "shade leaves," and can survive deep shade for several years waiting for the next tree death to bring back the sun flecks; then they make small (less than 2 inches wide) thick "sun leaves" again, even from the same twig that bore shade leaves last year. During the deep shade period, the salal thicket thins out, letting many of its stems and rhizomes die. When it finds itself in a gap again it re-densifies, sending up new root sprouts.

Snowbrush

Ceanothus velutinus (see-an-OATH-us: thistle, a misleading name; ve-LU-tin-us: velvety). Also tobacco-brush, cinnamon-bush, sticky-laurel. Flowers tiny, white, in dense, fluffy 2- to 5-in. clusters; petals, sepals, and stamens each 5; seedpods of 3 separating, 1-seeded cells; leaves 1½–3½ in., broadly oval, minutely toothed, often tightly curling, spicy-aromatic, shiny and sticky above, pale-fuzzy beneath (or nearly smooth on a variety found w-side below 2600 ft.), with 3 main veins from base nearly to tip; robust shrubs 2–6 ft. Dry, sunny clearings, abundant e-side. Rhamnaceae.

Snowbrush

Snowbrush invades burns and slash-burned clearcuts. Its seeds lie dormant and viable in the soil as long as 300 years, waiting to be reawakened by the heat of a fire and the increased soil warmth of a new clearing. The reappearance of a full-blown snowbrush community centuries after snowbrush was shaded out of the forest will seem miraculous. The young shoots grow slowly, but crowd out annuals like fireweed in three or four seasons. The roots host nitrogen-fixing bacteria, a big advantage where the soil has lost most of its organic nitrogen. Snowbrush often grows dense enough to discourage conifer establishment, especially in southern Oregon where it rose high on foresters' hit lists. But like the once-maligned red alder, it actually aids conifer growth a few years later, with the nitrogen. In between fires, snowbrush reproduction is largely vegetative. Snowbrush may have been smoked once or twice, but I think it's called "tobacco-brush" for its fragrance in the afternoon sun. Herbalists gather it as "red root," for medicinal use.

Snowbrush

Oregon-Grape

***Berberis* spp.** (BER-ber-iss: the Arabic name). Also barberries, mahonias; *Mahonia* spp. Flowers yellow, in a terminal group of 3- to 7-in. spikes amid a cluster of sharp ½- to 2-in. bud scales; petals or sepals in 5 concentric whorls of 3, outer whorl(s) greenish; berries ⅜ in., grapelike, purple with a blue bloom; leaves compound, crowded at top of stem, 8–16 in. long; spiny-margined (like holly), pointed-oval; inner bark yellow. Berberidaceae.

Cascade Oregon-grape, *B. nervosa* (ner-VO-sa: veiny) Leaflets 11–21, each with several main veins branching palmately; 4–40 in. tall. Abundant in w-side forests; almost ubiquitous at low to mid-elevs in w OR mtns.

Tall Oregon-grape, *B. aquifolium* (ak-wif-OH-lium: holly leaf). Leaflets 5 or 7 (rarely 9), pinnately veined, shiny; 2–10 ft. tall. Open forest, mainly e-side and low elevs.

Creeping Oregon-grape, *B. repens* (REE-penz: creeping). Also *B. aquifolium* var. *repens*. Like tall Oregon-grape, only short: 4–18 in. Open forests e of CasCr.

Though Northwesterners today may take them for granted, in his quest for English garden plants David Douglas rated tall

Creeping Oregon-grape

Cascade Oregon-grape

Cascade Oregon-grape

Tall Oregon-grape

Oregon-grape and salal each like striking gold. Though the leaves are evergreen, a few may burst crimson at any time of year. The stamens snap inward at the lightest touch to shake their pollen onto a bee.

The berries (not grapes, by a long shot) have an exquisite sourness not balanced by much sweetness. Both jelly and wine from Oregon-grapes are traditional since pioneer days, but decreasingly popular. Gourmands may gag, but those with a penchant for wild plant foods still smack their lips. They're juicy, and refreshing in their way. Indians mashed them with sweeter berries for winter storage in dry cakes. Tall Oregon-grape is Oregon's state flower.

The roots were gathered for yellow dye, and used medicinally, especially for stomach ills and dysmenorrhea. Today, one ingredient (berberine) is a recognized antibiotic and shows promise for treating antibiotic-resistant staph infections.

Disagreement over whether to split genus *Berberis*, putting the Oregon-grapes in their own genus *Mahonia*, has gone on at least since 1825, when Douglas pooh-poohed a rival thus: "Nuttall's division into *Mahonia* is trifling." His condescension reverberates in the 1997 *Flora of North America* treatment: "*Mahonia* is often recognized in horticultural works, but it is seldom recognized by botanists." Botanists at E-Flora BC and the USDA would take exception. USDA separates *Mahonia* from *Berberis*, but then oddly puts them back together by giving them all "barberry" for a common name.

Oregon Boxwood

Paxistima myrsinites (pa-KIS-tim-a: thick stigma; mir-sin-EYE-teez: myrrh-like). Also Oregon boxleaf, myrtle-boxwood, mountain lover, false box. Flowers 1/8 in. across, clustered in leaf axils, dark red petals, whitish stamens, and sepals each 4; capsules splitting in two; leaves opposite, 1/2–1 1/4 in., elliptic, shallowly toothed, glossy, dark above; twigs reddish, 4-angled; 8–24 in. Dryish forests, mainly at mid-elevs. Celastraceae.

Oregon boxwood

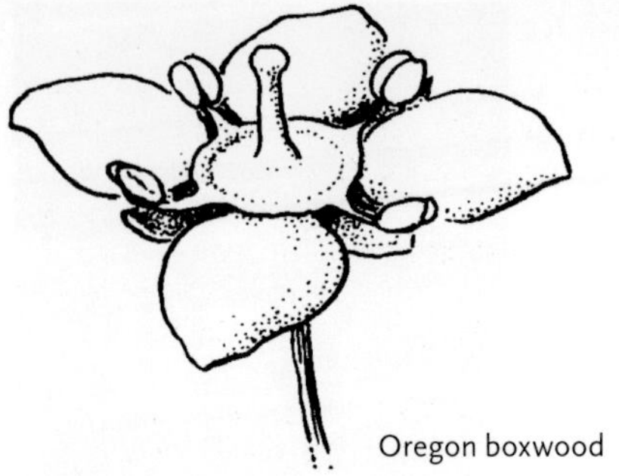
Oregon boxwood

Opposite evergreen leaves distinguish this plant from our heath shrubs other than tiny *Kalmia*, and from pretty much anything else in our range. They aren't truly opposite, though; botanists look at them closely and find them to be alternate, but on casual inspection they pass for opposite. Otherwise Oregon boxwood looks much like the heath family; florists use it interchangeably with evergreen blueberry from the coast, and few customers notice the difference. Deer and elk browse it in winter when there are few other green leaves around.

Green manzanita

Manzanita

***Arctostaphylos* spp.** (arc-to-STAF-il-os: bear grapes). Flowers pinkish to white, jar-shaped, 5-lobed, in small clusters; berries reddish brown, dry, mealy; leaves broadly elliptic, 1–2 in.; larger branches smooth, red, with peeling flakes; dense shrubs 3–10 ft. Pumice, lava flows, rocky exposed sites at all elevs. Ericaceae.

Green manzanita, *A. patula* (PATCH-u-la: spreading). Leaves bright yellow-green, hairless or with minute hairs. E-side as far n as Lake Chelan, WA.

Hairy manzanita, *A. columbiana* Leaves, leafstalks, and young twigs grayish with long fine hairs. W-side and CGorge, as far n as Desolation Sound, BC.

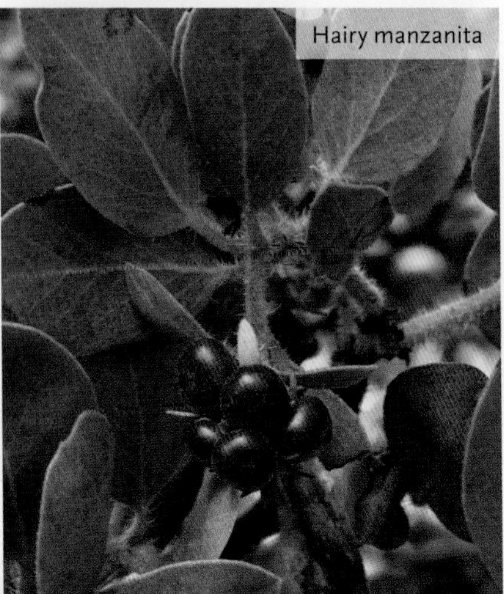
Hairy manzanita

More than thirty species of manzanita conspire in the making of California's notorious chaparral, a dense brushfield community adapted for taking over mountain slopes after fires. Manzanita seeds lie dormant in the soil until awakened by ground-fire heat; between fires, the plants spread by layering. After the chaparral burns, manzanita sprouts like crazy from the root crowns.

Our manzanitas are remote outliers of the chaparral, and they lack chaparral's monopolistic success. In fact, they probably help forests recover after fires, because heath shrubs share with conifers many of the same mycorrhizal partner species; the resprouting manzanitas sustain the mycorrhizal community, which conifers will need as soon as their seedlings germinate. Otherwise the soil might be taken over by fungi that associate with grasses, say, or rose-family shrubs—not as good for conifers.

In lowlands where their ranges overlap, hairy manzanita hybridizes with kinnickinnick, producing a red-fruited low erect shrub popular in cultivation.

LOW SHRUBS: BROADLEAF EVERGREEN

These shrubs are generally just inches tall, though a few are sometimes seen reaching 2 feet. A woody stem is hard to detect in very small plants, but if you see firm, dark, waxy-looking leaves held up off the ground, you know the stem holding them up has to be a year-round, woody stem. But when evergreen leaves are in rosettes right upon the ground, the woody stem is vanishingly short, so I won't ask you to discern it; look in the next chapter for rattlesnake-plantain (p. 179) and pyrolas (p. 243).

Some plants also fudge evergreenness. Many small species whose closest relatives are clearly deciduous have adapted to long-lasting snowpacks by keeping leaves in place and green through one winter, and then letting them slowly wither as they are replaced by new foliage the next summer. This way there is green foliage ready to photosynthesize, however meagerly, from the first snow-free day to the last. Foliage on this schedule can be called "persistent" or "wintergreen," as opposed to "evergreen" leaves that function during more than two summers. A couple of species with the common name "wintergreen" are actually evergreen shrubs; most of our other wintergreen plants are treated as herbs, in the next chapter.

All but three in the following group are in the heath family, Ericaceae. When in doubt as to evergreenness or shrubbiness, think of other plants your specimen resembles and may be related to.

Kinnickinnick

***Arctostaphylos* spp.** (arc-tos-TAF-il-os: bear grapes in Greek). Flowers pinkish to white, jar-shaped, 5-lobed, clustered; berries 1/4 in., dry and mealy, flat-tasting; leaves 1/2–1 1/4 in., widest past midlength; thin gray bark flaking, revealing smooth red bark underneath. Rocky, exposed sites. Ericaceae.

Kinnickinnick, *A. uva-ursi* (oo-va-UR-sigh: grape of bears in Latin). Also bearberry. Berries bright red; leaf tips rounded; prostrate trailing shrubs rarely 6 in. high. All elevs.

Kinnickinnick

Kinnickinnick

Pinemat manzanita

Pipsissewa

Little pipsissewa

Pinemat manzanita, *A. nevadensis* (nev-a-DEN-sis: of the Sierra Nevada). Berries dull splotchy red-brown; many leaves point-tipped; dense shrubs 4–20 in. tall. Upper mid-elevs, CasR as far n as Rainy Pass, WA; one record from OR CoastR.

Kinnikinnick was an eastern intertribal trading word meaning "smoking herbs." Hudson's Bay Company traders brought the word west. Often mixed with tobacco, the species was smoked everywhere it grows, and it grows from coast to coast.

The berries were starvation fare, or adulterants mixed in with sweeter berries. Small mammals cherish them, though, and deer and elk sometimes rely on them in midwinter, as they last for months on the bush. These species are valuable pioneers on volcanic or glacial soils, and excellent groundcover ornamentals in the cities.

Pipsissewa

***Chimaphila* spp.** (kim-AF-il-a: winter loving). Also prince's-pine. Stamens and pink-to-white petals flat-spreading, pistil fat, hub-like; flowers ½ in. across, nodding; leaves very dark, 1–3 in., narrowly elliptic, saw-toothed, in quasi-whorls on lower half of stem. Forests. Ericaceae.

Pipsissewa, *C. umbellata* (um-bel-AY-ta: bearing flowers in umbels). Flowers 4–12; leaves widest past midlength; plants 4–10 in. tall.

Little pipsissewa, *C. menziesii* (men-ZEE-zee-eye: for Archibald Menzies, p. 136). Flowers 1–3; leaves widest below or near midlength; plants 2–6 in.

These are rather habitat-indifferent forest plants, growing in virtually every type of west-side forest and in closed forests on the east-side as well. Their success under shade suggests dependence on mycorrhizae, which can lead to spotty distribution. The little one is slightly more common higher up, and is confined to the Northwest, whereas the circumboreal *umbellata* ranges across all northern coniferous forests. Their leaves used to sit on apothecary shelves as a remedy for bladderstones. Herbalists still harvest them, sometimes excessively, in the Northwest.

Mountain Heather

***Cassiope* and *Phyllodoce* spp.** (ca-SIGH-a-pee, fil-OD-a-see: two females in Greek myth). Ericaceae.

White heather, *C. mertensiana* (mer-ten-zee-AY-na: for Karl H. Mertens, opposite). Also moss heather. Corolla bell-shaped,

Lütke and the Mertenses

Karl Heinrich Mertens accompanied the Russian Count Fyodor Litke (born Lütke) on his globe-circling voyage of 1826–1829. In London in 1829 their tales so impressed David Douglas that Douglas became obsessed with completing his second trip to the West by sailing from the Russian colony at Sitka to Siberia. He would then have walked the length of Siberia, collecting plants.

Mertens died the following year, at age 34. His plant discoveries at Sitka, southeast Alaska, include the partridgefoot, *Luetkea*, several species named *mertensiana*, *mertensianus*, or *mertensii*, and as many more named *sitchensis*. (They do not include *Mertensia*, the bluebell genus that was named earlier in honor of his father, botany professor Franz Karl Mertens.) On the entire voyage he collected well over a thousand plants, many of them new to science.

white; flowers pendent from axils near branchtips; capsules erect; leaves tiny (1/8 in.), densely packed along the stem in 4 ranks with rounded (not grooved) backs; spreading, mat-forming shrubs 2–12 in. Alp/subalpine.

White heather

Four-angled heather, *C. tetragona* (teh-TRAG-a-na: four sided). Like the preceding, but with a pronounced groove down the center of each rank of leaves. Alpine rocks; BC and nc WA.

Pink heather, *P. empetriformis* (em-pee-trif-OR-mis: crowberry shaped). Corolla pink, bell-shaped; flowers 5–15 in apparent terminal clusters, erect in bud, pendent in bloom, then erect again as dry capsules; leaves needlelike, 1/4–1/2 in.; dense matted shrubs 4–10 in. or up to 15 in. Alp/subalpine.

Yellow heather, *P. glanduliflora* (gland-you-lif-LOR-a: glandular flower). Like the preceding, but corolla cream yellow to off-white, narrow-necked jar-shaped. Alpine.

Four-angled heather

Mountain heather is an old friend, always there to welcome you back to the high country. Loosen your bootlaces, sit still, see how much you can take in.

Scattered patches of pink and white

Pink heather

Yellow heather

Oregon wintergreen

heathers are a common denominator of the subalpine zone throughout the greater Northwest; both reach the alpine zone as well. In subalpine parkland, the heather community typically grows on stony soils with moderately late snowmelt. It is vulnerable to conifer invasion when there is a series of years with earlier snowmelt—something that may be the new normal. As trees grow taller than the annual snowpack, they have a "black body effect," absorbing sunlight and melting snow around them. This creates a feedback loop favoring tree seedlings in surrounding pockets of early melting. Fire, on the other hand, takes out trees and can sometimes restore heather.

Cassiope foliage is somewhat like clubmoss, while *Phyllodoce* foliage is more like common juniper; still, heathers share an obvious mutual resemblance in their flowers and habitat. Vast "heath" communities—species of *Cassiope, Phyllodoce, Erica,* and especially *Calluna*—took over much of Scotland following deforestation and sheep grazing hundreds of years ago. The "Scottish heather" in gardens is *Calluna vulgaris.*

Wintergreen

***Gaultheria* spp.** (galth-EE-ria: for Jean-Francois Gaultier). Flowers white to pinkish, bell-shaped, about 1/8 in. long, from leaf axils; berries red, up to 1/4 in., delicious; leaves oval, somewhat pointed; spreading shrubs 1–6 in. tall. Not in CoastR. Ericaceae.

Oregon wintergreen, *G. ovatifolia* (o-vay-ti-FOE-lia: oval leaf). Sepals and berries hairy; leaves 3/4–1 3/4 in.; mid-elev forest.

Alpine wintergreen, *G. humifusa* (hue-mi-FEW-sa: trailing). Sepals and berries hairless; leaves 1/2–3/4 in.; trailing subshrubs up to 1 1/4 in. tall; around timberline.

Aromatic wintergreen oil comes from the eastern checkerberry, *Gaultheria procumbens,* giving this genus a better claim than

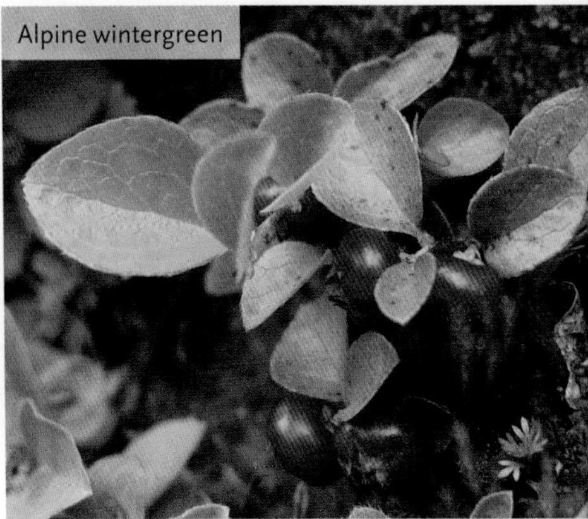
Alpine wintergreen

Pyrola or *Chimaphila* to the common name "wintergreen." However, modern wintergreen gum, candy, and snuff usually get their wintergreen oil (methyl salicylate) either synthetically or from black birch twigs. Wintergreen oil has long been popular both as a flavoring and as a medicine whose best use is as a topical counter-irritant—a balm that soothes aches by heating up the skin. Internally, your body turns it into salicylic acid, the same as it does with aspirin, and in high doses it is toxic. This versatile volatile is released by many plants when aphids attack them, by tropical orchids to attract bees, and by butterfly males upon females after mating, to decrease the female's chance of mating again. The spicy little berries have some of it in them, so eat them with restraint.

Alpine laurel

Alpine azalea

Alpine Laurel

Kalmia microphylla (KAHL-mia: for Per Kalm; micro-FILL-a: small leaf). Also western bog-laurel. Corolla pink, bowl-shaped, ½ in. across; sepals tiny, green; flowers 3–8 in terminal clusters; capsules 5-celled, with long style; leaves opposite, ½–¾ in. long (longer on a coastal bog variety), often with rolled-under edges; spreading subshrub to 6 in. Wet alp/subalpine soils. Ericaceae.

These profuse pink blossoms brighten up high seasonal bogs and soggy alpine slopes right after snowmelt. Look closely: ten little bumps on the odd-shaped buds hold the ten stamen tips. When the flower opens, the stamens are spring-loaded to throw their pollen on the first insect to alight.

This plant and its relatives are toxic. Laurel is a common name for *Kalmia* of all sizes, though they're unrelated to the laurel tree (*Laurus*), whose limbs wreathed champions in ancient Greece. Pioneers also called rhododendrons "mountain laurel."

Alpine laurel

Alpine Azalea

Kalmia procumbens (pro-CUM-benz: prostrate). Also *Loiseluria procumbens*. Corolla pink, flaring bell-shaped, 5-lobed, ¼ in. long; 5 sepals tiny, crimson; flowers 1–6 in terminal clusters; leaves opposite, ¼ in. long, with rolled-under edges; mat-forming subshrub up to 4 in. tall. Low bogs to alpine tundra; w-side in BC; one record from Skagit County, WA. Ericaceae.

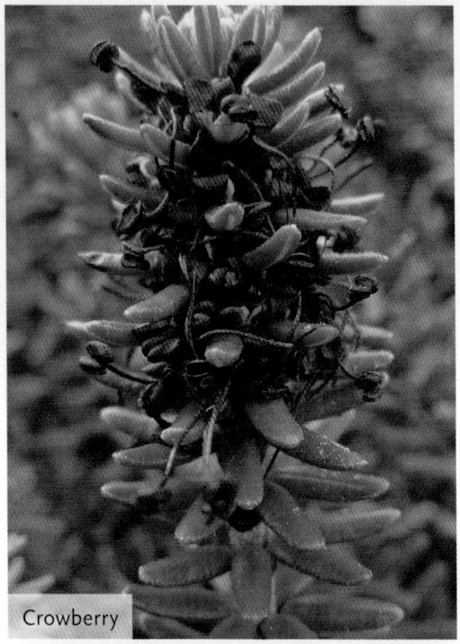
Crowberry

Crowberry

Empetrum nigrum (em-PEE-trum: on rock; NYE-grum: black). Flowers tiny, brownish purple, in leaf axils, parts in 3s (maximum of 3 stamens, 3 petals, 3 sepals, 3 bracts), stamens twice as long as other parts, or sometimes stamens or pistil lacking; berries blue-black, 1⁄8–1⁄4 in., juicy, 6- to 9-seeded; leaves needlelike, crowded, 1⁄4–1⁄2 in., with rolled edges; mat-forming prostrate shrubs, erect stems to 6 in. Rocky alpine slopes. Ericaceae.

Crowberry grows in coastal bogs up north, and sometimes as far south as Oregon, but skips intermediate elevations in our mountains. The berries stay fairly sweet and juicy all winter on the plant under the snow blanket, making them a crucial resource for ptarmigan, grouse, bears, and Alaskan Inuit. For my taste, they are minute, scarce, and insipid. They're extremely high in healthy anthocyanins, though, as we would expect the deepest-colored berries to be.

Olympic rockmat

Olympic Rockmat

Petrophytum hendersonii (petro-FIE-tum: rock plant; hen-der-so-nee-eye: for Louis Henderson). Flowers white, 1⁄4 in. across, many, in a dense spike 3⁄8–2 in. tall, often curving, bristling with the numerous stamens; 5 petals often persist after withering; 5 calyx lobes without intervening bracts; leaves evergreen, thick, oblanceolate, silky, up to 1 in. long, alternate but crammed against the ground in dense low mats; stems woody, flower stalks (but not the leaves) may reach 6 in. tall. Rock crevices, mainly alpine and subalpine, in the OlyM. Rosaceae.

Squawcarpet

Squawcarpet

Ceanothus prostratus (see-an-OATH-us: thistle, a misleading name). Also mahala-mat. Flowers whitish to blue, tiny, with parts in fives, in round-topped clusters from leaf axils; capsules of three 1-seeded cells; leaves opposite or in pairs of oppo-

Carolus Linnaeus

Linnaeus in traditional Sami dress, painted by Hendrik Hollander.

Carl Linnaeus is considered the "Father of Systematic Biology" or taxonomy. Until his day, naturalists often improvised Latin descriptions many words long for any plant or animal under discussion. Linnaeus made everyone's life easier with his idea that the name should be a two-word binomial that all scientists would agree upon for each type (species) of organism, with the first word (genus) being a broader category often embracing several species. During his lifetime (1707–78) he published more than 7000 species, including most of our genera that occur in Europe and quite a few New World genera. He took many genus names from classical Greek or Roman natural history authors like Theophrastus, Pliny, and Dioscorides. In many cases, exactly what plant the name referred to was no longer known, so when I translate a genus name as "the Greek name," I mean it was a name that ancient Greeks used for some plant, but not necessarily the plant Linnaeus gave that name to.

Linnaeus's system for classifying plants was "sexual" in that he based it on the numbers and arrangement of female and male flower parts. In promoting his system he tried out every anthropomorphic sexual metaphor he could think of—"husbands" "promiscuously" sharing the "bedroom" with "wives and concubines"—scandalizing the British.

Carl's father invented the family name by putting a Latin ending on the Swedish word for linden, a tree growing on the family farm. Swedish peasants up until then had not had surnames that passed from generation to generation. Carl was born "Carl Linnaeus," Latinized it to Carolus Linnaeus for his publications, and Swedified it to Carl von Linné when he was appointed to the nobility.

site whorls, spiny-edged (holly-like), ½–1½ in.; mat-forming prostrate shrubs, freely rooting from branch nodes. Infrequent here, e-side CasR from Mt. Adams s. Rhamnaceae.

Twinflower

Linnaea borealis (LIN-ee-a: for Linnaeus, p. 151; bor-ee-AY-lis: northern). Flowers pink to white, two per stalk, conical, pendent, ⅜–1 in. long; 2 shorter and 2 longer stamens; leaves 2 to 6, opposite, glossy, dark, ¼–1 in., usually with a few slight teeth, spicy- or anise-fragrant especially in warm sun; stems 3–5 in., reddish; from long leafy runners. Moist forest at low to mid-elevs. Linnaeaceae or Caprifoliaceae.

Carolus Linnaeus, who chose the scientific names for thousands of plants, asked a colleague to name this one after him. He then wrote, "*Linnaea* was named by the celebrated Gronovius and is a plant of Lapland, lowly, insignificant, flowering but for a brief space, after Linnaeus who resembles it." He liked to hold a sprig of it when posing for portraits. His charming humility was perhaps devious: though small and simple, the twinflower circles the globe and is widely admired.

Twinflower

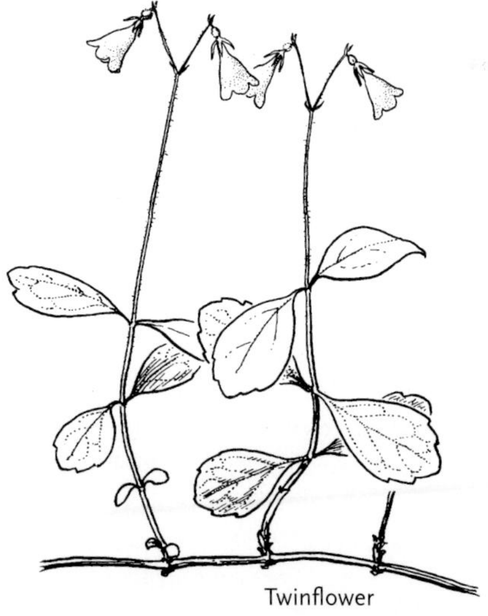
Twinflower

FLOWERING HERBS

Defined simply as seed plants without woody stems, the flowering herbs include most plants thought of as "wildflowers," as well as grasses and similar plants. But some wildflowers, even small ones, are shrubs. Since distinguishing between herbs and shrubs can be tricky. I've placed subshrubs in the flowering trees and shrubs chapter if they have noticeable woody twigs or stiff canes—except for some penstemons placed with their penstemon sisters here.

HERBS: GRASSLIKE

Grasses, sedges, and rushes are the three huge families of grasslike plants. Grasses proper are outnumbered by sedges above timberline here. To identify the family, roll a stem between thumb and forefinger; the rules of thumb:

sedge stems are triangular in cross-section, with V-shaped leaves in 3 ranks along the 3 edges ("sedges have edges");

grass stems are round and hollow, with a swollen node at the base of each leaf; and

rush stems are round and pith-filled; their leaves too are often tubular, especially near the tip; the pistils and seedpods are 3-celled.

The "sedges have edges" mnemonic applies to genus *Carex* (most of our sedges), but a few sedges such as cottongrass (p. 156) have somewhat rounded stems, often triangular only near the top.

Grasslike plants have wind-pollinated flowers that, as flowers, fall well short of being corsage-ready. Positive identification of grasslike plants requires a whole new vocabulary of grass parts, and a microscope. This book includes a representative handful of species, out of hundreds growing here, and describes them in brief. If both habitat and description fit what you're looking at, then you have an educated guess of what it is.

Beargrass (p. 175) is a lily you might mistake for a sedge when its flowers are absent, as they usually are; its leaves are V-shaped in section, dry, pale, abrasive, and robust, in abundant thick clumps. Blue-eyed grass (p. 178) is a slender iris that blooms early and briefly, and then goes unnoticeable in grassy east-slope meadows.

HERBS: GRASSLIKE, WITH TRIANGULAR STEMS

Sedges

***Carex* spp.** (CAIR-ex: Roman name). Cyperaceae.

Genus *Carex* includes the overwhelming majority of Cyperaceae in North America and the greatest number of species in any plant genus in the Pacific Northwest. Other genera in the sedge family include cottongrass (p. 156), bulrushes (or tule), and papyrus, which ancient Egyptians made into paper.

Many sedges like saturated or submerged soil, but others prefer cold, dry meadows. The common denominator is the suppression of grass competition by environmental stresses. High altitudes and high latitudes both have a lot of sedges.

When a *Carex* sedge blooms, a mop of stamens in conspicuous disarray adorns portions of the flowering spikes. Typically these start as yellowish anthers on whitish filaments, but later the anthers fall off. The stamen-bearing parts of the spike are male flowers, and their location is diagnostic: the male flowers are either at the spike's tip (androgynous) or at its base (gynecandrous, in a clever twist of jargon). Or some spikes are

Showy sedge

unisexual. Most spikes have several or many flowers, and most flowering stems bear several spikes.

After male filaments lose all their anthers, they can perhaps be mistaken for stigmas on female flowers, but stigmas are generally shorter and less shriveled up, and are consistently either two or three per flower on any given species. Each female flower on a sedge is behind a single scale, usually dark, and each bears a single seed.

Showy sedge, *C. spectabilis* (spec-TAB-il-iss: showy). Several spikes 3/8–1 in. long, top one ♂, lower ones ♀, increasingly long-stalked, drooping; scales nearly all dark, needle-tipped with tiny awns; leaves bluish; 6–20 in. tall. Lush high meadow slopes.

Showy sedge, the most abundant grasslike plant of subalpine meadows in moist parts of the range, is an important food for mountain goats and rosy finches.

Black alpine sedge, *C. nigricans* (NYE-grik-enz: blackish). Flower spike single, ♂ flowers above ♀; scales conspicuously blackish when young (sometimes hidden under a mop of fresh stamens) but maturing straw-colored; 3 stigmas per ♀; 4–9 leaves per stalk, often curling; 2- to 5-in. plants form a dense turf in alp/subalpine depressions.

Black alpine sedge

Dense, turfy concave beds of black alpine sedge underlie the latest-melting patches of snow around timberline. Once they dry out in late summer, they offer a spot for basking, tumbling, or napping. What's good for you is in this instance tolerated by the flora, too, as these sedges are relatively resilient. Not even sedge turf is immune to trampling damage, though; no subalpine plant community should be turned into a campsite.

To suit its extremely short growing season, black alpine sedge is a speed demon among grasslike plants, setting seed as soon as 13 days after its release from snow (nearby subalpine plants typically take 42–56 days). Even that is rarely quick enough, so it spreads mainly by rhizomes, producing a turfy, rather than clumpy, growth habit. The only even later-lying snowbed communities (ones that survive some dormant years when they don't melt out at all) are largely mosses and lichens; next to a black sedge bed you often see a strip of haircap moss.

Dunhead sedge, *C. phaeocephala* (fee-o-SEF-a-la: dun head). Also alpine hare sedge. Flower spikes 3–6, crowded together; ♀ flowers hidden by reddish to brown scales with pale translucent edges; 2 stigmas; ♂ flowers few, located at the bases of some spikes; plants 4–16 in. tall, in tufts. Dry alpine tundra or rock fields.

Dunhead sedge

Mertens sedge, *C. mertensii* (mer-TEN-zee-eye: for Karl H. Mertens, p. 147). 4–9 dense, cylindrical, grasslike spikes hang along the tall stem's elegant nodding arc; ♂ flowers are at the base of the terminal spike; ♀ flowers have 3 stigmas and densely overlapping dark scales; stem 16–40 in., rough-edged. Clearings, mainly mid-elev to low subalpine.

Mertens sedge stems arch gracefully under the weight of its nodding spikelets. It does well even without mycorrhizal assistance, enabling it to colonize trailsides, roadsides, and Mt. St. Helens' pumice plain.

Mertens sedge

Elk sedge, *C. geyeri* (GUY-er-eye: for Karl A. Geyer, p. 156). Just 1 spike per stem, consisting of 1–3 large ♀ flowers beneath a narrow 3/8- to 1-in. ♂ spike; leaves as tall as the 6- to 20-in. stems, in clumps. Common, an herb-layer dominant in much open forest e of CasCr from Chelan County s.

This sedge is unusual in its few-flowered inflorescence, its dry forest habitat, and its high forage value to deer and elk—equal to the better grasses. Under its modest clumps hides a huge fibrous root system, commonly 6 feet deep and 5 feet across.

Water sedge, *C. aquatilis* (a-QUA-til-iss: of water). Also Sitka sedge. Spikes up to 2½ in. long, the terminal one ♂ or ♂-tipped, lateral ones ♀, erect, with numerous neatly overlapping mostly dark brown scales; stems 1–4 ft., from horizontal rhizomes in standing water or saturated meadow soil.

The commonest sedge of Cascades marshes, water sedge is important waterfowl forage.

Ross sedge, *C. rossii* (ROSS-ee-eye: for polar explorer John Ross). Also hardscrabble sedge. 2 bracts embrace and rise above the upper flowers, which are few: one tight terminal spike of a few ♂, then 1–4 lateral spikes of just a few rotund ♀ flowers with 3 stigmas; other ♀ spikes hide near the ground among leaf bases; 3–12 in. tall. Dry slopes including burns, clearcuts, roadsides, steppe.

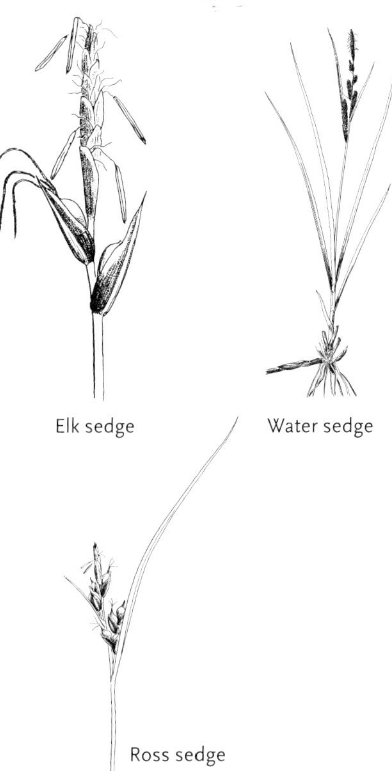
Elk sedge

Water sedge

Ross sedge

Karl Andreas Geyer

Karl Andreas Geyer came west with Sir William Drummond Stewart's 1843 expedition, the first pleasure trip to the American West. The party camped on Persian carpets under crimson canopies. Geyer left the party in Wyoming, carrying on westward, at first alone but soon with Jesuit missionaries—a giant step downscale: "the hospitality the Jesuits showed to me was scant and beggarly." From their Montana mission to Idaho was "one of the most terrible journeys I have ever made, especially in the midst of winter, crossing 76 times streams. Some we had to swim. . . . Owing to the difficulties . . . I could not pay proper attention to the vegetation. But this much I do know, that I saw [a coast redwood]."

Inattentive to the vegetation? No kidding. Usually a diligent and competent botanist, Geyer was, on the other hand, short on charm and ethics. He reneged on a contract to deliver his collections to eminent botanist Georg Engelmann in St. Louis; overstayed his welcome (a missionary's wife wrote "we are determined to be rid of him"); and left Chief Factor McLoughlin scrambling to find out whose credit line Geyer had been charging supplies on.

The basal flowers protect seeds from grazers—bears, sheep, and bighorn sheep—while making them easy-to-reach for ants, which disseminate them.

Tall Cottongrass

Eriophorum angustifolium (airy-AH-for-um: wool bearing: ang-gus-tif-OH-lium: narrow leaf). Also Alaska cotton; *E. polystachion*. Flower spikes 2–5, becoming white cottony tufts 3/4–1 3/4 in. long in seed; several bracts just below the flowers; leaves flat except V-folded near tips; stems triangular to round, 8–36 in. tall. High bogs. Cyperaceae.

Up in Alaska, the sight of mile after mile of cottongrass blowing in a breeze is hard to forget. Cottongrass stem bases were a food for Inupiat people. Patches of it here are much smaller, but fairly common. The less common slender cottongrass, *E. gracile*, bears one bract (rarely two) just below the flowers.

Tall cottongrass

Tall cottongrass

HERBS: GRASSLIKE, WITH ROUND, PITH-FILLED STEMS

Rushes

***Juncus* spp.** (JUNK-us: the Roman name). Flowers of 6 dry brown or green tepals and 2 outer bracts; many seeds, within a 3-celled capsule; leaf blades (if present) flat or tubular, dark green like the tubular, pith-filled stems. Juncaceae.

Mertens rush, *J. mertensianus* (mer-ten-zee-AY-nus: for Karl H. Mertens, p. 147). Flowers numerous, dark brown, tiny, in a single dense round cluster atop the 4- to 12-in. stem; 1–4 tubular leaves, the uppermost one angled off just below inflorescence. In or next to water, alp/subalpine.

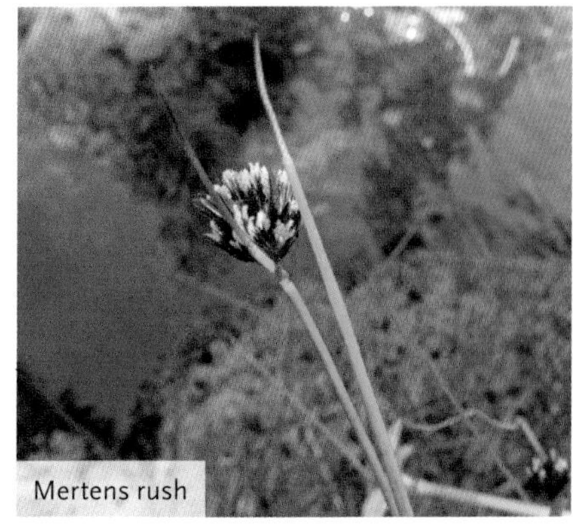

Mertens rush

Drummond's rush, *J. drummondii* (dra-MON-dee-eye: for Thomas Drummond). Tepals 1/4 in; flowers green, 1–4, in an apparently lateral cluster; stems 6–14 in., apparently leafless because the uppermost leaf, borne just below the inflorescence, looks like a continuation of the stem, and the lower leaves are reduced to sheaths.

Drummond's rush

Parry's rush

Parry's rush, *J. parryi* (PAIR-ee-eye: for Charles Parry). Flowers 1–4, narrow, seemingly borne partway up the stem because the 1- to 5-in. upper bract looks like more stem; capsule sharp-tipped; tepals 1/4 in.; 4- to 12-in. stems in clumps together with some 1- to 3-in. leaves. Streambanks to dry meadows, mainly alp/subalpine.

Swordleaf rush, *J. ensifolius* (en-sif-OH-lius: sword leaf). Flowers numerous, dark brown, tiny, in several dense round clusters; stem 8–24 in., exceeding the flat or folded basal leaves; uppermost leaf (bract) usually extends several inches above flower clusters. Moist ground at all elevs.

Rushes are tough, reedy, deep green, round-stemmed, round-leaved plants with chaffy tufts, sometimes nearly black, for flowers.

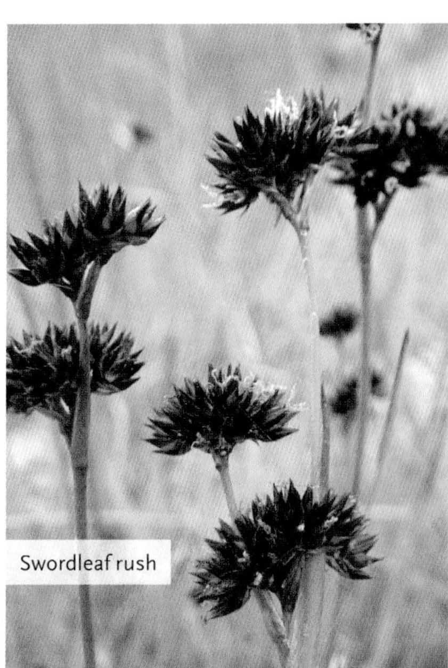

Swordleaf rush

Ours are small; big bulrushes or tules are not rushes but sedges. Rushes generally grow in wet places, including bogs and marshes. Some of them turn up as early pioneers on raw ground below retreating glaciers. Coast tribes made string out of the stems of larger coastal rushes.

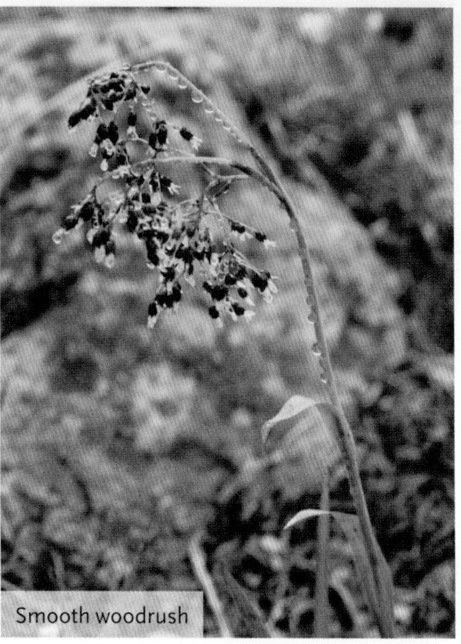
Smooth woodrush

Smooth Woodrush

Luzula hitchcockii (LUZ-you-la: light—; hitchcock-ee-eye: for C. Leo Hitchcock). Inflorescence sparse, often arching; flowers tiny, dry, green to brown, with 6 tepals and 2 sepal-like bracts; seed capsule has 3 cells with 1 seed in each; leaves grasslike, wide, flat, finely hair-fringed, becoming red-tinged or heavily red-brown-splotched; leaf bases sheath the stem but do not originate from a swollen node; plants 6–20 in. Rather dry alp/subalpine meadow, fellfield, or open forest. Juncaceae.

This plant often seems to be the most abundant subalpine grass, but it actually isn't a grass.

Like a glacier lily, a woodrush can melt its own hole in snow, to bloom through. Its ancient name, *gramen luzulae,* honored a humble plant for bearing dewdrops that refract morning light.

A smut fungus may produce growths on the seed heads, similar to the smut that grows on ears of corn and is eaten as a delicacy called *huitlacoche.* I've heard no reports on the edibility of woodrush smut.

Similar small-flowered woodrush, *L. parviflora,* is almost as common in the subalpine and also ranges down to sea level, where it may exceed 3 feet tall. Flower tepals (and later the seed capsules) are at most 1/10 inch on small-flowered, a bit longer than that on smooth woodrush.

The rush family, Juncaceae, is represented in our region by two genera, rushes and woodrushes. The tight inflorescences of the three rushes above contrast with the open, delicate, spray-like ones of these two woodrush species, yet each genus includes other species with those characteristics reversed. A stronger across-the-board distinction is that a woodrush has a three-celled seed capsule with one seed in each cell, while a *Juncus* rush has a three-celled, many-seeded capsule. Grasses and sedges have one-celled, one-seeded fruits.

HERBS: GRASSLIKE, WITH ROUND, HOLLOW STEMS

Grasses

Family Poaceae

GRASSES PRIMARILY OF THE HIGH COUNTRY

Green fescue, *Festuca viridula* (fest-YOU-ca: the Roman name; vee-RID-you-la: green). Spikelets of 3–7 florets forming a 4- to 7-in. spikelike panicle, without awns; leaves narrow, wiry, dark green; plants 16–32 in. Subalpine and e side in CasR.

Green fescue

Small sheep fescue

Alpine timothy

Spike trisetum

Spike trisetum

Small sheep fescue, *F. saximontana* (saxi-mon-TAY-na: of the Rocky Mtns). Also Rocky Mountain fescue; *F. brachyphylla, F. ovina*. Spikelets of 3–4 florets forming a 1- to 3-in. spikelike panicle; awns less than 1/8 in.; plants 2–8 in. Alpine.

Alpine timothy, *Phleum alpinum* (FLEE-um: Greek name for some grass). Short-awned, often purplish spikelets form a single dense, neatly cylindrical 1/2- to 1 3/4-in. spike; leaves flat, edges feel raspy; 4–20 in. High streambanks and wet meadows.

Spike trisetum, *Trisetum spicatum* (try-SEE-tum: 3-awned; spic-AY-tum: spiked). Also downy oatgrass. Spikelets of 1–3 florets forming a 1- to 3-in. spike; awns 1/4 in., bent outward; plants 4–16 in., fuzzy all over. Common on alpine ridges, sporadic elsewhere.

Purple hairgrass, *Vahlodea atropurpurea* (va-LOAD-ia: for Martin H. Vahl; at-ro-pur-PEW-ria: black purple). Also *Deschampsia atropurpurea*. Purplish spikelets of 2–3 florets in a wide, sparse panicle 2–4 in. tall; awns less than 1/8 in., bent inward, hidden within floret; leaves flat; stem 6–24 in. Abundant, subalpine.

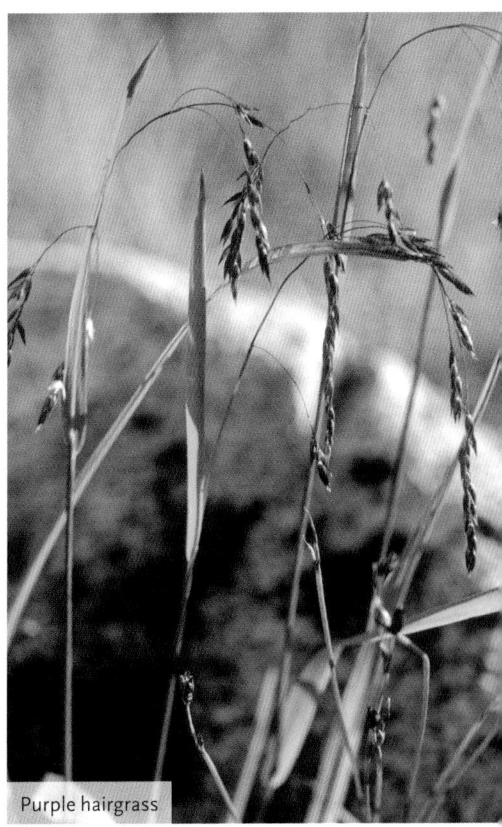
Purple hairgrass

GRASSES PRIMARILY OF THE EAST-SIDE

Bluebunch wheatgrass, *Pseudoroegneria spicata* (soo-doe-reg-NAIR-ia: after another genus; spic-AY-ta: spiked). Also *Elymus spicatus, Agropyron spicatum*. Large (6–8 florets) spikelets spaced out along stem to form a 3- to 6-in. intermittent spike; awnless and (¼- to ¾-in.) long-awned types occur; 24–40 in., in clumps. Pine or steppe border; once the chief grass of e OR and WA, now largely displaced by weedy grasses.

Tufted hairgrass, *Deschampsia cespitosa* (desh-AMP-sia: for J. L. A. Loiseleur-Deslongchamps; see-spit-OH-sa: grows in bunches). Spikelets of 2–3 florets in a wide, sparse panicle 4–10 in. tall; awns barely protruding from floret; leaves creased; plants 8–48 in. High open forests and meadows e of CasCr.

Columbia needlegrass, *Achnatherum nelsonii* (ac-NATH-er-um: awned scale; nel-SO-nee-eye: for Aven Nelson). Also *Stipa occidentalis*. One-floret spikelets held tightly erect against the main stem, in a 3- to 14-in. spike; awns ¾–1½ in. long, twice-bent, spreading at various angles; leaves often inrolled; plants 8–48 in. All elevs.

Pinegrass, *Calamagrostis rubescens* (cal-a-ma-GRAH-stiss: reed grass; roo-BES-enz: reddish). Flowering stems few or absent, the plant spreading mainly by rhizomes; 3- to 6-in. spikelike panicle of 1-floret spikelets; awns bent, barely protruding; leaves narrow, flat to inrolled (not creased), rough to touch; plants 16–40 in. All elevs e of CasCr; dominant herb in many pine forests, often with elk sedge.

Bottlebrush squirreltail, *Elymus elymoides* (EL-im-us: the Greek name; el-im-OY-deez: like *Elymus*, an absurd name now that this species is placed in that genus). Also *Sitanion hystrix*, a beautiful name I am loath to part with. Spikelets of 2–6 florets in a 1½-

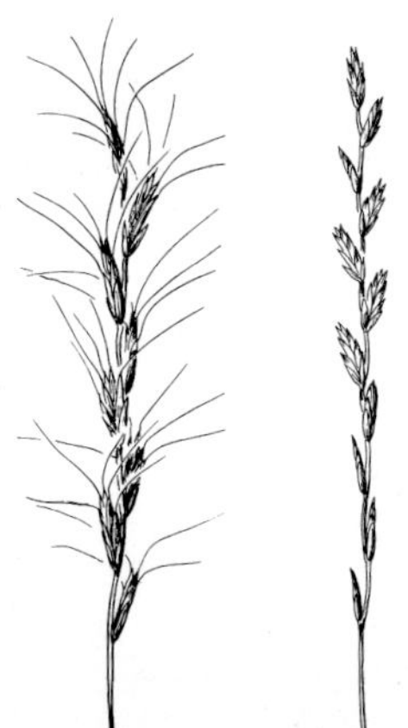

Bluebunch wheatgrass

Tufted hairgrass

Columbia needlegrass

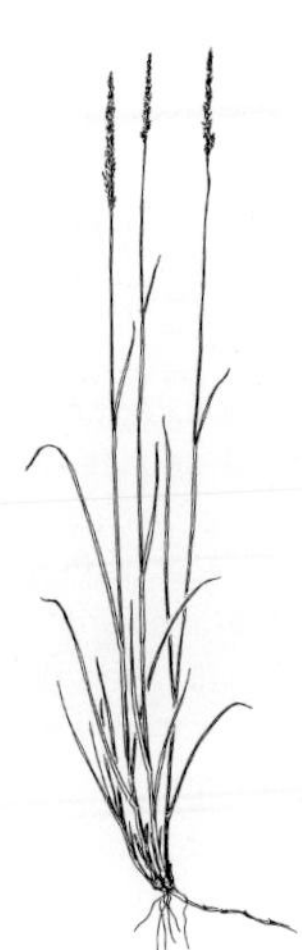

Pinegrass

Bottlebrush squirreltail

Bluebunch fescue

Cheatgrass

Blue wildrye

to 6-in. spike that looks brushlike thanks to the many awns ¾–4 in. long; plants 4–20 in. Pine forest with bitterbrush; also on alpine pumice.

Bluebunch fescue, *Festuca idahoensis* (fest-YOU-ca: the Roman name). Also Idaho fescue. Spikelets of 3–7 florets forming a 4- to 7-in. spikelike panicle, with short (⅛ in.) awns; leaves narrow, wiry, dark green; plants 16–32 in. All elevs.

Cheatgrass, *Bromus tectorum* (BRO-mus: Roman name; tec-TOR-um: of roofs, once a common habitat in Europe). Also downy brome, downy chess. Delicate 8- to 26-in. tufts, finely hairy all over; lower panicle branches often droop; awns about as long as florets, ½ in.; annual plant comes up in winter or spring, dries out by midsummer. European weed on dry rangeland.

WIDESPREAD GRASSES

Bearded fescue, *Festuca subulata* (sub-you-LAY-ta: awl-shaped). 3- to 4-floret spikelets in a 6- to 12-in., typically nodding panicle; awns ⅛–½ in.; leaves flat, ⅛–⅜ in. wide, blades 4–12 in.; plants 2–3 ft. Low forest up to subalpine meadows; a gracefully arching grass scattered in w-side forest is likely this one.

Blue wildrye, *Elymus glaucus* (GLAW-cus: bluish pale). 3- to 5-floret spikelets in a 2- to 8-in., often nodding spike; awns vary from 1 in. long to absent; leaves flat, ⅛–½ in. wide; plants 16–40 in. W-side clearings, gravel bars, CoastR grass balds.

Sandberg bluegrass, *Poa secunda* (PO-a: Greek name for grass; se-CUN-da: with florets all to one side, a misleading name). Also curly bluegrass; *P. sandbergii, P. scabrella, P. gracillima*. 3- to 5-floret spikelets in a 1- to 6-in. erect panicle, briefly open-branching but narrowing at maturity; no awns; leaves ⅛ in. or narrower, blades small and withering in some habitats; plants in tufts, 6–36 in., often purple in the panicle—and reddish overall by early summer when it withers; starts new growth in fall. Common at all elevs; meadow, tundra, clearcuts, and especially steppe.

Sandberg bluegrass

Often personified as humble, grasses are in fact taking over the world. Going by their rate and breadth of genetic diversification in geologically recent time, you would have to call them the most successful plant family. The ascendency of grasses is reflected in, and has been magnified by, the development of agriculture, which has always focused on grains (grass seeds) and on grazing (grass-eating) mammals. Of course, wild animals also coevolved with grasses, and make great use of them, but it's we humans and our livestock that have really gone to town with them, literally and figuratively.

Grasses dislike shade, so our region is not their favorite. Typically, our meadows are maintained by extreme snowiness, wetness, or infertility; the first two favor sedges and rushes over grasses. New clearings here are mostly made by fire, and quickly reoccupied by stump-sprouting shrubs and plants with windborne or fireproof seeds. (Grasslands do excel at regenerating after fires, but the grasses have to be there before the fire to spring up after it.) This is not to say there are few grasses here, just fewer than elsewhere. Our chief grass habitats are open forests and steppe margins on the lower east slope, dry meadow types at timberline and above, and gravel bars and river terraces at early stages of plant succession. Periodic soil drought seems to be a factor in each.

Identification of grasses requires a special vocabulary. Keeping it to a minimum, grasses are flowering plants with simplified, undecorated, single-seeded dry flowers (florets), each with three stamens and a usually two-styled pistil (these sexual parts are short-lived and easily overlooked). The florets are flanked by any number of scales or bracts with cool names: paleas, lemmas, and glumes. (Don't worry, those will not be on the test). Since the bracts are arranged alternately, in two ranks, rather than whorled, they are not sepals or tepals like the six whorled, scalelike tepals of a rush flower. In many species, certain bracts bear stiff hairs (awns), a conspicuous feature for identification. One or more florets and their bracts along a single axis make a spikelet. Several

Cattail

spikelets attach to the main stalk either directly, making a spike, or by small stalks (often branched) making a panicle. The thirteen species descriptions above are intended to suggest educated guesses on the identity of the grasses you will see most often.

The fourteen native grasses I describe are perennial, and several are excellent forage. Tufted hairgrass is so sought out by sheep and cattle that its presence indicates a meadow in virgin condition; once grazed out from a meadow, it returns slowly, if ever. Across numbingly vast portions of the West, nonnative annual grasses including cheatgrass have taken over from native perennial grasses over the past 150 years. Few of them are much good as forage, and cheatgrass changes the fire regime, with disastrous effects on sagebrush and sage grouse. Being annual seems to give the invaders a competitive edge. It's unclear how perennials ever came to dominate the region's grass flora in the first place, but it was nice while it lasted.

Cattail

Typha latifolia (TIE-fa: the Greek name; lat-if-OH-lia: broad leaf). Flowers minute, chaffy, in a dense round smooth spike of two distinct portions, the upper (♂) thicker when in flower but withering as the lower (♀) thickens and turns dark brown in fruit; stalks 3–10 ft.; leaves half as tall by 1/4–3/4 in., smooth; from rhizomes in shallow water. Typhaceae.

Big lowland cattail marshes are sought out by migrating waterfowl and by hunters thereof. Few such marshes lie among our mountains, though; the Quinault used to travel all the way to Gray's Harbor to pick cattails. Like all Northwest tribes, they wove the stalks (never the leaves) into thick, spongy mats for mattresses, kneeling pads in canoes, packsacks, baskets, rain capes, and temporary roofs in summer. Oddly, only a few of the tribes reported eating cattails, though the rhizomes and inner, basal stalk portions are pretty good baked, raw, or ground as flour.

HERBS: SHOWY MONOCOTS

Monocots and dicots are named after their respectively single or paired seed leaves, or "cotyledons"—the first green part(s) to sprout from a newly germinated seed. Since those leaves don't stick around for long, to aid identification, monocots are often detected by two less reliable traits: parallel-veined leaves and flower parts in threes (generally three petals and three sepals, though these are sometimes nearly identical, in which case we call them six "tepals" in an inner and an outer whorl). The monocots that follow are distinguished from the grasslike monocots by (for most of them) broader leaves and (for all of them) moist, delicate flower parts evolved for visual attractiveness—in a word, showy. The great majority were long treated as a large family, the Liliaceae, but research now shows that these "lilies" are not all closely related, and belong in several families.

Very few dicots reliably have petals or sepals in threes. Only three such genera are in this book, and they are easy to spot as dicots since they don't have parallel leaf veins: inside-out flower, wild-ginger, and buckwheats (pp. 267–269).

HERBS: SHOWY MONOCOTS, WITH 4 TEPALS, 4 STAMENS

Skunk-Cabbage

Lysichiton americanus (lye-zih-KITE-on: loose tunic). Flowers greenish yellow, 1/8 in., many, in a dense spike 2½–5 in., partly enclosed or hooded by a yellow, parallel-veined spathe; leaves all basal, net-veined, oval, eventually up to 3 ft. × 1 ft. or even bigger; from an enlarged fleshy vertical root, in wet ground. Araceae.

Many plants evolved sweet fragrances that attract sugar-loving pollinators, like bees. Others evolved putrid smells that attract flies and beetles. Our skunk-cabbage gets skunkier when its leaves are damaged. Its main pollinators, a species of rove beetle,

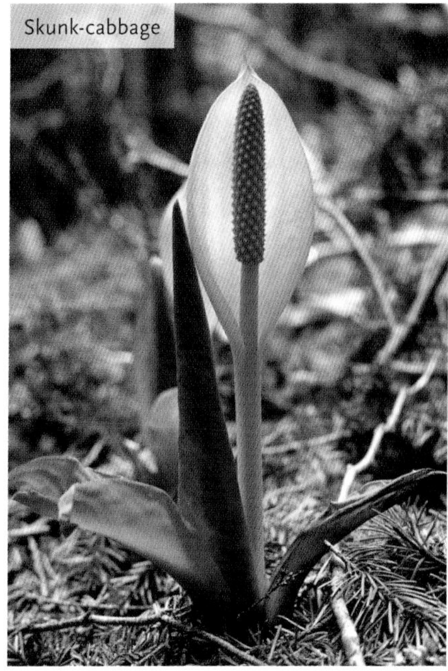
Skunk-cabbage

congregate in skunk-cabbage flowers to eat pollen and to mate. The flowers are at first functionally female, then become male (producing pollen, not nectar) a few days later.

The calla lily family, Araceae, has a characteristic inflorescence called a spadix (the fleshy spike of crowded flowers) and spathe (the large bract enfolding it). In the case of our skunk-cabbage, spathe and spadix thrust up from wet ground in early spring. Leaves come later, and keep growing all summer to reach sizes unmatched north of the banana groves; they were universally used as "Indian wax paper" to wrap camas bulbs, salal berries, and other foods for steam pit baking or for storage. The leaf bases and the roots are themselves edible after long cooking or storage breaks down the irritating, "hot" oxalate crystals. Some tribes ate them during the hard times of late winter. Tales told that in the bad old days before salmon came, the people had nothing to eat but skunk-cabbage roots. Elk and bears eat skunk-cabbage, with no complaints recorded.

Food or not, skunk-cabbage was regarded as strong medicine—for example, to induce labor, either timely or abortive. Later, some white man patented and sold it under the name "Skookum."

May Lily

Maianthemum dilatatum (my-ANTHEM-um: May flower; dil-a-TAY-tum: widened). Also false-lily-of-the-valley. Flowers white, 1/4 in. across, spreading tepals in a single whorl; berries 1/4 in., ripening red, in a 1- to 3-in. raceme; 2 (1–3) leaves, 2–4 in., heart-shaped but clearly parallel-veined, shiny dark green; plants 4–14 in., slender, from rhizomes. W-side forest up to 3500 ft., often on nurse logs. Asparagaceae.

The insipid berries were eaten unenthusiastically by most tribes, but in the woods you rarely see a full stalk of them even half-ripe, which shows that small mammals cherish them.

HERBS: SHOWY MONOCOTS, WITH 6 STAMENS ("LILIES")

False-Solomon's-Seal

***Maianthemum* spp.** Also *Smilacina*. Flowers white, fragrant, many, in a single terminal inflorescence; berries 1/4 in., round; leaves heavily veined, pointed, oval to narrowly elliptical, 2–7 in.; stems arching, unbranched, often zigzagging at leaf nodes; from horizontal rhizomes. Widespread in forest. Asparagaceae.

Starry false-Solomon's-seal, *M. stellatum* (stel-AY-tum: starry). Tepals 1/4 in., flat-spreading; flowers 6–18; berries longitudinally striped, ripening dark red to blackish; stems 8–24 in.

Starry false-Solomon's-seal

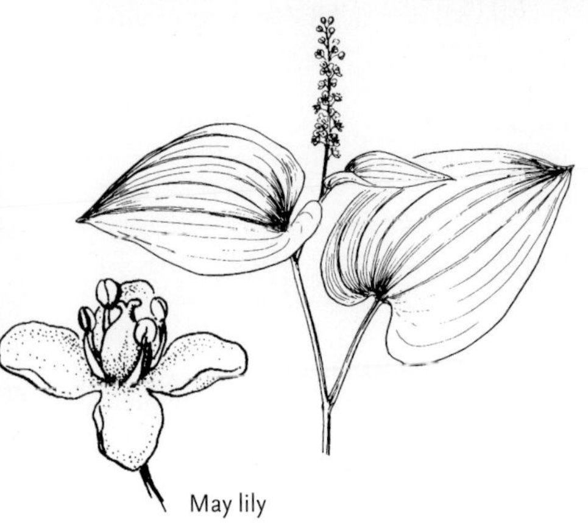
May lily

Plumed false-Solomon's-seal

Plumed false-Solomon's-seal

Crown brodiaea

Plumed false-Solomon's-seal, *M. racemosum* (ras-em-OH-sum: bearing flowers in racemes, a misleading name for this plant). Tepals minute, stamens longer (1/8 in.); flowers numerous in a conical fluffy panicle; berries speckled at first, ripening red; stems 1–3 ft.

False clues galore: This genus bears too little resemblance to Solomon's seal (genus *Polygonatum*) to justify the "false" in its common name. *Racemosum* isn't racemose, it's paniculate; but *stellatum* is racemose. I find false-Solomon's-seal berries sometimes delicious (and not purgative, as some authors report) but often insipid. Both species are locally abundant in deep west-side woods, but also look happy in clearings or even dry open slopes. Form varies with environment. In the silver fir zone, *stellatum* spreads its leaves flat from a bent-over stem; on the sunny east-side, it holds its stem upright, grows narrower leaves, angles them upward, and folds them sharply at the midvein.

Crown Brodiaea

Brodiaea coronaria (bro-DEE-a: for botanist James Brody; cor-a-NAIR-ia: worth making into garlands). Flowers several, erect, on unequal stalks; tepals 3/4–1 1/4 in., violet to blue with deeper-colored midrib, fused at the base; 3 white stigmas emerge from between 3 broad sterile stamens that hide 3 very short fertile stamens; 1–3 leaves basal, grasslike, drying before the flowers bloom; 4–10 in. tall. Grassy slopes, low to moderate.

The similar harvest brodiaea, *B. elegans*, overlaps crown brodiaea in the Oregon Cascades. They differ in the shapes of their sterile stamens and their corolla bases.

Douglas's Brodiaea

Triteleia grandiflora (try-tel-EYE-a: 3 perfect, referring to all flower parts in 3s; grand-if-LOR-a: big flower). Also gophernuts; *Brodiaea douglasii.* Flowers 1/2 in. long, sky blue, purplish blue, or white, narrow bell-shaped, several, on stalklets all from one spot between narrow bracts; 6 tepals fused more than half their length; 6 stamens attached at unequal heights on the tepals' inner faces; leaves 1 or 2, flat, grasslike; 8–30 in. tall. Dry low slopes. Asparagaceae.

Triteleia species resemble onions, taste somewhat like onions, and were once a major food resource for native people. For gophers, they still are. A similar

Douglas's brodiaea

Camas

white-flowered species, *T. hyacinthina,* is less common.

Camas

Camassia quamash (ca-MASS-ia QUA-mosh: two versions of the Chinook Dialect name for camas, from an originally French word). Tepals blue-violet, ¾–1½ in., narrow, the lowermost one usually noticeably apart from the other five; inflorescence roughly conical; capsule ½–1 in., splitting three ways; leaves narrow, basal or sheathing, shorter than the 8- to 24-in. stem; from a deep-set ½- to 1-in. bulb. Seasonally moist meadows, up to 4500 ft. Asparagaceae.

Camas bulbs were the prized vegetable food of most tribes of Oregon and Washington. The Nez Perce War was touched off by white settlers plowing up camas prairies for pastures. Camas cakes were second only to dried salmon in trade volume, especially northward along the British Columbia Coast, where no camas grows. Indians may have spread camas to some areas they didn't find it in. A family would mark out, "own," and maintain a camas patch year-round for generations, weeding and burning it. These practices indicate an agricultural economy, but may have been unique to camas. Year-round tending made it possible to weed out death camas when it's easy to recognize, blooming; that made it safe to dig camas in spring before flowering, when the bulbs are best. Nevertheless, many people died from eating death camas. Camas bulbs are not recommended to hikers.

David Douglas described quamash cuisine:

> A hole is scraped in the ground, in which are placed a number of flat stones on which the fire is placed and kept burning until sufficiently warm, when it is taken away. The cakes, which are formed by cutting or bruising the bricks and then compressing into small bricks, are placed on the stones and covered with leaves, moss, or dry grass, with a layer of earth on the

Clasping twisted-stalk

Rosy twisted-stalk

Rosy twisted-stalk

> outside, and left until baked or roasted, which generally takes a night. They are moist when newly taken off the stones, and are hung up to dry. Then they are placed on shelves or boxes for winter use. When warm they taste much like a baked pear. It is not improbable that a very palatable beverage might be made from them. Lewis observes that when eaten in a large quantity they occasion bowel complaints. . . . Assuredly they produce flatulence: when in the Indian hut I was almost blown out by strength of wind.

Lewis's original complaints are, let's say, not repeatable in polite company. The problems trace to inulin, an indigestible sugar that abounds in camas bulbs, balsamroot, agave, and Jerusalem artichokes. In smaller doses insulin is good for your intestinal flora.

Twisted-Stalk

***Streptopus* spp.** (STREP-ta-pus: twisted foot). Flowers bell-shaped, one (sometimes two) beneath each leaf axil; berries red, 1/4–1/2 in., juicy, sweetish but insipid; leaves 2–5 in., tapered, elliptical. Liliaceae.

Rosy twisted-stalk, *S. lanceolatus* (lan-see-o-LAY-tus: narrow-leaved). Also *S. roseus*. Tepals 3/8 in., variably streaked rose with white, slightly reflexed at the tip; style 3-branched; flower-bearing stalklets straight to curved; stems 6–14 in., rarely branched, arching. Higher (3000 ft.+) forests.

Clasping twisted-stalk, *S. amplexifolius* (am-plex-if-OH-lius: clasping leaf). Tepals 1/2 in., dull white, reflexed from near mid-length; style unbranched; flower stalklets with a sharp kink; stems 12–40 in., much branched.

Twisted-stalk discretely hides its flowers under its leaves—quite a trick, since the the crotch above each leaf bears the flower. Look closely to see the flower stalk where, fused to the stem, it runs up it to the next leaf base (the first leaf can't have a flower under it). The berries were called "snakeberries" by the Quileute, "frogberries" by the Kwakiutl, "owl-" or "witchberries" by the Haida—and inedible by all. Yet Makah women chewed the roots to induce labor.

Fairy Bells

***Prosartes* spp.** (pro-SAR-teez: appended). Also *Disporum* spp. Flowers bell-shaped, pendent from branch tips, white; berries red, egg-shaped, 1/4–1/2 in., juicy, sweetish but insipid; leaves 2–5 in., long-tapered,

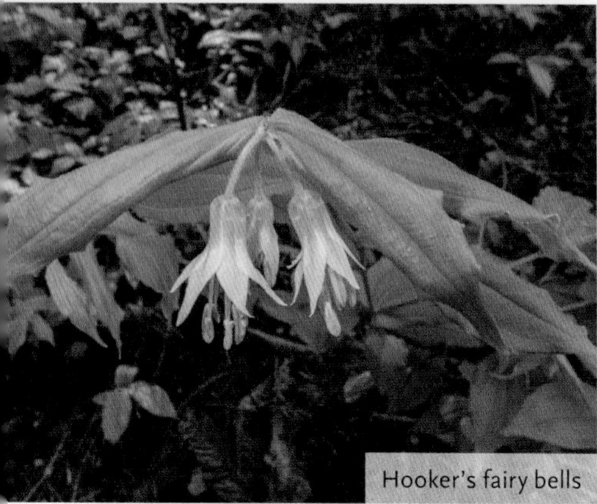
Hooker's fairy bells

Fairy lanterns

Bead lily

oval, wavy-edged; stems 14–40 in., much branched. Liliaceae.

Hooker's fairy bells, *P. hookeri* (HOOK-er-eye: for Sir Joseph Hooker). Tepals ¼–½ in., flaring; stamens exposed; flowers usually in pairs. Widespread in forests, sometimes together with fairy lanterns.

Fairy lanterns, *P. smithii* (SMITH-ee-eye: for Sir James E. Smith). Tepals ½–1 in., nearly straight, hiding the stamens; flowers in clusters of 1–5. Forests, CasR from Mt. Rainier s, and all our coastal ranges.

Bead Lily

Clintonia uniflora (clin-TOE-nia: for DeWitt Clinton; you-nif-LOR-a: one flower). Also queen's-cup, bride's-bonnet. Flowers single, white, face-up, broadly bell-shaped to nearly flat-spreading; tepals ¾–1 in.; berry intensely blue, ⅜ in., many-seeded, inedible; two or three leaves 3–6 in. × 1–2 in., heavy, smooth, shiny, basal, sheathing the 2- to 4-in. stalk; from slender rhizomes. Moist forest, mainly 2500–5000 ft. Liliaceae.

This mid-elevation plant makes a sweet indicator of upward progress. The beady blue berry—more striking than the formal white blossom—was used sometimes as a stain, never as a food.

Glacier Lily and Avalanche Lily

***Erythronium* spp.** (air-ith-ROE-nium: red—, the flower color of some species). Tepals 1–1½ in., spreading to reflexed either in an arc or from the base; flowers often nodding, single or sometimes 2–6 on a 6- to 12-in. stalk; capsule erect, 1 in. tall, 3-celled and -sided; 2 leaves 4–8 in., basal, wavy-edged; from a scallion-like bulb. Abundant around timberline, scattered at lower elevs. Liliaceae.

Glacier lily, *E. grandiflorum* (gran-dif-LOR-um: large-flowered). Flowers yellow.

Glacier lily

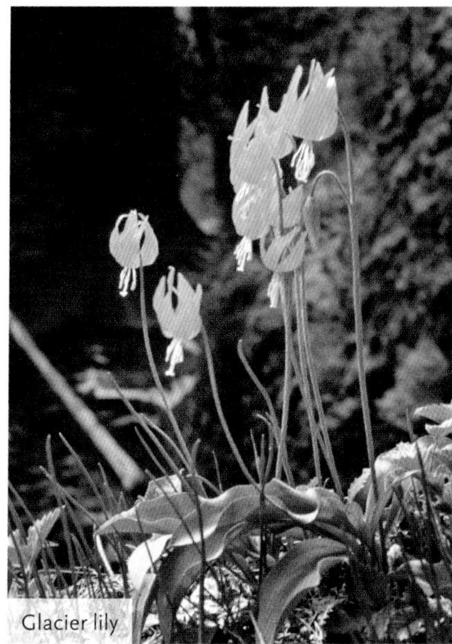
Glacier lily

The same glacier lilies a few hours apart, showing response to sun and heat.

Avalanche lily, *E. montanum* (mon-TAY-num: of mountains). Flowers white with a yellow center, often drying pink.

The snowy names refer to two amazing abilities—these lilies can generate enough heat to melt their way up and bloom through the last few inches of snow, and they proliferate into overwhelming drifts of white, or yellow. Fluttering with illusory fragility in subalpine breezes, they seem ideal vehicles for those anthropomorphic virtues we love to foist on mountain wildflowers—innocence, bravery, simplicity, perseverance, patient suffering, and so on. They toil not, neither do they spin, and they don't taste half bad either. (Bulbs, leaves, and flowers are edible, but not a good idea except when far from trails.) Ranging over much of the Rocky Mountains, glacier lilies are vital to grizzly bear diets in some areas. Bears are described as "gardening" lilies in Glacier National Park.

After the very early snowmelt of 2015, many of the glacier lilies at the south end of our range bore their flowers face-up, on stalks just 2–3 inches tall—possibly an indication of one way a plant may adapt to 21st-century climate trends. Glacier lilies flex their tepals upward as the day warms up or the humidity drops.

Glacier lilies are more common north of Mt. Rainier and south of Mt. Hood; avalanche lilies prevail from Rainier to Hood, and in the Olympics. In either case, lush

Avalanche lily

Subalpine cat's-ears

Lyall's cat's-ears

Tolmie's cat's-ears

subalpine meadows are preferred, though glacier lilies find their way down to near sea level along the Columbia. Two less common species, called trout or fawn lilies because of their mottled leaves, grow below 2500 feet: pink fawn lily, *E. revolutum,* in Olympic and coastal lowlands; and great white fawn lily, *E. oregonum,* mainly near the Puget-Willamette lowlands.

Cat's-Ears

***Calochortus* spp.** (cal-o-COR-tus: beautiful grass). Also mariposa lilies. Petals 5/8–1 in. long, almost as broad, usually with a fine purple arc at base; sepals pointed; flowers 1–5+; seedpods 3-winged, with persistent 3-branched styles; the only large leaf basal, flat, grasslike; from a small bulb. Liliaceae.

Subalpine cat's-ears, *C. subalpinus* Flowers creamy yellow; sepals have a purple dot near base; petals have long hairs over most of inner face; 6 stamens have sharp anthers longer than the filaments; flowers usually stem from one point high on the stalk; seedpods nodding; leaf taller than 3- to 12-in. stem. Subalpine in OR and s WA CasR.

Lyall's cat's-ears, *C. lyallii* (lie-AH-lee-eye: for David Lyall, opposite). Flowers white or pink-tinged; petals have an outer fringe of hairs, and a fringe just above the purple crescent; sepals almost as big as petals, and may also have purple crescent; seedpods erect; main leaf not as tall as the 6- to 18-in. stem. CasR lower e slope in WA and just barely into BC.

Tolmie's cat's-ears, *C. tolmiei* (TOLE-me-eye: for William Tolmie, p. 216). Flowers cream to purplish; petals have long hairs all over inner face; sepals much smaller, unspotted; seedpods nodding; stems often branching; leaf taller than 3- to 12-in. stem. Uncommon; rocky open slopes, w CasR in OR.

"Cat's ears" is the most pictorial of many flattering names given to these sensuous blossoms, all the more admired for being

David Lyall

David Lyall was the last of the rugged Scots prominent in early exploration of our region. After a pioneering botanical trip to the San Juan Islands in 1853, he was appointed surgeon-naturalist to the British contingent of the Northwest Boundary Survey of 1857–1862. The survey comprised separate British and American parties that often came up with different boundary locations. Following an arbitrary beeline across the unknown, precipitous North Cascades was a staggering task, and they did well to find energy and enthusiasm for science along the way. Lyall published a *Botany of Northwest America* in London in 1863.

The American party included George Gibbs as naturalist, geologist, and ethnographer; and Henry Custer, a topographer who was the first explorer to write passionately of the beauty of the North Cascades. Lyall and Custer have Cascade peaks named after them. Poor Gibbs got only a shrew-mole.

prohibitively hard to cultivate. Most species need bone-dry soil before the bulb goes into winter dormancy. There was an era when gardeners and nurseries attempted cultivating them on a grand scale; some species were nearly loved to death. The leading *Calochortus* taxonomist was also a leading collector: he actually boasted of his "record" pace of 4000 bulbs dug per day! Plainly there was little awareness of the risk of losing a species.

Beetles frequently pollinate *Calochortus*, apparently drawn by such features as off-white hair-filled bowls, which collect and hold heat; large glands on the petals, which beetles feed from; and prominent stamens and pistils.

The hairs can be extremely long, as in *C. longebarbatus*, which ranges from Yakima County south. Several members of the genus (including sego lily, the Utah state flower) are desert flowers, with lavender to white flowers and not much hair.

Wild Onion

***Allium* spp.** (AL-ium: ancient Roman for garlic). Flowers 1/4–3/8 in. long, several, on stalklets all from one spot between pointed, onionskin-like segments of the spathe that encased the inflorescence in bud; stems often bunching; from small onions with the trademark aroma. Amaryllidaceae.

Hooker's onion, *A. acuminatum* (a-cue-min-AY-tum: pointed). Also taper-tip onion. Tepals pointed, magenta to lavender or white with a fine red central line, the outer whorl spreading, bell-shaped, inner whorl smaller, narrowly jar-shaped; leaves 2–5,

Hooker's onion

Nodding onion

Olympic onion

Columbia lily

withering before flowers open, much shorter than the 4- to 12-in. tubular stem. Dry foothills.

Nodding onion, *A. cernuum* (sir-NEW-um: nodding). Inflorescence nodding (but often erect in fruit); tepals deep pink to white, oval, much shorter than stamens, all alike but in separated inner and outer whorls; leaves several; stems 8–20 in., often bunching. Dryish openings w of CasCr.

Olympic onion, *A. crenulatum* (cren-you-LAY-tum: scalloped). Tepals pink, narrow, pointed, all alike, 1/4–3/8 in.; leaves 2, much longer than the stem but spreading or sprawling; stem 2-angled, 2–3 in. High gravels in OR, OlyM, ec WA CasR, and VI.

An onion is easy to recognize—indeed, often hard to miss—because it smells like an onion. If it doesn't, don't try a taste test; it might be death camas. If you want it to season your food, just clip a few leaves. Digging up the puny bulb isn't worth the trouble, and kills the plant. We have several onion species of conservation concern.

Columbia Lily

Lilium columbianum (LIL-ium: Roman name; co-lum-be-AY-num: of the Columbia River). Also tiger lily. Tepals orange with small maroon spots, 1½–2½ in. long but strongly recurved; capsule fleshy, 1½–2 in.; flowers or fruit nodding, several, on long stalks; leaves 2–4 in., narrow, the ones near mid stalk biggest; stem 2–4 ft.; from a large, many-cloved bulb. Clearings and thickets up to timberline. Liliaceae.

The rather bitter bulbs were eaten by most tribes.

Cascades Lily

Lilium washingtonianum (washing-tony-AY-num: allegedly for Martha Washington). Tepals white, often purple-tinged or -spotted, and aging pink, 2½–3½ in.; flowers fragrant, bell-shaped, several, slightly nodding on short stalks all near the top of the 2- to 5-ft. stem; capsules fleshy, 1 in.; leaves 2–4

Cascades lily

in., narrow elliptical, often wavy, many of the upper ones in distinct whorls; bulbs large, many-cloved. Clearings and thickets, OR High CasR.

Our grandest lily grows only south of the Columbia, *washingtonianum* notwithstanding.

Chocolate lily

Chocolate Lily

Fritillaria affinis (frit-il-AIR-ia: checkered; af-EYE-niss: related). Also rice-root lily, checker lily, mission bells, fritillary; *F. lanceolata*. Tepals ¾–1½ in., inward-curving, brownish purple mottled with yellowish green; flowers pendent, 1–2+; capsule ¾ in., 6-winged; leaves 2–5 in., narrow, both whorled and single; stem 8–30 in.; from a bulb of a few large garlic-like cloves with many tiny rice-like bulblets. Moist clearings up to 5000 ft. Liliaceae.

These elegant flowers sell themselves short, with camouflage coloring and a fetid smell. The bulbs with their rice-like bulblets were universally eaten in the old days; they're too rare and too bitter to dig up now. When the Haida were introduced to rice, they named it "fritillary-teeth."

Yellow bell

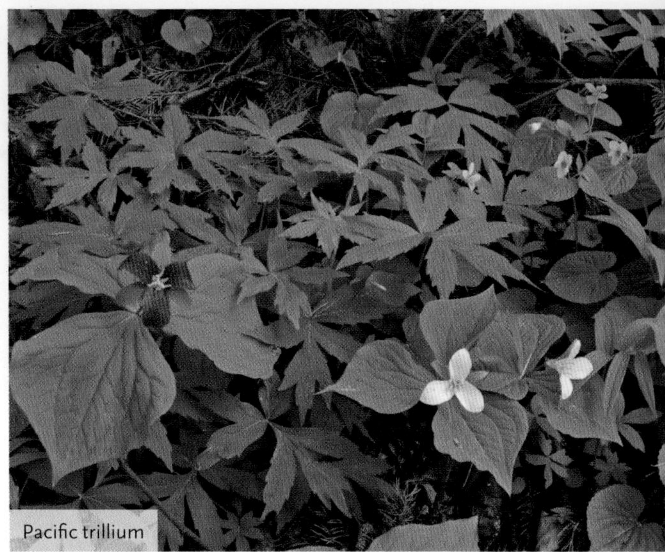
Pacific trillium

Yellow Bell

Fritillaria pudica (PEW-di-ca: modest). Flowers single (or rarely up to 4), yellow, pendent, narrowly bell-shaped, 7/8 in. long; tepals all alike; leaves grasslike, either 2 or several; stem succulent, 4–12 in. Blooming very early in grassy slopes e of CasCr.

Pacific Trillium

Trillium ovatum (TRIL-ium: triple; oh-VAY-tum: oval). Also wake-robin. Petals 1–3 in., white, aging through pink to maroon; sepals shorter, narrower, green; flowers single, on a 1- to 3-in. stem from the whorl of 3 leaves, 3–7 in., often equally broad, net-veined except for the 5 or so main veins; plants 6–16 in., rhizomatous. Low forest, or rarely up to tree line. Melanthiaceae.

What a joy, seeing the year's first trilliums in March or April, just when the winter rains feel like forever! Quinault elders used to warn youngsters that picking trillium would bring rain—a safe bet in Quinault country at that time of year. Whites spun the less reliable tale that picking the flower will kill the plant. It's true, though, that several parts of the country have seen sad declines in populations of their trillium species, partly due to overpicking. Let's not let that happen here. If you want trilliums in your yard or house, wait til the blooms are gone and collect the seeds. They need to be chilled twice before germinating; you can use your refrigerator for one of them in fall, then plant and let winter provide the second. The seeds come packed in a gummy oil that ants, the usual disseminators, find tasty.

For most flowers that shift color as they age, as trilliums do, the advantage is in using the aging blooms to help make a grander display to attract pollinators from afar, and then directing them toward the whiter blooms with more viable pollen.

Bronze Bells

Anticlea occidentalis (antic Leah: in Greek Myth, the mother of Odysseus; ox-i-den-TAY-lis: western). Also western featherbells; *Stenanthium occidentale*. Flowers several, pendent, narrowly bell-shaped, 3/8 in. long, varying from burgundy red to greenish cream; 6 tepals all alike; 2–3 leaves basal, up to 1 in. wide; 8–15 in. tall. Moist to wet high places. Melanthiaceae.

Death Camas

Toxicoscordion venenosum (toxic-oh-SCOR-de-un: toxic garlic; ven-en-OH-sum: poisonous). Also *Zigadenus venenosus.* Flowers white, saucer-shaped, in a tall raceme; tepals less than ¼ in., with a greenish oval spot near base, persisting after withering; capsules ½–¾ in., splitting, 3-celled, 3-styled; most leaves basal, narrow, sheathing, but often 2 or more along the 8- to 30-in. stem; bulb 1 in. Grassy places, primarily lower. Melanthiaceae.

Back during camas-digging days, death camas undoubtedly killed more people in the Northwest than any other plant ever will. Today it maintains its reputation with an occasional sheep death. No one would mistake the small white flowers of death camas for the big blue ones of camas, but mistakes occur when populations of the two are intermixed and both have gone to seed or withered—and camas bulbs are ripest for eating.

Beargrass

Xerophyllum tenax (zero-FILL-um: dry leaf; TEN-ax: holding fast). Stamens longer than tepals; flowers white, either fragrant or musty, saucer-shaped, ½ in., many, in a bulbous inflorescence 3–4 in. across, at first nippled, slowly elongating up to 20 in., the lowest flowers setting seed before the highest bloom; capsules 3-celled, dry; leaves narrow, tough, dry, V-folded, with minutely barbed edges, basal ones 8–30 in. in a dense clump; stalk up to 60 in., covered with small leaves. Dry forests and clearings at and w of CasCr, mainly at 4000–5800 ft.; also low elevs near coast. Melanthiaceae.

In optimal meadows, beargrass blooms abundantly most years. But the plant is at least as successful under partial forest cover, where it blooms rarely but reproduces year after year by producing new clumps from the rhizomes. It monopolizes many understories in the volcanic Cascades where ridges are thickly mantled in pumice from volcanic eruptions. This light soil is easy to root in, but very well drained, becoming too dry in summer for a lot of plants. When a clump does flower, it will soon die, but it likely has already reproduced vegetatively.

Hover flies predominate among beargrass's many pollinators. Spring's tender leaf bases figure in gopher, deer, elk, and bear diets (hence "beargrass"); but the neatly clipped leaf bases you see here and there are

Bronze bells

Death camas

Beargrass

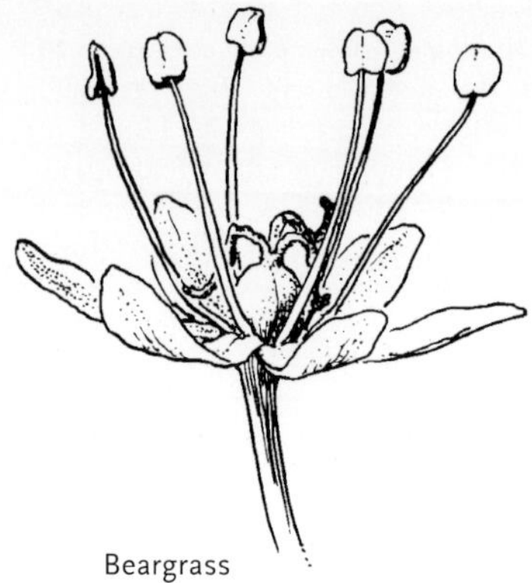
Beargrass

the work of a brushpicker gathering foliage for the florist trade. Beargrass was flown to Europe for years before trending among Northwest florists. For bouquets, extra long, dark, wide leaves are preferred. Longer leaves are found in forest than in meadow. For basketry, extra long, pale, thin, pliable leaves are best; they occur when beargrass regrows after a fire. Cultivating the best kind of beargrass leaf was one objective of Indian burning.

The leaves' strength made them an important material for Northwest tribes, who wove them into all kinds of baskets and hats. As David Douglas crowed,

> Pursh is correct as to their making watertight baskets of its leaves. Last night my Indian friend Cockqua arrived here from his tribe on the coast, and brought me three of the hats made on the English fashion, which I ordered when there in July; the fourth, which will have some initials wrought in it, is not finished, but will be sent by the other ship. I think them a good specimen of the ingenuity of the natives and particularly also being made by a little girl, twelve years old. . . . I paid one blanket (value 7 shillings) for them.

Douglas's imaginative biographer, William Norwood, later read between the lines of that and other journal entries to argue that Douglas, with his praise for a little girl's ingenuity, was disguising a romance with a "Chinook princess."

Corn Lily

***Veratrum* spp.** (ver-AY-trum: true black). Also false-hellebore. Flowers saucer-shaped, numerous; styles 3, persisting on the 1-in.-long 3-celled capsules, but usually lacking from lower flowers; leaves mostly 5–12 in., coarsely grooved along the veins, oval, pointed; stem 3–7 ft., from a thick black rhizome. Wet meadows, mainly subalpine. Melanthiaceae.

Green corn lily, *V. viride* (VEER-id-ee: green). Flowers pale green, 1/2–3/4 in. across, in a loose panicle with drooping branches. From n OR CasR n.

California corn lily, *V. californicum* Flowers dull white, or only slightly greenish, 3/4–1 1/2 in., in a dense panicle with ascending branches. WA CasR and s.

Heavy beds of snow lying on steep meadows tend to creep downslope through the winter, scouring vegetation from the surface. Woody seedlings are frustrated year after year, while herbs with fat storage roots and fast spring growth are favored, perpetuating the meadow. On many wet slopes, blunt corn lily shoots are the first plants to thrust

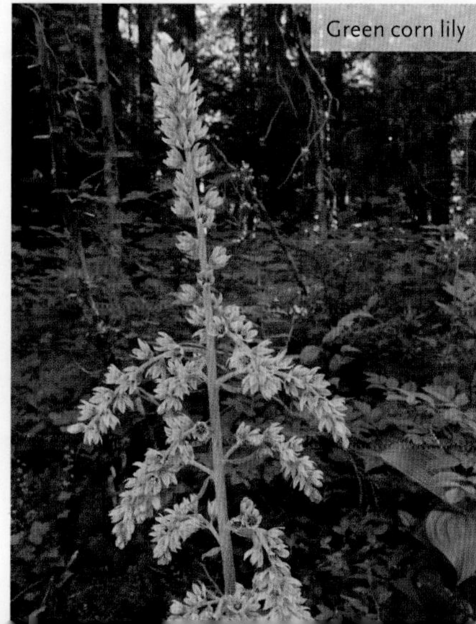
Green corn lily

upward as snow recedes, and they were the only herbaceous shoots robust enough to push up through six inches of new ash near Mt. St. Helens. Looking almost Venusian—startlingly clean and perfect—when they first unclasp from the stalk, before long they are often ragged, with help from foraging elk and insects.

Conspicuous signs of browsing do not prove the plant safe to eat. Idaho ewes that ate too much *V. californicum* gave birth to one-eyed lambs that were not long for this earth. Scientists traced the problem to an alkaloid they named cyclopamine, after the one-eyed Cyclops of Greek myth. They recognized cyclopamine as a potent carcinogen, but later realized that it could also be used to fight cancer. In contrast to older chemotherapy drugs that are cell toxins, and do a lot of damage, cyclopamine is part of the new class of anticarcinogens that works mechanically, switching intracellular communication pathways off and on. So corn lily extract has caused much excitement and study. Keep posted, but don't munch on the plant: both roots and young shoots are toxic, and used to be ground up for a crop insecticide (by farmers) or for a sinus-clearing snuff (by several tribes.) Every tribe that knew the plant used some part of it, sometimes burned as a fumigant, sometimes worn around the neck as a charm to ward off evil.

Tofieldia

Triantha occidentalis (try-ANTH-a: 3 flower; ox-i-den-TAY-lis: western). Also false-asphodel; *Tofieldia glutinosa*. Tepals white, 1/8–1/4 in., persistent while the 3-styled pistil grows out past them into a fat, reddish, 3-celled capsule; flowers or fruit in a dense cluster atop a 6- to 20-in., sticky, hairy stem; 1–3 grasslike basal leaves, 2–6 in., and sometimes 1–2 smaller stem leaves. Wet places, mainly subalpine. Tofieldiaceae.

Current analysis of the plant family tree finds *Triantha* on a branch rather far from the lilies—not just in its own family, but in a different order, Tofieldiales, closer to the pond-lilies than to the lilies.

HERBS: SHOWY MONOCOTS, WITH 3 STAMENS (IRISES)

Iris

***Iris* spp.** (EYE-ris: rainbow). 3 sepals spreading, 3 petals erect, and 3 smaller petallike parts (pistil branches) resting on the sepals and hiding the stamens; leaves grasslike, mostly basal; capsule 3-celled, splitting; from horizontal rhizomes. Iridaceae.

California corn lily

Tofieldia

Oregon iris

Oregon iris, *I. tenax* (TEN-ax: holding fast). Flower usually single, violet (or blue, rarely white, yellow, or pinkish) with fine dark lines; stem 4–12 in., with 1–4 small stem leaves. Open woods, w-side lowlands of OR and sw WA.

Western iris

Western iris, *I. missouriensis* (Missou-ri-EN-sis: of the Missouri River). Flowers usually 2, pale blue with fine dark lines; stem 10–24 in., usually without mid-stem leaves. Open woods, e-side of CasR and OlyM.

Yellowleaf iris, *I. chrysophylla* (cris-a-FILL-a: golden leaf). Flowers usually 2, pale yellow with fine darker lines; stems 3–8 in., with 1–4 small stem leaves, in clumps. Open woods, c to s OR. Hybridizes naturally with all seven *Iris* species of the Klamaths, producing flowers with varying amounts of blue or purple.

David Douglas found Indians braiding Oregon iris leaves into snares for large game, even elk: "It will hold the strongest bullock and is not thicker than the little finger." Such tenacity in a slender leaf suggested the name *tenax*. Iris was the Greek goddess who flashed across the sky, bearing messages—the rainbow.

Blue-Eyed Grass

Sisyrinchium idahoense (sis-er-INK-ium: the Greek name, derived obscurely from "pig snouts"; idaho-EN-zee: of Idaho). Tepals blue to purple, with yellow base, ¼–¾ in., all alike; stamens fused into a single, 3-anthered column; flowers 1 or a few; leaves

Yellowleaf iris

Blue-eyed grass

grasslike, basal, plus bracts at base of flower stalks, the longer bract looking like a continuation of the stem above the flowers; stem 6–14 in., 2-edged. Dry grassy sites that are briefly moist in spring; in BC and n WA it's scarce and mainly in lowlands. Iridaceae.

Grass Widows

Olsynium douglasii (ol-SIGH-nee-um: the author claimed it means "barely united," referring to the stamens; da-GLASS-ee-eye: for David Douglas, p. 56). Also purple-eyed grass, satinflower; *Sisyrinchium douglasii*. Tepals magenta, ¼–¾ in. long, all alike; stamens fused together for less than half their length; flowers 1 or a few; leaves grasslike, near-basal (plus two bracts below flowers, one of which may look like stem continuing upward) shorter than the 4- to 12-in., 2-edged stem. Dry grassy sites that are briefly moist in spring, mainly near CGorge. Iridaceae

This brilliant color spot is a spring ephemeral, meaning that it completes its active season in wet soil in a few weeks of spring, then withers into dormancy for the rest of the year. There's a nice patch of grass widows on a mountaintop in the Olympics—so far outside the plant's normal range that I suspect a fire lookout of doing a little gardening, decades ago.

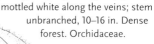

Grass widows

HERBS: SHOWY MONOCOTS, WITH IRREGULAR FLOWERS (ORCHIDS)

The orchid's flower structure is a snap to recognize; one petal, lowermost and thrust forward, is always utterly unlike the others and usually much larger. It's called the "lip" and serves as a platform for insect pollinators. Above the lip is a combined stamen and pistil structure called the "column."

Irregular dicots (pp. 205–221) have no more than five petals.

Orchid flowers are among the most elaborate insect lures on earth; but while the flowers evolved outlandishly, the roots mostly degenerated: a majority of the 500 or so genera of orchids are rootless lianas living on air and dripwater in tropical rainforest canopies. Our orchids are tenuously rooted, with vestigial root systems that tap into preexisting networks of fungal hyphae.

Rattlesnake-Plantain

Goodyera oblongifolia (GOOD-yer-a: for John Goodyer; oblong-gif-OH-lia: oblong leaf). Flowers greenish white, many, in a one-sided spike up to 5 in.; lip shorter than and hooded by the fused, ¼-in. upper petals, all connected to the stalk by a twisted ovary; leaves 1½–3 in., in a basal rosette, thick, evergreen, very dark glossy green, mottled white along the veins; stem unbranched, 10–16 in. Dense forest. Orchidaceae.

Rattlesnake-plantain

Rattlesnake-plantain

Rattlesnake-plantain

Ladies-tresses

> The Klallam informant, who is a devout Shaker, said that since she is a Christian she should not think of such matters, but formerly women rubbed this plant on their bodies to make their husbands like them better.
>
> —Erna Gunther

The intensity of the snakeskin pattern on the leaves varies. Sometimes only the mid-vein is white, but usually there is enough white pattern to tell these leaves from those of white-veined pyrola. This is one orchid with enough leaf area to make it nearly independent, when mature, of its mycorrhizal partners.

Ladies-Tresses

Spiranthes romanzoffiana (spy-RANTH-eez: coil flower; roman-zof-ee-AY-na: for Count Rumiantzev, p. 230). Flowers whitish, ½ in. long, seemingly tubular, in (usually 3) ranks in a 2- to 6-in., dense, coiled-looking spike (perhaps suggesting a 4-strand braid); leaves sheathing, mostly basal; stem up to 24 in.; from swollen roots. Wet meadows and streambanks, up to timberline. Orchidaceae.

Bog Orchid

***Platanthera* spp.** (plat-ANTH-er-a: broad anther). Also rein orchids. Flowers in a tall spike; lip (lower petal) narrow, with a pendent spur to the rear; 2 sepals horizontal, the other sepal and 2 petals erect, hooding the column. Orchidaceae.

White bog orchid, *P. dilatata* (dil-a-TAY-ta: broadened). Also *Platanthera leucostachys, Limnorchis dilatata, Habenaria dilatata.* Flowers white, spicy-fragrant, in a fairly dense 4- to 12-in. spike; spur usually longer than lip; leaves clasping the stem, up to 10 in. × 2 in., smaller upward; 8–40 in. tall. Wet ground, often subalpine.

Round-leaved bog orchid, *P. orbiculata* (or-bic-you-LAY-ta: circular leaf). Also *Habenaria orbiculata.* Flowers white to greenish

White bog orchid

Round-leaved bog orchid

Slender bog orchid

or yellowish, in a loose spike; basal leaves typically 2, broadly oval to nearly round, 2–6 in.; stem 8–24 in., leafless except for a few tiny bracts. Deep forest, n Cascades and CoastM.

Slender bog orchid, *P. stricta* (STRIC-ta: drawn tightly together). Also *Habenaria saccata.* Flowers pale green, sometimes purple-tinged, in a loose tall spike; lip longer than the sack-shaped spur; 1- to 6-in. leaves clasping the stem, oval to elliptic; 8–20 in. tall. Wet places.

The distinguishing feature of bog orchids is a narrow nectar-filled pouch or "spur" projecting rearward from the lip. The spur is a key element in the grand pattern of orchid evolution, which allies each variety and species of orchid with one, or at most a very few, species of insect. The right insect is not only powerfully attracted, but also physically unable to extract nectar from two successive blooms without picking up pollen from the first and leaving a good dose of it on the stigma of the second. Bog orchids' devices include: proboscis-entangling hairs to engage the insect for a little while; adhesive discs that stick to the insect's forehead while instantly triggering the stamen sac to split open; and little stalks that each hold a cluster of pollen to the adhesive disc (now on the insect's head), at first in an erect position that keeps the pollen away from the stigma of that same flower, but then (when the insect flies on) drying out and deflating into the right position to push the pollen onto the gluey stigma of the next flower of the same species, where the insect repeats her routine exactly in order to extract more nectar. All this just to minimize waste of pollen in the wrong places.

White bog orchid

The inch-long apparent stalk between the flower and the stem is actually the flower's ovary; a 180 degree twist in it shows that the lip evolved from what was originally the uppermost petal.

Calypso Orchid

Calypso bulbosa (ca-LIP-so: hidden, the name of a Greek sea nymph; bulb-OH-sa: from a bulb). Also fairy slipper, deer's-head orchid.

Flower single, pink; lip slipper-shaped, almost white, magenta-spotted above, magenta-streaked beneath; other petals and sepals all much alike, narrow, 3/4 in.; leaf single, basal, growing in fall, withering by early summer; stem 3–7 in., from a small round corm. Moist, mature forest, mainly lowland. Orchidaceae.

A close look reveals these little orchids to be just as voluptuously overdesigned as their corsage cousins, which evolved bigger to seduce the oversized tropical cousins of our insects. Get down onto their level to see and smell them; use a magnifying glass if you like; just don't pick them. Their bulblike corm is so shallowly planted that it's almost impossible to pick them without ripping the corm's lifelines. A calypso is dependent on its fungal and plant hosts (p. 318); its single leaf withers and is gone early in the growing season. Like other orchids, it produces huge numbers of minute seeds (3,770,000 seeds were found in one tropical orchid's pod) with virtually no built-in food supply, and an abysmal germination rate. They germinate only if particular species of fungi are already there to supply nutrients.

The black specks filling vanilla beans and vanilla ice creams are familiar examples of orchid seeds.

Mountain Lady's-Slipper

Cypripedium montanum (sip-rip-EE-dium: Venus's slipper; mon-TAY-num: of mountains). Also moccasin flower, Venus slipper. Flowers 1–3; lip 1 in. long, bulbous, white with purplish veins and a yellow staminate structure at its base; upper sepal and lateral petals brownish purple, about 2 in., slender, often twisted; stem 6–24 in., clasped by several broad leaves 2–6 in. long, plus a small bract beneath each flower. Open forest, e CasR slope, or rarely w-side in OR, and one record from VI. Orchidaceae.

Twayblade

***Neottia* spp.** (nee-OT-ia: bird's nest). Also big-ears, *Listera* spp. Flowers several, in an open, short-stalked spike; lower petal (lip) largest; slender upper 2 petals resemble the 3 sepals; stamens and pistil combine in a hoodlike shape; leaves 2, 1½–3 in., apparently opposite, clasping mid-stem; stem 4–14 in. Moist forest and wet meadows. Orchidaceae.

Broadlip twayblade, *N. convallariodes* (con-va-larry-OY-deez: resembling lily-of-the-valley). Flowers pale greenish; lip petal 5/8 in., narrow at base, widening to two broad short round lobes, like a narrow inverted heart; leaves oval to almost round with pointed tip.

Calypso orchid

Mountain lady's-slipper

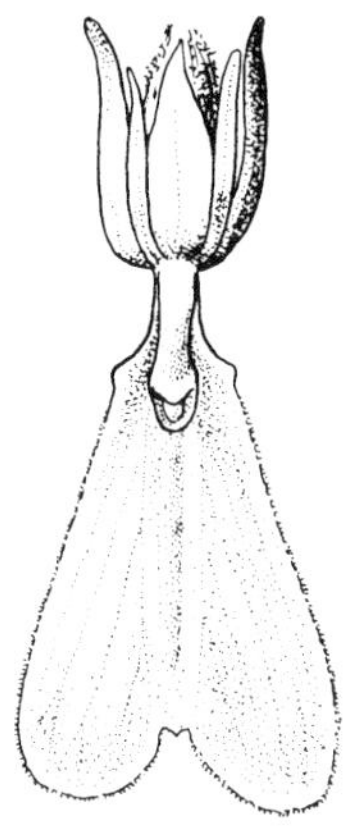
Broadlip twayblade

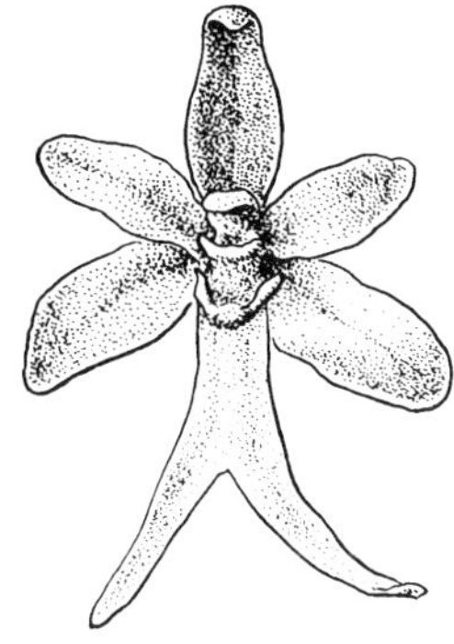
Heartleaf twayblade

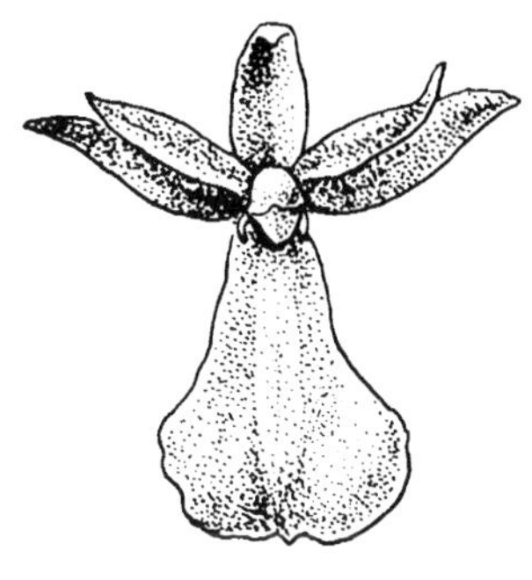
Northwestern twayblade

Heartleaf twayblade, *N. cordata* (cor-DAY-ta: heart-shaped). Flowers yellowish green ranging to red-stained or maroon; Y-shaped lip petal splits into two long pointed lobes, 3/8 in. long; leaves heart-shaped at base and stalkless, thus overlapping each other slightly.

Heartleaf twayblade

Northwestern twayblade, *N. banksiana* (banksy-AY-na: for Sir Joseph Banks). Also *Listera. caurina*. Flowers pale greenish; broad lip petal 3/8 in. long, with two tiny but long and pointed side-lobes at its base, and almost no notch at tip; leaves broad with pointed tip.

Though diminutive and dull, a twayblade is every inch an orchid, as testified by its glues and mechanisms for sticking pollen onto visiting insects—often mosquitoes. (And who better than an orchid to testify? Those two words derive from *orchis* and *testis*, the Greek and Latin words, respectively, for testes.)

Coralroot

***Corallorhiza* spp.** (coral-o-RYE-za: coral root). Entire plant pink to brown, or rarely pale yellow (albino); flowers 3/4–1 1/4 in. long (half of that being the tubular ovary), 6–30 in a loose spike; leaves reduced to inconspicuous sheaths on the 6- to 20-in. stem. Forest. Orchidaceae.

Spotted coralroot, *C. maculata* (mac-you-LAY-ta: spotted). Lip usually white with many magenta spots (sometimes also on petals).

Nongreen Orchids and Heaths

Some of our most intriguing herbs lack chlorophyll, and obtain all their nutrients from fungi. Since chlorophyll is the green pigment in plants, these plants are not green. They were long called "saprophytes," meaning that they obtain their carbohydrates from dead organic material, but that's incorrect. Their carbohydrates come from living green plants via living mycorrhizal fungi (p. 318), which pass them along to the nongreen plants below ground.

The word "saprophyte" (decay plus plant) was well established for over a hundred years for decay fungi and nongreen plants, because both were sometimes thought to be plants that live by decaying things. Now we know that fungi are not plants, and that plants cannot decay things (they lack the enzymes for it) so saprophytes don't exist. Organisms that rot things are now saprobes or saprotrophs. Words used by scientists for the plants formerly known as saprophytes range from the technical (mycoheterotrophs or epiparasites) to the casual (cheaters). This guide simply calls them nongreen plants, with the caveat that we also have nongreen direct parasites like broomrape. (A few authors still use "saprophyte" by giving it a new meaning, but that's misleading at best, because its old definition is still widely understood, is the one found in dictionaries, and is built into the word's etymology.)

The mycorrhizal symbiosis must have evolved because it lets fungi and plants utilize each other's strengths—the fungus's efficient uptake of water,

Western coralroot, *C. mertensiana* (mer-ten-zee-AY-na: for Karl H. Mertens, p. 147). Lip redder than plant, often with one or two spots or blotches.

Striped coralroot, *C. striata* (stry-AY-ta: striped). Petals and sepals brownish to purplish striped. Not reported from CoastM or VI mtns.

Coralroots usually grow in forest stands with few herbs or shrubs. They blend in with the duff and sticks until a shaft of sunlight hits, suddenly incandescing their eerie, translucent flesh. Their rhizomes do resemble coral—curly, short, knobby, and entirely enveloped in soft fungal tissue. As in other orchid genera, a seed's embryo develops only if penetrated, nourished, and hormonally stimulated by a minute strand (hypha) from a fungus in the soil. Fungal hormones suppress root hair growth and stimulate the orchid to produce mycorrhizae instead. In the case of coralroots, no root hairs ever form.

Spotted coralroot

phosphorus, and nitrogen, and the plant's ability to make carbohydrates out of air, water, and sunlight. Some mycorrhizal plants, it seems, gradually contributed less and less to this exchange, and got away with cheating as long as there were other plants feeding the same fungus. As the cheaters evolved, organs they no longer needed atrophied. They ended up with vestigial leaves, little or no chlorophyll, and no real roots—nothing but a stalk of flowers reproducing, while using the trees above for leaves and the fungi below for roots.

Proof of whether this symbiosis is mutualistic or parasitic has resisted most efforts, so far. Nongreen plants do produce chemicals that some researchers call "vitamin-like" because they stimulate growth of both the fungal and green hosts. But that doesn't prove beneficence: parasites like mistletoe commonly stimulate growth in their hosts, but that saps the hosts, it doesn't energize them.

Nongreen plants often show up during phases in forest development when competition among trees (for light and water, especially) is most intense, and consequently few understory plants remain and the weaker individual trees die. Forestry plans that use repeated thinning to mimic fire, bypassing those phases on the way to big marketable trees, may also short-circuit development of the nongreen community, which does have at least one economic value: candystick helps mushroom hunters find its host, the valuable matsutake mushroom.

Western coralroot

Striped coralroot

The vestigial leaves do not photosynthesize; oddly, the flowers' ovaries do, but not in significant quantities.

Phantom Orchid

Cephalanthera austiniae (sef-a-LANTH-er-a: headlike stamen tip; aus-TIN-ee-ee: for self-taught botanist Rebecca M. Austin). Also *Eburophyton austiniae.* Entire plant ivory white (aging brown) except for a yellow spot in the lip pouch; sepals, petals ½–¾ in., lip shorter; flowers 5–20; leaves mostly just sheaths, but one or two may have blades; stem 8–20 in. Forests; infrequent; not reported from CoastM or VI mtns. Orchidaceae.

"Phantom" here refers to the ghostly color, but also fits with this being the most elusive of our nongreen orchids.

Candystick

Allotropa virgata (a-LOT-ra-pa: turned various ways; veer-GAY-ta: striped). Also sugarstick. Entire plant fleshy, bright red and white; 5 white petals shorter than the 10 dark red stamens and dark red pistil; usually no sepals; flowers in a dense spike; stem thick, 4–16 in. (or rarely to over 6 ft.), sharply striped, with small white leaves. Infrequent, in dense lowland forests. Ericaceae.

The genus *Allotropa* grows its only species only here. This plant bursts paradoxically—at once candy-like and gothic—from the drab shady duff and litter.

Matsutake mushroom pickers learned to look for dried candystick stalks in fall as a marker for a patch of matsutakes. A scientist then investigated whether there was a mycorrhizal association between the two, and sure enough, all the mycorrhizae he found on candystick looked much alike, and all had that unique matsutake aroma. One scientist who did the math using then current prices for matsutake determined that many Northwest forests could be managed more lucratively for "special forest products" than for timber. Unfortunately, those prices turned out to be a bubble.

HERBS: DICOTS, WITHOUT GREEN PARTS

Pinedrops

Pterospora andromedea (tair-OS-por-a: winged seed; an-drom-ed-EE-a: a name from Greek myth). Entire plant gummy or sticky, monochromatically brownish red except for the amber, 5-lobed, jar-shaped corollas; flowers many, on downcurved stalks; capsules pumpkin-shaped; leaves brown, small and sparse on the 12- 48+ in. stem. Lower montane forests. Ericaceae.

Phantom orchid

Candystick

Pinedrops

Indian pipe

Pinesap

This year's glowing amber stalks of pinedrops shoot up alongside last year's still-standing dry brown stalks. They're our tallest nongreen plants: I measured one at 5½ feet. As the name implies, they may be found under (and mycorrhizally linked to) ponderosa pines, but also under Douglas-fir or many kinds of trees all across the continent. For their direct fungal hosts, in contrast, they apparently accept only one species.

This plant is also called Albany beechdrops in the east; it was near Albany, New York, that David Douglas, a year before coming to the Northwest, sought it out and was excited to find it, accurately observing that in "soil so dry that every other vegetation refused to grow . . . it seems to be a sort of parasite like *Monotropa* or *Orobanche*." Enthusiastically, but less accurately, he went on to write, "I have no doubt but it will cultivate."

Indian Pipe

Monotropa uniflora (ma-NOT-ra-pa: flowers turned one way, a meaningless name for a one-flowered plant; you-nif-LOR-a: one-flowered). Also ghost-plant, corpse-plant; *Monotropastrum uniflora*. Entire plant fleshy, white or pink-tinged, drying black; lobes and stamens usually 5, sometimes 4 or 6; flower single, narrowly bell-shaped, ½–¾ in. long, pendent, turning erect in fruit—a soft round capsule; leaves translucent, small; stems clustered, 2–10 in. tall. Dense forest. Ericaceae.

A strange plant, but a familiar one all across the continent. Mushrooms in the russula family are the usual cosymbionts here, and Douglas-fir is often at the far end of the pipeline. Don't pick Indian pipes—they'll just turn black and ugly within hours.

Pinesap

Monotropa hypopitys (hye-POP-it-iss: under pine). Also *Hypopitys monotropa*. Entire plant fleshy, yellow to straw or red, tinged with pink, drying black; flowers narrowly bell-shaped, ⅜–¾ in., mostly 4-lobed (rarely 5), several, initially all downturned in one direction from any one stem, turning erect in fruit; seed capsules round, soft; leaves translucent, small; stems clustered, 2–10 in. tall. Dense forest. Ericaceae.

Digging up a pinesap (don't!) would reveal a soft mycorrhizal rootball only a couple of inches deep. Species of *Boletus* (p. 388) are common partners of this species, and a pine or other conifer is almost always hooked up to the same bolete.

Generations of taxonomists quarreled over this little plant's name, *Hypopitys monotropa* vs. *Monotropa hypopitys*. At issue: how closely related is pinesap to Indian pipe? Studies of their DNA now find the two plants far from being each other's closest kin, so they shouldn't be in the same genus. The *Flora of North America* treatment acknowledges this, yet keeps pinesap within *Monotropa* for now because the paper properly realigning the two and their relatives has yet to be written. Realignment may prove more complex than simply reverting this species to *Hypopitys monotropa*. The latest proposal I have seen keeps it as *Monotropa hypopitys* but moves Indian pipe into genus *Monotropastrum*, home of a similar-looking Japanese species.

Naked Broomrape

Orobanche uniflora (oro-BAN-kee: vetch choke, referring to its root parasitism on plants such as vetch; you-nif-LOR-a: single flower). Entire plant purplish to yellow, with rarely a tinge of green, bristling with sticky hairs; corollas purple, pale lavender, or less often yellow, tubular, 5/8–1 5/8 in., with 5 short lobes; flowers 1 per stem; leaves reduced to scaly bracts. Found among its host plants—stonecrops, saxifrages, and woodland star. Orobanchaceae.

Broomrape stands accused of botanical violence in both its scientific and its common name. It lives as a direct parasite on plant roots (in contrast to most of our nongreen plants, which obtain their photosynthates indirectly, via fungi). Broomrapes each specialize in a narrow range of hosts. Similar clustered broomrape, *O. fasciculata*, has more numerous flowers and they're yellow, sometimes red-tinged, but not true purple.

Until recently, the family Orobanchaceae

Naked broomrape

was small and limited to parasites. Wildflower aficionados may be dismayed to see their beloved paintbrushes reclassified as Orobanchaceae. However, the two families were always seen as very closely related. The parasitic mode does not warrant family-level distinction, as it evolves easily and repeatedly. Partial parasitism is rife among paintbrushes.

HERBS: DICOTS, COMPOSITE

Picture a daisy. Seeming petals radiate from a cushiony disk. On closer examination, the base of each petallike ray enwraps a small pistil. The ray and pistil together constitute a ray flower, not a petal; the petallike length is an entire corolla of petals, fused then split down one side and flattened. The central disk turns out to be lots of little flowers too—disk flowers; each has a (usually two-branched) style poking out of a minute tube of five fused stamens, within a larger tube, which is the (usually five-lobed) corolla. What we saw at first as one flower is a composite flower head, the characteristic inflorescence of the family Asteraceae, or composites. An involucre of green bracts cups the head as the calyx of sepals cups many other kinds of flowers. True sepals may also be present in the form of a pappus—a brush of hairs, scales or plumes that remain attached and grow as the seed forms, usually to provide mobility via wind or fur.

Some composites, dandelion-like, have only ray flowers and no disk. In these the ray flowers are bisexual, having stamen tubes as well as pistils. Other composites have only disk flowers; others *appear* to have only disk flowers because their inner and outer flower types are equally unshowy; either way, I'll call them "thistle-like."

The tight fit of the stamen tube around the style is a mechanism that prevents self-pollination. As the pistil grows, it plunges all the pollen out of the tube; once its tip has grown free of the tube, it can split, exposing stigmas on the inner faces of its two branches.

Composite flowers excel at producing copious fat, well-nourished seeds. The family tends to be adept at rapid invasion; year-to-year survival in severe cold is not its forte, and in shady boreal habitats even less so, so composites are fewer here than in many mountain regions. Still, they are conspicuous in our meadows, providing color in late summer when most flowers have gone to seed and huckleberry foliage isn't incandescing yet.

Composites can be tough to identify. With somewhere between 15,000 and 20,000 species (several hundred in our range) they are even more diverse than grasses.

HERBS: DICOTS, COMPOSITE, WITH DISK AND RAY FLOWERS (DAISY TYPE)

Fleabane

***Erigeron* spp.** (er-IDGE-er-un: soon aged). Also daisy. Rays 40–80; disk yellow; heads usually single; leaves narrow, mostly basal; stem leaves get smaller upwards (few and tiny on alpine plants). Asteraceae.

Subalpine fleabane, *E. glacialis*. Also *E. peregrinus*. Rays violet to pale blue, pink, or white, 3/8–1 in.; involucre uniformly woolly or sticky from top to bottom. Abundant in subalpine meadows, especially in WA.

Alice's fleabane, *E. aliceae* (AL-iss-ee: for Alice Eastwood). Rays violet, 3/8–5/8 in.; lower half of involucre has long white hairs, upper half sticky or fuzzy; leaves both basal and alternate, elliptic to spoon-shaped, entire or lower ones with a few coarse teeth; stem 12–32 in., not sticky. OlyM, OR CasR.

Golden fleabane, *E. aureus* (AW-ree-us: golden). Rays bright yellow, 1/4 in.; involucre woolly; plant 2–7 in. tall, covered with fine wool—not sticky hairs. Alpine.

Subalpine fleabane

Alice's fleabane

Golden fleabane

Arctic-alpine fleabane

Cutleaf daisy

Arctic-alpine fleabane, *E. humilis* (HUE-mil-iss: humble, i.e., low-growing). Rays white to blue-purple, 50–150, 1/4 in. long, narrow; disk yellow; involucre purple, 3/8–3/4 in. tall, the bracts all one length; basal leaves spoon-shaped or oblong; 1–8 in. tall, bristling all over with white hairs. Seeps and wet meadows at mid to alpine elevs in BC.

Cutleaf daisy, *E. compositus* (com-POZ-it-us: compound). Rays white (may be pinkish or bluish, or absent), up to 3/8 in. long; disk yellow; involucral bracts all one length; leaves basal, compound, usually fine and lacy, with slender leaflets in threes. Sandy or rocky soils, mid-elevations and higher.

Daisies generally bloom during the spring flowering rush, earlier than most composites, which could be the implication of the Latin name. Insecticidal properties implied by "fleabane" are medieval superstition, or perhaps conflation with *Pyrethrum* daisies. The name "daisy" (originally for the English daisy, *Bellis perennis*) traces back to "day's eye" in Old English.

Cutleaf daisies commonly put out rayless-form flowers. These will probably set seed without pollination. The population presumably comes out ahead when some individuals take this safe route to reproduction, while others go for the benefits of cross-fertilization at the risk of going unpollinated and setting no seed at all.

Aster

Spp. formerly in *Aster*. Rays lavender to blue, pink, or white, 1/4–3/4 in.; disk yellow. Asteraceae.

Cascade aster, *Eucephalus ledophyllus* (yew-SEF-a-lus: good head, praising the "elegant calyx"; leed-o-FILL-us: rockrose

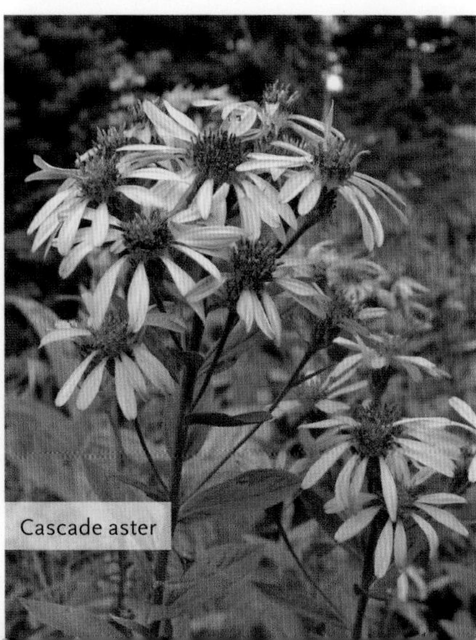
Cascade aster

leaf). Rays usually 13–24; several heads; involucral bracts slender, pointed, inner ones usually reddish; leaves 1–3 in., lanceolate, entire or with a few teeth, with thick gray wool underneath; lower stem lacks full-size leaves; 8–24 in. tall. Abundant in mid to subalpine clearings from Chelan County s.

Engelmann's aster, *Eucephalus engelmannii* (engle-MAH-nee-eye: for Georg Engelmann). Rays often white, usually 8 or 13; several heads; involucral bracts slender, pointed, inner ones usually reddish; leaves 2–4 in., lanceolate, entire, usually hairless; lower stem lacks full-size leaves; stem 2–5 ft. tall, ribbed. Moist, open forest, CasR in WA and BC.

Leafy aster, *Symphyotrichum foliaceum* (sim-fee-a-TRICK-um: joined hairs; fo-lee-AY-shum: leafy, referring to leaflike bracts). Rays 15–60; several heads; involucre has 3 rows of nonsticky bracts dramatically bigger, looser, and more leaflike than on most similar flowers, the lowest row much the biggest; leaves both basal and alternate, lanceolate to ovate, 2–5 in., usually entire; 8–24 in. tall.

Tundra aster, *Oreostemma alpigenus* (al-PIDGE-en-us: alpine). Single-flowered stems 1–3, 2–12 in., often leaning, often numerous in a clump; leaves linear to lanceolate, basal ones 2–4 in., stem leaves tiny. Alp/subalpine.

Asters tend to bloom later than daisies and to have fewer, broader rays. Until recently, most flora books treated North American "asters" as species of a large genus, *Aster*, but that name is now applied only to several species native to Europe. Cascade aster joined the subalpine elite that came up in large numbers through inches of Mt. St. Helens ash in 1980.

Arnica

***Arnica* spp.** (AR-nic-a: lambskin, referring to leaf texture). Heads yellow, single to few; rays ½–1¼ in.; 4–8 opposite leaves, plus some leaves nearby in nonflowering whorls from the rhizome; stems 4–24 in. Asteraceae.

Broadleaf arnica

Engelmann's aster

Leafy aster

Tundra aster

Hairy arnica

Arrowleaf groundsel

Lambstongue groundsel

Broadleaf arnica, *A. latifolia* (lat-if-OH-lia: broad leaf). Rays 8–15; leaves more or less toothed, heart-shaped to broadly oval, smooth to the touch. Abundant in meadows and open forest.

Hairy arnica, *A. mollis* (MOL-iss: soft). Also cordilleran arnica. Rays 12–20; disk flowers large, 5-lobed; involucre sticky-hairy from base to top; leaves lanceolate to elliptic; green parts usually hairy and sticky. Mid-elev to subalpine meadows; not in CoastR.

Several tribes used arnicas as a plaster for sore or injured muscles or joints; European herbalists made similar use of their *Arnica montana*. Broadleaf arnica hybridizes with its equally widespread and abundant look-alike, heartleaf arnica, *A. cordifolia*. Both readily resprout from deep roots after a fire. They are hard to tell apart.

Groundsel

***Senecio* spp.** (sen-EE-she-oh: old man). Also ragwort. Rays 4–10 (or rarely none), 1/4–1/2 in., sparse and disorderly; disk yellow; heads several; stem 1–6 ft. Asteraceae.

Arrowleaf groundsel, *S. triangularis* Rays yellow; leaves narrow-triangular, 3–7 in., usually toothed, all on stem. Widespread in lush meadows.

Lambstongue groundsel, *S. integerrimus* (in-te-JER-im-us: very smooth-edged). Rays yellow (var. *exaltatus*) or white as in photo (var. *ochroleucus*); leaves elliptical, basal ones 3–10 in. including their long leafstalks, much smaller upwards, usually entire but sometimes heavily crinkle-edged; tangled white hair on all green parts. Mainly e-side; not on VI.

Alpine Meadow Butterweed

Packera subnuda (PACK-er-a: for John G. Packer; sub-NEW-da: almost hairless). Also *Senecio cymbalarioides*. Heads single

Alpine meadow butterweed

Dwarf alpinegold

Woolly-sunflower

(or few), yellow; rays about 13, 3/8–1/2 in.; deep involucre with one row of bracts, purple-tinged or not; basal leaves often scalloped, spoon-shaped; stem leaves few and small; 2–12 in.; green parts usually hairless. Moist alp/subalpine sites; not in OlyM or VI. Asteraceae.

Several species in this genus poison livestock, and several have been used medicinally.

Bolander's Ragwort

Packera bolanderi (bo-LAN-der-eye: for Henry N. Bolander). Several heads, yellow; rays 8 or 13, 3/8–1/2 in.; leaves distinctive: heart-shaped overall, sharply incised into several lobes, each in turn divided into a few teeth, mainly basal; 4–20 in. Moist forest from CGorge s. Asteraceae.

Bolander's ragwort

Dwarf Alpinegold

Hulsea nana (HUL-see-a: for Gilbert Hulse; NAY-na: dwarf). Head yellow, single, 1/2–1 1/4 in., facing up; 15–28 rays short relative to the broad disk and robust goblet-shaped involucre; involucre, stem, and leaves covered with long, dense sticky hair; leaves primarily basal, with short lobes; 2–8 in. tall. Alpine volcanic slopes from Mt. Rainier s. Asteraceae.

Woolly-Sunflower

Eriophyllum lanatum (area-FILL-um: woolly leaf; lan-AY-tum: woolly). Heads yellow, 1 per stem; 8–13 rays 1/3 in. long; involucral bracts broad, few, all of one length; leaves alternate, linear or linear-lobed; all green parts thickly white-woolly; stems 5–24 in., many, weak, in thick clumps or sprawling mats. Dry meadows at all elevs. Asteraceae.

Carey's Balsamroot

Balsamorhiza careyana (balsam-o-RYE-za: balsam root; carey-AY-na: for John Carey). Heads all yellow, single, 2 1/2–4 in. across; leaves basal (plus 1–2 bracts on stem), triangular, 12 in. × 6

Carey's balsamroot

in., on long leafstalks; plant grayish and sandpapery with stiff hairs, especially under leaves when young; 10–30 in., in thick clumps. In sun, lower e-side from Chelan s. Asteraceae.

Balsamroots are spectacular in the spring, and they are also a major food plant. Deer and elk eat the leaves, and Indians ate the young shoots, the seeds, and the fat, fragrant, slightly woody taproot. It requires prolonged cooking, and even then provokes indigestion.

Carey's balsamroot provides the crazy yellow displays in the eastern Columbia Gorge and along the eastern side of the Cascades in Oregon and southern Washington. North of there—as well as everywhere eastward, across the Rockies—it is supplanted by arrowleaf balsamroot, *B. sagittata*. The two overlap abundantly in Chelan and Kittitas Counties, and are tricky to tell apart. The key is in the nature of the hairs all over the plant. On arrowleaf these are woolly; the leaf feels like felt, not at all like sandpaper, and looks whiter than the gray-green Carey's.

Spring gold

Spring Gold

Crocidium multicaule (cro-SID-ium: downy nap on cloth; multi-CAUL-ee: many-stemmed, a misleading name). Heads all yellow, 1 per stem; rays about 8, ⅓ in.; one involucral bract under each ray; leaves basal (plus a few on stem), lanceolate to linear, somewhat fleshy, ½–1 in.; stems 2–8 in., usually unbranched, often woolly near leaf axils; small annual plant. Rock ledges that dry out in summer, or sagebrush steppe; lowlands of WA, OR, e VI. Asteraceae.

Western Canada Goldenrod

Solidago elongata* and *S. lepida (so-lid-AY-go: healing, a misleading name; LEP-id-a: scaly). Also cascade goldenrod; *S. canadensis*. Heads yellow, 100+, in a tall fluffy cluster; rays 10–17, less than ⅛ in.; leaves alternate, narrow elliptic, largest near mid-stem; stem grayish-hairy, more so upwards; 1½–5 ft. Moist meadows and clearings. Asteraceae.

The widespread and familiar Canada goldenrod—a scapegoat for a lot of hay

Western Canada goldenrod

Northern goldenrod

Yarrow

fever—has been split into three species, with most of our populations falling into these two extremely similar species. The two occupy much the same range, and the only firm distinction between them is a coat of almost microscopic sticky hairs on parts of *S. lepida*.

Northern Goldenrod

Solidago multiradiata (multi-ray-dee-AY-ta: many-rayed). Also Rocky Mountain goldenrod. Heads yellow, several, in a small rounded cluster; rays 10–18, ¼ in.; leaves both alternate and basal, oblanceolate, with fine teeth and a fringe of hairs on the leaf stalks; stems minutely hairy, 2–18 in. Rocky sites, mostly high; infrequent s of Mt. Rainier. Asteraceae.

In the alpine zone of the Cascades or Olympics, a similar plant without hairs along the edges of its leaf stalks is likely dwarf goldenrod, *S. simplex* var. *nana*.

Yarrow

Achillea millefolium (ak-il-EE-a: for Achilles; mil-ef-OH-lium: thousand leaf). Rays 3–5, white (rarely pink), ⅛ in. long and wide; disk yellow; heads many, in a flat to convex inflorescence; leaves narrow, extremely (though variably) finely dissected, fernlike, aromatic; to 3 ft., or dwarfed (alpine). In sun. Asteraceae.

Achilles, the Greek hero in the Trojan war, was taught by Chiron the Centaur to dress the wounds of battle with yarrow. Northwest Indians also used yarrow poultices, and drank yarrow tea for myriad ailments. They steamed the homes of sick people with the pungent smell of yarrow leaves—rather like rosemary and sage. In China, the yarrow stalk oracle was systematized by Confucius and his followers in the I Ching. Europeans still use yarrow both medicinally and as a flavoring in bitters and beer. Herbalist Gregory Tilford says it will repel insects, at least briefly, when rubbed on the skin, but warns that it will irritate sensitive skin.

Some *Achillea* species have perfectly smooth-edged linear leaves. Our "thousand-leaf" species was once divided into several species on the basis of varying degrees of leaf dissection, but it was found that transplanted specimens would within a few years alter their leaf shape to fit their new environment, nearly matching the yarrows around them.

Edible thistle

Pearly everlasting

HERBS: DICOTS, COMPOSITE, WITHOUT RAYS (THISTLE TYPE)

Edible Thistle

Cirsium edule (SIR-shium: swollen veins, for which thistles were prescribed Medievally; ED-you-lee: edible). Flowers bright pink to purple; involucral bracts ending in long spines, cobwebby-haired at the base; leaves very spiny, pinnately lobed, up to 10 in. long, narrow, all on the 1½- to 7-ft. stem. Widespread in sun, mainly w-side. Asteraceae.

Native thistles are herbaceous biennials, storing starches in their taproot their first summer, dying back to the ground, and then resprouting to flower, fruit, and die in their second year. Three European thistles, including the misnamed "Canada thistle," are nasty weeds.Thistle taproots and peeled stems are nutritious and tasty, highly rated in both ethnobotanical and survival-skills texts. Meriwether Lewis wrote that "when [roasted] for uce it becomes black, and is more shugary than any fruit or root that I have met with in uce among the natives; the sweet is precisely that of the sugar in flavor." Even horses may—very carefully—munch the sweet-nectared flowers. The plant branches profusely after its main stem gets munched.

Edible thistle

Pearly Everlasting

Anaphalis margaritacea (an-AF-a-lis: the Greek name; margarite-AY-see-a: pearly). Yellow disks are surrounded by innumerable tiny papery white bracts (not ray flowers); heads 3/8 in. across, many, in a convex cluster; leaves 2–5 in., linear, woolly (especially underneath), all on the 8- to 36-in. stem, the lowest ones withering. Widespread on roadsides, burns, and clearcuts; also alpine. Asteraceae.

Woolly pussytoes

Dark pussytoes

Rosy pussytoes

What you might mistake for ray flowers are dry white involucral bracts that persist everlastingly, in the field or in a vase. Pearly everlasting's light wind-disseminated seeds made it an early dominant on devastated ground at Mt. St. Helens. It thrived and persisted only on sites that had been improved—most often by dwarf alpine lupine adding soil nitrogen and then getting out of the way by dying.

Pussytoes

***Antennaria* spp.** (an-ten-AIR-ia: antenna—). Disks whitish, soft-fuzzy, deep, surrounded by numerous sepal-like scaly bracts (not ray flowers); heads several, ¼ in.; leaves woolly, mainly basal. Asteraceae.

Woolly pussytoes, *A. lanata* (lan-AY-ta: woolly). Bracts whitish; basal leaves 1–4 in.; stems 4–12 in., in clumps, often broad, without runners. Abundant on dry rocky ground at all elevations; increases with overgrazing; not on VI.

Dark pussytoes, *A. media* (ME-dia: medium). Bracts blackish green, sometimes white-tipped; leaves rarely even 1 in.; stems rise 2–4 in. from leafy runners, forming mats. Subalpine meadows to alpine fellfields.

Rosy pussytoes, *A. rosea* (ROSE-ia: rose-colored). Bracts pink to white; leaves rarely over 1 in.; stems rise 6–18 in. from leafy runners, forming mats. Dry rocky ground at all elevations; increases with overgrazing.

Alpine forms of many composites, including rosy pussytoes, usually reproduce asexually, the ovules maturing into seeds without being fertilized by pollen. Any given patch is likely a female clone, perhaps with interconnecting runners. These plants are adapted to a severe climate in which the blooming season all too often zips by in weather too nasty for small insects (pollinators of minute flowers like these) to be out and about.

Since each clone's flowers look alike over a wide area while differing from other clones, many clonal populations were named as species. Some taxonomists felt that this situation demanded weeding out unwarranted species; but *Flora of North America* took the opposite tack—splitting, not lumping.

Sweet Coltsfoot

Petasites frigidus (pet-a-SIGH-teez: hat-shaped). Also alpine butterbur; *P. palmatus*, *P. sagittatus*. Flower heads white to pinkish, numerous, in a round cluster; ♂ heads have short rays; ♀ rayless; stalks 4–24 in.,

Sweet coltsfoot

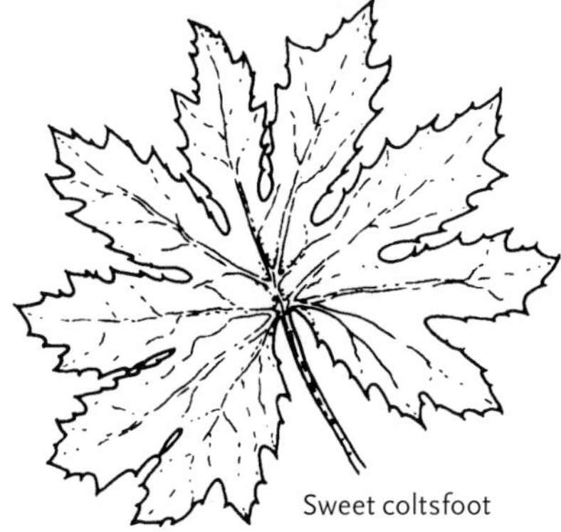
Sweet coltsfoot

with a few bracts 1–2 in. long; true leaves, ranging from triangular to deeply palmate-lobed, up to 12 in. × 16 in. wide, grow nearby, on fat 16- to 24-in. leafstalks. Wet places, mainly lowland. Asteraceae.

Fast-growing coltsfoot flower stalks appear in February in lower forests, providing the earliest nectar for bees. Leaves are separate and come later, maturing as the flowers go to seed. Parts of the plant are edible, and salty enough that ash prepared from them was valued as table salt. They were also used medicinally (for a really wide variety of uses, including making you throw up) and find a market among herbalists today, mainly for cough medicine. The alpine variety *frigidus*—smaller, with shallow-lobed leaf blades longer (up to 8 inches) than wide—grows from Mt. Hood north.

American Saw-Wort

Saussurea americana (so-SURE-ee-a: for Horace and Theodore Saussure). Disk flowers usually 13, dark purple, narrow-tubular, protruding haphazardly from a fluffy mass of pappus bristles; heads several, crowded; leaves triangular, neatly sawtoothed, narrow, the lower ones up to 6 in., all on the 10- to 40-in. stem. Lush low-subalpine meadows, WA and VI. Asteraceae.

Silverback

Luina hypoleuca (lu-EYE-na: anagram of genus *Inula*; hypo-LEW-ca: white underneath). Heads cream-colored, several; 10–24 large disk flowers have protruding yellow stigmas with 2 curling tips; leaves all along stem, 1–2 in., oval, white-woolly on lower or both sides; plants 8–24 in., often in dense patches. Rocky high elevs; BC, WA, and Tillamook County, OR. Asteraceae.

Silvercrown

Cacaliopsis nardosmia (ca-cay-lee-OP-sis: resembling genus *Cacalia*; nar-DOS-mia: nard aroma). Also *Luina nardosmia*. Heads bright yellow, ½–1¼ in., several; 20+ large

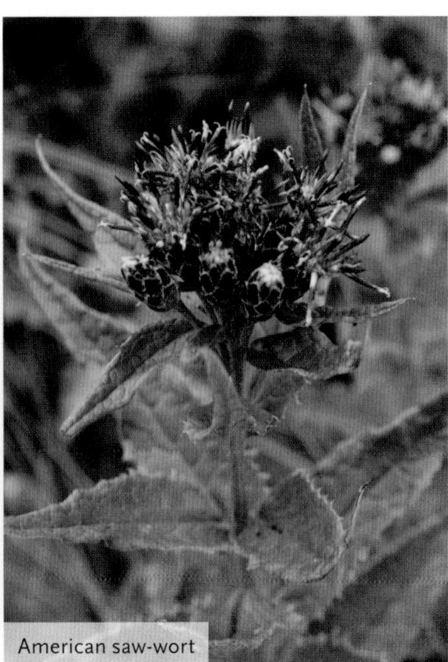
American saw-wort

disk flowers have protruding stigmas with 2 curling tips; leaves deeply palmate-lobed, round in outline, the bigger ones basal on long stalks, 8–14 in. across; plants 24–42 in. tall. Meadows and open forest e of CasCr and in OR CoastR; locally abundant. Asteraceae.

On this handsome plant, the individual flowers in the composite head are big enough for you to see them as flowers, with five petal lobes and two stigma branches.

Trail-Plant

Adenocaulon bicolor (a-den-o-CAW-lon: gland stem; BY-color: two color). Also pathfinder. Flower heads tiny, white, several, in a very sparse panicle on a 10- to 32-in. stalk; leaves all on lowest part of stem, triangular, 4–6 in., dark green on top, white-fuzzy underneath. Forest up to mid-elevs. Asteraceae.

Unlike most of its family, trail-plant is adapted to shade. The leaves are large, thin, flat-lying, and easy to recognize by their shape, while the flowers are rarely noticed (they attract small flies by their smell, not their looks). The combination of weak leafstalks and high contrast between upper and lower leaf surfaces led to the common name; a good woodsman tracking a large animal through the woods appreciated a conspicuous series of overturned trail-plant leaves. The sticky seeds also "trail" us by adhering to our legs. And then again, there are often tiny circumlocuitous trails etched across many trail-plant leaves over the summer by leaf-mining insect larvae.

Wormwood

***Artemisia* spp.** (ar-tem-EE-zhia: the Greek name). Also sagewort, mugwort. Flower heads many, small, pale, within cups of fuzzy bracts, in tall inflorescences; plants gray-woolly or fuzzy. Mid to high meadows and open forest. Asteraceae.

Western wormwood, *A. ludoviciana* (lu-doe-vis-ee-AY-na: of the Louisiana Purchase area). Also white sagebrush. Heads 1/8 in.; leaves 1–4 in., alternate, spicy-aromatic when crushed, silvery-fuzzy on both sides,

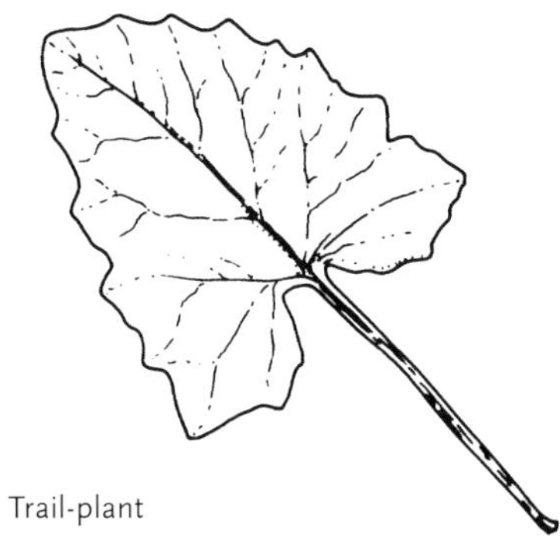

Trail-plant

Silverback

Silvercrown

Trail-plant

Western wormwood

Michaux's wormwood

Mountain sagewort

highly variable but most with a few irregular, fingerlike lobes; 1–5 ft. tall.

Michaux's wormwood, *A. michauxiana* (me-show-zee-AY-na: for Andre Michaux). Also lemon sagewort. Heads 1/8 in., often purple-tinged; leaves lemony-aromatic, alternate, usually hairless and bright green on at last one side, the bigger ones many-lobed; 8–30 in. tall. WA and BC CasR.

Mountain sagewort, *A. norvegica* (nor-VEDGE-ic-a: of Norway). Also boreal sagebrush; *A. arctica*. Flower heads larger, up to 3/8 in. across; leaves only mildly aromatic, basal ones much the largest, 1 to 3 times dissected pinnately; 8–24 in. tall. WA and BC.

Many Western tribes valued western wormwood above all other plants for ceremonial and purification purposes, right down to wiping bowls after eating. Burned for its smoke, infused in grease or water, or just tied up to waft about, wormwoods were variously reported to drive away evil spirits, mosquitoes, weakness, snow blindness, colds, headaches, menstrual irregularity, tuberculosis, underarm odor, eczema, and dandruff. Shrubs of this genus perfume half of the West. That's right, sagebrush.

In Europe, use of *Artemisia* to repel midges led to the old name "mugwort," a *mucg* being a midge. Wormwoods of Europe include the intoxicating absinthe, the bitter *vermouth* ("wormwood" in German) that flavors wines, and the culinary herb tarragon, which is native here as well; the Crow tribe called it "wolf perfume." It has been used medicinally in China for thousands of years. In the 1990s its active ingredient artemisinin, used in combination with another drug, became the leading medicine for malaria. Alarmingly, this therapy is already beginning to fail as the malaria parasite evolves resistance to it.

HERBS: DICOTS, COMPOSITE, WITHOUT DISK FLOWERS (DANDELION TYPE)

Mountain-Dandelion

***Agoseris* and *Nothocalaïs* spp.** (a-GAH-ser-iss: goat chicory; noth-o-ca-LAY-iss: false *Calaïs*). One 1-in. flower head per stem; plants milky-juiced; leaves basal, linear to lanceolate, often with a few widely spaced teeth. Asteraceae.

Pale agoseris

Orange agoseris

Alpine lake mountain-dandelion

Pale agoseris, *A. glauca* (GLAW-ca: silvery). Rays pale waxy yellow, drying pinkish; highly variable as to leaf shape, stature, and hairiness; 4–32 in. In sun, all elevs.

Orange agoseris, *A. aurantiaca* (aw-ran-TIE-a-ca: orange). Rays red-orange, drying purplish; 4–20 in. In sun, mid-elevs to alpine.

Alpine lake mountain-dandelion, *N. alpestris* (al-PES-tris: alpine). Also *Agoseris alpestris, Microseris alpestris.* Rays dandelion-yellow; leaves 1–6 in., hairless except on their edges; plants 2–10 in. Alp/subalpine, CasR from Mt. Rainier s.

These are related to dandelions (*Taraxacum* spp.) and resemble them in their seed-parachutes as well as their flower heads, which on *Agoseris* tend to close up on hot days. You may see either the common dandelion, a European invasive, or native species of *Taraxacum* high in our mountains. Flimsy hollow stems distinguish dandelions from these native mountain-dandelions.

Hawkweed

***Hieracium* spp.** (hi-er-AY-shium: hawk—). Flower heads several, ½–1 in. across, involucres slender, in a sparse panicle leaves long-elliptical, hairy. In sun. Asteraceae.

White hawkweed, *H. albiflorum* (al-bif-LOR-um: white flower). Heads white; 12–30 in. tall. Forest openings.

Scouler's hawkweed, *H. scouleri* (scoo-ler-eye: for John Scouler, p. 112). Also woollyweed. Heads yellow; leaves, stems, and involucres bristle with white hairs; leaves 2–4 in.; 6–36 in. tall. Rocky dry meadows.

Long-bearded hawkweed, *H. longiberbe* (lon-jib-ER-be: long beard). Like Scouler's,

White hawkweed

Scouler's hawkweed

Long-bearded hawkweed

Wall lettuce

but the white hairs are even longer; 6–24 in. tall; stems and leaf veins often magenta in spring. Limited to the CGorge at low to mid-elevs.

The milky juice of hawkweeds and mountain-dandelions dries into "Indian bubble-gum," which was chewed for mouth entertainment or cleaning.

Similar slender hawkweed, *H. triste*, is on the small side with yellow flowers, hairy involucres, but hairless leaves.

Wall Lettuce

Mycelis muralis (my-SEE-lis: meaning unknown; mew-RAY-lis: grows on walls). Also *Lactuca muralis*. Rays consistently five, yellow, from a tubular involucre; flower heads very sparse, blooming a few at a time; leaves coarsely pinnate-lobed, with "ears" clasping stem; plant milky-juiced, 2–3½ ft. tall. Low forest; Eurasian weed. Asteraceae.

This common garden weed turns up in more Cascadian wilderness forest stands than any other weed I've seen, but fortunately it doesn't take over.

It was formerly placed in genus *Lactuca*, along with cultivated lettuce. Because it consistently has five rays, it's easy to mistake wall lettuce for a five-petaled flower (as opposed to a composite flower head). If you have sharp eyes or a magnifying glass, reveal its true nature by splitting a ray back to its tubular base, where a pistil and stamens hide within each ray. While you're focused on fine details, note the five tiny teeth across the squarish tip of each ray. Those are corolla lobes—proof that technically, like most Asteraceae, this actually *is* a five-petaled flower.

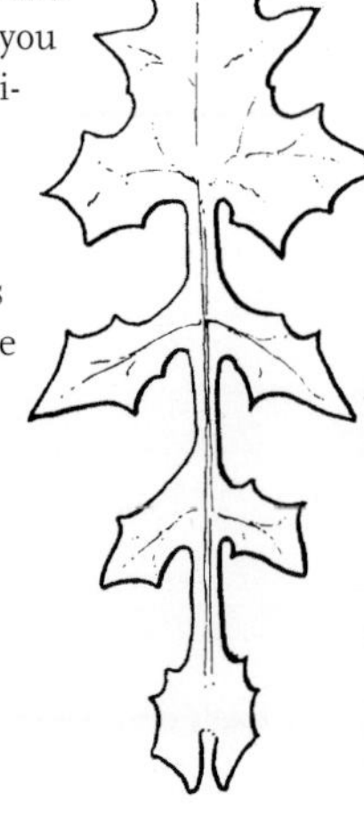
Wall lettuce

HERBS: DICOTS, FLOWERS WITHOUT PETALS OR SEPALS

Stinging nettle has four tiny, obscure sepals, but getting close enough to see them would likely prove painful. Aside from that, "without sepals" is applied pretty strictly to this group of oddities, not to betray readers who look closely enough to see and count minute sepals.

Marginally countable sepals or petals are on mountain-sorrel and pussypaws (p. 214), skunk-cabbage (p. 163), bunchberry (p. 265), desert-parsleys (p. 258), goatsbeard (p. 246), and baneberry (p. 270).

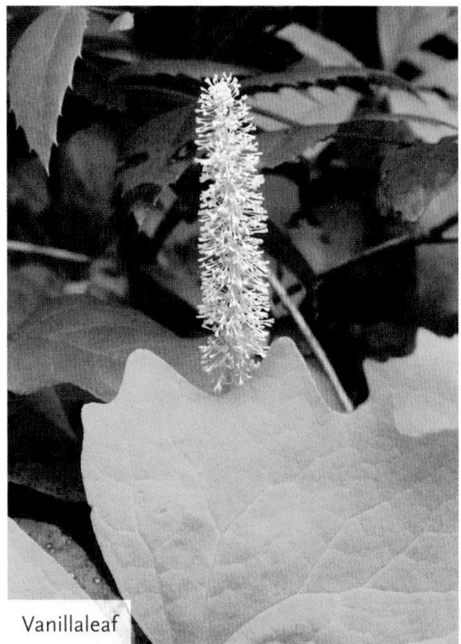
Vanillaleaf

Vanillaleaf

Achlys triphylla (AY-klis: a night goddess; try-FILL-a: 3 leaf). Also deerfoot, sweet-after-death. Flowers cream-white, minute, in a dense spike 1–2 in. × 1⁄4 in., on a leafless stalk a little taller (8–16 in.) than the one that bears 3 flat-lying leaflets (6- to 10-in. total diameter), each with 2 straight sides and a wavy-lobed outer arc. Forest types at neither the dry nor the wet extreme; locally abundant. Berberidaceae.

The vanilla fragrance is indetectable in growing leaves, but you should get it if you pick a few and let them dry. The odd leaf shape makes a good Rorschach pattern; where some see a deer foot, this writer sees Bullwinkle Moose.

Vanillaleaf

Western Dwarf Mistletoe

Arceuthobium campylopodum (ars-youth-OH-be-um: life on junipers; cam-pil-o-PO-dum: bent stem). Tiny, much-branched, orange-brown to olive-green growths (technically shrubs) on pine branches; flowers budlike, same color as stems; berries bicolored, with bluish-coated base and paler tan outer half; no recognizable leaves; stems 1–4 in. long. On lodgepole or ponderosa pine branches; similar *Arceuthobium* spp. grow on other conifers. Viscaceae or Santalaceae.

Western dwarf mistletoe

False-bugbane

Sitka burnet

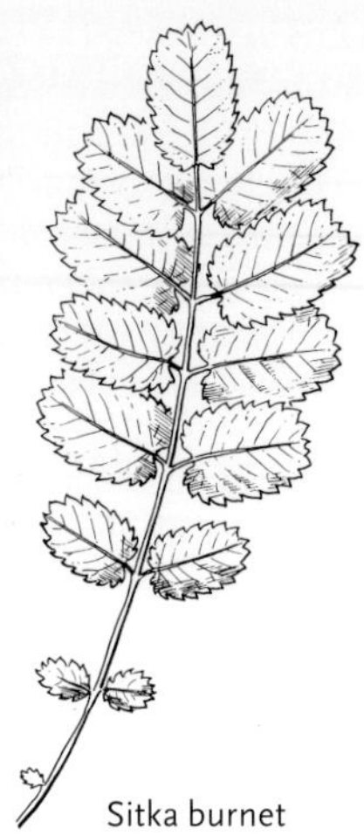
Sitka burnet

Occasionally you spot dwarf mistletoe on branches near eye level, but what you see more often is "witches' brooms"—big lumps in conifer crowns, consisting of massed unhealthy twiggy branches. A parasite, dwarf mistletoe extends threadlike roots inside tree limbs, inducing the tree to branch way too much. Mistletoe sucks the tree's energy, stunting its growth and slowly killing it.

Dwarf mistletoe berries explode when ripe, shooting the single seed as far as 40 feet. Some 70,000 seeds per year may get shot from one infested conifer. Gummy-coated, they stick if they hit another branch. When rain comes along, the gum dissolves, letting the seed slide down a needle to the twig. The berries are eaten enthusiastically by all of our grouse species and several songbirds, but are destroyed by digestion—unlike the bigger berries of Christmas mistletoes, which are disseminated mainly via bird droppings.

Several dwarf mistletoe species look much alike, but specialize in one or two species of host tree. The only one common on the west-side is hemlock dwarf mistletoe, *A. tsugense*. They are a serious economic problem in our region. After selective logging is used in an effort to mimic natural fire, mistletoe often spreads (actual fires don't spare much mistletoe, since brooms are ferociously flammable). Sometimes the only cure is to log the infected tree species completely out of the stand. From an ecological standpoint, mistletoe fosters plant diversity and creates great nest sites for animals. Northern spotted owls, accipiters, woodrats, and flying squirrels all benefit.

False-Bugbane

Trautvetteria caroliniensis (trout-vet-EE-ria: for Ernest Rudolf van Trautvetter; carol-in-ee-EN-sis: of the Carolinas). Flowers white, in broad rough clusters, consisting mainly of many stamens (up to 1/4 in.), the 4 (3–7) sepals falling off as the flower opens; leaves predominantly basal, 4–10 in. wide, deeply 5- to 7-lobed; 20–36 in. W-side streamsides; wet forest. Ranunculaceae.

The flowers closely resemble baneberry and the leaves resemble cow-poison (larkspur), but this one is harmless.

Sitka Burnet

Sanguisorba stipulata (sang-gwis-OR-ba: soaks up blood, an early medicinal use; stip-you-LAY-ta: with stipules). Also *S. canadensis*, *S. sitchensis*. Flowers many, minute, lacking petals but with conspicuous disorderly long white stamens sticking out all around the dense cylindrical inflorescence; leaves mainly basal, pinnately compound, the 9–17 leaflets oval and sawtoothed; 1–3 ft. tall. Wet or submerged soil at low to mid-elevs in BC and WA; abundant on VI. Rosaceae.

Stinging Nettle

Urtica dioica (UR-tic-a: burning; die-OY-ca: with ♂ and ♀ flowers on different plants, a name untrue of our nettles). Flowers minute, pale green, many, in loose panicles dangling from leaf axils, ♀ panicles higher on the plant than ♂ panicles; leaves opposite, sawtoothed, pointed or oval, 2–6 in.; stem and leaves lined with fine stinging bristles; from rhizomes; 2–6 ft. Streamsides, moist forest and clearings. Urticaceae.

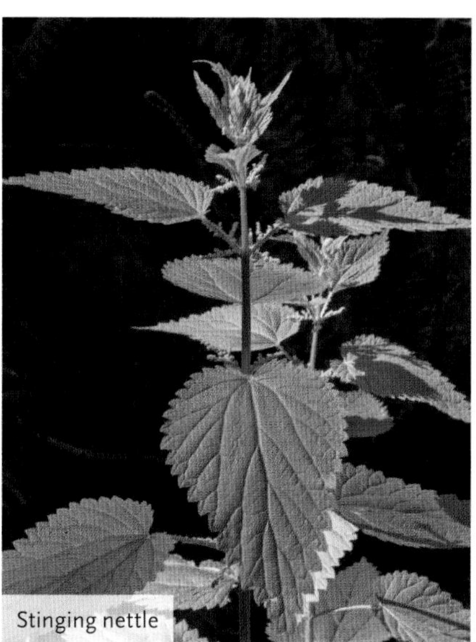
Stinging nettle

Nettles are back in style. "Really big in Oregon," writes Toro Bravo chef John Gorham, "like double-green spinach with more chlorophyll and flavor . . . a blood and liver cleanser. If you try your hand at all of our cocktails, you'll need that." In earlier times they were also used for fiber: the mature stems were made into good twine, cloth, and paper, substituting for flax in wartime as recently as World War II, and several tribes here made nettle-twine nets for ducks and fish. Medicinally, their sting helped stoical hunters stay awake through the night, and nettle tea has earned medicinal reputation worldwide.

Nettle stingers are miniature hypodermic syringes, like bee and ant stingers. The bee-sting toxin, formic acid, was long but erroneously believed to be the main toxin in nettles, which inject a cocktail of acetylcholine, hydroxytryptamine, and a histamine. They evolved as a defense against browsing (but they don't save nettles from Milbert's tortoiseshell and other caterpillars). One folk remedy holds that if you pull up the nettle that bit you, you can soothe the sting by crushing juice onto it from the nettle root.

Thorough steaming or drying renders nettles harmless. If you camp in April or May near a bed of nettle shoots less than 2 feet high, cook them up. Wear long sleeves and gloves (or socks) over your hands, lop them with your knife, and steam them limp in half an inch of water (if cooked only al dente, they have enough bristle left to worry your lips and tongue).

HERBS: DICOTS, WITH STRONGLY IRREGULAR FLOWERS

Irregular flowers are those in which the petals (or the sepals, if they are the showy parts) are not all alike. You might think of them as bilaterally—as opposed to radially—symmetrical, but their are exceptions; some louseworts are twisted and have no symmetry at all.

Irregular flowers display advanced specialization of form. Each species matches a particular form and size of insect, for pollination.

Flowers are not placed here if the irregularity consists of modestly unequal, but otherwise similar, petals or lobes. For example, veronica (p. 267) and kittentails (p. 263) each have four unequal blue to lavender

Purple monkeyflower

Subalpine monkeyflower

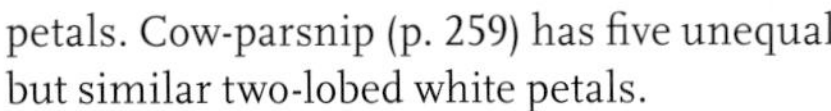
petals. Cow-parsnip (p. 259) has five unequal but similar two-lobed white petals.

Monkeyflower

Erythranthe **spp.** (air-ith-RANTH-ee: red flower). Also *Mimulus* spp. Flowers snapdragon-like—corolla with a long (3/4–2 in.) throat, hairy inside, and 2 upper and 3 lower lobes; calyx 5-lobed; 4 stamens; leaves opposite; dense clumps grow from rhizomes. Wet places. Phrymaceae.

Purple monkeyflower, *E. lewisii* (lew-ISS-ee-eye: for Meriwether Lewis, p. 262). Flowers deep pink to violet; leaves sessile, pointed, 2–3 in.; plants 12–36 in., sticky-hairy. Mid-elev to subalpine; not in CoastR.

Yellow monkeyflower, *E. guttata* (ga-TAY-ta: spotted). Flowers yellow, red-spotted, 1/2–3/4 in. long; upper calyx lobe bigger than the other 4; at least some leaves bigger than the petals, 1 1/2–5 in. long, with 3 or 5 main veins; stems mostly erect, 4–30 in. Low to subalpine.

Elegant monkeyflower, *E. decora* (DEC-or-a: elegant). Also *M. guttatus, M. tilingii.* Flowers yellow, 5/8–1 1/4 in., throat often red-spotted; leaves 1–2 1/4 in. long, broad but pointed, with 5 or 7 palmate veins and abrupt bases; stems mostly erect, 4–20 in. OR and WA, 3200–5500 ft.

Subalpine monkeyflower, *E. caespitosa* (see-spit-OH-sa: in clumps). Also *M. tilingii.* Flowers yellow, 3/4 in., throat often red-spotted; leaves only about 3/8–5/8 in., with 3 main veins, leaf bases tapered to the leafstalk; 2- to 4-in. plants in sprawling mats. 3600–7000 ft.

Both "monkey" and the "mime" in *Mimulus* are impressions of this fat irregular blossom as a funny-face. David Douglas coined the name *Erythranthe,* "red flower," to separate a bright red California flower from all its *Mimulus* relatives; little did he know that it would one day be the name of all those yellow, pink, or lavender relatives. Other botanists did not agree that the red flower needed its own genus, so the name was all but forgotten for more than a century. Then a 2012 paper broke up genus *Mimulus,* leaving only 7 species under that name and transferring 111 species to the oldest available name, *Erythranthe.*

Yellow monkeyflower

Lousewort

***Pedicularis* spp.** (ped-ic-you-LAIR-iss: louse—). Corolla fused, with two main lips, the upper lip long-beaked, the lower usually 3-lobed; calyx 2- to 5-lobed; capsule asymmetrical; leaves (except on sickletop lousewort) fernlike, pinnately compound; flowers many, on an unbranched stem. Orobanchaceae.

Sickletop lousewort, *P. racemosa* (ras-em-OH-sa: bearing racemes). Flowers (our variety) pale bronze-pink, beak curled strongly sideways, so inflorescence looks pinwheel-like from above; leaves reddish, linear, fine-toothed, all on stem; 6–18 in. Openings near forest line; or alpine.

Birdbeak lousewort, *P. ornithorhynca* (or-nith-o-RINK-a: bird beak). Flowers purple-pink, few, in a short round inflorescence; beak bent down and to the right, so inflorescence looks pinwheel-like from above; leaves almost all basal; 4–7 in. Moist alp/subalpine gravels in BC and WA.

Bracted lousewort, *P. bracteosa* (brac-tee-OH-sa: with bracts). Flowers yellow (rarely purple to dark red), scarcely beaked, in a robust tall spike; stem leaves as big as basal ones, aging purplish; 24–36 in.; lush meadows, mid-elevs to alpine; not in CoastR.

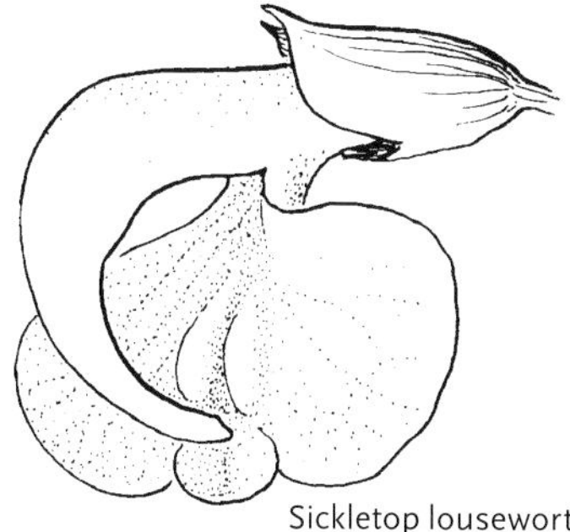
Sickletop lousewort

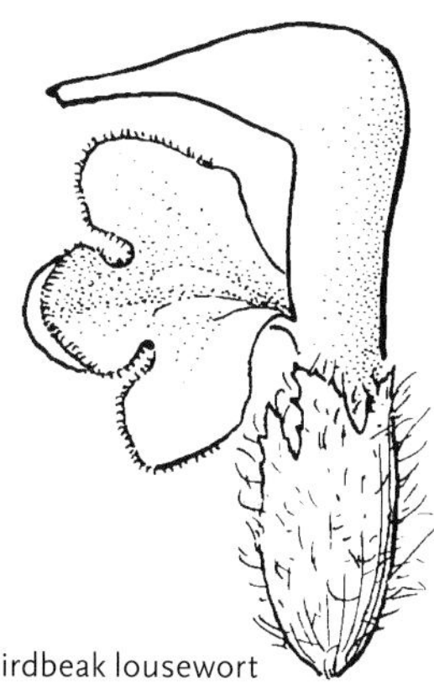
Birdbeak lousewort

Sickletop lousewort

Birdbeak lousewort

Bracted lousewort

Mt. Rainier lousewort

Coiled-beak lousewort

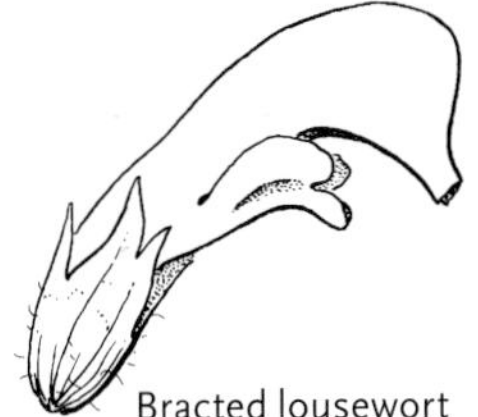
Bracted lousewort

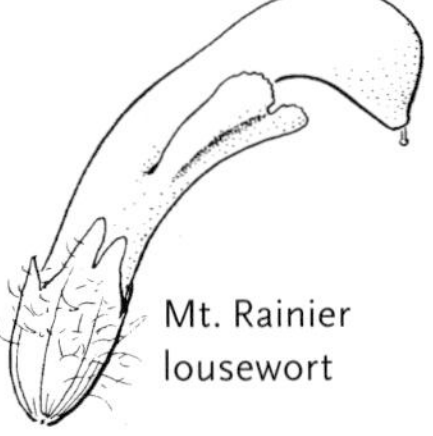
Mt. Rainier lousewort

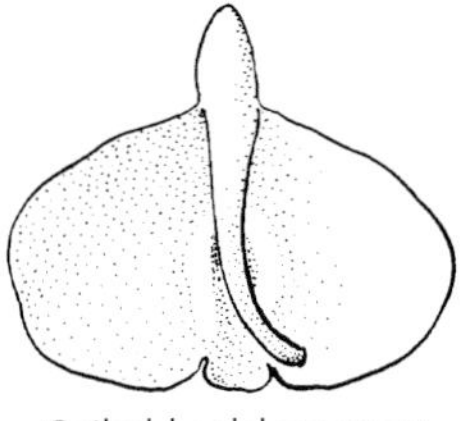
Coiled-beak lousewort

Mt. Rainier lousewort, *P. rainierensis* (ra-near-EN-sis: of Mt. Rainier). Flowers yellow to cream, scarcely beaked, in a robust spike; stem leaves much smaller than basal ones; 6–16 in. Meadows near Mt. Rainier.

Coiled-beak lousewort, *P. contorta*. Flowers (our variety) pale yellow to white, in a loose spike; beak semicircular, arching back into lower lip; leaves mostly basal; 8–14 in. Alp/subalpine turfs.

Elephant's head, *P. groenlandica* (green-LAN-dic-a: of Greenland). Flowers purple-pink, in a dense spike, elephant-like (upcurved beak as the trunk, lateral lower lobes as the ears); leaves mainly basal; 8–16 in. Subalpine rills and boggy meadows; not in CoastR.

Elephant's head

The name "lousewort" dates from an ancient superstition that cattle got lousy by browsing louseworts. Each lousewort flower shape

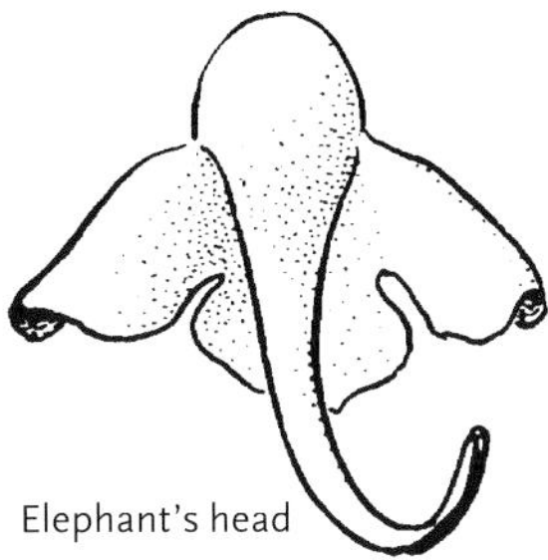
Elephant's head

suits the anatomy of one or more species of bumble bee—pollinators of the hundred or so species of lousewort. The tip of the beak (or "trunk" in one case) positions the stigma to catch pollen from the bee's legs or abdomen. The louseworts are as curiously irregular and varied a genus of flowers as you could ask for.

Scarlet paintbrush

Indian Paintbrush

***Castilleja* spp.** (cas-til-AY-a: for Domingo Castillejo). True flowers largely hidden by bracts that are brightly colored at least at their tips, grading to green at the bases of lower bracts; calyx narrowly 4-lobed, color similar to bracts; corolla a thin tube, dull green; leaves (and colored bracts) often narrowly 3-, 5-, or 7-pronged, elliptical, their main veins parallel; stems usually several, unbranched, from a woody base. In sun. Orobanchaceae.

Scarlet paintbrush, *C. miniata* (mini-AY-ta: lead-red, like old lead pigments). Bracts and calyx usually scarlet; colored bracts and calyx tipped with slender, sharp-tipped lobes; leaves entire, without lobes; 8–30 in. Foothills to treeline.

Small-flowered paintbrush, *C. parviflora* (parv-if-LOR-a: small flower). Bracts and calyx may be dusty rose-purple, red, creamy white, or gradients of those; bracts and leaves have 2 or 4 side lobes; 6–12 in. Abundant in subalpine meadows and clearings.

Small-flowered paintbrush

Cliff paintbrush

Harsh paintbrush

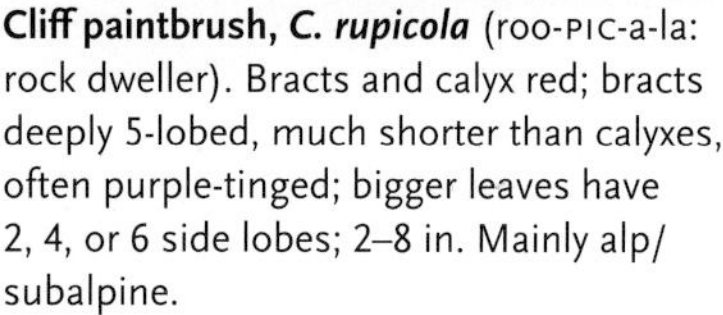

Cliff paintbrush, *C. rupicola* (roo-PIC-a-la: rock dweller). Bracts and calyx red; bracts deeply 5-lobed, much shorter than calyxes, often purple-tinged; bigger leaves have 2, 4, or 6 side lobes; 2–8 in. Mainly alp/subalpine.

Harsh paintbrush, *C. hispida* (HISS-pid-a: bristly). Bracts red- to orange-tipped, typically with a long green basal portion; bracts and upper leaves broad, with 2 or 4 side lobes; lower leaves entire; leaves have stiff white hairs; 8–24 in. Dry forest or grassland from foothills to lower alpine.

Paintbrush is easily recognized as a genus, hard to identify to species. Neither color nor hairiness are reliable. Hybrids abound.

The Makah used scarlet paintbrush to lure hummingbirds into traps, for use as charms for whaling.

Paintbrushes are partially parasitic, often on grasses and composites (they also photosynthesize). By late summer they may seem to hog all the water, staying green and turgid while their hosts wither.

Blue-Eyed Mary

***Collinsia* spp.** (ca-LIN-zia: for Zaccheus Collins). Also innocence. Corolla blue to violet, the upper 2 lobes fading to white; lobes seemingly 4, the 5th being the inconspicuous central lower lobe, creased shut to enclose the stamens and style; calyx 5-lobed, green; flowers in axils of upper, often whorled leaves; lower leaves opposite, linear; plants annual, 2–14 in. Sunny low to mid-elevs. Plantaginaceae.

Giant blue-eyed Mary

Rosy plectritis

Foxglove

Cascade penstemon

Giant blue-eyed Mary, *C. grandiflora* (gran-dif-LOR-a: big flower). Corolla at least ½ in. long, bent over at right angles to the calyx.

Small blue-eyed Mary, *C. parviflora* (par-vif-LOR-a: small flower). Corolla usually much less than ½ in., bent at an oblique angle to calyx.

Rosy Plectritis

Plectritis congesta (plec-TRY-tis: plaited; con-JES-ta: crowded, that is, clustered flowers). Corolla deep pink or white, ⅛–¼ in. long, with a rearward spur and 5 unequal lobes all about as long as the corolla tube; no sepals at time of flowering; flowers many, in a ball-like cluster; 3 stamens; leaves opposite, ⅜–1⅜ in., entire, elliptic, except lowest ones spoon-shaped; annual herb 4–24 in. Locally abundant on moist sites with some sun, coastal low to mid-elevs; WA, OR, VI. Valerianaceae or Caprifoliaceae.

Foxglove

Digitalis purpurea (digit-AY-lis: finger—; pur-PEW-ria: purple). Corolla pink (or purplish or white), tubular, 1½–2 in., with 5 very shallow lobes; sepals 5; stamens 4, paired; flowers many, in a showy one-sided spike; leaves oval, pointed, up to 20 in. × 6 in.; stems fuzzy and sticky, 2–6 ft.; biennial. Roadsides and scarified clearcuts. Plantaginaceae.

Our most beautiful European weed, foxglove is the age-old source of digitalin, used as a heart stimulant in cases of cardiac arrest. Consider it toxic.

Penstemon

***Penstemon* spp.** (PEN-stem-un: almost a stamen). Also beardtongue. Corolla typically blue or violet to pink or sometimes yellow-white, swollen-tubular, with 5 (2 upper, 3 lower) short rounded flaring lobes, and a broad, hairy sterile stamen resting on the throat; fertile stamens 4, paired; sepals 5, hardly at all fused; leaves opposite, often basal-clustered in part. Rocky places and drier meadows; common. Plantaginaceae.

Cascade penstemon, *P. serrulatus* (sair-you-LAY-tus: with tiny teeth). Flowers blue-purple, ¾–1⅛ in.; corolla hairless; leaves all on stem, lanceolate to ovate, ⅜–1½ in. wide, sharp-toothed; no part of plant has sticky hairs; 8–28 in. tall. Moist sites with some sun, low to subalpine.

Creeping penstemon, *P. davidsonii* (david-SO-nee-eye: for George Davidson). Flowers

Creeping penstemon

blue to lavender, ¾–1½ in., tending to all face one way; leaves crowded, minutely toothed or not, thick, evergreen, ¼–¾ in.; stems woody, forming dense mats, 3–6 in. High rock outcrops, not in CoastR.

Shrubby penstemon, *P. fruticosus* (fru-tic-OH-sus: shrubby). Flowers blue to lavender, 1–2 in.; leaves crowded, minutely toothed or not, thick, evergreen, ¾–2½ in.; stems woody, generally erect, 6–16 in. Outcrops at all elevs e of CasCr.

Rock penstemon, *P. rupicola* (roo-PIC-a-la: rock dweller). Flowers scarlet to pink, ¾–1½ in., tending to all face one way; leaves whitish-coated, thick, evergreen; stems woody, forming dense mats, 3–6 in. High rock outcrops; CasR from c WA s.

Rock penstemon

Shrubby penstemon

Small-flowered penstemon

Small-flowered penstemon, *P. procerus* (PROSS-er-us: tall and slender). Flowers blue to purple, 1⁄4–1⁄2 in. long, in 2–6 whorls; leaves lanceolate, basal ones largest, up to 3 in. long; stem 4–24 in. Rocky places at all elevs; not in CoastR.

The Greek word *penstemon* is usually translated as "five stamen," but "almost a stamen" is more plausible. The *pen*, as in penultimate, has no *t*, and with so many five-stamened genera around it would be strange to give the name "five-stamen" to one with the appearance of four stamens.

Mat-forming shrubs with tiny leaves perform a valuable role on talus slopes. The mats capture fine sediment as it drifts downslope, creating a deeper, more stable soil. The stems grow to keep up with the increasing depth. Look for coarser gravel dammed against the upslope side of the mat and slipping past it on both sides, while a downslope "shadow" area forms, made of finer sediment that contrast with the surroundings and can become a seedbed for more delicate plants.

Woodland Penstemon

Nothochelone nemorosa (noth-a-key-LOW-nee: false turtlehead; ne-mor-OH-sus: of the woods). Also *Penstemon nemorosus.* Flowers pink to purple, 1–13⁄8 in. long, single or in small clusters both terminal and from leaf axils; corolla roughly conical, sticky-hairy outside, with 5 (2 upper, 3 lower) short rounded flaring lobes; calyx small, 5-lobed; leaves opposite, lanceolate, sparsely sharp-toothed, 11⁄2–4 in.; stems 12–32 in., horizontally inclined. Open forest, mainly mid-elev. Plantaginaceae.

Corydalis

Corydalis scouleri (cor-ID-a-lis: the crested lark; scoo-ler-eye: for John Scouler, p. 112). Flowers light pink, 15–35, variously angled in an open spike; petals 4, upper one with a rearward spur at least as long as the forward part; inner 2 hidden; sepals 2, falling off early; stamens 6; seedpod splits explosively to propel seeds; leaves large, much compounded, round-lobed; plants 11⁄2–4 ft. Seeps and streambanks, lower w-side. Fumariaceae.

The name *corydalis*, used by the ancient Greeks for a bird, the crested lark, derives from "helmet." I think they saw the bird's crest as helmetlike, and the flower as helmet crest–shaped, not lark-like.

Woodland penstemon

Corydalis

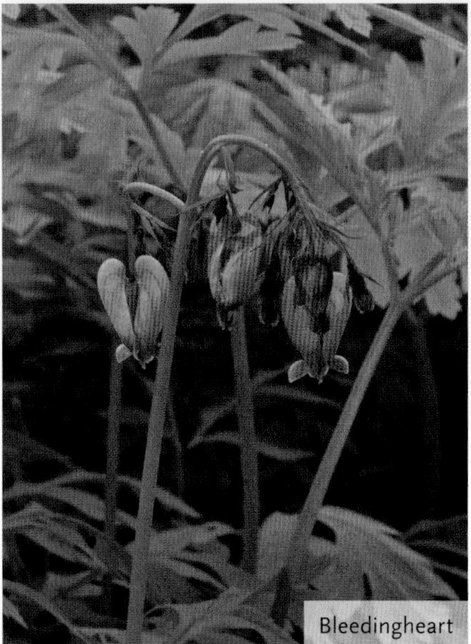
Bleedingheart

Steer's head

Mountain-sorrel

Bleedingheart

Dicentra formosa (di-SEN-tra: two spur; for-MO-sa: beautiful). Corolla pink, 3/4–1 in. long, pendent, shaped like an elongate heart made of two fused petals, hiding a smaller pair of fused petals inside; sepals 2, falling off early; stamens 6; seedpod growing as long as 2 in. out through the corolla mouth; stalks several-flowered, 12–20 in.; leaves fernlike, compound and incised. Open spots low to mid-elevs, w of CasCr. Fumariaceae.

Steer's Head

Dicentra uniflora (you-nif-LOR-a: one flower). Bizarre little drab pinkish flower resembles a horned skull, 5/8 in. long, with 2 petals fused (the muzzle) and 2 curved back (the horns); 2 sepals; 6 hidden stamens; 1 flower per stem; leaves many-fingered, compound, on 2- to 4-in. stalks attached to flowers below ground. Toxic. Blooms soon after snowmelt on moist gravels at any elev; CasR from Wenatchee River s. Fumariaceae.

Mountain-Sorrel

Oxyria digyna (ox-EE-ria: sharp—; DIDGE-in-a: two ovaries). Flowers tiny, brownish red to yellowish green, of 2 erect and 2 spreading lobes, 2 stigmas and 6 stamens, in rough spikelike panicles; fruit rust red, tiny, 2-winged; leaves kidney-shaped, 1–2 in. broad, on long basal leafstalks, coloring brilliantly in fall; stalks several, 4–18 in. Rocky streambanks and wet talus; alp/subalpine. Polygonaceae.

Mountain-sorrel leaves added a lemony note to salmon roe when boiled and pressed into cakes. Their tart acids include ascorbic (good for you) and oxalic (a little bit bad for you). Snack in moderation.

Pussypaws

Calyptridium umbellatum (cal-ip-TRID-ium: with a cap over the seed—not true of this species; um-bel-AY-tum: with flowers

Pussypaws

Hedge-nettle

Self-heal

in umbels). Also *Spraguea umbellata*, *Cistanthe umbellata*. Flowers rust-pink to white, in fluffy, chaffy heads on prostrate stalks reaching well past the basal rosette of tiny, obovate, semi-succulent leaves; sepals 2, round, 1⁄8–3⁄8 in. wide, sandwiching and nearly hiding the 4 small petals and 3 stamens. Rock crevices and gravels, especially pumice; alp/subalpine in CasR. Portulacaceae.

Hedge-Nettle

Stachys cooleyae (STAY-kis: ear of grain; coo-lee-ee: for George Cooley). Also *Stachys chamissonis*. Corolla purplish red to pink, 1⁄2–1 1⁄4 in. long, with a round upper lip and a longer, 3-lobed lower lip; calyx 5-pointed; stamens 4, paired; flowers in an open spike of several whorls; leaves opposite, elliptic, toothed; stem square, 1–4 ft.; fetid when bruised. Wet low to mid-elevs. Lamiaceae.

Like the English, Northwest Indians named this stingless plant after nettles, and sometimes mixed the two in infusions. Hedge-nettles often grow near stinging nettles, but claim mints for family relations, as evidenced by their flowers and square stems.

Self-Heal

Prunella vulgaris (pru-NEL-a: purple, small; vul-GAIR-iss: common). Also all-heal. Corolla blue-purple, 1⁄4–3⁄4 in., 4-lobed; upper lobe hoodlike, lower lobe liplike, fringed; calyx half as long; stamens 4 (rarely lacking); flowers bloom sequentially upward, in a crowded broad-bracted spike of opposite pairs neatly offset 90 degrees; leaves opposite, elliptical, 1–3 in.; stem squarish, 4–16 in. tall, or sprawling. Low to mid-elevs. Lamiaceae.

The mint family is loaded with medicinal, poisonous, and culinary aromatic herbs, including catnip, pennyroyal, horehound, oregano, sage, savory, thyme, and of course peppermint. Europeans once believed in self-heal as a panacea; in tribal and modern herbal lore it's prescribed to heal sores, chapped skin, and stomach ills.

Youth-On-Age

Tolmiea menziesii (TOLE-me-a: for William Tolmie, p. 216; men-ZEE-zee-eye: for Archibald Menzies, p. 136). Also piggyback plant. Calyx purplish to brownish green, bell-shaped but cut away on one side, 1⁄2 in., with 3 large and 2 small lobes; petals longer, threadlike, red-brown, 4 (or 5); 3 stamens; flowers many, in a raceme; leaves shallowly palmate-lobed, 1 1⁄2–3 in. broad, mostly basal on long leafstalks; entire plant hairy; stems several, 1–3 ft. Moist w-side forest. Saxifragaceae.

William Frazer Tolmie

Arriving at Fort Vancouver in 1833, William Frazer Tolmie was a young Scot fresh out of medical school and into the employ of the Hudson's Bay Company. At his suggestion, the company established there the Northwest's first lending library. In September, while waiting for a ship north out of Fort Nisqually, he set off to collect alpine plants from Mt. Rainier. Ankle-deep in fresh snow on a precipice directly facing the mountain (more likely Mt. Pleasant than the present Tolmie Peak) he decided to forget scaling Rainier. No white man had seen it so close.

Like many early naturalists, he studied medicine as a path to biology, as botany and human physiology were not yet separate branches of natural science.

He remained in the Northwest all his life, a company physician and later supervisor. His son became premier of British Columbia.

This anomalous saxifrage has several quaint names referring to its way of producing aerial offset plants from its leaf axils. These may take root when the mother stem reclines.

Specimens south of Corvallis are now treated as a very similar species, *T. diplomenziesii*.

Youth-on-age

Youth-on-age

Lupine

Lupinus **spp.** (lu-PIE-nus: the Roman name). Flowers blue to purple (sometimes white), pealike, small (½ in.), many; calyx 2-lobed; pods hairy; leaves mostly basal on long leafstalks, palmately compound; leaflets 5–9, center-folded. Fabaceae.

Broadleaf lupine, *L. latifolius* (lat-if-OH-lius: broad leaf). Also *L. arcticus* var. *subalpinus*. Plant bushy, with more than one branch flowering, 6–36 in. Subalpine (so abundant you can see its blue half a mile away) and also widespread in mid-elev openings.

Bigleaf lupine, *L. polyphyllus* (poly-FILL-us: many leaves). Also *L. prunophilus*. Flowers in a very tall columnar raceme (1 per plant) of rather separate whorls; up to 5 ft. tall. Moist mid-elev to subalpine openings in WA CasR, marginal and infrequent elsewhere.

Dwarf alpine lupine, *L. lepidus* var. *lobbii* (LEP-id-us: charming; LOBB-ee-eye: for collector William

Broadleaf lupine

Bigleaf lupine

Dwarf alpine lupine

Lobb). Also prairie lupine; *L. lyallii, L. sellulus.* Plant semi-prostrate, the leafstalks and flower stems radiating horizontally but the racemes fairly erect; leaves 1 in. across. Alpine gravels and tundra; rare and marginal in BC.

Dwarf alpine lupine attained celebrity status as one of the first photogenic flowers blooming in the gray ash wasteland of post-eruption Mt. St. Helens. By 1988 it was the most abundant flower on the ash barrens.

Botanists, who flocked to the area to see plant life develop on a clean slate, were in some ways surprised by its success. Most colonizing species were, as expected, plants with light, far-traveling, wind-dispersed seeds. Dwarf alpine lupine is not one of those. Its heavy little peas don't travel far at all. A lucky few dwarf alpine lupine plants got established in the very year of the eruption, 1980. At least some of them likely grew from root fragments broken and dispersed in the violence of May, rather than from seeds. Around 20 such individuals seeded the entire lupine boom. The lupine's nitrogen-fixing partners (bacteria) provided its main advantage in the nitrogen-poor volcanic ash. Lupines built up nitrogen-enhanced ash mounds, and outcompeted new arrivals on the mounds for as long as they lived. A year after each one died, its mound became a conspicuous seedbed for other species.

Botanist Jeff Braatne looked at the post-eruption benefits of fine hairs. While dwarf alpine lupine colonized in rugged solitude, broadleaf lupine also recolonized early, but only where mixed with other species. Both lupines fix nitrogen. Both quickly send taproots to draw water from at least ten inches down. Both have leaf adaptations to minimize water loss. Dwarf alpine lupine relies on its thicker coat of shiny silky hairs that deflect some of the intense light and hold drying winds away from the leaf surface. Broadleaf lupine seems more sophisticated, drawing its leaves up into a cone shape when it gets hot and dry, incurring the trade-off of lowered photosynthesis.

While broadleaf lupine gave up photosynthesis at around 86°F, dwarf alpine lupine kept going to 104°F (temperatures near the surface are much hotter than the air temperatures we normally measure). Dwarf lupine turns its leaves to face the morning and evening sun, maximizing photosynthesis at cooler times of day, and it stays green through winter, making the most of early- and late-season sun. Hairs and waxy coatings also protect plants by reflecting ultraviolet radiation, which damages tissue and is extra strong at high elevations.

Obviously, thick volcanic ash deposits can discourage plant growth, but before long ash proves itself as a fertilizer. At Goat Rocks, 41 miles downwind of Mt. St. Helens, five years after the blast, 1985 was a phenomenal year for wildflowers. For millennia, farmers around the world have braved the hazards of living near volcanoes to reap the benefits of young volcanic soils.

A bumble bee in search of lupine nectar might be overwhelmed by too many choices, so the lupines help her out: the upper petal has white spots that act as nectar guides. As a blossom ages, the spots turn magenta. Bees learn to skip those blossoms, since their nectar is depleted. Efficiency is increased for the flower as well as the bee, since stale pollen is kept out of circulation.

We don't know why the Romans named these flowers after wolves ("lupine" means "of wolves" or "wolf-like" in English, too). Maybe they felt an affinity: in their myths, a she-wolf was the mother, or at least the wet nurse, of Rome. Or "wolf" may have implied "sheep killer." Sheep have died from grazing lupines, which generally are more or less toxic.

Notice the way a little sphere of dew or rain is held on the center point of each leaf.

Sweetpea

***Lathyrus* spp.** (LATH-er-us: the Greek name). Petals 5, the upper one largest, the lower 2 partly fused, creased, enclosing pistil and 10 stamens; stigma bristly on upper surface; fruit a pea pod; leaves pinnately compound, often tendril-tipped; stems angled, 4–32 in. Fabaceae.

Sierra pea, *L. nevadensis* (nev-a-DEN-sis: of the Sierra Nevada). Flowers lavender, aging blue or tan, 2–10; calyx hairless; leaflets 6–10. Clearings mainly at lower elevs.

Leafy pea, *L. polyphyllus* (poly-FILL-us: many leaves). Flowers 5–15, purple to red or pink (aging blue), lower petals often nearly white; calyx finely hairy; leaflets 10–16. Dry woods, lower w-side from Port Angeles s.

Tendrils (tiny extensions on the leaf tip that twine and grasp things) are often short, straight, and nonfunctional on these two peas, which usually stand on their own. Tendrils help separate Lathyrus from two

Leafy pea

Sierra pea

Leafy pea

related large genera: locoweeds and crazyweeds (*Oxytropis* and *Astragalus* spp.) lack tendrils at the ends of their compound leaves. Their leaf terminates in a leaflet instead. Vetches (*Vicia* spp.) do have tendrils, like peas; their key difference is in the tiny pistil, which on a vetch is hairy near its tip on all sides, like a bottlebrush as opposed to the toothbrush-shaped pistil on a pea.

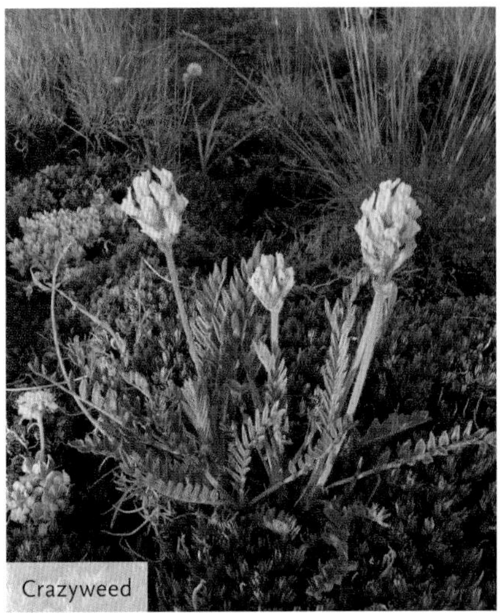
Crazyweed

Crazyweed

Oxytropis campestris (ox-IT-ra-pis: sharp keel; cam-PES-tris: of fields). Also stemless locoweed. Flowers pealike, pale yellow (our variety), 8–12; calyx black-hairy; pod very thin-walled; leaves near-basal, densely silky-hairy, pinnately 13- to 25-compound; stalks several, 3–15 in. Alpine and arid meadows. Fabaceae.

Crazyweeds and their close cousins the locoweeds, genus *Astragalus*, got their nasty names and ill reputes from their several rangeland species that sabotage the muscular coordination and vision of cattle that graze them in quantity. However, the many mountain goats that graze this sweet alpine variety don't appear any crazier than other mountain goats, and you'd think an uncoordinated purblind mountain goat wouldn't still be around.

Stream violet

Violet

***Viola* spp.** (vie-OH-la: the Roman name). Petals 5, the lowest one largest, with a rearward spur, usually with dark purple guide lines; sepals 5; stamens 5, short; capsules split explosively to propel seeds; leaves (these spp.) mostly heart- to kidney-shaped. Violaceae.

Stream violet, *V. glabella* (gla-BEL-a: smooth). Flowers yellow; stem 4–12 in., branched, bearing multiple leaves and flowers. Widespread, low forest to subalpine meadow.

Evergreen violet

Evergreen violet, *V. sempervirens* (semper-VEE-renz: ever green). Flowers yellow;

Hook-spur violet

Flett's violet

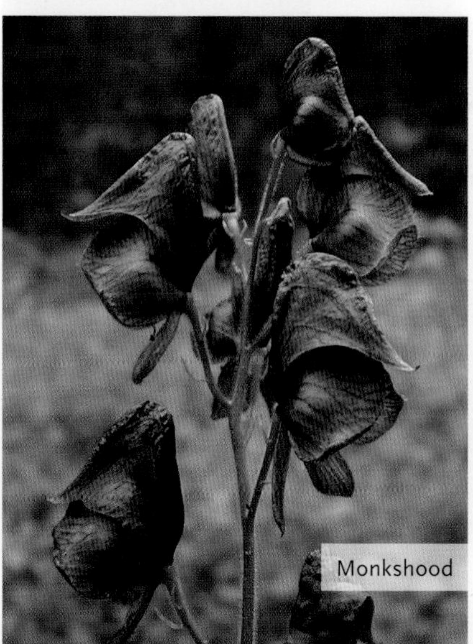
Monkshood

leaves rather firm, persistent through winter; each flower and each leaf on an unbranched 1- to 4-in. stalk from the runner. Widespread in w-side forest.

Hook-spur violet, *V. adunca* (a-DUNK-a: hooked). Flowers lavender to blue; leaves heart-shaped to elliptical; 1–5 in. Common in wet montane meadows.

Flett's violet, *V. flettii* (FLET-ee-eye: for J. B. Flett). Flowers lavender to blue; leaves kidney-shaped, often purple-tinged; 1–6 in. High rocky slopes; only in Olympics.

Our yellow violets bloom soon after the retreat of snow, often so early and chilly that pollinators are not yet on the wing. When they go unpollinated, violets respond with a second kind of flowers (cleistogamous, meaning "closed marriage"): greenish, low and inconspicuous, and able to pollinate themselves and produce seed without ever opening.

Monkshood

Aconitum columbianum (ac-o-NIGH-tum: the Greek name; co-lum-be-AY-num: of the Columbia River). Flowers blue-purple (or rarely white), 3/4–1 1/2 in. tall, in an open raceme atop the 1- to 7-ft. stem; 5 petallike sepals, the upper one hooding, helmetlike, hiding the two small true petals; leaf blades 2–5 in. across, deeply cut into 5, 7, or 3 palmate lobes, and also toothed. Moist sites in CasR, e-side in WA and BC, both sides in OR. Ranunculaceae.

Monkshood

Blue irregular flowers are typically pollinated by bumble bees. Monkshood's odd-shaped flower excludes from its nectary all insects except highly motivated, smart bumble bees, whose advantage to the plant is their fidelity; having been once well-rewarded with monkshood nectar, they will visit only monkshoods, not wasting the pollen on diverse flower species. Monkshood is considered toxic to humans and stock, but one study found lots of it in elk scats in the the Blue Mountains.

Larkspur

Delphinium **spp.** (del-FIN-ium: the Greek name, from "dolphin"). Flowers deep blue to violet, 3/4–1 1/4 in. across; sepals 5, petallike, spreading, the upper one with a long nectar-bearing spur behind; petals 4, much smaller; upper 2 petals, often much paler, have spurs within the sepal spur; in most species the lower 2 petals hide the numerous stamens; leaf blades round in outline, narrowly palmate-lobed (sometimes compound). Ranunculaceae.

Menzies larkspur, *D. menziesii* (men-ZEE-zee-eye: for Archibald Menzies, p. 136). 6–20 in. tall. Low w-side clearings.

Rockslide larkspur, *D. glareosum* (glare-ee-OH-sum: on gravel). Somewhat fleshy basal leaves form a rounded mound; 6–12 in. tall. Alp/subalpine rocks.

Upland larkspur

Upland larkspur, *D. nuttallianum* (nuttle-ee-AY-num: for Thomas Nuttall, p. 102). Stamens exposed below deeply 2-lobed lower petals; 6–16 in. tall. Steppe, pine forest, sometimes alpine; e-side.

Cow poison, *D. trolliifolium* (troll-ia-FOE-li-um: leaves like globeflower). Leaves mainly on stem, 4–8 in. across; 2–5 ft. tall. Low forest or rarely in moist subalpine meadow; CGorge and OR w-side.

Menzies larkspur

Rockslide larkspur

Cow poison

Though lethal only when eaten in quantity, larkspurs have killed more cattle than any other western genus. The seeds have for millennia been ground up to poison lice.

HERBS: REGULAR DICOTS, WITH 5 PETALS

These typically have 5 sepals and 5, 10, 15, or more stamens in addition to their 5 petals or corolla lobes (fused petals); the female parts aren't in fives. Also included here (p. 252) are flowers with just one set of main flower parts in fives—either petals or sepals but not both, and not the stamens. These variables run in families: Rosaceae mostly have 15 or 20 stamens; Polemoniaceae 5; Primulaceae have 2 sepals and Apiaceae have none. If you have a 5-petaled flower you can't locate here, try these leads: shrubs include many 5-petaled genera, and some are quite small. Gentian and starflower (pp. 271–272) have 5 petals in some of their blossoms, but have 6 or 7 on at least as many others nearby. Irregular dicots (p. 205) mostly have 5 corolla lobes, but these lobes are unlike each other. Composites (p. 189) have tight heads of tiny florets which are technically 5-parted, and sometimes apparently so, as in wall lettuce (p. 202) with its 5 rays per flower head.

HERBS: REGULAR DICOTS, WITH 5 FUSED PETALS, 5 (OR 4) STAMENS

Columbia Puccoon

Lithospermum ruderale (lith-o-SPERM-um: stone seed; roo-der-AY-lee: of waste places). Also western gromwell, stoneseed, lemonweed. Flowers pale yellow, 3/8 in. across, clustered at top and in leaf axils; 5 corolla lobes spread flat from a narrow tube; 5 short stamens don't quite emerge; leaves all on stem, linear, 1–4 in. long, many, hairy; stems several, rough-hairy, 8–28 in. E-side near lower timberline. Boraginaceae.

Use of the roots for red dye or, mixed with grease, for face paint was so widespread that settlers called puccoon "Indian paint." The Okanagan dyed fishing lines, believing that puccoon masked human odors. Some women consumed puccoon to suppress fertility; lab work confirms that puccoon suppresses some reproductive hormones.

Deer Cabbage

Nephrophyllidium crista-galli (nef-fro-fil-ID-ium: kidney leaf; CRIS-ta-ga-lee: cockscomb). Also *Fauria crista-galli*. Corolla white, with ragged fringes; 5–30 flowers in a loose cluster on a leafless 8- to 20-in. stalk; leaves kidney-shaped, blunt-toothed, 2–5 in. wide, each on its own 6- to 12-in. stalk from the rhizome. Wet places, low to subalpine; abundant on VI; also in OlyM, s-most CoastM, and Linn County, OR. Menyanthaceae.

Columbia puccoon

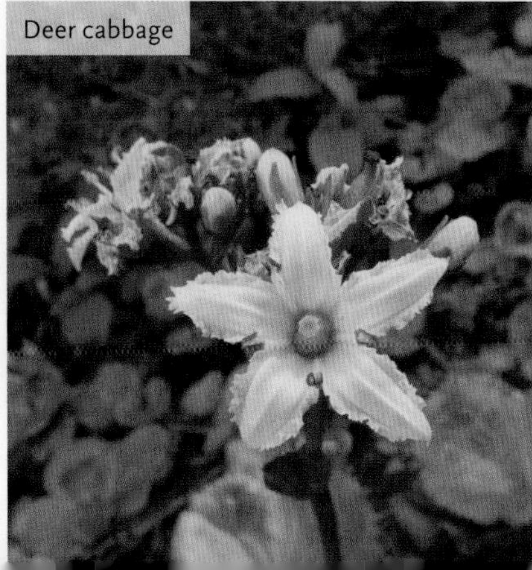
Deer cabbage

Spreading Phlox

Phlox diffusa (flocks: "flame," a Greek flower; dif-YOU-sa: spreading). Corolla white, pink, pale blue, or violet, 3/4 in. across, with 4–6 flat-spreading lobes at the end of a straight tube; stamens do not protrude past corolla mouth; flowers single on numerous leafy stems; leaves 1/4–3/4 in., linear, pointed but not stiff, crowded in dense mats 2–4 in. thick. Rocky sunny spots at all elevs. Polemoniaceae.

High ridges colonized by phlox fail to retain much soil or snow; both blow away. Without a snow blanket through winter, plants there are exposed to ferocious drying winds, and to hundreds of freezing or thawing cycles; the plants withstand frost action whose powers of pulverization are amply displayed on nearby rocks. Though the rocks continually break up, their particles tend to blow away as they reach soil size, preventing soil from accumulating.

Spreading phlox typifies the cushion plants adapted to this extreme environment. The smooth convex surface eases the wind on over with a minimum of resistance, and even more so when the plant contours itself in the lee of a large rock or a crevice between rocks. The tiny, crammed leaves live in a pocket of calm partly of their own making, and there they trap windblown particles that will slowly become a mound of soil. Mt. St. Helens provided a million little exhibits of this phenomenon. Miles downwind, an inch-thick blanket of ash was largely incorporated into the top soil layer within five years, but from the alpine ridges it was completely removed by wind except for what lay in deep crevices—or in sharply contrasting gray aureoles around the cushion plants.

Cushion plants tend to have really long taproots (say, 8–15 feet), an adaptation to dry soils. Ridgetops receive their share of snow, but wind and the coarse rocky substrate allow little of it to stay there.

Spreading phlox

Collomia

Collomia **spp.** (col-OH-mia: glue—). Corolla trumpet-shaped, 1/2–1 in., lavender-streaked or white to pink; stamens sometimes blue-tipped; each flower subtended by a green bract; leaves sticky-hairy, crowded in dense cushions 2–3 in. deep. Unstable alpine and subalpine gravels; see discussion of cushion plants under Phlox, above. Polemoniaceae.

Alpine collomia, *C. debilis* (DEB-il-iss: weak). Leaves oval, not lobed. WA CasR.

Talus collomia, *C. larsenii* (LAR-sen-ee-eye: for Lars John Larsen, an obscure assistant).

Alpine collomia

Talus collomia

Mountain trumpet

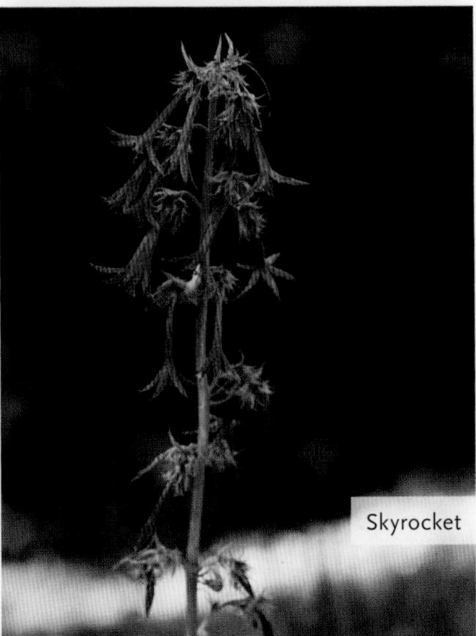
Skyrocket

Also *C. debilis*. Leaves deeply 3- to 7-lobed with the lobes often further divided. WA, OR.

Mountain Trumpet

Collomia grandiflora (GRAND-if-lor-a: large flower). Also large-flowered collomia. Corolla trumpet-shaped, 3/4–1 1/4 in., salmon-orange to almost white, fanning out from ball-shaped clusters of green bracts; stamens often blue-tipped, often unequal in length; seeds gluey when moist; leaves linear, alternate, 1–3 in.; plants annual, often leggy, 8–40 in. Dry clearings at low to mid-elevs.

Skyrocket

Ipomopsis aggregata (ip-a-MOP-sis: like morning-glory; ag-reg-AY-ta: clustered). Also scarlet gilia; *Gilia aggregata*. Corolla scarlet, trumpet-shaped, the slightly flaring tube twice as long (1/2–1 1/4 in.) as the slightly recurved, pointed lobes; stamens borne near mouth of tube; leaves much-dissected, lobes linear; stems to 3 ft., many-flowered, or dwarfed (4 in.) at high elevs. Dry clearings near and e of CasCr. Polemoniaceae.

The long tubular corolla and bright red color are both clues that this flower evolved with hummingbirds as pollinators. Most insects cannot see red, but hummers crave it.

Jacob's-Ladder

***Polemonium* spp.** (pol-em-OH-nium: the Greek name). Also sky-pilot. Corolla light blue with yellow center, 1/2 in. long; leaves pinnately compound, mostly basal; plants often skunky-smelling. Subalpine. Polemoniaceae.

Jacob's-ladder, *P. pulcherrimum* (pool-KER-im-um: most beautiful). Flowers wider than long; 11–25 leaflets 1/4–3/8 in. long; 4–8 in. tall. Subalpine.

Low Jacob's-ladder, *P. californicum*. Also moving polemonium; *P. pulcherrimum* var. *calycinum*. Flowers wider than long; 8–20 leaflets ¼–1 in. long, the 3 terminal leaflets often fused into one 3-lobed leaflet; several 8- to 20-in. stems, often flopping. Mid-elevs to low subalpine; OR, WA.

Elegant Jacob's-ladder, *P. elegans* (EL-eg-anz: elegant). Flowers longer than wide; 13–27 leaflets scarcely ¼ in. long, crowded; 3–6 in. tall. Mainly alpine; WA; rare in BC and OR.

Like most flowers, Jacob's-ladders produce a sweet flowery fragrance in their nectaries to attract nectar-feeding insects as pollinators. In many individuals, however, this is drowned out by a skunky aroma on sepals and bracts below the flowers. A researcher of a Rocky Mountain *Polemonium* thinks the foul smell serves to repel ants; she smells it only in plants at elevations where ants abound. Unlike bees and hover flies (good pollinators), nectar-feeding ants slip right past the pollen-bearing stamens on their way to robbing the nectary, and often also destroy the pistil in the process. See if you can find both skunky and sweet-smelling Jacob's-ladders in our mountains, and any pattern of either ant presence or elevation separating them.

Jacob's-ladder

Low Jacob's-ladder

Douglasia

***Douglasia* spp.** (da-GLASS-ia: for David Douglas, p. 56). Also *Androsace* spp. Rounded corolla lobes spread flat from the end of a narrow tube, where the stamens barely emerge; leaves entire or with a few teeth, in rosettes aggregating in low mats. Primulaceae.

Smooth douglasia, *D. laevigata* (lee-vig-AY-ta: smooth). Corolla crimson to deep pink; ½ in.; leaves narrow, ½ in. long, their faces hairless. Alpine rocks, common in OlyM; also on CGorge bluffs.

Snow douglasia, *D. nivalis* (niv-AY-lis: of snow). Corolla magenta to burgundy, ⅜ in.; leaves gray-hairy, elliptic, ¼–1¼ in. long. Alpine rocks, often of serpentine minerals; c and n WA Cascades.

Elegant Jacob's-ladder

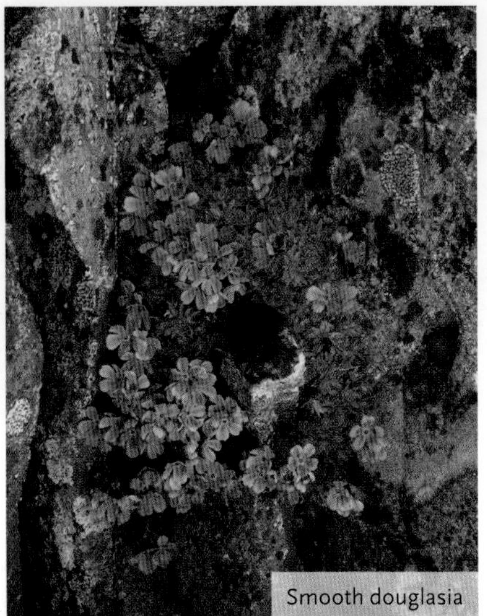
Smooth douglasia

Snow douglasia

Tall mountain shooting star

Smooth douglasia resembles and often grows near a commoner cushion plant, spreading phlox (p. 223). Douglasia's deeper-red flowers are on branched, leafless stalks, and each have a single, unparted stigma. Massed brilliant pink flowers are common to several early-blooming alpine cushion plants. They may be an efficient way to catch the eye of a bumble bee at a season when they are scarce.

The genus was first collected by David Douglas and then named for him by his friend John Lindley. That first specimen is a snow douglasia, and Lindley recorded the Canadian Rockies as its site, but the species has never again been found in Canada. Most likely Douglas collected it in central Washington and his labels got mixed up.

Shooting Star

Dodecatheon **spp.** (doh-de-CAYTH-ee-on: twelve gods). Corolla and calyx bent sharply back, ½–1 in. long; corolla includes a short fused collar part; stamens tightly clasping the pistil, or just slightly spreading; flowers several, many facing down (their petals thus pointing up) but all turn erect in fruit; leaves basal, long-stalked; 4–20 in. Seeps, streamsides, wet meadows. Primulaceae.

Tall mountain shooting star, *D. jeffreyi* (JEF-ree-eye: for John Jeffrey, opposite). Also *Primula jeffreyi*. Petals 4 or 5, pink, their fused collar mostly white; stamens dark red, close together. Abundant in the subalpine; CasR, OlyM, VI.

Darkthroat shooting star, *D. pulchellum* (pool-KEL-um: beautiful). Also *Primula pauciflora*. Petals pink to purple (or white, rarely) with yellow collar; fused base of the stamens is also yellow; stem smooth, not sticky. All elevs.

Poet's shooting star, *D. poeticum*. Also *Primula poetica*. Petals pink to purple, with yellow collar; stamens dark red, fused; leaves, stems, and sepals sticky-hairy. Low

John Jeffrey

John Jeffrey was our most mysterious early plant hunter. A group of Scottish gentlemen, thrilled by the garden plants Menzies and Douglas exported, incorporated "The Oregon Association" expressly to finance this little-known youngster, hoping to make him the next David Douglas. He explored the Okanagan, Similkameen, Fraser, Willamette, and Umpqua drainages in 1851–1853, arriving overland from Hudson's Bay, then continued south. His work habits fell far short of Douglas's. His employers were already fuming over his lackluster output of specimens by 1854—the height of the gold rush—when he sent off his last shipment, from San Francisco, before disappearing. Colorful but baseless rumors of his murder proliferated.

Darkthroat shooting star

White shooting star

Poet's shooting star

to mid-elevs in e CGorge (where common) and n to Yakima County.

White shooting star, *D. dentatum* (den-TAY-tum: toothed). Also *Primula latiloba*. Petals white with magenta collar and stamen base; leaves broadly oval. Low to mid-elevs in CasR, mainly e-side; infrequent.

The flower shape we call "shooting stars" and botanists call reflexed is also common in the nightshade family (tomatoes, potatoes, belladonna, and so on). These flowers are buzz pollinated: their stamens spew pollen in response to furious vibration. Bumble bees visiting the flowers land briefly on the robust column provided for that purpose, vibrate their wings, and are rewarded with a shower of pollen. For the plant, there is efficiency in making bumble bees learn a flower-specific trick, because they will be faithful: on any given day they just visit one species of flower over and over again, and thus don't waste pollen by leaving it on the wrong kind of flower. The bee does exact a substantial fee in pollen she eats, but apparently she's well worth the price. Lupine, lousewort, and monkshood win bumble bee fidelity another way—with robust irregular flower shapes that only bumble bees of a particular size can unlock.

Phacelia

***Phacelia* spp.** (fa-SEE-lia: bundle—the dense inflorescence). Flowers crowded, bristling with stamens about twice as long as corollas; calyx hairy; leaves gray-silky-coated. Boraginaceae or Hydrophyllaceae.

Silky phacelia

Silky phacelia, *P. sericea* (ser-ISS-ia: silky). Flowers purple (to blue or white) in a dense round spike; stamens pale-tipped; leaves deeply pinnately lobed, mostly basal, cushion-forming; stem 4–10 in. Alpine to mid-elev rocks; WA and BC.

Silverleaf phacelia, *P. hastata* (hass-TAY-ta: halberd-shaped, referring to the pair of leaf lobes). Also *P. leptosepala*. Flowers drab whitish (rarely lavender); leaves narrow elliptical, often with a pair of small lobes or leaflets at the base; 3–20 in. tall. Alpine to mid-elev rocks; not in CoastR.

Each of our several *Phacelia* species has alpine (compact) and mid-elevation (leggy) varieties. The silky is most striking, with ornate leaves and a compact, colorful inflorescence. The unrelated but similar-looking cutleaf kittentails (p. 263) grows on alpine gravels in the Olympics.

Waterleaf

***Hydrophyllum* spp.** (hydro-FILL-um: water leaf). Flowers in compact heads bristling with black-tipped stamens twice as long as the 3/8-in. corollas; calyx bristly; leaves

Silverleaf phacelia

Fendler's waterleaf

basal, pinnate, typically rising higher than flowers. Boraginaceae or Hydrophyllaceae.

Pacific waterleaf, *H. tenuipes* (ten-YOU-ip-eez: slender foot, referring to the stem). Flowers dull or greenish cream, or purple; usually 5 leaflets coarsely toothed, leaves 6–8 in. long and wide, with soft white hair underneath; 8–32 in. tall. Low to mid-elev clearings and thickets, w-side.

Fendler's waterleaf, *H. fendleri* (fend-ler-eye: for August Fendler). Flowers white, or purple; usually 7–11 leaflets, coarsely toothed, leaves 6–12 in., with soft white hair underneath; 8–32 in. tall. Lush thickets, e-sides in BC and WA, CasR in OR.

Ballhead waterleaf, *H. capitatum* (cap-it-AY-tum: flowers in heads). Flowers lavender to white, in spherical head; leaves 4–10 in., leaflets 5–11, with a few lobes, hairy; flower stalk 1–3 in. (a CGorge variety is taller). Moist open e-side forest.

Sitka Mist Maiden

Romanzoffia sitchensis (romans-AH-fia sit-KEN-sis: found at Sitka, Alaska, by botanists funded by Count Rumiantzev, p. 230). Flowers white, funnel-shaped with round corolla lobes, ¼–½ in. across, in loose racemes; leaves basal on long stalks, round,

Pacific waterleaf

Fendler's waterleaf

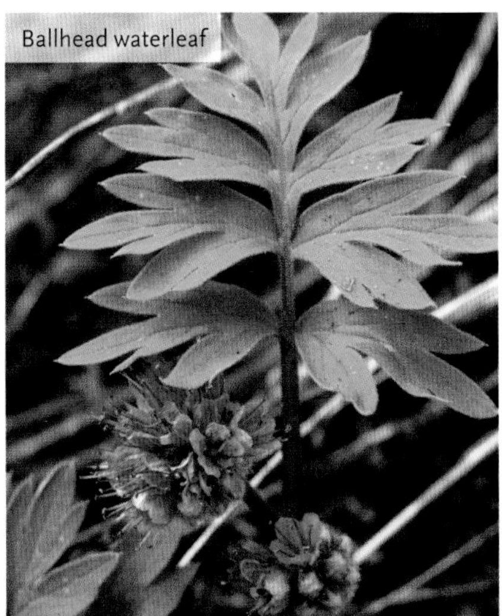
Ballhead waterleaf

Rumiantzev and Eschscholtz

Count Nikolai Rumiantzev (or Romanzoff) financed Captain Kotzebue's Russian exploration of 1815–18. Johann Friedrich von Eschscholtz and Adelbert von Chamisso were the naturalists. They collected extensively in Alaska and California, but apparently sailed right past Washington and Oregon. Chamisso, a poet from Berlin, was the primary botanist while Eschscholtz, an Estonian doctor, preferred insects.

Sitka mist maiden

Dogbane

½–1½ in. wide, with short round lobes; 4–8 in. tall, almost hairless. Seepy rock ledges, cliffs, or talus at all elevs. Boraginaceae or Hydrophyllaceae.

Dogbane

Apocynum androsaemifolium (a-POS-in-um: away dog!; an-dro-see-mif-OH-lium: leaves like *Androsaemum*.) Flowers pink, fragrant, ¼–⅜ in. long, bell-shaped with flaring corolla lobes, clustered; short stamens hiding deep within; leaves opposite, oval, pale beneath, spreading flat or sometimes drooping; stems milky-juiced, smooth, often reddish, much branched, resembling a shrub; seeds cottony-tufted, in paired, slender, 3- to 6-in. pods; 1–2 ft. Dry, rather shady sites, up to tree line. Apocynaceae.

To humans and perhaps also to dogs, dogbane is purgative, diuretic, and may cause heart irregularities. Baneful enough?

It attracts a wide assortment of butterflies and bees.

Pacific Hound's Tongue

Cynoglossum grande (sin-a-GLOSS-um: dog tongue). Also *Adelinia grande*. Flowers sky blue (or partly violet), ½ in. across, in clusters that uncoil upward; corolla lobes spread flat from a tube; 5 notched white bulges by the tube mouth; short stamens hide within; hairy sepals; round seeds in tidy clusters of 4, with short prickles; leaves pointed-elliptic, blades up to 7 in., hairy underneath, on leafstalks from lower stem; 8–36 in. Lowlands of e CGorge. Boraginaceae.

Pacific hound's tongue

Bluebells

Bluebells-of-Scotland

Bluebells

Mertensia paniculata (mer-TEN-zia: for Franz Karl Mertens, p. 147; pa-nic-you-LAY-ta: flowers in panicles). Also lungwort. Corolla blue, pink-tinged at first, short-lobed, narrowly bell-shaped, pendent, 1/2–3/4 in.: stem leaves pointed-elliptical, basal leaves oval on long leafstalks, both often with bluish bloom; plants many-flowered, robust, 1½–5 ft. Subalpine streamsides and meadows. Boraginaceae.

These flowers start out pinkish while they are producing and accepting pollen, and shift to pure blue as they switch to producing nectar instead. Bees bite through the bases of blue flowers and "rob" the nectar. (The flower's narrow throat locks them out at the front door, anyway.) Though it is sometimes assumed that nectar robbers replace mutualism with parasitism, close study disproved that in the case of this species. The same bumble bees come for both pollen and nectar. The postfertile flowers reward bees with nectar; the bee then goes to pinkish flowers for pollen on the same trip. Giving away nectar thus increases the number of pollination visits to the plant as a whole. The colors are signs that make the bee's work more efficient.

Bluebells-of-Scotland

Campanula rotundifolia (cam-PAN-you-la: small bell; rotund-if-OH-lia: round leaf). Also bluebell bellflower. Flowers several, usually nodding; corolla blue, bell-shaped, 5/8–1¼ in. long, with 5 short lobes; pistil 3-forked; stem leaves alternate, linear, entire; basal leaves round to heart-shaped on long stalks, often withering before flowers open; leggy plant 6–30 in. tall. Dry meadows, rocks, woods, mid-elevs to subalpine. Campanulaceae.

Olympic Bellflower

Campanula piperi (PI-per-eye: for Charles V. Piper). Flowers 1 to 3, erect; corolla 1–1¼ in. across, pale blue (ranging rarely to pure white), saucer-shaped, with lobes much longer than the fused portion; 5 calyx lobes with a few fine teeth; pistil initially a purple "candle," then splits into 3 white stigmas;

Olympic bellflower

Pale bellflower

Sibbaldia

Gordon's mousetail

leaves finely sharp-toothed, oblanceolate to spoon-shaped, both basal and opposite; 1–4 in. tall, in small clumps. Alpine rocks; only in OlyM. Campanulaceae.

Pale Bellflower

Campanula scouleri (SCOO-ler-eye: for John Scouler, p. 112). Flowers several on longish stalks, nodding to ascending; corolla ¾–1 in. across, pale blue to white, with recurved slender lobes longer than the fused portion (not bell-shaped); pistil longer than corolla, initially a "candle," then splits into 3 stigmas; leaves sparsely toothed, egg-shaped to lanceolate, both basal and alternate; 4–16 in. Outcrops or dry forests at low elevs; OR, WA, VI. Campanulaceae.

HERBS: REGULAR DICOTS, WITH 5 SEPARATE PETALS, 5 STAMENS

Sibbaldia

Sibbaldia procumbens (sib-AHL-dia: for Sir Robert Sibbald; pro-CUM-benz: prostrate). Petals tiny, yellow, sitting on top of 5 slightly longer green bracts alternating with 5 much larger (up to ¼ in.) green calyx lobes; leaves ternate; leaflets wedge-shaped, ½–1½ in., 3- or 5-toothed at the tip, white-hairy; leafstalks and flower stems rising 2–4 in. from rhizomes or prostrate stems. Alp/subalpine gravels, and down to mid-elevs in BC. Rosaceae.

Gordon's Mousetail

Ivesia gordonii (IVE-zia: for Lt. Joseph Christmas Ives; gor-DOE-nee-eye: for Alexander Gordon). Yellow flowers in ball-shaped clusters; petals smaller than the 5 yellowish-green calyx lobes alternating with 5 narrow bracts; leaves basal, 1–3 in. long, pinnately compound, leaflets divided into fingers ¼–⅜ in. long, all radiating from the axis in a bottlebrush shape; 2–6 in. tall. Dry ridges, ec WA CasR, Mt. Adams, and Iron Mtn, OR. Rosaceae.

Similar Tweedy's mousetail, *I. tweedyi*, with bigger petals, grows on similar Washington sites, especially on serpentine.

Grass-of-Parnassus

Parnassia fimbriata (par-NAS-ia: for Mt. Parnassus, referring poetically to holy heights; fim-bree-AY-ta: fringed). Petals white, ¼–½ in., fringed along the narrow

Grass-of-Parnassus

base; flower single; 5 stamens about half as long as petals, plus 5 short yellow clusters of sterile stamens; leaves heart-shaped, basal on long stalks, plus one small stalkless leaf halfway up the 6- to 16-in. stem. Wet soil, especially subalpine; late summer. Parnassiaceae or Celastraceae.

Brewer's mitrewort

Complaints about the misnomer "grass" for this flower have gone unheeded for a very long time. Witness John Gerard's *Herball* of 1597:

> The Grass of Parnassus hath heretofore been described by blinde men; I do not meane such as are blinde in their eyes, but in their understandings, for if this plant be a kind of grasse, then may the Butter-burre or Colte's-foote be reckoned for grasses, as also all other plants whatsoever.

Mitrewort

***Mitella* spp.** (my-TEL-a: mitre). Also bishop's cap. Petals branched, threadlike, sticking out between the calyx lobes; flowers 10–20 along a 6- to 14-in. stalk; leaves kidney- or heart-shaped, scalloped to toothed, basal, on long hairy leafstalks. Moist subalpine forest or meadow. Saxifragaceae.

Five-stamen mitrewort

Brewer's mitrewort, *M. breweri* (BREW-er-eye: for Wm. Brewer). Also *Pectiantia breweri*. Petals yellow-green, 5- to 9-branched; calyx saucer-shaped; stamens aligned with the spaces between petals.

Five-stamen mitrewort, *M. pentandra* (pen-TAN-dra: 5 stamens). Also *Pectiantia pentandra*. Petals yellow-green, 5- to 9-branched; calyx saucer-shaped; stamens aligned with the fine-branched petals.

Three-toothed mitrewort, *M. trifida* (TRIF-id-a; 3-forked). Also *Ozomelis trifida*. Petals white or purplish, 3-branched; calyx bell-shaped.

Three-toothed mitrewort

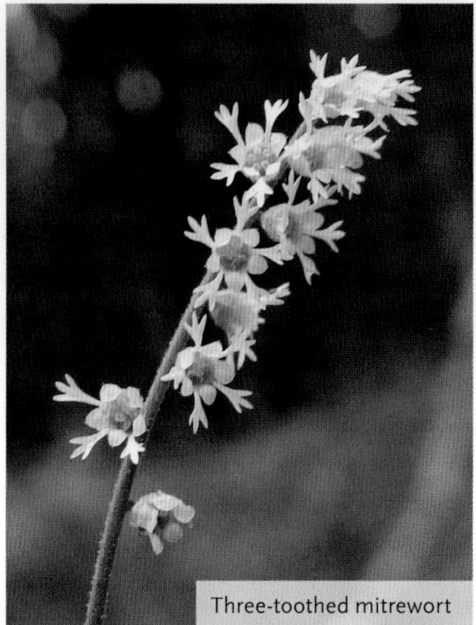

Three-toothed mitrewort

The seed capsule looks like a mitre—a bishop's tall, deeply cleft hat—until it splits open to resemble a chalice of caviar (in the five-stamen photo they're unripe, so call them mini-grapes). This splash cup invites a raindrop to knock the seeds out and away.

A scientist in Japan reports that the slender pinnate-lobed petals are adapted to support landings by fungus gnats, the pollinators of the species he studied; this may turn out to be the case here as well.

Roundleaf Alumroot

Heuchera cylindrica (HOY-sher-a: for botanist Johann Heinrich von Heucher). Flowers cup-shaped, in a crowded cylindric inflorerscence, dull cream to greenish or pinkish, lacking petals (technically, 1 to 5 minuscule petals may be present initially); stamens hidden within the 5-lobed calyx; 2 styles emerge as seeds grow; leaves basal, oval with coarse lobes and teeth, on long stalks; stem 6–32 in., leafless. E-side rock crevices, low to mid-elevs.

Alum is an astringent chemical long used to stop bleeding. European colonists learned from Native Americans to use the roots of *H. americana* for that purpose (and others), hence the name alumroot. Roundleaf alumroot roots were made into decoctions and poultices for bleeding, sores, rheumatism, sore throats, diarrhea, tuberculosis—and for the liver. North America has 37 species of *Heuchera*; *H. sanguinea* is the coral bells of gardens.

HERBS: REGULAR DICOTS, WITH 5 PETALS, 10 STAMENS

Fringecup

Tellima grandiflora (TEL-im-a: anagram of *Mitella*; grand-if-lor-a: big flower). Petals white, often aging deep pink, slender with

Roundleaf alumroot

Fringecup

many threadlike branches, reflexed around the lip of the jar-shaped, greenish white calyx; flowers 12–25 along one side of stalk; leaves kidney-shaped, shallowly lobed and toothed, mostly basal, on long hairy leaf-stalks; 16–40 in. Moist forest or meadows. Saxifragaceae.

Family resemblances among the saxifrages are so strong that it seems the same features are just reshuffled from genus to genus. Some members, like *Mitella* and *Tellima*, have reshuffled spellings.

Tiarella

Tiarella trifoliata (tee-ar-EL-a: crownlet; try-fo-lee-AY-ta: 3-leaved). Also foamflower, coolwort; *T. unifoliata*, *T. laciniata*. Flowers tiny, white, many, in a sparse raceme on an 8- to 16-in. stalk; petals threadlike, unbranched, less visible than the stamens; ovary and capsule of 2 very unequal sides; leaves mostly basal on short stalks, hairy, toothed, 3-lobed to ternate and incised, 2–4 in. Abundant in dense forest. Saxifragaceae.

By midsummer, many tiarella leaves display pale curlicues, the tracks of leaf miner larvae (any of several unrelated insects). Look closely to see the larva at the front end of the track.

Woodland Star

***Lithophragma* spp.** (lith-o-FRAG-ma: stone break, like "saxifrage" in not-quite-correct Greek). Petals lavender-pink to white, spreading flat, around ¼ in. long; stamens deep within calyx; leaves finely hairy underneath, mostly basal, palmately lobed and divided; delicate sticky-hairy plants 4–12 in. tall. Sagebrush, rocky slopes, forest openings at all elevs. Saxifragaceae.

Small-flowered woodland star, *Lithophragma parviflorum* (parv-if-LOR-um: small flower). Petals deeply 3-lobed, often unequal in length.

Bulbous woodland star, *Lithophragma glabrum* (GLAB-rum: hairless, a misleading name). Petals usually deeply 5-lobed; bears minute maroon bulbs in place of some or all flowers in upper leaf axils. E-side.

The tiny bulbs on bulbous woodland star can germinate and grow after the stem topples—a method of clonal reproduction. Some individuals produce lots of these bulbils and few or no flowers.

Tiarella

Tiarella

Bulbous woodland star

Leatherleaf Saxifrage

Leptarrhena pyrofolia (lep-ta-REE-na: slender anthers; pyro-lif-OH-lia: *Pyrola* leaf). Petals white, minute; stamens longer; flowers in a tight cluster; seedpods red, paired within flattish clusters; leaves toothed, oval to elliptic, thick, crinkly leathery, shiny bright green, 1–5 in., basal, plus 1 small leaf clasping the dark red, 8- to 18-in. stem. Alp/subalpine streambanks and wet meadows. Saxifragaceae.

When massed along rocky streambanks, the maroon seed heads and stems can be recognized from hundreds of yards away.

Leatherleaf saxifrage

Leatherleaf saxifrage

Saxifrage (taller species)

***Saxifraga* and *Micranthes* spp.** (sac-SIF-raga: stone break; my-CRANTH-eez: small stamen). Petals white (sometimes pinkish), ⅛ in. long; swollen white stamens; pistil of 2 horns (rarely 3 to 5); several flowers in a loose raceme; leaves 1–3 in., round to kidney-shaped, basal on long stalks. Wet rocks and gravels, low to subalpine elevs. Saxifragaceae.

Wood saxifrage, *S. mertensiana* (mer-ten-zee-AY-na: for Karl Mertens, p. 147). Pink anthers; leaves with shallow lobes each divided into 2 to 5 blunt teeth; stalks, leafstalks, and leaf undersides often bristling with sticky hairs; 6–16 in.

Heartleaf saxifrage, *M. nelsoniana* (nel-so-nee-AY-na: for Aven Nelson). Also *Saxifraga nelsoniana*, *S. punctata*. Petals elliptic with a short slender neck, white to pink, rarely with orange spots; leaves have large, even teeth; stem 4–10 in., hairless near bottom, fine-woolly near top.

Wood saxifrage

Wood saxifrage

Heartleaf saxifrage

Rusty-hair saxifrage

Brook saxifrage, *M. odontoloma* (o-don-ta-LO-ma: tooth fringe). Also *Saxifraga odontoloma, S. arguta*. Petals nearly round except for a short slender neck, white with 2 yellowish-green spots near base; swollen white stamens; leaves have large, even teeth, slightly fleshy; stalk sticky-hairy near top, 6–12 in.

Rusty-hair saxifrage, *M. rufidula* (roo-FID-you-la: reddish). Also *Saxifraga rufidula, S. occidentalis*. Petals oval with a distinct slender neck, without spots; stamens only slightly swollen; yellow to dark red anthers; inflorescence flat-topped; leaves tapering to flattened leaf-stalks 1½–3 in. long, the blades oval to triangular with tangled rusty hairs beneath, rather fleshy with coarse, even teeth, as if cut by a cookie cutter; 2- to 8-in. stems may redden. Meadows or steep rocks where wet in spring, low to subalpine.

Brook saxifrage

Alpine Saxifrage

Micranthes tolmiei (TOLE-me-eye: for William Tolmie, p. 216). Also *Saxifraga tolmiei*. Petals white, ¼ in. long; stamens white, flattened (petallike), red-tipped; flowers 1–4 on nearly leafless 2- to 4-in. stems; leaves fleshy (about as thick as wide), hairless, linear, ¼–½ in. long, basal, densely matted. Wet alp/subalpine gravels. Saxifragaceae.

This cute plant has tubby, succulent leaves resembling stonecrop. It earns its name "rock-breaker," pioneering in rock crevices of alpine talus where release from snow is too brief (annually) and too recent (geologically) for a mycorrhizal fungus community to have developed. It may be virtually the only plant on a nearly barren gravel bed, or it may join other scarcely mycorrhizal organisms like woodrushes, sedges, mosses, and lichens.

Alpine saxifrage

Spotted saxifrage

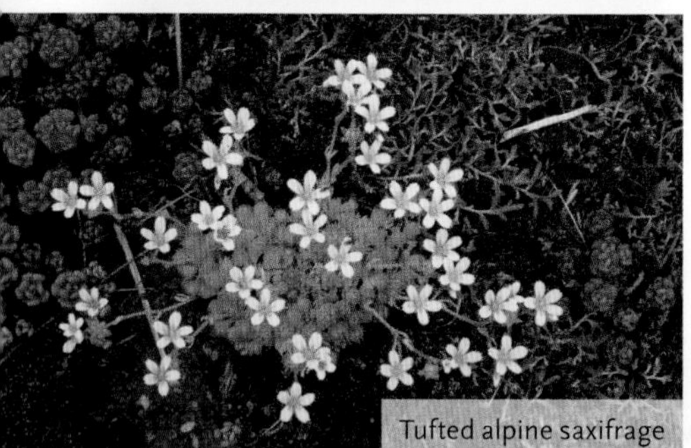
Tufted alpine saxifrage

Purple saxifrage

Saxifrage (mat-forming species)

***Saxifraga* spp.** (sac-SIF-ra-ga: stone break). Petals white, 1/4 in. long, flat-spreading, sometimes notched; slender white stamens; conical pistil; leaves 1/4–1/2 in., somewhat fleshy, mainly on nonflowering stems, crowded, forming a low cushion; a few small leaves on the 1- to 6-in. stem. Rocks and gravels. Saxifragaceae.

Spotted saxifrage, *S. bronchialis* (bronk-ee-AY-lis: windpipe, referring to inflorescence branches). Petals speckled with red or orange spots; leaves narrow, spine-tipped, with coarse hairs along their margins. Mid- to high elevations.

Tufted alpine saxifrage, *S. cespitosa* (cease-pit-OH-sa: growing in clumps). Petals unspotted; filaments and pistil often yellow; leaves of 3 linear lobes. All elevs but commonly alpine.

Saxifrages in their native habitat seem to live up to their "rock breaker" moniker, but the name actually derives from the medieval herbalists' doctrine of signatures: because their little bulbs were said to resemble bladderstones, a few European species were prescribed for breaking up bladderstones.

Purple Saxifrage

Saxifraga oppositifolia (opposite-if-OH-lia: opposite leaves). Petals pink to purple; flowers single, bell-shaped, 1/4–1/2 in. long; calyx cup-shaped; tiny semi-evergreen leaves in scalelike opposite pairs, borne on their own sprawling stems, crowded, forming a dense mat; minute hairs along leaf edges; 1–2 in. tall. Alp/subalpine rockfields from Mt. Rainier n. Saxifragaceae.

Stonecrop

***Sedum* spp.** (SEE-dum: the Roman name, derived from "sitting"). Petals yellow (except *S. oregonense)*, pointed, 1/4–3/8 in.; flowers several, clustered; seedpod 5-celled,

Spreading stonecrop

Lanceleaf stonecrop

Broadleaf stonecrop

starlike; leaves thick, fleshy, crammed together, often turning red; plants low (3–8 in.), spreading by rhizomes or runners. Sunny rocks. Crassulaceae.

Spreading stonecrop, *S. divergens* (di-VER-jenz: spreading) Seed cells spread flat; leaves opposite, rotund, many crowded on short nonflowering stems. Mid-elevs to alpine.

Lanceleaf stonecrop, *S. lanceolatum* (lan-see-o-LAY-tum: lance—). Leaves tubular-lanceolate, pointed, alternate but may appear basal. WA and BC.

Broadleaf stonecrop, *S. spathulifolium* (spath-you-lif-OH-lium: spatula-shaped leaves). Petals spread flat, seed cells curve outward; flowers in candelabra-like broad clusters; leaves spoon-shaped with a slight point, often strongly bluish, in crowded basal rosettes or on short nonflowering shoots. Low to mid-elevs on VI and WA, up to subalpine in OR.

Wormleaf stonecrop, *S. stenopetalum* (steno-PET-a-lum: narrow petals). Flower clusters flat-topped; seed cells spread flat; leaves tubular, pointed, many of them in bristling clusters in axils of bigger leaves (these fall off and can take root as new plants) or as nonflowering shoots.

Oregon stonecrop, *S. oreganum* (or-eg-AY-num: of Oregon). Petals and seed cells more narrowly erect; flowers in relatively vase-shaped clusters; leaves alternate, flattened oval, not very bluish, up to 1 in. Mainly w-side.

Wormleaf stonecrop

Oregon stonecrop

Creamy stonecrop, *S. oregonense*. Petals cream white; petals and seed cells more narrowly erect; leaves bluish, alternate, flattened, some notch-tipped, most in basal rosettes, many over 1 in. long and ½ in. wide. Mid-elevs in OR.

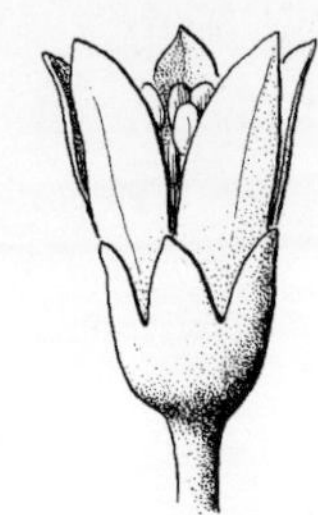
Creamy stonecrop

Like cactus stems, fat succulent leaves maximize the ratio of volume to surface area, and thus the ratio of water capacity to water loss through transpiration. But even with succulent storage tanks, stonecrops grow only while water is available, and store water to subsidize flowering and fruiting. Water-filled leaves might be vulnerable to frost damage, but stonecrops resist freezing and do very well in the alpine zone. You can squeeze liquid water out of stonecrop leaves at temperatures that will freeze it immediately.

Broadleaf stonecrop is a popular rock garden plant with many named horticultural varieties, notably "Cape Blanco" from the Oregon coast.

Western Roseroot

Rhodiola integrifolia (ro-dee-OH-la: rose—, referring to fragrance; in-teg-rif-OH-lia: untoothed leaf). Also king's crown, midsummer-men; *Sedum roseum*. Petals deep red, ⅛ in.; stamens protruding on ♂ plants, lacking on ♀ plants; seed capsules 5 per flower, deep red; flowers several, crowded; leaves thick, fleshy, elliptic, ¼–¾ in. long, either bright green or grayish-coated; 2–16 in., in clumps. Alp/subalpine, often where wet; WA CasR, possibly BC. Crassulaceae.

Western roseroot is very closely related to the roseroot (*R. roseum*) much studied as a remedy for stress fatigue, anxiety, depression, and cancer, and as an endurance performance enhancer. The two share some but not all of their essential oils, and our roseroot has not been studied on its own. Inuit and others described both plants as good "salad greens," but reported surprisingly little interest in them as medicine.

Wood-Sorrel

Oxalis oregana (OX-a-liss: the Greek name, from "sharp"; or-eg-AY-na; of Oregon). Petals white, usually with fine red veins; flowers single, ¾–1½ in. across; leaves cloverlike, of 3 leaflets, folding down at times; stems and leafstalks 4–7 in. Moist w-side forest up to 4000 ft. Oxalidaceae.

Herbs of deep shade habitats typically hold their leaves horizontal to maximize the sunlight that hits them. Wood-sorrel does this, but at times creases them sharply downward, taking about six minutes to fold up

Wood-sorrel with leaves folded

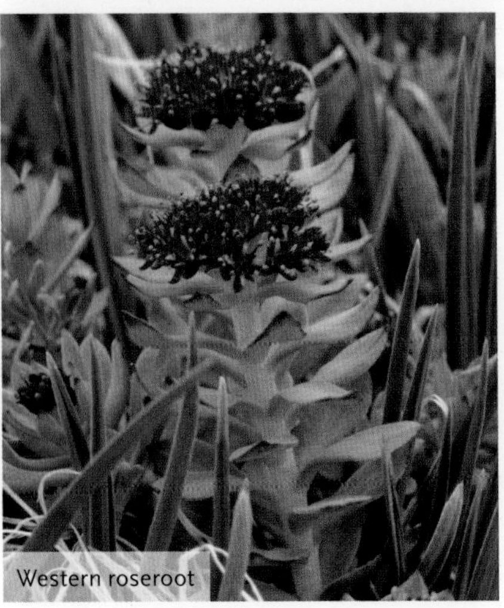
Western roseroot

and thirty minutes to flatten them again later. It responds this way to a puzzling variety of stimuli. When a patch of sunlight comes along, folding up conserves moisture and avoids sun-scorch. At night the reason may be similar: there is no photosynthesis to be lost by closing up shop, and there is at least a small amount of evaporation to be curtailed. However, folding up in the rain has to have a different reason. It may be to reduce some damage from raindrop impact.

Wood-sorrel makes good mouth entertainment. Kids all seem to love it. Though unrelated to French garden sorrel, *Rumex acetosa*, wood-sorrel tastes a lot like it as well as like mountain-sorrel, also unrelated. All get their tartness from oxalic acid, which is mildly toxic, so don't let those kids overdose.

Threadleaf sandwort

Sandwort

Eremogone **and** ***Cherleria*** **spp.** (air-em-OG-un-ee: child of the desert, perhaps; shair-LAIR-ia: for Johann Heinrich Cherler). Petals white, 1/4–1/2 in.; sepals scarcely 1/4 in., blunt (pointed in some other sandworts); 3 styles; leaves linear, mostly basal, plus 2–4 opposite pairs of stem leaves. Alp/subalpine gravels and crevices. Caryophyllaceae.

Threadleaf sandwort, ***E. capillaris*** (cap-il-AIR-iss: hair-leaved). Also fescue sandwort, slender mountain sandwort; *Arenaria capillaris*. Several flowers; basal leaves 3/4–1 1/2 in. long, needle-thin; capsule splits six ways; 2–6 in. tall. Also in steppe e of CasR.

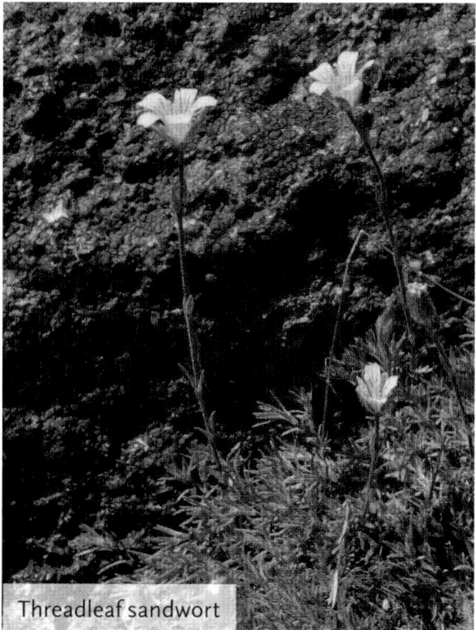
Threadleaf sandwort

Alpine sandwort, ***C. obtusiloba*** (ob-too-si-LO-ba: blunt-lobed). Also *Minuartia obtusiloba, Arenaria obtusiloba*. Flower usually single; leaves up to 3/8 in. long, dense, on mat-forming prostrate stems; capsule splits three ways; 1/2–2 1/2 in. tall.

Field Chickweed

Cerastium arvense (ser-AST-ium: horn—; ar-VEN-see: of fields). Petals white, each with 2 round lobes; styles usually 5; calyx

Field chickweed

White catchfly

White catchfly

Douglas's campion.

5-lobed; flowers 3–8 per stem; leaves linear, ½–1¼ in., opposite; tufts of leaves sprout from the larger leaf axils; 2–16 in. tall, sometimes forms broad mats. Dry sunny sites at all elevs. Caryophyllaceae.

White Catchfly

Silene parryi (sigh-LEE-nee: an associate of Dionysus who was portly and generally soused in suds, describing sticky secretions on the plant; PAIR-ee-eye: for Charles Parry). Petals white or lavender-tinged, each deeply 4-lobed, plus an inner whorl of 10 shorter lobes; calyx 5-lobed, hairy and very sticky; leaves narrowly elliptical, 1–3 in., 2 or 3 pairs opposite, the rest basal; 6–15 in. Mainly subalpine, BC, WA, and Mt. Hood. Caryophyllaceae.

Catchflies are not carnivorous plants, but small bugs can get caught on the sticky surfaces around the inflorescence. These blooms are at their best at night, when moths pollinate them.

Douglas's campion, *S. douglasii*, is similar but not sticky, just hairy, and with just two shallower petal lobes. It is widespread (including in Oregon) but not alpine.

Moss-Campion

Silene acaulis (ay-CAW-lis: stalkless). Also moss pink, cushion pink, carpet pink. Petals pink (to white), separate though they form an apparent tube, bent 90 degrees to spread flat; 3 styles or 5 of the 10 stamens often protruding; calyx shallowly 5-lobed; leaves linear, pointed, thick, crowded, to ½ in., mostly basal in mosslike mats 2 in. thick. Alpine. Caryophyllaceae.

This genus and the two preceding are in the pink family, so called not because the petals are pink but because they are pinked, or notched at the tip. Pinked petals do run in the family, but other family traits such as 10 stamens and unfused petals are more reliable. These flowers otherwise resemble phlox and douglasia, but are smaller (see p. 223 on cushion plants).

Moss-campion

Sidebells pyrola

Pink pyrola

White-veined pyrola

Single delight

Sidebells Pyrola

Orthilia secunda (or-THILL-ia: straight, small; se-CUN-da: with flowers all to one side). Also *Pyrola secunda*. Flowers greenish white, bell-shaped, with long straight style sticking out, 5–15 all on one side of stem; leaves 1–2½ in., light green, variably egg-shaped with small rounded teeth, on the lower half of the 3- to 7-in. stems. Forest shade. Ericaceae.

Sidebells pyrola also grows in the Northeast, but is less genetically diverse there. The Northwest was a valuable Ice Age refugium for preserving rich gene pools.

Pyrola

***Pyrola* spp.** (PIE-ro-la: little pear-shaped leaf). Flowers 5–25 in a tall spike; style bends sharply down or sideways, then curves up at its tip; leaves evergreen, dark, basal on stalks, entire or finely toothed, 1–3 in. long; stem reddish, 4–16 in. Low to mid-elev forest. Ericaceae.

Pink pyrola, *P. asarifolia* (ass-a-rif-OH-lia: leaf like wild-ginger). Petals pink to red; leaves oval to heart-shaped.

White-veined pyrola, *P. picta* (PIC-ta: painted). Petals pale greenish to purplish; leaves egg-shaped, white-mottled in a pinnate pattern along veins; some individuals lack leaves.

When the West was first botanized, reports came back of totally leafless but healthy specimens resembling *Pyrola*. They were named *P. aphylla*. Whether they are genetically distinct or merely a form of white-veined pyrola (and another species) has been debated ever since. The same-species camp finds leafless and leafy plants attached to each other by their rhizomes, and believes that an individual stem may lack leaves one year, and bear them the next. The distinct-species camp finds whole leafless populations with no leafy specimens nearby, and finds molecular evidence of *P. picta* and *P. aphylla* as genetically distinct. The British Columbia and Oregon online plant databases now recognize *P. aphylla*.

What I see is a plant hedging its bets between doing its own photosynthesis (autotrophic) and getting its photosynthates from other plants via fungal intermediaries (mycoheterotrophic). They have a new word for this: mixotrophic.

Single Delight

Moneses uniflora (mo-NEE-sees: single delight; you-nif-LOR-a: one flower). Also *Pyrola uniflora*. Flower single, ½–1 in. across, waxy-whitish, sometimes pinkish, fragrant; 5 petals spread flat; pistil stout, straight, 5-tipped (like a chess rook), persisting on the round seed capsule; leaves oval,

Weeds

Our mountains have fewer invasive plants than other North American regions. Once we leave roads and clearcuts behind, most nonnatives we see—wall lettuce, clover, thistles, certain buttercups and many grasses—are concentrated along trails and in old horse pastures, and outnumbered even there. Closed forests in the Northwest have resisted unfriendly takeovers—but currently it looks like either stinky Bob or garlic mustard may have begun to crack their defenses.

Nonnative *disease* organisms, on the other hand, have already had devastating impacts throughout our range, notably in wiping out our five-needle pines (p. 87). We will be incredibly lucky if the ancient forests remain even somewhat pure as they take on the cumulative stresses of climate change and species invasions of ever greater diversity.

Climate change and pollution will favor weeds. Most projections of 21st-century climate predict increases in fire and forest pests—disturbances that weedy plants commonly take advantage of. Since weeds tend to be heavy nitrogen consumers (and natives more efficient and conservative) they also benefit from global nitrogen deposition, which derives from agricultural fertilizers and waste. Many invasive plants additionally can adapt to climate change by timing their growth and flowering in accord with temperature. Many temperate-zone natives time their season according to day length, which could make them slower to adapt.

Most problem weeds are not particularly "weedy" or aggressive in their native lands. Without human help, species rarely travel around the globe very fast, and as long as they migrate slowly, fungi, bacteria, and grazers that consume them, as well as competitors, coevolve with them, maintaining a level of control so that a single species rarely takes over. Scientists who seek ways to control a weed look to that plant's native lands to see what eats it there. They choose a few promising consumers (insects, usually) and set them up in quarantined tests for several years to see which ones could be introduced without undue risk to native plants. The process is slow, expensive, and far from foolproof.

Invasives may sound less apocalyptic, and get less media coverage, than global warming or toxic pollution, but they are a grave threat to the biosphere. Promoting "free trade" based on political or economic theory alone, without looking at biology, is so myopic it's deranged. Trade in unprocessed logs and wood chips introduces pests and diseases whose potential for economic harm dwarfs any potential profits.

usually toothed, ½–1¼ in., from lowest part of 2- to 6-in. stem; often on rotting wood. Low to mid-elevs. Ericaceae.

Yerba de Selva

Whipplea modesta (WHIP-lia: for Amiel Weeks Whipple). Also whipplevine. Flowers ¼ in. wide, in a fluffy head; petals white, becoming greenish, sticking out flat between the calyx lobes; petals, calyx lobes, stamens, and styles all typically 5 but sometimes 6; leaves opposite, ½–1 in., elliptic with sparse rounded teeth, 3-veined, often persisting through winter; stem 1–6 in. tall from leafy woody runners. Dry w-side forest, c and s OR and disjunct in OlyM. Hydrangeaceae.

Yerba de selva means "forest herb" in Spanish.

Yerba de selva

Stinky Bob

Geranium robertianum (jer-AY-nium: crane—; robber-tee-AY-num: obscure reference to some damned Robert). Also herb robert. Flowers ½ in. across; pink petals spread flat from a tubular base enclosed in sepals; usually 2 flowers per stem; sepals and stems have straight white hairs; stems deep red to green, the whole plant often turning red after going to seed; leaves twice dissected, parsley-like, with rank peanut butter odor when crushed. Annual herb up to 1 ft. tall. CGorge and other w-side forest up to 2000 ft. Geraniaceae.

Botanists I know all call this weed stinky Bob. They hate it. Don't fall for its demure charm. Bob is the one weed (so far) that can take over the herb layer of a shady west-side forest without the aid of logging or fire. It actually achieves greater dominance in 90 percent shade than in more open forest. It can shoot its seeds 15 or 20 feet; it can overwinter as a rosette (even under snow) after germinating in fall; it can also germinate in spring, as the seeds are viable for five years; and it produces allelopathic chemicals to poison herbaceous competition.

Stinky Bob

Then there's that heavy aroma, which may discourage some herbivores. If you spot it anywhere in small numbers before it goes to seed, by all means yank it. However, we'll probably have to get used to it.

HERBS: REGULAR DICOTS, WITH 5 PETALS, 15 OR MORE STAMENS

St. John's Wort

Hypericum scouleri (hi-PER-ic-um: Greek name for it, meaning "under heath"; scoo-ler-eye: for John Scouler, p. 112). Also *H. formosum*. Flowers deep yellow, orange in bud, many; stamens showy, as long (¾–1½ in.) as the petals; capsule 3-celled; leaves opposite, oval, clasping-based; stems many, 4–30 in. Uncommon; wet thickets, especially low subalpine. Hypericaceae.

St. John's wort

Goatsbeard

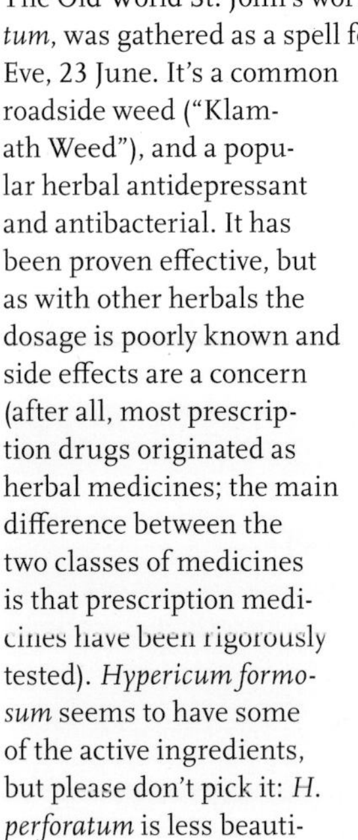

The Old World St. John's wort, *H. perforatum,* was gathered as a spell for St. John's Eve, 23 June. It's a common roadside weed ("Klamath Weed"), and a popular herbal antidepressant and antibacterial. It has been proven effective, but as with other herbals the dosage is poorly known and side effects are a concern (after all, most prescription drugs originated as herbal medicines; the main difference between the two classes of medicines is that prescription medicines have been rigorously tested). *Hypericum formosum* seems to have some of the active ingredients, but please don't pick it: *H. perforatum* is less beautiful and more available as well as more potent. Its leaves have unique tiny translucent dots that you can just barely see if you hold the leaf up against the light (a magnifying glass helps).

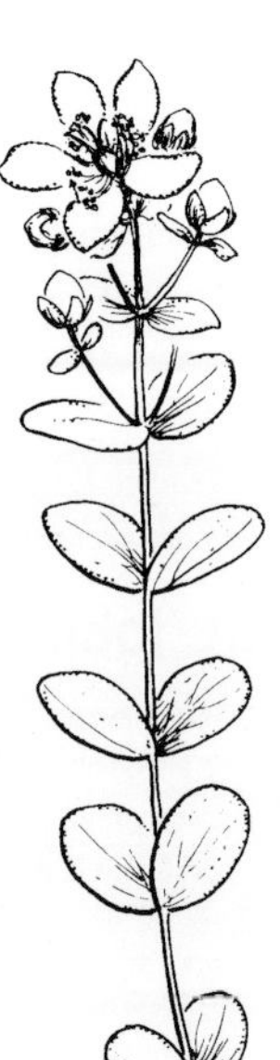
St. John's wort

Goatsbeard

Aruncus dioicus (a-RUNK-us: beard of goat; die-OY-cus: two houses, that is, with ♂ and ♀ flowers on different plants). Also bride's feathers; *A. sylvester.* Flowers cream white, minute, in large (to 14 in.) stringy panicles, the ♂ (on separate plants) much fluffier than the ♀, since the 15–20 stamens are the largest flower part; leaves twice- or thrice-compound, to 20 in., leaflets fine-toothed, long-pointed oval, 3–6 in.; plant 3–6 ft., easily mistaken for a shrub. Moist thickets up to subalpine avalanche tracks. Rosaceae.

Goatsbeard roots and leaves made medicine for sores and sore throats among the Northwest tribes.

Partridgefoot

Partridgefoot

Luetkea pectinata (LOOT-key-a: for Count Lütke, p. 147; pec-tin-AY-ta: cockscomb—, referring to leaf shape). Flowers white to cream, ¼ in., in a compact raceme; leaves of about 9 fine, narrow lobes, mostly basal from runners or rhizomes, often carpet-forming, often persistent in winter; 3–8 in. Abundant, subalpine and lower alpine. Rosaceae.

Partridgefoot surrounds many of the sunken beds of black alpine sedge that emerge from late-melting snowbeds. That indicates a need for a slightly longer snow-free season than the sedge, or slightly less tolerance for standing water, or both.

Purple Avens

Geum triflorum (JEE-um: the Roman name; try-FLOR-um: 3-flowered). Also prairie smoke, old-man's-whiskers. Flowers usually pendent, in 3s, dull reddish, 1 in. long, vase-shaped, scarcely opening; petals yellow to pink, mostly hidden by the 5 reddish calyx lobes; seeds long-plumed; leaves mostly basal, finely cut (fernlike), hairy;

Purple avens

8–16 in. Dry sties from steppe to subalpine ridges; e of CasCr, e OlyM, and Saddle Mtn, OR. Rosaceae.

Dwarf Raspberry

***Rubus* spp.** (ROO-bus: the Roman name). Petals ⅜ in. long, narrow; fruit of 1–5 glossy red one-seeded drupelets ¼ in. long; flower stems and toothed leaves rise 1–2 in. from woody runners. W-side forest, especially mid-elevs. Rosaceae.

Strawberry bramble

Dwarf bramble

Strawberry bramble, *R. pedatus* (ped-AY-tus: 5-leafleted). Petals white; 5 leaflets (rarely 3, the lateral 2 not quite fully divided); runners smooth.

Dwarf bramble, *R. lasiococcus* (lazy-o-COC-us: shaggy berry). 3 leaflets; runners smooth. US and n to Hope, BC.

At their best, these berries miniaturize the essence of raspberry flavor as wild strawberries do the essence of strawberry. More often, the ones we sample are flat-tasting and hard, perhaps because small rodents beat us to them as they ripen.

Wild Strawberry

***Fragaria* spp.** (fra-GAIR-ia: the Roman name). Petals white, nearly circular, 1⁄4–1⁄2 in.; sepals apparently 10–12; stamens 20–25; berry red, up to 1⁄2 in. long; leaves ternate, toothed coarsely and evenly, on hairy leafstalks; 3–8 in. tall, from runners. Forest openings. Rosaceae.

Wood strawberry, *F. vesca* (VES-ca: thin). Seeds on surface of berry; most leaves minutely hairy on top, veins slightly recessed.

Blueleaf strawberry, *F. virginiana* (vir-gin-ee-AY-na: of Virginia). Seeds imbedded in pits on berry surface; most leaves hairless and flat on top, bluish green; runners red.

Mountain tribes used the leaves and the roots, mainly as poultices and as antidiarrheal teas.

Commercial strawberries are a complex hybrid derived beginning 250 years ago from these two species and *F. chiloensis* of the Northwest coastal lowlands. None of them had big berries before the breeding began.

A 2012 paper described the higher-elevation strawberries of the Oregon Cascades as a new species, *F. cascadensis*. It has hairless leaf uppersides, like wood strawberry; but like blueleaf strawberry it has one tooth at the leaf tip shorter than all the other teeth. On wood strawberry the leaf-tip tooth is usually longer than the others.

Wood strawberry

Wood strawberry

Wood (left) and blueleaf (right) strawberry leaves.

Fanleaf cinquefoil

Blueleaf cinquefoil

Subalpine buttercup

Cinquefoil

Potentilla **spp.** (po-ten-TIL-a: small but mighty). Petals yellow, usually notch-tipped; 5 true sepals alternate with 5 shorter bracts; leaves compound, leaflets 1–1½ in.; stem 4–12 in. Not in CoastR. Rosaceae.

Fanleaf cinquefoil, *P. flabellifolia* (fla-bel-if-OH-lia: fan leaf). Also high mountain cinquefoil. 3 leaflets thin, coarse-toothed. Subalpine meadow.

Blueleaf cinquefoil, *P. glaucophylla* (glaw-ca-FILL-a: leaves with grayish bloom). Also varied-leaf cinquefoil; *P. diversifolia*. 5 leaflets deeply toothed. Alp/subalpine from Mt. Hood n.

One cinquefoil is easily overlooked, but a few thousand of them in the high-country ultraviolet can take your breath away. Fanleaf cinquefoils are among the earliest subalpine meadow flowers to bloom in quantity, following close upon springbeauties and glacier lilies. Both *cinquefoil* (French for "five-leaf") and *Potentilla* (medicinally potent) were names originally cut to fit European species.

Subalpine Buttercup

Ranunculus eschscholtzii (ra-NUN-cue-lus: froglet; ess-SHOLT-zee-eye: for Johann Friedrich von Eschscholtz, p. 230). Petals glossy yellow; seeds in a tight conical head; leaves generally 3-lobed to compound, but highly variable; 3–8 in. Subalpine meadows or scree, especially where wet. Ranunculaceae.

Snow buttercups are solar trackers, bending to face the sun as it crosses the sky. Their sensors and bending mechanism are in the upper stem, which will bend with the sun even if the flower has been clipped off. Tracking to focus the sun's heat on the flower's sexual organs dramatically improves the fertility of the pollen. Insects that come to bask in the warmth may leave dusted with pollen.

Smoothness is the key to mirror-quality reflective layers. A buttercup petal's glossy surface is a layer of thin, flat, very smooth, oily, translucent yellow pigment cells covering a layer of paper-white starch cells—a structure that excels at reflecting ultraviolet light as well as yellow light. A flash of ultraviolet doubtless attracts pollinators. Children aim the yellow glow on the undersides of each other's chins, claiming that it reveals a love for butter.

Glossy petals are your first clue for telling snow buttercups from cinquefoils. The surer clue is buttercups' 5 sepals as opposed to an appearance of 10 sepals on cinquefoils.

Buttercup stem juices are blistering irritants. Mountain tribes used them as arrowhead poisons and also (cautiously, you would think) as poultices for sore joints and toothaches.

Columbine

Aquilegia formosa (ak-wil-EE-jia: the Roman name, possibly referring to water-bearing or to eagle claws; for-MO-sa: beautiful). Flowers nodding, several, the petal spurs and spreading ¾–1¼ in. petallike sepals red, while the stamens and short, cuplike petal blades are yellow; leaves mostly basal on tall leafstalks, compound with 9 round-lobed leaflets; 6–40 in. Lush subalpine meadows to lower clearings. Ranunculaceae.

Species of columbine share an unmistakable flower shape, while their colors vary. A pale yellow Rocky Mountain columbine, *A. flavescens*, enters the northeast fringe of our range, where it is sometimes flushed with pink after messing around with our red species. Different columbines are interfertile and often grow together; they owe their separate identities to the fact that pollinators that go for red flowers are uninterested in blue flowers, and so forth. The red-yellow combination is preferred by hummingbirds, some bees, and this writer. Bees nip the bulbous spur-tip to get the nectar, and also go around by the front door for pollen. Moths like the blue and white of the Colorado state flower, *A. coerulea*, and have very long tongues to reach the bottoms of the long spurs.

Columbine

HERBS: REGULAR DICOTS, WITH 5 PETALS, 2 SEPALS

Western Springbeauty

Claytonia lanceolata (clay-TOE-nia: for John Clayton; lan-see-o-LAY-ta: narrowleaved). Also lanceleaf springbeauty. Petals ¼–½ in., white (rarely yellow, in n CasR), usually with fine pink lines; 1 opposite pair of stem leaves narrow-elliptical, ½–3 in., basal leaves 1–4 or none; stems 3–6 in., rather succulent, hollow, weak, several-flowered. Common in meadows at all elevs, especially subalpine. Montiaceae.

Springbeauty owes its success to timing rather than brute size. It begins growing at its bulb tip in September, just when its neighbors are dying back. While snow insulates it for the next eight months, holding the soil close to freezing, the shoot inches up to the soil surface. Very few plants—all arctic or alpine specialists—are active at such low temperatures. Without the snow

Western Springbeauty

blanket it would be even colder, and growth would be impossible.

As soon as the snow melts away from the shoot in spring, springbeauty bursts to its full height of 3 or 4 inches, expending in a few days its disproportionately large reserve of starches. It can even push through the last inch or two of snow by combusting some of the starch to melt itself a hole. It has two to four weeks to complete its life cycle—blooming, setting seed, and photosynthesizing like mad to store up starches for the next spring. Then it withers, existing only underground for late July and August, the peak growing season for its neighbors.

Plants on this sort of schedule are called spring ephemerals. Many, such as blue-eyed grass, are common on semiarid land with just a few weeks of wet soil following snowmelt. Springbeauty does well on such sites on the lower east slope, but in subalpine meadows its timing has a different purpose—jumping the gun on bigger, leafier plants that will monopolize the light later in the season.

The thin-fleshed hollow stem acts as an internal greenhouse. When stored carbohydrates are burned off during its quick burst of growth, some of the heat produced is retained in the stem, making the internal air warm enough for photosynthesis even when the outside air is not. Waste carbon dioxide from respiration also stays inside, available for synthesis into new carbohydrates.

With their concentrated starches, springbeauty bulbs are good edibles; Meriwether Lewis rated them tops among Indian root vegetables. They taste radishy. Unfortunately, they're depleted when in bloom and hard to locate at other times, so leave them in peace unless starvation impends.

Similar broadleaf springbeauty, *C. cordifolia*, has entirely white petals and broader leaves, the basal ones up to 2½ inches wide, on long leafstalks.

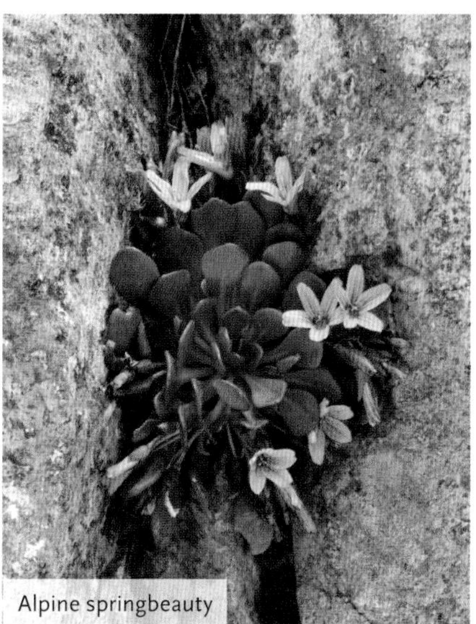
Alpine springbeauty

Alpine Springbeauty

Claytonia megarhiza (mega-RYE-za: big root). Petals 5, deep pink to white, usually with fine darker lines; basal leaves numerous, fleshy, spoon-shaped; opposite stem leaves small or lacking; stems numerous, often reddish, 2–10 in., tending to sprawl. Alpine rocks, Chelan and Kittatas Counties, WA, and on Three Sisters and Three-Fingered Jack, OR.

Populations of alpine springbeauty are widely scattered over the northern Rockies and a few small areas of the Cascades. The photo above shows the deep pink form that grows on serpentine soils in Washington. It has sometimes been treated as a distinct variety or even a species named *nivalis*.

Candyflower

Claytonia sibirica (sib-EE-ric-a: Siberian). Also miner's lettuce, Siberian springbeauty. Petals ¼–½ in., notch-tipped, white with fine pink veins; sepals 2; stamens 5; stem leaves 2, opposite, usually pointed-oval, 2–4 in., clasping; basal leaves many, at least as large, on long leafstalks; stem rather succulent, several-flowered, 5–16 in.

Candyflower

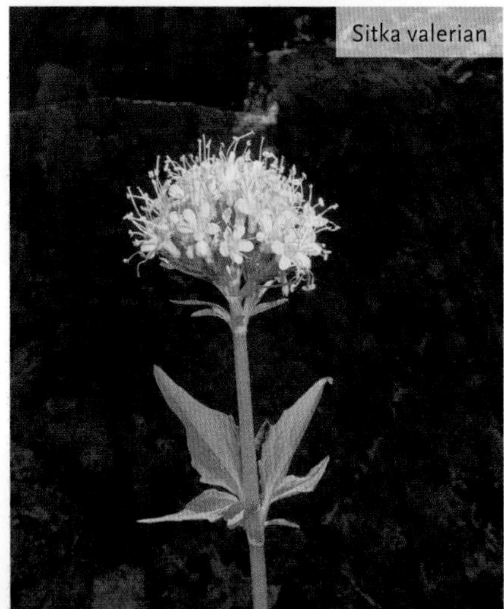
Sitka valerian

Hooker's valerian

Moist forest; sometimes on moss mats on trees. Montiaceae.

Candyflower is one of our few common annuals—plants that grow from seed and die within a single growing season. Where it grows, you may find it germinating and blooming at any time of spring or summer. To eat like a forty-niner, find young unbloomed ones. They're mild and tender.

HERBS: REGULAR DICOTS, PETALS OR SEPALS TOTAL 5

The definition of petals and sepals states that if they're in just one whorl, they're sepals, no matter how colorful or tender. Technically, then, there are no flowers with 5 petals and no sepals, but in appearance there are quite a few. Parsley family flowers have a vestigial whorl or fleshy ring barely perceptible below the 5 petals. This ring is a calyx, but its lobes are so reduced as to be indetectable. Another apparent instance is valerian: sepals unfurl only as the flower goes to seed, so the flower in bloom lacks them.

Valerian

***Valeriana* spp.** (va-lee-ree-AY-na: strong—). Corolla white or pinkish, lobes flaring from a slightly asymmetrical tube; 3 stamens protruding; calyx a "parachute" of plumes on the maturing seed; flowers form a rounded head; leaves compound; 3 or 5 leaflets elliptical, pointed, vaguely toothed. Valerianaceae or Caprifoliaceae.

Sitka valerian, *Valeriana sitchensis* (sit-KEN-sis: of Sitka, Alaska). Corolla ¼ in. long; leaves opposite, usually all on stem; plant 2–4 ft., rank-smelling especially when it dries out in late summer. Lush subalpine meadows and nearby forest.

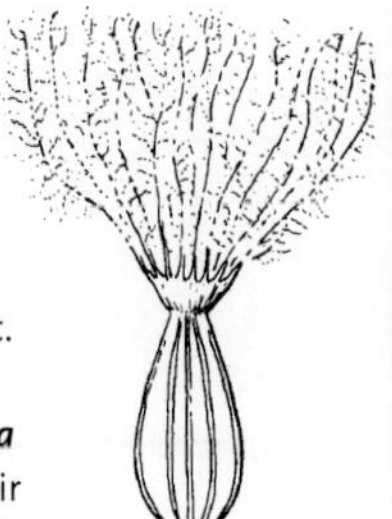
Sitka valerian

Hooker's valerian, *Valeriana hookeri* (HOOK-er-eye: for Sir William Hooker). Also Scouler's valerian; *V. scouleri*. Corolla white, 1/4–3/8 in. long; leaves both basal and opposite; terminal leaflet largest by far, up to 3 in. long; 8–28 in. Low to mid-elev forest.

As snowmelt releases subalpine meadows, reddish shoots of Sitka valerian shoot up. The redness disappears as the foliage matures, lingering in the budding flowers but disappearing as they mature. Most redness in plants comes from anthocyanin, a complex carbohydrate pigment that ranges from red to blue, depending on acidity.

Anthocyanin is suspected of several functions in high-elevation plants. It filters out ultraviolet radiation, which can damage plant tissue. Ultraviolet is more intense at high altitude, with less atmosphere to screen it, and more intense in June, when sunlight is at its peak. In June the plants are still snowbank-chilled and tender; that's when anthocyanin goes into action.

Second, anthocyanin absorbs and concentrates infrared radiation, heating the plant. Third, it is an interim form for carbohydrates on their way up from storage. To bloom and fruit within the short high-country growing season, plants store carbohydrates in their roots and then move them up fast after snowmelt, or even before. In dereddening, valerian stuffs itself with preserves from the root cellar.

Valerian root has regained its ancient reputation as an herbal sedative. More potent than some species, Sitka valerian fetches good prices for brushpickers, and has been overpicked locally. "It is most effective," writes herbalist Michael Moore, "when you have been nervous, stressed, or become an adrenalin basket case, with muscular twitches, shaky hands, palpitations, and indigestion." I'll keep that in mind.

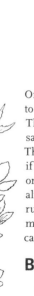

Sitka valerian

Bastard toadflax

Bastard Toadflax

Comandra umbellata (co-MAN-dra: hairy stamens; um-bel-AY-ta: flowers in umbels). Also *C. pallida*. Calyx lobes white to purplish, petallike, still conspicuous on fruits; 5 short stamens; no petals; flowers in round clusters; fruit 1/4 in., 1-seeded, berrylike, blue, purple, or brown; leaves bluish-coated, somewhat fleshy, narrow elliptic, untoothed, alternate; stems unbranched, 2–14 in., often clustered. Sandy soil, foothills to timberline; e of CasCr in WA and BC, both sides in OR. Comandraceae.

Once you get past the name, there are things to like about this plant. Thoreau admired it. The oily fruits are tasty when green, though said to be nauseating when eaten in bulk. There are also things to dislike, especially if you're a plant. It is a partial root parasite on nearby plants of many kinds, and it is an alternate host for *Cronartium comandrae*, a rust fungus that attacks pines. The fungus makes yellow bumps on toadflax leaves, and can turn the whole plant yellow.

Bistort

***Bistorta* spp.** (bis-TOR-ta: twice twisted, referring to the rhizome). Flowers white, tiny, chaffy, fetid; 5 unequal calyx lobes; no petals; 8 equal stamens usually protruding; stem leaves few, sheathing; basal

American bistort

Alpine bistort

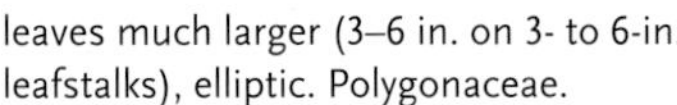

leaves much larger (3–6 in. on 3- to 6-in. leafstalks), elliptic. Polygonaceae.

American bistort, *B. bistortoides* (bis-tor-TOY-deez: resembling bistort). Also *Polygonum bistortoides*. Flowers in a dense ball, its width at least half its 1- to 1½-in. height. Abundant in alp/subalpine meadows.

Alpine bistort, *B. vivipara* (viv-IP-a-ra: giving birth to live young, referring to bulblets). Also *Polygonum viviparum*. Flowers in a dense narrow spike, its width about one-third of its 1-in. height, with tiny pink bulbs in place of flowers in its lower half. Moist sunny sites, mainly alp/subalpine, n Cascades and BC.

Bistort flowers stink, probably to draw flies for pollination. Bears and elk eat the roots and shoots anyway, as did the Blackfoot and Cheyenne. A hover fly is visiting the flower in the photo above.

The absurd scientific name—"bistort resembling a bistort"—came about by a mundane path. The scientist who named it saw it as a species of *Polygonum,* but one that resembled another genus, *Bistorta,* hence *Polygonum bistortoides.* A century later, further study found that in fact it belongs in *Bistorta,* to which it was transferred (though not by every authority).

Newberry Knotweed

Aconogonon davisiae (a-con-a-GO-non: whetstone, that is, rough, seed; da-VIS-ee-ee: for Nancy Jane Davis). Also Newberry's

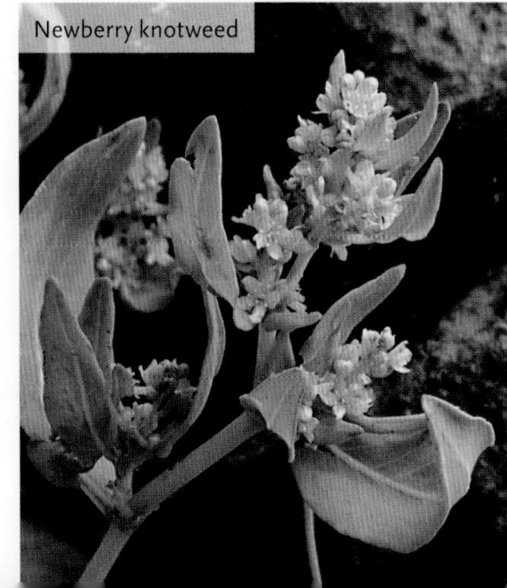
Newberry knotweed

fleeceflower, Davis's knotweed; *A. newberryi, Polygonum newberryi, P. davisiae*. Flowers tiny, greenish, in short spikes wedged in leaf axils; 5 unequal calyx lobes; no petals; 8 short stamens; leaves alternate, gray-green, oval, 3/4–2 in., with flaring papery sheaths above each leaf; stems up to 16 in., often partly prostrate. High gravels, usually pumice or serpentine; CasR and OlyM. Polygonaceae.

Newberry knotweed comes up in spring as rich red buds and shoots. The redness may disappear, and then return in late summer. It and its cousin, dirty socks, were early pioneer dominants on Mt. St. Helens mudflows and pumice. They typify pumice desert habitats, which look desertlike even where they get lots of precipitation, because pumice retains moisture poorly. The plants there don't so much tolerate drought as win a race with it by growing and flowering early.

The thick taproots outweigh the aboveground parts several times over, and are a major food for pocket gophers. They often extend far upslope from the plant's stem. On unstable scree, the top few inches of fine gravel creep downslope much faster than the next layer down; to survive there, plants have to allow their roots to stretch (and also grow) in a downslope direction. When its roots are severed by soil creep, this species can sometimes sprout new plants from the root fragments.

Anemone

***Anemone* spp.** (a-NEM-a-nee: ancient Greek name for it, honoring the god Adonis under an alternate name, Na'man). Also windflowers. Sepals 5 (sometimes 6), petallike; no petals; many stamens; 3 stem leaves in a whorl 3/4 of the way up; similar but flowerless whorls of 3 leaflets may stand nearby, from the rhizomes; 2–12 in. Low to mid-elev forest and clearings. Ranunculaceae.

Oregon anemone, *A. oregana* Flowers blue-violet (occasionally pink or white), 1–2 in. across; 30–75 stamens; stem leaves

Oregon anemone

Three-leaf anemone

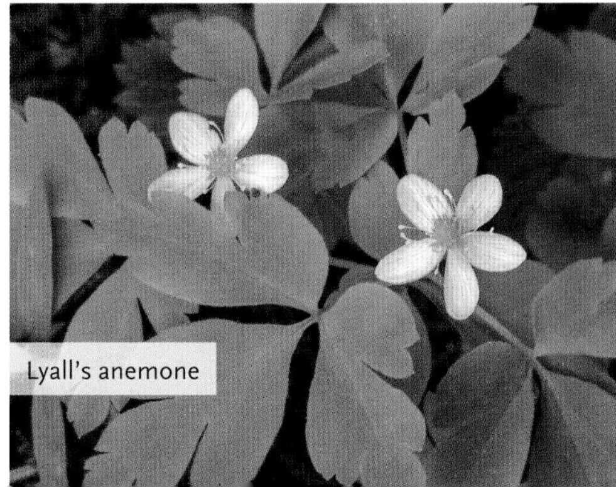
Lyall's anemone

3- to 5-compound and lobed, on leafstalks. OR, n to Chelan County and OlyM in WA.

Three-leaf anemone, *A. deltoidea* (del-TOY-dia: triangular). Flowers white (occasionally pinkish), 1–2 in. across; stem leaves coarsely toothed, oval, without leafstalks. OR and s WA CasR and CoastR.

Lyall's anemone, *A. lyallii* (lye-AH-lee-eye: for David Lyall, p. 171). Flowers white to pink or bluish, 3/4 in. across; 10–30 stamens; stem leaves ternate, toothed, on leafstalks. Low prairies and up to timberline; infrequent.

Our woodland anemones look like each other, and quite unlike our subalpine anemones (p. 269).

Sweet Cicely

***Osmorhiza* spp.** (os-mo-RYE-za: odor root). Also sweetroots. Flowers minute, in a very open inflorescence; seeds slender, bristly; leaflets usually 9, oval, toothed; plant licorice-fragrant, leggy, 1–3 ft. Apiaceae.

Purple sweet cicely, *O. purpurea* (pur-PEW-ria: purple). Flowers pink to maroon. Moist mid-elev openings.

Mountain sweet cicely, *O. berteroi* (bare-TARE-oh-eye: for Carlo Giuseppe Bertero). Also *O. chilensis*. Flowers greenish white. Lower forests.

Mountain sweet cicely

Herbalists praise sweet cicely as a fungicide, and the Salish used to smoke it. Avoid any internal use, though, because of deadly relatives.

Water-parsley

Oenanthe sarmentosa (ee-NANTH-ee: wine flower; sar-men-TOE-sa: twiggy) Flowers white, tiny, in rounded inflorescences 2–4 in. across; 5 petals, no easily visible sepals, 5 stamens; leaves both alternate and basal, twice-pinnate; leaflets 3/4–2½ in., toothed; side veins lead from the midvein to the tooth points; stem branching, hollow, weak, tending to sprawl and to root where in contact with earth; up to 2 ft. Marshes, wet places in low to mid-elev forest.

You should not eat water-parsley because of the risk of confusing it with deadly toxic water hemlock. That said, the

Mountain sweet cicely

Water-parsley

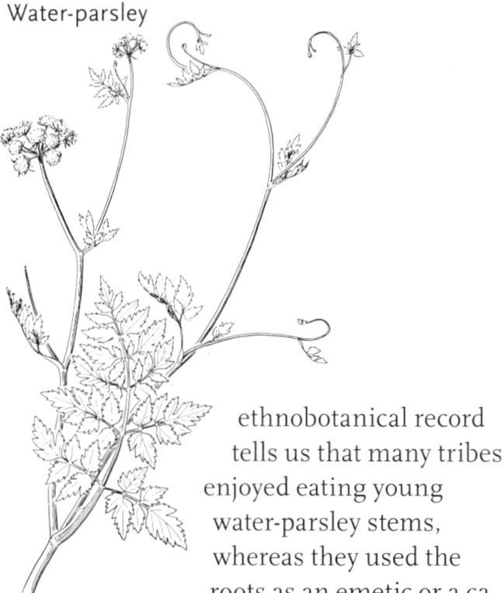
Water-parsley

ethnobotanical record tells us that many tribes enjoyed eating young water-parsley stems, whereas they used the roots as an emetic or a cathartic, or to induce labor, or else simply called them poisonous.

If you search online, you'll find the roots (the emetic part) described as a "dainty dish of the Oregon Indians . . . which has a sweet, cream-like taste." Mmmnn, irresistible. A search for the first-hand report goes back 165 years to Karl A. Geyer, the same explorer-botanist who reported coast redwoods in Idaho (p. 156). His "sweet, cream-like" root, it turns out, grew on dry upland hillsides in eastern Oregon. Definitely not water-parsley; probably yampah. Geyer used the wrong scientific name, and in fact he corrected himself two years later, but his mistake had already blasted off into the 19th-century infosphere, to be repeated in fat tomes decade after decade. And now here it is on websites. Mistakes live forever.

The moral is, Don't believe everything you read on the internet—and not in antiquarian bound media either. Don't eat water-parsley unless you're a professional botanist.

Sharptooth Angelica

Angelica arguta (an-JEL-ic-a: angelic, see below; arg-YOU-ta: sharp-toothed). Also Lyall's angelica. Petals 5, white or pinkish, tiny; 5 stamens; no easily visible sepals; flattish inflorescences 3–6 in. across; leaves

Sharptooth angelica

usually twice-compound; leaflets 2–5 in. × ½–3 in., toothed; 2–7 ft. Low to mid-elev forest. Apiaceae.

Sharptooth angelica, whose flowers often swarm with beetles or flies, is not known to share the potency of two famous relatives—*dong quai* of Chinese apothecaries and angelica of European ones. The Archangel Raphael allegedly revealed angelica to humans as a remedy, hence its name, *Angelica archangelica*; it is cultivated today as a fragrance in cosmetics, as a seasoning, and to some extent for medicines.

Gray's Lovage

Ligusticum grayi (lig-us-tic-um: Roman name, referring to Liguria; GRAY-eye: for Asa Gray). Also licorice-root. Flowers white

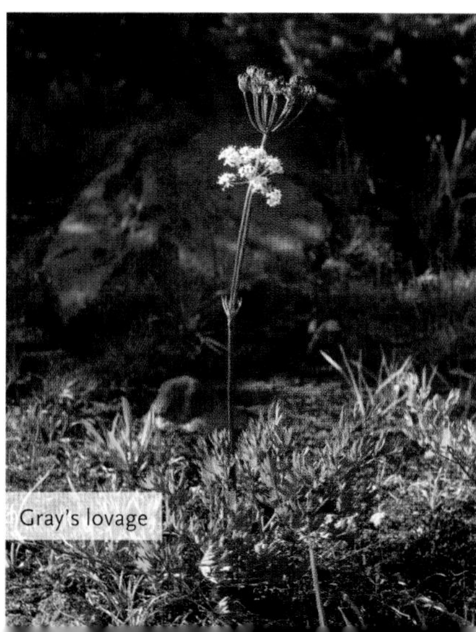
Gray's lovage

(sometimes purple-tinged), in 1–3 slightly rounded inflorescences 2–4 in. across; leaves like Italian parsley, nearly all basal; 8–24 in. Blooms into September in lush subalpine meadows. Apiaceae.

Lovage is the "Queen Anne's lace" look-alike common in subalpine meadows in late summer. Lovage is edible but not recommended because of deadly toxic relatives. Some *Ligusticum* species are now overcollected for the herbal trade. This "osha has been sensationalized beyond its true usefulness," according to herbalist Gregory Tilford.

Columbia Gorge desert-parsley

Desert-Parsley

***Lomatium* spp.** (lo-MAY-shum: hemmed seeds). Also hog-fennels. Flowers minute; leaves lacy, at least twice pinnate, mainly basal; stem hollow. Dry places. Apiaceae.

Cascade desert-parsley, *L. martindalei* (martin-DAY-lye: for Isaac C. Martindale). Flowers yellow, in ½" clusters on ray-like stems from the root crown; leaves form a nearly flat rosette. Dry rocky ground (often pumice) at higher elevs.

Columbia Gorge desert-parsley, *L. columbianum*. Flowers purple to pink, in rounded clusters 3–8 in. across, blooming before leaves are fully grown; leaflets linear, up to ¾ in.; stem aromatic, hairless, 12–30 in. Dry meadows, e CGorge and n to Yakima County.

Cascade desert-parsley

Chocolate-tips

Chocolate-tips, *L. dissectum* (dis-EC-tum: finely cut). Also fernleaf biscuitroot. Flowers purple-brown or else yellow, tiny, in many ½-in. balls on rays (like fireworks) from a common point; 20–60 in.

Lomatium is a large and tricky genus in a large and tricky family—though it's easy to recognize at the family level. The parsley family includes carrots (called "Queen Anne's lace" when growing wild), parsnips, celery, fennel, and dill. Robust taproots in the family range in edibility from staple foods of several tribes to deadly poison hemlock. Some tribes reportedly ate young chocolate-tips roots, but others poisoned fish and lice with them. Scientific studies of its medicinal value are also ambiguous, though it appears active against some pathogenic bacteria and fungi.

Cow-Parsnip

Heracleum maximum (hair-a-CLEE-um: the Greek name, for Hercules). Also *H. lanatum*. Petals 5, white, those near edge of inflorescence much enlarged and 2-lobed; 5 stamens; 1 or several nearly flat inflorescences 5–10 in. across; leaves alternate; 3 (occasionally 5) leaflets 6–16 in. wide, palmately lobed and toothed; stems juicy, aromatic, hollow, 3–10 ft. Moist thickets up to low subalpine. Apiaceae.

Cow-parsnip

Cow-parsnips, avidly eaten and widely eradicated by cows, are also browsed by wild herbivores. The fetid flowers draw flies. Native Americans ate the young stems, either raw or cooked but always peeled first to remove a weak toxin that causes skin irritations in reaction to sunlight. They taste milder and sweeter than the rank odor leads you to expect. Poultices and infusions of the leaves and the purgative roots held high repute as medicines.

Cow-parsnip's three huge leaflets offer an easy way to tell it from its deadly poisonous relatives with innumerable small leaflets: water hemlock and poison-hemlock, *Cicuta douglasii* and *Conium maculatum*. Nevertheless, foragers have managed to mistake them, and paid the price; poison hemlock

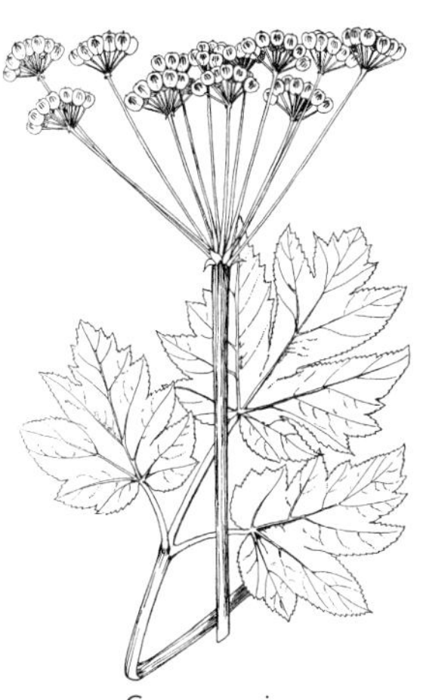
Cow-parsnip.

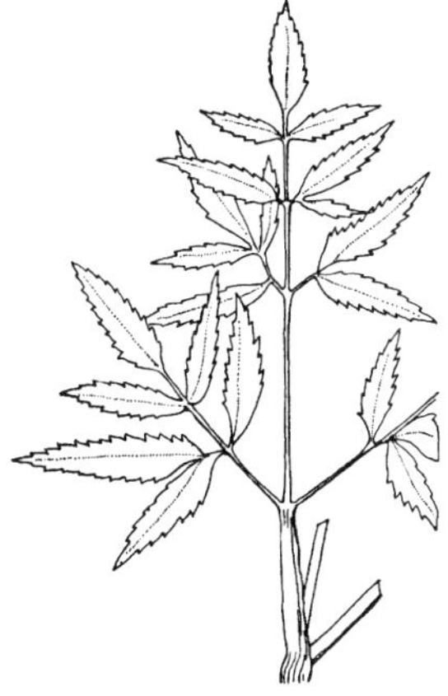
Water hemlock

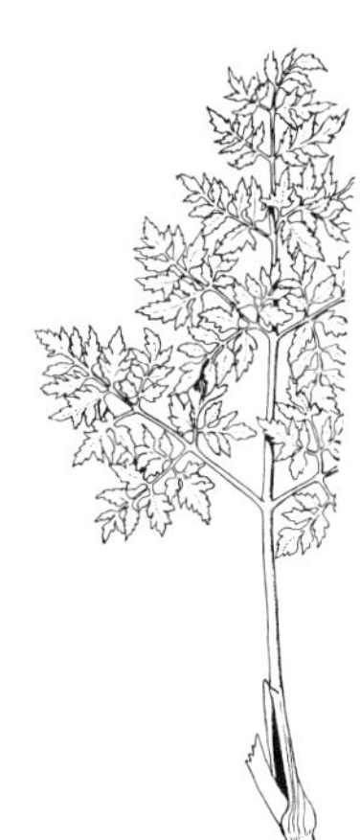
Poison hemlock

Coastal manroot

Enchanter's nightshade

causes more accidental fatal poisonings than any other wild plant. To be safe, never eat any part of any wild "carrot-topped" plant with dissected or compounded leaves.

Coastal Manroot

Marah oregana (MAR-a: bitter, biblically). Also Oregon bigroot. Flowers white, ¼–½ in. across, ♂ in racemes from leaf axils, with 1 ♀ flower at raceme base; 5 (or fairly often 6–8) spreading corolla lobes; 3 stamens; microscopic sepals; fruit green, usually spiny, egg-shaped, 1–3 in.; leaves alternate, palmate-lobed, rough-hairy, up to 8 in. long; weak-stemmed vine clambering by corkscrew-shaped tendrils. Moist open slopes; lowlands of w WA and VI, reaching a little higher in OR. Cucurbitaceae.

Colloquially called "wild cucumber," this plant is the only Northwest representative of the family of cucumbers, melons, and squash. Don't taste it. It's very bitter, and several tribes considered it poisonous. They found medicinal uses for the "big man" root, where the bitterness reaches ferocious levels. Children stuck twigs into the cucumbers to make toy animals.

HERBS: REGULAR DICOTS, WITH 2 OR 4 PETALS

Stonecrop and roseroot (p. 238) occasionally have flower parts in fours, but usually in fives in our region. There are a few monocots with flower parts in fours: skunk-cabbage and may lily (p. 163).

Enchanter's Nightshade

Circaea alpina (sir-SEE-a: of the goddess Circe) Flowers minute, white, several; 2 petals, 2 sepals, 2 stamens; leaves opposite, elongated heart-shaped, shallowly toothed or not, juicy, 1–2½ in.; 4–16 in. tall. Common (though inconspicuous) in moist forest shade. Onagraceae.

There's no record of magical use of this species in North America, nor is it related to nightshade. The names refer to myths associating the genus with Circe, the witch deity who turned Odysseus's men into beasts. "Lest the unwary be enchanted by the name," wrote Hitchcock in 1961, "it should be pointed out that it easily rates among the worst weeds among our native plants." I can't say I've had that experience either.

Willow-Herb

***Epilobium* spp.** (ep-il-OH-bium: upon pod, because the flower is on top of an ovary looking much like the pod it will become). 4 petals, 4 sepals, and 4 stamens borne at the tip of an extremely slender ovary 1–5 times as long as the petals; the ovary matures into a seedpod that splits into 4 spirally curling thin strips, releasing tiny downy seeds; leaves narrowly elliptical, all on stem, often opposite. Onagraceae.

Alpine willow-herb

Yellow willow-herb

Fireweed

Alpine willow-herb, *E. anagallidifolium* (ana-gal-id-if-OH-lium: with leaves like *Anagallis*). Also *E. alpinum*. Flowers deep or pale pink, eventually opening nearly flat, 1/4–1/2 in. across; petals 2-lobed; seedpod maroon; leaves 3/8–1 in.; plant 4–8 in. Alp/subalpine streams and seeps.

Yellow willow-herb, *E. luteum* (LOOT-ium: yellow). Flowers pale yellow, bell-shaped; petals 1/2–3/4 in. long, deeply 2-lobed, crinkly; leaves 1–3 in., fine-toothed; 8–24 in. Mid-elev to subalpine streambanks and wet meadows.

Alpine willow-herb and mountain monkeyflower often bloom together, either in or right next to ice-cold running water, as shown in the book's frontispiece.

Alpine willow-herb is one of five species that were long treated as one species, *E. alpinum*. The distinctions among the five are subtle. Deep red seedpods, which I've always loved, are noted for *E. anagallidifolium*.

Yellow willow-herb

Fireweed

***Chamerion* spp.** (ca-ME-ree-on: contraction from *Chamaenerion*, dwarf oleander). Also *Epilobium* spp. Flower/seed structures as in *Epilobium*. Onagraceae.

Fireweed, *C. angustifolium* (ang-gus-tif-OH-lium: narrow leaf). Flowers pink to purple, nearly flat, 1 1/4–2 in. across, blooming progressively upward in a tall conical raceme; leaves 3–6 in. × 3/4 in.; plant 3–8 ft. tall. Avalanche basins, recent burns, lakeshores, clearcuts, roadsides, and other sites at all elevations.

Dwarf Fireweed, *C. latifolium* (lat-if-OH-lium: wide leaf). Also river beauty, red willow-herb. Flowers deep pink to purple, nearly flat, 1–1 1/2 in.; leaves 1–2 in. × 1/2–3/4 in.; 3–16 in. tall. Mtn river bars to alpine talus, from Mt. Rainier n (OR CasR has one record, s of our range).

With its copious plumed seeds that fly in the wind, fireweed is a major invader of burns, from Northwest clearcuts to bombed urban rubble in Europe. If that makes it a "weed," so be it, but it is native, beautiful, and nutritious, and it yields to later-successional plants after a few years. Unlike many pioneer herbs, it seems to need mycorrhizal partners: lacking them, fireweed seedlings on deep Mt. St. Helens

Meriwether Lewis and William Clark

Lewis and Clark's voyage of 1804–1806 is so well known it needs no lengthy description here. Less well known is that biological discovery, not exploratory heroics, was its great distinction. After all, Alexander Mackenzie had crashed on through to the Pacific at Bella Coola in 1789, but he and others in the Northwest were interested in little but fur profits. Lewis and Clark were briefed intensively on natural history, taxidermy, and cartography before they set out, and they did their natural history well. Lewis rivals Douglas and Nuttall in the number of first collections of Western plants credited to him, and far surpassed them in writing down all he could learn about plants from the tribes he met, including results from testing their herbal medicines on his men.

The medicine Lewis personally needed was an antidepressant. Near the Continental Divide, the apex of his superlative grand adventure, he turned 32 and pondered,

> I have in all human probability now existed about half the period which I am to remain in this Sublunary world. I have as yet done but little, very little, indeed, to further the hapiness of the human race or to advance the information of the succeeding generation. I view with regret the many hours I have spent in indolence.

Not true, Meriwether!

His mysterious death just four years later may have been murder, but his friend Thomas Jefferson believed it was suicide.

Dwarf Fireweed

ash in 1981 died without flowering.

Fireweed is more abundant northward, beautifying vast areas of Alaska where trees don't grow. It was mainly northerly tribes that ate its inner stems as a staple food in spring (caution: may prove laxative). Its dwarfed (but large-flowered) version earns the name "river beauty" in the Canadian Rockies, covering miles and miles of river bars, but here its elevational range is generally too high for sizable rivers.

Farewell-to-Spring

Clarkia amoena (CLAR-kia: for William Clark, above; a-ME-na: delightful). 4 petals intense lavender to violet, with white streaking and often a carmine splotch at center; calyx shallowly 4-lobed, seemingly only 1 sepal; 8 yellow stamens; 4 cream stigmas; leaves alternate, linear, 1–2 in.; annual plant 4–32 in. tall, can be slender or much-branched. Sunny, well-drained slopes, low w-side; barely reaches BC. Onagraceae.

Farewell-to-spring

Ragged Robin

Clarkia pulchella (pool-KEL-a: most beautiful). Also pink fairies. Dramatic, unique flowers: 4 fuchsia petals each have 3 squarish lobes on a long slender base, their overall arrangement usually slightly asymmetrical; calyx bent off to one side, 4-lobed; 4 fertile stamens plus 4 stunted ones; pistil resembles a small white 4-petaled flower near the center of the 4 petals; leaves alternate, linear, 3/4–3 in.; annual plant 4–20 in. tall. Open e-side pines or sagebrush in OR and WA.

Ragged robin

Kittentails

***Synthyris* spp.** (SYNTH-er-iss: fused doors, referring to seedpod). Corolla unequally 4-lobed; 2 stamens protruding; leaves basal, 1–3 in. Plantaginaceae.

Snow queen, *S. reniformis* (ren-if-OR-mis: kidney-shaped). Corolla pale blue, 3/8 in.; several flowers in a loose raceme; leaves heart-shaped, with coarse blunt teeth; stems sprawling. Forests of w OR and sw WA.

Snow queen

Mountain kittentails, *S. missurica* (miz-oo-ric-a: of the Missouri River). Corolla blue to lavender, 3/8 in.; several flowers in a loose raceme; leaves round to kidney-shaped, with coarse blunt teeth; stems erect, up to 12 in. CGorge; otherwise e of our range.

Featherleaf kittentails, *S. pinnatifida* (pin-a-TIF-id-a: with finely cut leaves). Corolla

Snow queen

Mountain kittentails

Featherleaf kittentails

Slender toothwort

purple, 1/4 in. long; many flowers, in a dense raceme; leaves white-woolly, finely pinnate-lobed; 3–8 in. tall. Alpine, rare, in ne OlyM; otherwise well e of our range.

Snow queen has been known to bloom as early as December in mild winters.

Slender Toothwort

Cardamine nuttallii (car-DAM-in-ee: the Greek name; nut-ALL-ee-eye: for Thomas Nuttall, p. 102). Flowers pink to lilac, 1/2–1 in. across, several; stem leaves 1–3, with 3 or 5 uneven narrow lobes, purplish underneath; roundish basal leaves rise from the rhizomes separately; 4–14 in. tall. Lowlands. Brassicaceae.

Toothwort is is one of our earliest-blooming flowers, along with springbeauty (p. 250), and is called springbeauty in some books, confusingly. Springbeauty has five petals.

Lyall's Rockcress

Lyall's rockcress

Boechera lyallii (BUSH-er-a: for Tyge Böcher; lye-AH-lee-eye: for David Lyall, p. 171). Also *Arabis lyallii*. Petals 4, purple, rounded, 1/4–3/8 in.; 4 sepals, often purplish; 6 stamens; seeds in erect slender pods up to 2 in.; leaves both alternate and basal, firm, the basal ones 5/8–1 1/4 in., pointed-oblanceolate; stem leaves smaller, with 2 earlike lobes at their bases; 4–10 in. tall. Alp/subalpine dry meadows or rocks, more common e of CasCr. Brassicaceae.

Wallflower

***Erysimum* spp.** (er-ISS-im-um: ancient Greek name). Petals brilliant yellow, round, 5/8–1 in. across; flowers many, in a round-topped cluster; seedpods narrow, splitting lengthwise; leaves narrow, often shallowly

Cascade wallflower

Rough wallflower

Alpine smelowskia

toothed, most in a basal rosette, a few on the stem. Brassicaceae.

Cascade wallflower, *E. arenicola* (air-en-IC-a-la: sand dweller). Leaves 1–3 in.; plant 10–20 in. Mid-elev to alpine rocks from Mt. Rainier n, and disjunct on Saddle and Onion Mtns, OR CoastR.

Rough wallflower, *E. capitatum* (cap-it-AY-tum: flowers in heads). Also *E. asperum*. Leaves 2–5 in.; plant grayish-hairy, 16–40 in. Hot, dry grassy sites, mainly low.

Alpine Smelowskia

Smelowskia americana (smel-ow-skia: for Timotheus Smelowsky). Also *S. calycina*. Flowers cream white or purple-tinged, 3/8–3/4 in. across, several, in roundish clusters; sepals falling off as flower opens; 6 stamens; leaves crowded, basal, 1–4 in., pinnately compound or lobed, gray-fuzzy; low mat or cushion plants. Alpine in WA and BC CasR and OlyM. Brassicaceae.

A similar flower, but with its sepals persisting through flowering, would be short-fruited smelowskia, *S. ovalis*. It's in the Cascades only.

Bunchberry

Cornus unalaschkensis (COR-nus: horn; oona-lash-KEN-sis: of Unalaska, AK). Also ground-dogwood; *C. canadensis*. True flowers minute, of 4 petals, in a dense head 1/2–3/4 in. across, which is surrounded by 4 or more white bracts often mistaken for petals, each 1/2–1 in. long; berries red-orange, several, 1-seeded, 1/4 in.; leaves pointed, oval, 1–3 in., in a whorl of 6 beneath each flower head, and in whorls of 4 on flowerless stems nearby, from the rhizome; 2–8 in. Moist forest at low to mid-elevs. Cornaceae.

When you see those big white floral bracts, you can't miss the Mutt-and-Jeff resemblance between the dogwood tree and this

Bunchberry

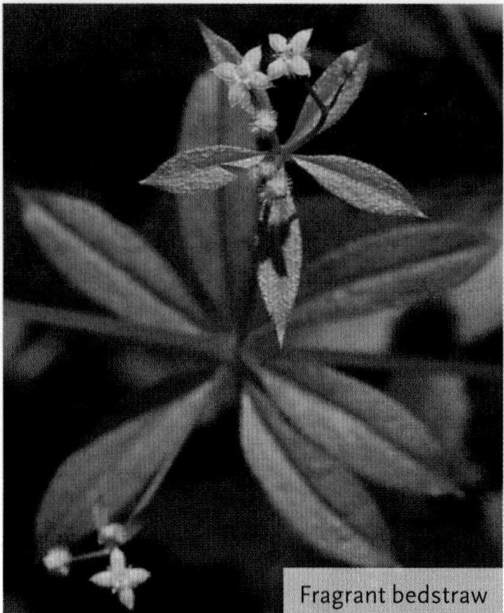
Fragrant bedstraw

6-inch subshrub. The true flowers, on the other hand, are tiny but mighty: they explode pollen into the air on spring-loaded stamens. Researchers proclaim this snap action the fastest plant motion yet measured, and call the mechanism a trebuchet, referring to a compound-action medieval catapult with a flexible strap to flick the payload. Advantages include selecting for farther-traveling pollinators (those heavy enough to trigger the explosion) and then blasting pollen onto body parts where they won't be able to eat it, but may still rub some of it onto another bunchberry flower. It also shoots some pollen up into breezes.

LEFT: Male meadow-rue flowers. RIGHT: Female meadow-rue flowers.

Fragrant Bedstraw

Galium triflorum (GAY-lium: milk—referring to old use for clabbering cheese; try-FLOR-um: 3-flowered). Corolla white, 4-lobed, flat, 1⁄8 in. across; no sepals; flowers usually in sparse threes branching from leaf axils; leaves in whorls of 5 or 6, linear to lanceolate, slightly vanilla-scented; seeds in pairs, globular, clinging to clothes with minute barbs; stems 4-angled, weak and sprawling, lined with minute bristles angled downwards. Lower forest and thickets. Rubiaceae.

Where other plants barb their fruits to cling to passing animals, bedstraw also barbs its entire stem, and breaks off at the roots. Its clinging tangles are irresistibly easy to uproot by the fistful. In days of old it was put in straw mattresses to perfume them. Several less common *Galium* species here differ in ways such as 4-leaved whorls, fuller inflorescences, less fragrance, or a more erect stature.

Western Meadow-Rue

Thalictrum occidentale (tha-LIC-trum: the Greek name; ox-i-den-TAY-lee: western). Sepals 4 (or 5), greenish, 1⁄4 in.; no petals; ♀ and ♂ flowers on separate plants, the ♂ with numerous stamens of long yellow anthers dangling loosely by purple filaments; ♀ less droopy, with several reddish pistils that mature into a starlike rosette of capsules; leaves twice- or thrice-compound; leaflets 3⁄4–1½ in., round-lobed (similar to columbine); 20–40 in. tall. Open forests to subalpine meadows. Ranunculaceae.

I often see male meadow-rues associating exclusively with other males, and females with females—an apparent inefficiency that I cannot explain.

The Blackfoot used meadow-rue seeds as both a spice and a perfume. Meadow-rues have found wide medicinal use, and some of their alkaloids have shown promise in laboratories.

Veronicas

***Veronica* spp.** (ver-ON-ic-a: from a Greek name). Also speedwell. Corolla blue-violet with yellow center, unequally 4-lobed, nearly flat, 3/8 in. across; in a small raceme; leaves opposite, lanceolate; stem 2–6 in. Alp/subalpine, in drier meadows or with heather or krummholz.

Cusick's speedwell, *V. cusickii* (cue-ZIK-ee-eye: for William Cusick). Style and stamens longer than petals; leaves crowded, 3/8–1 in.; stem 2–8 in. CasR and OlyM.

American alpine speedwell, *V. wormskjoldii* (vormsk-YOL-dee-eye: for Morten Wormskjold). Style and stamens shorter than petals; leaves scattered, 1/2–1 1/2 in.; stem 3–12 in. All but CoastR.

Cusick's speedwell

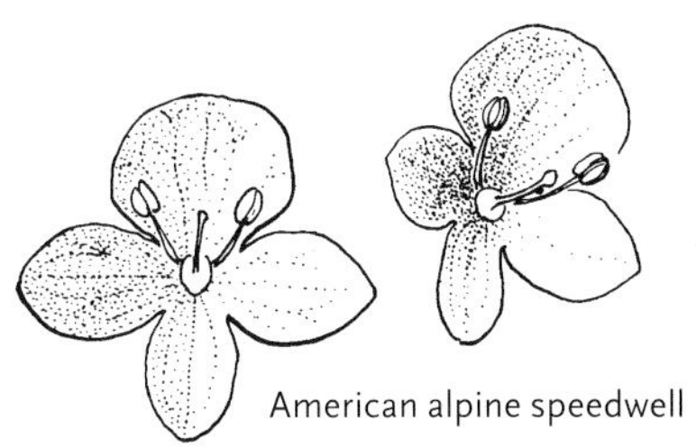
American alpine speedwell

HERBS: REGULAR DICOTS, WITH 3, 6, OR SEVERAL PETALS OR SEPALS

This is a small, oddball group of dicots, as most 3- or 6-petaled flowers are monocots (with 6 or fewer stamens, a total of 6 petals and sepals, and parallel-veined leaves). "Several" petals means a variable number between 5 and 13. Most apparently several-petaled flowers are composites (p. 188); their seeming petals are ray flowers.

Buckwheat

***Eriogonum* spp.** (airy-OG-a-num: woolly joints). Calyx 6-lobed; petals lacking; stamens 9; flowers small, many, above whorls of usually hairy bracts; leaves basal, oval, on short leafstalks, often woolly underneath. Rocky dryish places, alpine to steppes; CasR. Polygonaceae.

Dirty socks, *E. pyrolifolium* (pi-roe-lif-OH-lium: pyrola leaf). Also alpine or Shasta buckwheat. Flowers dull pinkish or off-white, reddish-fuzzy, foul-smelling; only 2 bracts below inflorescence; stems often red, 2–5 in. Commonest on pumice.

Dirty socks

Oval-leaf buckwheat

Sulphur-flower

Wild-ginger

Oval-leaf buckwheat, *E. ovalifolium* var. *nivale* (oh-val-if-OH-lium: oval leaf; niv-AY-lee: of snow). Flowers dull cream yellow, deep rose, or a mixture; leaves silvery white (scarcely at all green), tiny, densely matted; 1½–4 in. tall. Alpine from Mt. Hood n.

Sulphur-flower, *E. umbellatum* (um-bel-AY-tum: flowers in umbels). Flowers cream or reddish to bright yellow; leaves whitish beneath, often red above; 2–12 in. On Marys Peak, OR, as well as CasR.

Genus *Eriogonum* turns up frequently on lists of hosts favored by butterflies. It's one of North America's largest genera—250 species, of which around 35 grow in the Northwest. Sulphur-flower has 41 varieties. Oval-leaf, with its curly white mass of foliage, is my favorite alpine cushion plant.

Wild-Ginger

Asarum caudatum (ASS-a-rum: the Greek name; caw-DAY-tum: tailed). Calyx brownish purple, with 3 long-tailed lobes 1–3 in.; no petals; 12 stamens crowded against pistil; flower single on a prostrate short stalk; leaves heart-shaped, 2–5 in., finely hairy, spicy-aromatic, firm, persistent in winter, on hairy 2- to 8-in. leafstalks. W-side forest. Aristolochiaceae.

This odd plant is unrelated to ginger, and even the tangy fragrance isn't really close, yet its stems as a seasoning won approval from cooks of the trapping, pioneering, and wild-food-stalking eras alike. The earthbound, camouflaged flowers are less fragrant. They attract creeping and crawling pollinators.

Wild-ginger

Inside-Out Flower

Vancouveria hexandra (van-coo-VEE-ria: for George Vancouver, p. 136; hex-AN-dra: 6 stamen). Also duckfoot. Apparent petals and sepals each 6, white, sharply reflexed, ¼ in.; another 6–9 outer bracts fall off as the flower opens; 6 stamens; many flowers, mostly pendent (points down) in a very sparse panicle; leaves at least twice compound, the 9 to 27 leaflets ¾–2 in., vaguely 3-lobed; 8–20 in. W-side forests from Tacoma s—nope, nowhere near Vancouver, BC. Berberidaceae.

Inside-out flower

White Marshmarigold

Caltha leptosepala (cal-tha: goblet; by-flor-a: two flower). Also elkslip; *C. biflora*. Sepals 6–11, a few often 2-lobed, white, petallike, ½–¾ in.; petals lacking; stamens and pistils many; flowers usually 2 on a forked 3- to 10-in. stem; leaves basal on 2- to 3-in. leafstalks, kidney-shaped, 2–4 in. across, fleshy, edges scalloped, often curling. Wet places (often in streams), especially subalpine. Ranunculaceae.

White marshmarigold

Towhead Baby

Anemone occidentalis (a-NEM-a-nee: ancient Greek name for it, honoring the god Adonis under an alternate name, Na'man; ox-i-den-tay-lis: western). Also western pasqueflower; *Pulsatilla occidentalis*. Sepals 5–8, white, petallike, ½- to 1-in.; petals lacking; stamens and pistils many, styles growing to 1–2 in. and feathery as seeds mature; stem 1–2 ft., hairy, 1-flowered, with a whorl of 3 leaves at mid-height, plus larger basal leaves, all finely twice- or thrice-compound, fernlike. Subalpine meadows. Ranunculaceae.

The most strangely lovely of subalpine "flowers" is actually the seed head of this anemone. It looks like something Dr. Seuss would have dreamed up—or more traditionally, "the old man of the mountains," or a hirsute towhead. The flower attracts less attention,

Towhead baby

Towhead baby seed head

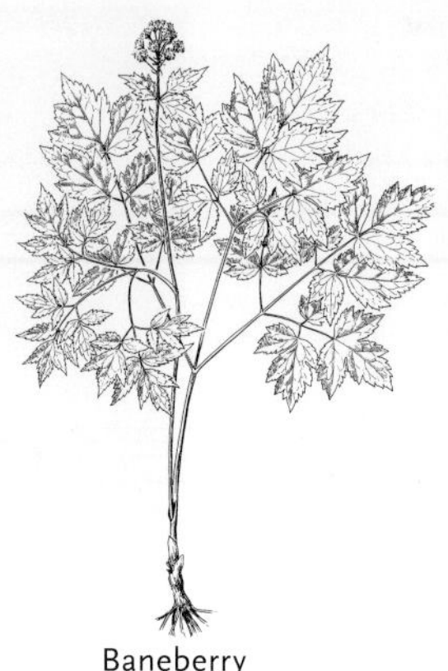
Baneberry

Baneberry

blooming early when the plant is 2–6 inches tall and lingering snow is keeping many hikers away. After the petals fall, growth of the stem, leaves, and styles takes off; the styles become plumes on the seeds, to catch the wind. Drummond's anemone, *A. drummondii,* and cutleaf anemone, *A. multifida,* are similar species mainly of the alpine zone, with much shorter, straight plumes, and sepals sometimes blue-stained on the outside.

Baneberry

Actaea rubra (ac-TEE-a: elder, for the similar leaves; ROOB-ra: red). Numerous ¼-in. white stamens are the showy part of the flower; 5–10 petals (sometimes lacking) white, smaller than the stamens; 3–5 sepals petallike but falling off as flower opens; flowers (and berries) in a roughly conical raceme; berries ⅜ in., glossy bright red, or pure white on some plants; leaves compound, 9 to 27 leaflets pointed-oval, toothed and lobed, 1–3 in.; stem 16–40 in. Low to mid-elev forests. Ranunculaceae.

Even our most toxic native berries (these) are less than deadly. A handful could render you violently ill, but the first one should be enough to start you spitting, saving your stomach the troubles.

Goldthread

***Coptis* spp.** (COP-tiss: cut—). Petals and sepals similar, each 5–8, greenish white, threadlike, ⅛–⅜ in. long; petals shorter than sepals, with a tiny gland on a broad spot near the base; stamens many; leaves

Baneberry berries

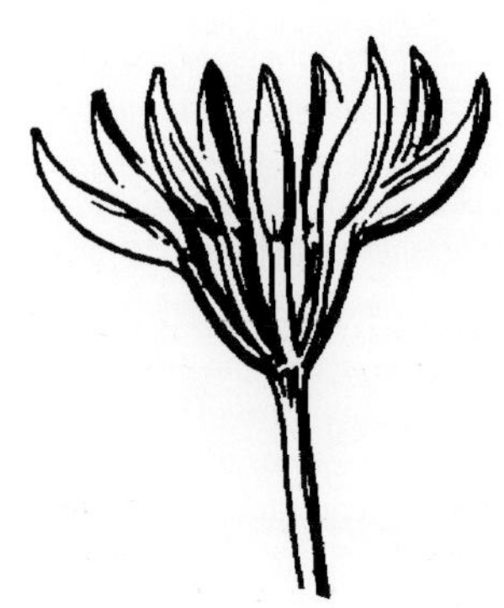
Fernleaf goldthread

Oregon goldthread

Oregon goldthread

shiny, persistent, very fernlike, at least thrice-compound, toothed, incised; roots bright yellow beneath their bark; 2–6 in. Ranunculaceae.

Fernleaf goldthread, *C. aspleniifolia* (a-splee-nee-if-OH-lia: spleenwort leaf). Flowers above leaves. Wet forest and bogs; common in BC, rare in OR CoastR and nw WA.

Oregon goldthread, *C. laciniata* (la-sin-ee-AY-ta: cutleaf). Lfeaves above flowers. Forests, w-side OR and sw WA.

Western starflower

Goldthread solutions were long used for mouth sores in both Anglo and native cultures. There do seem to be antibiotics present, but the plants should be left alone because they are not abundant and cannot survive harvest of their roots. The main active ingredients can be obtained from abundant plants, including Oregon-grape.

Western Starflower

Lysimachia latifolia (lies-im-AH-kin: loose mache; lat-if-OH-lia: broad leaf). Also *Trientalis latifolia, T. borealis.* Flowers white to pink, 1 to few, ½ in. across; petals, sepals and stamens each 5–8 (most often 6); leaves pointed-oval, 1½–4 in., lying flat in a single whorl on the stem; capsule spherical; stem 3–8 in. Forests. Primulaceae or Myrsinaceae.

Yellow Pond-Lily

Nuphar polysepala (NEW-far: from the Arabic name for it; poly-SEE-pa-la: many sepals). Also wokas. Bright yellow, heavy, waxy, roundish 1½- to 3-in. petallike sepals 4–8; smaller green outer sepals 4; true petals and stamens numerous, much alike, crowded together around the large parasol-shaped pistil; leaves heavy, waxy, elongated heart-shaped, 6–18 in., usually floating. Ponds and slow streams up to about 6 ft. deep. Nymphaeaceae.

Yellow pond-lily

Many tribes ate either the spongy rootstocks or the big hard seeds—parched, winnowed, ground up, and boiled into mush—and some still do today. Oddly, Nancy Turner's Okanogan informants said the roots were considered poisonous, while the stems could be used to alleviate toothache. Many tribes mashed the roots as a poultice to relieve pain.

Recent studies find that water-lilies are among the closest living relatives of the very first flowering plants that ever evolved.

Mountain Bog Gentian

Gentiana calycosa (jen-she-AY-na: Greek name, for King Gentius; cay-lic-OH-sa: cuplike). Also explorer gentian, who knows why. Corolla profound indigo blue, 1½ in. tall, with 4–7 shallow lobes, and fine teeth on the pleats between lobes; same number (4–7) calyx lobes and stamens; leaves opposite, oval, ½–1½ in.; stems 3–16 in., clumps. Mainly subalpine, where wet. Gentianaceae.

Of roughly 360 species of gentian worldwide, many are collected for medicines and for flavorings in bitters, liqueurs, and a soft drink, Moxie. I've seen no records of Native American use of mountain bog gentian. Thanks to it—one of the latest late bloomers—September hikes don't entirely miss the subalpine wildflower season. Leave it alone, it's fragile.

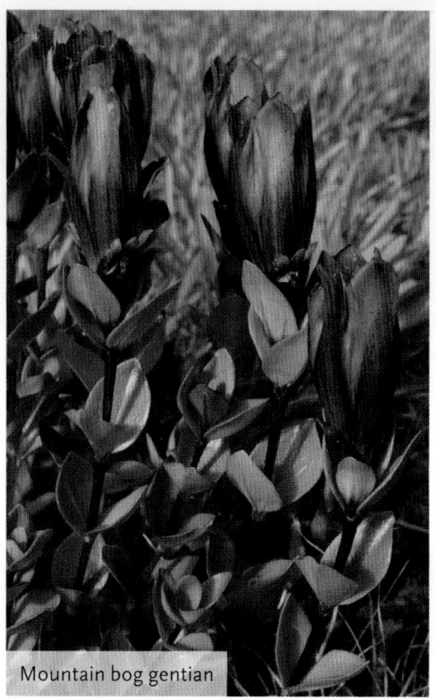
Mountain bog gentian

Bitterroot

Lewisia rediviva (lew-ISS-ia: for Meriwether Lewis, p. 262; ree-div-EYE-va: reborn). Numerous petals and equally showy sepals pink, apricot, or white; flowers 2–2¼ in. across, very low to ground, 1 per stem, in small clumps; leaves basal, linear, initially fleshy but withering often by time of flowering. Arid gravels at the eastern margins of our range. Portulacaceae.

Each spring when bitterroot was first dug, Salish and Kootenai bands held their great feast event, the First Roots ceremony. Prizing bitterroot above all plant foods, the Salish were willing to barter a horse for a full basket of roots. The root is so small and the plant so sparse that it took a few days to fill a bag. They believed they mollified the bitterness by digging bitterroot in spring when the leaves first appear; or by digging only in locales known for relatively mild roots; or by discarding the roots' cores; or by eating them after a year or two in storage.

Bitterroot

Columbia lewisia

Meriwether Lewis tried some and wrote that they "had a very bitter taste, which was naucious to my pallate, and I transfered them to the Indians who had ate them heartily." He greatly preferred the root of spring-beauty. Despite this bad first impression, he made a point, when he returned to the river known for bitterroots, of collecting specimens. That sweet Montana river became the "Bitterroot" along with the plant.

Several years later in Philadelphia, one of Lewis's dried roots got planted and watered. It sprouted green leaves and lived for some months. Privileged to name the plant for science, botanist Friedrich Pursh (p. 119) determined that it was not just a new species but a new genus, naming it for Lewis, whose life by then had come to an early and bitter end. Pursh did not state whether by combining *rediviva* ("revived") with *Lewisia* he was hinting wishfully at bringing Lewis himself back to life. More likely, *rediviva* refers to that undead dried specimen, reminding us that many plants were scientifically named by botanists who never saw them bloom gloriously in their habitat, but knew only a pressed, desiccated relic in a dim herbarium far away.

Columbia Lewisia

Lewisia columbiana Petals 7–9, almost white with fine pink veins, ranging to solid deep pink in the OR CoastR, ¼–½ in.; 2 green sepals; 5 or 6 stamens; flowers in sparse inflorescences; leaves in a basal rosette, rather fleshy, oblanceolate, 1–4 in. long; stems several, often red, 4–12 in. Alp/subalpine rocks; WA, VI, BC CasR, and rare in OR in CGorge and n CoastR.

About 7 percent of plant species, including cacti, *Lewisia* species, and many other succulents, have a nifty adaptation to drought. Plants have to open up their pores to take in carbon dioxide for photosynthesis, but they inevitably lose moisture through open pores. What if they could avoid the heat of the day and just open their pores at night? Since photosynthesis requires light, they can do that only if they take in CO_2 at night and store it until morning. These plants store it as malic acid and then quickly photosynthesize it daily.

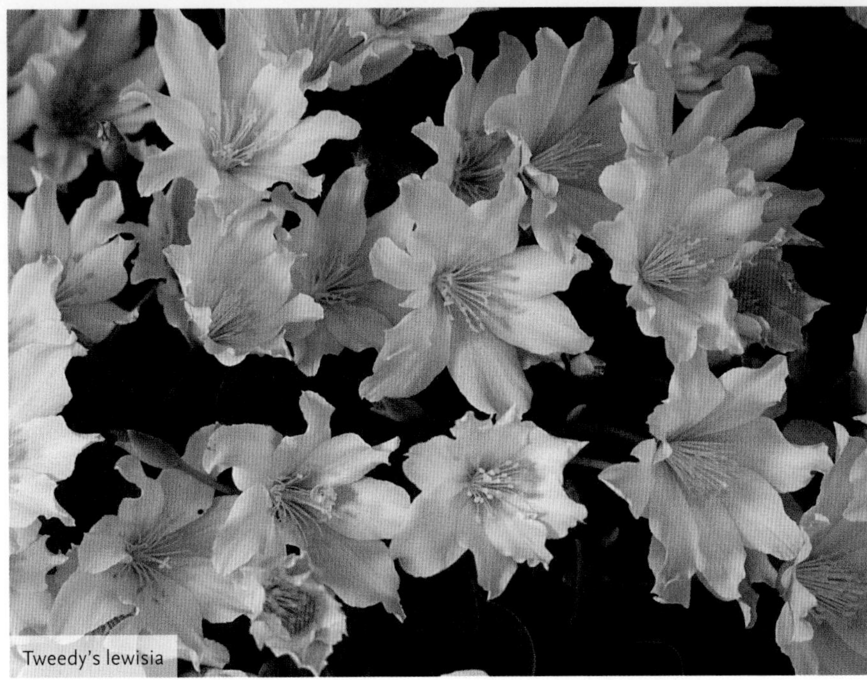
Tweedy's lewisia

Tweedy's Lewisia

Lewisiopsis tweedyi (lewis-ee-OP-sis: looks like *Lewisia*; TWEE-dee-eye: for Frank Tweedy). Also *Lewisia tweedyi*, *Cistanthe tweedyi*. Petals 7–11, ranging in a beautifully smeared fashion from white or cream to apricot and pink, 1–1¾ in. long; 2 green sepals; many orange-tipped yellow stamens; leaves basal, somewhat fleshy and heavy, blades 4–8 in., elliptic narrowing to a broad leafstalk; plants 4–10 in., in large clumps. In sun at low to mid-elevs in e WA CasR mainly in and near Wenatchee Mtns; reported also in BC CasR. Portulacaceae.

I saved the best for last.

Though you may luck out and find a great display of Tweedy's lewisia, its entire range is so restricted that its total numbers are small.

It is not overly difficult to grow in a rock garden, if provided with very well-drained sandy soil. Starts are occasionally available from native plant specialty nurseries.

After it spent a lifetime under the name *Lewisia tweedyi*, a 1990 paper moved this flower, along with the pussypaws (*Calyptridium umbellatum*), into the South American genus *Cistanthe*. The USDA list-makers, apparently liking plants in the same genus to share a common name, coined a "common" name, "Tweedy's pussypaws," that fits this Lewisia about as well as . . . as a mattress fits on a bottle of wine. In a rare display of uppitiness, the Oregon and Washington botanists did not follow *Flora of North America* in adopting the *Cistanthe* names. Even *Flora of North America* had noted that for *tweedyi* the placement is "equivocal and it might best be treated as a distinct genus." Bingo! Such a genus, *Lewisiopsis*, had in fact been published for *tweedyi* in 1999.

If they had asked me, I would have suggested *Spectaculopsis*.

FERNS, CLUBMOSSES, AND HORSETAILS

Land plants that spread by means of spores, not seeds, are traditionally divided into those with and those without vessels, the tubes that conduct water and the materials water can dissolve. Vessels are small, but their effects are large. Spore plants without vessels—mosses and liverworts—are only a few inches tall because without vessels they can't raise vital fluids any higher. With vessels, on the other hand, spore plants grew to tree size and dominated the globe during the Mesozoic era. Their modern descendants are smaller, typically 6 to 48 inches, but still larger and palpably much more robust than mosses.

Spore plants are sometimes called cryptogams ("hidden mating"). Yes, they have a sexual process, it's just less conspicuous than in seed plants with their showy flowering and fruiting. More significantly, it doesn't produce seeds capable of extended dormancy or travel. The traveling function is left up to an asexual stage in the cryptogam life cycle—a one-celled spore, more of a prototype of a pollen grain than of a seed.

In ferns, the dustlike spores are borne in and released from sori—tiny clusters appearing as dark spots, lines, or crescents in patterns on the leaf underside. In some ferns each sorus is shielded by a tiny membrane, in some others by a length of rolled-under leaf margin.

Each fern frond and its stalk from the rhizome is one leaf; it is pinnately compounded or divided into pinnae. A pinna—a unit branching directly from the central leaf stalk—may be compounded an additional one to three times.

The twelve genera of ferns below were all in one family in *Flora of the Pacific Northwest* in 1976. *Flora of Oregon* now divides them among nine families.

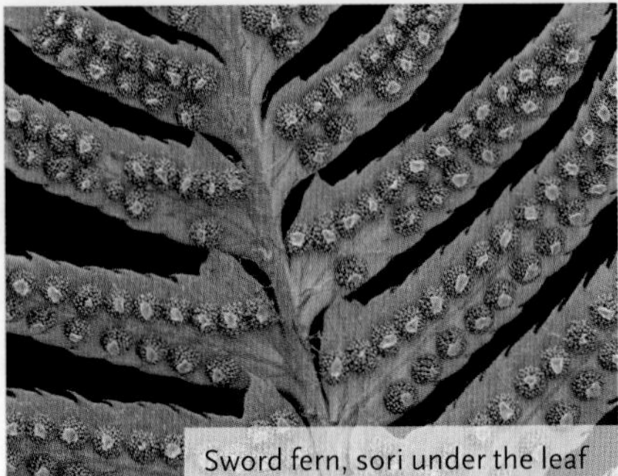
Sword fern, sori under the leaf

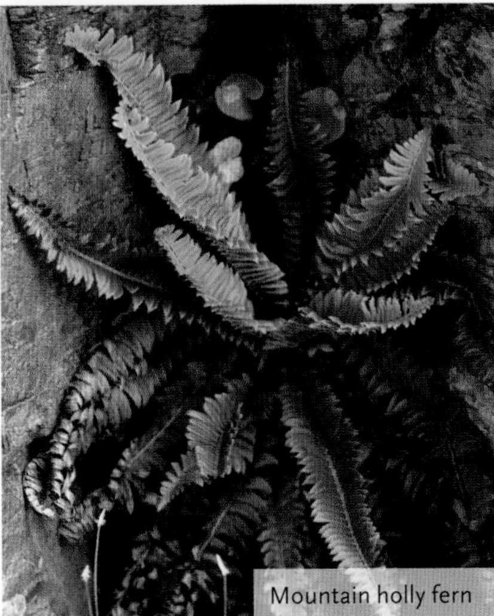
Mountain holly fern

Deer fern

FERNS: EVERGREEN

Sword Fern

Polystichum munitum (pa-LIS-tic-um: many rows; mew-NIGH-tum: armed). Leaves 20–60 in., dark, leathery, once-compound, in huge clumps; pinnae 1–5 in. long, asymmetrical at base, with an upward-pointing coarse tooth; stalks densely chaffy; sori round, with a membranous shield attached centrally. Widespread in forest; abundant in moist w-side forest. Dryopteridaceae.

Sword ferns are not favored for food or forage, but florists prefer their fronds for funerals, gathering them in great numbers with little threat to their abundance. Indians sometimes bundled them up as mattresses. Makah children made a game of peeling off as many sword fern pinnae as they could on one breath, saying *pila* ("sword fern" in Makah tongue) once for each pinna.

Sword Fern

Mountain Holly Fern

Polystichum lonchitis (lon-KITE-iss: spear—). Leaves 4–20 in., dark, leathery, once-compound, in clumps; pinnae less than 2 in. long, edged with holly-like sharp teeth, asymmetrical at base, upper edge with 1 coarse tooth; lowest pinnae triangular; sori round. Rock crevices at mid- to high elevs. Dryopteridaceae.

Deer Fern

Blechnum spicant (BLEK-num: the Greek name; SPIK-ent: spiky). Leaves 12–50 in., dark, in clumps; pinnae slender, broadening toward the base and not separated all the way to the stalk; stalks dark brown, smooth. Common in moist w-side old-growth. Blechnaceae.

Deer ferns are important winter forage for deer, elk, and cattle. The rhizomes were eaten, but not highly prized, by people. Their leaves are plainly of two types—fertile (spore-bearing) leaves, and sterile vegetative leaves. The fertile leaves are taller, and stand segregated at the center of each clump; their pinnae, narrower and more widely separated than the sterile pinnae, roll tightly around sori crowded on their undersides. The sterile leaves, which lack sori, fan out in a circle around the fertile centerpiece.

Maidenhair spleenwort

Maidenhair Spleenwort

Asplenium trichomanes (a-SPLEEN-ium: spleen—; trick-AH-ma-neez: ancient Greek name for a fern, possibly from "hair mania"). Leaves 2–10 in., dark, leathery, once-compound, in clumps; pinnae less than 5/8 in. long, oval, asymmetrically attached; 4–8 eyebrow-shaped sori; stalk reddish. Moist rock crevices at low to mid-elevs, mainly west of CasCr. Aspleniaceae

Licorice fern

Licorice Ferns

***Polypodium* spp.** (poly-POE-dium: many foot). Leaves green through winter, dark, smooth; pinnae broadening toward the base and not separated all the way to the stalk; sori exposed. Polypodiaceae.

Licorice fern, *P. glycyrrhiza* (gly-sir-EYE-za: licorice, from "sweet root"). Leaves 4–30 in.; spores in late fall and winter; stalk green, tastes licorice-sweet at least initially. Typically among mosses upon rocks or trees; w-side lowlands.

Irregular polypody

Irregular polypody, *P. amorphum* (ay-MOR-fum: misshapen). Leaves 4–12 in.; spores in summer and early fall; stalk often white-coated, tastes bitter. Rock crevices, not usually in moss mats; montane, up to 6000 ft., w of CasCr.

The flavor we call licorice occurs in many unrelated plants, including star anise, fennel or sweet anise, this fern, and licorice, *Glycyrrhiza glabra*. Worldwide, people have found this flavor and the chemical behind it, glycyrrhizin, to be good for the appetite,

Lace fern

Lace fern underside with rolled margins.

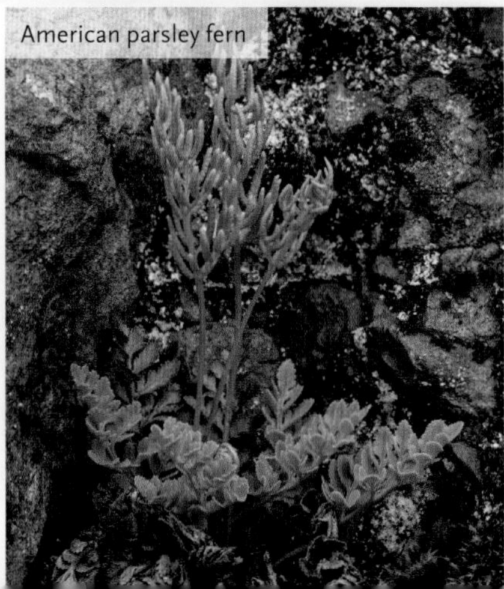
American parsley fern

the digestion, the spirits, the breath, and the dreams. In the Northwest, licorice fern rhizomes were sucked by hungry hunters or berry-pickers along the trail, or fed before meals to finicky young eaters. In quantity they may prove laxative, but the bitter edge stops most snacking before that point anyway.

Licorice ferns grow on rocks, logs, and tree trunks like maples and alders, preferably in a good bed of mosses to keep their roots moist. On all but the moistest sites here the leaves are usually less than 8 inches tall, and die back in summer when the moss mat dries out. New leaves sprout with the fall rains.

Lace Fern

Cheilanthes gracillima (kye-LANTH-eez: margin flower; gra-SIL-im-a: slenderest). Also lip fern. Leaves 3–10 in. tall, slender, evergreen, pale, at least twice-compound, in clumps; leaflets tiny, reddish-woolly underneath, with margins rolled under; upper part of stalk hairy. Rocky sites in sun. Pteridaceae.

Not all ferns are particularly moisture-demanding. The little lace fern and parsley fern are drought-tolerant, living almost exclusively in crevices of cliffs and rockpiles. Lace fern is partial to igneous rocks.

FERNS: DECIDUOUS

American Parsley Fern

Cryptogramma acrostichoides (crypto-GRAM-a: hidden lines; across-tic-OY-deez: top row—). Also *C. crispa*. Vegetative leaves 3–8 in. × 2–4 in., rather leathery, evergreen, slightly paler on back side, at least twice-compound, in clumps; fertile leaves 7 to 12 in. tall, pinnae slender, tightly rolled. Rocky sites in sun at all elevs, but mainly low. Pteridaceae.

Cascades Parsley Fern

C. cascadensis. Also *C. crispa*. Leaves 3–8 in. × 2–4 in., thin, withering in fall, same shade front and back, at least twice-compound, in clumps; fertile leaves 7 to 12 in. tall, pinnae slender, tightly rolled. Dry to fairly moist rocky sites in mountains.

Cascades parsley fern

Parsley ferns are important in pika diets. Like deer ferns, they have spore-bearing leaves very different from their vegetative leaves—twice as tall, fewer, not fine-toothed or parsley-like.

Western Maidenhair Fern

Adiantum aleuticum (ay-dee-AN-tum: not wetted; a-LEW-tic-um: of the Aleutian Islands). Leaf blades 4–16 in., fan-shaped, broader than long, twice-compound; sori under rolled edges; stalks black, shiny, wiry. Saturated soil or rocks in shade; or sunny rock crevices in serpentine soils. Pteridaceae.

Easily recognized maidenhair pinnae fan out on striking shiny black stalks that split into two slightly unequal branches. The stalks kept their dark shine well in decorative patterns in Makah and Quinault basketry. Women used infusions of this fern to enhance the sheen of black hair; yet Anglo

Western maidenhair fern

Western maidenhair fern on serpentine

sources trace the common name to the masses of fine dark root hairs.

Maidenhair fern is common in serpentine areas like the Wenatchee Mountains, where it takes a more upright, less broadly fanned form (illustrated above), and does not seem to favor wet soil or shade.

Bracken

Pteridium aquilinum (teh-RID-ium: from the Greek term for fern, derived from "feather"; ak-wil-EYE-num: eagle—). Also brake fern. Leaves 24–80 in. tall, triangular, twice- to thrice-compound, undersides fuzzy; sori under rolled edges. Widespread in part or full sun. Dennstaedtiaceae.

Bracken has the widest native distribution of any vascular plant. No fern grows taller or faster—up to 16 feet tall in Washington, at speeds of inches a day. Its best Cascade habitats are lower subalpine slope meadows annually scoured by avalanches or snow creep. It owes its success partly to "allelopathy," or secretion of chemical compounds that are somewhat toxic to other kinds of plants, and partly to vegetative reproduction, sending numerous new shoots up from the rhizomes. In some burns and clearcuts it seems able to hold off conifer reproduction for years.

Many Northwest tribes ate bracken rhizomes or young shoots, called fiddleheads. They taste like asparagus with a dash of almond extract and an unnervingly mucus-like interior. But don't eat them. If you must, try just one or two (being sure of your ID, as highly toxic monkshood shoots are slightly similar). Bracken turns out to be an ancient traditional plant food that causes cancer. A certain rare stomach cancer occurs more frequently in parts of Japan and Wales where bracken is popular. The carcinogen in bracken has been identified and proven, and is somewhat concentrated in the fiddleheads.

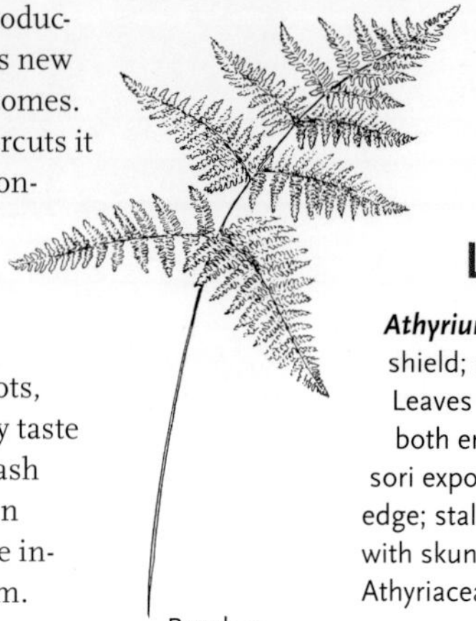

Bracken

Most fiddleheads sold as food today are lady fern or ostrich fern, which are not carcinogenic. (Ostrich fern may rarely cause stomach distress. It grows in a few spots low in the British Columbia Cascades, and eastward across Canada and into the northeast United States.) The US Forest Service still issues a few permits to gather bracken fiddleheads, and I can't rule out their appearance at a farmer's market or an Asian market.

Ranchers have long known bracken to be toxic, aside from being carcinogenic. Six hundred dry pounds of bracken consumed within a six-week period are enough to kill a horse via the enzyme thiaminase, which breaks down vitamin B_1; vitamin B_1 is the antidote. Thiaminase has the exact same effect on humans, but humans are not known to stuff down that much bracken. Additional toxins affect cattle.

Lady Fern

Athyrium filix-femina (ath-EE-rium: no shield; FIE-lix FEM-in-a: fern-woman). Leaves 16–80 in. tall, narrowing toward both ends, twice- or thrice-compound; sori exposed, or initially shielded on one edge; stalk base scaly. Wet ground, often with skunk-cabbage and devil's club. Athyriaceae.

Medieval herbalists associated the female principle with this very large fern (larger than the male fern, *Dryopteris filix-mas*, which grows east of the Cascades). They prescribed powdered roots and leaf infusions of lady fern for such diverse ailments as jaundice, gallstones, sores, hiccups, and worms; only since 1950 have male fern rhizomes fallen from pharmaceutical favor as a dewormer. Northwest tribes used both lady and male ferns medicinally, and baked the rhizomes of these and other ferns for dinner. You can cook and eat young spring shoots, called fiddleheads, after rubbing off the brown chaff.

Lady fern

The alpine lady fern, *A. alpestre*, is similar, but smaller (8–32 inches tall) and more finely incised. Common in open subalpine country, it can monopolize patches of wet talus.

Wood Fern

Dryopteris expansa (dry-OP-ter-iss: oak fern; ex-PAN-sa: broad spreading). Also shield fern; *D. austriaca*. Leaves 8–36 in. tall, broadly triangular, thrice-compound, in small clumps; sori round-shielded; stalk bases scaly. W-side forest. Dryopteridaceae.

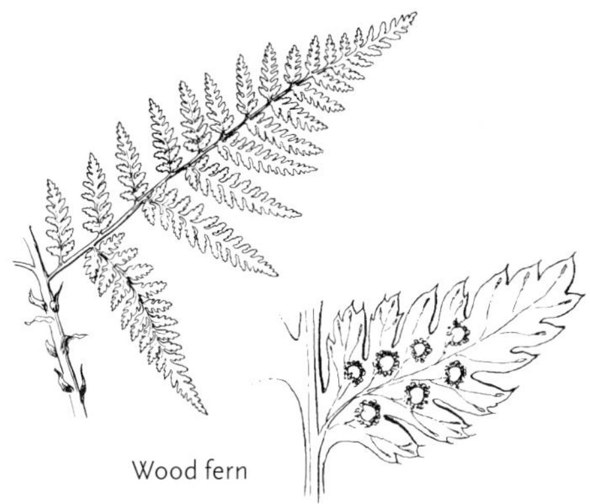
Wood fern

Indians ate wood fern rhizomes. Some said they clean the system after eating poisonous plants or red-tide shellfish. Pharmacognosies call them laxative.

Oak Fern

Gymnocarpium disjunctum (gym-no-CAR-pium: naked fruit). Also *G. dryopteris*. Leaves 6–18 in., broadly triangular, thrice-compound, rising singly from runners; sori exposed; stalks pale, slightly scaly. W-side forest. Cystopteridaceae.

Oak fern appears to have three similar leaves on each stalk. Technically, this is a single leaf with two basal pinnae, left and right, each nearly as big and as dissected as all the remaining pinnae put together.

Oak fern

Fragile fern

Fragile Fern

Cystopteris fragilis (sis-TOP-ter-iss: bladder fern, referring to sorus coverings; fra-JIL-iss: fragile). Also brittle bladderfern. Leaves 5–14 in., twice- or thrice-compound, somewhat strung out along the rhizome; sori enfolded in a membranous sheath resembling a wall sconce. Often in shady rock crevices. Cystopteridaceae.

Rocky Mountain Woodsia

Woodsia scopulina (WOODS-ia: for Joseph Woods; scop-you-LIE-na: of the Rockies). Leaves 3–14 in., twice- or thrice-compound, in clumps together with last year's broken bases; sori when first opened have starlike remnants of their membranous cover; stalks reddish brown; stalks and leaf undersides have long white hairs. Among rocks, all elevations but not abundant. Woodsiaceae.

Rocky mountain woodsia

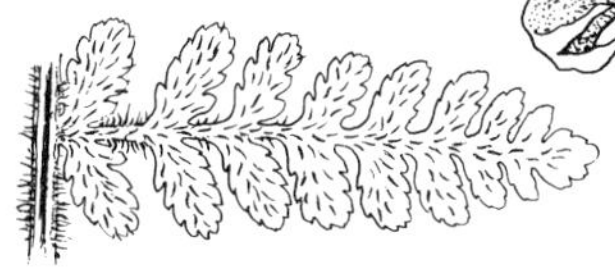

CLUBMOSSES AND HORSETAILS

Clubmosses

Lycopodium **and** ***Diphasiastrum*** **spp.** (lye-co-POE-dium: wolf foot; di-fay-zee-ASS-trum: resembling genus *Diphasium*). Also ground-pines. Mosslike plants; green leafy stems arise at many points along a horizontal runner; spore-bearing "cones" straw-colored, usually erect, often separated from green leafy stems by a slender stalk. Lycopodiaceae.

Alpine clubmoss, ***L. alpinum.*** Also *D. alpinum*. Cones 3/8–1 in., arising directly without a stalk from the leafy stem; lateral leaves curled and larger than the minute dorsal and ventral leaves. Alp/subalpine.

Alpine clubmoss

Stiff clubmoss, ***L. annotinum*** (an-o-TIE-num: of last year). Cones 5/8–1 3/8 in. tall, on unbranched 4- to 8-in. erect stems; leaves 1/4–1/2 in. (longer than other spp), shiny, rather stiff. Forest.

Running clubmoss, ***L. clavatum*** (cla-VAY-tum: club-shaped). Cones 3/4–3 in. tall, on long, often branched stalks. Forest.

Running clubmoss

Ground-cedar, ***D. complanatum*** (com-pla-NAY-tum: flattened). Also *L. complanatum*. Cones 3/8–1 1/4 in., on branched stalks; foliage flattened, cedarlike, leaves of 3 distinct shapes, in 4 linear ranks. Forest.

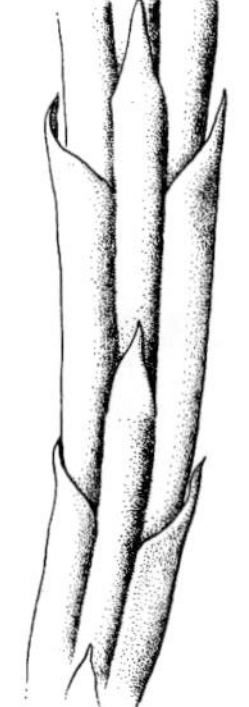

Ground-cedar

Sitka clubmoss, ***D. sitchense*** (sit-KEN-zee: of Sitka, Alaska). Also *L. sitchense*. Cones 3/8–1 in., arising without a stalk; 4 ranks of leaves much alike; in dense clumps. Alp/subalpine.

Like mosses, these fern relatives look shriveled and dead when they dry up, then quickly resurrect as soon as they're wetted.

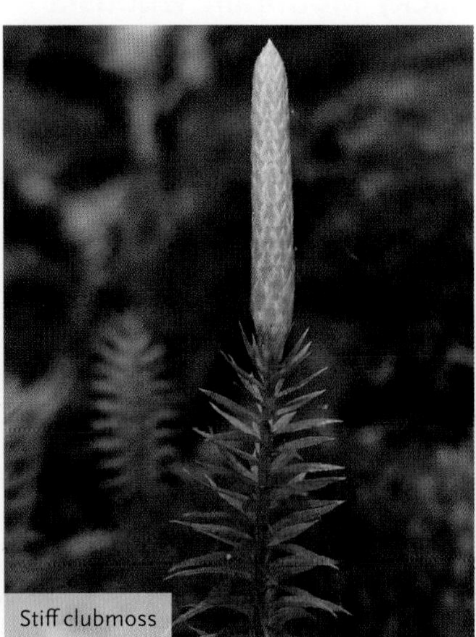

Stiff clubmoss

Sitka clubmoss

Having vessels (which mosses lack) enables their leaves to be more robust than moss leaves, so they look a bit like heather, and go unnoticed among heathers in the high country. Most species have erect fertile portions loosely termed "cones" terminating some of their branches. Cones are completely distinct from the leafy portions in clubmosses, less so in spikemosses.

Spores are extremely fine, smooth, slippery, chemically nonreactive, water-repellent, and nonclumping. You may have noticed these qualities in pollen, which descended from spores through evolution. Pollen and spores need to be water-repellent and nonclumping to maximize air travel in the rain. Of all plant and fungal spores, clubmoss spores are the ones that have entered commerce, partly because they're easiest to collect. The cones were cut off, dried, pounded, rubbed, and sifted to collect spores, used for centuries to dust wounds, pills, and babies' bottoms, and also as flash powder.

Oregon spikemoss

Oregon spikemoss

Spikemosses

***Selaginella* spp.** (sel-adge-in-EL-a: from the Roman name). Mosslike plants; spore-bearing portions of stems just as green and leafy as sterile portions, and not separated from them, but more neatly four-ranked and closer-packed, and often turning erect. Selaginellaceae.

Oregon spikemoss, *S. oregana* Pendent up to 6 ft. long from trees. Rainforest in CoastR, OlyM, and VI.

Douglas's spikemoss, *S. douglasii* (da-GLASS-ee-eye: for David Douglas, p. 56). Foliage flattened, resembling a more robust leafy liverwort, leaves in the dorsal or ventral and two lateral ranks differ in shape. Talus slopes, low in CGorge.

Rocky Mountain spikemoss, *S. scopulorum* (scop-you-LOR-um: of the Rocky Mtns). Also *S. densa*. Cones single; leaf color same as stem color; often forms dense mats. Rocky or dry sites, mainly alpine.

Douglas's spikemoss

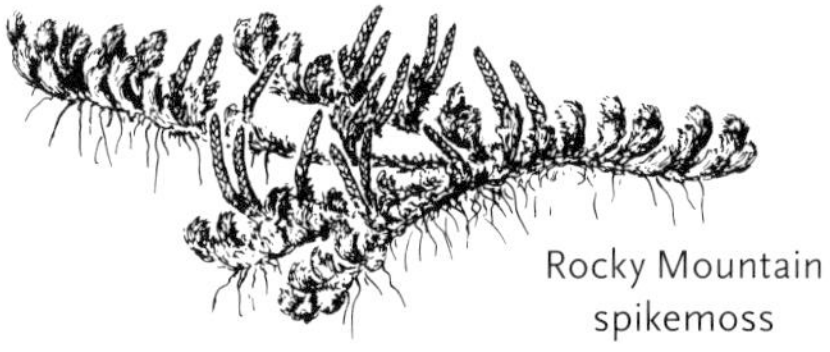
Rocky Mountain spikemoss

Wallace's spikemoss, *S. wallacei*. Cones often paired; leaf color distinct from stem color. Rocky sites, low to subalpine.

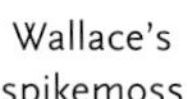

Wallace's spikemoss

Giant horsetail

Horsetail and Scouring-Rush

***Equisetum* spp.** (ek-wis-EE-tum: horse tail). Thickets of hollow vertical stems with many sheathed joints. Equisetaceae.

Common horsetail, *E. arvense* (ar-VEN-see: of fields). 1- to 3-ft. green stems of summer have jointed, wiry, whorled branches that you might mistake for leaves, and have 8–10 shallow vertical ridges; reddish tan to almost white spore-bearing stems come up in early spring, soon wither. Moist ground at all elevs; weedy on roadsides.

Giant horsetail, *E. telmateia* (tel-ma-TIE-a: of marshes). Like common horsetail, but 2–10 ft. tall; stems have 15–40 shallow ridges. Forms colonies on marshy ground or roadsides, w-side, mainly low-elev.

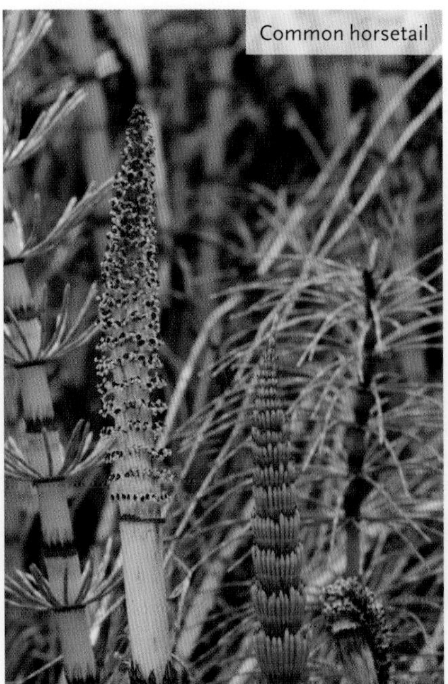

Common horsetail

Marsh horsetail, *E. palustre* (pa-LUS-tree: of marshes). All stems branched and green (but die back in winter); main stems and some branches bear blunt-tipped spore cones in summer. In shallow water, low to subalpine.

Scouring-rush, *E. hyemale* (hi-em-AY-lee: of winter). Stems evergreen, unbranched, 1/8–1/2 in. thick × 1–5 ft. tall; cones sharp-pointed. Wet ground, low to mid-elevs. (Smaller *E. variegatum* is low to alpine in WA and BC.)

Marsh horsetail

Long ignored as primitive, common, and monochromatic, horsetails won their hour of glory for sending the first green shoots up through Mt. St. Helens' debris of May 1980. They can crack their way up through an inch of asphalt on highway shoulders. No wonder Quileute swimmers felt strong after scrubbing themselves with horsetails! And some Northwest gardeners feel weak after weeding them.

Leaves on *Equisetum* are reduced to sheaths made up of fused whorls of leaves, often straw-colored, growing from nodes at

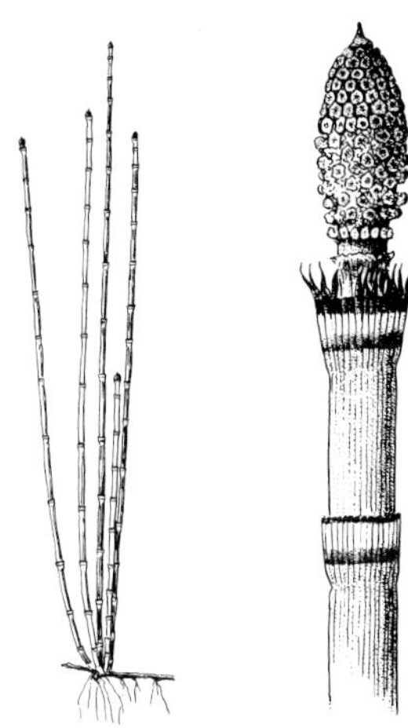
Scouring-rush

regular intervals along the stem. On horsetails, whorls of slender green branches grow just below the leaf sheaths, from the same nodes, producing a bottlebrush shape. The branches themselves have little nodes and sometimes little branchlets.

Northwest Indians eagerly ate the new fertile shoots and heads of common and giant horsetail—spring's first fresh vegetable, succulent beneath the fibrous skins that were peeled or spat out.

Scouring-rushes and some horsetails have been picked worldwide for scouring and sanding thanks to silica-hardened gritty bumps on their skins. Northwest cultures report using them to polish arrow shafts, canoes, and fingernails.

MOSSES AND LIVERWORTS

These spore-bearing plants lack vessels, leaving them with little ability to conduct water and dissolved nutrients up into their tissues; in many of them conduction takes place mainly along the outside of their stems, aided by surface tension. They compensate with an ability to pass water through their leaf surfaces—either in or out—almost instantly. After a few dry days in the sun, a bed of moss may be grayish, shriveled, and brittle, and look quite dead. But let a little dew or drizzle fall on it, or a little water from your bottle, and see how the leaves revive before your very eyes, softening, stretching out, and turning bright green. In freezing weather, they can give up their free moisture to crystallize on their surface rather than inside, where it would rupture cells.

Lichens (p. 322) share many of these characteristics with mosses and liverworts, and may lead similar lives. All three abound on trees and rocks, undergoing countless alternations between their dried-out and their moist, photosynthetically active states. When growing as epiphytes ("upon-plants"), they use a plant to hold them up off the ground, but draw little or no material out of it.

Mosses that grow on the forest floor stake out a seasonal niche, living their active season in spring and (where there's no snowpack) winter. Quick recovery from morning frost is essential. By late spring these mosses are so heavily shaded by leaves above them that they must go nearly dormant until fall.

The sexual life cycles of spore-bearing plants evolved before those of seed plants, and are more primitive, but not simpler; they're so complex and varied that I won't even attempt to describe them. Many mosses and liverwort species propagate vegetatively from fragments much more often than from spores. Some produce multicelled asexual propagules called gemmae just for this purpose. In mosses (as well as many seed plants) life in arctic and alpine zones often entails virtually abandoning sexual reproduction in favor of cloning, either vegetative or by unfertilized spore or seed formation.

The "fruits" of mosses are spore capsules, usually borne on slender fruiting stalks. To release spores, most open at the tip after shedding first an outer cap, the calyptra, and later an inner lid, the operculum. Most keys to the mosses first separate two primitive families, Sphagnaceae and Andreaeaceae, with spore capsules that don't fit that description at all, and then divide the remainder into two growth forms based on where on the stem the fruiting stalks sprout: fruiting from the tip of the leafy shoot, and typically growing upright in crowded masses or small tufts; or fruiting from midpoints along the year's new leafy shoot, which typically arches, trails, or hangs.

Season of fruiting varies with species, but usually lasts several months. Positive identification of most mosses requires not only fruiting specimens but also a microscope and a technical key. The following pages offer tentative identifications of a few common species, with or without the help of a 10× or 12× magnifying glass or monocular. A basic magnifying glass doesn't cost much, and the plant forms it reveals are gorgeous.

MOSSES: UPRIGHT, FRUITING AT THE TIP

Haircap Moss

Family Polytrichaceae Stems wiry, rarely branched, vertical, in dense colonies; leaves ⅜ in. average, narrow, sheathing the stem at their bases; stem and stalk (or sometimes entire plant) rich reddish; capsule single, initially cloaked (except Lyall's) in a densely long-hairy cap; some plants (the ♂) tipped with flowerlike splash cups.

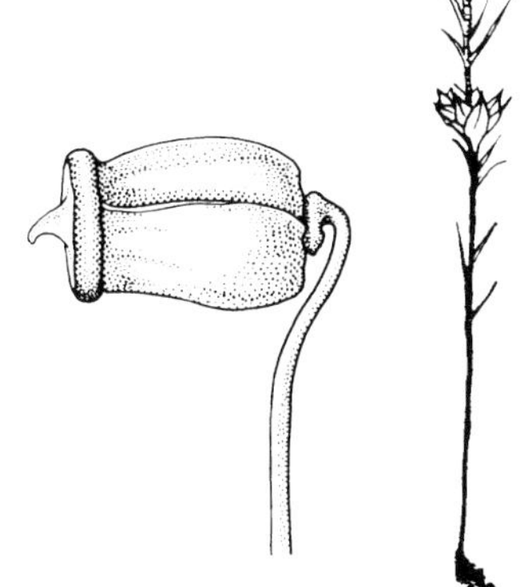

Common haircap moss, *Polytrichum commune* (pa-LIT-ric-um: many hairs; com-MEW-nee: common). Leaves often arched, toothed (under 10× lens); leafy shoots 2–6 in. tall (rarely up to 18 in.) + 1½- to 4-in. fruiting stalk; capsule horizontal, 4-angled (after dropping the hairy cap). Can form large patches on organic soils in sun, e.g., bogs.

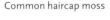

Common haircap moss

Juniper haircap moss

Juniper haircap moss, *Polytrichum juniperinum* (jew-NIP-er-eye-num). Leaves straight, often bluish, untoothed (under 10× lens), with a short reddish hair-tip; leafy shoots 1–4 in. + 1- to 3-in. fruiting stalk; capsule (after dropping the hairy cap) 4-angled; ♂ cups tan to red. Poor soils in sun; weedy on disturbed soil, abundant on St. Helens ash.

Hair-tipped haircap moss, *Polytrichum piliferum* (pil-IF-er-um: hair-bearing). Leaves untoothed, with whitish translucent hair tips; shoots just ¼–1¼ in. + ¾- to 1¼-in. stalk; ♂ stalks tipped with membranous splash cups like little flowers. Sunny rock outcrops.

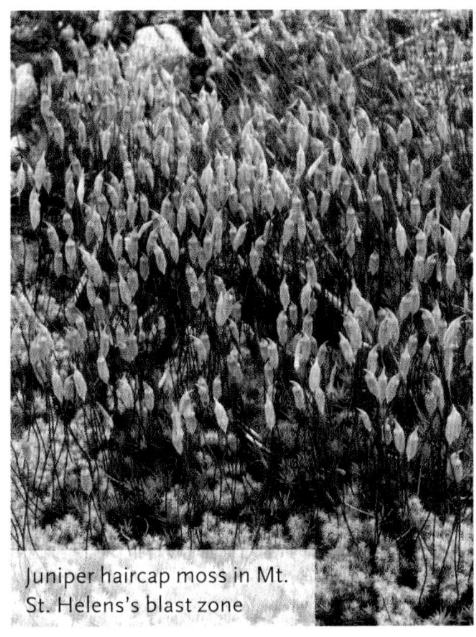

Juniper haircap moss in Mt. St. Helens's blast zone

Flowerlike male plants of hair-tipped haircap moss.

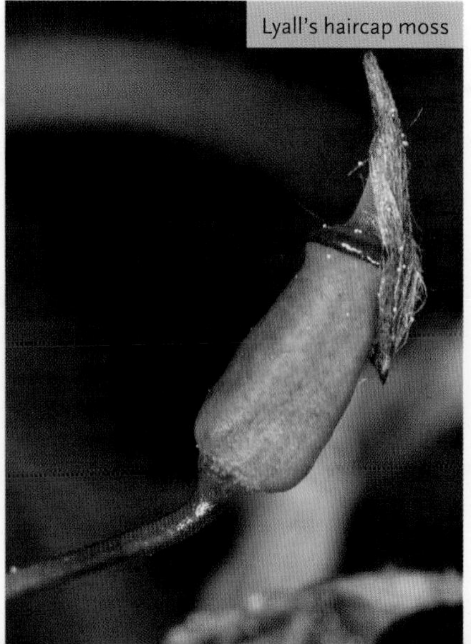

Lyall's haircap moss, *Meiotrichum lyallii* (my-OT-rick-um: less hair; lye-AH-lee-eye: for David Lyall, p. 171). Also *Polytrichadelphus lyallii.* Leaves dark green, tapered gradually, toothed near the tip (under 10× lens); shoots ½–2 in. + 1½- to 2½-in. stalk; capsule 4-angled, held horizontal, cap only sparsely short-hairy. Subalpine, abundant near black alpine sedge or alpine saxifrage; also in lowland forest.

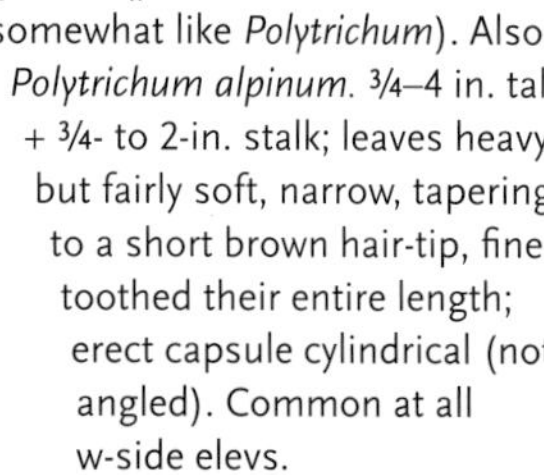

Bearded haircap moss, *Polytrichastrum alpinum* (pa-lit-ric-AST-rum: somewhat like *Polytrichum*). Also *Polytrichum alpinum.* ¾–4 in. tall + ¾- to 2-in. stalk; leaves heavy but fairly soft, narrow, tapering to a short brown hair-tip, fine-toothed their entire length; erect capsule cylindrical (not angled). Common at all w-side elevs.

Six-angled haircap moss, *Polytrichastrum sexangulare* (sex-ang-you-LAIR-ee: six angled). Also *Polytrichum sexangulare, P. norvegicum.* Leaves untoothed, blunt-tipped; shoots ½–¾ in. + ¾-in. stalk; capsule (under the hairy cap) has 5 or 6 angles. Mainly subalpine, in late-snowbed sites.

Bearded haircap moss

Haircap mosses are palpably more substantial than other mosses, almost resembling small evergreen shrubs like heather or juniper. Their stems contain some woody tissue and primitive vessels. They can even store carbohydrates in underground rhizomes, like higher plants. The leaves, too, are more complex and thicker than the translucent, one-cell-thick leaves of most mosses. Several species of haircaps have translucent leaf margins that, in drying, curl inward to protect the chlorophyllous cells. These traits generally adapt the haircaps to sunny sites, as well as to human use—the tough stems were plaited for baskets or twine, and the whole plants used for bedding. Linnaeus reported sleeping well on a haircap moss mattress on a trip to arctic Scandinavia.

Menzies' Tree Moss

Leucolepis acanthoneuron (lew-COL-ep-iss: white scale; ay-canth-o-NEW-ron: thorn vein). Also *L. menziesii.* Dark brown stem, 1½–3 in., lower stem with scattered white leaf-scales, upper stem with fine branches bearing minute deep green leaves; fruiting stalks usually 2 or 3, 1½–2 in. tall, reddish, not twisted when dry; capsules nodding, pear-shaped, smooth, sometimes colorful; ♂ plants terminate in flowerlike green rosettes. On soil, bark, or rotting logs, w-side below 3000 ft. Mniaceae.

Menzies' tree moss

Where tree mosses grow crowded together, you may need to separate one to see it as a tree with leafy horizontal branches from a vertical stem. Menzies' tree moss yields a yellow dye once used in Salish basketry. A more northerly tree-shaped moss, *Climacium dendroides,* is paler, with upswept branches and erect capsules.

Badge Moss

Plagiomnium insigne (play-gee-ohm-NYE-um: slant moss; in-SIG-nee: badge). Leafy shoots 1¼–3 in. tall, unbranched; leaves bright green, large (up to ⅜ in.) and broad, edges minutely toothed (under 10× lens), crumpling up when dry; fruiting stalks usually 3 to 6, 1–1¾ in. tall, reddish grading upward to yellow; capsules nodding, yellow, smooth; ♂ plants terminate in a "badge," a green rosette around a fuzzy disk. Logs or soil up to timberline. Mniaceae.

Badge moss

Howell's broom moss

These are some of the largest leaves you'll see on moss, but they're still just one cell thick. At 12× magnification, held up against light, their cells can be discerned.

Howell's Broom Moss

Dicranum howellii (die-CRAY-num: two head; how-EL-ee-eye: for Thomas Jefferson Howell, author of the first flora of the PNW). Also *D. scoparium.* Stems ¾–3 in., unbranched, often woolly; leaves ⅜ in., long-pointed, often all arcing sideways in the same direction; fruiting stalks single, ¾–1½ in., capsule angled upward, curving downward, maturing in spring. Logs, soil, and tree bases in moist forest. Dicranaceae.

As the capsule sheds its cap, it may look like a heron's bill. At higher elevations *D. scoparium* may join this one. The two are almost indistinguishable, and indeed E-Flora BC currently chooses not to distinguish them. Rainforest conifers often have *D. howellii* on their bases and then the similar but smaller, darker *D. fuscescens* a little higher on the trunk.

Alpine Schistidium

Schistidium apocarpum (shis-TID-ium: split—; ap-o-CAR-pum: fruiting at the top). Also common beard moss; *Grimmia apocarpa*. Tiny cushions in rock crevices, deep green when wet, drying almost black, with a silvery surface sheen from whitish translucent hair tips on the leaves; stems about ½ in.; spore capsules less than ⅛ in. tall rarely protrude above the leaf tips. Alpine rocks. Grimmiaceae.

Alpine Schistidium

Reflective whitish hair tips on moss leaves, like the silvery hairs all over some higher plants, conserve water on sunny sites by reflecting heat. In an experiment, clumps of a similar *Grimmia* with all their hair tips clipped off lost half again as much moisture in a day as the unclipped controls. Alpine rock surfaces can be ferocious habitats, surpassing 150°F on some summer afternoons.

Hoary Rock-Moss

Racomitrium lanuginosum (ray-co-MIT-rium: ragged hat; la-noo-jin-OH-sum: woolly). Also frayed-cap moss. Stems 1–3 in. in large mats, sprawling but typically erect near the tips; most leaves on short branches in 2 opposite ranks; spore capsules vertical, on ½-in. stalks that twist to the right (upward) when dry; leaves taper to whitish translucent hair tips that cast the whole mat ash-gray when dry. On rocks, abundant at lower elevs in CGorge. Grimmiaceae.

Hoary rock-moss

A similar moss on sandy soil would likely be *Niphotrichum elongatum*, formerly treated as *R. canescens*. It moved aggressively into the Mt. St. Helens blast zone, as seen in the foreground of the photo of massed juniper haircap mosses on page 287.

Shaggy Peat

Sphagnum squarrosum (SFAG-num: Greek name; squa-RO-sum: a particular way to be shaggy). Whitish-green massive spongy mats, the stems crowded, supporting each other; leaves tiny, bristling outward from the many ¼- to ¾-in. branches; fruiting stalks short, several per shoot tip, each bearing a round blackish capsule which releases spores all at once, explosively. Moist forest floor and subalpine meadows. Sphagnaceae.

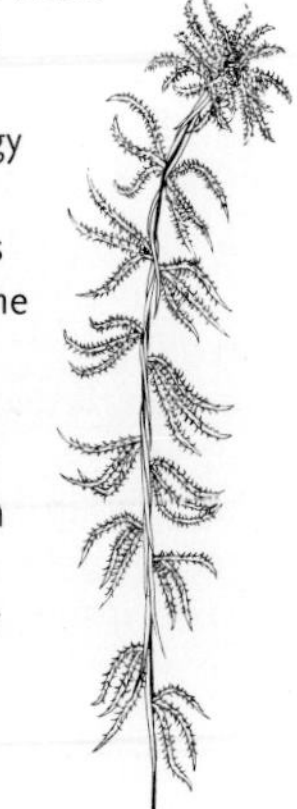

Shaggy peat

The most important mosses, both ecologically and

Shaggy peat

economically, are peat mosses. Estimates have them covering 1 percent of the earth's land—among the most extensive of all dominant plant types. They can take over by changing their environment to suit themselves and discourage others. Growing in slow-moving cold water, they draw oxygen and nutrients out of the water and replace them with hydrogen ions, creating uronic acids. The water becomes too acidic and too poor in oxygen and nutrients to support most kinds of plants. The new, peat-dominated plant community is a mire or peat bog as opposed to a non-acid fen or marsh. (Though bog peats thrive in the acids they create, they die in the sulfuric acids resulting from acid rain.)

Sphagnum species specialize. Some of them love acid, others like fens. Few grow on unsaturated forest soils—mainly this one and *S. girgensohnii*, which is also whitish green but has silky-smooth rather than bristly branches, and rarely has any black spore capsules. Some acid-loving species are pink to deep red when growing in sun; our most common red peats are *S. rubrum* at low elevations and *S. capillifolium* higher; the latter often spreads over rocks, forming mounds.

In a bog, the bacteria that normally perform decomposition duties underwater are suppressed—by cold, lack of oxygen, and antibiotics produced by the mosses. Very little decomposition takes place. The floating mass of peat moss lives and grows at the top, in the air, and dies bit by bit just below. The dead part, failing to decompose, gets thicker and thicker beneath the waterline. In some places (like western Ireland and northern Minnesota) this can go on indefinitely, the dead peat compressing and becoming a concentrated deposit of biomass suitable for fuel—the leading economic use of peat, at least historically. The ascendant use is in garden and greenhouse soils. Peat's inimitable contribution to whiskies falls in the fuel category: peat fires dry the malted barley, flavoring it with both peat and smoke.

Peat bogs are not always an ecological dead end. The peat moss surface may grow or float high enough above water to become a seedbed for dry-land plants. That's one way for glacial cirque tarns to end up as forests. Most cirques, though, have plenty of streamflow to avoid ever creating a bog: tarns silt up and turn into glorious meadows after a marshy (not boggy) transitional phase. Still, peat bogs are fairly common in our mountains.

Peat moss was an invaluable material to some Northwest tribes, especially upcoast, where *Sphagnum* muskeg bogs abound. Expectant mothers used to gather quantities of peat moss, sometimes lining the entire lodge where the baby was to be born. Its phenomenal water-absorbing capacity suited it for diapers, cradle lining, and sanitary napkins. Most tribes' languages didn't distinguish types of moss other than peat moss. Where peat moss was unavailable, other mosses were substituted for sponging, padding, and wiping.

Granite Moss

Andreaea rupestris (ahn-dray-EE-a: for G. R. Andreae; rue-PES-tris: on rocks). Also *A. rothii*. Plants brownish black even when wet (unlike schistidium; check with a few drops of water), in tight tufts usually less than 1 in. high; leaves minute; capsule hardly raised above the foliage, black, much less than 1/8 in. tall, opening by 4 lateral slits rather than at the tip. On rock (especially igneous) in full sun. Andreaeaceae.

The granite mosses are a primitive family set apart by their capsule structure and their

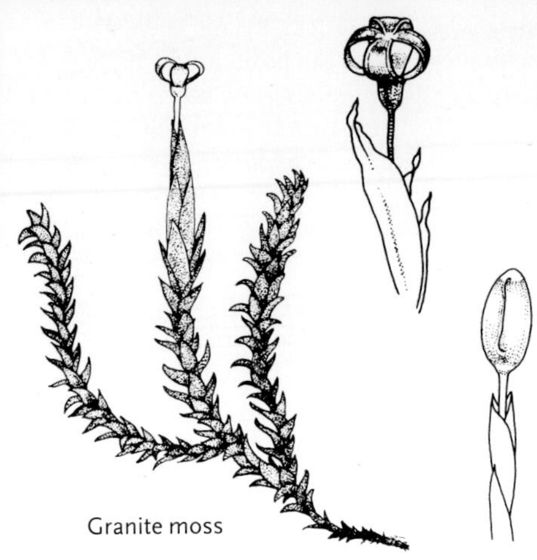
Granite moss

leaf cells. The sooty pigmentation of this odd species consists mainly of red anthocyanins on top of green chlorophylls; the former are there to protect the latter from the intense ultraviolet radiation that blasts exposed high-altitude sites.

MOSSES: SPRAWLING, FRUITING FROM MIDPOINTS

Oregon Beaked Moss

Kindbergia oregana (or-eg-AY-na: of OR). Also *Eurhynchium oreganum*. Leaves green to gold, in strands often 12 in. or longer, with branches mostly on one plane, featherlike, because branches are very close and regular; leaves 1–2 mm long; fruiting stalks ½–1 in. tall appear in late fall, the lower portion minutely roughened under 10× lens; luxuriant mats on ground, logs and tree bases below 4000 ft. on the w-side; the most abundant forest-floor moss in wetter w-side valley bottoms. Brachytheciaceae.

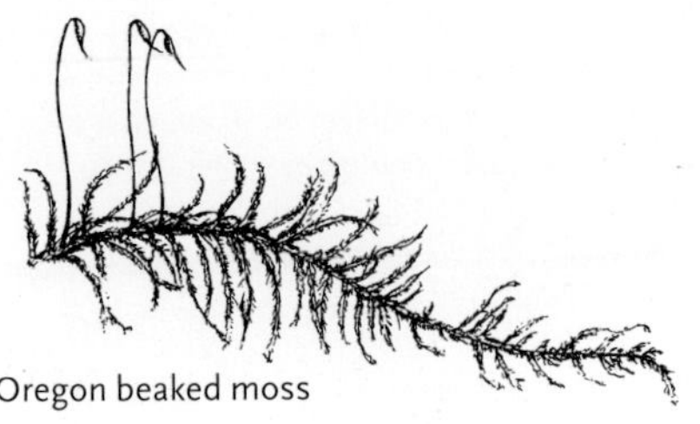
Oregon beaked moss

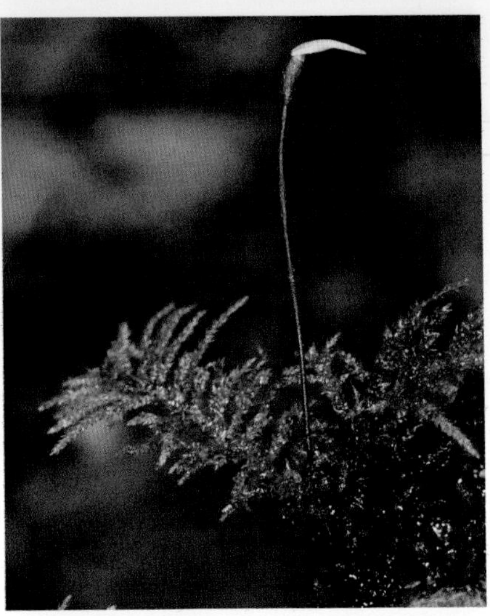
Kindbergia praelonga.

Abundance in general, and on accessible low maple branches in particular, makes these target species among moss collectors (see yellow shaggy moss, p. 294). A very similar moss common on streamside rocks is *K. praelonga* (pre-LONG-ga: elongated). Its branches are more irregular, and some are sub-branched; its leaves are smaller, up to 1 mm long.

Rope Moss

Rhytidiopsis robusta (rye-tiddy-OP-sis: like genus *Rhytidium*). Also pipe-cleaner moss. Yellow-green to brownish moss in loose mats; the strands look thick and ropy due to close-packed leaves and minimal branching; stems yellow-green; leaves ¼ in., irregularly deeply wrinkled (under lens),

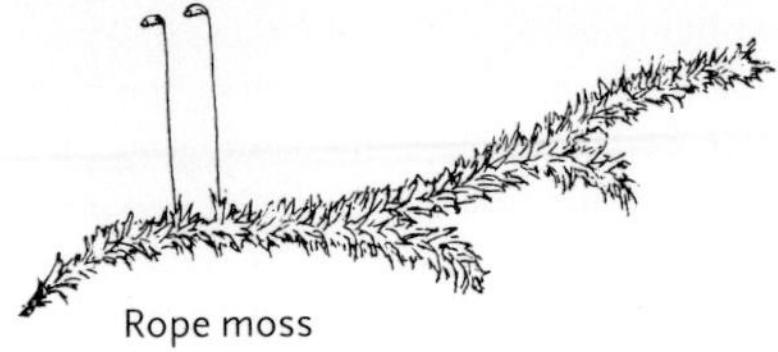
Rope moss

tending to curve all to one side of stem; fruiting stalks 1 in., red-brown; capsules often sharply crooked downward. Abundant on higher w-side forest floors; rare below 2000 ft. Hylocomiaceae.

Rope moss

Fern Moss

Hylocomium splendens (hi-lo-COE-mium: forest hair; SPLEN-denz: lustrous). Also stair-step moss. Glossy gold to brownish green mosses in a distinctive stepwise growth form—each year's growth, shaped like a tiny (1½ in.) twice-pinnate fern, rises from a midpoint on the previous year's stem, grows vertically and then bends to horizontal; specimens 10+ years are common, but only the upper 1–3 steps look very alive; fruiting stalks few, ½–1 in. tall, red, not twisted; capsules ⅛ in., horizontal; leaves minute. Luxuriant mats on rocks, logs, and earth. W-side low to mid-elevs. Hylocomiaceae.

Fern moss

This cosmopolitan moss grows in New Zealand and Africa, and is very common across the globe's boreal zone where, along with one other feather moss, it hosts nitrogen-fixing bacteria that are the mainstay of the boreal forest nitrogen cycle. Partly thanks to first grabs at the nitrogen supply, these moss mats apparently produce more biomass (per acre per year) than the trees above them.

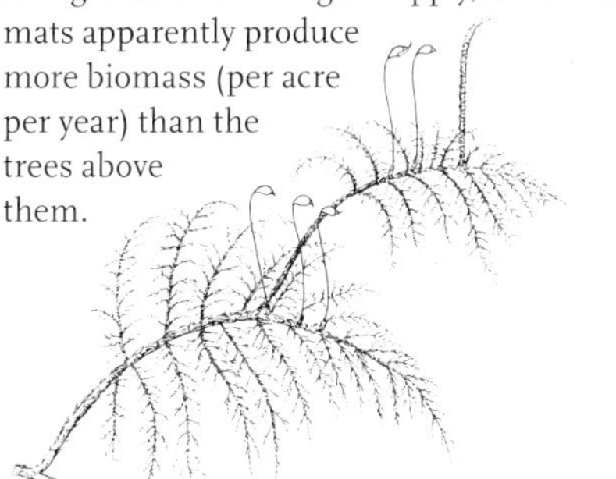
Fern moss

Wavy-leaved Cotton Moss

Buckiella undulata (bucky-Ella: for William R. Buck). Also *Plagiothecium undulatum*. Whitish-green moss in loose mats, the shoots ropy but flattened: about ¼ in. wide by less than ⅛ in. thick; leaves shiny,

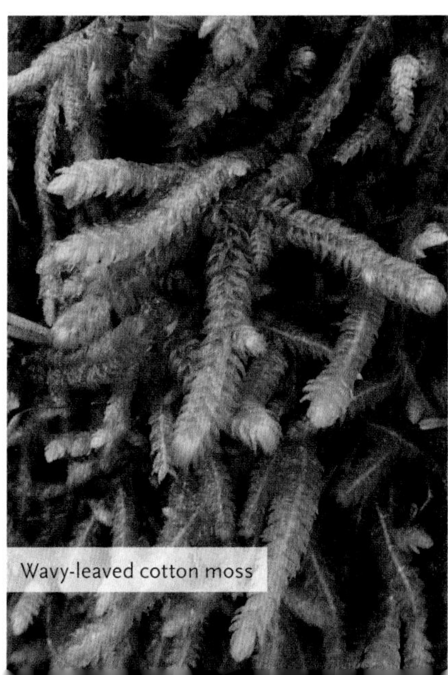
Wavy-leaved cotton moss

Aspects of Tree Trunks

According to the old saw, mosses grow on the north sides of trees. Actually they grow on the wet sides. These might well be north sides due to shade, all other things being equal—on flat terrain with trees straight as plumb lines, for example. But trees around here mostly grow on slopes, and lean downslope. Their upper sides (which would be south sides of trees on a north-facing slope) catch most of the rain and grow most of the moss.

Moist bark also favors lichens. In luxuriant habitats, however, only a few big lichens, such as the green dog lichen, can hold their own in direct competition with mosses. Better sites for lichens on these trees will likely be higher on the wet side of the trunk, and in a fringe transitional between wet and dry sides. The dry side may be coated with crust lichens, which, being easily shaded out, are last in line for good microhabitats. Stumps, buttresses, and the tops of larger limbs make outstanding microhabitats because they accumulate litter, which breaks down into humus and eventually forms soil.

Up on the tree trunks and branches, these sorts of differences determine a whole set of zones for different epiphytes; see page 328.

crinkled in crosswise waves (visible with naked eye, but a lens helps); fruiting stalks 2 in., reddish; capsules sloping, slender, grooved. Moist forest on soil, rotted wood, or alder bark. Hypnaceae.

The distinctive almost bluish white cast makes this an easy moss to spot.

Big Shaggy Moss

Rhytidiadelphus triquetrus (rye-tiddy-a-DEL-fus: brother of genus *Rhytidium*; try-KWEET-rus: 3-cornered). Also electrified cat's tail; *Hylocomiadelphus triquetrus*. Light green moss in coarse mats; stems red-brown, sprawling or partly upright; leaves triangular, 1/4 in. × 1/8 in., faintly but neatly pleated (under 12× lens), sticking out all ways from the stem for the shaggy look; fruiting stalks few, 1 in., at right angle to stem; capsule bent, maturing in autumn. Widespread on lowland humus, logs, rocks, maple trunks and limbs, mainly w-side. Hylocomiaceae.

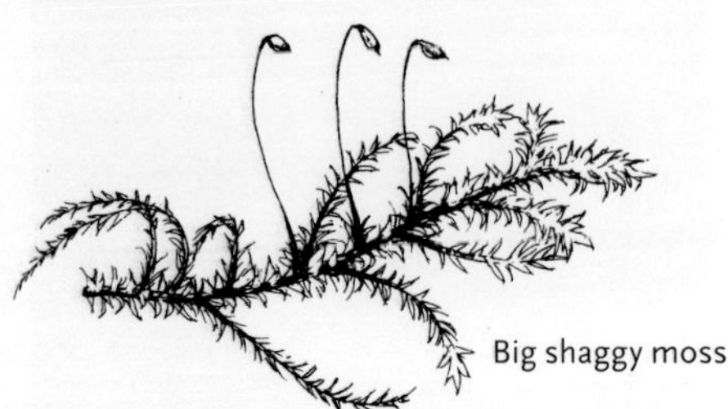

Big shaggy moss

MOSSES: SPRAWLING OR HANGING

Yellow Shaggy Moss

Rhytidiadelphus loreus (LOR-ee-us: strap). Also lanky moss. Light green, fine moss in luxuriant mats, irregularly branched or featherlike (but not as finely so as beaked moss); stems red-brown; leaves about 1/8 in., pleated near their bases (under 12× lens), curving all to one side of shoot; fruiting stalks 1½ in., capsule short and tubby, tilted, maturing in spring. Abundant in moist w-side forests on logs, trees, or humus. Hylocomiaceae.

Yellow shaggy moss turns up more than other species in bags of moss harvested for florist and nursery use. That suggests that much of the harvest is taken from logs. USFS regulations allow moss to be harvested only from branches, which would be less damaging ecologically, since moss mats on logs serve as nurseries for tree seedlings. It's hard to enforce any regulation of moss or mushroom harvests, and the science on sustainability of these resources is in its infancy. The available studies find that Northwest moss harvest levels are already several times what they should be. It takes 25 to 100 years to regrow a nice thick moss mat on a maple limb.

Douglas's Neckera

Neckera douglasii (NECK-er-a: for Noel M. J. de Necker; da-GLASS-ee-eye: for David Douglas, p. 56). Yellow-green moss with flattened shoots that first descend and then curve outward; numerous short fruiting stalks descend from near branch tips, bearing red-brown capsules; leaves rather shiny, crinkled in crosswise waves (barely visible with naked eye); dense mats on maple and other tree trunks. Lower w-side. Neckeraceae.

Douglas's neckera

Like the preceding one, this moss is heavily harvested. Similar *M. menziesii* is a darker, browner green, and its flowering stalks are so short they're hidden among the leaves.

High Branch Moss

Antitrichia curtipendula (ant-i-TRICK-ia: opposing hairs; curti-PEND-you-la: short hanging). Also hanging moss. Robust, rotund orange-green growths on rain-forest branches; some strands pendent, to 6 in.; side branches sparse, some with whiplike tips with minute root hairs; leaves 1/8 in.; fruiting stalks scarce, 3/8–1/2 in.; capsules mature in winter. On bark in w-side old-growth forest. Leucodontaceae.

High branch moss

This moss builds up huge biomass in the oldest, moistest forests, but most of that is up on canopy limbs. We don't know exactly why it waits for the forest's second century to thrive, and for the third to sixth century to really take off. We can guess that it has something to do with light coming into the middle canopy, thanks to the death of some of the taller trees, while the epiphytes themselves are making their own microclimate moister by intercepting and holding on to cloud moisture. Red tree voles and marbled murrelets both burrow into these luxuriant pillows to make their nests, which is one reason those two species are old-growth dependent.

You're most likely to see high branch moss as fragments that litter the forest floor, sometimes taking hold and growing there, but rarely flourishing. It often mixes with icicle moss; tell them apart by this one's bigger leaves, coarser branching, and less pendulous form.

Icicle Moss

Isothecium myosuroides (eye-so-THEECE-ium: equal capsules; my-o-soo-ROY-deez: mousetail-like). Also cattail moss; *I. stoloniferum.* Glossy yellow-green festoons; strands plume-like with close branches, typically pendent, often 8 in. or longer; leaves minute, straight; fruiting stalks ¼–½ in., dark red; capsules mature in winter. Moist forest; abundant on branches. Lembophyllaceae.

Icicle moss

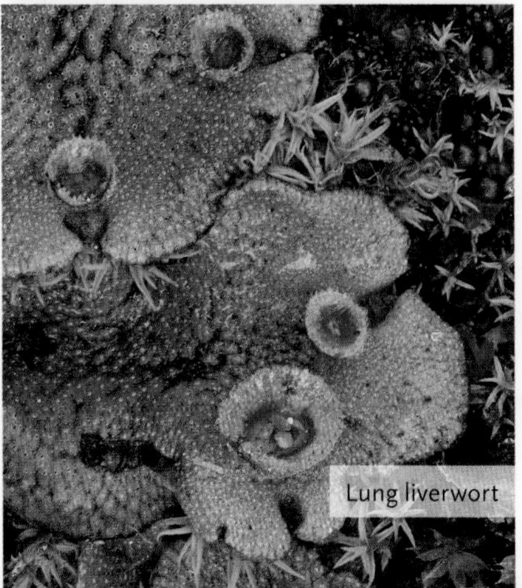

Lung liverwort

Of the long dangling plants you might think of as the "Spanish moss" in our rain forests, this is the main one that's actually a moss. Olympic rainforest festoons also include abundant Oregon spikemoss (a fern relative) and old-man's-beard (a lichen). Louisiana's Spanish moss is a seed plant in the pineapple family. (Compared to icicle moss, Oregon spikemoss has stronger stems and very uniform awl-shaped leaves.) These four organisms could hardly be less related, but all live as epiphytes. They rarely suck anything from their host trees, though they do utilize nutrients leached by dripwater from the tree's surface, and some trees actually compete with them for this resource by extending rootlets among the epiphytes on their own bark.

Curly-leaf Moss

Hypnum circinale (HIP-num: Greek name; sir-sin-AY-lee: coiled). Very fine, delicate mosses in thin waterfall-like mats most often on conifers; stems reddish; leaves minute, narrowing (under 12× lens) to slender points in long arcs (to nearly complete circles) all to one side of stem, giving the shoot a braided look; fruiting stalks ¼–½ in., not twisted when dry; capsules very short (much less than ⅛ in.), maturing in winter. Abundant low on conifer trunks, w-side below 4000 ft. Hypnaceae.

Curly-leaf moss

LIVERWORTS

Thallose Liverworts

Class Marchantiopsida Flat, leathery, green lobes textured with small pale bumps; ¾- to 4-in. fruiting stalks appear briefly in spring.

Lung liverwort, *Marchantia polymorpha* (mar-SHAHN-tia: for Nicolas Marchant;

poly-MOR-fa: many forms). 1–2½ in. long; surface often bears splash cups holding a few gemmae (vegetative propagules); short fruiting stalks umbrella-like, the ♀ ones 9-fingered. Streambanks or burned or disturbed earth.

Conehead liverwort, *Conocephalum conica* (co-no-SEF-a-lum: cone head). Our largest common liverwort, 3–8 in.; surface bumps large, close-packed, vaguely hexagonal; no splash cups; tall fruiting stalk has a conical head fringed with spherical spore capsules; menthol-aromatic when crushed. Moist earth, streambanks.

Conehead liverwort

Thallose liverworts bear no obvious resemblance to either leafy liverworts or mosses. You're more likely to confuse them with foliose lichens, but their "liver-like" surface differs from either the patternless black speckles on green dog lichens (p. 294) or the ridges of lungwort. Liverwort, lungwort, and dog lichen are all names bestowed by medieval herbalists who looked for images of body parts—God's drug prescriptions—in the plant world. The bumps that give liverworts their alleged liver texture are air chambers, each opening to the outside by a tiny pore. They offer a good environment for photosynthesis. Thallose means that the main green part of the plant is a thallus or body, as opposed to branches and leaves.

In *Conocephalum*, the female "cone head" rests on the liverwort's surface for several weeks in spring, waiting for liverwort sperms to swim to it through a film of rain or dew or in the splash of a raindrop. When the spores are ripe and weather permits, the head is raised several inches into the air in the space of a few hours by a stem of special cells that don't grow or multiply; they simply balloon lengthwise upward. This unorthodox manner of growing a stalk offers speed but not durability. You'll be lucky to ever catch one of these cute but short-lived fruitings.

Rarely do ecologists pinpoint the site requirements of a plant as confidently as Alsie Campbell describing where *Marchantia* grows on Oregon Cascade streamsides: "Occasionally a semiporous barrier will be deposited upon a slightly sloping, nonporous surface across which water seeps all year, such as a small log impeding drainage from an almost flat rock. If there is no disturbance, organic matter and extremely fine inorganic particles build up and form an aqueous muck." Campbell concluded that the *Marchantia* has "practical" importance in treacherously hiding slick footing.

Leafy Liverworts

Class Jungermanniopsida. Mosslike growths of branched, flattened ribbonlike strips of leaves neatly overlapping in 2 to 5 ranks. (You need a magnifying glass or even a microscope to see them well.) These 4 spp. mainly w-side, low to mid-elevs, rarely subalpine.

Yellow ladle liverwort, *Scapania bolanderi* (sca-PAY-nia: shovel; bo-LAN-der-eye: for Henry Bolander). Leaves minutely toothed all around (just visible under 10× lens), in 4 ranks all visible on top side, but only 2 apparent from underneath. Abundant on logs and wet sides of conifers.

Tree ruffle liverwort, *Porella navicularis* (por-EL-a: pore—; nav-ik-you-LAIR-iss: little boat, referring to leaf shape). Leaves glossy olive green, lateral ones bowl-shaped, smooth-margined; 3 additional ranks of

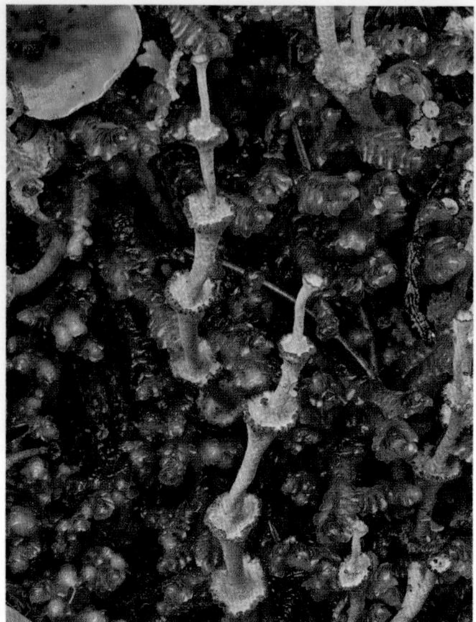

Yellow ladle liverworts surround two ladder lichen stalks.

smaller leaves underneath are visible at 20×; mild aroma and taste, in contrast to strongly peppery taste of similar *P. roellii*. Abundant on hardwoods and conifers, up to mid-canopy.

Hanging millipede liverwort, *Frullania nisquallensis* (fru-LAH-nia: for Leonardo Frullani; nis-qual-EN-sis: of the Nisqually River, WA). Also *F. tamarisci*. Plant dark red-brown (rarely green); 4 ranks of leaves are visible underneath but require at least 12×, as they're half the size of leaves in the 2 preceding spp. Vertical surfaces; especially on hardwoods in rainforest.

Hanging millipede liverwort

Little-hands liverwort, *Lepidozia reptans* (lep-id-OH-zia: scaly branches; REP-tenz: creeping). Leaves bright green, in 3 ranks, each with 3 long fingerlike lobes. On heavily rotted logs and stumps.

Little-hands liverwort

Leafy liverworts are easily mistaken for mosses at first glance, but tend to look kind of weather-beaten and flattened. Under a microscope, the foliage arrays seen are elegant, beautiful, and diagnostic of species. Whereas the spore-bearing stalks of mosses are sturdy and conspicuous several months out of the year, the watery, insubstantial stalks of liverworts are rarely seen, lasting only for a few spring or summer days.

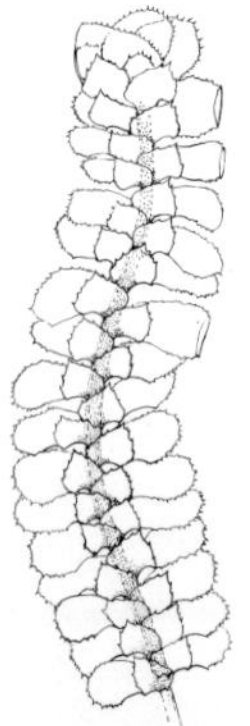

Yellow ladle liverwort

Tree ruffle liverwort

FUNGI AND LICHENS

The mushroom is not the fungus—at least not by itself. Neither is a puffball, or a shelf fungus on a tree. Each is essentially a fruit produced by a fungus organism that is many times larger and longer-lived. As an apple tree produces apples to carry its seeds, the fungus produces mushrooms or other fruiting bodies to spew spores.

A graphic illustration is provided by a "fairy ring"—a circle or partial circle of mushrooms that comes up year after year. These mushrooms are fruits of one continuous fungus body whose perimeter they mark; it expands year by year through the soil, often dying out in the center. In some years the mushrooms may fail to appear, but the fungus is still alive and growing; it merely didn't get the conditions it needed for fruiting that year. The largest fairy rings are over 600 feet across. Divided by the observed rate of growth, that yields a likely age of five to seven centuries. Still larger rings made by honey mushrooms are visible from airplanes over forests—circular dents in the canopy, consisting of sick and dying trees attacked by the fungus. Certain map lichens are calculated, extrapolating from diameter, to be 4000 years old, rivaling the oldest trees. Each of these fungal circles is a genetic individual, but can't exactly be compared with an individual as we understand the term for animals and most plants. In any case, a mushroom is not an individual. The body of the fungus is a network of tiny tubular hyphae too fine to see or handle except when they aggregate in bundles or in fruiting bodies.

A fungus is also not a plant. It's more closely related to an animal. Fungal cell walls, like insect skeletons, get their strength from chitin; they contain no cellulose, the characteristic fiber of the plant kingdom. Also in common with animals, fungi obtain their complex hydrocarbon foods from photosynthetic (green) organisms—animals by eating, fungi through any of four nutritional modes:

- **Mycorrhizal:** linking up with plant roots for exchange of nutrients and water
- **Lichenized:** enclosing and "farming" algae and cyanobacteria
- **Saprobic:** decomposing (rotting) dead organic matter
- **Parasitic:** drawing nutrition out of living plants or animals

The first two modes, embracing a majority of the multicelled fungi, are mutualistic symbioses, meaning that they commonly benefit both the fungal and the green partners in the relationship. The third and fourth modes do not benefit host plants or animals as individuals, but they certainly benefit biotic communities. Rotting is necessary for clearing away dead material, recycling nutrients, and, one might add, for keeping the world from bursting into flame due to excess plant-produced oxygen in the air. Even parasitic fungi, usually considered diseases, are often beneficial when viewed from a whole-systems point of view (see p. 314).

Some saprobic fungi could be called omnivorous, since they supplement their diet of dead things by catching live microscopic animals (p. 319).

The key point on fungus-plant relations

is that, with minor exceptions, symbiosis between them is what makes the world go around. When life first moved from the sea onto the land, it likely did so by means of partnerships between primitive fungi and algae. The algae evolved into the first plants, and plants coevolved with fungi up to the present day. About 90 percent of plant species are known to form mycorrhizae, and other mutualisms prevail among the remaining 10 percent. Sedges, for example, rarely have mycorrhizae, but are commonly infested by microscopic internal fungi called endophytes, which protect them from pathogenic microorganisms. Fungal endophytes are very common in leaves. One study found that only a single gene mutation is required to turn a pathogenic microfungus into a beneficial one.

Switching from being a plant's foe to its friend can benefit the fungus, which can live longer in a healthy host than a dying one. Conifers, the backbone of Cascadian ecosystems, work with all kinds of friendly fungi: conifers are all mycorrhizal, they're widely infested with needle endophytes, and ours are copiously festooned with lichens, many of which fix nitrogen.

FUNGI: WITH PAPER-THIN GILLS UNDER CAP

Fly Amanita

Amanita muscaria (am-a-NIGHT-a: Greek name for some fungus on Mt. Amanus; mus-CAIR-ia: of flies). Also fly agaric. Cap typically bright red; sometimes orange, yellow, or nearly white; usually sprinkled with whitish warts; stem white, with skirtlike ring near the top and a bulbous (not quite cuplike) base, which has a few slight rings, diminishing upward, just above bulb; gills and spores white. On soil, in fall.

The gorgeous fly amanita is the archetypal mushroom. Or perhaps it's the archetypal malevolent toadstool (a British word for any inedible mushroom). William Rubel and David Arora use it as a case study of the biases of field guides, which tend to err on the side of caution when it comes to mushroom toxicity (I'm guilty as charged). They consider *A. muscaria* a delicious edible, and they regularly share it with dinner guests. They concede it is toxic, but they detoxify it by boiling it in water. (Slice the mushrooms first, drain them well after boiling, discard the water, then cook the mushrooms.) I don't recommend it. Symptoms reported from the raw mushrooms include hallucinations, ataxia, hysteria, myoclonic jerking, hyperkinetic behavior, stupor, seizures, and coma. The next day, subjects often don't remember what they went through. Nevertheless, some individuals sign up for this potluck in hopes of hallucinations. There are said to have been Siberian tribes who ate them ritualistically.

The fly amanita has several close relatives with warts on the cap that are apparently more toxic (and that's before we get to the more distant relatives without warts, which are killers; next entry). Mushrooms answering the description at the top are *A. muscaria* if it's late summer or fall and the cap is bright red. The close relatives fruit in various seasons and have caps ranging from pale tan through deeply blushing yellow. *Amanita muscaria* itself may or may not also range to

Fly amanita

yellow and tan; the taxonomy is unsettled. Whatever the species, trailside specimens are a scenic resource to be left untouched.

Dogs and cats must be more sensitive: some have died from eating it. In times past, fly amanitas were left around the house in saucers of sugared milk, to kill flies—children beware! Mode of fly death may have been drowning while inebriated; no harm to flies has been verified experimentally.

Death Cap and Destroying Angel

***Amanita* spp.** Flesh, gills, and stem white; stem cylindrical or slightly smaller upward, slender, with a tattered skirtlike ring (sometimes missing) and a usually bulbous base in a white cup (requires careful excavation to see; the cup often barely emerges from ground, and may have a dirty surface); spores white; becomes fetid with age. Do not taste, no, none at all, never.

Death cap, *A. phalloides* (fal-OY-deez: phallus-like). Cap light yellow-green to tan, rarely white. Late summer and fall. Introduced from Europe, found so far mostly near cultivated filberts, chestnuts, and oaks, but may continue its spread into new habitats.

Destroying angel, *Amanita ocreata* (oc-ree-ay-ta: sheathed). Cap white. In spring.

Destroying angel

Lovely but monstrously poisonous, these are our most dangerous fungi, and they seem to be on the increase, especially in the suburbs. It's worth knowing their characteristics even though they're still uncommon here. All North American amanitas have white spores and more or less white gills. Most have a definite ring around the stem, the remnant of a partial veil that extended from the edges of the cap, sealing off the immature spores to keep them moist. More distinctively, most also emerge from a universal veil, an additional moisture barrier that wraps the entire young mushroom, from under its base to all over its cap. As a young button, each amanita fruiting body in its universal veil is egg- to pear-shaped, resembling a puffball but with the outline of cap and gills visible in cross-section. Remnants of this veil usually persist as a cup or lip around the base of the stem, or on top of the cap in the form of warts, crumbs, or broad patches. But absence of these remnants doesn't disprove any amanita, since the stem easily breaks off above the cup, and the cap crumbs can wash off.

The genus *Amanita* contains many good edible species, some of them long popular in Europe, but the chance of misidentifying a deadly one leads most American guidebooks to caution against all amanitas (and leads this guidebook away from recommending any gilled, stemmed mushrooms at all).

These amanitas and the little-brown-mushroom genus *Galerina* share one of the most insidious poisons found in nature. It attacks the liver within minutes of ingestion, but symptoms don't appear for 10 to 96 hours, by which time the liver is seriously—often mortally—damaged. As many as half of the poisonings recorded in America by these species have been fatal. Hospitals can greatly improve the odds if they know they're dealing with amanita poisoning before symptoms are advanced.

Autumn galerina

Autumn Galerina

Galerina marginata (gal-er-EYE-na: helmeted). Also *G. autumnalis.* Caps mostly ¾–1¾ in. across, slightly tacky and deep yellow-brown when wet, dull tan when dry, radially striped near the edge when moist; gills pale, becoming brown with spores; stem thin, brown, darkening toward base, with a thin whitish ring; rusty brown spores may dust the ring. Typically clustered on rotting (sometimes buried) wood, often among mosses, in late fall or sometimes spring.

This unprepossessing "LBM" (little brown mushroom) contains the same cyclopeptide poisons as the deadly amanitas, and is just as deadly. It is less of a danger because it's so small, and people don't normally bother with LBMs (unless they are hunting psilocybin mushrooms).

Short-stemmed russula

Short-Stemmed Russula and Lobster Mushroom

Russula brevipes (RUSS-you-la: red—; BREV-ip-eez: short foot). Cap 3–10 in., white, bruising brown or yellowish, dry, concave, margins initially rolled under; gills fine, crowded; spores white to cream; flesh odorless, bland to slightly peppery; stem white, cylindrical, rigid, brittle, can be snapped, leaving rough, chalk-like, fiberless broken surfaces. Mycorrhizal with conifers; often partly buried in forest duff; fall.

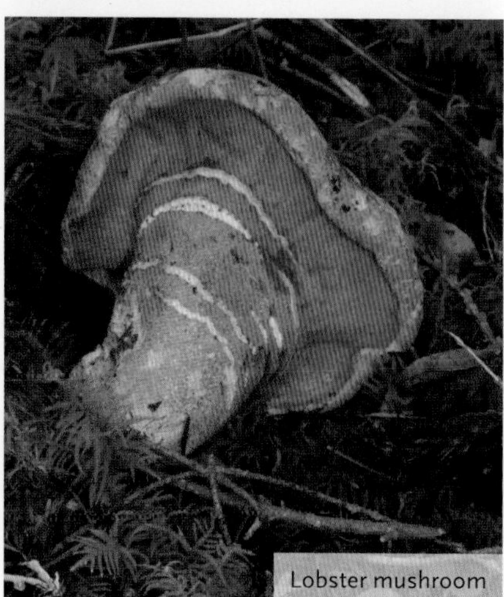
Lobster mushroom

These two species tell a charming Frog Prince story. Well, not exactly: as the mushroom morphs into the object of our desire, it turns from virginal white to enflamed and pimply. Anyway, our story begins with a rather attractive mushroom that, due to its abundance and blah flavor, was voted "most boring mushroom" at one mycophagist convention. It likes to sturdily push thick duff up from underneath, and usually has a great many crumbs on its face. It belongs to a huge and abundant genus nicknamed JARs ("just another Russula"); on several species, the pure white, brittle flesh and gills contrast with a cap skin—often quite peelable—that may be carmine red, green, or black. There are so many russulas, so few are tasty, and identification is so difficult, that many mushroom hunters don't bother to identify them.

Some russula mushrooms host a parasitic fungus, *Hypomyces lactifluorum*, inside them. Think of it as a bright orange mold. The mold prevents paper-thin gills from developing, alters the graceful form to a crude knob and the delicate, brittle flesh to spud-like firmness, and wraps the whole thing in a scurfy deep orange skin. *Voilá*, it's a marketable delicacy, a lobster mushroom.

Is it safe to eat? The host mushroom is so transformed that it can only be identified with chemical and genetic analysis. It seems to always be a species of *Russula* or *Lactarius*, and in our area usually *R. brevipes*. Toxic species occur in those genera, and cannot be ruled out; yet lobster mushrooms have a safer gastrointestinal record than lobster. They also keep longer than normal mushrooms, apparently killing or repelling bugs and rot.

Shoestring Root Rot or Honey Mushroom

Armillaria solidipes (ar-mil-AIR-ia: banded; so-LID-ip-eez: solid foot). Also *A. ostoyae*, *A. mellea*. Cap yellow-brown to brown, with coarse fibrous scales radiating from the center; gills white, stained rusty in age; stalk has stringy white pith, and a substantial, up-flaring, brown-edged ring; clustered on wood or ground, caps often coated with spores where overlapped; spores white; coarse black threadlike rhizomorphs often visible around base, or netting across nearby wood, often under bark. Fall.

Mushroom hunters know this an edible of long standing. Tree farmers know it as a deadly pathogen on trees. Some of the species live peaceably as saprobes; some become deadly parasites where the trees are stressed—in highly competitive stands, in logged and roaded regions, and during drought, which suggests that climate change could exacerbate them. Close study has found that this mushroom with many faces is actually several species. They vary in

Honey mushroom

Cautious Mushroom-Eating

A small minority of mushrooms are seriously poisonous. A greater number may make you sick in the stomach, or uncomfortable somewhere else. Still more are considered edible by most who have tried them, but their reputations are tainted by a few reports—allergic reactions, possibly. Even the supermarket mushroom, *Agaricus bisporus*, upsets some tummies. Many other mushrooms go unrecommended on the grounds of flavor or texture. Again, one person's "edible and choice" is another's "Bleccch!"

Though the odds favor mushroom eaters, the risks are extreme. There are old mushroom hunters, the saying goes, and there are bold mushroom hunters, but there are no old bold mushroom hunters. Actually, there was at least one old, bold mycologist: Captain Charles McIlvaine lived 69 years while routinely tasting mushroom species on first encounter. He claimed to have tried well over 1000 and liked most of them.

Mushroom identification is more subtle and technical than most plant identification, often requiring chemical reagents and a microscope, or even DNA sequencing. Since this book describes only a few fungi and doesn't use those tools, I restrict the "edible" recommendation to some that either lack paper-thin gills or lack a distinct stem. Each of the species I recommend can be separated from poisonous species on the basis of a careful look at field characters alone. All the same, you must assume responsibility for your own results, gastronomic and gastrointestinal.

Try a small nibble before eating a quantity. Give your stomach at least two hours to test it. The test nibble can be raw (except morels), but otherwise, cook all fungi before eating.

Eat modest quantities, of only one species, when trying any species for your first time.

Very small children are more susceptible to mushroom poisoning and allergies, and should not eat wild mushrooms.

Excessive bugginess or worminess occasionally causes stomach upset. If the stems but not the caps show larval bore holes, leave the stems behind so they won't infect the caps.

Carry in paper bags, not plastic. Keep mushrooms as cool as possible.

Deer chomp marks are not evidence of safety.

Spore color is useful for identification. Make a spore print by laying a cap flat on a piece of paper for an hour or so. Put part of the cap over inked or colored paper to make white spores visible.

Gentle, thorough sauteing, without a lid, is rarely a bad way to cook a fungus. Scrambled eggs, toast, or crackers rarely fail to complement.

pathogenicity to trees, and in flavor quality, but none are toxic to eat.

Broadly, *Armillaria* is a leading agent of white rot in wood. In ecological terms, that makes it a valuable recycler of nutrients and facilitator of animal habitats. White rot breaks down both cellulose and lignin, in contrast to brown cubical rot, which breaks down only cellulose, turning dead wood into, yes, those rotten brown cubes we often see. Quoting an unusually sensual sentence from the Forest Service tome on *Armillaria*, "the crunch of collapsing compartments of pseudosclerotial tissue when one walks on logs decayed by the fungus adds an audible dimension to its saprophytic activities."

The evolution of the first white rot fungi was a very big deal for life on earth. For 60 million years, plants ("tree ferns" in particular) had been evolving to grow much bigger and faster, thanks to using lignin; there were no organisms that could decompose lignin, so masses of lignin were accumulating, eventually getting buried and turning into coal. (That geologic period is named Carboniferous, or "coal-bearing.") The removal and burial of so much carbon was making the atmosphere very oxygen-rich, which led to ice ages and presumably would, if unchecked, have eventually caused the land biota to catch fire. The earth was fortunate that the atmospheric carbon to oxygen ratio was corrected not by a global fireball but by *arriviste* white rot fungi, ending the Carboniferous Period. (This compelling hypothesis, from 1990, was corroborated in 2012 by a molecular clock study that placed the origin of white rot acceptably close to the end of the Carboniferous at 299 million years ago.)

Getting back to our present-day fungus, the "shoestrings" in its name are black rhizomorphs—hyphae bundled in protective black sheaths that enable them to reach across inhospitable stretches in search of the next hospitable site, usually the roots of another stressed tree. They enhance *Armillaria*'s ability to spread, which seems to set a new record every time I turn around. The media anointed the honey mushroom the World's Largest Living Thing in 1992, when Michigan mycologists found a honey mushroom that spread over (or rather under) 37 acres. Not to be outdone, researchers here mapped one underlying 1500 acres near Mt. Adams, and then another across 2200 acres in eastern Oregon. We aren't talking about Godzilla mushroom caps, but about networks of tiny hyphal tubes. The researchers matched the *Armillaria* genes at widespread spots in their forest, and found that a single mushroom clone had spread across 2200 acres, all starting a couple of thousand years ago from one spore. There is every reason to doubt that all these hyphae are still interconnected. If a clone can be World's Largest Living Thing, there are doubtless larger mushroom clones in the world, and even they might not tip the scales against Pando, the 6000-ton aspen clone.

Violet Cortinarius

Cortinarius violaceus (cor-tin-AIR-ius: curtained; vye-o-LAY-see-us: violet). Cap and stem almost uniformly purple to blackish; cap 2–5 in., shiny even when dry, covered

Violet cortinarius

with fine fibrous scales; cinnamon-brown spores soon color the gills; distinctive fragrance somewhat like cedar. On ground in moist old-growth, late summer and fall.

I admire this mushroom's amazing deep color, but I can't recommend it for eating because positive identifications in this huge and risky genus are beyond the scope of this book. Several of the more than 600 species of *Cortinarius* have rusty spores and varying shades of lavender caps. The genus is named for its veil or cortina, which stretches out like a filmy curtain as the cap expands, and later leaves cobwebby remnants rather than any substantial ring on the stem.

FUNGI: WITH WRINKLES UNDER CAP

Lobster mushrooms sometimes have crude wrinkles, but are placed with their gilled host species on page 302.

Chanterelle

***Cantharellus* spp.** (canth-a-REL-us: small vase). Vase-shaped mushroom, cap not sharply distinct from stem, margin often irregular; spore-bearing surface consists of rounded ridges (not paper-thin gills) sometimes with slight cross-wrinkles, netlike; slight peppery aftertaste when raw. On soil, in fall.

White chanterelle, *C. subalbidus* (sub-AL-bid-us: almost white). Cap white, bruising yellow to (eventually) rusty orange; often very stout and short; spores white. Old-growth forest.

White chanterelle

Pacific golden chanterelle, *C. formosus* (for-MO-sus: beautiful). Also *C. cibarius.* Cap yellow-orange, smooth, underside paler; spores ochre. Most abundant under conifers 40 to 80 years old.

The chanterelle leads the Northwest's wild mushroom trade in pounds; in dollar value only morels (and, in some years past, matsutakes) surpass it. Its popularity owes much to its rich color, easy and safe identification, abundance, resistance to bugs, and the established place in French cuisine of its smaller cousin, *C. cibarius.* We used to call all our yellow chanterelles *C. cibarius;* first the Pacific Golden was separated out, and then another nearly identical species, *C. cascadensis.* It will be a while before there's definitive information on their respective distributions. All are great edibles. The one that's easy to tell apart from the others is the white chanterelle, which may be the best of the lot. The only poisonous mushroom sometimes mistaken for a chanterelle (aside from the unrelated woolly chanterelle) has paper-thin gills.

Debates continue over the sustainability of mushroom harvesting. Chanterelles

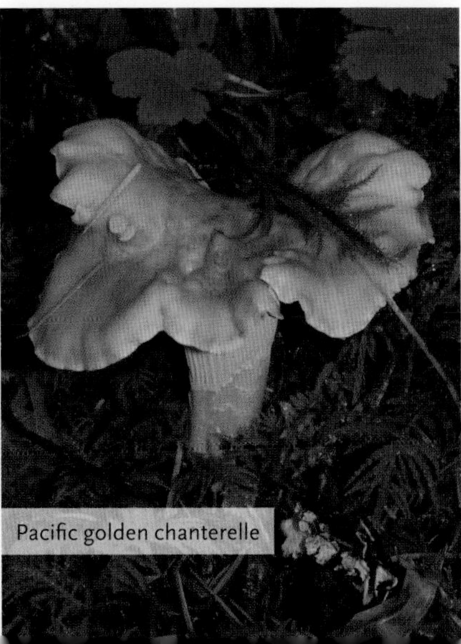

Pacific golden chanterelle

were found to fruit slightly *more* abundantly where they're harvested year after year, as of 13 years into an unpublished study by the Oregon Mycological Society in the Bull Run watershed. In the longer term, who knows? The No Worries side of the debate likes to say mushrooming is like picking the apples from an apple tree: mushrooms are the fruits, not the organism. The Worry side points out that the aboveground-fruiting fungi wouldn't have evolved to disseminate staggering numbers of spores if that didn't have significant value to them.

Woolly chanterelle

Woolly Chanterelle

Turbinellus floccosus (tur-bin-EL-us: small top; flock-OH-sus: woolly-tufted). Also scaly vase chanterelle; *Gomphus floccosus*. Orange trumpet-shaped fungus; cap undifferentiated from stem; often deeply hollow down the center; inside surface roughened with big soft scales; outside surface paler and irregularly, shallowly wrinkled (no paper-thin gills); spores ochre. On ground, late summer and fall.

Mushroom guides, over the years, batted this pretty species back and forth between the "edible" and "poisonous" lists. Let's call it "highly questionable."

Hedgehog mushroom

FUNGI: WITH FINE TEETH UNDER CAP

Hedgehog Mushroom

Hydnum repandum (HID-num: truffle; rep-AND-um: wavy-edged). Also sweet tooth mushroom; *Dentinum repandum*. Cap yellow-orange to buff or nearly white, only vaguely differentiated from stem; underside covered with fine pale teeth of mixed lengths (average ¼ in.) in lieu of gills; spores white. Mycorrhizal with Douglas-fir and other trees; on ground, summer through fall and even winter.

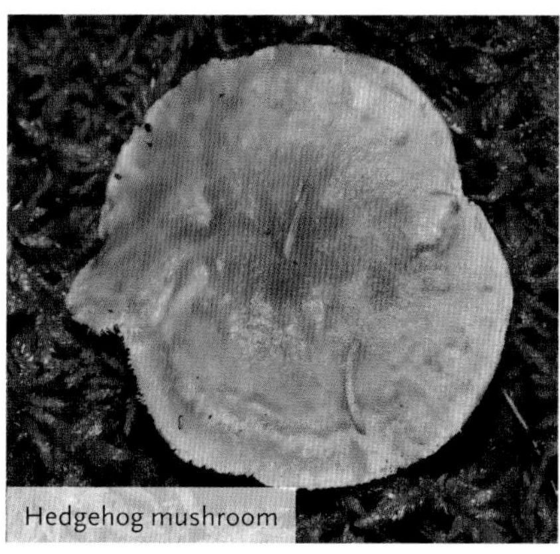
Hedgehog mushroom

Eyes scouring the ground for the soft gold of chanterelles may jump at this similar cap; fingers will be in for a surprise when they reach underneath to pluck it and find a

Cautious Bolete-Eating

Many good edibles are easily classed as boletes, members of a group that may or may not constitute a family. The defining character is a spore-bearing undersurface consisting of a spongy mass of vertical tubes. If you tear the cap, you will see that the tubes are distinct from the smooth-textured flesh above them, and can usually be peeled away. Most boletes range between choice and merely edible, and none are commonly deadly. The relatively few toxic species can be ruled out rather simply, so the rest can be eaten without necessarily identifying them to species. Boletes begin fruiting in midsummer, earlier than most edibles, and are often large, supplying good eatings from few pickings. Their main drawback is rapid susceptibility to insects, decay, and mold.

Here are the three things to avoid:

Red-orange or pinkish-tinged tube openings; this trait characterizes several moderately toxic species.

Bitter, burning, or peppery tastes, which you can check for with a tiny nibble of the cap.

Tubes that turn deep blue where handled, within a minute or two. A few species that cause stomach upset show this sharp reaction. Many good edibles may also bruise bluish, at least slowly, at least sometimes or in some of their parts, so expert Northwest mycophagists are undeterred by the blue bruising unless it is intense and quick, or the tube-mouths are at all reddish.

If the cap has a gelatinous or sticky skin, remove this. It upsets some people's bowels. You may also want to peel and discard the tubes from mature specimens, unless you're drying them.

Look closely for larval pinholes by separating the stem from the cap; you hope to find just a few. Slice through the mid-stem, and look again. A stem with few or no holes or discolorations can be eaten along with the cap. Discard buggy stems before the larvae spread into the cap. Don't expect boletes to keep longer than overnight, except perhaps clean young specimens in chilly weather or a refrigerator. Carry in paper bags, out of direct sun.

curious soft, spiny texture. Don't be disappointed—this mushroom is edible, and hard to confuse with anything poisonous. Some toothed mushrooms, however, are bitter (and turn out not to be closely related). The tiniest taste will tell you.

FUNGI: WITH A SPONGY LAYER OF CLOSE-PACKED TUBES UNDER CAP

King Bolete

Boletus edulis (bo-LEE-tus: clod; ED-you-lis: edible). Also porcini, cep, steinpilz. Cap 3–12 in. across, skin tan to red-brown,

King bolete

Admirable bolete

often redder just under surface, often bumpy, but not fibrous, sticky when fresh; flesh white, firm; pores very small, white, becoming olive to tawny yellow with age or bruising, but never blue; stem often very bulbous, white with brown skin, upper part finely net-surfaced; spores olive-brown. On soil; mycorrhizal with various conifers. Late spring to early fall.

This is as fabulous an edible as you can find. Just don't let it sit around at room temp for long, and don't eat specimens with white or mustard-colored mold.

Admirable Bolete

Boletus mirabilis (mir-AH-bi-lis: admirable). Also *Aureoboletus mirabilis, Boletellus mirabilis, Xerocomus mirabilis.* Cap 2–6 in. across, with dark red-brown skin minutely fibrous-roughened, and cream-white flesh red-stained just under the skin; tubes yellow, bruising darker yellow, not bluish; stem shaggy, streaked with the same red-brown shade as cap; spores olive-brown. Usually on rotting wood, under hemlocks; in fall.

I love the lemony taste of this bolete, which is much less heralded than the king.

Boletes are generally mycorrhizal. The admirable forms mycorrhizae with hemlock roots in rotting wood, but it doesn't do the rotting itself. An abundance of potentially mycorrhizal hyphae in rotten logs may help explain why nurse logs are the main seedbed for hemlocks here (p. 76).

Suillus

***Suillus* spp.** (sue-ILL-us: piglet, i.e., porcini).

Western painted suillus, *S. lakei* (LAKE-eye: for E. R. Lake). Cap rough with red-brown flat scales, yellow and sticky under the scales; flesh and tubes yellow, maturing orange, may bruise reddish; tubes angular and radially stretched when mature; stem has whitish ring when young; base bruises blue-green; spores brown to cinnamon. Always near Douglas-fir. Edible, tasty to some.

Hollow larch suillus, *S. cavipes* (CAV-i-peez: hollow foot). Cap dry, with reddish to

Western painted suillus

brown scales; flesh and tubes pale yellow, not bruising blue; tube mouths angular, strongly radial-arranged when mature; stem reddish-scaly below ring, smooth white and slightly narrower above ring, while the white-fibrous ring itself may disappear; stem becoming hollow; spores dark brown. Always near larches. Ranges from a good edible to mediocre or bitter.

Grainy slippery Jack, *S. granulatus* (gran-you-LAY-tus: granular, a misleading name). Cap with a tacky to slimy skin, tan to cinnamon, faintly mottled; flesh white to cream; tubes tan to yellow, very small, "dewy" in youth, staining or speckling brown with age; no veil or ring; stem white, developing brown dots or smears with age; spores cinnamon to ochre. Usually under pines, often abundant. Good edible.

Short-stem slippery Jack, *S. brevipes* (BREV-i-peez: short foot). Like *S. granulatus*, but cap starts deep red-brown and pales to ochre with age, and the short stem remains pure white except, rarely, for faint dots in great age; and pores don't stain. Choice edible.

Hollow larch suillus

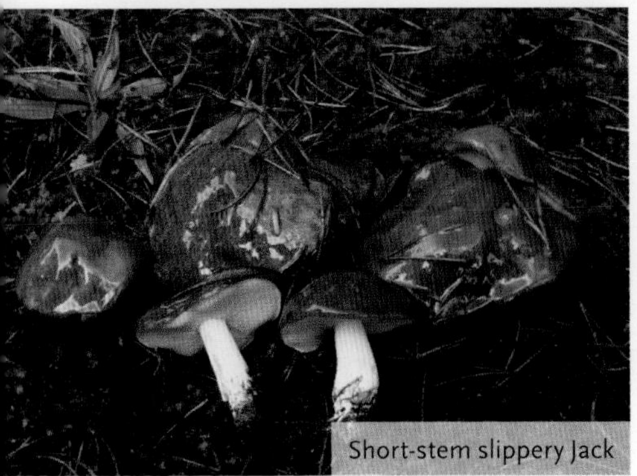
Short-stem slippery Jack

Most boletes were long placed in two large genera, *Boletus* and *Suillus*—names used by the Romans for certain mushrooms. One name derives from the Greek for "a lump of earth," which boletes sometimes resemble, and the other from the Latin for pigs, which are fond of eating them. Italians still name boletes *porcini*, little pigs.

Suillus species almost all live mycorrhizally with conifers; several require pines or larches as partners, and are common east of the Cascades. No American *Suillus* is reported as poisonous, aside from warnings about numerous allergic reactions often blamed on the skin of the cap, which can be peeled before cooking. No single field trait distinguishes *Suillus* from *Boletus*, so do check the notes on cautious eating (p. 308). Many *Suillus* have, in addition to an association with conifers, at least two of the following traits: yellow tubes; tube-mouths stretched out and aligned in a direction radial from the center; a partial veil that persists as a ring, at least for a while; a glutinous skin on the cap, slimy when wet, tacky when dry; glandular dots on at least the upper part of the stem, at maturity.

FUNGI: WITHOUT A DISTINCT CAP AND STEM

Oyster Mushroom

Pleurotus pulmonarius **and** ***P. populinus***
(ploor-OH-tus: side ear; pull-mun-AIR-ius:

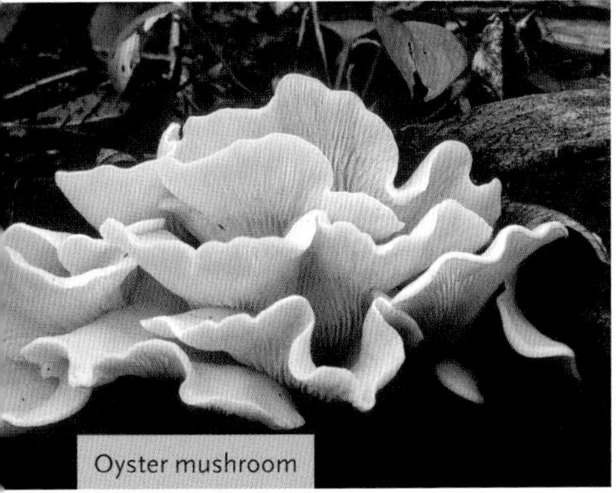

Oyster mushroom

Angel wings

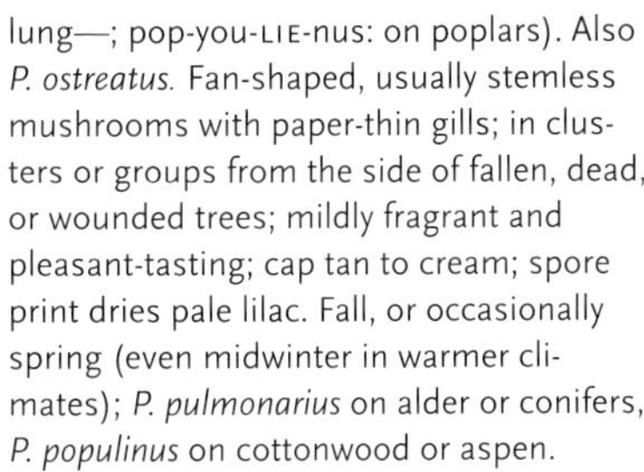

lung—; pop-you-LIE-nus: on poplars). Also *P. ostreatus*. Fan-shaped, usually stemless mushrooms with paper-thin gills; in clusters or groups from the side of fallen, dead, or wounded trees; mildly fragrant and pleasant-tasting; cap tan to cream; spore print dries pale lilac. Fall, or occasionally spring (even midwinter in warmer climates); *P. pulmonarius* on alder or conifers, *P. populinus* on cottonwood or aspen.

Carnivorous plants like Venus flytrap may be notorious, but carnivorous fungi are news. Tiny nematode worms have long been observed tunneling in mushrooms for dinner. Many saprobic fungi, it now turns out, turn the tables and "eat" their nematodes. *Pleurotus* has specialized cells that splash poison onto nematodes that touch them; hyphae then seek, invade, and digest the immobilized worm. Without nitrogen-rich foods such as animals and nitrogen-fixing soil bacteria, a saprobic diet is nitrogen-poor.

Oyster mushrooms occasionally have a short, semihorizontal stem from one edge of the cap—never from the center. But it's the stemlessness that makes oysters and angel wings the only gilled mushrooms that I can recommend for eating without more technical identification. Several undesirable species share the stemless or offcenter-stemmed habit, but can be excluded by at least one of these traits: tough, leathery, thin flesh; saw-toothed gills; yellow gills or brown spores or a dark, drab cap; intense bitter or peppery taste (take small nibbles, don't swallow).

Angel Wings

Pleurocybella porrigens (ploor-oh-si-BELL-a: a compound of two other genera; POR-i-jenz: spreading). Fan-shaped, usually stemless mushrooms with paper-thin gills; white, aging cream-colored; flesh thin; spores white; in clusters or groups on rotting wood; mildly fragrant and pleasant-tasting. Usually on hemlock logs.

If you find oysters or angel wings, search the log for more: the fungus inhabits the entire tree and tends to fruit here and there all over it. Slice them off rather than ripping them out. Tiny beetles between the gills can be knocked loose by tapping briskly.

Purple-Tipped Coral

Ramaria botrytis (ra-MAIR-ia: branched; bo-TRY-tiss: bunch of grapes). Cauliflower-like structure, the fat white bases (often clustered) more massive than the branchings on top; the blunt branch tips brownish rose to red, dulling with age; base typically submerged in duff or moss, leaving only the tips exposed; delicately fragrant; spores ochre. Under mature conifers in early fall.

This species has provided me with fine camp appetizers. Eat it in small quantities, as it is laxative for some people. Coral fungi—a large group that generally grows on

Medicinal Shrooms

Ötzi, the man who froze to death on a glacier in the Alps and was found 5200 years later, had two kinds of mushrooms in his bag. He was probably using one of them to treat his intestinal worms. We deduce that because it is one of dozens of mushrooms with specific medicinal uses that are very well known to ethnobiologists (and because he had whipworms). More recently, countless studies find cholesterol-lowering, anti-cancer, antioxidant, anti-fungal, and anti-microbial properties in various mushrooms including the cauliflower, the hedgehog, and the king bolete. Mushroom-based medicines are marketed in China, and one is officially approved in Japan, yet they remain on the alternative medicine shelf in North America. It's especially odd because fungi practically invented modern pharmacology. First there was ergot, then *Penicillium*, and it went on and on from there. Go figure.

And go eat some mushrooms. Safe ones.

the ground or on rotten wood—tend to be stomach-upsetting to varying degrees and inferior to this one in flavor.

Cauliflower Mushroom

Sparassis radicata (spar-ASS-iss: lacerated; rad-ic-AY-ta: rooted). Also *S. crispa*. Large (typically 5–24 in. across) fragrant cream-white leafy structure resembling a bowlful of ribbon noodles; spores white. On conifer stumps or trunks quite near the ground, usually in late fall.

This looks less like cauliflower than the preceding species, and more like fettucine begging for Alfredo sauce. Before that sauce, give it long slow cooking. Beauty, fragrance, size,

Purple-tipped coral

Cauliflower mushroom

and moderate rarity make this a great prize for the mushroom hunter. Smart ones carefully note the location and return a year later.

Bear's Head Tooth Fungus

Hericium abietis (her-ISH-ium: hedgehog; ay-bih-EE-tiss: of fir trees). Also coral hydnum. Large (6–12 in., or rarely up to 30 in. high × 16 in.) white to cream fungus consisting of many branches and sub-branches ending in fine teeth all pointing down; rounded overall, with crowded short branches from a massive, solid base; spores white. Saprobic on conifer logs or stumps; late summer, early fall.

Spectacular appearance puts this in the "Scenic Resource" category unless you find one well away from a trail; leave trailside specimens intact. Though popular with small mammals, it gets mixed reviews from people: fragrance and flavor are lovely, but the texture bothers some. The larger branches can be tough and hard to digest. Soak them in water to float any beetles out from the crevices, then mince and saute gently. Very similar *H. coralloides* grows on dead hardwoods.

Chicken-of-the-Woods

Laetiporus conifericola (lee-TIP-or-us: bright pores; conifer-ICK-a-la: residing on conifers). Also sulfur polypore; *L. sulphureus*. Thick, fleshy shelflike growths 2–12 in. wide, typically in large overlapping clusters; orange above, yellow below. On conifers, summer through fall (long-lasting).

Shelf fungi grow simple fruiting bodies that release spores through tiny pores on their smooth undersides. The pores are never separable from the cap flesh. Dense, rather woody flesh makes these fungi much longer-lasting than mushrooms and hence more often seen than numbers alone warrant—but it doesn't do a thing for their edibility. The one relatively tender exception is chicken-of-the-woods, a good edible when young. The texture can resemble chicken; the taste is a bit lemony. A mycophagist convention once voted it the top edible mushroom; but a 2015 mushroom book calls it too sour.

Bear's head tooth fungus

Chicken-of-the-woods

No serious toxins have been found among the shelf fungi; occasional adverse reactions to this species have been blamed on allergies, excessive consumption, or overly mature specimens. To make sure of eating it young enough, take only the outer edges, and only if your knife finds them butter-tender, lemon-yellow rather than deep orange, and fat and wavy rather than thin and corrugated. New tender margins may grow in their place. Don't cut off enough to put you in danger of overeating, and don't cut lovely shelves right by a trail.

Most shelf fungi live as heart rot in either dead or living trees. In either case the cells they attack are dead cells (only the thin outer layers of a tree trunk are live cells) so they are technically saprobes, but they kill trees indirectly by weakening them to wind breakage, and they spoil the lumber. From an ecological point of view, killing a tree here and there in the forest is beneficial: it provides habitat, lets in light, and altogether enhances plant and animal diversity.

Laminated Root Rot

Phellinus sulphurascens (fel-EYE-nus: cork—; sulfur-ASS-enz: turning yellow). Also *P. weirii*.

Laminated root rot is surely Cascadia's worst fungal disease in the eyes of the timber industry. It grows in tree roots and then up into the tree, slowly, inexorably, passing from tree to tree when the roots touch each other. After many decades, the infested tree dies, often with a bark beetle attack as the proximate cause.

The easy way to see laminated root rot is from an airplane. Look for patches where the continuous conifer canopy is broken by many smaller trees and shrubs, their colors indicating a conifer-hardwood mix. You aren't likely to see it at ground level, so we'll skip the ID characters and the illustration. It's related to chicken-of-the-woods, but it rarely produces fruiting bodies, and when it does, they're dark brown and on the undersides of rotting logs.

Laminated root rot infests at least 2 percent of west-side forest soils. It is so incurable and so inexorable in its growth that we can reasonably ask why it isn't everywhere. First, it moves very slowly. Second, it has preferences. Douglas-fir is the chief victim. Mountain hemlock and true firs are also susceptible; western hemlock less so, pines and larches still less; and hardwoods immune. So every time a fire comes along it comes to a standstill, or retreats if the post-fire stand is hardwoods or pines. It advances fastest where Douglas-fir abounds. The climate that let Doug-fir take over the Northwest arrived only 11,000 years ago. More recently, logging exacerbated root rot by increasing the proportion of Douglas-fir. Climate change exacerbating it remains a hypothesis at this point.

Though about as popular as anthrax within the timber industry, root rot is respected by forest ecologists as an agent of biodiversity. It provides refugia where species can persist that might otherwise disappear from dense conifer forest; they can spread out again after disturbances come along. In northwest California it was found to actually benefit Douglas-fir by opening gaps in the white firs. Beneficiaries include broadleaf trees and shrubs, western redcedar, and many animals. Root rot patches are ideal deer and moose habitat, richly mixing shrubs with a few tall trees. They have snags for cavity nesters, which helps the surrounding forests by keeping cavity-nesting insectivorous birds around and ready to take on pest insect outbreaks.

Dyer's Polypore

Phaeolus schweinitzii (fee-OH-lus: dusky—; SHWIGH-nit-zee-eye: for Lewis de Schweinitz). Also velvet-top fungus. Fleshy rosettes 3–16 in. across, flaring out upward from a thick central point or short stalk; bands of color initially include rich yellow or orange near margin, but darken to browns; surface woolly or velvety; underside covered with fine greenish-yellow pores; flesh soft and moist in youth, later brittle and light; resembles a shelf fungus and grows sometimes as shelves on stumps or trees, but more often from soil near its conifer host. Growing in fall, persisting to spring.

As the most common cause of heart rot in Northwest conifers, dyer's polypore is a serious pathogen, yet it isn't a terrible scourge like some diseases. It's essentially normal for trees to get heart rot if they live long enough (some species sooner than others) and then many trees live with it for a very long time. Eventually the trunk snaps.

This is one of many mushrooms and lichens that make beautiful dyes, and have been used in that way since biblical times.

Dyer's polypore

Gemmed Puffball

Lycoperdon perlatum (lie-co-PER-dun: wolf fart; per-LAY-tum: pearled). Pear-shaped or spherical fruiting bodies with neither cap, stem, nor gills; white or tinged with tan; top surface patterned with tiny pyramidal warts which can be rubbed off. On soil, usually in groups; July–October.

Gemmed puffball

The maturing puffball skin either splits open or opens a small hole at the top, and spores come puffing out by the millions, mostly when raindrops strike. Spores, like pollen, are hydrophobic or resistant to wetting, so their flight is undamped by rain or fog. Puffball spores, a hundred times smaller than fern spores and pollen grains, are barely even subject to gravity; squeeze a ripe puffball on a breezy day, and you may truly send a few spores around the world. One good-sized gemmed puffball produces around four billion spores. Native Americans used puffball spores to dress wounds; but take care not to inhale clouds of spores, which can infect the lungs.

While the puffball's puff of spores is doubtless helpful, it turns out that gilled mushrooms also manage to give their spores a lift. Constant evaporation from their moist surfaces chills the air, creating eddies that send many spores upward as soon as they fall free.

No true puffballs are poisonous to eat, but young deadly amanitas can be mistaken for them, so you must slice each puffball through its center vertically, and eat only those that are undifferentiated white inside, from tip to toe. Amanita buttons in cross-section reveal at least a faint outline of developing stem and gills. Other telltales for the discard pile would be a green-, brown-, or yellow-stained center (a puffball starting to mature into a bag of spores) or a punky center distinct from a smooth ⅛-inch outer rind (a risky *Scleroderma*). Puffballs take a couple of weeks to mature, so you stand a good chance of catching them young. They

Mycocuisine Around the World

Attitudes toward mushrooms are strikingly culture-bound. The mycophobic English traditionally regarded only species of *Agaricus* (like the supermarket mushroom) as deserving either the term "mushroom" or a place on the table. French go for truffles, morels, chanterelles, and boletes; and Slavs are eclectic, intimate with species in dicey genera like *Russula* and *Lactarius*. And then there's East Asia: leathery "tree-ears," resiny "pine mushrooms," "straw mushrooms" grown in bottles for legginess, and "black fungus" cured in brine.

Japanese prices have exceeded $200 a pound for northwest matsutakes, *Tricholoma magnivelare*. (Matsie prices seem to have peaked years ago, before China and other countries fully exploited the matsie market.) Lorelei Norvell assures us we can identify matsutakes by their "delicious" fragrance, but *Mushrooms of Northeast North America* mutters that the emperor has no clothes: "odor like dirty gym socks but usually described as spicy-sweet, aromatic, fruity, or fragrant." There may be a chance convergence between matsutake vapors and human pheromones (analogous to the one between French truffles and pig pheromones). Yes, they do smell kind of like delicious dirty gym socks. I've fed them to uninitiated eaters with results ranging from "nothing special" to "no more of those, please."

aren't for everyone: the texture is slippery where sliced, a bit rubbery within.

Warted Giant Puffball

Calbovista subsculpta (cal-bo-VIS-ta: bald foxfart; sub-SCULPT-a: somewhat sculptured). Stalkless, slightly flattened 3- to 6-in. ball, white patterned with brownish raised polygons. (Positive identification is technical, but similar species are all equally edible.) Commonly subalpine among grass, or sometimes under conifers; summer.

Warted giant puffball

Most puffballs are smaller than golf balls, but *Calbovista* is baseball-sized, and some *Calvatia* species can grow to basketball size. The name *Calbovista* is a compound of two other genera: *Calvatia* is Latin for "baldhead," while *Bovista* ("fox fart") is old German vernacular for a puffball.

One day I just had to stop and get out my stove for a *cuisine sauvage* lunch, a warted giant puffball sandwich—half-inch slices fried in butter with garlic, on crackers thinly layered with anchovy paste and cheese.

Oregon White Truffle

Tuber gibbosum* and *T. oregonense (TOO-ber: Latin for truffle; jib-OH-sum: swollen;

oregon-EN-zee). Knobby firm lumps ¾–2½ in. (rarely 5 in.) across, with cheesy, garlicky, or eventually metallic odor developing at maturity; skin pale brown, bruising reddish and darkening in age; interior marbled shades of white, aging to brown with white veins. Below soil surface, usually in groups, under young Douglas-fir. *T. gibbosum* January–June; *T. oregonense* October–March.

Truffles live mycorrhizally just like many mushrooms, but instead of giving their spores to the wind to carry, they use distinctive aromas to entice mammals to eat them (see p. 352). Some of them also get by with tiny fruits that get moved around accidentally by burrowing animals.

Hundreds of truffle-like (that is, aromatic underground-fruiting) species abound in our forests. Oregon white truffles have led the way into fine restaurants, aided by being in the same genus as the white and black truffles of Italy and France. European truffles are harvested with the help of dogs or sow pigs that sniff them out, and hence are found at their aromatic peak. Dogs need to be trained (and prevented from urinating on the truffles they find), but sows come preprogrammed, and merely have to be restrained from eating: the truffle shares an aromatic compound with boar pheromones, which the sows find highly attractive. Few human noses can zero in on truffles underground. Some trufflers rake all over in appropriate habitat, but raking is bad for forests and wastes many immature truffles with neither aroma nor culinary value. Christmas tree farms with good-sized Douglas-firs are good potential habitat for Oregon white truffles. European truffles are now cultivated in several parts of the world, and cultivation is underway in Northwest filbert orchards.

An early effort at cultivating them was commissioned by the King of Prussia in the 1880s. Professor Albert B. Frank failed to grow truffles, but he looked so closely at how they work that he made perhaps the greatest advance in mycology: the discovery and naming of mycorrhizae.

Oregon white truffle

Truffles of genus *Rhizopogon*—small, drab, and of no gastronomic interest—are almost ubiquitous in forest. Their genes are so similar to *Suillus* species that they may end up combined in one genus—an example of genetic relationships among fungi not fitting the old classifications based on fruiting body morphology and spores.

Morel

***Morchella* spp.** (mor-KEL-a: from their Old High German name). Cap conical or rod-shaped to egg-shaped or round, gray-brown or somewhat yellowish; exterior honeycombed with narrow ridges with

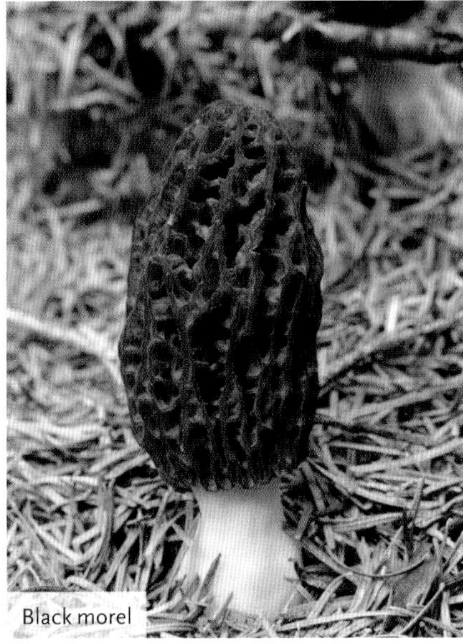
Black morel

The Fungus-Root Symbiosis

The Web of Life is not a metaphor, the Wood-Wide Web is not a joke. It's really out there, and it's made of fungi. Simply put, the job of root hairs in plants is actually performed mostly by fungi, working symbiotically with plants.

Soon after a plant germinates from seed, its rootlet is likely to meet up with its fungal counterpart, a hypha. Some plants, including most orchids, won't germinate until they're penetrated by a hypha. The plant and fungus each contain hormones that stimulate and alter the growth of the other, forming a joint fungus-root organ that immediately goes to work as a nutrient loading dock. This fungus-plant organ is a mycorrhiza, a word coined in 1885 that simply means "fungus root."

In one type of mycorrhiza, hyphae grow as a net around the root tip. In another they digest root cell walls, and penetrate and inhabit the cells, which eventually digest them. Either way, the hyphae hormonally suppress the formation of plant root hairs, but provide a preestablished network of root hair surrogates finer and more efficient than the plant's own. (A root hair is about 1 mm in diameter; a hypha is about 0.003 mm; a hypha can thus provide about 300 times as much absorptive surface area for a given investment in biomass.) In addition, mycorrhizal fungi deliver nitrogen and phosphorus that would otherwise be unavailable to plants. They can even bore into solid rock to extract nutrients.

In exchange, the fungus gets its food, or carbohydrates, from the host plant. Most mycorrhizal fungi are totally dependent on their plant partners. Few plants are equally dependent on fungi, since most plants have the genetic information for making root hairs to obtain water and minerals. Planted in a rich, moist, nutritious substrate, a seedling may do just that, and repel mycorrhizal infection. But given real-world challenges, nonmycorrhizal seedlings often fail to thrive. On a hot logged-over slope, Douglas-fir seedlings proved more likely to survive if planted right next to certain heath-family shrubs that partner with suitable fungi. In another study, seedlings survived only if they were inoculated with a teaspoonful of forest soil. The active ingredients in that elixir are poorly known, but mites, nematodes, bacteria, and other microorganisms are present in great numbers and variety, and surely share credit with the 100 miles or so of hyphal tubes per teaspoon of soil.

Most plants have many mycorrhizal species as potential partners. Our conifers each have hundreds if not thousands. A tree forms mycorrhizae with several species at a time, and grows best if it has a range available for changing conditions, even changing them with the seasons.

While the typical barter is carbohydrates from the plant in return for water and minerals from the fungus, there's much more. Root rots (parasitic fungi) have a harder time attacking roots mantled in healthy mycorrhizal hyphae, which form both a physical and a chemical barrier. Many fungi compete with other fungi by secreting selective toxins, and they secrete antibiotics that fight bacteria, including some plant pathogens. Mycorrhizal fungi exude carbohydrates into the soil, making the soil more cohesive, more porous, and better aerated (and sequestering carbon while they're at it).

Then there's the all-important nitrogen cycle. Some fungi have the ability to break proteins into amino acids and deliver these to their plant partners. Mycorrhizal plants can meet their nitrogen needs in substrates where it had been thought that all the nitrogen was organically bound up, unavailable to plants. Other fungi attack and digest live animals—a nitrogen source available to few plants. John Klironomos and Miranda Hart measured nitrogen transfer to white pine seedlings from springtails (tiny soil insects) killed and consumed by mycorrhizal partners. These seedlings were getting as much as 25 percent of their nitrogen this way. He had started out intending to observe springtails eating fungi. The reversal was "as shocking as putting a pizza in front of a person and then having the pizza eat the person."

Finally, the mycorrhizal web is a social safety net, carrying carbs from plants to other plants, related or not. Typical beneficiaries are small plants growing in shade where they cannot photosynthesize enough to survive. Suzanne Simard measured transfer of carbohydrates to Douglas-fir seedlings from birches above them; the nurture increased when the seedlings were made needier by shading them. Herbs can also receive support from trees and, surprisingly, sometimes return the favor. In eastern Canada, trout lilies were found to borrow sugars from sugar maples in summer when the lilies store sugars in their bulbs, but to actually give up sugars to the maples in spring when the lilies are leafed out but the maple leaves are just emerging. Does this trade demonstrate trust between unrelated plants?

Nongreen orchids and heaths (p. 184) are plants that seemingly get away with cheating the system their whole lives long.

deep pits in between; flesh brittle; interior hollow; no gills; cap is attached very near its bottom to the stalk (except in cottonwood morel); stalk smooth or wrinkled, whitish; odor slight or pleasant. Abundance peaks in late spring.

Black morel, *M. eximia* and *sextelata* (ex-IM-ia: excelling; sext-ee-LAY-ta: sixth type in the *M. elata* group). Also *M. elata, M. conica, M. septimelata.* Cap 1–3 in.; color variable, cap usually darker than stem, ridges may blacken with maturity; main ridges are all vertical. Montane conifer forest in the first spring after a fire.

Fuzzy-foot morel, *M. tomentosa* (toe-men-TOE-sa: fuzzy). Also gray morel. Cap 1–4 in.; young specimens dark gray, coated with fine velvety hairs; fades to any of several shades with age, but with cap and stalk a roughly similar shade at any time; ridges vertical. Conifer forest in the late spring to summer after a fire.

Yellow morel, *M. americana* Also *M. esculenta, M. esculentoides.* Cap 1–5 in. or more, typically tan colored; ridges more erratically oriented (not so strongly vertical), not darkening much with maturity. Most common under low-elev hardwoods.

Cottonwood morel, *M. populiphila* (pop-you-LIF-il-a: poplar-loving). Also half-free morel; *M. semilibera.* Cap 1–2 in., fairly dark, conical, skirtlike, i.e., separate from the stem for much of its length. Under cottonwoods.

Black and fuzzy-foot morels rise phoenixlike from the ashes of burned areas. They were there in the soil already, waiting to bear fruit after fire. They may be mycorrhizal and saprobic at different points in their life cycles, or possibly just saprobic. Scientists debate whether these phoenicoid fruitings are a response to a flush of new nutrition or to the impending loss of old nutrition when their conifer partners die. Insect-killed trees also promote rich fruitings, but those seem more to be of the nonphoenicoid species. Black morels popped up on barren ash at Mt. St. Helens, and where they rotted back into the ash, algae and mosses soon flourished.

Both black and yellow morels are tricky to spot, camouflaged against their respectively burnt and unburnt forest floors. (There are other blackish species that are not burn-related.) All morels are somewhat toxic raw; most people can safely eat them cooked. To make sure they are morels, sniff their pleasing odor and slice one lengthwise to see how the honeycombed cap is attached at its bottom—there's no underside, only the full-length hollow interior shared with the stem. Often sandy, morels benefit from washing. They are the most lucrative class of wild mushroom in the greater Northwest (meaning Oregon to Montana; the greatest harvests are in the Blue Mountains and Northern Rockies.)

Fuzzy-foot morel

Yellow morel

Like other fungi, morels have many "sexes" (mating types, properly). Unlike typical mushroom fungi, their cells have many, genetically distinct nuclei, with the result that adjacent morels in the same cluster are genetically distinct, even though they probably arose from the same mycelium, or network of hyphae. This complexity has made it especially difficult to classify morels. Two new sets of morel scientific names came out in 2012, and their conflicts were resolved, for the time being, in 2014. Most are new names, because many American morels had previously been considered conspecific with European ones. No longer. *Morchella sextelata* and *eximia* are a cryptic pair, distinguishable only by DNA sequencing, and there are additional new species within the "black morel" type. The fuzzy-foot was not officially a species until 2008, but morel pickers had long recognized and named it.

Snowbank False-Morel

Gyromitra montana (jye-ro-MY-tra: round hat; mon-TAY-na: montane). Also snow mushroom; *G. gigas*, *G. korffii*. Cap dull yellow-brown, convoluted, lacking gills, flesh in cross-section thin, white, brittle; stem white, largely hidden by cap, nearly as big around as the cap and with similarly convoluted, thin, brittle flesh enclosing many irregular hollow spaces. Under high-elev conifers immediately after snowmelt.

Gyromitra toxicity is a persistent mystery. Countless people, over centuries, happily ate the so-called edible false-morel, *G. esculenta*. A few of them died. The toxin (after metabolizing in your body) is the same chemical as a rocket fuel that sent astronauts into space—a well-studied chemical known to be both poisonous and carcinogenic. However, it is volatile enough to be removed by either drying or boiling, and it typically produces no symptoms until a victim exceeds a threshold level, presumably by eating lots of inadequately boiled *Gyromitra* over a period of a few days. Now that the explanation is known, mushroom guides say "POISONOUS" right under the name *esculenta*, meaning "good to eat." Some people still eat *G. esculenta* after scrupulous parboilings.

As for snowbank false-morels, chemical testing has generally found either no toxin or just a trace. Consequently, some guides call it toxic and compare eating it to Russian roulette, while others call it a good edible that requires parboiling as a precaution. I have eaten it happily. Steve Trudell and Joe Ammirati hedge judiciously: "We recommend that it be cooked well and not eaten frequently or in large amounts."

Scorched-Earth Cup

Geopyxis carbonaria (geo-PIC-sis: earth goblet). Also fire-following fairy cup. Half-inch smooth light brown cups with pale, perhaps ruffled, rims; usually on very short stalks (often not visible until picked); no gills. Abundant in burns in the first year after fire; spring to fall.

Snowbank false-morel

Scorched-earth cup

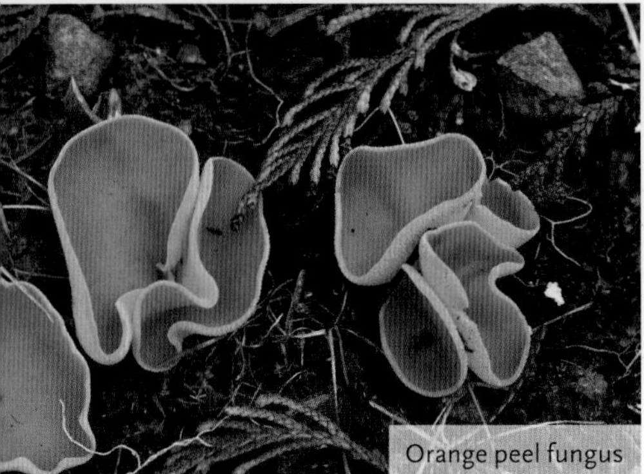
Orange peel fungus

These tiny cups could be looked at as hot tips, coming up in many of the same spots as black morels—typically in fire-thinned duff very near fire-killed trees—and often before the morels. In Sweden, scientists found that in the rare instances where a forest burned and no scorched-earth cups turned up afterward, forest failed to reestablish. Though that suggests it's a valuable mycorrhizal species, some studies find it to be primarily saprobic.

Orange Peel Fungus

Aleuria aurantia (a-LOO-ria: flour; aw-RAN-tia: orange). Bright orange thin-fleshed cups ½–4 in. across; underside paler; no stalk; brittle, not tough. Gravelly soil, e.g., road shoulders, or grass or moss, often grouped; summer and fall.

This common fungus, edible but insipid, can release visible puffs of spores.

LICHENS

A lichen is a sophisticated organism in which one or more kinds of fungi enclose and "farm" photosynthetic one-celled organisms—algae, cyanobacteria, or both. The lichen produces organs, tissues, and chemicals that are never seen in nonlichenized fungi, algae, or cyanobacteria. Unlike other fungi, lichens grow in the open and are tough, durable, and perfectly able to revive after drying out. The lichen symbiosis seems to have evolved separately in seven branches of the fungus family tree. Its original occurrence may have been the breakthrough that life needed in order to move from the sea onto the land.

Lichen fungi get their food from their photobionts—the algae or cyanobacteria—which benefit by being able to grow on sites far too severe for free-living relatives. It's kind of like farming in that irrigation enables plants to grow in climates too dry for them, and barns and hay let cattle live in climates too snowy. The lichen offers physical shelter and also chemical protection: the best-understood function of lichen chemicals is to repel herbivores, microbes, and competing plants. You could say we have here counterparts to a farmer's greenhouse, pesticides, herbicides, and deer repellent. Most lichenologists agree to call this symbiosis a beautiful mutualism, but some have floated extreme views: that the fungus is slowly killing the algae, or that the alga hijacks the fungus to build a perfect house for it, just as a gall wasp induces a plant to build a gall for the wasp larvae.

It can be misleading to single lichens out as combo organisms. Simpler organisms working as symbionts inside bigger organisms are the rule, not the exception. For example, photosynthesis is performed by chloroplasts, which originated as cyanobacteria that survived inside bigger one-celled organisms that tried to consume them. Most green plants benefit from fungal or bacterial endophytes in their leaves, or mycorrhizae invading their roots. The mycorrhizae also include bacterial partners, whose symbiotic role remains poorly known. Then there's the human body: nine out of ten cells in it are bacteria, most of which benefit us. Lichens arc a variation on this common theme in the diversity of life on earth.

The photobiont, with only about 7 percent of the tissue mass of a typical lichen, is very much the junior partner. (Partly on those grounds, the International Code of Nomenclature classifies and names lichens as fungi.) It was once thought that a lichen spore can't begin to farm unless it happens to land near a free alga of the right type. It turns out that a spore can grow into a sort of slight smudge called a prethallus, and can survive for years waiting for the right alga to turn up, and then for the two to develop their relationship and form an actual lichen. For food, the prethallus may consume algae, or it may parasitize a tree or shrub it's growing on.

To varying degrees, different lichens do release spores that can reproduce in that fashion. (Their spore-producing organs are the fruiting disks in the species descriptions.) While sexual propagation via spores is important for genetic diversity, it is far less common than propagation from fragments that include both partners together. These may be just any old fragment that happens to break off, or they may be specially evolved propagative bundles (propagules) in the form of powders, grains, or tiny protuberances.

Lichens are loosely sorted by growth form. Field guides use anywhere from three to seven forms. I'll use four:

Crust lichens are thin coatings or stains on or in rock or bark surfaces—so thin that you could not pry them up.

Leaf lichens are also thin, ranging from salad-like heaps attached to their substrate in only a few spots to almost paint-like sheets with distinct, thick, margins that can be pried from the substrate.

Shrub lichens are three-dimensional—either erect or pendent—and much-branched.

Twig lichens stand up, with some or no branching, often above a mat of scales.

Of all familiar, visible organisms, lichens have perhaps the most modest requirements—a little moisture, any amount of sunlight from minimal to extreme, and solid materials that even the cleanest air carries. From minimal input comes modest output; growth rates measured in lichen species range from 0.0012 inch to about 4 inches per year.

Success in lichen niches is a matter of making hay while there's moisture—rain, snow, dew, fog, or even just humidity—and then drying up, suspending all activity. Dry, lichens can survive temperatures from 150°F (typical of soil surfaces in the summer sun) down to near absolute zero (in laboratories). Drying out and suspending respiration is the only way they can get through hot days in the sun. At 32°F or a bit colder they remain active and unfrozen, thanks to complex chemistry including alcohols. Our alpine lichens get some of their photosynthesizing done while buried in snow, which keeps them moist and lets sunlight in. While alpine rocks with their extremes of sunlight and temperature are no problem, far more of our lichen biomass, and much faster growth rates, occur in an environment with moderate temperatures, low light levels, and high rainfall: the bark of rainforest trees. There, too, the lichens dry out many times a year when the rain and fog lapse. Most lichens will actually die if they don't dry out periodically.

Lichens that colonize bare rock may, after centuries of life, death, and decomposition, alter the rock enough for plants to grow, initiating the long, slow succession of biotic communities. This scenario has captivated countless naturalists, from Linnaeus to our high school biology teachers, but in fact it is not a common path of primary succession on barren, newly exposed ground. Since pioneer plants need usable nitrogen, associations with nitrogen fixers are typical: mosses loosely coated with cyanobacteria pioneer on rock, and nodulated trees and shrubs like alders sprout from crevices that hold a bit of fine gravel or dust. On barren ash at Mt. St. Helens, nitrogen-fixing herbs like lupine pioneered; the small lichen patches that did make an appearance were more likely to inhibit than to nurture plant growth.

Lichens secrete acids that dissolve minerals from rock, but this chemical etching is one of nature's slower tools for disintegrating rocks. Slightly faster is lichens' physical crumbling of rock—effective on soft limestone and shale, and also on old stained glass of cathedrals. Lichens' gelatinous gripping surfaces expand and contract, crumbling tiny bits of rock, as they moisten and dry out—an effect that has been experimentally replicated using plain gelatin. Bottom line: lichens' ability to break down rock is negligible compared to that of frost.

A second appealing myth proposes lichens as candidates for restarting succession, or even evolution, after a global ecocatastrophe. This idea may have been inspired by arctic lichens that accumulated radioactive fallout and survived, while passing harmful amounts of it into the bones of lichen-eating caribou and caribou-eating Inuit and Saami. There may be something to this myth. Lichen lineages are so old that they must have survived three of the big five mass extinctions.

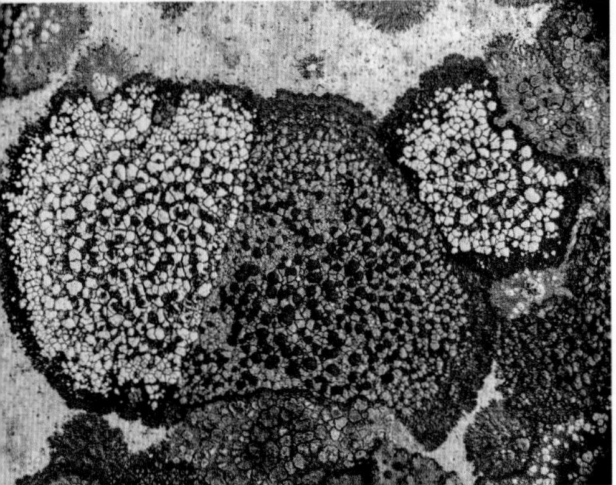

Rhizocarpon geographicum and a less-colorful relative, *R. macrocarpon*.

CRUST LICHENS

Map Lichen

Rhizocarpon geographicum (rye-zo-CAR-pon: root fruit). Chartreuse yellow patches broken by fine black lines and surrounded by a wider black margin. On rocks; abundant in exposed situations.

Crust lichens grow at slow but steady rates. Especially steady, and ubiquitous on arctic and alpine rocks, map lichen dominates the science of lichenometry, which uses lichen growth to measure time—for example, the time since glaciers retreated from rocks that now bear lichens. Radial growth rates of 3 and 3⅓ mm per century, after a slightly faster initial growth spurt (ha ha) typify map lichens in the US Rockies: 3000-year-old lichens are 4–4½ inches in diameter.

Bloody-Heart Lichen

Mycoblastus sanguinarius (my-co-BLAS-tus: fungus bud; sang-gwin-AIR-ius: blood red). Also clot lichen. Gray patches without sharp edges, on bark, texture grainy to warty, with clusters of blackish fruiting disks 1–2.5 mm across; under each disk, if it's sliced off, is a bright red spot in the lichen cortex. Dry tree bark microsites.

Bloody-heart lichen

Saucer Lichen

***Ochrolechia* spp.** (oh-kro-LEK-ia: ochre bed?). Also pumpkin pie lichen, donuts. Light gray patches without sharp edges, on bark, with small (up to ⅛ in.) salmon-pink fruiting disks.

Smooth saucer lichen, *O. laevigata* (lee-vig-AY-ta: smooth). Crust very thin, often smooth; disks small, their rims thin, white. Abundant on red alder.

Double-rimmed saucer lichen, *O. oregonensis* (oregon-EN-sis: of Oregon). Crust thicker, finely warty; disks abundant, with a rough outer ring which matures orange. Abundant on young firs.

These lichens lend their ghostly whiteness to the bark in young forests. Of many whitish crust lichens on red alder bark, saucer lichens are the ones with distinctive white-rimmed disks like tiny pumpkin pies.

Brilliant purples, reds, and rich browns once made *Ochrolechia* valuable. The Scots scraped "corkir" or "cudbear," *O. tartarea,* from rocks to make a dye for Harris Tweeds and litmus paper. Our two species can't be used because they're inseparable from the bark, whose tannin would ruin the color. *Ochrolechia laevigata* permeates the bark like a stain more than a crust, with only its disks sitting upon the surface. Many lichens yield yellow, olive, or brown dyes when boiled in water. The transformation to purple and red comes when lichens containing gyrophoric acid, such as *Ochrolechia* or *Umbilicaria,* are cured for several weeks in warm ammonia. Stale human urine was the form of ammonia used from the beginning (more than 2000 years ago, around the Mediterranean) through the 19th century. Yet the dyed fabric came out with a fine fragrance, even longer-lasting than the color.

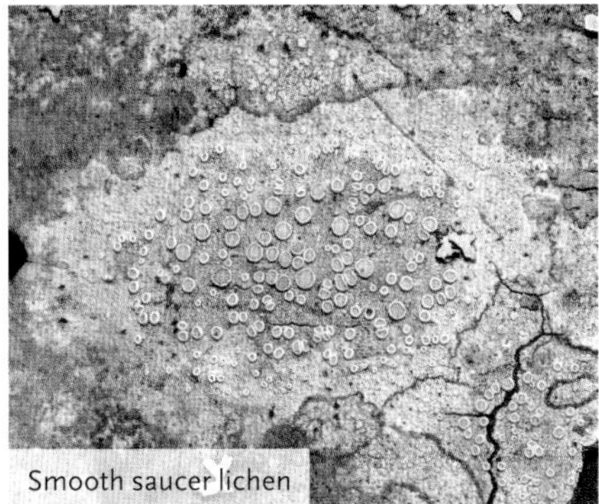
Smooth saucer lichen

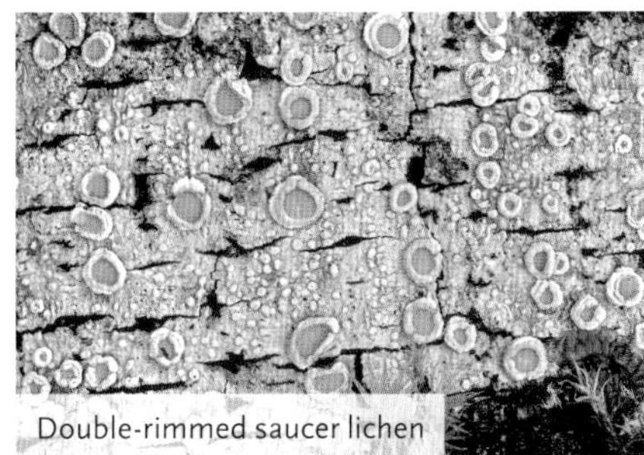
Double-rimmed saucer lichen

Spraypaint lichen

Spraypaint Lichen

Icmadophila ericetorum (ick-ma-DOFF-il-a: mudlover; er-iss-et-OR-um: among heathers, a misleading name). Also pixie barf. Pale blue-green (moist) or nearly white (dry) grainy crust dotted with white-rimmed, raised pink fruiting disks; the disks are on short stalks if you look closely enough. On rotting wood, or growing over mosses.

Dust Lichen

Black alpine dust lichen, *Lepraria neglecta* (lep-RAIR-ia: leprous, i.e., scurfy). A speckly

Biological Crusts

In alpine and cold steppe environments, soil surfaces are often a structured mix of small bits of lichens, cyanobacteria, mosses, and fungi. The resulting crust, ranging from an eighth of an inch to over an inch thick, often goes unnoticed, but is vital to plants. It stays relatively cool and moist in the sun, resists erosion, and in many cases fixes nitrogen.

The crust, called either biological or cryptobiotic ("hidden life"), is easy to damage and slow to repair itself. A footprint in it can last for decades. If you hike off-trail above treeline, watch for nubbly, crusted sandy earth and avoid walking on it. Detour onto snow or bare rock; in a pinch, even raw gravels or dense sedge turf are less fragile than crusted soils.

bluish pale gray coating. All elevations; abundant on alp/subalpine soil or moss.

Gold dust lichen, *Chrysothrix candelaris* (CRIS-o-thrix: gold thread; candle-AIR-iss: luminous). Bright yellow scurfy granular coating on bark.

Sulfur dust lichen, *C. chlorina* (chlor-EYE-na: greenish yellow). Bright greenish yellow scurfy granular coating, typically on moist, shaded cliff rocks.

This degenerate lichen growth form (also known as imperfect lichen or powdery paint lichen) is just a powdery layer of fungi and algae bundled together in little clumps called soredia. Many lichens bear soredia as reproductive propagules. (They're the either "granular" or "powdery" stuff in several species descriptions.) Apparently dust lichens evolved repeatedly (in several unrelated lichens) when some soredia learned the trick of propagating more soredia without bothering to propagate the rest of the lichen. Lacking the continuous cortex layer that most lichens have, dust lichens are more vulnerable to drying out, but better able to absorb moisture from the air: they live by absorbing humidity from the air, but actually repel raindrops and drips, being unable to absorb liquid water. They specialize in rain-deprived substrates like the undersides of limbs, and rock overhangs. They like foggy climates, and go crazy in shaded waterfall spray zones.

Sulfur dust lichen

Black alpine dust lichen seems to fill in bare spaces in almost any sort of alpine community, frosting moss turf or bare soil with white, and typically producing a nubbly texture of 2-inch mounds. It also abounds on bark, specializing in twigs and in dry sides of trees. Sulfur dust lichen, less extensive, is spectacular on wet basalt cliffs beside Columbia Gorge waterfalls.

Early naturalists filed dust lichens under *Lichenes Imperfecti* within Deuteromycetes, two taxonomic dustbins indicating the naturalists' inability to categorize fungi that had never been seen with sexual organs. Modern molecular techniques allow transferring them from these dustbins to their rightful places all over the fungus family tree.

LEAF LICHENS

Lungwort

***Lobaria* spp.** (lo-BAIR-ia: lobed). Big "leaves" pale, dull green above when dry, bright green when wet, ridged in a branching pattern (on underside, these ridges become valleys, as opposed to the raised veins under dog lichens); cream-colored underneath when dry, mottled with brown in the furrows; margins deeply lobed, curling; occasionally has red-brown fruiting disks. On w-side trees.

Lungwort, *L. pulmonaria* (pul-mon-AIR-ia: lung—). Has loose gray-brown granules on some ridges and margins.

Lettuce lungwort, *L. oregana* (or-eg-AY-na: of Oregon). Lacks loose granules.

Massive proliferations of lungwort grow in thick salad-like beds up on top of limbs in the conifer canopy. Lungwort litter on the forest floor gives a hint of the abundance above, but the true quantity went unappreciated until rock-climbing hardware was brought to bear on forest science. It was then calculated that this species supplies up to half the nitrogen input in the oldest west-side forests, at least at mid-elevations in the western Cascades. (Lungwort mass is substantially higher on 700-year-old trees than on 400-year-old trees, and higher in very cool moist valleys than in average west-side forests.) Cyanobacteria in the lichen pull nitrogen out of the air; their fungal cosymbionts appropriate it; and it moves on in the nutrient cycle when it leaches out in rainwater, or when the lichen is eaten by insects, red tree voles, or decomposing bacteria. To intercept nutrients before they wash away, alders, maples, and cottonwoods may extend roots among the lichens and mosses on their own bark.

The word "lungwort" derives from the medieval Doctrine of Signatures, which prescribed this lichen for lung ailments because of its textural resemblance to lung tissue. *Mertensia* and at least six other green plants were also called lungwort and prescribed for lung ailments.

Dog Lichen

***Peltigera* spp.** (pel-TIDGE-er-a: shield bearer). Also veined lichen, pelt. Broad sheets with lobed and curled-up margins; fruiting bodies on lobe edges, somewhat tooth-shaped, tan or reddish tan except on *P. collina*; underside netted with branching veins, raised from surface, bearing hairlike rhizines.

Membranous dog lichen, *P. membranacea* (mem-bra-NAY-cia: thin). Also diamond pelt. Gray to brownish, covered (at least near edges and on underside veins) with feltlike wool; rhizines very coarse, long (often 3/8 in.); fruiting bodies reflexed. Forest floor, low w-side.

Lungwort

Membranous dog lichen

Canopy Zones

Canopy scientists find that old-growth trees offer epiphytes just as wide a range of habitats as the wet-to-dry sides of the Cascades. Upper canopy branches receive the most moisture, but quickly turn arid in the intense wind and sun. They support thick beards of pendulous lichens, which excel at intercepting fog and dew and taking advantage of the few moist or bright minutes per day that result. At the other end, jungles of thick moss thrive on the north sides of tree bases, where the sun never shines and the wind scarcely blows.

Broom moss and high branch moss gradually take over the tops of large branches at all heights. They need a moist microclimate and are good at creating it for themselves, intercepting and condensing far more fog and rain moisture than a bare branch can, and sponging it up, releasing it slowly after the foggy or rainy weather passes. Eventually an actual soil results. Red tree voles live out their lives on this lofty earth, as do some clouded salamanders; fireweed, devil's-club, hemlock, and salal have been seen taking root and growing in it; and the host tree itself, if it is an alder or maple, may extend aerial roots into it for a share of its fertility.

Epiphyte habitats vary along three gradients: from the top to the bottom of a forest, from drier to wetter forest locations, and through time as the forest matures. Succession continues past 400 years of stand age, giving truly ancient forests ecological traits they don't share with the mere 200-year-old forests usually defined as "old growth."

Starting at the high, dry, young end, the sequence goes:

1. Witch's-hair, horsehair, and beard lichens
2. Tube and ragbag lichens
3. Lungwort, flaky freckle pelt, and other lichens with cyanobacteria; also coral lichen
4. Mosses and leafy liverworts

Carpet pelt, *P. neopolydactyla* (neo-polly-DAC-til-a: new many-fingers). Also undulating pelt. Upper surface olive gray to brownish, hairless; veins not felted; rhizines long (often 3/8 in.); moist forest floor.

Tree pelt, *P. collina* (co-LYE-na: on hills). Gray to brownish; edges rimmed with pale granules like salt on a margarita-glass rim; underside pale, felted, with slight veins and fine rhizines; fruiting bodies black but uncommon. On bark, or sometimes rock, all elevs.

Flaky freckle pelt, *P. britannica* Bright green above when wet, pale green to tan when dry; upper side freckled with raised dark bumps that can be flicked off with your fingernail. Abundant on w-side soil, bark, rocks, and in moss mats on high limbs of old conifers.

Freckle pelt, *P. aphthosa* (af-THO-sa: blistered). Also silver-edge pelt. Bright green above when wet, pale green to tan when dry; upper side freckled with barely raised dark bumps that are not easily flicked off. On soil and rocks, both sun and shade.

"Frog's blankets," my favorite name for these lichens, is a translation of what British Columbia's Gitxsan people called them. The European name dates from the medieval Doctrine of Signatures, which looked in nature for semblances of body parts and read them as drug prescriptions in God's own handwriting. In the dog lichen's erect fruiting bodies they saw dog teeth, so they prescribed dog lichen for dog-bite disease: the decoction for rabies, right up until the last century, was ground dog lichen and black pepper in milk. The doctrine was a wrong turn in the history of herbal medicine. Lichens do have medicinal value, and they were used more appropriately in pre-Christian Europe.

Carpet pelt

Tree pelt

Flaky freckle pelt

The Pacific Northwest has at least 25 gray and 4 green species of *Peltigera*, more than any other part of the world. Dark gray lichens have nitrogen-fixing cyanobacteria, often of genus *Nostoc*, as their chief photosynthesizing partners. Green species like *P. britannica* employ green algae throughout, and cyanobacteria only within their "freckles." Some *P. britannica* individuals may lack the green alga, and be gray; some day those individuals may catch some green algae and sprout green lobes.

Ragbag Lichen

Platismatia glauca (plat-iss-MAY-sha: broad—; GLAW-ca: pale). Fluffy wads of small sheets (up to 1 in. wide) with strongly ruffled edges; pale greenish gray above; un-

Ragbag lichen

derside patchy with white, greenish brown, and black; surface often granular-coated.

This cosmopolitan species, native to six continents, tolerates pollution and is common on urban trees. Along with several tube lichens (opposite), it grows throughout young forest conifers, but shifts into the mid-canopy as the forest ages. In ancient forests you see it mainly where it has fallen on the ground.

Blistered Rock Tripe

Umbilicaria hyperborea (um-bil-ic-AIR-ia: navel—; hyper-BOR-ia: of the Far North). Black to brown leafy lichen attached to a rock by a single, central "umbilical" holdfast; tough and leathery wet, hard and brittle when dry; upper side very rough, like miniature lava; underside smooth, lacking the hairs (rhizines) found on some other rock tripes. Abundant on exposed rock.

Along the coast, boiled rock tripe was sometimes added to herring eggs, a prized delicacy, to make the eggs go farther. In Asia, people fry it up to eat like potato chips, or relish it tender in salad or soup, always drying and boiling it first to leach out dark and bitter flavors. After boiling it for three hours, Ernest Thompson Seton found it "the most satisfactory of all the starvation foods" and credited it with saving Franklin and Richardson (p. 500) on their desperate Arctic trek in 1821: "Their diet was varied with burnt bones when they could find them and toasted leather and hide; but the staple and mainstay was rocktripe."

Orange Chocolate-chip Lichen

Solorina crocea (so-lor-EYE-na: sun—; CRO-sia: crocus, i.e., saffron yellow). Upper surface bright green (wet) to pale dull green (dry) with dark brown fruiting disks; upturned edges reveal the bright orange underside, which has fine wool, brown veins, sparse rhizines. Alp/subalpine soil.

This lichen excels on late-lying snowbed sites, often alongside mosses that get started there with the help of nitrogen-fixing cyanobacteria on their leaves. The lichen can then incorporate those same bacteria, but may remain quite small for years before the right green algae blow in and enable it to realize its full potential.

Elegant Sunburst Lichen

Xanthoria elegans (zan-THOR-ia: yellow; EL-eg-enz: elegant). Bright orange patches adhering tightly to rocks, easily mistaken for a crust lichen, but with slightly raised flakes and distinct, lobed edges; fruiting disks deeper orange, small, concentrated near center of patch. On sunny rocks fertilized with nitrogen or calcium.

This lichen marks habitual perches of rock-pile-dwelling animals like pikas and marmots, where it is fertilized by the nitrogen in urine. More conspicuous than the pika itself, this orange splash may help us spot the source of the "eeeenk." The orange pigment, parietin, is a sunblock protecting the lichen algae from excessive ultraviolet light.

Blistered rock tripe

Orange chocolate-chip lichen

Elegant sunburst lichen

Air Pollution Indicators

Lichens have discriminating tastes for airborne solids and solutions that, after all, they live on. Along with natural aerosols, they accumulate air pollution in their tissues, and it can kill them. Since different lichens tolerate different amounts and types of pollutants, scientists can use them to monitor an airshed's pollution by analyzing tissue samples in the lab, or simply by checking which species are still present. Compared to testing air samples directly, this has the advantage of averaging pollution levels over several years.

A few lichens thrive on some kinds of pollution. Concerned about ancient rock art fading rapidly in Hell's Canyon, archaeologists asked lichenologist Linda Geiser to find out if air pollution could be the culprit even in that remote wilderness. The telltale clue she spotted was not any missing lichen species, but abundant ones—a belt of bright orange *Xanthoria* low on the canyon walls near rapids. That genus needs extra nitrogen or calcium, and typically gets it, at least in wilderness, from urine or guano. Here, nitrogen probably came down the river from Idaho's feedlots, fertilized fields, and fish farms, and went airborne as acidic spray or fog, feeding the lichens and eating the petroglyphs.

SHRUB LICHENS

Tube Lichen

***Hypogymnia* spp.** (hypo-JIM-nia: naked underneath). Also puffed lichen, bone lichen. Tufts of hollow branches, sharply two-toned, pale greenish gray above with black specks, blackish brown beneath, lighter brown at the tips; caramel-colored fruiting cups or disks ⅛–⅜ in. across. On small limbs, wood, or sometimes rock.

Gut lichen, *H. enteromorpha* (enter-o-MOR-fa: intestine shaped). Branches alternately puffed and constricted, usually crowded in a flattened cluster; interior surfaces dark.

Wishbone lichen, *H. inactiva* (in-AC-tiv-a: not chemically reactive). Also mottled tube. Branches slender, widely spaced, often erect; interior surfaces dark (if white, it's the similar forked tube lichen, *H. imshaugii*).

Gut lichen

Wishbone lichen

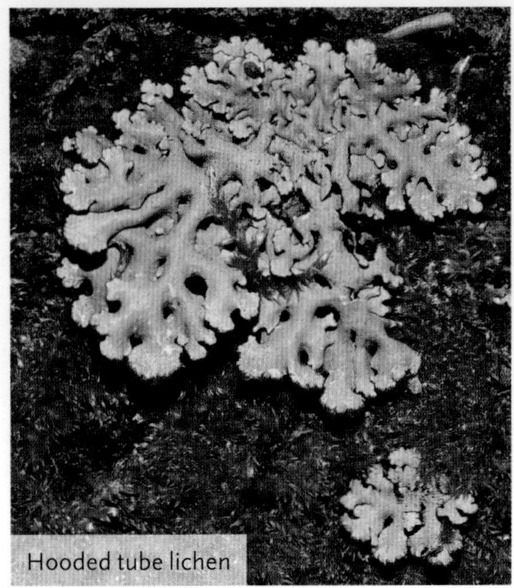
Hooded tube lichen

Hooded tube lichen, *H. physodes* (fie-zo-deez: bladder-like). Also monk's hood. Branches flattened, tips look like they've burst open, erupting granular propagules; fruiting cups rare.

Wolf Lichen

Letharia columbiana* and *L. vulpina (leth-AIR-ia: death—; co-lum-be-AY-na: of the Columbia River; vul-PIE-na: of foxes). Also includes the proposed *L. lupina.* Brilliant sulfur-yellow stiff tufts; profuse branches often pitted, black-dotted; brown fruiting disks ¼ in. (up to ¾ in.) across are common on *columbiana*, absent or rare on *vulpina* (shown here). On pines and junipers.

Wolf lichen

Somewhere there was a tradition of collecting this intense-colored lichen to make a poison for wolves and foxes. My American sources say this used to be done in Europe, while a British source writes it off as an American barbarism. There is a recent record of a dog death from eating wolf lichen as litter on snow, but no records of human poisonings.

Wolf lichen imparts to fabrics a chartreuse dye close to its own color. Northwest tribes dyed moccasins, fur, feathers, wood, porcupine quills for basketry, and their own faces.

Iceland-Moss

***Cetraria* spp.** (set-RAIR-ia: shield—). Shrub-like clumps 1–3 in. tall by 2–8 in. wide, of narrow flattened lobes with sparsely fringed edges. On soil, mostly alpine.

Heather Iceland-moss, *C. ericetorum* (er-iss-e-TOR-um: among heaths). Brown to olive when dry; edges rolled nearly into tubes; with white specks (under 10× lens) aligned under edges.

Iceland-moss, *C. islandica* (iss-LAND-ica: of Iceland). Brown to olive; with white specks scattered across backsides; lobes scarcely rolled up.

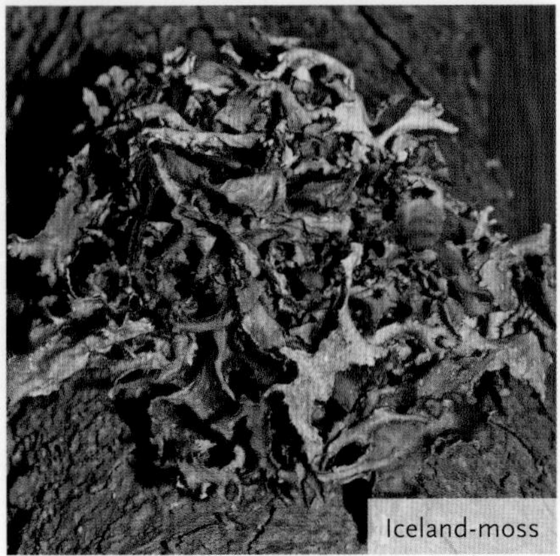
Iceland-moss

Crinkled snow lichen, *C. nivalis* (niv-AY-lis: of snow). Also ballroom dervish; *Flavocetraria nivalis.* Pale yellow; some white specks beneath; lobes scarcely rolled up.

The misleading but time-honored common name "Iceland-moss" comes from Europe, where this is the best-known lichen eaten by people. You can find it in herbal medicines in Sweden, and in teas and throat lozenges in Switzerland. Scandinavian sailors used to bake Iceland-moss flour into their bread to extend its shelf life at sea. The lichen had to be parboiled with soda before milling, or it would have been unspeakably bitter. In North America it was popular among the Inuit.

Methuselah's-Beard

Usnea longissima (US-nee-a: Arabic term for a lichen; lon-JIS-im-a: longest). Pale greenish gray pendent strands commonly 2–6 ft. long, with short perpendicular side branches. Infrequent.

Restricted to low, rainy, mature conifer forest, Methuselah's beard is scarce enough that current levels of harvesting (for the florist's moss market) may threaten it. Several other *Usnea* species are more common and widespread. Some are small, bushy, and erect; a few are pendent and can be mistaken for witch's hair, except that they have some short perpendicular branches. All *Usnea* species share one distinctive feature: when stretched gently, the thicker branches (unless extremely dry) reveal an elastic, pure white inner cord inside the brittle, pulpier skin—like wire in old cracked insulation.

The genus abounds throughout boreal regions, inspiring schemes to convert lichen starches into glucose for food, or alcohol for fuel or drink. Even abundant lichens are quickly depleted, though, due to slow growth, and cannot sustain a starch industry.

Witch's Hair

Alectoria sarmentosa (alec-TOR-ia: rooster?; sar-men-TOE-sa: twiggy). Pale gray-green festoons on trees; wispily pendulous, 3–30 in. long; branches are pendent, not perpendicular; when pulled, strands snap straight across (compare with *Usnea*). On trees; copiously abundant from mid-elevs to timberline.

In heavily browsed areas like Olympic valleys, witch's hair may show a browse line at the maximum height elk can reach. What may look like a similar browse line of witch's hair in higher forests is actually a marker of spring snowpack depth. Spring is the prime

Crinkled snow lichen

Methuselah's-beard

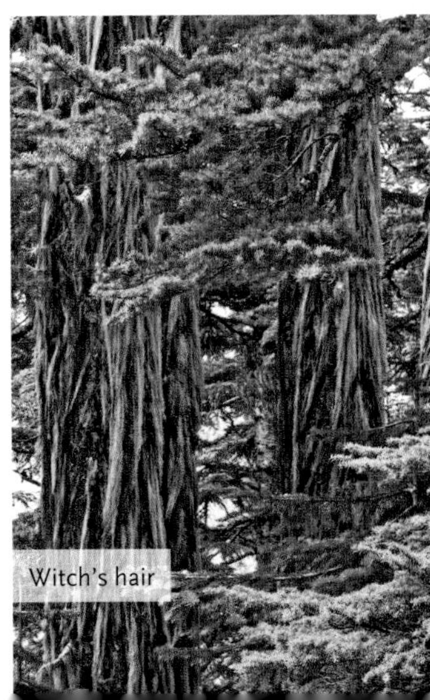
Witch's hair

growing season for high-elevation lichens, optimizing rain with temperature and day length, and the light is better above the snowpack.

Edible Horsehair Lichen

Bryoria fremontii (bry-OR-ia: moss—; free-MONT-ee-eye: for John C. Frémont). Also tree hair, black tree lichen. Blackish brown 2- to 16-in. festoons of extremely fine, weak, matted fibers, sometimes speckled with pale, powdery propagules; on high-elev trees, krummholz, and rarely rock surfaces.

These black visual accents add drama to weather-bonsai'd trees. Don't confuse them with ugly old snow mold, *Herpotrichia nigra* ("black creeping hair"), a pathogenic fungus that turns mountain hemlock and silver fir branches into mats of smutty needles, mainly during late-snowmelt years. Horsehair and other lichens are neither pathogenic nor parasitic.

This horsehair is relatively edible because it lacks the chemicals that defend its relatives from herbivores. For flying squirrels and woodland caribou it is a winter staple; for deer and elk it is a minor food that helps them get more nutrition out of conifer needles. Indians ate horsehair lichen, especially in cold interior areas where carbohydrate foods were scarce in winter, and some bundled it to make a sort of shoe. Reports vary as to whether it was delicious or starvation fare, bitter or soapy or sweet or bland. Taste tests distinguish it from a bitter, yellow form that does produce the toxic chemicals. DNA sequencing shows that the two forms have the exact same algal and main fungal partners; but a 2016 study discovered a third symbiotic partner, a yeast fungus, whose abundance correlates with toxin production. This order of yeasts, new to science in 2015, is found in many lichens, and only in lichens. It appears to demand a new taxonomy of lichens that names the entire symbiotic package, not just the primary fungus.

Fragmenting Coral Lichen

Sphaerophorus tuckermannii (sphere-AH-for-us: sphere bearer; tucker-MAN-ee-eye: for Edward Tuckermann). Also globe lichen; *S. globusus*. Robust (not hairlike), brittle, stiffly bushy 1- to 3-in. tufts, light red-brown to gray when dry, greenish wet; fruiting bodies, if present, are tiny (2 mm) globes filled with sooty black spores, on branch tips. On trees, from base well up into canopy.

Green Reindeer Lichen

Cladonia mitis (cla-DOE-nia: branched; MY-tis: mild, in flavor). Also *C. arbuscula* subsp. *mitis*, *Cladina mitis*. Profusely fine-branched lichens 2–4 in. tall, in dense patches, on soil but barely attached to it; yellowish when moist, sometimes with bluish bloom. Increasingly common northward, among alpine sedges and heathers.

Though found at all elevations here, reindeer lichens of several species are best

Edible horsehair lichen

Fragmenting coral lichen

Green reindeer lichen

Whiteworm lichen

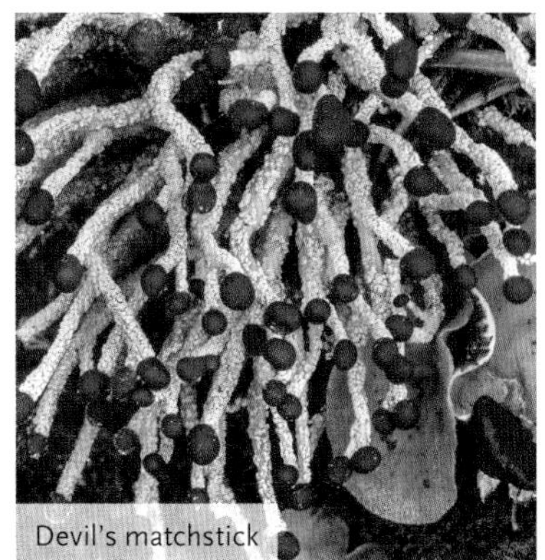
Devil's matchstick

Toy soldiers

known for covering vast areas of arctic tundra, where they are the winter staple of caribou and their domesticated form, reindeer. They aren't all that digestible or nutritious; even caribou prefer green leaves when they can get them, but to occupy that particular range they adapted to wintering on lichens. This requires ceaseless migration, since the slow-growing lichens are eliminated where grazed for long. The Saami people (or Lapps) even harvest lichens for their reindeer herds. Some Inuit relish a "salad-like" delicacy consisting of half-digested lichens from the stomachs of caribou killed in winter.

Closer to home we encounter them, dyed green and softened in glycerine, as fake trees and shrubs in architectural models. They also supply extracts for commercial uses including perfume bases and antibiotics. Along with *Usnea* species they are a chief source of usnic acid, an antibiotic potent against ailments ranging from severe burns and plastic surgery scars to armpit odors and bovine mastitis—and potentially MRSA, a dangerous form of staph infection.

TWIG LICHENS

Whiteworm Lichen

Thamnolia vermicularis (tham-NO-lia: bushy, a misleading name; ver-mic-you-LAIR-iss: wormlike). Also rockworm. White tapering tubes 1–2½ in. tall, without fruiting cups, typically in lackadaisical clumps of standing tubes with some reclining tubes and a few branched tubes. Alpine.

The whiteworm has neither spore-bearing organs nor vegetative propagules. Propagating only from broken bits of stalk—a snail's-pace mode of travel—it is has reached every continent but Africa.

Several variable *Cladonia* species may be worm-like or awl-like when they fail to fruit, but are gray-green or tan-brown in contrast to the bone white of *Thamnolia*.

Devil's Matchstick

Pilophorus acicularis (pil-AH-for-us: hair bearing; a-sic-you-LAIR-is: needlelike). Pale gray stalks ⅜–1 in. long, rarely branched, with fat rounded black fruiting tips; standing or reclining in dense clumps, on rocks in forest.

Toy Soldiers

***Cladonia* spp.** (cla-DOE-nia: branched). Greenish gray stalks ½–2 in. tall, some bearing scarlet fruiting heads; often from a mat of flakes.

Toy soldiers, *C. bellidiflora* (bel-id-if-LOR-a: martial flower). Also floral pixie. Stalks flaky-coated; scarlet heads large, often lobed. On rocks, soil or logs.

Powdery soldiers, *C. transcendens*. Also graduated pixie. Stalks granular-coated; scarlet heads small and more round. On rotting wood or tree bases.

The huge genus *Cladonia* tends to have a two-part growth form. The primary growth is a mat of flakes (squamules) resembling some leaf lichens, only finer. After a while, fruiting twigs may rise from this mat. Sometimes the mats of squamules just persist and spread without fruiting; at the other extreme, in species like *bellidiflora* the mat of primary squamules may die and disappear, while thick coats of squamules develop up on the twigs.

Frosted Cladonia

Cladonia ecmocyna (ec-mo-SIGH-na). Also orange-footed pixie. Messy mini-forests of greenish gray 1- to 4-in. stalks, some orange-tinged basally, some branched, some with turreted brownish heads, others tapering to a point; usually lacking a bed of squamules. On sunny soil or talus.

Trumpet Lichen

Cladonia fimbriata (fim-bree-AY-ta: fringed). Also pixie goblets. Clustered greenish gray golf tee–like fruiting stalks ½–1¼ in. tall, from a thick flaky mat; "baby tees" may sprout from rims of main ones. On soil, stumps, fenceposts, etc.

Many *Cladonia* species produce "golf tees" or, if you like, pixie goblets. The name is catchy enough that some would call all Cladonias pixies of one sort or another. The original Pixie Goblets, *C. pyxidata* (uncommon here), was named for resembling a *pyxis*, an ancient Greek goblet-shaped container with a lid. *Pyxis* is the root word of "box," not of "pixie." The golf tees (or pixies) sometimes stand on each other's shoulders in several tiers; in the ladder lichen, *C. verticillata* (pictured on p. 298), is especially good at that, with its proliferations growing most often from the center of cups.

Frosted cladonia

Trumpet lichen

MAMMALS

Do we even need an introduction to mammals? We *are* mammals. We're well schooled in the salient characteristics of mammals. Most mammals give birth to live young; yet egg-laying platypuses are mammals and live-bearing snakes are not. We are all warm-blooded, that is, we maintain a constant relatively warm body temperature; but so do the birds and, arguably, the bees.

In mammals only, a coat of keratinous hairs serves to insulate the body, so hair may be the definitive mammalian body part, since only half of mammals (the females) produce milk. Whales, armadillos, and other mammals even less hairy than we are all have at least a few hairs at some developmental stage. Mammal coats come mainly in shades of brown and gray. Even on the few mammals, like skunks, with "showy" rather than cryptic coloring, no fur is bright blue or green, as some feathers are. Most mammals need to be inconspicuous. They achieve that by wearing camouflage colors, by being quiet and elusive, and by being nocturnal. That makes mammal-watching a less popular pastime than bird-watching, and makes mammal tracks, scats, and other signs the key to being woods-wise to mammals. Mammals learn to avoid popular hiking trails. I've often begun to see more of them as soon as I got even a hundred yards off trail. The mammals we see most often each have reasons to be unafraid: porcupines are spiky, bears are big, squirrels go up, marmots and pikas go down, and National Park–dwelling deer, elk, and goats take advantage of their protected status. Watch out for them!

Small mammals are especially limited to the murky corner of the spectrum. Experienced field naturalists can sometimes recognize the species they study, using color differences they have learned in a particular locale. They may report these shades as "dusky" or "buffy," "tawny" or "ochraceous"—terms less useful to nonscientists. The animals themselves vary. In a given species, there may be different shades for different seasons, for juveniles versus adults, for infraspecific varieties and color phases, for the paler underside and darker back, and between the hair tips, underfur, and guard hairs. Among closely related mammals, populations of dry regions are often paler than their wet-side relatives, each tending to match the color of the ground so as to be less visible to predators (especially owls) that hunt from above in dim light. Dry country has pale dry dirt, whereas moist forests have dark humus and vegetation.

Positive identification of small mammals utilizes the number and shape of molar teeth, and caliper measurements of skulls and penis bones (a feature of most male mammals); the creature must first be reduced to a skeleton. Don't worry, this chapter will not go into molar design or the meaning of "dusky," but will offer size, tail:body length ratio, form, habitat, and sometimes color, to facilitate educated guesses as to small mammal identities. Our typical glimpse of a shrew, mouse, or vole, unless we trap it or find it dead, is so fleeting and dark that we can only guess based on habits and habitat.

MAMMALS: LAGOMORPHA (RABBITS)

Pika

Ochotona princeps (ock-o-TOE-na: their Mongolian name; PRIN-seps: a chief). Also cony. 8 in. long if stretched out, but appearing a thickset 5–6 in. long in typical postures; no tail; brown; ears round, ½ in. across. On talus, in CasR and CoastM. Ochotonidae.

A cryptoventriloquistic nasal "eeeenk" in the vicinity of coarse talus (rockpile) identifies the pika for you. Look carefully for it on the rocks. You might see it as a rodent, but the posture is rabbit-like— the sharply nose-down head angle, the neck drawn back in an S curve.

Pikas are year-round (nonhibernating) warm bodies in cold climates, clad in appropriately warm fur coats. There's a down side

Pika

Pika haystack.

to that: being out and about for more than a few minutes on a hot day kills them. They stay cool by retreating deep into the talus, where it is never hot, even during most forest fires. So they are absolutely dependent on talus. The question is whether they are dependent on cold climates. If so, they could be poster children for species threatened by climate change. It's true that nearly all populations of this species are up at high elevations, and that a few Nevada mountain ranges have lost their pikas within recent decades.

Here in Cascadia, most of our pikas are up high, but numerous colonies thrive close to sea level in the Columbia Gorge, where there have been 90°F days nearly every year for as long as records have been kept. Close study finds that Gorge pikas and alpine pikas lead very different lives. Alpine pikas spend many months a year under the snow, eating "hay"—vegetation they spend summer industriously gathering from nearby meadows and curing in "pika haystacks." A hotter climate may not allow them enough hours aboveground in summer to harvest the several bushels of hay each pika needs. Gorge pikas, in contrast, eat a lot of moss, which is about as fresh and available in winter as in summer, so they don't store much hay. The moss grows right on the talus, too, so that they can find some even under snow or ice (which they only suffer for a few weeks a year) as well as in the heat of summer. Mammals don't generally eat much moss, which isn't very nutritious. Exactly how that challenge affects Gorge pikas is not known; I doubt they could increase the moss portion of their diet from what it is now.

The big question is whether pikas elsewhere will adapt to warming by forging new lifestyles. It's a tall order. Young pikas dispersing from their natal talus have to find talus habitat soon—a severe restriction on migration, as it prevents crossing most lowlands. (Pikas never managed to reach the Olympics after the last ice age.)

The young disperse and make their

Coprophagy

The high fiber content of a diet of leaves, twigs, and mosses is a challenge to digestive systems. Cud-chewing grazers meet the challenge with multiple stomachs; they can chew away at their leisure on food that their first stomach has already partially broken down. Pikas, rabbits, and several other small mammals have a way of rechewing food that's already been in their stomachs, without having to squeeze extra stomachs into their small frames. They defecate lumpy soft pellets of lightly digested food and eat them, sometimes in winter after leaving them stored, or sometimes immediately. Their hardcore waste comes out as neatly formed hard pellets. (Pika hard pellets are spherical, a bit bigger than peppercorns, and often aggregated in huge latrines.) Pikas also eat marmot scats, and sometimes store them in their haypiles.

The benefits go beyond shorter chew times. Soft pellets commonly have higher nutrient value than the foods that go into them, suggesting that symbiotic bacteria have been working their magic. There are nutrients pikas can't absorb until they've been worked on first in the stomach, then in the caecum (a pocket between the stomach and the intestine), and then in the stomach again. Some coprophagists have been found to culture their food with a bacterium that completes its digestive work when exposed to sunlight.

own hay their first summer, even if they're only half grown. A youngster's prospects are favorable only when there's room for them somewhere on that rockpile they call home—typically near the pile's center, since outer sites near the meadow belong to dominant individuals. Trying to disperse farther is fatal more often than not.

You're most likely to spot haystacks under rock overhangs in talus; others are deep in the rockpile. Haystacks are prone to rotting, and pikas include some highly phenolic (mildly toxic) plants to inhibit rot. The phenols degrade with age, allowing the cured hay to be eaten. Pikas graze on grasses in summer, but turn to more phenolic perennials and even woody plants for haymaking.

"Eeeenk" calls carry far, for such a small creature. They can express either territoriality or alarm—the two salient features of a pika's so-called social life. Pikas are intensely antisocial, attacking other pikas that infringe on their territories (except of course when they're ready to mate).

On the other hand, the colony is critically important, if only for the alarm system embodied in "eeeenk!" The alarm call is used for larger predators but not for weasels and martens; they're small enough to chase pikas in rockpiles, so it's better to quietly disappear into the maze. According to more than one report, a pika may be aided by other pikas coming out from refuge to distract the weasel by running around like crazy. Such reports set naturalists to arguing over whether it's altruism (evolved traits endangering individual lives for the benefit of the genetic group) or merely foolish nervous agitation.

"Pika" derives from the way Siberian Tungus tribespeople say "eeeenk," so it should be pronounced "peeeeka." I hear that pronunciation in Canada, but south of the 49th I've mostly heard "pike-a," perhaps due to confusion with "pica" or "piker."

Snowshoe Hare

Lepus americanus (LEP-us: their Roman name). Also varying hare. 16 in. when stretched out, + 1½-in. tail; gray-brown to deep chestnut brown in summer; in winter, High Cas and e-side race turns white, with dark ear-tips; w-slope race stays brown; ears slightly shorter than head. Nocturnal and secretive; widespread in mainland forest. Leporidae.

Thanks to their "snowshoes"—large hind-feet with dense growth of stiff hair between the toes—these hares can be just as active in the winter, on the snow, as in summer. They neither hoard nor hibernate, but molt from brown to white fur, and go from a diet of greens to one of conifer buds and shrub bark made all the more accessible by the rising platform of snow. They make the animal tracks we see most often while skiing. They also become the staple in the winter diet of several predators—foxes, great horned owls, golden eagles, bobcats, and especially lynxes. Though the hares' defenses (camouflage, speed, and alertness) are good, the predator pressure on them becomes ferocious when the other small prey have retired beneath the ground or the snow. Hares can support their huge winter losses only with equal summer prodigies of reproduction, which we call "breeding like rabbits." Several times a year, a mother hare can produce two to four young. She mates immediately after each litter, and gestates 36 to 40 days.

Drastic population swings in 8- to 11-year cycles are well known in northerly parts of showshoe hare range, but not here. The other kind of varying the hare is named for—from summer brown to winter white pelage—is true of some hares here. The semiannual molt is triggered by changing day length. In years when autumn snowfall or spring snowmelt come abnormally early or late, the hares find themselves horribly conspicuous and have to lay low for a few weeks. Permanently brown races have evolved in lowland areas that fail, year after year, to develop a prolonged snowpack—for example our west-side foothills and mid-elevations. These brown hares stand out during the occasional snows. The rest of the year they make the most of their camouflage, foraging by dawn and dusk, and sometimes on cloudy days in deep forest. Snowshoe hares don't use burrows, but retire to shallow forms under shrubs.

Snowshoe hare

Though infrequently vocal, snowshoe hares have a fairly loud aggressive or defensive growl, a powerful scream perhaps expressing pain or shock, and ways of drumming their feet as their chief mating call. A legendary courtship dance, in which they may literally somersault over each other for awhile, appears to crescendo out of an ecstatic access of foot-drumming.

Several other kinds of hares and rabbits live in Northwest lowlands and steppe, venturing into the margins of our range. Physical differences between hares and rabbits are arcane, but there's a big difference in life history: hares (*Lepus* spp.) are born fully furred, ready to run and eat green leaves within hours; rabbits, born naked and blind, nurse for 10–12 days before leaving the nest.

MAMMALS: SORICOMORPHA (SHREWS AND MOLES)

Shrew

Sorex **spp.** (SOR-ex: their Roman name). Mouse-like creatures with long, pointed, wiggly, long-whiskered snouts, red-tipped teeth, and hairless tails. Soricidae.

Dusky shrew, *S. monticolus* (mon-TIC-o-lus: mountain-dweller). 2¾ in. + 1¾-in. tail; dark brown. Forests from n OR north.

Wandering shrew, *S. vagrans* (VAY-grenz: wandering). 2½ in. + 1½-in. tail; fur dark gray frosted brown on back, pinkish on sides, and pale on belly. Wet forest and meadows both low and high.

Western water shrew, *S. navigator*. Also *S. palustris*. 3 in. + 3-in. tail; blackish above, paler beneath; tail similarly bicolored. In and near high-elev marshes and lakes.

Marsh shrew, *S. bendirii* (ben-DEAR-ee-eye: for Charles Bendire, p. 342). 3½ in. + 3-in. tail; blackish all over. W-side lowlands, often in water.

Trowbridge shrew, *S. trowbridgii* (tro-BRIDGE-ee-eye: for William P. Trowbridge). 2½ in. + 2¼-in. tail; gray-black except white underside of tail. Lower w-side forests; not on VI or CoastM.

Masked shrew, *S. cinereus* (sin-EE-rius: ashen). 2¼ in. + 1¾-in tail; brown with tan underside. Drier mtn forests, WA and mainland BC.

Shrews, our smallest mammals, lead hyperactive but very simple lives. As shrew expert Leslie Carraway writes, "*S. vagrans* exhibits some behavior that tends to indicate it does not perceive much that transpires in its microcosm." Day in and night out, shrews rush around groping with their little whiskers, sniffing, and eating most everything they can find. This goes on from weaning, between April and July of one year, until death, generally by August of the next.

Wandering shrew

They eat insects and other arthropods (often as larvae), earthworms, and a few conifer seeds and underground-fruiting fungi; they have been known to kill and eat other shrews, and mice. They have cycles of greater and lesser activity, but as a rule they can't go longer than three hours without eating, and the smaller species eat their own weight equivalent daily. As with bats and hummingbirds, such a high caloric demand is dictated by the high rate of heat loss from small bodies: at two grams, masked shrews approach the lower size limit for warm-blooded bodies. Baby shrews nurse their way up to this threshold while huddling together so that the combined mass of the litter of four to ten easily exceeds two grams. Whereas bats and hummingbirds take half of every day off for deep, torpid sleep (p. 358), shrews never do. Nor do they hibernate. It's hard to imagine how our shrews meet their caloric needs during the long snowy season when insect populations are dormant, and heat loss all the more rapid. But they do—or at least enough of them do to maintain the population.

One cause of mortality seems to be a sort of Shrew Shock Syndrome triggered, for example, by capture or a sudden loud noise. Some scientists relate it to the shrew's extreme heart rate (1200 beats per minute have been recorded) and others to low blood sugar caused by even the briefest shortage of food.

Charles Bendire

Karl Emil Bender, as he was originally known in Germany, watched birds and other creatures while stationed near Harney Lake in 1874–1877. He reported what he saw in copious letters to eminent eastern naturalists. To them he was a diamond in the rough, an army major previously noted only as the intrepid Indian-fighter who dissuaded Cochise from returning to the warpath. His reports were published as *Birds of Southeastern Oregon* and later as a thick *Life Histories of North American Birds*. He was first to unmask the kokanee salmon as a landlocked form of sockeye.

At any rate, it is common to see little shrew corpses on the ground. With poor eyesight and hearing, shrews are ill-adapted to evade predators. Their defense is simply to be unappetizing. Owls, Steller's jays, and trout are on the short list of predators known to have a taste for shrews.

Marsh and water shrews, the ones most likely to tempt trout, spend much of their time in the water, going after aquatic insects and larvae, snails, leeches, and so on. Their fine, dense fur traps an insulating air layer next to the skin, giving them enough buoyancy to scoot across the water surface for several seconds. When they dive and swim, they have to paddle frenetically to stay under, aided by stiff, hairy fringes on the sides of their hind feet. As soon as they stop, they bob to the surface. Yet marsh shrews can stay down for three minutes and more. Underwater, they have a silvery coat of little bubbles coming out of their fur.

Our more terrestrial shrews may run on the ground or even climb trees, but more of the time they are subsurface. Dusky and vagrant specialize in the duff layer; others use existing vole runways; and the bigger, stronger Trowbridge's burrows in mineral soil.

The first four species listed above are all part of a closely related group that is not yet well sorted out. New species names in the group have been assigned, but it remains difficult to assign old behavior and distribution records to the correct new name.

Shrews are ferociously solitary. In order to mate, they calm their usual mutual hostility with elaborate courtship displays and pheromonal exchanges—a real-life "taming of the shrews."

Shrew-Mole

Neurotrichus gibbsii (new-ROT-ric-us: hairy wire, i.e., tail; GIB-zee-eye: for G. Gibbs, p. 171). 3 in. + 1½-in. tail; gray-black; tail hairy (unlike any other shrew or mole); teeth not red-tipped; eyes tiny; no visible ears; forefeet and claws larger than rear ones, but less so than in moles; snout long, whiskered. Mainly in w-side forest; not on VI. Talpidae.

The shrew-mole is barely bigger than shrew-sized, yet it is a mole, genetically. Behaviorally, it's less into burrowing and more into life above ground, even climbing bushes in search of bugs.

Shrew-mole

Mole

***Scapanus* spp.** (SCAP-an-us: digger). Burrowing animals, blackish with pink, naked tail and snout; eyes and ears barely visible; forefeet huge, turned-out, heavily clawed. Talpidae.

Coast mole, *S. orarius* (or-AIR-ius: coastal). 5 in. + 1¼-in. tail. Widespread in OR and WA, barely into BC.

Townsend's mole, *S. townsendii* (town-ZEND-ee-eye: for John Kirk Townsend, p. 350). 7 in. + 1½-in. tail. W-side meadows, up to subalpine; CoastR and OlyM.

Moles are so specialized for burrowing that they practically swim through loose soil. Their forelimbs are hyperdeveloped, while the pelvis and hindlimbs are small and weak. Eyes and ears are both almost entirely overgrown with skin and fur so as not to clog up with dirt. While the eyes barely function at all, the ears are quite sharp at receiving earthborn sounds, enabling the mole to detect and hunt earthworms (its main food) by sound.

These two moles are commonest in lowland pastures, but the coast mole also inhabits forests in most parts of our range, and both species are sometimes found in subalpine meadows. Each individual defends its own network of tunnels, which lack entrance holes. Coast moles usually tunnel just below the surface, pushing up sinuous ridges of soil. Townsend's moles tunnel several inches down, and get rid of the dirt by pushing it up to form numerous mole hills. These are symmetrically volcano-shaped, in contrast to fan-shaped gopher mounds; they may have a vertical hole in the center, or you may be able to expose one by digging a little.

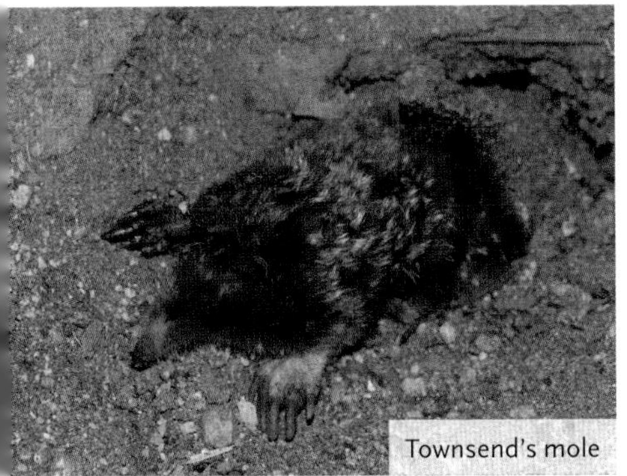
Townsend's mole

MAMMALS: CHIROPTERA (BATS)

Bat

Bat

As evening gets too dark for swifts and nighthawks to continue their feeding flights, bats and owls come out for theirs. Though our largest bats and smallest owls overlap in size—around 5½ inches long with a 16-inch wingspread—bats are easy to tell from owls by their fluttering, indirect flight. Our species never venture out in the daytime, so you are unlikely to see one well and I won't identify our ten or twelve species individually.

Among mammal orders, only rodents are a larger population than bats, which probably take a bigger slice out of the insect population than any other type of predator. Bats catch flying prey either in the mouth or in a tuck of the small membrane stretched between the hind legs; the mouth then plucks it while the bat tumbles momentarily in mid-flight. Each wing is a much larger, transparently thin membrane stretched from the hindleg up to the forelimb and all around the four long "fingers." Since the wing has no thickness to speak of, it is less effective than a bird or airplane wing at turning forward motion into lift. To compensate, bats generally have much greater wing area per weight than birds, and use a complex stroke resembling a human breaststroke to pull themselves up through the air. Bats are slower flyers than birds, but much more maneuverable, able to pursue flying

Animal Sonar

You have probably heard that bats use a sort of ultrasonic radar to find their way around and to locate and catch prey. This is rather recent information. In 1794 it was first observed that bats get around fine with their eyes blocked, but become helplessly blind with their ears blocked. The obvious deduction—that bats hear their way around as competently as other animals see theirs—was too strange to win acceptance for over a century. Not until 1938 were instruments able to detect bats' high-frequency squeaks, whose echoes bats hear in a sonar-like perceptual capacity, echolocation.

A typical bat "blip" lasts a thousandth of a second, during which time it drops an octave and spreads out from a focussed sound to a nearly omnidirectional one. These precise shifts, and the very short wavelength, tune the echoes so finely that the bat not only locates objects but perceives their texture and their exact motion. It's a snap for a bat to nab a mosquito, distinguishing it from a shower of cottonwood fluff amid an obstacle course of branches.

From a casual blip rate of several per second in the open air, the bat steps up to over fifty per second when closing within a yard or so. That's as far as it can echolocate, since high-pitched sounds don't carry far. (Contrast with the great carrying power of a grouse's low booming.) To compensate for the short range, the bat's reactions must be extremely quick, and its blip extremely loud; the decibel level an inch from a bat's mouth is several times that of a pneumatic drill at 20 feet. Those god-awful earsplitting nights in the country! (Well, they would be, if our hearing were sensitive to 80,000 cycles per second instead of a mere 15,000.) To protect the bat's own hearing from damage, its auditory canals vibrate open and shut alternately with the blips, admitting only the echoes. To communicate, bats squeak at a lower (humanly audible) pitch.

The nocturnal aerial hunting made possible by echolocation is key to most bats' success. By day, bat wings are at a competitive disadvantage to feathered wings, which can fly much faster. Yet there are a few kinds of diurnal bats (none in this part of the world) that see pretty well and echolocate poorly.

Aspects of echolocation have been found in many unrelated animals. Porpoises and toothed whales echolocate as sophisticatedly as bats. Some moths evade bats by emitting bat-like blips to scramble the bats' radar. Some shrews echolocate, crudely. Cave-dwelling birds have learned to do it. The ability may be latent in most mammals; sightless humans often learn to echolocate impressively, though rarely developing special calls for the purpose. The human auditory system, according to one hypothesis, also vibrates shut to save us from the racket of our own voices.

insects rather than just intercepting them.

Bats roost upside down, hanging from one or both feet, often in large groups. Daytime roosts during the active season include caves, but more often tree cavities and well-shaded branches. They sleep all day and hibernate all winter upside down. (A few species fly south instead.) Our bats typically hibernate in caves, which provide stable above-freezing temperatures and high humidity. Some males mate very aggressively, others so sneakily that the female appears unaware that anything is going on. Our bats mate in autumn, then typically delay fertilization and bear a single pup in spring. Still hanging upside down, for a few weeks the mothers nurse almost constantly except while out hunting. Coming in from the hunt to a colonial roost, they are fairly accurate in picking out their own pup.

Bats may carry rabies, but even rabid ones rarely bite people.

Since 2006, a fungal disease called white-nose syndrome has afflicted bats in eastern North America, nearly wiping out entire cave populations. Though there are few records of it, so far, from west of the eastern Great Plains, a single bat crippled by white-nose turned up in the west-side Cascade foothills in 2016. White-nose appears to be a Eurasian pathogen that Eurasian bats are resistant to, most likely brought to North America by humans. It's going to be hard times for North America's bats, but there is hope that selected bat caves could be fumigated to offer refugia where species can persist long enough to evolve resistance.

MAMMALS: RODENTIA (RODENTS)

Out of the 4000-plus species of mammals living today, almost 1700 are rodents, and almost 1300 of those, or 32 percent of all mammalian species, are myomorphs, or mouselike rodents. As with insects, songbirds, grasses, and composite flowers, such disproportionate diversification bespeaks great success in recent geologic times.

Of the numerous rodent families, seven appear in this section.

Boomer

Aplodontia rufa (ap-lo-DON-sha: simple teeth; ROO-fa: red). Also mountain-beaver, sewellel, chehalis. 12- to 14-in. rotund body; tail vestigial, inconspicuous, 1–2 in.; dark brown above, slightly paler beneath; with blunt snout, long whiskers, small eyes and ears, long front claws. Shrubby moist habitats; OR, WA, BC CasR. Aplodontidae.

Boomers are big, slow, nearly tailless, partly arboreal, mostly burrowing rodents. They achieve several distinctions, all rather ludicrous. They host the world's largest (3/8 inch) species of flea. They are the only surviving species in the most primitive living family of rodents, having changed little since they first appeared, very early on in the evolution of rodents. Naturalists never quite know what to call them, apart from "living fossils." Most manuals list them under mountain-beaver, but then apologize that this is neither a beaver nor especially a mountain-dweller. Everyone in my end of the county that has boomers calls them "boomers," despite their relentless failure to boom. Well, they might "moom" from time to time—sort of a low moan, repeated.

Boomers prefer wet, scrubby thickets and forests at all elevations. They thrived in the 20th century, with the proliferation of second-growth timber. They honeycomb their half-acre home ranges with shallow burrow systems, making molehill-like dirt

Boomer

heaps and marmot-like burrow entrances with fanned-out porches. Mainly nocturnal, they are active year-round, eating sword ferns and bracken, vine maple and salal bark, and Douglas-fir seedlings. The latter makes them unpopular with foresters, of course, but their digging does a lot for soil drainage and friability, and disseminates spores of desirable underground-fruiting fungi.

American Beaver

Castor canadensis (CAS-tor: their Greek name). 25–32 in. + 10- to 16-in. tail; tail flat, naked, scaly; hind feet webbed; fur dark reddish brown. In and near slow-moving streams. Castoridae.

The beaver is by far the largest North American rodent today, and was all the more so 10,000 years ago, when there was a giant beaver species the size of a black bear. Of all historical animals, the beaver has had the most spectacular effects on North American landforms, vegetation patterns, and Anglo-American settlement. If that's not enough, it's also Oregon's state animal.

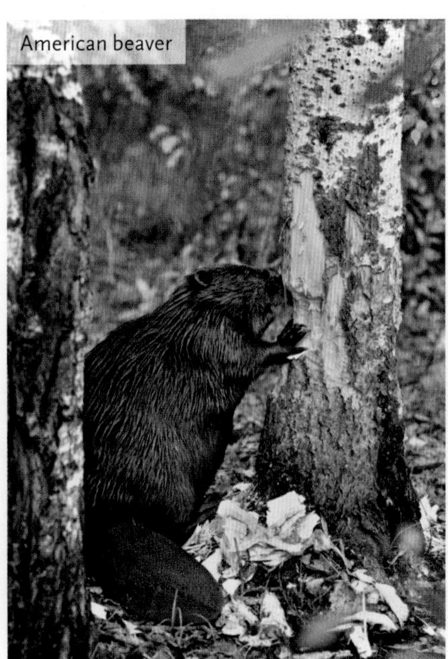
American beaver

Though beavers themselves are infrequently seen by hikers, they leave conspicuous signs—beaver dams, ponds, and especially beaver-chewed trees and saplings.

The sound of running water triggers a dam-building reflex in beavers. They cut down poles with their teeth and drag them into place to form, with mud, a messy but very solid structure as large as a few yards wide and several hundred yards long. Rather inconspicuous dams are more common in our range. A beaver colony may maintain its dam and pond for years, adding new poles and puddling fresh mud (by foot agitation) into the interstices.

Most beaver foods are on land; the adaptation to water is for safety's sake. The pond is a large foraging base on which few predators are nimble. In much of beaver range, pond ice in winter walls them off from predators. Living quarters, in streambank burrows or mid-pond lodge constructions, are above the waterline, but their entrances are all below it, as are the winter food stores—hundreds of poles cut and hauled into the pond during summer, now submerged by waterlogging. Cottonwood, willows, and aspen are favorites. Beavers can chew bark off the poles underwater without drowning, thanks to watertight closures right behind their incisors and at their epiglottis. They maintain breathing space just under the ice by letting a little water out through the dam. They are well insulated by a thick fat layer just under the skin, plus an air layer just above it, deadened by fine underfur and sealed in by a well-greased outer layer of guard hairs.

The typical beaver lodge or burrow houses a pair, their young, and their yearlings. Two-year-olds must disperse in search of new watersheds, where they pair up, commonly for life, and found new lodges. While searching, they may be found far from suitable streams.

When beavers dammed most of the small streams in a watershed, as they once did throughout much of the West, they stabilized river flow more thoroughly, subtly, and effectively than concrete dams are able to do today. Beaver ponds also have dramatic local effects. First off, they drown a lot of trees. Eventually, if maintained by successive generations, they may fill up with silt, becoming first a marsh and later a level meadow with a stream meandering through it. Such parks well below treeline are abundant and much appreciated in the Rockies, but less common in our range.

Beavers were originally almost ubiquitous in the United States and Canada, aside from desert and tundra. Many tribes considered beavers kin to humans, showing them respect in lore and ritual, while also hunting them for fur and meat. Europeans, in contrast, trapped Eurasian beavers (*C. fiber*) nearly to extinction just to obtain a musky glandular secretion used as a perfume base. There was a busy trade in this castoreum for centuries before the beaver hat craze hit Europe in the late 1700s and the demand for dead beavers skyrocketed, not letting up until the supply of American beavers became scarce around 1840. Beaver pelt profits provided the main impetus for westward exploration and territorial expansion, including the Louisiana Purchase.

Changing fashions dropped beaver far below carnivore furs in value. Populations recovered about as much as they can, reaching even into central Seattle and Portland, but will never foreseeably regain their natural level because so much beaver habitat has been lost, and the beaver's considerable ability to rebuild it is not easily tolerated by an agricultural economy.

If we judge the charisma of fauna by the number of geographic names, then beavers rank third in the United States, after bears and deer.

Deer Mouse

Peromyscus maniculatus (per-o-MISS-cus: boot mouse; ma-nic-you-LAY-tus: tiny-handed). 3½ in. + 3- to 4-in. tail (length ratio near 1:1); brown to (juveniles) blue-gray above, pure white below including white feet and bicolored, often white-tipped tail; ears large, thin, fully exposed; eyes large. Ubiquitous; nocturnal. Cricetidae.

Deer mouse

The deer mouse is far and away the most widespread and numerous mammal on the continent. Not shy of people, it makes itself at home in forest cabins, farmhouses, and many city houses in the Northwest. It remains less urbanized than the house mouse, *Mus musculus*, which spread from Europe to cities worldwide together with its relatives the black rat and Norway rat. (Those three invasive urbanites are easily distinguished from our native mice, rats, and voles by their scaly, hairless tails.)

The deer mouse builds a cute but putrid nest out of whatever material is handiest—kleenex, insulation, underwear, moss, or lichens—in a protected place such as a drawer or hollow log. In winter it is active on top of the snow. Omnivorous, it favors larvae in the spring and seeds and berries in the fall. Such a diverse diet adapts it well to burns and clearcuts; as the forest matures, deer mice are gradually displaced by more specialized fungus-eating voles. After Mt. St. Helens' 1980 eruption, they were common in the blast zone so soon that they are presumed to have survived the blast in their homes, and to have found food under the ash.

Dear mice carry the hantavirus, whose flu-like symptoms in humans can turn deadly if untreated for a few days. The greatest danger is in dry, dusty cabins with deer mice; people can become infected by breathing mouse-contaminated dust. It's a good idea to minimize handling deer mice, and to wash your hands promptly and thoroughly if you do handle one. They also carry Lyme disease, but don't transmit it to humans directly and don't apparently carry it very much in our region, at least not yet.

Many deer mice in western British Columbia and Washington forests with tails at least 3¾ inches long are now separated as the northwestern deer mouse, *P. keeni*.

Bushy-Tailed Woodrat

Neotoma cinerea (nee-AH-ta-ma: new cutter; sin-EE-ria: ashen). Also packrat. 8–9 in. + 7-in. tail covered with inch-long fur, hence resembling a squirrel as much as a rat; brown to (juveniles) gray above, whitish below; whiskers long; ears large, thin. Can either run or, if chased, hop like a rabbit. Mainland; patchy in nonalpine sites with rock outcrops or talus; nocturnal. Cricetidae.

For some strange reason, packrats love to incorporate human-made objects, shiny ones especially, into their nests. Possibly some predators are spooked by old gum wrappers or gold watches, or perhaps the packrat's craving is purely aesthetic or spiritual. She is likely to be on her way home with a mud pie or a fir cone when she comes across your Swiss Army knife, and she obviously can't carry both at once, so there may be the appearance of a trade, though not a fair one from your point of view. Packrats have other habits even worse than trading, often driving cabin dwellers to take up arms. They spend all night in the attic, the woodshed, or in the walls noisily dragging materials around—shreds of fiberglass insulation, for example. Or they may mark unoccupied cabins copiously with foul-smelling musk. The males mark rock surfaces with two kinds of smears, one dark and tarry, one calcareous white and crusty.

Our common species, the bushy-tailed, is an active trader. It nests in crevices of trees, talus, cliff, mine, or cabin, and sometimes assembles piles of sticks to cache food in. In caves in arid climates, packrat nests and stick piles can last for millennia, held together and perhaps preserved by rock-hard calcareous deposits of dried urine, enabling paleobotanists to study vegetation shifts as far back as the last ice age. Bushy-tailed woodrat middens are studied at Yellowstone.

Heather Vole

Phenacomys intermedius (fen-ACK-o-mis: impostor mouse). 4¼ in. + 1⅜-in. tail (length ratio 3:1); gray-brown above, paler beneath; tail distinctly bicolored; feet white, even on top. Sporadic, mainly subalpine. Cricetidae.

The heather vole lives around the low heath shrub community—heathers, subalpine blueberries, kinnickinnick, and manzanita. You may spot a heather vole's nest shortly after snowmelt: a 6- to 8-inch ball of shredded lichens, moss, and grass, typically

Bushy-tailed woodrat

Heather vole

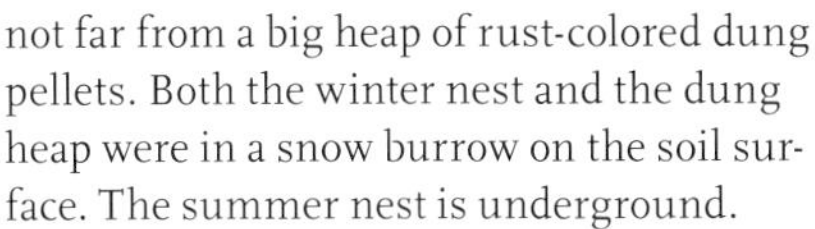
Heather vole's winter latrine exposed by snowmelt.

not far from a big heap of rust-colored dung pellets. Both the winter nest and the dung heap were in a snow burrow on the soil surface. The summer nest is underground.

Sometimes called meadow mice, voles are casually distinguished from mice by smaller, even inconspicuous, ears and eyes. Taxonomists differ over whether to separate them from our native mice at the family or the subfamily level.

Creeping Vole

Microtus oregoni (my-CRO-tus: small ear). 4½ in. + 1⅜-in. tail (length ratio 3:1); gray-brown fur exceptionally short, dense. W-side forests, clearcuts, dry meadows, and deciduous woods; CasR, CoastR, OlyM. Cricetidae.

Our smallest vole stays within an inch one way or the other of the ground surface, either burrowing shallowly in loose dirt or plowing little runways through turf, under logs, or inside rotten logs. This offers some protection from hawks, but not from weasels. Creeping voles maintain sparse populations in forests, ready to multiply rapidly, along with grasses and herbs, after a disturbance.

Long-Tailed Vole

Microtus longicaudus (lon-ji-CAW-dus: long tail). 4¾ in. + 3-in. tail (length ratio 3:2); ears barely protruding; fur gray-grizzled,

Long-tailed vole

feet pale, tail bicolored. Brushy streamsides, clearcuts, etc.; mainland.

Voles of this large genus, related to arctic lemmings, are known for drastic population swings on a three- or four-year cycle, with each species synchronized over much or all of its range. Mysterious hormonal or behavioral mechanisms, rather than either starvation nor predation, seem to curb the population explosions somewhat short of mass starvation—though not always in time to prevent serious damage to seed or grain crops. The Northwest's most notorious vole "plagues" have been of *Microtus montanus* in Klamath and Deschutes Counties.

Townsend's Vole

Microtus townsendii (town-ZEND-ee-eye: for John Kirk Townsend, p. 350). 5½ in. + 2¼-in. tail (length ratio a little over 2:1); ears distinctly protruding. Moist to marshy meadows at all elevs w of CasCr, including VI but just a short way into mainland sw BC.

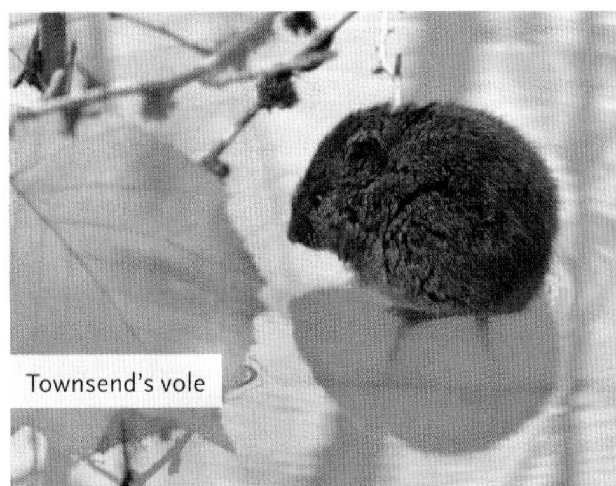
Townsend's vole

Rodents and Fungi

Underground-fruiting fungi—truffles, broadly speaking—are a mainstay of rodent diets in Western conifer forests.

Rating the nutrition in these morsels has proven tricky. Laboratory analysis finds them high in protein, very low in fats, moderate in carbohydrates, and very high in some vitamins and minerals. But digestibility turns out to be abysmal. After all, the principal contents are spores, and passage of spores through the rodent's digestive tract intact and viable is the whole point of the relationship, from the fungus' point of view, so spores have to be pretty indigestible. After adjusting for digestibility, truffles seem barely worth eating. Two factors tip the scales in their favor: they fruit in late fall and winter, when green foods are least nutritious; and finding them consumes fewer calories than finding plant foods because it's done with the nose, a small mammal's most effective sense organ.

Moisture content is another big plus; eating fungi is often less taxing than making the trip to a stream or puddle to drink, thereby reducing exposure to predators. Moist fungi thus enlarge the fungivores' habitat by freeing them from having to live near creeks. (On the other hand, some rodents like Douglas's squirrels hang fungi up to dry, preserving them for winter when, according to more than a few reports, moisture tends to be in good supply around here.)

Fungal spores aren't the only potent stowaways in vole and squirrel droppings. Nitrogen-fixing bacteria, which live in the truffles, also pass unharmed through the rodents' bowels, as do yeasts, which contribute nutrients the bacteria need in order to fix nitrogen. Since nitrogen fertility is often a limiting factor on conifer growth, the conifers may be as dependent on the bacteria and yeasts as on their mycorrhizal partners the truffles. It adds up to a five-way symbiosis, including the rodents that disseminate all four other partners.

digestive system. A fraction of the resulting debris (100 needles may be consumed per hour) is used to line the nest, an airy edifice enlarged over the generations to include several rooms and escape tunnels. The only known escape tactic appears to consist of a leap and free fall from the conifer canopy, with legs spread wide like a flying squirrel prototype. The vole almost always lands on its feet.

Researchers find tree voles hard to get to and impossible to count: you can't bait them into a trap because the only thing they eat is always copiously available. Still, it's clear that they prefer old-growth. Young forests are short on thick limbs for nests, and on the massive moss growths (p. 328) that intercept fog and retain liquid water even through dry spells. Tree voles rely on these for their water.

Muskrat

Ondatra zibethicus (ahn-DAT-ra: Huron tribe's name for muskrat; zi-BETH-ic-us: civet- or musk-bearing). 9–13 in. + 7- to 12-in. tail; tail scaly, pointed, flattened vertically; fur dark glossy brown, paler on belly, nearly white on throat; eyes and ears small; toes long, clawed, slightly webbed; voice an infrequent squeak. In or near slow-moving water up to mid elevs. Cricetidae.

Muskrat

We are tempted to think of the muskrat as an undersized beaver, but its anatomy unmasks it as an oversized vole. Leading similar aquatic lives, beavers and muskrats grow similar fur, which was historically trapped, traded, marketed, and worn in similar ways. (The guard hairs are removed, leaving the dense, glossy underfur.) Several million muskrats are still trapped annually—more individuals and more dollar value than any other US furbearer. In the South, the meat also finds a market as "marsh rabbit."

They are smaller than beavers—half the length and rarely a tenth the weight—and their teeth and jaws aren't robust enough to cut wood, so they build no dams or ponds. Soft vegetation like cattails, rushes, and water-lilies makes up the bulk of their diets, their lodges, and the rafts they build to picnic on. They stray from the vegetarianism typical of the vole family, eating tadpoles, mussels, snails, or crayfish. Their interesting mouths remain shut to water while the incisors, out front, munch away at succulent stems underwater. They can take a big enough breath in a few seconds to last them 15 minutes underwater. Both sexes, especially when breeding, secrete musk on scent posts made of small grass cuttings. Neatly clipped sedge and cattail stems floating at marsh edges are a sign of muskrats. East of here, many muskrats build domed lodges, but in our area the norm is a burrow in a mud bank. The entrances, usually underwater, lead upslope via tunnels to chambers above the water line.

The South American nutria, *Myocastor coypus*, a similar rodent about twice as big, is occasionally seen in the lowlands, especially in Oregon. Nutria fur farms were established in the early 1930s in response to an aggressive, deceptive promotion campaign. When profits failed to materialize, many hard-up farmers just turned their rodent herds loose illegally. Nutria locally threaten some crops and native competitors, particularly muskrats.

Jumping Mouse

***Zapus* spp.** (ZAY-pus: big foot). 4 in. + 5- to 6-in. tail (longer than body); sharply two-toned, with back dark brown to black, sides paler; belly buff white; hind feet several times longer than forefeet; ears small. Thickets and meadows near streams, mainland, May to September. Dipodidae.

Western jumping mouse

Western jumping mouse

Pacific jumping mouse, *Z. trinotatus* (try-no-TAY-tus: 3-striped back). Sides washed with orange. Mainly w-side.

Western jumping mouse, *Z. princeps* (PRIN-seps: a chief, perhaps ironically). Sides washed with yellow. Mainly e-side.

The jumping mouse can run on all fours, but it prefers to hop along in tiny hops, or to swim. If you flush one it's likely to zig-zag off in great bounding leaps of 4 or 5 feet. This unique gait gives you a good chance of recognizing them, even though they're mainly nocturnal. The oversized feet are for power, and the long tail for stability: jumping mice that have lost or broken their tails tumble head-over-heels when they land from long jumps. While none of our other mice or voles hibernate at all, this one hibernates deeply for more than half the year. It eats relatively rich food—grains, berries, insects, and tiny truffles that grow on maple roots.

Porcupine

Erethizon dorsatum (er-a-THIGH-zon: angering; dor-SAY-tum: back). 28–35 in. long, including 9-in. tapered tail; large girth; blackish with long coarse yellow-tinged guard-hairs and long whitish quills visible mainly on the rear half; incisors orange. Mainland, mainly e of CasCr. Erethizontidae.

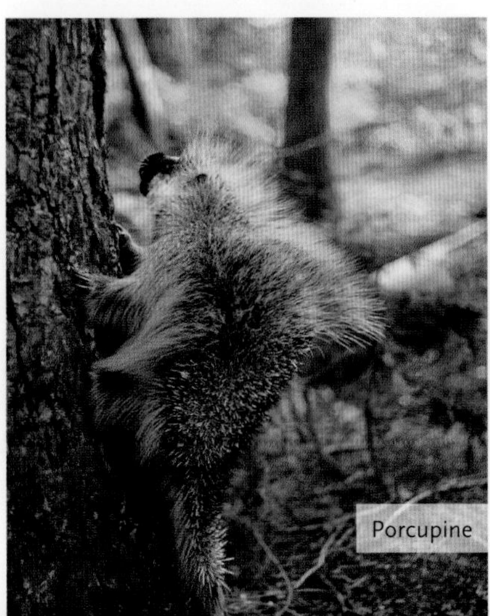

Porcupine

Porcupines' bristling defenses permit them to be slow, unwary, and too blind to obtain a driver's license. This is both good and bad news, for you. Though they're mainly nocturnal, you stand a good chance of seeing one some morning or evening, and possibly of hearing its low murmuring song. And you stand a good chance of having your equipment eaten by one during the night. Porcupines crave the salts in sweat and animal fat, and don't mind eating boot-leather, rubber, wood, nylon, or for that matter brake hoses, tires, or electrical insulation, to get them. (Marmots also consume car parts occasionally.) When camping in east-side valleys, always sleep by your boots, and make your packstraps hard to get at, too. Fair warning.

Quills and spines are modified hairs that have evolved separately in many kinds of rodents, including two separate families both called porcupines. On American porcupines they reach their most effective form: hollow, only loosely attached at the base, and minutely, multiply barbed at the tip. The barbs engage instantly with enough grab to detach the quill from the porcupine; quickly swell in the heat and moisture of flesh; and work their way farther in (as fast as one inch per hour) with the unavoidable twitchings of the victim's muscles. Though strictly a defensive weapon, quills can occasionally kill, either by perforating vital organs or by starving a poor beast that gets a noseful. More often they work their way through muscle and out the other side without causing infection, since they have an antibiotic greasy coating.

So, just maintain a modest safe distance while the porky, most likely, retreats up a tree. "Throwing their quills" is a myth; in fact, they just thrash their tails, whose range sometimes takes people by surprise.

Since quills are their only defense, porcupines have to be born fully quilled and active in order to survive infancy in good numbers. This requires long gestation (seven months) and small litters (one or rarely two). But still, how to get little spikers out of the womb? Answer: the newborn's soggy quills are soft, but harden in about half an hour as they air-dry. And then again, how to get mama and papa close enough to mate? Or baby close enough to nurse? Solving these problems has given porcupines their Achilles' heel, or rather, soft underbelly. With a quill-less underside including the tail, a porcupine can safely mate with her tail scrupulously drawn up over her back. (They mate in late autumn, but are otherwise solitary.) The soft underbelly actually has very tough skin, to hold up through months of dragging up and down tree bark. Genitalia of both sexes are protected from abrasion by withdrawing entirely behind a membrane. This makes it hard to tell the sexes apart.

If it weren't for that unarmed belly, predators would have no place to begin eating. And predators there are, mainly fishers and cougars; rarely coyotes, bobcats, and even great horned owls. The soft underbelly is safe as long as porky is alive enough to stay right side up. Fishers attack the head. Follow their example, with a heavy stick, if you ever find yourself lost and starving and near a porcupine. Some states protect porcupines on the grounds that they are easy edible prey for unarmed humans lost in the woods. They are not choice fare. They were sometimes eaten by Indians, who also turned the quills into an elegant art medium on clothing and baskets

Porcupines eat leaves, new twigs, and catkins in summer, and tree cambium, preferably of pines, in winter. They select cambium near the top of the tree, where it is sweetest. Bright patches of stripped bark high up in pines are a sign of porcupine. When they kill a tree's top by girdling it, the tree turns a branch upward to form a new main trunk, leaving the tree kinked and diminished in lumber value. So foresters are alarmed at the increasing porcupine populations that resulted mainly from human persecution of predators.

Like the red tree vole, the porcupine reveals the nutritional stress of subsisting on this all-you-can-eat cafeteria. Porcupines inexorably lose weight in winter, even while keeping their big guts stuffed with bark. In summer when trees offer tender new foliage, they defend it with toxically high potassium levels. For the porcupine kidney to keep up with the task of eliminating potassium, the porcupine is driven to find low-acid, low-potassium sources of sodium. Your sweaty boots and packstraps fit the bill, as do the coolant hoses and wire insulation it can find at the trailhead. For the same reason deer and elk eat the mud around soda springs, and mountain goats go after human urine.

Pocket Gopher

***Thomomys* spp.** (THO-mo-miss: heap mouse). 5½ in. + a scarcely hairy 2½-in. tail; highly variable gray-brown tending to match the local soil; front claws very long, eyes and ears very small, incisors large and always showing. Open areas with loose soil. Geomyidae.

Mazama pocket gopher, *T. mazama* (ma-ZA-ma: the Crater Lake volcano). OlyM and OR CasR.

Northern pocket gopher, *T. talpoides* (tal-POY-deez: mole-like). CasR of WA and BC.

Pocket gophers spend their lives underground, and have much in common with moles: powerful front claws, heavy shoulders, small weak eyes, small hips for turning

Northern pocket gopher

Gopher Teeth

To see top-notch work from nature's design shop, check out a cleaned rodent skull. Carefully slide out one of the four incisor teeth. It's a long skinny arc, and slides out of an arcuate socket the full length of the skull or the jaw. Throughout life, new material is added at the back end and hardens as it moves forward, continually making up for wear. The outer side of the arc gets thicker enamel, resisting wear differentially to create a self-sharpening chisel edge. Iron oxides further harden the enamel, while staining it orange.

Porcupines wear away roughly 100 percent of the tooth length every year. That's a lot of gnawing. No wonder the word *rodent* derives from "gnaw."

This is a rootless tooth, neither fixed nor ever done growing. Some rodents have rootless molars as well as incisors. Porcupines do not. Chewing on trees their entire lives inflicts heavy wear on their molars, limiting their lifespans. Occasionally, a rodent dies of malocclusion, where an upper and a lower incisor don't quite meet head-on, so they keep growing and either pierce the skull or lock the jaw.

around in tight spaces, and short hair with reversible "grain" for backing up. But moles live on worms and grubs, and gophers are herbivores. They can suck a plant underground before your very eyes, making hardly a dent on the surface. They get enough moisture from their food that they don't even go to water to drink. In fact, only two occasions always draw them into the open air. One is mating, in spring. That takes only a few minutes, and draws out only the males. Afterward, they return to mutually hostile solitude, plugging up burrow openings behind them. The other is the eviction of young gophers from their mothers' burrows.

Gopher "esker" exposed by snowmelt.

Gophers sustain their populations on just one small litter per year, attesting to the safety of life underground. Badgers and gopher snakes are well equipped to take gophers, but rarely venture very far into our range. At the same time, the low reproduction rate signals severe energy costs. Burrowing ten feet takes about 1000 times more energy than walking ten feet. To power that, gophers eat roots and tubers, the most energy-rich part of a meadow.

Our *T. mazama* does go out on occasion, mainly at night. Also, any gopher that lives where it gets snowy may, without exactly going out, eat aboveground foods like bark and twigs by tunneling around through the snow. In spring (July or so in the high country) you find gopher eskers—sinuous ridgelets about 3 inches wide of dirt and gravel that came to rest on the ground during snowmelt. Shortly before snowmelt, the gopher resumed burrowing, and used the abandoned snow tunnels as dumps for newly excavated dirt. Gophers' summer throw mounds are fan-shaped.

When Mt. St. Helens blew, some gophers survived in their burrows under plants that got buried in ash. When they dug out to the surface afterward, they churned old soil into the new ash, helping new plant seedlings contact mycorrhizal spores that were essential to plant survival in the nitrogen-poor ash.

A pocket gopher's pocket is a cheek pouch used, like a squirrel's, to carry food. Unlike a squirrel's, it opens to the outside. Fur-lined and dry, it turns inside out for emptying and cleaning. The big protruding "gopher teeth" are used for digging. The lips close behind them to keep out the dirt.

Marmot

***Marmota* spp.** (mar-MOE-ta: their French name). Also rockchuck, whistle pig. Heavy-bodied, thick-furred, large rodents of mountain meadows and talus, known for their piercing whistles. Sciuridae.

Hoary marmot, *M. caligata* (cali-GAY-ta: wearing boots). 20 in. long + 9-in. tail; grizzled gray-brown, with black feet and pale belly and bridge of nose. Alp/subalpine, WA and BC CasR and CoastM.

Olympic marmot, *M. olympus* Like hoary marmot but face and feet markings less contrasty; back often yellowish by late summer, perhaps bleached by urine-soaked burrow walls. Alp/subalpine, OlyM.

Vancouver marmot, *M. vancouverensis*. 16 in. + 8-in. tail; becoming rich dark brown after the midseason molt; white nose and chest. Alp/subalpine on VI; rare (endangered).

Yellow-bellied marmot, *M. flaviventris* (flay-vi-VEN-tris: yellow belly). 16 in. long + 6½-in. tail; yellowish brown, often gray-grizzled, with yellower throat and belly; feet darker. From CasCr e, mainly lowlands, but sometimes subalpine (as it is in Rockies and CA).

It's hard to feel you're really in the high country until you've been announced by a marmot, with a sudden shrill shriek. If you hear no shrieks in what looks like good marmot habitat, and maybe even has some marmot burrows with their 4-foot porches, it may be because the day got too warm for them and they're all taking a siesta below ground. The shriek (done with the vocal chords and thus not a true whistle) is a warning that may send several other marmots lumping along to their various burrows. The shrieker probably moved to safety near a burrow entrance before deciding whether to shriek. The others then look around, perhaps standing up like big milk bottles, to appraise the threat level. From the inflection of the shriek they know whether to look for the predator in the sky or on the ground. In your case, they may after a while become nearly oblivious to you, or even quite forward and interested in your goods. You may get to watch them scuffle, box, and tumble, or hear more of their vocabulary of grunts, growls, and chirps. They often greet each other with hugs and kisses—well,

Hoary marmot

Yellow-bellied marmot

Torpor and Hibernation

Most warm-blooded species have normal body temperatures about as warm as our 98.6°F, but many spend much of their time at sharply reduced metabolic levels: they become torpid. Torpor is deep sleep, with very slow breathing (one per minute) and heartbeat (four to eight per minute) at body temperatures close to the ambient temperature, down to a limit a few degrees above freezing. Its purpose is to conserve calories at times when they are hard to come by. It follows several patterns:

Seasonal torpor, usually called either hibernation (from the Latin for "winter") or aestivation (for "summer"); the animal may or may not wake up occasionally to excrete, stretch, eat stored food, or go out and forage.

Daily torpor is used by bats daily and by hummingbirds nightly; ordinary sleep would waste too many calories through heat loss from tiny bodies like these, in temperate climates.

Occasional torpor is used by many, many small mammals in response to calorie shortage, or even to shock, as in "playing possum."

Torpor helps animals adapt to severe environments. Some species of jerboas include subarctic races that hibernate, desert races that aestivate, and in-between races active year-round. Some chipmunks vary from year to year, as well as with elevation and latitude, as to whether they will hibernate or forage through the winter, and they may dehibernate if the weather turns better in midwinter. Ground squirrels and marmots of steppe country go into aestivation in the summer and don't come out until they dehibernate in early spring.

Hibernating is costly. The animal must put on a lot of weight—33 to 67 percent on top of its midsummer weight. Since obesity slows animals down, increasing vulnerability to predators, they squeeze their hyperphagia (overeating) into a short season, after the carbohydrate-rich seeds and berries ripen, and then go to ground as soon as they can. Much of the tissue

mouth-to-mouth, teeth-to-teeth, or nose-to-nose contact, and chewing each other's faces and necks.

Marmots need their early warning system because they're slow, and count all the large predators as enemies. They perforate their meadow with dozens of escape burrows. To protect themselves from digging furies—badgers—our yellow-bellied marmots locate many burrows in rockpiles. Our subalpine marmots, with no badgers to worry about, burrow in loose meadow soils. An entire hibernating family can be dug out and eaten by a bear, but that is rare. Coyotes have become the greatest threat overall. People rarely hunt them any more, though in the old days marmots earned high marks for fur, flavor, and fat content in fall. The Tlingit

gained is brown fat, which can oxidize to produce heat directly, without muscular activity. But burning off fat draws water out of the bloodstream, whereas burning off muscle adds water, and dehydration is a big problem during hibernation; muscle mass gets added, only to be burned off again. To conserve water, pituitary hormones suppress urine formation, but then with minimal urination, toxic urea accumulates in the blood, requiring another special process to convert the urea into harmless compounds.

For roughly one day per month, some long-term hibernators raise their temperature while remaining asleep and apparently dreaming. Their brainwaves indicate REM sleep (associated with dreaming) whereas in deep torpor they show little brainwave activity. They probably do this to maintain brain function.

Triggers for hibernation include scarcity of food, abundance of fat, outside temperature, day length, and absolute internal calendars. Once it's hibernating, a rodent is hard to rouse. To wake up, most species spend several hours raising their body temperature by violent shivering. Marmots hibernate in heaps, and the shivering of one will trigger the others to join in a group shiver.

Bears, in contrast, lower their body temperature only a little, can rouse into full activity quickly, and commonly do rouse in winter. Some people conclude that bears are "not true hibernators." A truer statement would be that bears are not squirrels. Bears reduce their metabolic rate about 75 percent (compared to 95–98 percent in small mammals) but they can do some things squirrels can't—like go without urinating or defecating for months, and maintain 100 percent of their muscle mass by recycling metabolic waste into protein. Perhaps bears are simply so much bigger and better-insulated that lowering their body temperature is difficult, and would serve no purpose.

measured wealth in marmot skins.

Squirrels wrote the book on hibernation, and these largest of all squirrels take hibernating seriously indeed. They put on enough fat to constitute as much as half their body weight, and then bed down for more than half the year, the colony snuggling together to conserve heat. Resist the temptation to think of seven-month hibernation as a desperate response to an extreme environment. It is just one strategy that can work here. Other small subalpine grazers like the pika and the water vole stay active beneath the snow at a comfortable constant 32°F, and long-legged browsers forage above the snow, either staying subalpine or migrating downslope. These different wintering strategies align with tastes for different plants, so the grazing species rarely compete directly for one food resource.

Marmots concentrate a year's worth of eating into a brief green season. The season doesn't have to be summer. Our three subalpine marmot species keep a winter schedule (hibernating late September to early May) similar to that of yellow-bellied marmots of the high Rockies; but our yellow-bellies, low on the Cascades' east slope, fatten in April and May and go down for their seven-month slumber in midsummer when the heat dries up spring's herbs and grasses. Summer torpor is aestivation as opposed to hibernation, but yellow-bellies have never heard of that distinction, and go from one to the other without pause.

Young yellow-bellies mature fast enough to disperse (leave their maternal burrow) at the end of their first or, more often, second summer. With an even shorter active season, subalpine marmots mature slowly, dispersing in their third or fourth summer. Young marmots and adult females alike suffer heavy casualties to winter starvation. Even more than a mother bear, a marmom is hard put to fatten enough for her nursing litter's hibernation as well as her own; females skip breeding in some years. (This used to be seen as rigid every-other-year breeding, but closer study found it to be variable: dominant, well-fed females commonly breed in consecutive years, but low-ranked females often skip years.) The colony often consists of an alpha *ménage à trois* surrounded by their young and a few "aunts and uncles" who help out. Most of the marmot tussles you see are youngsters at play. Those that end in a one-sided chase may be colony members evicting outsiders or nudging their own young adults to disperse.

The wild population of Vancouver marmots reached a low of around 35 individuals in 2004. Big human-influenced swings in predator numbers and behavior probably contributed, as did extensive clearcut logging, which created an illusion of extensive new marmot habitat. Colonies seemed to thrive in clearcuts, only to die out when the trees regrew. Since then, several hundred captive-bred Vancouver Island marmots have been released, and are surviving and reproducing. One study found that current colonies may be too small for the predator alarm system to work efficiently. Not only are too many marmots killed, but they spend so much time looking around for predators that they have trouble eating enough to be ready to hibernate.

Olympic marmots are also in decline, especially in the southern half of the park and the northeastern edge. Their decline is blamed on intense predation by the coyotes, which invaded here after wolves were killed off, and are now the marmots' chief predator.

While climate change didn't directly cause either of those declines, it's likely to harm most high-mountain specialists sooner or later. Many subalpine meadows are expected to shift to either forest or steppe vegetation, neither of which offers much marmot forage. However, studies of warming's effects on marmots to date yield mixed verdicts: shorter snow-free seasons benefit marmots in the Colorado Rockies (by giving them more to eat, sooner) but increase winter mortality in the Yukon. Apparently winter dens there got too cold when the insulating snow cover melted away before plant growth invited the marmots to come out and eat.

Golden-Mantled Ground Squirrel

***Callospermophilus* spp.** (calo-sper-MAH-fil-us: beautiful seed lover). Also copperhead; *Spermophilus* spp. 7 in. + 4-in. bushy tail; medium gray-brown with 2 dark and 1 light stripes along each flank; head and chest (the "mantle") tawny to yellow-brown, and not striped. Grass balds, subalpine, and e-side. Sciuridae.

Golden-mantled ground squirrel, *S. lateralis* (lat-er-AY-lis: sides, referring to stripes). In OR.

Cascade golden-mantled ground squirrel, *S. saturatus* (satch-er-AY-tus: dark). BC CasR, WA.

These ground squirrels occupy some of the same open-forest range as the yellow-pine chipmunk, but may avoid direct competition by being less arboreal and by hibernating for months, fattening grossly in the fall. They eat a smorgasbord of seeds, nuts, leaves, shoots, and fungi. Ground squirrel cheek pouches—the mucus-lined mouth interior that extends nearly to the shoulders—can hold several hundred seeds. Their alarm call is a single sharp whistle, higher-pitched than a marmot's (and used less often).

A 2009 study split the large genus *Spermophilus* eight ways. All the North American ground squirrels came away with new names, including three larger, stripeless species found at various grassy margins of our range: Columbian ground squirrel, *Urocitellus columbianus*, in Okanogan County, Washington, and adjacent British Columbia; Belding's ground squirrel, *U. beldingi*, on the east-side Cascades in Oregon; and California ground squirrel, *Otospermophilus beecheyi*, in grasslands in and near the Coast Range and southern Puget-Willamette Trough. Standing 10 inches tall in their milk-bottle posture, any of these could almost pass for marmots.

Golden-mantled ground squirrel

Northern Flying Squirrel

Glaucomys sabrinus (GLAWK-amiss: silvery-gray mouse; sa-BRY-nus: of the Severn). 7 in. + 5½-in. tail (broad and flat); large flap of skin stretching from foreleg to hindleg on each side; eyes large; red-brown above, pale gray beneath. Forest. Sciuridae.

Active in the hours just after dark and before dawn, these pretty squirrels are rarely seen. On a quiet night in the forest, you might hear a soft birdlike chirp and an occasional thump as they land low on a tree trunk. They can't really fly, but they glide far and very accurately, and land gently, by means of lateral skin flaps, which triple their undersurface. They can maneuver to dodge branches, and almost always land on a trunk and immediately run to the opposite side—a predator-evading dodge that includes a feint of the tail in the opposite direction. Large owls preying on them often pick off and drop the tail, so we sometimes find jettisoned tails on the ground.

Flying squirrels usually nest in old woodpecker holes, and have their young gliding at two months of age, around midsummer. They don't hibernate, nor do they store great

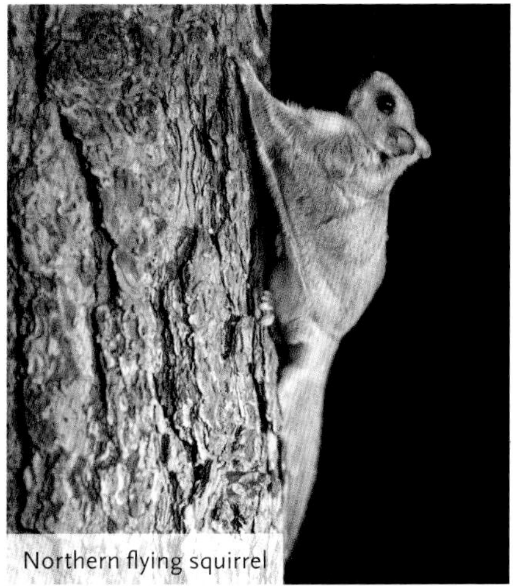
Northern flying squirrel

quantities of food for winter. Ours mainly eat truffles (underground-fruiting fungi), sometimes augmented in winter with horsehair lichens, which also insulate their nests. (Intensive fungivory seems unique to Pacific Northwest flying squirrels, and requires at least a small supplement of richer fare, like seeds or nuts.) The truffle / flying squirrel / spotted owl food chain may be a key to spotted owls' dependence on old growth forest, since truffles abound only in old-growth, especially within thoroughly rotted fallen trees. Logging methods that leave some coarse woody debris and some patches of old trees benefit flying squirrels, red-backed voles, and ecological health overall.

Sabrinus was a river nymph in Roman myth, but the squirrels didn't get their name for being river nymphets. The type, or first-described specimen, of the species lived by Ontario's Severn River, which was named after England's Severn River, originally named Sabrinus by the Romans.

Chipmunk

***Tamias* spp.** (TAY-me-us: storer). Rich brown with four pale and three dark stripes conspicuous down the back and from nose through eyes to ears. Sciuridae.

Townsend's chipmunk, *T. townsendii* (town-ZEND-ee-eye: for John Kirk Townsend, p. 350). 6 in. + bushy 5-in. tail; pale stripes grayish. Dense forest.

Yellow-pine chipmunk, *T. amoenus* (a-me-nus: delightful). 5 in. + bushy 4-in. tail; pale stripes yellowish brown. Open conifer forest and timberline areas; not on VI or in CoastR, rare in OlyM.

These small chipmunks are diurnal, noisy, and locally abundant. Their diverse chips, chirps, poofs, and tisks can be mistaken for bird calls. Townsend's is often heard without being seen, since it prefers heavy forest cover and is shy. Though sometimes seen together, these two species are more often separated by habitat if not by range; yellow-pine chipmunks require open forest, and tend to be either higher or farther east than Townsend's.

Our chipmunks are semi-arboreal, nesting either in burrows or up in trees. They forage terrestrially for seeds, berries, a few insects, and, increasingly toward winter, lots of underground fungi. To facilitate food-handling, they have an upright stance (like other squirrels and gophers) that frees the hand-like forefeet. They store huge quantities of food, carrying it to their burrows in cheek pouches. Their winter strategy varies with climate and genetics, but commonly they rely on stored food alone, without fattening up. They pass the winter with a series of torpid bouts at only moderately depressed

Townsend's chipmunk

Yellow-pine chipmunk

body temperatures; every four or five days they get up to excrete and eat from stores in the burrow. You may hear their chatter even in midwinter, and on milder days at lower elevations they are likely to go out and forage. The young, though born naked, blind, and helpless, mature fast enough to disperse and make their own nests for their first winter.

Douglas's Squirrel

Tamiasciurus douglasii (tay-me-a-sigh-oo-rus: chipmunk squirrel; da-GLASS-ee-eye: for David Douglas, p. 56). Also chickaree. 7 in. + bushy 5-in. tail; red-tinged gray-brown above; eye-ring and underside orange, with a black line separating the upper and lower colors. Forest. Sciuridae.

Noisy sputterings and scoldings from the tree canopy call our attention to this creature that, like other tree squirrels, can afford to be less shy and nocturnal than most mammals thanks to the escape offered by trees. Scolding lets all the neighborhood squirrels know there's a possibly dangerous animal nearby, but once they know about you they don't seem to consider you much of a threat. There are predators that take squirrels quite easily—martens, goshawks, large owls—but apparently they were never common enough to put a dent in the squirrel population, and are scarcer than ever today, in retreat from civilization. Unlike squirrels.

The similar red squirrel, *T. hudsonicus*, replaces Douglas's on Vancouver Island and in the eastern British Columbia Cascades (but *not* Coast Mountains) and Okanogan County, Washington; it is common eastward across the continent. Its dorsal color is slightly redder or darker, while its underside and eye-ring are whitish.

Sometimes in late summer and fall we know Douglas's squirrel by the repeated thud of green true-fir cones hitting the ground. Since fir cones are designed to open and drop their seeds while still on the tree, closed cones you see on the ground are likely a squirrel's harvest. The squirrel runs around in the branches nipping off cones, twelve per minute on Douglas-fir or up to thirty per minute for some smaller cones; then it runs around on the ground carrying them off to cold storage. True-fir cones are too heavy to drag or carry, so it gnaws away just enough of the outside of the cone to lighten it to a draggable weight, while leaving the seeds still well sealed in. Some day, it will carry the cones back up to a habitual feeding limb and tear them apart, eating the seeds and dropping the cone scales and cores in a heap we call a midden. Either the center of a midden or a hole dug in a streambank can be used to store cones for one to three years. The cool, dark, moist conditions keep the cone from opening and losing its seeds and also, incidentally, keep the seeds viable. Foresters learned to rob middens, and squirrels became the chief suppliers of conifer seed to Northwest nurseries by 1965. This scam is in decline now that nurseries want to pick particular trees for breeding.

Mushrooms and truffles, which must be dried to keep well, are festooned in twig crotches all over a conifer, and later moved to a dry cache such as a tree hollow. With such an ambitious food-storage industry, this squirrel has no need to hibernate. For the winter, it moves from a twig and cedar-bark nest on a limb to a better-insulated spot, usually an old woodpecker hole. This-year's

Douglas's squirrel

young winter in their parents' nest (unlike smaller chipmunks) since they need most of a year to mature.

The proportion of all conifer seeds that are consumed by rodents, birds, and insects is huge, exceeding 99 percent in some poor cone crop years. Foresters have long regarded seed eaters as enemies. But the proportion of conifer seeds that germinate and grow is infinitesimal anyway, and of those, the percentage that were able to succeed *because* they were harvested, moved, buried, and then neglected is significant. Trees coevolved with seed eaters in this relationship, and may depend on it (see p. 84). Additionally, all conifers are dependent on mycorrhizal fungi, many of which depend in turn on these same rodents to disseminate their spores. Conifers limit squirrel populations by synchronizing their heavy cone crop years. A few poor cone crop years bring squirrel numbers down, and then the trees produce a bumper crop with way more seeds than the reduced population can eat.

Western Gray Squirrel

Sciurus griseus (sigh-OO-rus: their Greek name, from "shade tail;" GRIS-ee-us: gray). 12 in. + very bushy 10½-in. tail; gray frosted with silver-white hair tips; belly white; ears reddish. Dry, open forest in OR; rare in WA, in Klickitat, Chelan, and Okanogan Counties. Sciuridae.

Scarcer than Douglas's squirrels and rarely vocal or bold, these gray beauties are infrequently seen or heard. With their huge tails, they are gracefully athletic to watch. Large size and good meat make them popular game. They are protected, as a threatened species, in Washington, but still hunted in Oregon even though they are declining. They live around oaks and pines, as they need acorns or pine nuts to augment their diet of truffles.

Western gray squirrel

MAMMALS: CARNIVORA (CARNIVORES)

Members of six families in the order Carnivora are described below. All six are household words: dogs, cats, raccoons, bears, skunks, and weasels. The order also includes seals and walruses.

Coyote

Canis latrans (CAY-niss: dog; LAY-trenz: barking). 32 in. + bushy 14-in. tail; shoulder height 16–20 in.; medium sized, pointy-faced dog with erect, pointed ears; blend of tan, gray, brown, or sometimes mostly black; runs with tail down or horizontal. Ubiquitous except on VI and CoastM. Canidae.

In pioneer days, wolves ruled the forests, leaving coyotes to range over steppes, brushy mountains, and prairies. Then during the 19th century, guns and traps tipped the scales in favor of coyotes by targeting the bigger predators—cougars and grizzlies as well as wolves. Where the big predators were eliminated, coyotes, bobcats, and eagles inherited the brunt of predator-hatred, even though they are too small to significantly limit deer or sheep numbers. Coyotes are America's most bountied, poisoned, and targeted predator, yet they uncannily persist, increase, and spread. Returning wolves may halt that trend, but reports are mixed as to whether that is happening yet at Yellowstone.

More often than you'll see coyotes, you'll hear them howling at night. You can guess that hair-filled scats in the middle of the trail are likely theirs, especially when placed smack dab on a stump, hummock, footlog over a creek, in an intersection, on a ridgetop, or any combination of the above. Coyote feces and urine are not mere "waste," like yours, but more like graffiti signatures full of olfactory data that later canine passers-by, even other species, can read. In Chinook myth, Coyote consulted his dung as an oracle! The male canine habit of fiercely scratching the ground after defecating deposits scents from glands between the toes. The long noses in the dog family really are "the better to smell you with, my dear," as the large olfactory chamber is loaded with scent receptors. Coyotes can detect the passage of other animals a mile or two away, or days earlier. They read scent posts to learn each other's condition and activities. Mates scent-mark together on the same spot. Territory is not a primary function of marking, as coyotes aren't particularly territorial.

When you're trying to identify scats, being full of hair easily distinguishes predator scats from those of herbivores or kibble-fed canids, and size separates coyotes from, say, martens. Further characteristics can tentatively identify the scatmonger; study these in *Wildlife of the Pacific Northwest* or other guides. Scat ID is trickier than you might expect: in one study, biologists collected 404 predator scats in Olympic National Park. (They were finding out who is eating Olympic marmots. Answer: mainly coyotes.) They field-identified the scats, then confirmed the ID using DNA. Their field accuracy rate was only 63 percent. Given that there were only three candidates—cougar, bobcat, and coyote—random guessing would have yielded 33 percent.

As for their spooky nocturnal cacophony, most people hearing it feel that it, too, conveys something above and beyond mere location—though helping a family group relocate each other is its best-understood function. Often it's hard to tell how many coyotes we are listening to; the Modoc used to say it's always just one, sounding like many. Coyote choruses mix up long howls with numerous yips; wolves howl without yipping.

Though preferring small mammals and birds, coyotes also eat grasshoppers, berries, mushrooms, and scavenged carrion. Stalking mice, they patiently "point" like a bird-dog, then pounce like a fox. Against hares they use the fastest running speed of any American predator. Though they

Coyote

commonly try to pick off fawns or elk calves, they hunt adult deer only rarely, locally, and usually in later winter when they gain an advantage from crusted snow as well as the winter-weakened condition of the prey. Usually they hunt alone or pair up, one mate perhaps decoying or flushing prey to where the other lurks. An unwitting badger, eagle, or raven may be briefly employed as a partner.

Pairs bond for many years, and display apparent affection and loyalty. To say they mate for life would be about as euphemistic as saying that Americans do. In years when coyotes are abundant and rodents are unusually scarce in a given area, as many as 85 percent of the mature females there may fail to go into heat, and those who do mate will bear smaller litters than usual. On the other hand, they reproduce like crazy when their own populations are depleted. Some coyotes remain with their parents as yearlings, helping to raise the new litter. Thus the most typical pack is a family, but coyotes vary, sometimes forming larger groups and sometimes remaining solitary or in pairs.

The fierce antagonism of wolf packs toward outsiders (including coyotes) has been key to maintaining wolves and coyotes as distinct species. Wolves, coyotes, jackals, and domestic dogs are all interfertile and beget fertile offspring, yet they are dramatically divergent, physically and behaviorally. The separation of wolves and coyotes broke down (producing "red wolves" and very large coyotes) in parts of the East where coyotes moved in after wolves were nearly extirpated; the tiny, stressed remnant wolf population presumably had no experience of coyotes, and allowed some interbreeding.

Coyote the Trickster is a ubiquitous, complicated figure in Indian mythologies, a devious intelligence undermined by downright humanoid carelessness, greed, conniving lust, and vulgarity. In some myths, Coyote exemplifies the bad, greedy ways of hunting that destroyed a long-gone Eden-like abundance. In others, he brought the poor starving people rituals and techniques they needed, like catching salmon. Each of those tells half the story that anthropologists reconstruct: the first people in North America found an Eden-like abundance; eventually their population in some regions, like the Northwest Coast, reached a saturation point for simple hunting and foraging, and the people had to learn to store salmon and roots. Some tribes, on learning about Jesus, saw Him as the white man's Coyote since He came to Earth to improve people's lot.

In other myths Coyote is the Creator. No wonder the world doesn't always work perfectly.

Gray Wolf

Canis lupus (LOOP-us: the Roman name). 52 in. + bushy 18-in. tail; shoulder height 26–34 in.; large gray to tan dog with massive (not pointy) muzzle, long legs; ears erect, tips rounded; blend of tan, gray, brown, or sometimes mostly black or rarely white; thicker-furred in winter; runs with tail down or horizontal. North CasR, VI, CoastM; expected elsewhere. Canidae.

Wolf, resurgent! Packs now roam the eastern North Cascades and the Wallowas, after several decades of absence from Washington and Oregon, and are likely to continue to spread in the Cascades. Vancouver Island's wolves—a paler subspecies—rebounded from a point so low that some people called them extinct to abundance sufficient to make them the chief predator of the endangered Vancouver marmot. The Coast

Gray wolf

Mountains supported wolves all along, though not as abundantly as central and northern British Columbia. Today's Oregon and Washington wolves descend from British Columbia wolves, and some opponents point out that they are thus nonnative. Their degree of genetic divergence from wolves that lived here in the past is not likely very significant. Certainly they are a native species, whose reinsertion into our food web should have far-ranging ecological benefits.

Wolves and coyotes are very closely related, and interfertile. What separates them reproductively, keeping their genetic lineages distinct in most areas is a trait called interference competition, which means that wolves attack every coyote they run across, often killing them.

Within a wolf pack, aggression is infrequent. A picture of ceaseless vicious competition over alpha status originated from observations of captive wolves thrust into pens together. Wolves in the wild were so wary of people that there was no way to observe their normal lives. David Mech overcame that obstacle by spending 13 summers on an arctic island with wolves that had never encountered humans and were unwary. His conclusion: a pack is a family. Rather than an "alpha female" and "alpha male," we might speak of the "mom and dad." The kids wouldn't think of challenging Dad's alpha status. Medium-sized packs include two or three years of offspring. Some add a male adoptee; occasionally a daughter and the adoptee become a second breeding pair within the pack.

Young wolves may disperse as young as ten months, when they are full-grown, or as late as three years, when their hormone levels begin to peak, and drive them to reproduce. They have several paths to breeding: adoption; replacing a breeder who has died; usurping one who is still alive; or most often pairing with another disperser to found a new pack on a new territory. Those paths can all lead to deadly aggression, as can efforts of neighboring packs to expand their territories when food is scarce.

Hunting as a pack (typically three to five mature pack members) facilitates taking prey as large as elk, moose, or bison. Large prey are dangerous, but a single wolf can actually take a moose. Economic analysis, in terms of meat per capita, suggests that the pack advantage may center not on the hunt but on holding ravens at bay afterward until most meat is consumed.

When the saber-tooth tigers and other Pleistocene megapredators went extinct, leaving only wolves, grizzlies, and humans to prey on the large herbivores, it destabilized North American ecology. Since grizzlies rarely prey on large herbivores, regional extirpations of wolves throw things way out of balance, with no regular predator at all for the large species.

In the 19th century, Euro-Americans despised and feared wolves. Some people still feel that way, but in much of the media wolves have gone from cruel to cuddly. Both views are exaggerations. Wolves are wild carnivores. Statistically, they rarely attack people but, like black bears, they can do so, and are more likely to if they are habituated to people, or if they have rabies. Wolf-dog hybrids and wolves that have been raised by people are especially dangerous.

Some time during the last ice age—probably many times, in many places—some wolves began hanging around humans to scavenge food scraps. At some villages this strategy fed them well, and their descendants thrived, or the mellower-tempered ones did while aggressive ones were driven away or killed. Over the generations, humans came to like these self-selected dogs while often finding ways to exploit them—for meat, or wool, or to haul loads. At some point, dogs began to participate in a hormonal response known for strengthening trust and bonding between human mothers and infants: if a dog and its owner gaze into each other's eyes, oxytocin levels rise in both of them. This doesn't happen in wolves, even ones raised by humans. The wolves that stayed wild back then continued to evolve, so that modern wolves are not as closely related to dogs as ancient wolves were. Dogs are thus not wolves, even thought they are officially *Canis lupus.* (Linnaeus named dogs *Canis familiaris*, but current taxonomists don't regard domestication as speciation.)

Red Fox

Vulpes vulpes (VUL-peez: the Roman name). Also *V. fulva*. 24 in. + 15-in. tail; shoulder height 16 in. (terrier size); various colors, with black legs and ear tips, white belly and tip of tail. Mainland, infrequent; the native subspecies are rare, subalpine, found around our biggest volcanoes. Canidae.

Foxes are little seen here—nocturnal, shy, elusive, and alert. They can bark and squall, but rarely make a concert of it. Their tracks and scats are hard to tell from small coyote ones, and their dens are most often other animals' work taken over without distinctive remodeling.

As wolf range shrank over the last century, coyote and red fox range expanded; red foxes took wolves' place as the world's most widely distributed wild land mammals. They apparently expanded into new range across much of the lower 48 states, and are now seen in Cascadia locales (Puget lowlands and the Olympic Peninsula) where pioneers and early explorers did not record any foxes. For 200 years, these range expansions were attributed to European foxes—said to be less shy, more adaptable, bigger, and redder—brought over by rich gentlemen for hunting. A 2002 paper wailed that invasive genotypes had almost finished wiping out the natives! In a stunning reversal, DNA study now finds that American foxes have no significant European ancestry, and a literature search found that the alleged importations for sport may be a myth. If imports did happen, their lineage died out.

Red fox

That said, transportation of foxes for fur farms likely played a role here. Foxes in the Puget and Fraser lowlands are descended from fur farm escapes bearing eastern North American genes. In contrast, those in the Willamette Valley are most closely related to our native foxes, which comprise two high-elevation subspecies, both quite rare and threatened: the Cascade red fox in Washington, and the Sierra Nevada red fox in Oregon. These subalpine-zone critters are adapted to cold habitats, and may be challenged by climate change. But maybe not: they persist in the Willamette Valley today, and the red fox as a species seems highly adaptable. They are clearly shy of humans—except in Mt. Rainier National Park, where they have become habituated, even loitering at parking lots for food. Don't give them any! Habituation to humans harms wild carnivores.

Red fox coats come in several different color schemes—even within the same litter. The color phases have no more taxonomic significance than hair color in humans. The phase called silver is blackish with some grizzling on the back and shoulders, and white tail tip. The red phase may be solid deep red in the East, but here it tends to be paler, yellowish, and grizzled with gray. The cross phase is a cross between the other two phases—gray-grizzled, washed with yellowish russet. (A gray-colored fox in Oregon

Paw Prints Simplified

5 toes: Bear, raccoon, and weasel families. Distinguish among these by size.

4 toes, with claw prints in front of most toes: Dog family. Wild canids indistinguishable from domestic dogs.

4 toes, mostly without claw prints: Cat family. Cougar prints are 3–3½ inches long and wide, bobcat about 1¾–2 inches. Claws are normally retracted (and don't show in the print) but may extend for traction in soft mud, and then show up in prints.

4 toes, the larger two paws side by side, alternating with staggered forepaw prints: Hare or rabbit.

The pad (ball of foot, behind the toes) of a cougar or bobcat print is indented or scalloped once in front and twice in back; dog pads are convex (not indented) in front, as are lynx pads though the fur often obscures this feature in a lynx print. Scratchings on trees, or on the ground aimed at scats, can also identify the cat family (p. 370). Skilled trackers know the patterns of how forepaws and hindpaws are placed in various gaits.

without the telltale white tip would be a gray fox, *Urocyon cinereoargenteus*. Gray foxes are not native to British Columbia or Washington, and are common in Oregon mainly south of our range.)

Red foxes mate in midwinter, bear their litters of four to seven in early spring, and commonly stay mated. In contrast to the cat and bear families, canids make good fathers. Foxes eat gophers and other small mammals, supplemented with insects, fruit, seeds, and birds' eggs. They hunt with devious opportunism and stealth, often culminating in a spectacular aerial pounce. The huge plumey tail offers balance, and also keeps the face warm when they curl up.

Bobcat

Lynx rufus (links: their Greek name; ROO-fus: red). Also wildcat; *Felis rufus*. 28 in. long + 6-in. tail; tawny to gray cat, often with visible darker spots, and bars on outside of legs and top (only) of tail; ears may show tufts, and cheeks ruffs, shorter than on lynx. Widespread on mainland, favoring brushy, broken, or logged terrain. Felidae.

The bobcat is another lovely creature we rarely see even though it inhabits most parts of our range, and is thought to be as abundant here as it ever was. You just might surprise one if you travel quietly, but generally they keep out of sight.

In bobcat diet studies, hares and then rodents predominate, but in the Oregon Coast

Bobcat

Range boomers were the preeminent prey. In winter bobcats may hunt fawns, but more often find carrion.

Wild cats all like to work out their claws and clawing muscles on tree trunks, like house cats scratching furniture. Bobcat or lynx scratchings will be 2–5 feet up the trunk, cougar scratchings 5–8 feet up. These gashes may be deep, but rarely take off much bark; tree-clawing that strips big patches of bark is bear work. Wild cats also scratch dirt or leaves to partly cover their scats. These scratchings are aimed at the scats—more so than the almost random pawings of dogs next to their fecal markers. Bobcat and cougar scats also tend to be more segmented than coyote scats.

To preserve their sharpness for slashing or gripping prey, cat claws are kept retracted most of the time, and rarely show in cat tracks. One toe (the first, or "thumb") has been lost from the hind foot, and on the forefoot has moved a short way up the paw, enlarging the grip. The hind legs are powerful, for long leaping pounces, but cats other than the cheetah aren't especially fast runners. The cat jaw is shorter and "lower-geared" than most carnivore jaws, and has fewer teeth. Mammals evolved from reptiles with many teeth, and the broad evolutionary trend is toward fewer, more specialized teeth. Cats have small, rather unimportant incisors, huge canines for gripping and tearing, and a quartet of enlarged, pointed carnassials that, rather than meeting, shear past each other like scissor blades for cutting up meat. Cat tongues are raspy with tiny recurved horny papillae, which can clean meat from a bone or hair from a hide. The cat nose is short, suggesting less reliance on smell than in the dog family. As in owls, the eyes are large, wide apart, and aimed straight forward to maximize three-dimensionality. They reflect fire or flashlight beams in the dark (again like owls) thanks to a reflective layer right behind the receptor cells on the retina, doubling light intensity at night. Most cat pupils narrow to vertical slits for maximum differentiation between night and day openness. Cougars, with round pupils, are an exception.

Canada Lynx

Lynx canadensis. Also *L. lynx, Felis canadensis.* 31 in. long + 4-in. tail; tawny-tinged gray cat, not clearly spotted or barred except the black tip of stubby tail; ears tufted, and cheeks ruffed, with long hairs. To confirm a lynx sighting, you would need to measure several footprints well over 2 in. long, or see a tail-tip black underneath as well as on top. CasR e-side from Chelan County n. Felidae.

Sometimes pictured as a larger sort of bobcat, a lynx in fact weighs about the same as a bobcat but looks larger thanks to longer fur and legs, and bigger feet—adaptations to deep snow and cold.

The lynx is listed as threatened in the lower 48 states. It is still fairly numerous, though declining, in Canada. Lynxes may be able to hold on in Washington's northeast Cascades and Okanogan Mountains, if the

Canada lynx

current area of little-visited roadless habitat can be maintained. They are very shy of people. They have shown up in the Oregon Cascades occasionally, but Oregon lynxes have probably always been male refugees from peaking population cycles up north, rather than reproducing populations.

The lynx may be our most single-minded predator, rarely preying on anything but snowshoe hares. Lynx populations in Canada rise and plummet cyclically in response to the hare population. Lacking lynxes to sustain the feedback loop, US snowshoe hare populations don't cycle much.

Cougar

Puma concolor (POO-ma: name for it in the Quechua language of Peru; CON-color: all one color). Also mountain lion, puma; *Felis concolor.* 4–5 ft. long + 2½-ft. tail; ours ruddy brown (deer-colored); no spots or ear tufts except on kittens; long, thick tail. Vocalizations (purrs, chirps, yowls) infrequent. Widespread, preferring steep forested terrain at low to mid-elevs. Felidae.

Cougars take diverse prey, from grasshoppers and mice on up through porcupines and coyotes to elk, but their staples are young deer and elk. A male (the larger sex) can eat about one deer every 10–14 days, up to 20 pounds at a time, burying the remains to come back to later. Buried meat, which may assault your nose, is a sign of cougar. She locates deer by smell or sound, stalks it slowly, crouching, freezing for periods in a position a deer might mistake for a log, then pounces the last 30 feet or so in a few bounding leaps. She bites the prey in the nape, and may either bite through the spinal cord or snap it by twisting the head back. If that fails, she tries to hang on until the prey suffocates. It's risky for cougars to hunt deer and elk, which outweigh them. They are sometimes trampled or thrown hard enough to kill them, and one starved to death pinned under an elk it killed.

Cougars are solitary, with large home ranges, the males' overlapping those of females. Males rarely fight over territory. They scent-mark by scraping piles of dirt mixed with their urine or scats. Near a cougar sighting I found scats on the trail in several piles a few feet apart, each with radiating claw marks in the dirt. Scent-markers help the sexes find each other when a female is

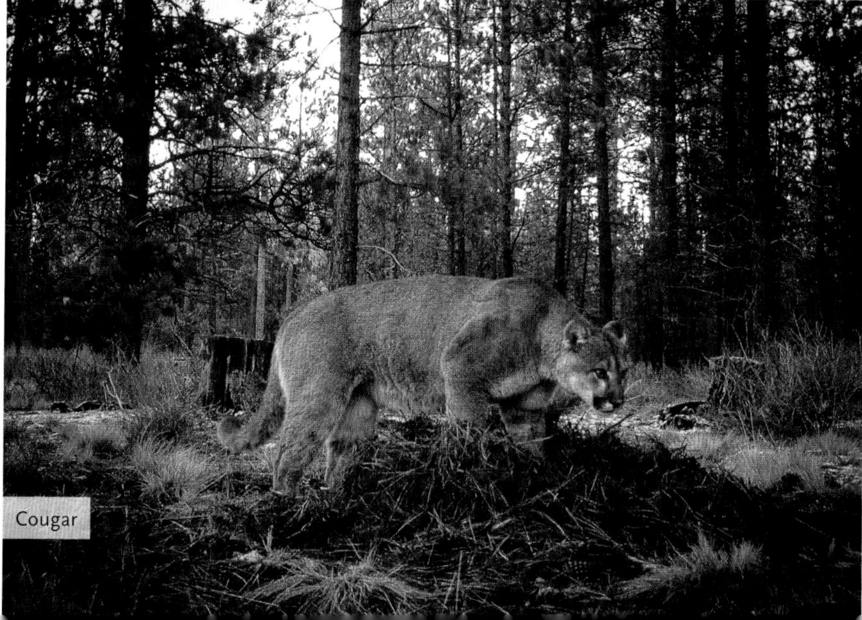
Cougar

in estrus, which may be at any time of year. A male roams with and sleeps near the female for about two weeks, but no longer: if she let him approach the kittens, he might eat them. She rears the young for well over a year, and breeds in alternate years. She has a loud, eerie mating scream that sounds strangely human.

Cougars sometimes follow solitary hikers, unseen, for days, but hardly ever let hikers catch a glimpse of them. Consider yourself lucky if you find so much as a clear set of cougar tracks.

Most game managers agree on the value of cougars as the remaining major predator of deer. Their chief benefit may lie in keeping deer and elk moving on their winter range, which helps avoid local overbrowsing. Cougars select young, old, or diseased herd members—the easiest and safest to attack—minimizing their impact on total deer and elk numbers, which are affected more by hunting.

After voters in Oregon and Washington banned the use of dogs to hunt cougars, the number of them killed by hunters in Washington immediately *increased*: state wildlife managers, trying to protect deer and elk populations (for hunters) as well as to scare cougars away from humans, started issuing far more cougar permits, for a much longer season. Twenty years later, managers and scientists are still arguing about whether the evolving cougar hunt plans are helping or hurting either the elk or the suburbanites. They even disagree over whether Pacific Northwest cougar numbers are up or down. Certainly they are up from 50 years ago.

Hunting pressure tends to disrupt cougar territories and to increase the proportion of young adult males—trends that may increase the threat to human safety. Nevertheless, attacks on humans peaked around the year 2000, both regionally and continent-wide, and fatalities remain very rare—fewer than one per year in North America, far fewer than fatal dog attacks, fatal snakebites, and so on. Most victims are children or solitary small adults. (Historically, about 25 percent of attacks—and of fatal attacks—on humans in North America were on Vancouver Island.) Pets also may be snatched from large campgrounds and even back yards.

Some safety rules apply (note that some are the opposite of safety rules for bears, p. 381): Don't leave small children or pets unattended in likely cougar habitat. If you see a cougar, pick children up immediately, stand tall and confident, and maintain eye contact. Move your arms and pack in any way that will make you look bigger. Act unlike prey. Do not run or turn your back. Retreat slowly. If the cougar still seems aggressive, throw things at it (without prolonged crouching to pick them up). Remain standing. If attacked, fight back aggressively with any weapon you can grab. The cat may give up in favor of easier prey.

Skunk

Western spotted skunk, *Spilogale gracile* (spil-OG-a-lee: spot weasel; GRASS-il-ee: slender). Also *S. putorius*. 10–11 in. + 5-in. tail (kitten-sized); glossy black with intermittent white stripes more or less lengthwise; tail ends in a rosette of long white hairs. Low to mid-elevs w-side. Mephitidae.

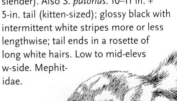

Western spotted skunk

Striped skunk, *Mephitis mephitis* (mef-ITE-iss: pestilential vapor). 18 in. + 11-in. tail (cat-sized); glossy black with 2 broad white stripes diverging at nape to run down sides of back, plus thin white stripe on forehead. Open low elevs. Mephitidae.

Skunk coloration is the opposite of camouflage; it's to a skunk's advantage to be conspicuous and recognized, since its defenses are so good. The rare animal that fails to stay clear may receive additional warnings such as forefoot stamping, tail raising, or (from a spotted skunk) a handstand with tail displayed forward like a big white pom-pom. Spotteds can spray from the handstand, but usually return to all fours. As a last resort, the skunk sharply bends its spine and fires its notorious defensive weapon—up to six well-aimed rounds of a musky liquid secreted just above the anus. This substance burns the eyes, chokes the throat, and of course stinks like hell. It can be shot either in an atomizer-style mist or, more typically, in a water pistol–style stream fanned across a 30- to 45-degree arc for greater coverage. Range is well over 12 feet. Folk antidotes to skunk spray include tomato juice, ammonia, gasoline, and incinerating your clothes; juice is the least unpleasant, fire the most effective. (Seriously, try a five-minute soak, avoiding your eyes, with hydrogen peroxide with a little baking soda and dish detergent mixed in.) The musk is extracted commercially, chemically stripped of scent, and used as a vehicle for perfumes. Talk about a silk purse from a sow's ear!

Only great horned owls—with built-in protective "goggles" and very little sense of smell—seem to prey on skunks regularly. Many big owls smell skunky and have skunk-bitten feet. As far as the oddsmakers of natural selection are concerned, skunk defenses are superlative. But like porcupines, skunks seem to be as vulnerable to tiny parasites as they are well-defended against big predators.

Skunk foods include insects and grubs, mice, shrews, ground-nesting birds and their eggs, berries, grain, carrion, and kitchen scraps. Our skunks remain active most winters. Farther north, they sleep torpidly for days or weeks during cold spells. Typical dens are burrows dug by other animals.

Long known as denizens of North America's farms more than its wilderness, skunks in this century are making their move on suburbs and cities. They're seen as a plague in parts of the East, and the Northwest is not far behind.

Weasel

***Mustela* spp.** (mus-TEE-la: their Roman name). Fast, slinky, slender, short-legged, long-necked animals; in characteristic running gait, the back is arched; ears inconspicuous; rich medium brown above, white to orange-yellow beneath, including feet and insides of legs and (long-tailed only) some of tail; most e-side and high-elev weasels turn pure white in winter, except black tip of tail; ♂ almost twice as heavy as ♀. Widespread up to subalpine. Mustelidae.

Long-tailed weasel, *M. frenata* (fren-AY-ta: bridled). 9–11 in. + 5- to 6½-in. tail (larger dimensions are ♂ average; smaller

Striped skunk

Long-tailed weasel

are ♀); deep cream to yellow underneath (in summer). Not on VI.

Ermine, *M. erminea* (er-MIN-ee-a: their Roman name). Also short-tailed weasel. 7–8 in. + 2½- to 3½-in. tail; white to light cream underneath.

Narrow, linear shapes like the weasel's are rare among the smaller warm-blooded animals because they are inefficient to heat. When asleep or torpid, weasels can roll up into, at best, a lumpy sort of disk, which takes 50–100 percent more calories to maintain at a temperature than a rodent of similar weight, which can roll up into a sphere. Weasels have to eat around 30 percent of their body weight daily, and more in winter. But there's no question of the shape being worth that price: when it needs to eat, the weasel can chase that rodent down any hole or through any crevice, or find it hibernating there. A weasel is thinner, faster, and fiercer of tooth and claw than any animal anywhere near its own weight. Though mouse-sized prey are their staple, long-tailed weasels can also run down squirrels in trees and snowshoe hares on snow—prey as much as ten times their size. In general, the smallest members of predatory families go after the most abundant prey, and are the surest of catching it. The food chain is really an extremely broad pyramid: few individuals can fit at the top as large predators.

Weasels are ferociously aggressive. Reports of "killing sprees" in which they kill far more than they can eat are numerous and confirmed. Granted, human observation may have inhibited or overlooked the weasel's efforts to cache the leftovers for later use. There are also cases of weasel cannibalism, including juveniles eating litter-mates, seemingly carried away with the taste or smell of blood. They nest in burrows of chipmunks, ground squirrels, moles, and so on, often lining these with fur plucked from the late homeowner. They may themselves fall prey to owls, foxes, bobcats, or snakes.

The name ermine is applied by naturalists to the short-tailed weasel only, but by furriers and the general public to the fur of both species interchangeably, so long as it's in the white, winter pelage. In fact, most ermine coats are made from long-tailed weasels because it takes fewer of them to make a coat. It still takes hundreds, though, so a single pelt commands a surprisingly low price. The black tail-tip on the otherwise white winter fur may serve as a decoy: the weasel can usually escape hawk or owl talons that strike this one body part that's conspicuous against snow.

American Mink

Vison vison (VICE-un: an archaic French name). Also *Mustela vison, Neovison vison.* 13–16 in. + 6- to 8-in. tail; long, narrow and short-legged; in characteristic running gait, the back is arched; dark glossy brown except variable white patches on chin, chest, belly; ears inconspicuous. In and near streams, marshes, and sometimes lakes; often in trees as well. Mustelidae.

Ermine

American mink

The mink, a semi-aquatic weasel, preys on fish, frogs, crayfish, ducks, water voles, and muskrats. Some populations become terrestrial for a while, subsisting on hares and voles; others line the British Columbia and Alaska coasts, preying on crabs. Too slow in the water to chase fish efficiently (unlike otters), they more often pounce on slow fish in shallow water. The muskrat may be a mink's most dangerous game—heavy enough to drown a mink by dragging it under. In deep water, muskrats even attack mink fearlessly. On the other hand, a duck that thinks it can shake a mink by taking to the air may be in for a fatal surprise: cases are on record of mink hanging on for the flight until the duck weakens and drops.

The mink version of delayed implantation (p. 377) allows the female to mate and conceive, and then a few weeks later ovulate and mate again. The ensuing litter may have multiple fathers.

Foul discharges from under the tail are characteristic of the weasel family, which used to include skunks. While skunks developed their marksmanship and range, optimizing the anal gland as a defensive weapon, mink evolved an even worse smell. They spray when angered, alarmed, or captured, when fighting each other (they are antisocial) and to mark territory or repel raiders of their meat caches. It may seem ironic that there is so much blood, gore, and stench in the natural milieu of a mink coat; but anyone watching a mink in the wild is likely to admire it. Modern mink coats come from mink ranches, where many novel fur coat colors have been bred. Escaped American mink are an invasive problem in South America and Europe.

Northern River Otter

Lontra canadensis (LOAN-tra: otter in Italian). Also *Lutra canadensis*. 27–29 in. + thick, tapering, muscular 17- to 19-in. tail; dark brown with silvery belly, pale whiskers, very small ears, webbed feet. In or near rivers, marshes, lakes or ocean. Mustelidae.

Otters are among the unlucky animals people are belatedly adoring—only after reducing them to near rarity. In both Europe and America they were trapped for fur or shot on sight as vermin, largely because anglers accused them of more predation on trout than they actually inflict. Ancient Chinese fishermen, in contrast, trained them to herd fish into nets. A few European hunters trained them to retrieve waterfowl.

Today, otters come up in arguments over the existence of nonhuman play. Reputable observers report them running up snowy hills again and again just to body-sled down, or body-surfing in river rapids for no apparent reason. Others claim these behaviors are simply efficient transportation, or youngsters honing their transportation skills. Otters need to spend a lot of time rolling around, to clean and align their fur to maintain its warmth when in water, and extended rolling can look playful. Oddly, the pups seem afraid of the water and have to be taught to swim. Their most efficient and powerful stroke is a lengthwise undulation, using the massive tail but not the paws. They can also swim with their hind paws or all four. On land, they look awkward, and would rather slide on their bellies than walk, especially on snow; nevertheless, they regularly travel many miles on land.

Otters have a low, mumbly chuckle while

Northern river otter

nuzzling. While mating, females may caterwaul like cats. Otters are relatively social, for weasels. Two main nonfamily social patterns are known: a female raising kits may have an unrelated female helper; and unrelated males may form groups that stay together for a long time, groom each other, hunt together, and share food—but of course do not want their buddies' company when a female in estrus is around. Even where large, tight brotherhoods have been studied (in coastal Alaska), a percentage of males and most females are solitary.

Fishermen here see otters regularly. Look on riverbanks and lakeshores for otters' slides, tracks, rolling sites or spraints. The latter are fecal scent-markers placed just out of the water on rocks, mud banks, or floating logs, often atop small debris piles and usually showing fish bones, scales, or crayfish shell bits under a greenish, gelatinous (when fresh) coating that smells distinctive but not unpleasant. Otter staples are crayfish and slow-moving fish, which are much easier to catch than trout. They commonly occupy beaver lodges, even sharing them with the beavers, a species they hardly ever prey on.

Pacific Marten

Martes caurina (MAR-teez: their Roman name; cor-EYE-na: Northwestern). Also pine marten; *M. americana*. 16–18 in. + 8-in. tail; body narrow, legs short, tail fluffy, nose pointy, ears triangular; reddish brown with bright orange or buff on chest and belly. Mainly in trees, in wilderness. Mustelidae.

Pacific marten

Martens have evolved a striking resemblance in form, color, and habits, to their favorite prey, tree squirrels. They even eat conifer seeds sometimes, like Douglas's squirrels, or a few berries, and raid birds' nests. Like weasels, they excel as predators because their prey is abundant and has only meager defenses against them. But unlike weasels, they have been reduced from infrequent to almost rare by trapping and by their aversion to civilization. They may already be gone from the Olympics and northern Coast Range, and are common only in mountain wilderness with conifers.

We rarely see them because they are usually up in the branches, where they are fast, camouflaged, and active mainly at dawn, dusk, or under heavy overcast. Still, curiosity and appetite sometimes lure one right into a hiker's camp. Winter forces them to the ground more, when they hunt voles and hares. They are light enough to move well on top of snow, and can also pursue prey in snow tunnels.

Their musk, so mild as to be almost undetectable to us, is used mainly to mark tree branches to ward off other martens—except of course briefly during summer when about 50 percent of other martens find the smell not repellent but, on the contrary, quite attractive. Like their weasel relatives, they are solitary and aggressively territorial vis-à-vis members of the same sex. Male and females whose territories overlap ignore each other except when ready to mate.

Fisher

Pekania pennanti (pec-AN-ia: from the Algonquin name for them; PEN-an-tie: for Thomas Pennant). Also wejack, pekan; *Martes pennanti*. 20–25 in. + 13- to 15-in. tail; long, thin, and short-legged; glossy black-brown, occasionally with small white throat patch; ears slightly protruding. Rare; mainland forest. Mustelidae.

Fishers don't fish. The name may derive from the Dutch *visse*, meaning nasty. Fishers eat a variety of mammals and birds, snowshoe hares predominating. They're fast enough to chase and kill martens. They can rotate their hind feet almost 180 degrees to run down tree trunks, and use that skill to force porcupines to the ground. Their special technique for porcupines (which outweigh them about two to one) features darting, dodging attacks to the face, with both tooth and claw, repeated for maybe half an hour, until the porcupine is too weak to flail with its tail. Fishers end up with quill bits scattered throughout their organs and musculature like shrapnel, though the majority soften in the stomach and pass safely through. Scats containing bits of quills are generally either fisher or cougar.

The only animals that significantly threaten the fisher are people. Fisher pelts, resembling Siberian sable, usually rank as the highest-priced North American pelt. Trapping and habitat loss virtually eliminated fishers from the lower 48 states. In our range their presence could no longer be confirmed, but central and northern British Columbia still have enough of them to supply fishers for reintroductions in Oregon and Washington. Ninety fishers released in Olympic National Park between 2008 and 2010 traveled all over the peninsula, and have given birth to many litters of kits. They even crossed farms and highways, though several died trying. Releases in southern and eastern Oregon began earlier and seem to have been partly successful, but to date there are no recent records of fishers in our range in Oregon. Reintroductions in the Washington Cascades began in 2015. Stay tuned.

Fisher

Reintroduction success rate is higher for fishers than for most carnivores, presumably because they were extirpated more by trapping than by habitat loss. Attempts to model fisher habitat under climate change produced increased habitat in Washington in one study, but decreases in others. Today, the main way Americans kill fishers is with rodent poisons, which fishers accumulate as they eat rodents. Their preference for remote wilderness tends to help fishers avoid areas where people poison rodents—with the exception of clandestine marijuana crops, a major problem for fishers.

Reproduction in the weasel and bear families usually involves delayed implantation: the fertilized ovum undergoes its first few cell divisions and then goes dormant for weeks or months before implanting in the uterus and resuming its growth in time for springtime births. Increasing day length triggers implantation. The delay is extra long in the fisher, producing a total gestation of up to 370 days, only around 60 of them active. Thus, the female often goes into heat just a few days before or after giving birth, and mates before weaning.

Wolverine

Gulo gulo (GOO-low: gullet or glutton). Also skunk-bear. 26–30 in. + 8- to 9-in. tail; somewhat like a small bear but with gray-brown to yellowish striping across the brow and down the sides to the tail; legs long, especially for the weasel family; fur thick and long. Near timberline; very rare. Mustelidae.

After their likely extirpation from the lower 48 states decades ago, wolverines have found their way back to the Washington Cascades—where a lucky few hikers have seen them or their prints—and the Oregon Wallowa Mountains. Only a handful live in our entire range, and they are equally rare in southeast British Columbia. A Vancouver

Island subspecies was once named, but is thought to be extinct. Northern and inland British Columbia have several thousand, and the province permits hunting and trapping them. Montana still allows trapping their wolverines, which probably number in the dozens.

Our joy at the return of a cool creature is tempered by their prognosis in a changing climate. One paper looked at climate models and predicted that by 2100 the climate they require will not exist in the lower 48 states. They seem (and this is just a hypothesis, but it looks well supported) to require a home that has a thick snowpack into mid-May. Sighting and trapping records suggest a broader range, but those appear to be far-wandering young males; all confirmed female sightings and den locations adhere to the May-snowpack rule. They may need the snow over their dens to keep the kits warm at night, or perhaps for refrigeration—seriously: females cache meat under snow in advance of giving birth, since litter survival through the nutritional demands of lactation may require more meat than can be obtained fresh in early summer.

Of all the sizable North American mammals, wolverines have been one of the most mysterious and hard to study because they scrupulously (and easily) avoid humans, as well as each other. Advances in radio-tagging have finally enabled closer study, especially in Montana's Glacier National Park. Perhaps the least surprising finding is that they are, after all, lovable, at least to their researchers. They are not as solitary as was once thought: after dispersal from the birth den, young wolverines were seen consorting with litter-mates, or even with their dads (for training in predation and survival, I suppose). The paths they take from A to B, just in the course of patrolling their territory, make mountaineers' jaws drop: a Glacier National Park male was GPS-tracked ascending 4900 feet in 90 minutes, crossing the park's highest summit—in January.

As they're the largest members of the weasel family, their reputation as the scrappiest fighters on the continent should come as no surprise. Even cougars and bears will sometimes yield their kills to wolverines, who like nothing better than to polish off another predator's dinner.

American Badger

Taxidea taxus (tax-EYE-dee-a TAX-us: both from the Roman name). 25 in. + 5-in. tail; very broad, low, flat animal with thick fur grizzled yellowish gray-brown; white stripe down face; forefeet heavily clawed for digging. Visitor on e slope, ranging to CasCr in OR and (rarely) to Fraser Gorge in BC. Mustelidae.

This squat, ungainly, but fantastically powerful burrowing creature lives mainly by digging ground squirrels, gophers, and

Wolverine

American badger

snakes out of their holes. It is common in the drier country just east and south of our range.

Raccoon

Procyon lotor (PRO-see-on: ancestral dog; LOW-tor: washer; both names are mistaken). 22 in. + 12-in. tail; gray with black mask across eyes and rings around tail; thick-set and bushy-furred; 5 toes long and clawed, visible in their tracks. Lower elevs. Procyonidae.

Northern outliers of a generally tropical family, raccoons are like us in the same two ways bears are. They are omnivorous, not just by habit but by tooth structure, with plenty of blunt molars for grinding plants rather than cutting meat. And they are plantigrade, meaning they place the heel of the foot on the ground. With long toes on all four feet, raccoons even rival our primate relatives in dexterity; they can turn doorknobs. They raid garbage cans, and are more abundant around town than in our mountains, where they concentrate around lowland lakes and streams. Their food includes berries, acorns, small mammals, frogs, bugs, fish, and crayfish. They climb trees for refuge, and are fond of large hollow trees for their dens, either at the base or in a crotch. Though not territorial, they are generally solitary and mutually hostile except when mating.

Raccoon

Black Bear

Ursus americanus (UR-sus: their Roman name). 4–6 ft. long (4-in. tail inconspicuous), 3–3½ ft. at shoulder; most often stunningly jet black, with a tan nose; also brown, tan, red-brown, or white (the spirit bear, local in CoastM); facial profile is straight; no hump over shoulder; claws dark, 1–1½ in. Widespread; largely diurnal except around human populations. Ursidae.

Perhaps even more than sneaky Coyote, smart Raven, and industrious Beaver, Bear has always been seen by humans as somehow kindred. Though Bear's reflection of human nature is at once darker and grander than Coyote's or Beaver's, it is hard to pin down the essential quality. Mammalogists would concede that bears are among the most humanoid of animals in terms of their feet and their diet. The feet are five-toed,

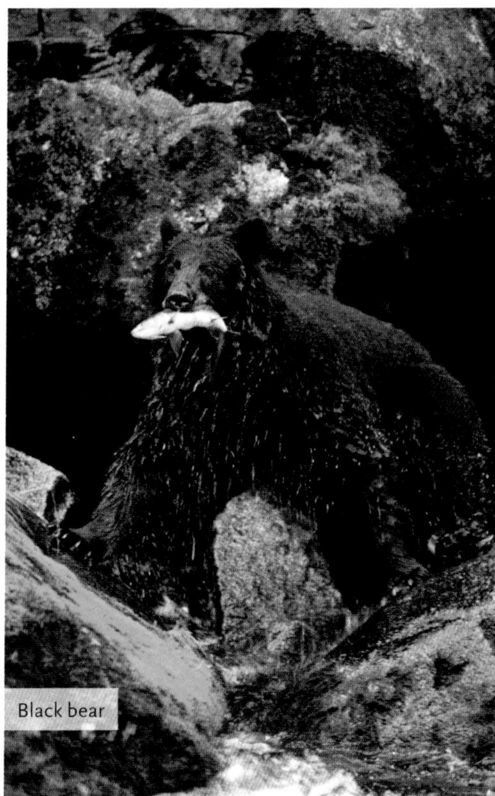

Black bear

plantigrade (putting weight on the heel as well as the ball and toes) and about as big as ours, so that the prints—especially the hind print—look disturbingly familiar.

The diet includes almost anything, and varies enormously by season, region, and individual. Plant foods predominate, starting in spring with tree cambium, horsetails, grass, bulbs, and all kinds of new shoots, and working up to berry gluttony in fall, the fattening-up season. Prey include small mammals, fawns, fish snatched from streams, and insects or larvae where they can be lapped up in quantity—anthills, grubby old logs, wasp nests, or bee hives, preferably dripping with honey. An adult bear can chase predators from their kills, but is less adept at hunting for itself, so large animals are eaten as carrion. Some bears learn to rob woodpecker nests, grain crops, fallen orchard fruit, garbage dumps, or hiker camps. During heavy berry-eating, bear scats become semiliquid like cow pies, and show lots of fruit seeds, leaves (blueberry), or skins (apple). Earlier in the season, they are thick, untapered cylindrical chunks, perhaps showing animal hair, but often closely resembling horse manure. Fresh, they are often as jet-black as the beast itself.

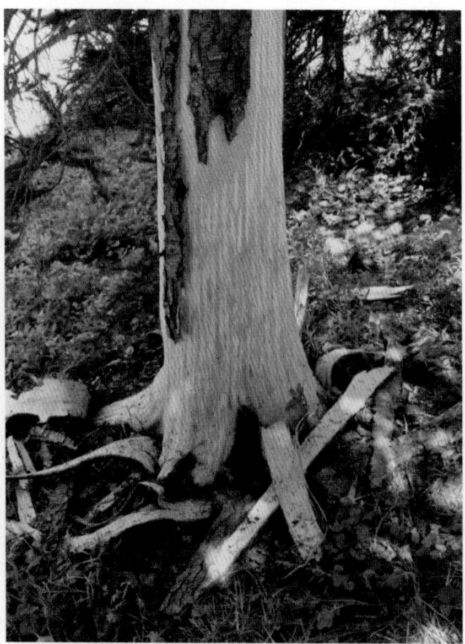
Cambium stripped by a bear.

Trees show several different kinds of bear markings. To eat conifer cambium, bears peel huge strips of bark, typically from around 5 feet down to the ground, with irregular incisor gashes. (Though not all bear-stripped trees die, a bear are serious tree-killers; during times when cambium seems like the best food available, a bear may strip 60 trees a day.) To assert territory, bears bite trees or claw them with long, parallel slashes 5–9 feet from the ground (compare with cat scratches, p. 370). They rub against rough bark, leaving diffuse abrasion and lots of bear hair 2–4 feet up. That may be either scratching an itch or another way of scent-marking. They also leave claw marks when they climb trees to eat catkins, nuts, or fruit. Cubs are often sent into trees for safety while Mom forages, or whenever a threat (such as a hiker) is perceived.

Bears are somewhat nearsighted, and when they stand on their hind legs it's usually to see farther. They have excellent hearing and a phenomenal sense of smell, able to detect carrion many miles away.

Black bears, especially the females, are aggressively territorial, but they tolerate each other's proximity occasionally at banquets, such as salmon runs or great berry crops. Once the ripe fruits are all gone in the fall, there is little bears can do to fatten up. They begin to slow down even before hibernating, and appear listless while preparing their dens—for example, building a nest of fluffy stuff such as cedar bark, which stays resilient a long time. The bear sleeps curled up in a ball with the crown of its head down. With insulative nest padding as well as thick fur, the bear loses little heat to the air of its den, and maintains a body temperature of about 88°F. But its heart rate may reach an astonishing low of just eight very weak beats per minute. (See p. 358 for more on hibernation.)

Two or three cubs are born around

January. The mother wakes up to give birth, then nurses them mostly in her sleep for the next few months. A den of cubs nursing emits a loud buzz or hum like a beehive, only deeper. About 25 percent of litters include half-siblings, indicating that females as well as males are promiscuous. Cubs are smaller at birth, relative to their adult weight, than almost any mammals short of marsupials. To nurse them to viable size, the mother may lose 40 percent of her weight during hibernation, in contrast to the 15–30 percent that hibernating males lose. The next year she will hibernate with her yearlings rather than breeding again. The ferocity of black bear mothers accompanying cubs likely evolved to protect cubs from males of their own species. Subadult bears also risk cannibalism if they are foolish enough to stand up to a big male.

Consider black bears dangerous. They normally withdraw from any contact with people; but the bears we encounter often fall under one of the two infamous exceptions—sows with cubs, and "problem bears" that have learned to scrounge for camper food. Human injuries from black bears have been extremely rare historically, but are bound to increase if naive campers leave food around.

Don't go backpacking in terror of bears, just be smart about them. If you follow game paths into thickets (where bears like to sleep through the day) make lots of cheerful noise as you approach. If a bear moseys into your camp vicinity, stand and bang pots and pans or break branches. If it continues to approach, distance yourself from your food. If you meet one in the open, observe and let your intuition tell you if the bear is threatening. If so, avoid eye contact and retreat discreetly. If a bear charges you, simply stand still; almost all charges are bluff-charges, and you have no chance of outrunning it anyway. (Bears being slow is an optical illusion.) If you're attacked, curl up face-down and play dead. That's the very very last, unlikely resort; don't worry about it, just worry about keeping your food inaccessible to them.

Some backcountry campsites have bear-proof vaults for your food, toothpaste, and cooking utensils. Otherwise, bring your own bear-resistant canisters or hang your food well out of reach. When car-camping, keep food and cookware in your car. (Black bears in the Sierra Nevada rip doors off of cars to obtain food, but fortunately have not yet passed that technological advance along to their Cascadian cousins.) Detailed advice on food storage and other recommended behavior are available from the national and provincial parks.

Grizzly Bear

Ursus arctos* subsp. *horribilis (UR-sus: their Roman name; ARC-toce: their Greek name; hor-RIB-il-iss: horrible). Also brown bear. 6–8 ft. long (3-in. tail invisible), shoulder height 4½ ft.; brown (rarely black) often grizzled with light tan; hump of muscle over front shoulder; facial profile is concave; claws pale, fore-claws typically 3 in.+ long. CoastM and n CasR.

The North Cascades are thought to have grizzlies in extremely small numbers. There have been several confirmations of their presence in the British Columbia Cascades in recent years, but years of efforts to snag a hair sample (identifiable by DNA) in Washington were fruitless. North Cascades

Grizzly bear

National Park is studying whether to translocate a few grizzlies into the park to give them a better chance. They're rarely seen in the southernmost Coast Mountains, but increase sharply north and west of Whistler.

The grizzly is the largest terrestrial carnivore, and one of the more intimidating. It's big and fierce enough to prey on deer or elk, but not fast enough to do so regularly. Its huge tongue is remarkably dextrous at sorting small foods. Its diet is much like a black bear's, with roots, berries, insect grubs, pine nuts, spawning salmonids, small mammals, and large mammal carrion each important, varying widely by season and geography: 90 percent vegetarian in Glacier National Park, 90 percent piscivorous or carnivorous in coastal Alaska, and 50/50 at Yellowstone. It was 60 percent salmon in three 19th-century bears in central Idaho; grizzly recovery there today would require an entirely different diet. (The 60 percent number comes to us thanks to measurements of marine isotopes in hair samples from museum specimens.) Their life cycle is fairly similar to black bears', except that sows breed only every 3 to 5 years and raise their cubs for up to 2½ years; and they do some serious digging, often moving a ton of dirt, for their hibernating dens.

Grizzlies avoid contact with people, and do not normally view people as food. On the other hand, they show little fear of people in close encounters. Avoid those.

Subspecies *horribilis*, the grizzly bear of the Western states and provinces, was once treated as a full species. Other *U. arctos* subspecies include the even larger Kodiak brown bear and the much smaller brown bears of Eurasia. The polar bear, *U. maritimis*, is a close enough relative that polar bears and grizzlies have produced fertile offspring together. Climate change could conceivable force them into more frequent proximity, producing extensive hybridization.

MAMMALS: ARTIODACTYLA (CLOVEN-HOOVED MAMMALS)

Members of the deer and cattle families are found here. The cattle family includes sheep and goats. Two smaller artiodactyl families, the pronghorns and peccaries, live in other parts of North America.

Mountain Goat

Oreamnos americanus (or-ee-AM-nos: mountain lamb). 58 in. long + 6-in. tail, 36-in. shoulder height; all white; extra-long hair forms a beard, a shoulder hump, and pantaloons; sharp, curved, black horns; black hooves. Tracks 2–3 in. long, like deer, but the 2 toes are each rather blunt and almost oblong; deer toes taper sharply. Alp/subalpine in WA and mainland BC. Bovidae.

Ridgecrest goat paths may coincide with hikers' high routes, but often betray us by leading out onto rock faces that require climbing technique or hardware. At least for us. Tufts of white floss on branch tips remind us whose paths they are.

Mountain goats are classified in a tribe with chamois, which lead a similar life in the Alps. True goats and sheep are a separate tribe, also in the cattle family. Mountain goat horns and skulls are not massive enough to sustain bouts of butting. Male mountain goats are reinforced at the other

Mountain goat

end instead: the skin of their rumps, where they may get gored in their flank-to-flank style of fighting, has been known to reach 7/8 inch thick, and was used by Alaskan tribes for chest armor. The males mostly avoid serious combat; the occasional pair of rivals who get carried away typically end up with broken horns or severe wounds, retiring them from further competition. Successful breeders are those who intimidate rivals with visual and olfactory displays. Pit wallowing is indulged in, as among elk, leaving the males' coats filthy, looking rattier still around June when these molt in big blankets, revealing immaculate new white.

Males commonly allow females and immature males, who aren't as inhibited from using their horns, to chase them around. A female may viciously gore other adults who come too close. During her brief estrus in fall, she may tolerate a creeping, submissive courtship. She typically bears a single kid in May or June. Mothers are famously protective—for example walking against a kid's downslope flank to prevent a fall in steep terrain. Kids become playful, apparently because mountain goat gymnastics require a lot of practice at balance and nimbleness. They even try to play with marmots.

Mountain goats are deservedly legendary creatures, and we're usually happy to see them. Unfortunately, many hiker and goat encounters take place in the northeastern Olympics, where the goats are not native and are pests. To alleviate damage to subalpine plant communities, the park braved tourist sentimentality and flew more than 300 goats out during the 1980s. In places the vegetation came back. The year 2010 brought the first known fatal goat-human encounter. A large male with a history of aggressive attitude was standing his ground on a park trail; a hiker tried to shoo him off the trail, and then began to retreat and was gored, severing arteries. The park is studying further ways to either reduce or strategically move its goat population.

Goat hair caught on twigs.

Mountain goats were introduced there for hunting, in the 1920s before it was a national park, and quickly multiplied, radiating from the north corner. (Introduced goats failed to survive on Vancouver Island, fortunately.) They seem reluctant to push west of the Bailey Range climatic divide except during very light snowpack years. Cold wind may not penetrate their insulation, but floundering through wet snow all day and night is a problem. Unlike goats in the Rockies, which seek bare windswept ridges in winter, Olympic goats move down to closed forests where they find thinner snow to paw through. They eat enough huckleberry twigs, lichens, subalpine fir needles, and snow to keep their stomachs busy, but extract scant nutrition from this winter fare, and survive on stored fat.

Apparently, mountain goats are nowhere limited primarily by predation. Eagles take a few kids and yearlings, dive-bombing to knock them off ledges, and cougars occasionally take even adults, but goats are fairly predator-proof with their proverbial evasive skills on cliffy terrain, as well as their defensive weapons, hooves and horns. The hooves have sharp outer edges and a hard, rubbery, corrugated sole for superlative grip. Mortality follows mainly from winter starvation, parasites, avalanches and, in fact, falling. Climate and forage limit goat populations. Reintroducing wolves to the Olympics could in theory reduce goat numbers by inhibiting their winter migration downslope.

Antlers

Horns are unbranched sheaths of keratin, like fingernails; they form from epidermal tissue at their bases, and slowly slide outward over small bone cores. They grow throughout life, generally on both sexes, in the cattle family (sheep, goats, antelope, cattle).

Antlers, a defining character of the deer family, are solid bone, usually branched, and in most species confined to males. They take form inside living skin—complete with hair and blood vessels—and stretch the skin outward as they grow. This skin, or velvet, dies and sloughs off before the antlers come into use in fall. In late winter the antlers weaken at their bases and are soon knocked off, and a new pair will begin to grow by early summer.

On the forest floor, tiny incisors set to work converting shed antlers to mouse bones. In recent years, humans increasingly compete with the mice for "sheds," which can be crafted into decor or sold into the Asian medicinal trade.

Cumbersome and easily entangled in brush, antlers make poor survival tools. Hooves are a deer's defensive weapon, not antlers. With the exception of the small antlers grown by some female caribou, antlers exist to establish dominance among males. Like bright plumages on small male birds, they are a fitness display evolved through sexual selection. (The fittest do survive—but as a genetic lineage, not necessarily as long-lived individuals.

Goats are hunted outside the national parks, but within them they have largely lost their fear of humans. Be careful to suspend your stashed gear and to pee only on the rocks. Mountain goats get too little sodium in their summer diets, so they crave the sodium in our urine and our sweaty boots, as well as in mineral springs. When they brazenly enter camps to eat freshly peed earth, they scrape and demolish precious alpine vegetation.

Mountain goats need not be confused with bighorn sheep, *Ovis canadensis*, which were widespread before 1900 on the steppes and mountains east of the Cascades. Then domestic sheep arrived, competing for the grass and carrying a disease that killed many bighorns. After dying out from the Cascades in the 1920s, they were reintroduced locally on arid grasslands along the Cascades' eastern fringe. These small bands persist tenuously, and are unlikely to spread far into our mountains. They are buff-colored with massive curled horns.

Mule Deer

Odocoileus hemionus (oh-doe-coe-ILL-ee-us: hollow teeth; hem-ee-OH-nus: half ass, i.e., mule). 4¼ ft. long + 6- to 8-in. tail (goat-sized or a bit larger); medium tawny brown or in winter grayish, with white patches on throat, inside of legs, and rump just under the tail; belly paler; ♂ grow antlers; fawns white-spotted; 8- to 9-in. ears rotate independently of each other. Adult tracks 2–3 in. long, the 2 toes each tapered their full length; scats ½- to ¾-in. oval pellets, or occasionally looser. Ubiquitous up to subalpine. Cervidae.

Large-antlered elk bulls tend to die younger than weak ones who rarely fight over cows, but the latter, leaving few offspring, are by definition less fit.)

Some scholars think antlers' chief value is visual—attracting females or intimidating rival males. Like boxing gloves, antlers can regulate and extend combat, reducing risk to life and limb; no doubt they're less deadly than smaller, sharper headgear would be; but this case has been overstated. Even though antlered males usually engage in restrained sparring, and far less often in serious fighting, combat injuries inflict a major portion of adult male mortality.

An elk or whitetail deer antler has one main beam from which all the other points branch, starting with a brow tine. On mule and blacktail deer, both branches off the first Y may again branch. The number of points increases with age, but also responds to nutrition, and thus advertises physical condition. Most yearling bucks east of the Cascades grow two-point forks, whereas most yearlings on the west-side, where the deep shade suppresses good deer browse, grow unbranched spikes. Rich feeding in captivity has produced five-point yearlings, while meager range can limit even dominant bucks to forks. Full-grown elk average five points; older bulls may grow six, seven, or rarely eight. While mature mule deer typically have four or five, British Columbia has seen freakishly large antlers—48 points on a mule deer, 25 on a white-tail.

Mule deer, *O. hemionus* subsp. *hemionus*. Tail pale with black tip. CasCr and e-side.

Blacktail deer, *O. hemionus* subsp. *columbianus*. Tail dark brown to black. W-side.

Browsing is sophisticated business. Spend a while sitting quietly near some deer and see exactly what they eat. (They tolerate a lot of watching in Olympic National Park, where they've been protected for generations.) They often show an intense preference for a particular bush, which must contain good levels of some nutrient. They lap up spring water—no matter how muddy it has become from trampling hooves—that contains mineral salts they crave. Overall, they seek a great variety of browse plants and fungi. They chomp mushrooms, "nature's salt licks," for other hard-to-find minerals. They strip horsehair lichen from tree limbs; it has low nutritive value on its own, but enhances digestibility of the austere winter diet of twigs and evergreen leaves such as salal.

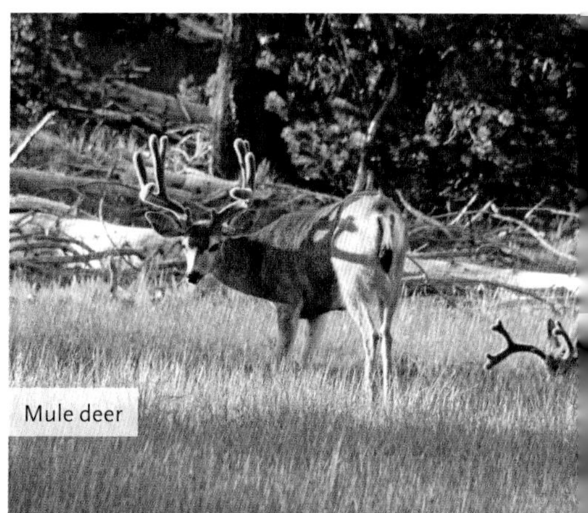
Mule deer

Like other cud chewers, deer can live on a high-roughage diet thanks to cellulose-digesting bacteria in their first (pre-cudchewing) stomach. They have to browse for the nutritional demands of the bacteria; insufficient protein kills the bacteria, malnourishing the browser even with its belly full. Deer populations sometimes approach a local limit, the carrying capacity of the habitat. Overbrowsed habitat isn't denuded, it's just short on plants that offer adequate fats, proteins, and trace minerals.

Cougars are the top nonhuman predators of US deer, now that wolves are nearly extirpated. Bobcats, coyotes, and bears also prey on fawns. Dogs, hunters, cars, and trains kill many deer.

An alarmed mule deer walks slowly, elegantly stiff-legged, head held high. If it decides to flee it breaks into a stiff-legged high-bounding gait called stotting or pronking. Many explanations of stotting have been offered over the decades. The current one is that is says to the predator, "Look how strong and quick I am! Wouldn't you be better off chasing a weaker deer?" Predators do in fact waste energy when they chase healthier-than-average individuals, and impressive stotting is hard for a weak animal to fake.

Whitetail deer, *O. virginianus*, have longer, wider, flashier tails. Rather than stotting in response to predators, they flash their tails by raising them upright, exposing the white. This may signal that "I know you're there and I'm ready to run," and may forestall some chases, but it seems less convincing than stotting. The Pacific Northwest has two whitetail subspecies: the Columbian whitetail is endangered, reduced to tiny west-side areas just outside our range. The Northwest whitetail thrives, pushing westward from the Rockies into the eastern edge of the North Cascades, chiefly on valley floors. For reasons that remain unclear, mule deer have decreased where whitetails have moved in.

Steep south slopes just above river bottoms are ideal winter range. The low elevation and the insulating tree canopy offer warmer temperature and much shallower snow, while the south aspect lets in a little of the low-angle sunlight, and tends to have more shrubs. In summer, many of our deer move upslope to meadows where they fatten on herbs.

The one tight social tie among deer is between a doe and her fawns and yearlings. Males are solitary or form loose small groups. During the rut, dominant bucks follow does, relentlessly checking their pheromones—with an approach that mimics a fawn going for milk—to catch the one day when each doe is receptive. Before and after giving birth, a doe seeks seclusion even from her yearlings; it's up to them to reunite with her afterward. For their first few weeks she hides the new fawns—separately, if there are two or three—in nest-like forms under brush. She browses in the vicinity, strives to repel other does, and comes back to nurse mainly at night. If a threatening large animal like you approaches, she will resolutely ignore the fawns, acting nonchalant. (She will meet a smaller threat, like fox or bobcat, with a bold counterattack.) Occasionally people come across the hidden fawn and not the foraging doe, and make the cruel mistake of "rescuing the abandoned" fawn. Unless you actually find the mother dead, assume a fawn is being properly cared for, and leave it in peace, untainted by human contact.

A nonnative louse has been afflicting Northwest deer since 1996. It causes hair loss (most visible in winter and spring) and a lot of scratching and licking, and exacerbates a modest long-term decline in mule deer numbers. Chronic wasting disease, a prion disease fatal to deer, elk, and moose, is spreading in many regions of the continent but has not been detected in British Columbia, Washington, or Oregon as of early 2016. It seems not to be transmissible to humans. The bacterium *E. coli* 0157:H7, which can be deadly to humans, is common in deer and elk. Hunter-bagged venison, including jerky, should be cooked to 165°F. Windfall apples are also suspect where they may have contacted deer scats.

Elk

Cervus canadensis (SIR-vus: Roman for deer). Also wapiti; *C. elaphus.* 7–8 ft. long + 4- to 6-in. tail (large cow-sized); overall color dark brown to gray-tan, tending to be darker near the coast and in winter; large, sharply defined cream patch on rump; darker tinges on neck, face, legs and belly; ♂ grow antlers; fawns white-spotted. Adult tracks 3–4⅝ in. long, more rounded than deer; scats ⅝- to 1¼-in. ovals in winter, patties in spring. Widespread. Cervidae.

Elk inhabit coniferous forests and high mountains of the West today. Before white settlement they were common all the way to Vermont and South Carolina. Great herds of them on the Plains were second only to buffalo both in sheer biomass and as a food and material for humans. They were shot in huge numbers for meat and hides, reducing both their range and their numbers by at least 90 percent. They held on, notably at Yellowstone, Vancouver Island, and the Olympics, until an alarmed public, rallying around a famous hunter named Teddy Roosevelt, got refuges and hunting restrictions enacted to allow their population to recover. The very idea of conserving species was novel to white culture; the object, as popularly understood, was to conserve them for future generations of people to hunt.

Our coastal ranges have native Roosevelt elk, formerly treated as a subspecies. Cascades populations descend largely from Rocky Mountain elk reintroduced here since 1900. Native elk may or may not have been completely extirpated from the Cascades, and we don't know exactly how their genes compared to those of today's population.

There have been long-running politicized controversies over the natural population levels of elk. Levels were suppressed by Indian hunting, beginning several thousand years ago, and rebounded a few hundred years ago when Indians were decimated by introduced diseases. They were thus high (would that be "naturally" or "unnaturally" high?) when white settlement began, and were then savaged by 19th-century hunters. They've done pretty well over the past century with regulated hunting, but became unnaturally dense in national parks with no hunting, no wolves, and reduced cougar numbers.

After Mt. St. Helens erupted, elk browsed photogenically on some of the first

Elk

plants to emerge in the devastated blast zone. Even before there was anything to browse, elk explored the blast zone, perhaps out of curiosity. They sped the revegetation process by bringing seeds of plants and spores of mycorrhizal fungi. Most plants would have had a hard time pioneering there without fungi.

Elk migrate vertically—valley floors in winter and spring, high meadows in late summer to the rutting season in fall. Most of the year they travel in herds segregated by sex, the mature bulls in bands of ten or fifteen, the females and young males in larger herds. In late summer, the bulls become mutually hostile, and the largest divide out harems from the cow herds. They tolerate yearlings, but drive away two- and three-year-old males. The harem's movements, like those of the cow herd in winter, are subtly directed by a matriarch apparently respected for her maturity more than her size or strength. The bull aggressively herds cows that try to stray, and may lose part or all of his harem if he lets himself be distracted. Other bulls will surely be distracting him, hoping to take over the harem by overcoming him in a clash of antlers staged at dusk or dawn.

Elk have a remarkably extravagant courtship system. Bulls challenging each other or working up their sexual or combative frenzies behave curiously:

Thrashing These attacks on small trees and brush (common also among deer bucks) have been called "polishing the antlers" or "rubbing off the itchy velvet" but are actually visual challenges, warm-up or practice for sparring, or autoerotic stimulation. Profligate urination typically accompanies thrashing, and antlers are used to toss urine-soaked sod onto their backs.

Pit-wallowing Shallow wallows are dug and trampled out and lined with urine and feces. Elk cows appear to get excited when exploring them. Wallows often become long-lasting pools.

Bugling This unique call includes a deep bellow and a farther-carrying whistle. Its clearest function is in herding cows. Elk cows occasionally bugle too, when calving in spring.

The reek of urine advertises the bull's physical condition. Others can smell how much he has been metabolizing fat as opposed to fresh food or, worse yet, muscle. A bull metabolizing only fat is one so well fed that he can devote all of his energy to the rut without weakening from hunger. Keeping track of a harem, defending it from other bulls, and reaping the sexual rewards are not only hard work, but so time-consuming that the bull can no longer eat or rest. Almost inevitably, primary bulls succumb in the same season to lesser but better-rested rivals, and often these secondary bulls yield in turn to tertiary bulls. Defeated dominants wander off alone, catch up on food and sleep, and show no further interest in sex that year. They may not last the winter. Smaller opportunistic bulls live longer. They spend the rutting season alone, but stand at least a chance of mating with a stray cow.

While Cascades elk cows may bear young every year, starting at age two, coastal elk only go into estrus every other year, and have poorer calf survival rates. Browsing techniques and care of the young are much like those of deer (pp. 385–386) except that to an elk cow, humans are puny meddlers to be chased from the nursery. Biologists who tag elk calves have to be quick tree-climbers. Fenced elk exclosures in the Hoh valley have shown that elk browsing greatly affects the vegetation of valleys where elk herds winter. It increases Sitka spruce, which is too prickly to eat; it thins vine maples and salmonberries, which elk love; it generally clears the understory; and it has tended to speed the invasion of weedy grasses, clover, dandelions, and buttercups.

In Europe, a relative, *C. elaphus,* is the red deer or stag that Robin Hood hunted. If you're thinking that the genus known to the English as a "deer" ought, in English, to be

Deer Pheromones

Deer are fine subjects for the study of pheromones—chemical messages conveyed among conspecifics. Mule deer are rather antisocial, using some pheromones apparently to repel each other (a function akin to territoriality, though mule deer are not territorial). A subordinate deer will sniff a dominant deer's tarsal patches, get the message, and retreat to a respectful distance. Tarsal glands are buried in patches of dark hair on the inside of the ankle joints, midway up the rear legs. To activate tarsal pheromones, deer of any age or sex urinate on these patches and rub them together. While most pheromones are secreted in sweat or sebum (skin oil), deer urine is itself pheromonal in that it reveals the animal's health and strength. Glands on the forehead are rubbed on shrub twigs to advertise the condition of a dominant buck, or to mark possession of a sleeping bed. Interdigitate glands, between the two toes, secrete an attractant pheromone, marking a deer's trail for other deer to follow. Metatarsal glands, on the outside of the lower hind leg, secrete a garlicky odor signaling fear or alarm.

Sensing pheromones looks like sniffing (or maybe something beyond mere sniffing, in the case of the male lip-curl). It is truly a sixth sense, and uses its own organ, the vomeronasal organ within the nose chamber. Whereas smelling detects chemical recipes made by combining six or seven basic odors, a vomeronasal nerve ending—1000 to 10,000 times more sensitive than an olfactory nerve ending—is lit up by only one pheromone. "Bingo! This female will be receptive in six hours."

a deer, you have a point. A different genus exists which we ought to call "elk," as Europeans do and had done for centuries before Americans dubbed it a "moose." The names were misplaced because American species of *Cervus* and *Alces* are larger than their European congeners. Colonists on these shores met whitetails about the size of European deer (*Cervus*) and wapiti about the size of European elk (*Alces*) and named them accordingly. The misnomers stuck, even through generations of texts trying to replace "elk" with the Shawnee name wapiti.

Moose

Alces americanus (AL-sees: Latinization of the same Norse word that became, in English, "elk"). Also *A. alces*. 9 ft. long + 7-in. tail; ♀ much smaller; dark gray-brown; long horselike head with loose overhanging upper lip; antlers have broad flat blades and many points; long dewlap hangs from throat, especially on ♂; pronounced shoulder hump. Adult tracks 5 in. or longer, more pointed than elk; scats 1½- to 2-in. ovals in winter, patties in spring. E-side river bottoms; BC and n Cas. Cervidae.

In northernmost Washington and southernmost British Columbia, moose went from almost unknown in 1920 to fairly common by 1950. Their continent-wide population explosion is attributed to post-logging increases in willow shoots, a moose's winter staple. Willow thickets with numerous broken, chewed, and bent-over tops are a sign of

Moose

moose. Moose evolved to take advantage of post-fire willow explosions by moving in and doubling their birth rate, and they respond the same way post-logging.

Moose are often described as docile, but "self-confident and relaxed" might be more accurate. They tolerate humans, up to a point. A skittish, unpredictable streak combines with sheer bulk to produce the surprising statistic that more people are killed by moose than by grizzly bears. While some deaths are in car crashes (moose being the one common species of roadkill hefty enough for mutual assured destruction) others result from aggressive behavior. Lowered ears and raised hair on the neck are warnings. Never try to "shoo" a moose.

BIRDS

Birds are winged, warm-blooded vertebrates with feathers. Wings first developed in some dinosaurs, of which birds are the surviving descendants. According to DNA evidence, birds and crocodilians are each other's closest living relatives—closer than crocodiles to lizards or birds to mammals.

In one conspicuous way, birds and mammals (which diverged from reptiles much earlier) evolved in parallel: both bird and mammal lines produced keratinous skin growths to serve as insulation and make warm-bloodedness possible. While mammals got hair, birds got feathers, whose light weight is ideal for flying. As you know from the sales pitch on down sleeping bags, bird plumage still has no equal among resilient, deformable, durable substances, in insulation value per weight.

In addition to insulating, feathers provide most of a bird's shape, size, and color: plucked, a duck, a crow, a hawk, and a gull would look surprisingly alike in form, and pathetically small. Body plumage as much as doubles a bird's girth. The "fat" gray jays you see while skiing aren't fat, they're fluffing out their plumage to maximize its insulation value. (Goosebumps on your skin are a lame vestige of a similar response.) Less fluffed out during flight, body plumage serves the equally crucial function of streamlining. The long outer feathers of wings and tail, meanwhile, provide most of the bird's airfoil surface at very little cost in weight. They constitute 35 to 60 percent of a typical bird's wingspread and 10 to 40 percent of its length. Feathers make the bird.

Color in most plumages—nearly all female and juvenile plumages and many fall and winter male plumages—emphasizes camouflage. Since pale colors make good camouflage against the sky, and darker colors against foliage or earth, birds tend to be paler underneath than on top. A mother and young in the nest especially need to be cryptic, since they can only sit tight when predators pass overhead. (The mother could fly, of course, but she stays to protect her flightless young.) Males are freer from the need for camouflage than females, and much freer than earthbound mammals. In them (and in the females of a very few species) sexual selection went wild evolving colorful plumage.

Even a bird that looks drab to us, or two species that look just alike to us, may actually look otherwise to a bird. Songbirds and a few other bird orders can see ultraviolet light quite well, and many have evolved markings that reflect ultraviolet. We don't see these at all. Raptors can't see ultraviolet very well, so these markings grab the attention of females but not of predators.

For efficient pairing up, conspecifics need to recognize each other quickly. A showy plumage doesn't look equally good to all female birds; it looks best to females of the same species. The same goes for bird songs, which are distinguished from calls as being longer and more complex, and characteristic of order Passeriformes, often called songbirds. Experienced birders can identify many species by song alone; females and juveniles in many genera are nearly impossible to identify when no males or songs are present. Females sing in many tropical species, but few species around here; only one partner is really needed for quick recognition of conspecifics. It may seem obvious to us that bird songs are a courtship communication, and some studies do find that females are attracted to superior singers, and that song quality advertises good health. But some scientists prefer alternate hypotheses, like assertion of territory. Most singing goes on at times when courtship is not in play.

Birds molt, or replace all of their feathers, at least once a year, and twice if they have different seasonal plumages, which serve to make the male showy for courtship and then camouflaged for the nonbreeding seasons. Molting has a different reason—camouflage—among ptarmigan, whose females, juveniles, and males all may go through two or three seasonal plumages (to match snow, no snow, or patchy snow). With a few exceptions like the mallard and the dipper, the large feathers of the wing and tail molt just a few at a time, leaving the bird tattered but still flightworthy.

Much time is spent on the vital task of preening with the toes or beak, applying oil from a preen gland. Aligning and oiling plumage optimizes it as an airfoil, as insulation, and as waterproofing.

To fly, birds had to evolve not only wings and feathers, but radically larger, more efficient respiratory systems. The stamina for a single day of flying, let alone for migrating across oceans, would be inconceivable in a mammal. It demands a lavish supply of oxygen to the blood and of blood to the muscles. Cooling also is done through the breath. Breathing capacity is augmented by several air sacs and, in many birds, by hollow interiors of the large upper leg and wing bones, all interconnected with little air tubes. Each breath passing through the lungs to the sacs and bones and back out through the lungs is efficiently scoured of its oxygen.

Hollow bones, their interiors crisscrossed with tiny strut-like bone fibers in accord with the best engineering principles, doubtless evolved to save weight, yet some birds lack them. Loons, for example, have solid bones—advantageous for a bird that dives for a living and doesn't fly much. But some diving birds have hollow bones, and a few soaring birds manage with solid bones.

A bird's sternum, or breastbone, projects keel-like in front of the rib cage to provide a mechanically advantaged point of attachment for the flight muscles. Known on the dinner table as breast meat, these muscles are a flying bird's largest organs. They power the wings and also guide flight by controlling the orientation of each and every feather along the wing edge through a system of tendons like ropes and pulleys. There is scant muscle in the wing and none in the foot, which is moved via tendons from upper leg muscles held close to the body. A flying animal ideally has nearly all its weight in an aerodynamic "fuselage" close to its center of gravity, and little weight in gangly limbs.

The wing is analogous at once to both wing and propeller of an airplane. This is no accident; pioneers of mechanical flight studied and tried to copy bird flight for centuries before Wilbur and Orville finally, albeit crudely, got it right by separating the propelling and lifting functions of the bird wing. Like a propeller, wings provide forward thrust by slicing vertically through the air while held at a diagonal—the rear edge angled upward on the downstroke and vice versa.

Once there is enough forward motion or headwind to provide strong airflow across the wings (bird or airplane), their shape provides vertical lift by creating a low-pressure pocket in the air curving over their convex upper surface, while the lower surface is effectively flat. This upperside-convex principle is common to all flying birds except perhaps hummingbirds; but wing outlines have diverged in many specializations. Read about swimming wings on page 396, soaring wings on page 403, speed wings on page 409, silent wings on page 412, little-used wings on page 398, and hovering wings on page 416.

Nomenclature of species follows the American Ornithologists' Union (AOU) Checklist, which is accepted as official throughout the continent. The size figure that begins each description is the length from tip of bill to tip of tail of an average adult male; most species' females are a little smaller, bird of prey females bigger. I use *Golden Guide*'s measurements of "live birds hand-held in natural positions." These run about 10 percent shorter than those in other bird manuals that, following taxonomic tradition, are measurements of long-dead specimens or skins forcibly hand-stretched. For a mental yardstick, I recommend thinking of sparrow size (4–6 inches), robin size (8½ inches), jay size (9–12 inches), crow size (17 inches), and raven size (21 inches). Unfortunately, it can be hard to get much sense of a bird's size when you see it against the open sky.

Habitat and behavior are often useful ID clues. Many small birds are faithful to certain plant communities or to levels within a forest—upper canopy, lower canopy, tall shrubs, low shrubs, or streamside thickets without a canopy over them. After the nesting season, many birds migrate either south or downslope. Ones that don't migrate may shift to a different habitat as the weather, their caloric needs, and the foods available all change.

Mallard

Harlequin duck

BIRDS: ANSERIFORMES (WATERFOWL), FAMILY ANATIDAE

Mallard

Anas platyrhynchos (AN-us: Roman for duck; plat-i-RINK-os: broad nose). 16 in.. ws 36 in.; breeding ♂ (September–June) have iridescent dark green head separated from red-brown breast and brown back by white neckband; bill yellow on ♂, black and orange on ♀; both sexes have a band of bright blue with black-and-white trim on upper rear edge of wing, and much white under wings; ♀, juveniles, and summer ♂ speckled drab. Loud quack. Marshy lakes, as in the c OR Cas.

The mallard exemplifies surface-feeding, or dabbling ducks. It is conspicuous over much of the Northern Hemisphere—except during duck-hunting season, when it makes itself scarce. Tasty flesh contributes to its renown. Domestic ducks were bred largely from mallards, centuries ago, and breed with them when given the chance; city park ducks often include mallards and hybrids together.

Dabbling ducks feed by upending themselves in shallow water and plucking vegetation from the bottom. They also eat a few mollusks and insects, and a very few small fish. They take flight abruptly and steeply, unlike diving ducks, which splash along the surface.

Unlike most birds, mallards molt their flight feathers all at once, leaving themselves flightless. To escape predators they hide out for the duration in large groups in marshes. In summer we see mallard mothers with chicks trailing behind, but no fathers. Newly hatched ducklings can swim a mile, but they can't fly for almost two months. At that point (late summer) it's the mothers' turn to molt. While flightless, they are "sitting ducks," but the rest of the time they can practice "sleeping with one eye open." If four mallards are asleep in a row, the two in the middle close both eyes while the two on the ends tend to keep the end-of-the-line eye open for predators. Brain scans on mallards in this state found that the brain hemisphere connected to the open eye remained semi-wakeful and capable of rousing the bird upon sighting a predator, while the other hemisphere experienced normal sleep.

Harlequin Duck

Histrionicus histrionicus (hiss-tree-ON-ic-us: jester). 12 in., ws 26 in.; breeding ♂ (October–June) plumed in a clown-like patchwork of slaty blue-gray, rich brown, and splotches of white with black trim; others dark brown with small white patches on head, and whitish belly. Usually silent. On fast streams with bedrock, March–August.

Whether in whitewater rivers or heavy surf, harlequins display great pluck and strength as swimmers. Many live on rocky seashores, diving for shellfish, and then migrate inland to build a grass-lined nest by a mountain

Bufflehead

stream, where they feed largely on insects.

Harlequins and buffleheads are carnivorous diving ducks, as opposed to dabbling ducks who merely tip or dip, feeding at the surface for their mostly plant diet. Divers tend to be smaller and chunkier, with shorter bills; birders are all familiar with these duck categories, but they no longer have any taxonomic status. Harlequin plumes were once prized for ladies' hats.

Bufflehead

Bucephala albeola (bew-SEF-a-la: buffalo head; al-BE-a-la: small white). 10 in., ws 24 in.; ♂ white with black back, black head with with big erectile white patch crossing crown behind eye; ♀ brown with long white patch behind eye; short, thick bill. Usually silent. On and near lakes: high OR CasR in summer, low throughout our range in fall through spring.

Buffleheads are the only ducks small enough to move right in to a flicker's old nest without alteration, and seem to depend on that convenience. A courting male flies over his target female and makes a splashy ski-landing, with white crest erect, just past her. Most of our buffleheads winter here or migrate through, and summer in interior British Columbia and farther north. A modest number are found around high lakes in the Oregon Cascades in summer, but not in our Washington mountains. They excel at diving, and mainly eat crustaceans, molluscs, and insect nymphs.

Common Merganser

Mergus merganser (MER-gus: diver; mer-GAN-ser: diving goose). 18 in., ws 37 in.; breeding (November–July) ♂ white beneath with black back and head, and red bill, the head greenish-iridescent in strong light, becoming red brown in August–October; ♀ gray with red-brown head sometimes showing slight crest on nape, and red bill, white throat. Hoarse croaks and cackling. Lakes and streams; common.

Instead of a Donald Duck–like broad bill, mergansers have a long, narrow bill with a hooked tip and serrated edges for gripping slippery fish and other aquatic prey. Of our three merganser species, the common is the largest, most montane, and most common. Many winter here and fly north to breed, but others move up to our mountain lakes to

Common merganser

breed, finding hollow trees or other cavities to nest in.

Canada Goose

Branta canadensis (BRAN-ta: Norse name for goose). 16–25 in., ws 68 in.; head and neck (held straight forward in flight) black, with white chin strap; body brown, thick; tail black and white; wings brown; belly white. Both sexes "honk"; migrating flocks form a V, and honk continuously. Lower-elev rivers and lakes.

The best-established explanation for the V formation of flocks in flight is that a goose saves energy (75 percent in one calculation, 3.5 percent in another) by flying in the draft of the goose ahead of it. Different birds, usually females, trade off in the leader spot, the only position that doesn't save any energy.

Canada goose

Common loon

Canada geese declined due to hunting and draining of wetlands in many areas, but then they found a lot of new habitat on lawns, golf courses, and croplands. Populations have increased perhaps ten-fold over recent decades, making geese equally unpopular among urbanites and farmers. Most geese of Pacific Northwest cities are year-round residents. Many of the migrators in spring and fall are the recently separated cackling goose, *B. hutchinsii*, which looks very similar but smaller, with a shorter bill.

BIRDS: GAVIIFORMES (LOONS), FAMILY GAVIIDAE

Common Loon

Gavia immer (GAY-via: the Roman term; IM-er: sooty). 24 in., ws 58 in. (variable size but generally bigger than ducks); bill heavy, tapered; breeding-season adults (both sexes) with iridescent green and black head, white collar, black and white checked back, white belly; winter plumage dark gray-brown above, white below; in flight, head is held lower than body, and feet trail behind tail. Lakes; rare.

The varied nocturnal "laughs" and "yodels" of loons have been called beautiful, horrible, hair-raising, bloodcurdling, magical, and maniacal. Unequivocally they are loud.

Loons resemble diving ducks in their feeding and locomotion skills. They eat mainly fish, plus some frogs, reptiles, leeches, insects, and aquatic plants. Like ducks they use wings as well as webbed feet to swim underwater. Diving either headfirst or submerging submarinewise, they can go deeper than any other birds (300 feet down!) thanks to their heavier bodies—only slightly less dense than water. Their heavy bones are a primitive trait that doubtless remains advantageous for diving. It is disadvantageous for flying; though loons can fly fast and far, they plop down gracelessly, and take off with great effort and splashing. Loons can become trapped for days or weeks on forest-lined lakes too small for their low-angle takeoff pattern. They wait for a gale to arise, which they can then take off into. On their feet they're still more inept and cumbersome; the extreme rear placement of their legs is great for swimming but awful for walking. They go ashore only to breed, on an island, and nest in soggy plant debris at the water's edge. She and he take turns on the eggs.

After wintering near the coast, some loons move to mountain lakes, arriving soon after the ice breaks up. Loons are sensitive to human disturbance during the breeding season, and have nearly disappeared from the Cascades as a breeding species.

Ruffed grouse

BIRDS: GALLIFORMES (CHICKENLIKE FOWL)

Ruffed Grouse

Bonasa umbellus (bo-NAY-sa: bull; um-BEL-us: umbrella). Also drummer. 14 in.; mottled gray-buff; tail red-brown or gray (two color phases) with heavy black band at tip and faint ones above; ♂ have slight crest; black neck ruff is erected only in courtship display. Distinctive "drumming" in lieu of a vocal mating call is common in late spring, occasional (territorial?) at other seasons; an owl-like hoot is sometimes heard. Low to mid-elev forest with alders. Phasianidae.

The male ruffed grouse makes a mysterious noise. Even Press Expedition men—the seasoned frontiersmen who made the first recorded trip across the Olympics—seem to have mistaken it for, of all things, geysers bubbling. It's an accelerating series of muffled thumps, known as drumming or booming. He does it with sharp downstrokes of his wings while perched on a log. You can't tell what direction or distance it's coming from. (Very low-pitched sounds carry farthest in forests, but they sound nondirectional.) An attracted female must have a tantalizing search in store for her. At the end of it, she can watch his fantailed, ruff-necked dance, and then mate with him, but that's all he has to offer her; she will incubate and raise the young by herself. She nests on the ground, like other grouse, and trusts her excellent camouflage up until the last second, when you're about to step on her unaware. Then she flushes explosively, right under your nose. She may actually try to scare you away, if there are young to protect, or to draw you away from them with her famous broken wing routine. You are touched. She knows a thing or two about psychology.

Sooty Grouse

Dendragapus fuliginosus (den-DRAG-a-pus: tree lover; foo-lih-jin-OH-sus: sooty). Also hooter, blue grouse; *D. obscurus*. 17 in.; adult ♂ mottled dark gray above, pale gray beneath, with yellow eyebrow-comb; others mottled gray-brown; both sexes have blackish tail. ♂ courtship call a series of 5 or 6 low hoots; hen with chicks clucks. All elevs in montane forest; fairly often seen, but on the NABCI Watch List. Phasianidae.

Sooty grouse spend the breeding season in relatively open habitats, enriching their diets with caterpillars, plant shoots, berries, and even mushrooms. For winter they move into dense conifer stands, which offer better thermal cover, visual cover, and plenty of needles, which are all they'll find to eat in winter anyway. To adapt to the poor diet,

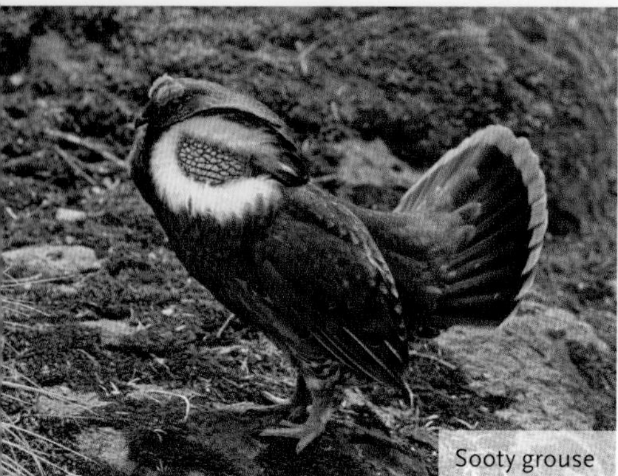
Sooty grouse

White-tailed ptarmigan

their intestine lengthens by about 40 percent each fall; they pack their digestive tracts full each evening and spend all night digesting, and still some 75 percent of the fibrous matter passes through undigested, creating a thick buildup under roost trees. In experiments they have been able to maintain their body weight on 100 percent Douglas-fir needles, but not on needles of other species.

Both the courting hoot and the chief visual display of the males—bare yellow patches on the neck—are performed by inflating a pair of air sacs in the throat.

Birds of the order Galliformes feed and nest on the ground, and fly only in infrequent short bursts. They have undersized wings and pale breast meat, indicating a scanty supply of blood to the flying muscles. After the fowl has been flushed a few times in quick succession, these muscles are too oxygen-short to fly again until they are rested. Tirelessness in flight is more the norm among other kinds of birds that, being infrequent walkers, have dark breast meat and pale and scanty leg meat.

A few miles east of the crest in northern Washington, sooty grouse gives way to dusky grouse, *D. obscurus*. The two are almost indistinguishable, and the AOU treated them as a single species until 2006. Spruce grouse, *Falcipennis canadensis,* also may turn up from the crest eastward in British Columbia and northern Washington. It has a red-orange eyebrow-comb and a pattern of bars across its breast. All three species were nicknamed "fool hens" for being preposterously fearless around humans—vulnerable even to sticks and stones.

White-Tailed Ptarmigan

Lagopus leucura (la-GO-pus: hare foot; loo-CUE-ra: white tail). Also snow grouse. 10 in.; underparts white; upper parts white in winter, mottled brown in summer, patchwork of brown and white in spring and fall; feet feathered; bright red eyebrow-comb on ♂ in spring. Soft clucks and hoots. Alp/subalpine, rarely lower during heavy snow seasons; WA CasR, VI, CoastM. Phasianidae.

Though smaller than their grouse relatives, ptarmigan are the largest creatures that make our alpine zone their exclusive home. Dwarf willows are their staple in winter, crowberries in fall. Like other grouse, they rely on camouflage to protect them from predators. For winter they molt to pure white plumage and stay on pure white snow as much as possible, plunging and swimming into it for nightly shelter and to reach willow buds. Occasionally they explode up out of the snow when a skier comes along on top of their snow blanket.

The *p* in ptarmigan is silent, and silly. It must have found its way into print long ago in the work of some pedant who assumed "ptarmigan" to be Greek. It's Gaelic.

Mountain Quail

Oreortyx pictus (or-ee-OR-tix: mountain quail; PIC-tus: painted). 9 in.; sexes alike; half gray, half reddish-brown, with white streak below eye, reddish brown throat and dramatic white bars on dark brown flanks; two long black plumes on top of head (may be intertwined to appear as one). On the ground in brush or woodland, e.g., in burns or clearcuts; w-side in OR mtns, also possible (rare) on OR e-side and on WA side of CGorge. Odontophoridae.

Mountain quail

The male quail's spring mating call—a short high, clear yelp repeated every 7 seconds or so—carries well and is easy to recognize, but these shy birds are rarely seen. The female lays two clutches averaging 11 eggs each, and each parent incubates one clutch and raises its chicks; by late summer, they may join forces. They typically migrate upslope and downslope seasonally, on foot. You're most likely to see a covey of them early or late in the day in autumn, when the chicks are nearly full-grown. The species is declining, but apparently less so here than in the rest of its range.

BIRDS: COLUMBIFORMES (PIGEONS), FAMILY COLUMBIDAE

Band-Tailed Pigeon

Patagioenas fasciata (pat-a-JEE-nus: ?; fas-ee-AY-ta: banded). Also *Columba fasciata.* 13½ in.; gray with purplish and whitish hues, broadly fanned gray tail, yellow legs and black-tipped yellow bill, thin white band across nape (adults only). Low w-side, openings near big trees. Call a low, owl-like "whoo-whoo"; call is a squawk, at once nasal and guttural.

Band-tailed pigeon

Flocks of band-tailed pigeons rove our west-side forests (and croplands as well) from April through October, then winter far to the south. Here they gorge on our tasty berries—salal, madrona, elder-, salmon-, and blackberries, among others—and, not coincidentally, become tasty and desirable game themselves. Back when passenger pigeons were hunted to extinction, band-tails very nearly shared their fate. A federal ban was placed on hunting them in 1916; after their numbers recovered somewhat, hunting was permitted again until the 1990s, when Washington and British Columbia both shut down their pigeon hunts.

They lay only one egg per nest, which tends to keep recovery slow. As many as 50 pairs may nest in one large conifer, with

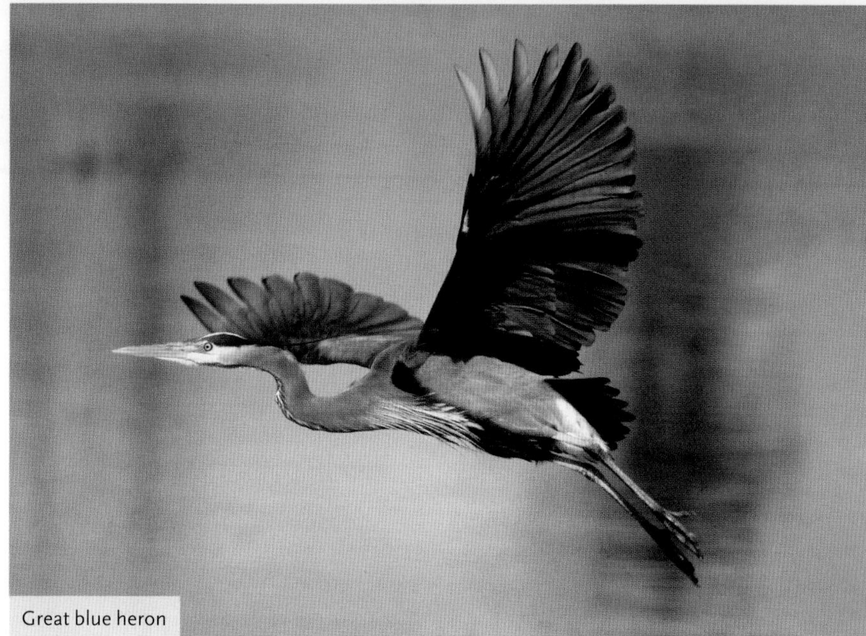
Great blue heron

as many again in the next tree over. Males tend the nest in the midday, females in the evening and overnight. Both sexes in their off-duty time frequent salty springs and brackish estuaries, replenishing their mineral salts.

BIRDS: PELECANIFORMES (HERONS), FAMILY ARDEIDAE

Great Blue Heron

Ardea herodias (AR-dia her-OH-dias: Roman and Greek names for heron). 38 in., ws 70 in.; bluish gray with some white, black, and dark red markings; bill, neck, and legs extremely long; neck held "goose-necked" in flight; huge birds seen in slow-flapping low flight over rivers and lakes are generally this species. Various loud, gutteral croaks.

The heron's way of life is to stand perfectly still in shallow water until some oblivious frog or small fish happens by, and then pluck or spear it with a quick thrust of the beak. The prey see little of the heron but its legs and shadow, and perhaps mistake it for an odd reed or cattail. A heron can nail prey even at night, as members of this order have excellent night vision.

BIRDS: CHARADRIIFORMES (SHOREBIRDS)

Spotted Sandpiper

Actitis macularia (ak-TIE-tiss: shore dweller; mac-you-LAIR-ia: spotted). Also teeter-tail. 6¼ in.; light brown above with

Spotted sandpiper

white eye-stripe and wing-bars, white below; summer adults dark-spotted white below, with yellowish legs and bill; dips and teeters constantly when on the ground; flies with wings stiffly down-curved. Call a high, clear "peep-peep," usually in flight or when landing. Single or in pairs, along subalpine streams and lakes, or in low meadows. Scolapacidae.

Like the dipper, which also feeds in frothy streams, the spotted sandpiper dips from the knees; it distinguishes itself in tipping forward and back, hence its nickname "teeter-tail." When threatened by a hawk it can dive like a dipper as well. To feed, it doesn't dive, but plucks prey from shallow water or the bank nearby, or from midair. Prey range in size up to trout fry, though insects predominate. No plant foods are eaten. Spotted sandpipers are widespread, breeding in almost any mountains north of Mexico and then wintering on seacoasts with mild weather—sometimes as far north as Washington.

Sex roles are reversed in this and a few other sandpipers. The females are larger, more aggressive, and dominant; they migrate to the breeding grounds first, establish and defend territories, court the males, initiate sex, do less than their share of sitting on the eggs, and do very little raising of the young aside from serving as a sentinel. They have less prolactin than the males, prolactin being a hormone that promotes parental caregiving. Many females are monogamous, but the fittest are serially polyandrous: a pair courts, bonds, builds a nest, and provisions it with four fertile eggs, and then she leaves that family and goes off to do it all over again with a second, a third, and even a fourth male in one season. It's different, but it makes sense. But, why sandpipers?

Marbled Murrelet

Brachyramphus marmoratus (breaky-RAM-fus: short bill; mar-mor-AY-tus: marbled). 8 in.; chunky thick-necked seabird, breeding (spring and summer) plumage mottled gray-brown all over; fall and winter plumage sharply 2-toned, white beneath, black above and on wings. Shrill "keer" call in rainforest near dawn is distinctive. Rainforest near coast or in WA CasR. Alcidae.

While these birds had long been a familiar sight on the ocean waves, their breeding habits were a mystery until 1974. As it turns out, they fly inland as far as the Washington Cascade Crest, or even a bit farther, to rear their young in thick moss on the high limbs of mature conifers. They are often seen paired up even in winter, when they are normally offshore but still make occasional visits to inland forests, possibly to maintain their pair bond. In spring, they take 24-hour turns sitting on the single egg, or tending the single chick while the partner flies to sea and back with a small, oily fish. Since eggs and nestlings are heavily preyed upon, the parents fly to and from the nest silently and in dim light, in contrast to their noisy circling in the broader vicinity. The first Washington nest was only found in 1990. Murrelet study has come a long way since then, as sustaining the threatened Oregon and Washington populations was a key goal of the Northwest Forest Plan. They seem stable in Oregon and Washington for now, but uncertain for the long term. Alaska has 91 percent of the total population, and British Columbia has 7 percent.

Marbled murrelet

BIRDS: ACCIPITRIFORMES (HAWKS AND EAGLES)

Turkey Vulture

Cathartes aura (cath-AR-teez: purifier; aura: breeze). Also turkey buzzard. 25 in., ws 72 in.; plumage black except whitish rear half of wing underside; head naked, wrinkled, pink (black when young); soars with wings in a shallow V, often tipping left or right, rarely flapping. Open country. Migratory: here late February through October. Cathartidae.

bird of rebirth
buzzard
meat is rotten meat made
sweet again and
lean

—Lew Welch

Linnaeus was perceptive when he named this creature "Purifier" to counter its unsavory reputation. Its digestive tract is immune to disturbance by the meat-rotting organisms that would sicken the rest of us. Its beak and talons are too weak to tear up freshly dead mammals, let alone to kill live ones. Predatory birds, in contrast, are equally ready to either kill or eat carrion. Vultures go long periods without food, and when they find it they gorge themselves. This may account for their lethargy on foot, and difficulty in taking flight. (If hungry enough, they'll fill their stomachs with plant foods.) Once on the wing, they are the best soarers of all land birds, rarely needing to flap.

A congregation of vultures wheeling usually means carrion below. Vultures take notice, and slowly gather from miles around. Several may gather around a carcass, but they eat one at a time, in order of dominance yielding occasionally to desperation. Dominant individuals have redder heads, and seem to flush even redder as a dominance display. Vultures locate their food by both sight and smell. Birds generally have little sense of smell, but turkey vultures almost

Turkey vulture

uniquely have a sharp sense at least for a few carrion odors. Natural gas pipeline companies found that by perfuming their gas with ethyl mercaptan they could get vultures to lead them to pipeline leaks.

A much larger vulture, the endangered California condor, *Gymnogyps californianus,* was common here in Lewis and Clark's day. It's the largest US bird. Condor range shrank inexorably until they survived only in captivity. Rerelease into the wild has been going on in southern California, but not here. Turkey buzzards, in contrast, have increased over the past century, are highly adaptable, and appear likely to be able to handle moderate climate change.

Osprey

Pandion haliaetus (pan-DIE-un: a mythic king; hal-ee-AY-et-us: sea eagle, the Greek term for osprey). Also fish hawk. ♂ 22 in., ws 54 in., ♀ larger; blackish above, with white crown; white beneath, with black markings most concentrated at wing tips and elbows; the "elbow" break is sharper both rearward and downward than on similar birds, suggesting a shallow M while soaring. Frequent calls include loud whistles and squeals. Near rivers and lakes. Pandionidae.

The osprey dives into water from 50–100 feet up, plucks a fish from a depth of 1–3 feet, and bursts immediately back into flight, gripping a squirming fish sometimes as heavy as itself. The soles of its feet are

Soaring Wings

Vultures, eagles, and *Buteo* hawks share a broad, spread-tipped wing and tail design specialized for soaring over land. This contrasts with the short wings and long tails of *Accipiter* hawks, the narrower wings of falcons, and the clean, linear wings of gulls and albatrosses that also soar superlatively, but on the very different air currents over the ocean.

The overland soarers stay aloft largely by seeking out thermals, or columnar upwellings of warm air—the daytime convection pattern of low, warm air rising to trade places with higher, cooler air. They don't try to cross large lakes, or travel at night or in the early morning, since thermal air is warmed by land absorbing and reradiating sunlight. Dry, sparsely vegetated land does it best, so steppes and prairies are popular with soaring birds. They also like mountains, which deflect prevailing winds upward, and they shift to using those updrafts more during windier weather. To travel long distances, they ride one thermal up in a spiral, then glide obliquely downward to the next thermal, and climb again. To migrate, they often wait for a low-pressure weather trough, or they follow the updrafts of long north–south mountain ridges. Tightly packed mountain topography, like ours, produces useful oblique thermals along creek headwaters.

toughened with minute barbules that help grasp wet fish.

The osprey is a nearly worldwide species comprising a genus and subfamily by itself. It is among several birds of prey that suffered heavy losses from toxic chemicals like DDT. Toxins from prey concentrate in the tissues of predators; birds are especially sensitive to them. Ospreys made a huge comeback after DDT was banned, and dams have given them a lot of new habitat.

Osprey

Bald Eagle

Haliaeetus leucocephalus (hal-ee-EE-et-us: sea eagle; lew-co-SEF-a-lus: white head). ♂ 32 in., ws 75 in., ♀ larger; adults blackish with entire head and tail white; immatures (1–3+ years) brown; ankles naked; wings held flat while soaring. Widespread; especially in BC, on OR High Cascade lakes, WA Nooksack and Skagit valleys. Calls: various weak chips and squawks, or almost gull-like louder shrieks. Accipitridae.

Despite being the national symbol, bald eagles have been shot on sight for most of America's history. Shooting them earned

Bald eagle

a bounty in Alaska until 1952, twelve years after it became illegal in the lower 48 states. Some Westerners still fear and hate eagles enough to break the law.

The Northwest is lucky to have plentiful bald eagles along the coast from the Aleutians to the Columbia, spilling inland along salmon streams and to high lakes where waterfowl concentrate. Fondness for fish and waterfowl tends to keep them near water, but they are sometimes sighted in our mountains, and seem less averse to deep forest than the other big soarers. Despite a public image as a fearsome predator, the bald eagle far more often scavenges carrion or takes the prey of other birds—ospreys, gulls, kingfishers, and smaller bald eagles. Most salmon it eats are spawned-out carcasses. At lambing time on sheep ranches, bald eagles eat afterbirths and stillborn lambs. Exaggerated fears of lamb and salmon predation fueled America's animosity toward eagles for the last two centuries.

Our bald eagles breed in mid- to late winter. That way the young, after an extraordinarily long time in the nest (six weeks incubating under both parents taking turns, and ten to twelve weeks from hatching to flying) will be ready to fly up the coast in time for the summer coho salmon runs in Alaska. Those that migrate work their way back down the coast in conjunction with salmon runs that follow heavy fall rains. They reach the Fraser, Squamish, Nooksack, and Skagit Rivers in November, and peak by around the New Year. Some of our birds stay put year-round.

In a spectacular courtship "dance" of bald eagles, the male dive-bombs the female in midair, she rolls over to meet him, they lock talons, and they plummet earthward, breaking out of their death-taunting embrace at the last possible instant. Juvenile bald eagles engage in every kind of courtship behavior short of mating, which waits for the fifth or sixth winter.

North American tribes associated the bald eagle with sickness, death, and healing, and considered it an ally of shamans. Eagle feathers were used in healing rituals, and it was variously said that an eagle would fly over a sick person, would eat a dead person, or would scream to a person soon to be killed by an arrow.

Golden Eagle

Aquila chrysaetos (AK-will-a: Roman for eagle; cris-AY-et-os: gold eagle). ♂ 32 in., ws 78 in., ♀ larger (up to twice as heavy); adults dark brown all over, with golden nape (and highlights on head); juveniles have white wing patch and tail base (but not an all-white tail, as in bald eagle, nor a white rear edge of wing); ankles feathered; soars with wings slightly raised. Call (rarely

Golden eagle

Raptors Reconfigured

Once long ago, the hawks, eagles, falcons, owls, and vultures comprised a single order, Raptores, from the Latin for "snatcher." It embraced nearly all birds that prey on things bigger than bugs. Later, owls were given an order of their own, but raptor persevered as a casual term that sometimes includes owls or vultures, and sometimes not. Starting in 1873, our New World vultures were said by some to belong among the storks, and to have separately evolved some traits in common with hawks. The AOU Checklist adopted that position in 1998.

But not for long! A series of DNA-based studies concluded that vultures are hawks after all, that owls are fairly closely related as well, and that the birds of prey that evolved far from the others on the family tree are the falcons, which are almost songbirds. The AOU Checklist switched to that view in 2010, recognizing a new order, Accipitriformes, for the hawks and vultures, leaving their previous order, Falconiformes, with nothing but falcons.

Raptors still offer a good case of convergent evolution, regardless of whether it's owls or falcons that converged with hawks over evolutionary history. The shared traits are heavy, hooked bills; large, heavily muscled feet; and females larger than males. (Female northern harriers outweigh males by as much as 3:2, and in golden eagles the ratio can reach 2:1. Among the other bird orders as well as mammals, males tend to be bigger than females; invertebrates tend to have bigger females.) The usefulness of beaks and talons in predation is clear, but correlating female size with predation had ornithologists wracking their brains for a century. It turns out to be a case of sexual selection, that same force that makes males grow bigger and bigger in so many species! Female birds are bigger than their mates in species where females choose mates largely on the basis of acrobatic courtship flights, with "rapid changes in flight direction, twists, rolls, and turns." As humans know, small size helps gymnasts. Even though acrobatic skill undoubtedly aids avian hunters, this trait has to result from sexual selection, not directly from success in hunting; otherwise both sexes would be small. Vultures do not share the trait: they are not stunt fliers, and their males are as big as their females.

used) is rapid chipping. Cliffy open country (alpine or steppe). Accipitridae.

Golden eagles inhabit any North American terrain (and much Asian, North African, and European terrain) that has plenty of vertical relief, few trees, and populations of both hares and large diurnal rodents like marmots or ground squirrels; the hares provide winter fare while the rodents hibernate. Winter may impel an eagle to attempt larger prey such as fox, or rarely coyote or deer. This can be accomplished with a falcon-like plummet; momentum multiplies the eagle's ten pounds into enough force to overpower heavier prey.

Normally, the golden eagle hunts from a low, fast-soaring cruise, using angular topography both for visual cover and for updrafts. It also robs hawks and falcons of their kills; hawks rarely venture, let alone nest, within half a mile of an eagle's aerie. The latter is a stick structure 4–6 feet across, and growing from 1 foot deep to as much as 5 feet with many years of reuse.

Red-tailed Hawk

Buteo jamaicensis (BOO-tee-o: the Roman term; ja-may-KEN-sis: of Jamaica). ♂ 18 in., ws 48 in., ♀ larger; brown above, highly variable in color beneath, from dark brown to (most often here) white with delicate red-brown patterning; tail (adults) red-brown above, pink below, fanned out. Any sort of open country. Call a scratchy descending scream. Accipitridae.

Comfortable around freeways, often perching on roadside fenceposts, the redtail may be America's oftenest-seen large bird of prey. It has been on the increase in nearly all regions, perhaps thanks to increases in things like utility poles and wires, fences, juniper trees, voles, and ground squirrels. Its preferred natural habitat is grassland with some trees, such as our east-side ponderosa pine timberline. It's easily the oftenest-*heard* bird of prey worldwide, at least in the movies. Sound editors have a sample that used to be labeled "red-tail hawk scream: for Westerns." Today they export it everywhere from the Alps to Antarctica, whenever the director says "dial up some of that wild and free lonesomeness."

Red-tailed hawk

Adaptability, opportunism, and economy are the keys to the redtail's success. Lacking the speed that makes falcons and accipiters perfect specialists, it employs patience, craft, and acute vision to hunt—mainly from a perch. Hares and ground squirrels may get an aerial swoop after a stealthy approach. Or the hawk may brazenly land between a rodent and its refuge, forcing the rodent into an end run; the hawk tries to snatch it. Band-tailed pigeons may be swooped upon while feeding in brush. Lizards, snakes, and slugs are easy, and form a large part of the diet in some seasons. Redtails are also pirates, robbing hawks and even eagles or great horned owls of their kills. In winter, individuals that remain in the snowy North are remarkably adept at conserving calories and subsisting on an irregular diet.

Northern Harrier

Circus cyaneus (circus: Greek name for a circling hawk; sigh-AY-nee-us: blue). Also marsh hawk; *C. hudsonicus*. ♂ 16¼ in., ws 42 in., ♀ larger; ♂ ash gray above, whitish underneath with black wing tips and tail bars; ♀ speckled reddish brown, paler beneath; white rump patch on both sexes; tail long; soars low, with wings held well above horizontal. Squawking "kek-kek" chatter. Marshes, fields, meadows, mainly in summer. Accipitridae.

The harrier cruises dry grasslands and wet meadows alike. It nests among tall grasses, and spends hours a day cruising just above the tops of the reeds, grasses, or low shrubs. When a vole takes off running, the hawk may harry it through dashes and turns before dropping on it. It is an unusual hawk in hunting primarily by sound; in experiments, harriers precisely locate and attack tiny tape players concealed in meadow grass peeping and rustling like voles. In this respect harriers evolved convergently with owls, developing an owl-like facial disk of feathers to focus sound.

In years of abundance some males take multiple mates and manage to feed two or three nests of about five young each. The mothers often leave the nest momentarily to take midair delivery of morsels from their harried breadwinners. A female, having paired and begun a nest, may dump that mate if he is turning out to be a poor provider, and join the harem of a better one. A male courts by means of a "sky dance" in a grand U pattern, culminating by landing on the nest site he proposes. Agile, vigorous dancers get more mates.

Northern harrier

Sharp-shinned hawk

Accipiter

***Accipiter* spp.** (ak-SIP-it-er: Roman name meaning a fast flier). Wings proportionately short and broad; tail long, often not fanned out, broadly barred (dark gray or white) its full length, with a pure white tuft under its base; both sexes slaty gray above, or brownish; underside pale with fine bars; yearlings brown above, pale beneath with red-brown streaking. Species are hard to tell apart, and size ranges overlap, ♀ being about as big as next bigger species' ♂. Calls cackling, infrequent. Accipitridae.

Sharp-shinned hawk, *A. striatus* (stry-AY-tus: striped). ♂ 10½ in., ws 21 in. (jay-sized); tail dark-tipped, feathers all same length; red-brown bars beneath. Often at forest or clearing edges, or alpine.

Cooper's hawk

Cooper's hawk, *A. cooperii* (COO-PER-ee-eye: for William Cooper). ♂ 15½ in., ws 28 in. (crow-sized); outer tail feathers shorter than middle ones; red-brown bars beneath. Forest understory, edges, or streamside brush.

Northern goshawk, *A. gentilis* (jen-TIE-lis: aristocratic). ♂ 21 in., ws 42 in. (red-tailed hawk size); outer tail feathers shorter; blue-gray bars beneath. Deep wilderness forest.

These hawks evolved in the forests. Their long tails lend maneuverability while the short wings avoid branches. Cooper's typically bursts out from a concealed perch; the sharp-shinned flies around more or less constantly and randomly, and chases the birds it happens to surprise; the goshawk also cruises, flushing grouse and ptarmigan, its chief prey, and also taking some squirrels and hares.

Each day while young are in the nest, a sharp-shinned father brings home about two sparrow-sized birds apiece for his family of seven or so. That's a lot of hunting. He seems to stay in shape with playful harassment of larger birds, even ravens. Accipiter males select a limb not far from the nest and take prey there to pluck it before eating it or delivering it to the nest. An indiscriminate scattering of thousands of small feathers may be a sign of one such pluckery in the branches above. Either parent may make a nasty fuss over an animal, such as yourself, happening near the nest. Accipiters are often described as nonsoarers, with a flight rhythm of five flaps and a short glide—sometimes a useful identifying trait. But in the strong sustained updrafts of rugged mountains they appear perfectly capable of soaring till hell freezes over.

BIRDS: FALCONIFORMES (FALCONS), FAMILY FALCONIDAE

American Kestrel

Falco sparverius (FAHL-co: the Roman term; spar-VER-ius: sparrow). Also sparrow hawk. ♂ 9 in., ws 21 in., ♀ slightly larger; red-brown above; wings blue-gray on adult ♂ only, and tail tipped with heavy black band and slight white fringe; brown-flecked white beneath; dark tail. Call a sharp, fast "killy-killy-killy." Open country.

American kestrel

The kestrel is one of the smallest, most successful, least shy, and most often-seen raptors. When not perched on a limb or telephone wire, it often hovers in place, wings fluttering, body tipped about 45 degrees, facing upwind, 10–20 feet above a field or roadside. From this vantage it can drop and strike prey quickly, as a larger, broader-winged hawk might do from a low soar. Grasshoppers and other big insects are staples; mice are also taken. If all these are scarce, the kestrel may fly down sparrow-sized birds.

Peregrine Falcon

Falco peregrinus (pair-eg-RYE-nus: wandering). Also duck hawk. ♂ 15 in., ws 40 in., ♀ larger; wings pointed, tail narrow; color variable, ours most likely slate blue to (immatures) dark brown above, white beneath with dark mottling and reddish wash except on pure white throat and upper breast; face has a distinctive high-contrast rounded dark bar descending across and below eye. Infrequent; perhaps near cliffs.

During the 1960s, use of DDT (as well as the capture of peregrines for falconry) was banned in the United States after it was shown that the severe worldwide decline of peregrines was caused chiefly by breakage of thin-shelled eggs from falcons contaminated

Speed Wings

Tell falcons in flight from other hawks by their pointed, swept-back wings and straight, or even slightly tapering, tails when in flapping flight. (Soaring, they fan their tails out as other hawks do.) This must be the optimal wing design for sustained speed, since so many of the fastest flyers—falcons, swifts, swallows, and nighthawks—evolved it independently.

The fastest of all falcons in level flight is said to be the largest falcon, the gyrfalcon, *Falco rusticolus*, of the Arctic (rarely reported seen here). In ancient falconry, only kings were entitled to fly gyrs. The slightly smaller peregrine edges out the gyrfalcon as world's fastest animal, when it stoops—not exactly flying but plummeting at an airborne target. To minimize drag the wings are cupped close to the sides—not pulled all the way in tight. Most hawks and eagles stoop occasionally, when presented with an irresistible target, but the peregrine specializes in midair prey, and has perfected the stoop.

The figure 180 miles per hour started making the rounds after 1930, when a small plane pilot reported a stooping peregrine passing him while he was diving at 175 miles per hour. He was disbelieved by some who maintained that the race belongs to the swifts. Ornithologist Vance Tucker retorts that swifts are probably no swifter than pigeons, whereas his instruments optically tracked a peregrine stooping at 157 miles per hour. Ken Franklin of Friday Harbor trains peregrines and sky-dives with them. He took Frightful, his fastest one, up to the perhaps abnormal height of 17,000 feet and clocked her stooping from there at 242 miles per hour.

Peregrine falcon

with DDT and related insecticides. Programs for captive breeding and release of peregrines were funded and a recovery process begun. Success is coming slowly, hindered partly by poaching (peregrines fetch astronomical prices from falconers, especially in the Middle East). Also it is likely that other pollutants cause some eggshell thinning. Peregrines have been exploiting a new habitat—large cities—where two of their favorite things abound: high ledges to perch and nest on, and pigeons to eat. They also commonly winter on the Northwest Coast, preying on shorebirds.

Peregrine eyesight is sharp enough for them to spot a small bird a mile away. They approach in a long arc (actually a logarithmic spiral) to use their best visual acuity for distance vision, which is at 45 degrees off to the side. They typically fly level, at a commanding height, until fairly close, and then stoop (dive with wings folded) at a moderate to steep angle of descent. At that point they can fly straight at the target, because a different part of the eye has the best acuity over shorter distances. They can simply snatch small prey, or they can stun larger birds with a blow of the talons, then loop around quickly to catch the tumbling victim and kill it with a bite through the neck. Their speed is a weapon: since momentum = velocity × mass, it enables them to stun a victim more massive than themselves. Very stiff tail feather shafts enable them to hit the brakes without breaking feathers.

BIRDS: STRIGIFORMES (OWLS), FAMILY STRIGIDAE

Owl

Great horned owl, *Bubo virginianus* (BOO-bo: the Roman term). ♂ 20 in., ws 55 in., ♀ larger; large "ear" tufts or "horns," yellow eyes, and reddish tan facial ruff; white throat patch, otherwise finely barred and mottled gray-brown. Long, low hoots (4–6 in series) year-round, but especially in January–February breeding season; pairs sing duets, the ♀ higher-pitched. Nocturnal; common and widespread, preferring open forest.

Northern spotted owl, *Strix occidentalis caurina* (strix: as in "strident," Greek name imitating screech owl; ox-i-den-TAY-lis: western). ♂ 16 in., ws 42 in., ♀ larger; no ear tufts; dark eyes, yellow bill; dull brown, white-spotted above and barred beneath. Strident quavery hoots in series of 3–4. Nocturnal; in mature conifers; rare in BC, uncommon in OR and WA.

Barred owl, *Strix varia* (VAR-ia: variegated). ♂ 17 in., ws 44 in., ♀ larger; like spotted owl, but the white flecking on back forms horizontal bars, and on chest is more a white field with vertical brown flecks. Strident quavery hoots, like a dog yelping at the moon, in series of 6–9. Nocturnal; in forest.

Western screech-owl, *Megascops kennecottii* (MEG-a-scops: big owl; ken-a-cot-ee-eye: for Robert Kennecott). Also *Otus kennecottii*. ♂ 8 in., ws 20 in., ♀ larger; finely brown-streaked near coast, or gray-streaked inland; dark-outlined facial disk; "ear" tufts sometimes show; yellow eyes. Series of short whistles accelerate while dropping in pitch, like a bouncing ball. Nocturnal, at low to mid-elevs.

Northern saw-whet owl, *Aegolius acadicus* (ee-JO-lius: a Greek name for owl; a-KAY-di-cus: of eastern Canada). ♂ 7 in., ws 17 in., ♀ larger; reddish brown above, white and brown smeared (adults) or golden (juveniles) beneath; yellow eyes, V-shaped white eyebrows. Short toots repeated in machinelike monotony, sometimes for hours, at night. Nocturnal; in conifers.

Northern pygmy-owl, *Glaucidium gnoma* (glaw-SID-ium: small owl, derived from "gleaming"; NO-ma: gnome). ♂ 6 in., ws 15 in., ♀ larger (barely robin-sized, but owl-shaped); brown with slight pale barring, 2 dark eyelike spots on nape; yellow eyes; longish tail often held cocked; flight swift, darting, audible, with rapid beats—qual-

Great horned owl

Northern spotted owl

Barred owl

ities atypical of owl flight. Short toots repeated in slow machinelike monotony, mainly in daytime. Mainly diurnal; infrequent, in semi-open forest.

Owls have universally evoked human dread, superstition, and tall tales with their ghostly voices and silent, nocturnal predatory flight. Various parts of their anatomies found their way into talismans and potions both medical and magical. Owl pellets are almost ready-made talismans, but to naturalists they offer precise information on owl diets and distribution. Pellets are strikingly neat oblong bundles coughed up by owls to rid them of indigestible parts of small prey (and anything else) they swallow. Hard, angular parts are smoothly coated with fur. A spot with many pellets indicates an owl's roost on a limb above. (Hawks make similar but smaller and fewer pellets, eating their prey in smaller pieces and digesting it more completely.)

While all owls are formidable hunters, evolution has specialized them for a broad spectrum of habitats and roles. The ferocious pygmy owl darts about catching insects and also birds up to its own size and bigger. Like some 40 percent of owl species, it hunts mainly by day. The nocturnal great horned owl can hunt mammals much heavier than itself, such as porcupines and large skunks, as well as almost any sort of creature down to beetles and worms. Cottontails, where common, are a diet staple.

Owls' sensory adaptations are the stuff of legend. They have the broadest skulls of any birds, separating their eyes and their ears as widely as possible to optimize

Western screech-owl

Northern saw-whet owl

Northern pygmy-owl

three-dimensionality of vision and directionality of hearing. Their ears pinpoint prey along the vertical axis as well as the horizontal, thanks to asymmetrical skulls. Some kinds of owls locate and catch mice by hearing alone, in pitch darkness or under several inches of snow. The facial ruff of feathers, plus ear flaps hidden under its outer rim, funnel sound to the highly developed inner ears. (The "ear tufts" or "horns" on top of some species' heads are unconnected with hearing, but are expressive and decorative.) Owls' eyes are the most frontally directed of any bird's; this narrows the field of vision but makes nearly all of it three-dimensional. The bill is squashed down out of the way for the same reason. (Try straining your eyes left, then right, to see the translucent profile of your nose on either side; only that portion—about a third—of your field of view lying between the "two noses" is seen in 3-D, by both eyes.) The tradeoff—narrower field of view than other birds', but all of it three-dimensional—favors zeroing in on prey, not watching out for predators. To look around, an owl can twist its neck in a split second to anywhere within a 270-degree arc. The eyeballs, which don't rotate in their sockets (the neck does it all) evolved an optimal light-gathering shape: somewhat conical, like a deep television tube, with a thick lens. The retina has a reflective backing behind the photoreceptor cells; that's what makes nocturnal mammals' eyes gleam in your headlights. The cells are almost all rods (high-sensitivity vision) and few cones (color vision). Owls' light perception threshold is between a thirty-fifth and a hundredth of ours. They have much sharper acuity for detail than we do, even by day, and a modicum of color perception as well.

Most owls practice utterly silent flight, a magical thing to witness. Their feathers are literally muffled, or damped, with a velvety surface and soft-fringed edges, incurring a tradeoff in efficiency and speed. Their flapping is slow and easy, thanks to low body weight per wing area. (With extra fluffy body plumage, owls are far slimmer and lighter than they look.) Silent flight enables owls in flight to hear the movements of small rodents who can't hear the owl coming for dinner. Do voles even know that owls exist? Or are they just your cousins disappearing, one by one?

Most forest owls depend on camouflage rather than escape when approached by large creatures; people alert enough to spot them can approach quite close. Spotted and great horned owlets seem to attempt flight from the nest before they are ready; landing on the forest floor, they must reside there until fully fledged. The parents continue to feed and guard them—aggressively in the case of the great horned. If you find an adorable, fluffy owlet on the ground, back off.

Northern spotted owls mainly live in dense, old forest. That's true of many animals, but was first proven of this subpecies, and once it was listed as threatened it became a powerful tool for slowing down logging in the Pacific Northwest. Even with greatly reduced logging on federal lands, spotted owl numbers continue to fall.

Decades of intense study have not really determined whether it was already too late to save the subspecies back when the Owl Wars began. They have shown that the owl is by no means rigidly confined to old-growth; the connection is really complicated. Climate change dims the owl's prognosis, and so does the arrival of the spotted owl's closest relative, the barred owl, which was all but unknown in our range before the 1980s. It has spread stunningly fast. Both species require forest, so the treeless Great Plains separated them, allowing them to evolve as two species. Barred owls began their end-run around the plains by 1912, perhaps because warming (then already underway) enabled expansion northward into boreal forests. By 1996 they were as numerous as spotted owls in Mt. Rainier National Park. They bear larger broods, are more aggressive, less dependent on old-growth, less picky about their diet, and require less territory per pair.

It's hard to think of a good reason why they wouldn't completely replace northern spotted owls and drive them extinct. I hope spotted owls have some advantage we haven't figured out yet. I would hate to lose them.

While some of the steps taken in the name of saving the owl may have been imperfect or unwise, there is absolutely no cause to regret (or to reduce) the preservation and maintenance of old-growth forests.

BIRDS: CAPRIMULGIFORMES (GOATSUCKERS), FAMILY CAPRIMULGIDAE

Common Nighthawk

Chordeiles minor (cor-DIE-leez: evening dance; minor: lesser, a false name since this is now the larger species of nighthawk). 9 in., ws 23 in.; wings long, bent backward, pointed, falcon-like; mottled brown and black, with white wing-bar; ♂ also have white throat and a narrow white bar across tail. Marshes and open areas, all elevs.

Nighthawks are most often seen at dusk: no self-respecting nighthawk would be on the ground at that hour, when insects are on the wing. Like swifts and swallows, they prey on insects by flying around with their mouths open. Their flight is wild and erratic like a bat's, but swift like a falcon's—though they aren't really any kind of hawk at all. Males may interrupt their erratic feeding flights with long steep dives that bottom out abruptly with a terrific raspy, farting noise of air rushing through the wing feathers. This is their courtship. The vocal call is a softer, nasal beep repeated while feeding. Nighthawks are our briefest breeding visitors, here only from June through early September. They nest on gravelly ground with very little construction work, and they have an odd style of perching, lying lengthwise along a branch. A population decline related to the general use of insecticides is suspected.

Common nighthawk

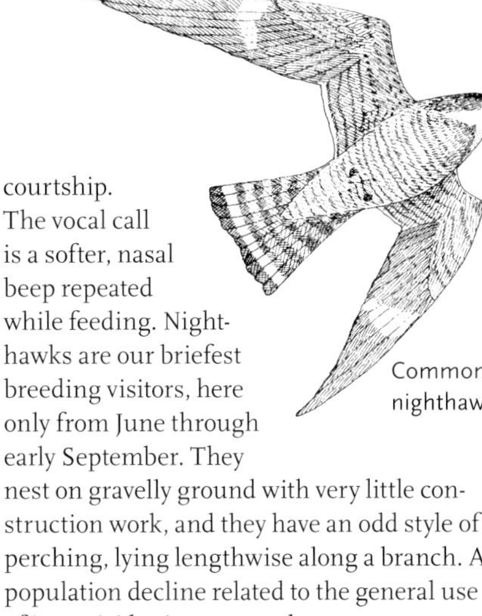
Common nighthawk

BIRDS: APODIFORMES (SWIFTS AND HUMMINGBIRDS)

Swift

Vaux's swift, *Chaetura vauxi* (key-TOO-ra: hair-thin tail; VAWX-eye: for William Sansom Vaux, p. 414). 4½ in.; slaty to brownish gray, somewhat paler beneath; wings long, pointed, gently curved; tail short, rounded. Rapid chipping. Widespread.

Black swift, *Cypseloides niger* (sip-sel-OY-deez: like *Cypselus*, the Old World swift; NYE-jer: black). 7 in.; black all over; wings long, pointed, gently curved; tail slightly forked. Call rarely heard. Subalpine; uncommon; on the NABCI Watch List. Apodidae.

> Flying before the storm, arcing so close
> that the sharp wing-whistle is heard.
> —Gary Snyder at Crater Mountain
> Fire Lookout, 1952

Swifts may not be among the swiftest after all, but they sure are impressive flyers. They do all their hunting, eating, and drinking in flight, and black swifts even mate while

The Vaux Family

William Sansom Vaux, president of the Zoological Society of Philadelphia, never saw the West; his niece and nephews Mary, George, and William did. They turned their western vacations into the first annual study of glacial retreat in North America. The idea began when Mary Vaux was shocked by the visible retreat of a glacier in Canada's Glacier National Park. They photographed it every year from 1897 to 1913, developing the big glass plate negatives in the Glacier House wine cellar, and they contributed to the growing science of glacial cycles and landscapes. When Mary's wildflower paintings were published in five volumes, a reviewer called her "the Audubon of American wild flowers."

Black swift

aloft. (They do stop flying, so they fall, then disengage after several seconds.) Some ornithologists go so far as to say swifts "roost" in flight. They often fly 600 miles in a day—and make it look playful, interspersing short glides between spurts of flapping, and creating their famous optical illusion of flapping left and right wings alternately. Unfortunately they do most of this, especially in fair weather, too high up for us to see in detail.

Swifts—"strainers of aerial plankton"—can only maintain their high metabolisms on a steady supply of flying insects. Few insects fly during cold weather, so when it's cold and gray, swifts may fly off for a few days, as far as they need to to find sun, or else stay home but go cold and torpid (p. 358). If Mom and Dad vacation in the sun, nestlings stay behind, in torpor. People sometimes mistake torpid swifts and nighthawks for dead, and pick them up, only to be startled when they fly off in perfect health as soon as they warm up.

Black swifts nest in steep wet places, like seepy cliffs or behind waterfalls. Wetness helps their nests adhere. Vaux's swifts glue their nests to the insides of hollow trees or chimneys. In Southeast Asia, swift nests are gathered for the famous curative delicacy "birdsnest soup," featuring filmy masses like boiled egg whites—actually the special saliva swifts work up for gluing nests. Stiff, spine-tipped tail-feathers help Vaux's swifts perch on sheer surfaces. In fall they roost by the thousands in a hollow tree or chimney for a few weeks, congregating for a mass migration. After sundown, they create a tornado-like Vaux vortex spiraling down into the roost.

Hummingbird

Rufous hummingbird, *Selasphorus rufus* (sel-us-FOR-us: light bearer; ROO-fus: red). 3½ in.; ♂ red-brown with iridescent red throat patch, and some white on belly and green on wings and crown; ♀ and juveniles mostly green with some reddish near base of tail. Flight makes a deep dragonfly-like hum. A common montane hummingbird here, but on the NABCI Watch List.

Calliope hummingbird, *S. calliope* (ca-LIE-o-pee: a Muse). Also *Stellula calliope*. 2¾

Rufous hummingbird

Calliope hummingbird

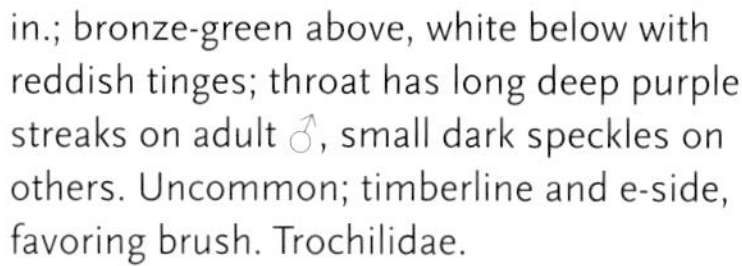

in.; bronze-green above, white below with reddish tinges; throat has long deep purple streaks on adult ♂, small dark speckles on others. Uncommon; timberline and e-side, favoring brush. Trochilidae.

Any bright red we wear, even as small as bootlaces, is likely to draw hummers in the alpine country in July. It takes them only an instant to discover my boots are no bed of columbine. I can only hope the pleasure they bring me doesn't cost them much.

Bright red flowers that bear nectar at the base of tubes 1–2 inches long are adapted to pollination by hummingbirds. Columbine and skyrocket are typical (and beloved of hummers) but many pinkish to red flowers offer valued nectaries: currants, fireweed, paintbrush, lilies, fool's-huckleberry.

Even hummers can't live on nectar alone. They need protein! They get it by zooming around with mouth agape, catching flies. Their relatives the swifts have mouths well adapted for that: short, wide bill, flexible jaw. Hummingbird bills, adapted for nectaring, are long and thin and have no mandibular joint at all. They're fused of slivers of bone so thin that the entire bill is elastic: the upper and lower bill bend wide apart and then snap back together in a hundredth of a second. Scientists don't yet know whether the snap action is triggered by flies, or only by being stretched so wide.

Rufous males may reach Washington as early as February; at such nectar-deprived times they have to subsist on bugs, supplemented with sap from sapsucker wells. Climate change is disrupting the timing of flowering: some plants bloom earlier in warmer years, and others don't, basing their timing on the solar calendar instead. This is a problem for pollinators, and especially for hummingbirds and others that evolved to migrate in time with blooming seasons.

The rufous ranges farther north than any other hummer—Valdez, Alaska—and the calliope migrates farther per gram of flesh than any other warm-blooded creature; at one tenth of an ounce, it is the smallest US hummer. Both of these species migrate in a counterclockwise loop, north along the Pacific, then inland in summer, and south along the Rockies to central Mexico. Habitat loss in Mexico is suspected of causing declines. The mystery of exactly how birds navigate on long migrations is finally beginning to yield. By day, they orient themselves by the polarization of sunlight (which they see, somehow) and use that to recalibrate their sense of the earth's magnetic field (which they somehow feel). By night they use the stars and the magnetic field.

The smallest of all birds, hummers have frantic metabolisms in common with shrews, the smallest mammals. Ounce for ounce, a hummingbird flying has ten times the caloric requirement of a person running—and we don't have to spend all day running, while hummingbirds do spend most of their waking hours flying around in search of nectar for those calories. They fly even to move a few inches or to turn around, as their feet are too weak for walking. Daily, they consume up to half their body weight in sugar, which they convert into body fat at shockingly high percentages, at least when migrating. A rufous can fly 610 miles before refueling. Hummers' hyperkinetic days are complemented by torpid nights (no, not torrid nights), with temperature and metabolism sharply lowered (see p. 358).

Their whirring flight, suggestive of a huge dragonfly, does in fact work a a bit like insect flight, and allows stationary and backward hovering, but no gliding. The wings beat many times faster than other birds' thanks to an extremely shortened wing with long feathers; there's very little mass to flap.

Hummingbirds are belligerent toward their own and larger species: calliopes have been seen dive-bombing red-tailed hawks. Harassment of large birds by small ones is called mobbing. There are records of predators actually being killed by mobs of smaller birds. But that's neither the norm nor the object. Studies show that small birds that mob—even when it's two or three little birds harassing a predator twenty times their size—are preyed upon less than those that don't. The predator may conserve energy by saving its killer moves for unwary prey.

Rufous hummingbirds' territoriality seems to concern food rather than sex. (Hummers don't pair up anyway, but mate freely.) Both sexes stake out their patch of the nectar resource even during two-week refueling stops during migration, and defend it with the same tall elliptical flights they use for courtship: a courting male swoops around and around in an ellipse hundreds of feet high, at the lowest point passing at high speed only inches from the demure object of his attentions, while eliciting a shrieking buzz from his tail feathers. These two species and their close relatives have evolved feathers that produce specific buzz frequencies that appeal to conspecific females, just as songs do in songbirds. Males flash their gorgets (iridescent, erectile throat patches) both in courtship and in aggression.

BIRDS: CORACIIFORMES (KINGFISHERS)

Belted Kingfisher

Megaceryle alcyon (meg-a-SER-i-lee AL-see-on: two Greek names for kingfishers, one with "big"). 12 in.; head looks oversized because of large bill and extensive crest of feathers; blue-gray with white neck and underparts and (♀ only) reddish breast band; in flight, white patches under wings may flash. Call a long, peculiar rattle. Along streams, year-round. Alcedinidae.

In Greek myth, the Halcyon, a kind of bird we presume was a kingfisher, floated its nest on the waves of the sea while incubating and hatching the young. Hence "halcyon days" are a fortuitous respite from the storms of life. Our kingfishers, in real life, raise their young amid a heap of regurgitated fish bones at the end of

Belted kingfisher

Belted kingfisher

a hole in a mud bank. Is "nest" too sweet a term for such debris? They look for their prey—fish, crayfish, waterbugs, and larvae—from a perch over a stream or lake. (They can hunt from a hover where branches are in short supply, but that's rarely the case on our streams.) After diving and catching a fish, they return to thrash it to death against their branch before swallowing it head first. Anglers have long resented kingfishers' success rate, but statistically the birds are unlikely to reduce trout numbers significantly. The kingfisher population has plummeted during the advance of civilization; there was once a pair of kingfishers for virtually every creek in the United States.

Hairy woodpecker

BIRDS: PICIFORMES (WOODPECKERS), FAMILY PICIDAE

Woodpecker

Hairy woodpecker, *Picoides villosus* (pic-OY-deez: like a *Pica*, a Roman name for magpies and woodpeckers; vil-OH-sus: woolly). 7½ in.; black and white except (♂ only) a small red patch on peak of head; wings strongly barred. Widespread.

Downy woodpecker

Downy woodpecker, *P. pubescens* (pew-BES-enz: fuzzy). 5¾ in.; like hairy only smaller. Less common: lowlands with some deciduous trees.

White-headed woodpecker, *P. albolarvatus* (al-bo-lar-VAY-tus: white mask). 7¾ in.; black all over except white head, throat, and patches near tip of wings; ♂ has small red patch on nape; often walks head-down or sideways on tree trunks. Ponderosa pine forest in US, locally common.

White-headed woodpecker

Black-backed woodpecker, *P. arcticus*. 8 in.; almost entirely black above and white below, with modest flecking on wings and sides; ♂ has small yellow crown. E-side pine forest in and near burns.

Black-backed woodpecker

American three-toed woodpecker

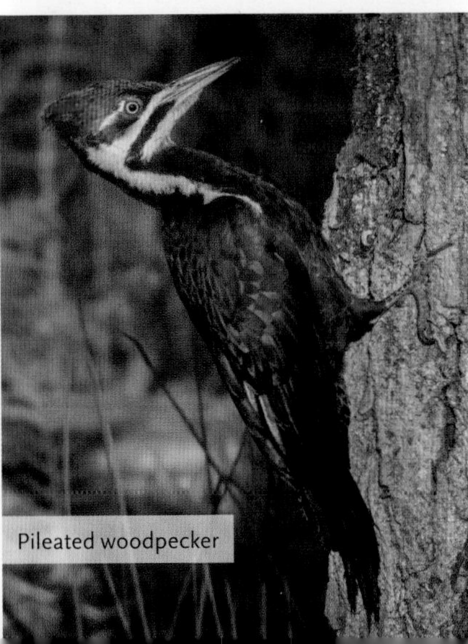
Pileated woodpecker

American Three-toed woodpecker, *P. dorsalis*. Also *P. tridactylus*. 7½ in.; generally black above and white below, back and wings are barred black-and-white; ♂ has small yellow crown. Infrequent; high forest in CasR.

Pileated woodpecker, *Dryocopus pileatus* (dry-OC-o-pus: tree sword; pie-lee-AY-tus: crested). 15 in.; black, with bright red, large, pointed crest, black or white-streaked head with (♂ only) red mustache and white underwing markings visible in flight; drumming loud, slow, irregular; call a loud rattling shriek slight rising in pitch. Deep forest with standing dead trees or snags.

Woodpeckers resemble songbirds (Passeriformes), but differ in several specialized traits. Most have two front and two rear toes, rather than 3-and-1. (Black-backed and three-toed have a 2-and-1 arrangement.) Strong sharp claws on their feet, together with short stiff tail feathers, give them the grip and the bracing they need for hammering the full force of their bodies into a tree. Naturally, they also have adamantine chisel-like beaks, and thick shock-absorbing skulls to prevent boxers' dementia. Before

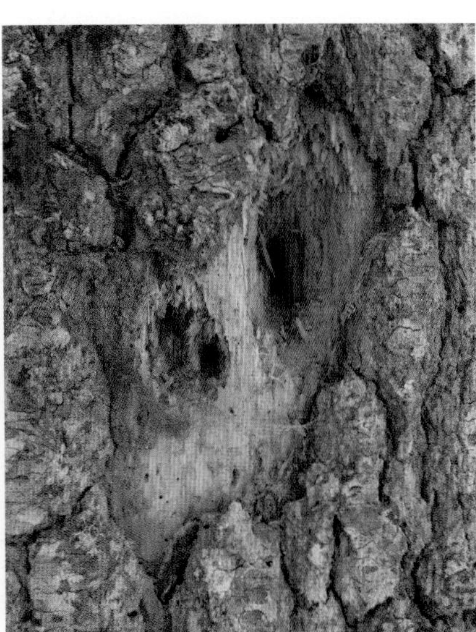
Pileated woodpecker excavation.

diving into work on a tree, they listen for the minute rustlings of their insect prey boring around under the bark. Insect larvae and adults provide the bulk of their diets, seeds and berries the rest. For snatching grubs out of their tunnels, the woodpecker has a barb-tipped tongue much longer than its head. The tongue shoots out and then pulls back into a tiny tubular cavity looping around the circumference of the skull.

Though jackhammering for food is the woodpecker norm, and was likely the first task woodpecking evolved for, not all woodpeckers forage that way. The white-headed relies heavily on pine nuts, and forages for insects by prying bark. Woodpecker females in general are thinner-billed than males, and pry bark perhaps more than they jackhammer it.

But all of these woodpeckers do use woodpecking for two other vital tasks. First, they chop large squarish holes for their nests, padding them with a few of the chips. Such nests are dry and easy to defend, allowing prolonged rearing—advantages that have led several other species to depend on abandoned woodpecker holes for their nests. Second, they drum—the classic woodpecker drum roll—on resonant trees to assert territory or to point out a nest site to a prospective mate. When you hear slower, irregular tapping on trees, it's exploration or spousal communication. Woodpeckers can also vocalize. The pileated, our largest woodpecker, has a strident call like a harsh, maniacal laugh, which it seems to use when disturbed—such as whenever you or I come around. When you recognize it you'll know to look around for one of our flashiest birds. It excavates the largest, squarest holes of any of our woodpeckers, but for a nest it saves effort by carving an entrance into an already-hollow rotten tree.

Pileateds eat ants primarily, and may chop many inches deep into rotten wood to dig out carpenter ant nests. Each bird requires lots of dead trees, so the species dwindled as old-growth forests vanished from most of the continent. It was also hunted. More recently it has recovered, and is quite willing to brave urban woods if they have enough snags. A few pileateds have become pests, chopping away at house and phone-pole timbers.

The black-backed woodpecker, specializing in insects of freshly fire-killed trees, is our top avian fire-follower. It declined during the decades of successful fire suppression, and is listed as sensitive in Oregon and Washington. Climate-related fire increases may alleviate that problem. The three-toed, restricted to high elevations and at least equally uncommon, also likes burns and may specialize in bark beetles.

Northern Flicker

Colaptes auratus (CO-LAP-teez: chiseler; aw-RAY-tus: golden). 11 in.; gray-brown with black-spotted paler belly, black-barred back, black "bib," and reddish crown, mustache (♂ only) and underside of wings and tail; flight dips down and up. Varied calls include a prolonged "nyuk-nyuk-nyuk." Widespread and common in semi-open and edge habitats. Picidae.

Flickers grab ants and preen with them, using their formic acid to kill parasites. They peck for insects in the soil or catch them in midair, as well as excavating bark for them. Outside of the breeding season, seeds and berries become major diet items.

Northern flicker

Red-breasted sapsucker

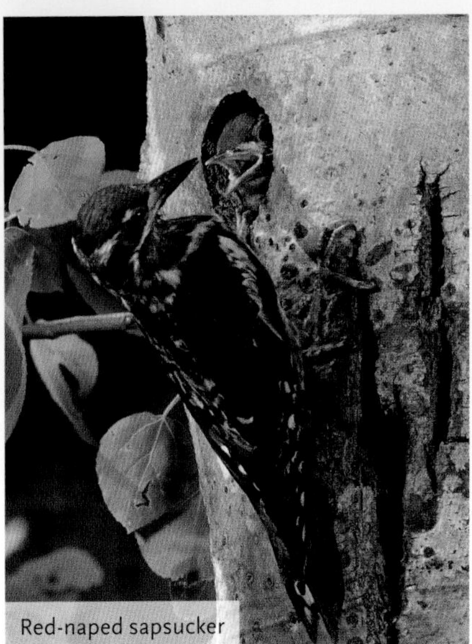
Red-naped sapsucker

Sapsucker

***Sphyrapicus* spp.** (sfie-ra-PIE-cus: hammer woodpecker). 7¾ in.; back and wings black and white. Taps in a syncopated rhythm, but does not jackhammer, on trees; calls are catlike mews and "cherrrrs." Picidae.

Red-breasted sapsucker, *S. ruber* (ROO-ber: red). Sexes alike; entire head and breast has scarlet overlay; short white mustache; yellow belly. W-side forest; year-round, moving to lowlands in winter. Picidae.

Red-naped sapsucker, *S. nuchalis* (noo-CAL-iss: nape—); Red forehead, nape spot, and throat; white mustache extends and curves onto breast; ♀ has white chin; dingy pale yellow belly. E-side woodland with aspen or cottonwood.

Neat horizontal rings of quarter-inch holes drilled through tree bark are the work of these deviant woodpeckers, which drill these "wells," leave, and come back another day. Time allows sap not only to flow, but also sometimes to ferment, and certainly to attract the sapsucker's main course, insects. Butterflies and moths in experiments prefer their foods fermented, and inebriated behavior has been observed in butterflies and sapsuckers alike. Other birds also dine at these sap wells. They are crucial for rufous hummingbirds that inadvertently migrate north too fast for adequate nectar supplies.

Damage to the bark is insufficient to kill the tree by girdling it, but any breaching of the bark increases the odds for fungal diseases to invade. On balance, though, sapsuckers are good for trees, because they're leading predators of spruce budworm moths, which are major pests. They can nab insects in midair, glean ants from bark crevices, and vary their diets with berries.

BIRDS: PASSERIFORMES (SONGBIRDS)

Olive-Sided Flycatcher

Contopus cooperi (con-TOE-pus: short foot; coo-per-eye: for James or William Cooper). 6¼ in.; olive-gray with pearly white smear down throat and breast; white downy tufts on lower back are visible in flight. Tyrannidae.

The olive-sided's song, usually asserted from some conifer pinnacle, has been transcribed as "Quick! . . . FREE beer" or "Tuck . . . THREE bears." These flycatchers summer throughout our forests, clearcuts, and timberlines. They eat winged insects, spotting individuals from their perch and darting out to snatch them. In contrast to the continual seining method of swifts and swallows, which nets small insects, flycatchers eat insects up to bee size.

Pacific-slope flycatcher

Pacific-Slope Flycatcher

Empidonax difficilis (em-PID-o-nax: gnat king; dif-ISS-il-iss: difficult). Also western flycatcher. 5 in.; olive brown above with 2 whitish wing-bars; pale yellowish olive beneath; teardrop-shaped eye-ring, two-toned bill. Abundant but inconspicuous in wet forest, less so e-side; usually in deciduous understory. Tyrannidae.

The specific name *difficilis* says that it's next to impossible to identify *Empidonax* birds in the bush. They are hard to see, staying camouflaged among foliage. This one has a recognizable call, though: a very high, rising "pseeeet." The song is similar to the call, but much repeated, with "pseet-eets" as well.

Warbling vireo

Vireo

***Vireo* spp.** (VEER-ee-oh: I'm green). 4¾ in.; greenish-gray above, dark gray wings, paler below. April–September here, wintering in Mexico and Central America. Vireonidae.

Warbling vireo, *V. gilvus* (VEER-ee-oh: green; GILL-vus: pale yellow). 4 in.; no wing-bars, dull white above and below eye; underside pale yellow. Call: 8- to 12-note phrases at 2- to 4-second intervals, final note higher. Around deciduous trees and shrubs.

Cassin's vireo, *V. cassinii* (cas-IN-ee-eye: for John Cassin). Also solitary vireo. White eye-ring and line in front of eye (spectacles); 2 white wing-bars; flanks yellowish, belly white. Call: varied 2- to 3-note phrases at 2- to 4-second intervals, second note accented. Dry conifer forest, High CasR and e-side plus drier lowlands w-side.

Female and male vireos take turns warming the eggs, and won't leave them even if approached and handled; they're oddly sluggish birds. The nest is a small cup of grasses lined with lichens, moss, or feathers, often decorated outside with bark, petals, or catkins held on with spiderwebbing. It dangles from a fork in horizontal branches not too high up in a conifer.

Gray Jay

Perisoreus canadensis (pair-i-SOR-ee-us: "I-heap-up"). Also Canada jay, camp-robber, whiskey-jack. 10 in.; fluffy pale gray with dark gray wings, tail, rump, nape, and crown; short black bill; juveniles dark gray with pale cheek-streak. Calls and songs include a whistled "whee-oh" and many others. Conifer forest and timberline. Corvidae.

Like their close relatives the crows, jays seem coarse and vulgar but are intelligent,

Georg Steller

Georg Steller was the first European naturalist-explorer on northeast Pacific shores. A German, he crossed Siberia to accompany Danish Captain Vitus Bering on a Russian ship built and launched from Kamchatka in 1741. They were just east of Cordova, Alaska, when they turned around late that year, and they didn't quite make it back to Kamchatka. Marooned for a terrible scurvy-ridden winter on small, rocky Bering Island, the Captain and many of the crew died. Steller survived, but took to drink and died in Siberia without ever reaching Europe again.

versatile, and successful. Their voices, though harsh and noisy, are capable of extreme variety and accurate mimicry of other birds. Equally versatile in feeding, ours eat mainly conifer seeds, berries, and insects, but also relish meat when they can scrounge some up or kill a small bird or rodent. Gray jays, or "camp robbers," would sometimes nip at a trapper's catch while he was still skinning it, and notoriously thronged logging-camp mess halls. They will descend noiselessly into your backcountry camp at dinner time, and even snatch proffered food from your fingertips, especially in winter when food is more scarce. But their nonchalance reminds skiers that winter here is perfectly livable for the well-adapted. Gray jays and Clark's nutcrackers are so comfortable in the cold that they nest and incubate their young with plenty of snow still on the ground—or even on their heads. To store food for winter, the jays glue little seed bundles with sticky saliva, and leave them in bark crevices or foliage.

Steller's Jay

Cyanocitta stelleri (sigh-an-o-SIT-a: blue jay; STELL-er-eye: for Georg Steller, <directional>). 11 in.; deep ultramarine blue with blackish shoulders and dramatically crested head. Widespread near conifers. Corvidae.

Birds of North America lists this vocal repertoire for the Steller's jay: creak; squawk; growl; rattle; song; Ut; Ow; Wah; Wek; Aap; Tjar; Tee-ar; gutteral notes; and mimicry. Mimicry includes an uncanny imitation of a

Gray jay

Steller's jay

red-tailed hawk's scream. This presumably tricks other birds into clearing out while the jay feeds, but perhaps it sometimes warns of an actual hawk. Jays and crows are the birds most often seen harassing or "mobbing" birds of prey—a defense of smaller birds against larger ones (p. 416). This jay is omnivorous, smart, and aggressive—traits that run in the crow family. It will commonly rob the caches of its cousin, Clark's nutcracker.

The smaller, paler blue jay proper, *C. cristata*, is an eastern bird that visits here rarely. Westerners sometimes say "blue jay" either for Steller's or for the western scrub jay, *Aphelocoma californica*, a crestless jay, blue above and white beneath, seen in and near the Willamette Valley.

Clark's nutcracker

Clark's Nutcracker

Nucifraga columbiana (new-SIF-ra-ga: nut breaker; co-lum-be-AY-na: of the Columbia River). 11 in.; pale gray (including crown and back) with white-marked black wings and tail (white outer tail-feathers and rear wing-patch); long thin bill; throat can bulge like a large goiter when full of pine nuts. Call a harsh "kraaa, kraaa." Around whitebark or lodgepole pines; not in CoastR, rare on VI. Corvidae.

Flashy black-and-white wings and tail distinguish Clark's nutcracker from the more numerous gray jay. Like the jay, the nutcracker has been known as the "camp-robber," but mainly in California, beyond the range of the gray jay.

Clark's nutcrackers coevolved with whitebark pines (p. 84). While many conifers hide or protect their seeds from seed-eaters as long as possible, the whitebark pine exposes them early and conspicuously, and enriches them with oils and proteins. It also fails to give them the membranous wings that other pine seeds have to help the wind carry them. Clark's nutcracker obliges by collecting the seeds compulsively, selecting the high-quality ones (most nutritious and most viable), eating some on the spot and burying all the rest, a few at a time, for retrieval in winter.

Though canny enough to remember cache locations for nine months, the birds are so industrious that they store two or three times as many as they can consume—well upwards of 20,000 per year. The remainder have thus been planted, often many miles from their source—a great advantage to the pines, especially in recolonizing large severe burns. The strong-flying nutcrackers have a typical foraging range of 14 miles from their caches, and can carry more than 150 whitebark pine seeds in a sublingual pouch that bulges conspicuously at the throat. Other conifer seeds are eaten, too. Poor pine-seed crop years cause irruptions of nutcrackers into far-flung lowlands in search of substitute fare, and the decline in whitebark pines due to white pine blister rust has caused a decline in nutcrackers.

Common Raven

Corvus corax (COR-vus: their Roman name, from COR-ax: their Greek name, imitating their voice). 21 in., ws 48 in.; black with purple-green iridescence, and shaggy grayish ruff at throat; bill heavy; tail long, flared then tapered; alternates periods of flapping and flat-winged soaring. Call a throaty croak. Timberlines (both upper and lower). Corvidae.

Common raven

You can tell raven from little sibling crow by raven's greater size, heavier bill, ruffed throat, more prolonged soaring, and by its voice: an outrageously hoarse guttural croak rather than a nasal "caw." At timberline in our mountains and near the east-side steppes you are more likely to see ravens. Their courtship flights in spring are a sight to remember: they do barrel rolls or chaotic tumbles while plummeting, then swoop, hang motionless, all the while exercising their vocabularies. The ensuing family group—four or five young are typically flying by June—often stays together through the following winter, and may flock with other families. Ravens mate for life (but see p. 434 before you get sentimental) and live as long as thirty years. The nest is high, solid, and cozy, perhaps lined with deer hair, but filthy and smelly by our standards, and often flea-ridden. Ravens eat anything crows eat and then some; by grouping up they can take live prey as large as hares.

Ravens were once abundant throughout the West, but westward settlement pushed them back to remote deserts and mountains.

Ravens were accepted members of tribal life in Northwest Coast villages. Raven was seen as at once a trickster and a powerful, aggressive, chiefly figure—much the equivalent of Coyote among intermountain tribes. He was a Creator in origin myths. His croaks were prophetic, and a person who could interpret them would become a great seer. To draw prophetic powers into a chosen newborn, the Kwakiutl would feed its afterbirth to the ravens. Myths almost universally depict ravens and crows as powerful, knowing, and a little bit sinister. French peasants thought that bad priests became ravens, and bad nuns, crows.

The raven is the largest bird in the Passeriformes, known as perching birds or songbirds. They are the most recently evolved avian order, with by far the greatest number of species, which indicates success and rapid evolution. The evolution of seed plants was accompanied by the specialization of seed eaters—songbirds and rodents, mainly—and a wave of predators specializing in eating seed-eaters. The raven rides the crest of both waves: it eats rodents, nestlings, and eggs, as well as seeds. By some accounts it is the most advanced bird.

Bernd Heinrich, who devoted years to close observation of ravens, casts doubt on one well-known anecdote said to prove raven intelligence: their teaming up to heist meat from coyotes. He does believe (as do many native tribes) that ravens will lead a wolf or a human hunter to prey, on the odds that they will end up with the scraps. Devising ingenious tests of raven intelligence, he showed that they remember where they cache seeds under snow, rather than smelling them out; moreover, they keep a corner of their eye open for where other ravens are caching seeds, and try to rob those caches first. To avoid being robbed, they fly much farther before caching when other ravens are within view.

Crow

Corvus spp. 17 in.; black with blue-purple-green iridescence; tail squared-off; rarely glides more than 2–3 seconds at a time. Lowlands. Corvidae.

American crow, _C. brachyrhynchos_ (brak-i-RINK-os: short beak). E-side, and w-side in OR and sw WA.

Northwestern crow, _C. caurinus_ (cor-EYE-nus: northwestern). W-side from Olympia north.

Northwestern crow

Most crow-like birds you see in our mountain wilderness are ravens; crows characteristically inhabit farmlands, and avoid both deep forest and cliffy terrain. You are most likely to see them here along lowland streams and meadows, or in part-deciduous forest. They scavenge carrion, garbage, fruit, snails, grubs, insects, frogs, and eggs and nestlings from birds' nests. Species as large as ducks, gulls, and falcons may be victims, and some songbirds count crows among their major enemies.

Crow populations in North America grew between 1966 and 1999, and then fell when West Nile virus arrived. Crows and their family are highly susceptible. West Nile trends since 2005 have been ambiguous, and this new threat to birds fell off the radar somewhat until 2013, when it caused a huge die-off of a relatively scarce species, eared grebes, at Great Salt Lake. As one of many serious threats to birds, it bears watching.

Morphological characters of northwestern and American crows overlap, such that even experts can barely tell them apart in the field.

Horned Lark

Horned lark

Eremophila alpestris (air-em-AH-fil-a: loving lonely places; al-PES-tris: alpine). 6½ in.; pinkish brown back, yellow face, whitish below; sharp black breast-band and cheek smear; tiny feather tufts ("horns") above eyes; white outer tail feathers show in flight. Nests and forages on ground, walking (not hopping). Song a long, twinkling twitter, starting by dawn. Alpine tundra (mainly WA and mainland BC), e-side short grasslands; listed as a common bird in steep decline. Alaudidae.

In his famous courtship display, the male spirals steeply to several hundred feet up, circles round and round singing, then plummets with wings held to his sides. One song type, the "recitative," lasts several minutes.

The horned lark is the only New World member of the lark family, and is widespread across North America, with many subspecies specializing in diverse habitats that all feature sparse low vegetation. For safety from predators, it just ducks into slight depressions and, I would imagine, prays.

Violet-green swallow

Tree swallow

Barn swallow

Swallow

Graceful flyers in flocks, with backswept pointed wings, deeply to shallowly forked tails. Breeding summer residents. Hirundinidae.

Violet-green swallow, *Tachycineta thalassina* (tacky-sin-EE-ta: fast moving; tha-LASS-in-a: sea-green). 4¾ in.; dark with green and violet iridescence above; white below, extending around eyes and up sides of rump to show as two white spots when seen from above; tail shallowly forked. High tweeting chatter. Open areas; in flocks; spring and summer.

Tree swallow, *T. bicolor* (BY-color: 2-colored). 5 in.; iridescent blue-black above, white below (not extending above eye or rump); otherwise like violet-green swallow. Near water and trees, but not closed forest.

Barn swallow, *Hirundo rustica* (he-RUN-doe: the Roman name; RUST-ic-a: rural). 6 in.; blue-black above; rusty below, dark at throat and forehead but pale (or even white) elsewhere; tail forked. Continuous "zip-zip" chatter with occasional fast rattle sounds.

A swallow's flight is graceful, slick, and fast, though not quite as swift as a swift's. A swallow's swallow, or more precisely its gape, is striking. The wide, weak jaws are held open almost 180 degrees while the swallow knifes back and forth through the air intercepting insects. It can react to a bug or a raindrop and turn its head fast enough to snag it, or pluck berries off of a bush while in flight. Even before daylight you may hear a twittering flock of violet-green swallows already up and feeding.

Swallows often nest in large colonies. Barn swallows build mud nests on porch roofs or eaves. *Tachycineta* swallows use tree holes and other ready-made crevices.

Chickadee

***Poecile* spp.** (PEE-sil-ee: many-colored). Also *Parus* spp. Paridae.

Chestnut-backed chickadee, *P. rufescens* (roo-FES-enz: reddish). 4¼ in.; black crown and throat, white cheeks and belly, rich red-brown back and sides. Rapid chipping calls are frequent, and may sometimes function as songs. Abundant year-round in most w-side habitats.

Black-capped chickadee, *P. atricapillus* (ay-tri-ca-PILL-us: black cap). 4½ in.; black crown and throat, white cheeks; grayish belly, gray-brown upper parts. Song a slow "fee-bee." Lower thickets, streamsides.

Mountain chickadee, *P. gambeli* (GAM-bel-eye: for William Gambel). 4¼ in.; black crown, eye-streak and throat; white eyebrow and cheeks, grayish belly, gray-brown upperparts. Song a faster "fee-bee-bee." Subalpine and e CasR slope.

Chickadees seem to display the chipper dispositions people want to see in songbirds, and they let us see it, being tamer than most. Gleaners of caterpillars and other insects from the branches, they reside here year-round, nesting in well-lined holes dug rather low in tree trunks either by woodpeckers or by themselves, in soft punky wood. They tend to partition the habitat vertically—chestnut-backed feeding in the canopy, black-capped in the shrubs. They also eat seeds, and cache them for winter.

"Chick-a dee-dee-dee" is an alarm call, or a call to arms, gathering chickadees and others to help mob a predator. For higher danger levels they speed up the "chick-a-dee" and add more "dee-dees." Researchers counted 23 "dees" once for a pygmy owl—more dangerous than a big owl because being close to chickadee size makes it agile enough to catch them.

Nuthatch

***Sitta* spp.** (SIT-a: their Roman name). Year-round residents. Sittidae.

Red-breasted nuthatch, *S. canadensis.* 4 in.; blue-gray above, rusty below; throat and eyebrow white; crown and eye-streak black

Chestnut-backed chickadee

Black-capped chickadee

Mountain chickadee

Red-breasted nuthatch

White-breasted nuthatch

Brown creeper

Pacific wren

(♂) or dark gray (♀). Song a lazy, a tinny "nyank." Forest, especially at higher elevs w-side.

White-breasted nuthatch, *S. carolinensis* (carol-in-EN-sis: of the Carolinas). 5 in.; blue-gray above, white below (may have a red tinge under tail); white face surrounds eye; crown black (♂) or gray (♀). Song a block of 6–10 rapid "wanks." Subalpine and e-side pine or oak woodland.

Nuthatches are known for walking headfirst down tree trunks, apparently finding that way just as right-side up as the other. They glean insects from the bark, and eat seeds in fall through spring. Their nest, in a hole in a dead snag, is inconspicuous but identifiable by the pitch smeared around it. Even in deep wilderness they aren't shy, and draw our attention with their penetrating song and call.

Brown Creeper

Certhia americana (SERTH-ia: the Greek name). 4¾ in.; mottled brown or gray above, white beneath; long down-curved bill. Call a single very high, soft sibilant note. On conifer trunks year-round; common but inconspicuous. Certhiidae.

You probably won't see a brown creeper unless you happen to catch its faint, high call, and then patiently let your eyes scour nearby bark. (The call is so high-pitched that many of us are literally deaf to it—a deficiency correlated with being male and with rock and roll.) This well camouflaged full-time bark dweller gleans its insect prey from bark crevices, and nests behind loose bark. In contrast to nuthatches, which usually walk down tree trunks, the creeper spirals up them, propping itself with stiff tail feathers like a woodpecker's. Crevices approached from above and below present different types of prey, putting creepers and nuthatches in different ecological niches.

Pacific Wren

Troglodytes pacificus (tra-GLOD-i-teez: cave dweller, a misleading name). Also winter wren; *T. troglodytes*. 3¼ in.; finely barred reddish-brown all over; tail rounded, very short, often (as in all wrens) held upturned at 90 degrees to line of back. Near the ground in forest with a dense herb or low shrub layer; abundant year-round. Troglodytidae.

Though we hear it often, the Pacific wren's song never ceases to amaze with sheer virtuosity. The notes go by too fast—ten per second—for us to catch them individually, but the singer knows his repertoire perfectly, and would be as defiant as the fictional Mozart if criticized for "too many notes." Each song, of up to 300 notes, is a permutation of

Recycling For Bird Brains

To the long list of weight-saving adaptations in birds, you can now add the ability to grow new brain cells. You may have heard that you can lose brain cells throughout life (when you overimbibe, perhaps) but never grow new ones. Not true. The discovery of newly formed neurons in chickadees led the way to a similar find in humans. In both species, the new cells are in the hippocampus, the brain part that's involved in learning and memory.

Chickadees grow new neurons in a big burst each fall, when they cache seeds in thousands of crevices they will have to find again if they are to survive winter. An even bigger hippocampal growth spurt benefits dispersing juveniles, who will have to learn the geography they will inhabit for the rest of their lives. But the total hippocampal neuron count does not increase over the chickadee life span. One hypothesis holds that each neuron stores one memory, and is resorbed and replaced at some point after that memory is no longer needed. In a tiny flying animal, a brain big enough for a lifetime of memories might never get off the ground.

Very small birds actually have a far higher percentage of their body mass in the form of brain than we do and they also cram the brain neurons in much more densely. The fact that natural selection produced big chickadee brains shows that brainpower is critical for food-caching birds, as brains are energy hogs compared to other kinds of tissue. Phenomenal ability to remember precise locations evolved separately in the chickadees and the jays that cache food for winter, and in many migrating species. Some of these species have nonmigratory or noncaching relatives whose powers of recall don't amount to diddley squat.

Another kind of memory that must be worth holding on to is a male warbler's memory of conspecific males' songs. As long as each singer remembers his neighbor's song from the year before, and stays on his own territory, both are spared a fight. They remember songs from year to year as they return from Central America to reclaim their old haunts.

short building blocks from a vocabulary of perhaps 80 blocks. He can repeat the song exactly, and so can his neighbor, showing that they learn each other's songs. He typically repeats it several times, with slight variations, before moving on to the next permutation, and he takes many days to go through his repertoire. (A recording is available of a Pacific Wren song slowed down to one-sixth speed. Lordy, lordy. . . .)

The wren moves in a darting, mouse-like manner, eats insects, maintains a low profile among the brush, and goes to great lengths to keep its nest a secret. Several extra nests are often built just as decoys, and the real occupied nest has a decoy entrance, much larger than the real entrance but strictly dead-end. Real and decoy nests are both also camouflaged.

American dipper

Golden-crowned kinglet

American Dipper

Cinclus mexicanus (SINK-lus: the Greek name). Also water ouzel. 5¾ in.; slate gray all over, scarcely paler beneath, often with white eye-ring; tail short; feet yellow. In or very close to cold mtn streams. Cinclidae.

It's no wonder that dippers make such an impression on campers throughout America's western mountains, considering how much trouble campers have keeping warm. Winter and summer, snow, rain, or shine, dippers spend most of their time plunging in and out of frigid, frothing torrents, plucking out invisible objects—actually aquatic insects such as dragonfly and caddis fly larvae, and sometimes tiny fish. Somehow they walk on the bottom, gripping with their big feet. They can also swim with their wings, quickly reverting to flight if they get swept out of control downstream. They can dive to considerable depths in mountain lakes, and occasionally they forage on snowfields. They show little interest in drying off. Even in flight they are usually in the spray zone over a stream, and they often nest behind waterfalls. In August they have a flightless molt period when swimming becomes their only escape from predators. Fledglings swim on their first day out of the nest, at around 25 days old. Dippers never really get soaked to the skin, thanks to extremely dense body plumage and extra glands to keep it well oiled.

They are named for their unexplained jerky genuflections, performed as often as once a second while standing, accompanied by blinking of their flashy white eyelids. Their call, "dipit dipit," is forceful enough to carry over the din of the creek. Even in midwinter they occasionally break into song. Both sexes are virtuosi, with long, loud, lyrical, bell-like, and extremely varied songs.

Kinglet

***Regulus* spp.** (REG-you-lus: small king). Regulidae.

Golden-crowned kinglet, *R. satrapa* (SAT-ra-pa: ruler). 3½ in.; gray-green above, whitish below, with 2 white wing-bars; central yellow (♀) or orange (♂) stripe on head is flanked by black and then white stripes at eyebrow. Very high, lisping "chee, chee" call. Widespread year-round in conifer canopy, often abundant.

Ruby-crowned kinglet, *R. calendula* (ca-LEND-you-la: larklet). 3¾ in.; gray-green above, whitish below, with white eye-ring and two white wing-bars; rarely visible scarlet spot on crown is displayed only by excited ♂, leaving the species almost indistinguishable from vireos. Scolding "jit-it" calls, and long, variable song of chatters, warbles, and rising triplets. Breeds at high elevs in CasR; winters in brush and lower canopy w-side.

Constant movement—wings twitching even when perched—characterizes kinglets.

They catch insects, sometimes in flight but mostly on foliage. To avoid competing directly with other foliage gleaners like chickadees, their tiny size and ability to hover enable them to forage on twigs too weak to support other birds. Insects are a less concentrated and less predictable food than seeds, and kinglets supplement with some seeds. Golden-crowned kinglets, chickadees, and woodpeckers commonly flock together in winter, as this seems to help them locate insect populations.

A kinglet weighs about as much as two pennies. Among birds and mammals, only a few kinds of hummingbirds and shrews are smaller, and not by much; and hummingbirds or shrews aren't usually exposed to such cold air as kinglets. In winter they spend nearly every waking minute foraging, raising their body fat daily from around 5 percent to 11 percent, enough to survive the night if they are lucky. When it gets too dark for foraging to produce a net gain, they plunge into the first insulative spot they see, such as soft snow under thick brush, twist their necks to wedge their eyes and bills in among their back feathers, and go to sleep. Occasionally several may huddle together overnight. It's a harsh existence. Mortality in northerly kinglets is estimated to be 87 percent per year. They compensate by producing 18 to 20 eggs per pair, in two broods per summer.

Ruby-crowned kinglet

Mountain bluebird

Bluebird

***Sialia* spp.** (see-AH-lia: the Greek name). Turdidae.

Mountain bluebird, *S. currucoides* (cue-roo-COY-deez: warbler-like). 6 in.; summer ♂ turquoise above, shading to paler blue or gray beneath; ♀ and winter ♂ gray-brown with varying amounts of blue on tail, rump, and wings. Song a long series of chips and descending warbles. Alp/subalpine in March–October, mainly e-side; OR pine forests year-round.

Western bluebird

Western bluebird, *S. mexicana* 5½ in.; summer ♂ deep blue above, rich russet breast and upper back, pale gray belly; ♀ and winter ♂ analagous but dull, head usually just gray. Song a long series of descending chips and "chi-chips." Open forest such as lower timberlines east of CasR and CoastR.

Bluebirds drop on insect prey from a low hover or perch. In fall they fatten up on berries. Western bluebird numbers declined notoriously by the mid-1900s, but seem tentatively to be heading up in recent decades, with the help of campaigns to build nest boxes for them. The mountain bluebird has prospered from clearcutting and ranching, as well as nest boxes.

Townsend's Solitaire

Myadestes townsendi (my-a-DES-teez: fly eater; TOWN-zend-eye: for John Kirk Townsend, p. 350). 6¾ in.; gray with white eye-ring; dark tail has white feathers on sides (like the more abundant junco, p. 436; solitaire is longer, slenderer, more upright, more arboreal); dark wings have buff patches, visible underneath in flight. Song a series of 2-second rapid warbles, heard at any season; call a high, ringing peep. Mid- to high-elev open forest. Turdidae.

The solitaire returns to the mountains early, searching the first snow-free areas for a nesting cavity in a stump or rotting log. It likes the edges of clearings, and apparently increased in the Cascades as patch clearcuts proliferated. In spring and fall solitaires gather in large flocks, belying their name. Many winter in juniper woodlands east of the Cascades, subsisting on juniper berries; a few manage to find sufficient winter-persistent berries on the west side. They defend their berry territories with fierce attacks on intruders of any species. In summer they eat insects.

Varied Thrush

Ixoreus naevius (ix-OR-ius: mistletoe mountain, referring to food and habitat; NEEV-ius: spotted). 8 in.; breast, throat, eyebrow, and wingbars rich rusty-orange (♂) or yellow-buff (♀), contrasting with slate-gray breastband, cheeks, crown, back, etc.; whitish belly; perches or walks with body more horizontal than the similar robin. W-side forest; listed as a common bird in steep decline. Turdidae.

The varied thrush sings a single note with odd, rough overtones; it's actually two slightly dissonant notes at once. After several seconds' rest, he sings another tone, similar but higher or lower by some irrational interval. Birds have two sets of vocal chords, one in each bronchus. Many songbirds alternate them rapidly to warble or burble euphoniously. Several thrush species use them for simultaneous note pairs instead, but only varied thrush performs just this one vocal trick in the starkest possible way. Prolonged early or late in the day, in deep

Townsend's solitaire

Varied thrush

forest and fog, this minimal music acquires powers of enchantment.

Foraging on the ground for insects and berries, varied thrushes can't stay after snow covers the ground, so they descend to the lowlands.

Similar American robin, *Turdus migratorius*, looks a bit drab in comparison, lacking the white wing-bars or the gray breast-band. It is fairly common in our mountains, and of course abundant in the developed lowlands.

Swainson's thrush

Swainson's Thrush and Hermit Thrush

***Catharus* spp.** (CATH-a-rus: pure). 6¼ in.; sexes alike, gray-brown above; pale eye-ring; belly white, breast spotted. Turdidae.

Swainson's thrush, *C. ustulatus* (ust-you-LAY-tus: singed). Back and head red-tinged; tail less so. Partly open low to mid-elevs; winters in Central America.

Hermit thrush

Hermit thrush, *C. guttatus* (ga-TAY-tus: spotted). Tail, but not back, is rusty red; tail is "nervously" raised and lowered every few seconds, while wings may twitch. Common subalpine; winters in w-side lowlands.

Thrushes of this genus are hard to see but easy to notice for their distinctive, lyrical songs. Hermit starts with its longest, loudest note, then warbles softer and downward, and performs variations at different pitches. Swainson's works its way upward in pitch, in a sort of spiral, and also may repeat at different pitches. Both species forage on the ground for earthworms, insects, and berries.

American pipit

American Pipit

Anthus rubescens (ANTH-us: Greek term for some bird; roo-BES-enz: reddish). Also water pipit. 5½ in.; sexes alike: gray-brown above, buff below, with white outer tail feathers and dark legs; bill slenderer than sparrows. Alpine in summer, shores at other seasons. Motacillidae.

Distinguish the pipit from two other common species with white outer tail feathers (junco and solitaire) by its habit of regularly jerking its tail down as it walks along foraging. It often finds invertebrate prey in shallow water or on snow. To attract a mate and, once he has one, to assert territory, the male flies straight up and then drifts down on spread wings, singing a rapid, high "chee-chee-chee" all the while. Often the song or

Extra-Pair Goings-On

Birds don't do it, bees don't do it,
WE are the only ones that fall in love.

The 1928 original Cole Porter version of this lyric shows poor grasp of bird behavior, compared to its 1987 send-up by Sly and Robbie. The DNA police have been looking into avian paternity, and they've demolished the faithful chirping couples stereotype that inspired centuries of bad verse. In many bird species a male may help build the nest, sit on the eggs, defend the territory, and bring food to the young, but that species' social monogamy rating bears little correlation with that male's likelihood of being the sire of all the young in that nest. There's a whole lot going on on the sly.

Patterns of extra-pair copulations (EPCs) vary widely among closely related species, or even populations of the same species. For example, a study of cliff swallows found that 2 percent of fertilizations were extra-pair, whereas the study of tree swallows found 44 percent. The EPC picture in swallow colonies is complicated by plenty of intraspecific brood parasitism, in which a female waits for a neighboring nest to be momentarily unattended, and then slips in and lays an egg. Her victims will feed her young along with their own. This gets worse: a male slips into an unattended nest and rolls an egg out, to its doom, perhaps to make room for his mate to lay an egg there, or perhaps to keep his female neighbor receptive to his seductions. Either way he's promoting his own genes.

Diverse strategies are being pursued here, and there are ongoing academic imbroglios—replete with anthropomorphic terms like "divorce," "harem," and "cuckold"—over how to interpret them. There are male strategies and female strategies; the latter are usually the key, since females apparently control the fertilization success of copulations. One scientist who watched black-capped chickadees in a small area over a 20-year period witnessed 13 extra-pair trysts; in each case the female actively sought out a male of higher social rank than her own mate. A later study using DNA fingerprinting corroborated that conclusion. A study in one warbler species found that males with larger song repertoires were able to seduce more females, and that the females were getting what they were looking for: fitter genes, as measured by the breeding success of her offspring.

the call can identify the bird while it flies too high to be spotted. The call note may occasionally suggest "pipit."

Warbler

Yellow-rumped warbler, *Setophaga coronata* (see-toe-FAY-ga: bug eater; cor-o-NAY-ta: crowned). Also *Dendroica coronata*. 4¾ in.; yellow in 5 small patches (mere tinges on ♀): crown, rump, sides; otherwise mostly gray and black (breeding ♂) to soft gray-brown (others), with white eye-ring and one vague wing-bar; formerly treated as two spp., Audubon's with yellow throat and myrtle warbler with white. Song a rapidfire "seedy-seedy" burst, loudest in the middle. Widespread and abundant.

Yellow-rumped warbler

Townsend's warbler, *S. townsendi* (TOWN-zend-eye: for John Kirk Townsend, p. 350). Also *Dendroica townsendi*. 4¼ in.; whitish beneath, greenish gray above, with two white wing-bars; crown black; sides of face (except dark cheek patch) and breast bright yellow. Song several high sweezes and then lower ones. Mid-elev to high forest and openings.

Townsend's warbler

Yellow warbler, *S. petechia* (pet-EEK-ia: red-dotted). Also *Dendroica petechia*. 4 in.; mostly yellow with some gray on wings and tail; ♂ breast red-streaked. 3 or 4 lower "swees" followed by higher, faster ones. Thickets.

Yellow warbler

Wilson's warbler, *Cardellina pusilla* (car-del-EYE-na: little goldfinch; pew-SIL-a: tiny) Also *Wilsonia pusilla*. 4¼ in.; bright yellow over almost entire head; black throat bib on breeding ♂; very white beneath, greenish gray above with two white wing-bars. Several rising then a few faster lower notes, all very fast. Brush and mixed forest; listed as a common bird in steep decline. Parulidae

Wilson's warbler

Sparrow-sized birds with some yellow on them are usually warblers. This large family is known for long winter migrations to the tropics and for distinctive (but not exactly warbling) songs. Birders try to learn the songs, since there are so many kinds of warblers and they all tend to keep themselves inconspicuous among foliage. Most are gleaners of insects; many also hawk at larger insects; some vary their diets with fruits and seeds.

The closely related Townsend's and hermit warblers have distinct ranges, and hybridize where they meet. The common one in western Oregon is hermit, but Townsend's apparently out-competes it, and is advancing southwestward from the North Cascades and from the Ochocos. The current front lines, or hybrid zones, are in the southern Washington Cascades and the central Oregon Cascades.

Song Sparrow

Melospiza melodia (mel-o-SPY-za: song finch). 5½ in.; brown with blackish streaking above, white below with brown streaking convergent at throat, above a mid-breast brown spot; pumps its tail in flight. Widespread year-round; thickets. Emberizidae.

"Sparrow" is a catchall term for a lot of common, drab brown birds which aren't really a taxonomic group—less so with each revision of bird taxonomy, it seems. This species is one of the most widely distributed birds in America, and is truly melodious. Its typical song—heard on spring and early summer mornings—is a few clear piping notes, then a lower, raspy buzz or series, ending with around three quick, clear notes.

Dark-Eyed Junco

Junco hyemalis (JUNK-oh: rush, a plant with no obvious connection; hi-em-AY-lis: of winter). Also Oregon junco. 5¼ in.; tail dark gray-brown except for white feathers at sides; belly white, throat and above variably gray and brown. Song a simple, rapid burst of chirps. Ground-foraging and -nesting; one of our most abundant birds. Emberizidae.

Though juncos migrate, we have them year-round: many migrate upslope from northwest cities and farms in early summer while others arrive from California, and still others, having wintered here, take off to breed in the Yukon. They eat seeds primarily, turning to insects in summer and feeding insects and larvae to their young. After the young leave the nest, they travel in loose flocks until the next summer.

Western Tanager

Piranga ludoviciana (pir-ANG-ga: name for it in the Tupi language, of Brazil; loo-do-viss-i-AY-na: of "Louisiana"). 6¼ in.; summer ♂ has bright red to orange head, yellow breast, belly and rump, black back-band, tail, and wings, and white wing-bars;

Song sparrow

Dark-eyed junco

others yellowish to greenish gray above, yellow beneath. Series of separate chirps, each consisting either of a squiggle or two very quick notes. Generally near treetops in open forest, in summer. Cardinalidae.

Lewis and Clark described many new plant species, but only three new birds: Lewis's woodpecker, Clark's nutcracker, and the western tanager, whose scientific name refers to the land they explored, the Louisiana Purchase. "Tanager" and "piranga" are native names for the birds from deep in the Amazon rainforest, where some tanagers winter. Wearing its dull winter plumage, this species travels as far as Central America. Back here, in breeding plumage, it looks like a gaudy jungle bird.

Tanagers switch from an insectivorous diet to one of ripe berries in late summer. Their beaks are intermediate between the insect-picking thin type and the heavy, seed-crushing beaks of finches. Taxonomists no longer see much significance in bill thickness, and mix thick- and thinner-billed birds in several families, including the two that "tanagers" are now divided between.

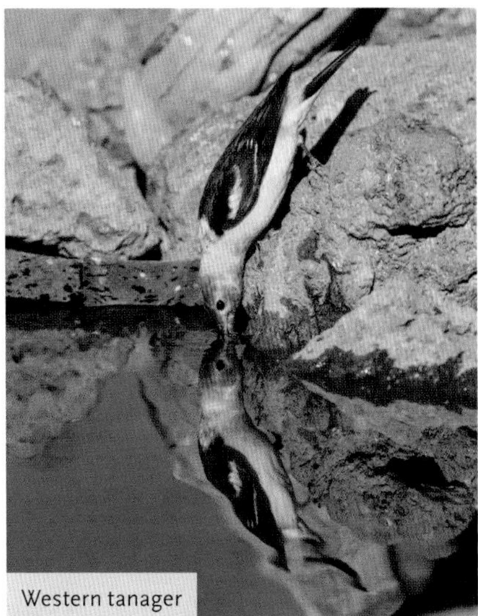
Western tanager

Gray-crowned rosy-finch

Gray-Crowned Rosy-Finch

Leucosticte tephrocotis (lew-co-STICK-tee: white patchy; tef-ra-co-tis: ashen head). Formerly rosy finch. 6¼ in.; brown with blackish face, gray crown or entire head, and (♂ especially) reddish tinges on rump, shoulders, and belly. Either squawky or high chip calls; song rarely heard. Arctic fellfields, snow, etc.; infrequent. Fringillidae.

The finch family name, Fringillidae, comes from the same Latin root as "frigid." Rosy-finches are the most alpine birds of the West, at least in summer, foraging as high as 11,000 feet on Mt. Rainier. They nest in high rock crevices, reportedly even in ice crevasses, and often forage on glaciers, utilizing a resource all climbers have noticed—insects that collapse on the snow, numbed by cold after being carried astray by diurnal up-valley winds. The bulk of their diet is vegetable, including seeds, white heather flowers, and succulent alpine saxifrage leaves. Most of our rosy-finches winter east of the Cascades, where they prove congenial with such lowland conveniences as window feeding-boxes, grain elevator yards, railroad beds where grain has spilled, and the company of dozens of other rosy-finches. Some entire flocks are male; for unknown reasons there are six times more male than female rosy-finches.

Cassin's finch

Red crossbill

Purple Finch and Cassin's Finch

***Hemorhous* spp.** (he-mo-ROE-us: blood—). Also *Carpodacus* spp. Mature ♂ reddish, especially toward late summer, with dark gray wings and white belly; ♀ (and ♂ up to breeding yearlings) a sparrow-like gray-brown with streaked to spotted white breast and belly. Bubbling, rapid, clear-toned songs. Fringillidae.

Purple finch, *H. purpureus* (pur-PEW-rius: purple). 5½ in.; ♂ dusky rose to wine red crown; red extends as a wash onto back and belly. Semi-open w-side forests.

Cassin's finch, *H. cassinii* (cas-IN-ee-eye: for John Cassin). 6 in.; ♂ red crown, pinkish breast and rump, little or no red on brownish back and white belly. Varied warble full of breaks and squeaks. Subalpine and e-side; on the NABCI Watch List.

When the red-flowering currant blooms, the purple finch is sometimes seen eating the flowers for their nectar-rich ovaries. Cassin's finch is more likely eating conifer buds. Both are primarily seed-eaters later in the year.

Red Crossbill

Loxia curvirostra (LOX-ia: oblique; cur-vi-ROS-tra: curve bill). 5½ in.; older ♂ red; ♀ yellowish beneath, greenish gray above; young adult ♂ often orange, in transition from yellowish to red; wings solid dark gray. "Chip, chip" call; warbling song. In flocks, in the coniferous canopy. Fringillidae.

A small shower of conifer seed coats and seed wings often means a crossbill flock is above. You have to be close to see the crossed bill: the lower mandible hooks upward almost as much as the upper one hooks downward. These odd bills can move sideways to efficiently pry cone scales apart. Evolution has specialized crossbills to clean up conifer seed crops when the remaining seeds are too sparse for larger seed-eaters like squirrels and woodpeckers, and too tightly encased in the cone for siskins and finches. They can keep cleaning up the leftovers from the fall crop well through winter and usually spring, depending on tree species; then in summer their jaws open wide to glean insects.

Different red crossbills have different sizes and styles of crossed bill, each specialized for one size of cone, from one species of conifer—a species that retains many of its seeds through winter and keeps many of them out of the tiny bills of siskins. To pass their bill size on to their offspring, the birds must find mates of similar bill size. Slight differences in their call notes enable them to do so, and thus the different-billed populations share range without interbreeding. That means that the red crossbill is really eight or ten different species, distinguishable by bill size and call note but not by plumage. Our region has at least four. (They aren't named yet, nor even recognized by the AOU.) The Douglas-fir or ponderosa pine eaters migrate sweepingly, because those trees produce a good cone crop in one area one year, then somewhere else next year. Specialists in western hemlock and lodgepole pine, which are consistent producers, get to stay put.

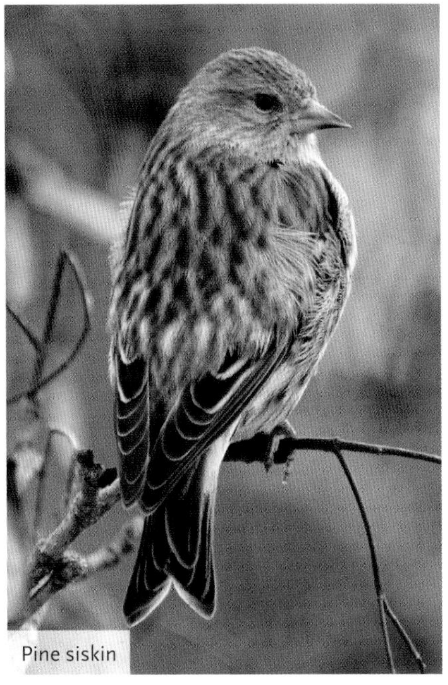
Pine siskin

Pine Siskin

Spinus pinus (SPY-nus: the Greek name). Also *Carduelis pinus*. 4¼ in.; gray-brown with subtle lengthwise streaking; yellow in wings and tail may show in flight. Various distinctive scratchy twitters and sucking wheezes. In large flocks in treetops, subalpine year-round; listed as a common bird in steep decline. Fringillidae.

Siskins' narrow, sharp bills (in contrast to the heavy conical ones typical of their family) limit them to light seeds—thistle, foxglove, and birch seeds, for example—along with insects and buds. Siskins hang upside down from catkins while extracting the seeds. The populations move around sweepingly, tending to be locally abundant in alternate years. Pine siskins look nondescript, but call and fly quite distinctively. Often a flock's twitterings seem to match its breathtaking undulations and pulse-like contractions and expansions in flight. Relative to that, the Navy's Blue Angel jets fly like clumsy novices.

REPTILES

We may say "reptiles and amphibians" in one breath, or lump them together as "herps," but they are very different, and probably aren't each other's closest relatives.

Early amphibians pioneered onto land with the use of two innovations: air-breathing organs (lungs or skin) and legs. Certain lunged amphibian ancestors later developed two more innovations—watertight skin and sturdy eggshells—and could exploit terrain farther from water. That evolutionary step eventually led to birds, mammals, and the groups traditionally called reptiles.

Snakes and lizards are generally well adapted to hot, dry climates. (Our mountains are therefore lizard-poor and amphibian-rich.) Nevertheless, some studies find that lizard populations are in sharp decline due to climate change. They share the climate problem that pikas and marmots have: they avoid the heat of the day by retreating underground; when the heat of the day gets longer, the time available for foraging gets shorter, and they are underfed. It doesn't kill lizards, but they fail to reproduce, and populations die out locally.

Because arid lands are relatively unproductive, warm-blooded thermoregulation is something of a handicap for mammals there, demanding frequent feeding. Cold-blooded lizards and snakes, in contrast, can go a very long time between meals, burning few calories. They can wait two years or more and then reproduce when a richer season comes along. But if it doesn't. . . .

Evolution turned egg-layers into live-bearers in dozens of separate events, starting long ago. Boas all bear live young, though they are one of the more primitive snake families. Eggs predominate in the tropics, and births in cooler climates, suggesting that carrying embryos around in her body helps a mother keep them warm. Genus *Sceloporus*, with more than 70 species, and genus *Elgaria*, with 2, are each evenly divided between egg layers and live bearers; their northerly species (like ours) bear live young.

Reptilian scales overlap rearward, so that a snake slides forward easily, but not at all easily backward. This key to slithering locomotion enables the entire body to slide forward following the serpentine path that a still photo captures. This mode, lateral undulation, is the norm for snakes on land. They continuously push off against bumps on the ground, and also briefly lift portions of their bellies that are leaping forward. Undulation takes just as much energy as a lizard takes to walk on four legs, so we can rule out energy savings as the reason snakes lost their legs in evolution (still a mystery). A completely different locomotion mode, side-winding, is more efficient, and yet only one kind of snake (a rattler called a sidewinder) specializes in it; several other species can do it, but save it for crossing surfaces too smooth for lateral undulation to work. Then there's rectilinear slithering, where they creep straight forward by alternately flexing and relaxing tiny muscles just under their scales, in waves that travel along the body. Very slow, and seven times costlier in energy used per distance traveled, it is used only for sneaking up on prey, and only by large snakes (including our largest, the gopher snake). Other modes of slithering are needed for swimming, for climbing trees, and for passing through narrow spaces.

The traditional class Reptilia comprises the scaly-skinned land animals—tortoises, crocodilians, tuataras, and snakes and lizards. Taxonomists have agreed for decades that those four groups originated separately and are not as closely related to each other as crocodiles are to birds. So Reptilia has to be either broken up or enlarged to include birds. No consensus has formed yet to resolve this issue. The least destabilizing solution would be to keep only snakes and lizards (currently the order Squamata) in the class Reptilia, while putting turtles and crocodilians each in their own new class.

Western Fence Lizard

Sceloporus occidentalis (skel-OP-or-us: leg pores; ox-i-den-TAY-lis: western). Also bluebelly. 6–8½ in. long; belly relatively wide, legs big, with very long toes on rear; scales spiny, abrasive; back olive brownish; belly pale, with many light blue flecks and patches; yellow-orange under legs; ♂ have two blue throat patches. Diurnal; in warm sunny habitats from c WA s. Iguanidae.

With their long toe-claws, fence lizards are agile climbers, fond of fenceposts. In winter they hibernate, perhaps in an old log. In spring, females lay clutches of 5–15 eggs in loose dirt. For courtship, territory assertion, and other communication they have a precise gestural language including pushups, head-bobbing, teeth-baring, throat-puffing, and side-flattening, much of it tailored to display their blue patches. Contact with you may alarm one enough to provoke several of these gestures—or a quick scurry to the far side of the tree or rock.

Male western fence lizard

Northern Alligator Lizard

Elgaria coeruleus (see-RUE-lius: blue). Also *Gerrhonotus coeruleus*. 8½–10 in. long; body thick, legs and toes slender; scales heavy, rough; dark olive back with light stripe; belly gray to bluish. Diurnal; mainly w-side to subalpine, including s VI. Anguidae.

Alligator lizards bear scales heavy enough to serve as armor, exacting a high price in terms of flexibility. They breathe with the help of a pair of large pleats along their flanks, and walk stiffly, somewhat snakewise, on legs too weak to get their bellies off the ground. If you pick up an alligator lizard you may encounter its other defenses—it can bite quickly and hard, albeit harmlessly, defecate all over your hand, or snap off its tail. Many lizards share this trait, fracture planes in the tail. It lets a lizard escape while a predator holds and likely consumes the still-writhing tail. A new tail

Northern alligator lizard

Common garter snake

Gopher snake

grows within weeks, but it's a cheesy knock-off of a tail, lacking vertebrae or high-quality muscles or scales.

Northern alligator lizards eat millipedes, snails, and other crawling things.

Common Garter Snake

Thamnophis sirtalis (THAM-no-fis: shrub snake; sir-TA-lis: garter). 18–54 in. long; long pale stripe down the entire center of the back, and usually two similar stripes the length of the two flanks; background color variable, most often dark gray, often patterned with regular red blotches. Widespread, but averse to dark forest. Colubridae.

Garter snakes like to bask in the sun, sometimes intertwined in groups. They eat worms, slugs, and small amphibians. They give birth in summer to 13–18 live, worm-sized snakelets. They try to repel attackers (and people who pick them up) by getting stinky musk and feces all over themselves. Being offensive does not seem to be the best defense in this case. Birds (which have little sense of smell) prey heavily on garter snakes, and mammals only a little less.

Any snake in our area with a nice pattern that includes a full-length back stripe is likely to be a garter snake. We have three species, the common being the largest and, yes, most common. Its typical colors in the Salish Sea watershed are pale blue stripes and flecks against a nearly black background. In Oregon, expect pale yellowish stripes and brick-red flecks. But all three species come in a range of colors and patterns. (The other two are the northwestern, *T. ordinoides*, and the terrestrial, *T. elegans*.) Identifying garter snakes to species is a tall order, requiring careful counting of scales.

Gopher Snake

Pituophis catenifer (pih-TOO-o-fis: pine snake; ca-TEN-if-er: chain-bearer). 48–66 in. long, heavy-bodied; tan (e-side) or gray-brown (w-side) with blackish blotches, largest ones along the back, flanked by two nearly solid narrow stripes. Sunny habitats; throughout our range in OR; low and well to the e in WA and BC. Colubridae.

The only snake you would likely mistake for a rattler around here is the gopher snake. The resemblance is probably a case of adaptive mimicry for fright value; it even includes puffing up the head to make more of a triangle shape, and vibrating the tail which, when it rustles dry leaves, can sound like a rattler. This snake is nonvenomous, killing its prey, including gophers, by constriction. (Constricting characterizes both the boas and one branch of the huge family Colubridae, which contains some 68 percent of all snakes.) It can also climb trees and prey on nestling birds.

Rubber Boa

Charina bottae (car-EYE-na: graceful; BOT-ee: for Paolo Botta). 18–27 in. long; solid dark greenish brown above, grading to dull yellowish belly; scales small, smooth, shiny; tail does not taper to a point, but is almost as broadly rounded as the head. Widespread, but unlikely in coastal rainforest or in our BC range. Boidae.

Rubber boa

Unlike reptiles that bask in the sun to warm up for activity, the boa avoids hot sun, and is active at dawn, dusk, night, and on cloudy days. Well, maybe "active" is a stretch: this is one sluggish snake. Somehow it manages to catch small mammals, especially the young in their nests. It kills by coiling and squeezing, like its relatives the tropical constrictors. This works by stopping the heart, not the breath, and is a quick death. A rubber boa may use its blunt tail as a "head" decoy, or as a club to fend off a mother vole while swallowing her progeny. You can safely pick one up—just plan on washing up afterwards. They give birth to live young in late summer.

Western Rattlesnake

Crotalus oreganus (CROT-a-lus: rattle; or-eg-AY-nus: of Oregon). Also *C. viridis oreganus*. 16–60 in. long, heavily built, with large triangular head; tail terminates in rattle segments; variable brown, black, gray, and tan colors in a pattern of regularly spaced geometric dark blotches against paler crossbars. Rocky places in US, lowest e-side and s Willamette Valley elevs. Viperidae.

Western rattlesnake

We're lucky in having no poisonous snakes except along the eastern and southern low fringes of our range, where the rattler may be found. Avoid it. This species can inject a dose of venom lethal to small children and many mammals, though sublethally painful, almost always, to adult humans. (A solitary victim might possibly be incapacitated long enough to die of hypothermia if warm clothes and food are far away.) Rattlesnakes hunt at dusk, dawn, and night. A brisk, dry buzz of the tail rattles is the typical warning to large intruders. Far from being aggressive toward humans, they will almost always flee if given the chance. Starting from any of various positions (not necessarily coiled), a snake's head can strike and pull back again faster than a mammal can react—literally in the blink of an eye. Even some nonvenomous snakes are as quick as rattlers. The quick pull-back does have a drawback: it limits the amount of venom injected.

AMPHIBIANS

Though often listed among the terrestrial vertebrates, amphibians barely qualify: they lack an effective moisture barrier in either their skins or their eggs, so to avoid lethal drying they must return to water frequently, venturing from it mainly at night or in the shade, and never far. Many of them hatch in water as gilled, water-breathing, legless, swimming larvae (for example, tadpoles), later metamorphose into terrestrial adults, and return to water to breed. Hence the word amphibious, from "life on both sides." Some individuals fail to make the move onto land, but reach full size and sexual maturity while still in the larval form. On the other hand, the lungless salamanders live their entire lives in moist terrestrial habitats like animal burrows, rotten logs, talus, or moss mats. Western Oregon and Washington, abounding as they do in moist habitats, may be weak on reptiles, but support ungodly numbers of unnoticed (quiet, nocturnal, largely subterranean) amphibians. At least until recently.

Among vertebrate animals, mammals and birds are "warm-blooded," whereas reptiles, amphibians and fish are "cold-blooded." This doesn't mean they're self-refrigerating, but they're never a lot warmer than their environment. Ambient heat definitely helps them be active, yet they can sustain activity in astonishing cold—long-toed salamanders in our high country typically breed in sub-40°F water with winter's ice still on it (after hibernating through most of the freezing season). At the other extreme, amphibians rarely survive heat over 100°F. Ironically, their intolerance of heat won salamanders and newts a superstitious reputation as fireproof. They do know how to survive a ground fire: they take refuge in a familiar wet crevice or burrow, just as they do from the midday sun. Most populations hold up quite well after forest fires. When Mt. St. Helens blew up it was mid-May; amphibians that were underwater at that season survived and carried on in the blowdown zone, while terrestrial amphibians died and were slow to return.

Amphibians are in serious decline worldwide, due to a tangled swarm of problems that vary by region and species, and interact in more ways than we know about. Why are amphibians hit especially hard? Their permeable skin (at all life stages) gives them little protection from pollutants, pathogens, or ultraviolet radiation. And they seem slow to adapt.

And why is it happening now? Climate undoubtedly plays a role, but perhaps not as large as some other anthropogenic processes: habitat loss such as draining of wetlands, introduction of predatory fish to high lakes, water pollution, increased ultraviolet radiation due to ozone depletion, and transport around the world of fungal diseases. A pandemic of Amphibian Chytrid Fungus, or Bd, is killing many species globally but does not seem to be the main problem in our region.

Rough-Skinned Newt

Taricha granulosa (TAIR-ic-a: mummy; gran-you-LOW-sa: grainy). 6–7 in. long; back warty-textured (except on breeding-season ♂) greenish black to almost translucent brown; underside orange to yellow; ribs not visible. W-side. Salamandridae.

Newts are a family of salamanders with relatively bright colors and toxic skin secretions. While many salamanders protect themselves with skin toxins and nocturnality, this newt is so toxic it doesn't need to be nocturnal. That makes it our most often-seen salamander, commonly foraging on gray summer days in forest not far from its retreat in a pond or marsh. When threatened, it goes into a rigid reflexive posture for two or three minutes. displaying its bright underside by curling up until its tail is near its upturned chin. This presumably deters predators by reminding them of the newt's poisonous skin. Newt toxicity varies from one population to another; for some reason Willamette Valley newts are intense and Vancouver Island newts are innocuous. Most small predators, in experiments, die quickly when force-fed bits of newt skin. Garter snakes are resistant to newt toxin, and prey on newts. Living newts don't release much toxin, and it's only toxic when consumed anyway, so handling a newt is not too risky, but I still recommend a thorough hand-washing afterward.

At breeding time (winter or spring) the male's skin smooths out, his tail flattens, his genital region swells, and his underside turns a brighter orange. Newts migrate accurately back to their natal pond. Some have proven sadly faithful to drained pond sites.

Torrent Salamander

***Rhyacotriton* spp.** (rye-a-co-TRY-ton: brook sea-god). 3–4½ in. long, slender, bug-eyed; olive to brown above, yellow-flecked beneath; ♂ have squarish anal lobes behind rear legs. Dicamptodontidae.

Olympic torrent salamander, *R. olympicus*
OlyM.

Cascade torrent salamander, *R. cascadae*
W-side CasR from Toutle to Mackenzie drainages; rare.

These delicate, pretty little salamanders generally stay in mountain creeks or within splash range of them. Two additional species occupy the Coast Range.

Coastal Giant Salamander

Dicamptodon tenebrosus (die-CAMP-ta-don: twice-curved teeth; ten-eb-ROE-sus: dark). 7–12 in. long, stocky; brown to purplish with dramatic black splotches; belly light brown; ribs indistinct. W-side forest; CasR, OlyM, and south. Dicamptodontidae.

Rough-skinned newt

Cascade torrent salamander

While other salamanders are limited to eating insects and other small invertebrates as food, this one—the largest terrestrial salamander—can catch and eat mice, garter snakes, and small salamanders. In some small mountain streams it is the main predator, outweighing all salmon and trout put together.

It is the only salamander with a real voice, variously described as a "yelp" or a "rattle." Salamanders have no eardrums or external openings to receive communications, but they do have inner ear organs apparently sensitive to vibrations transmitted up through the legs. Larvae have intricate plume-like red (blood-filled) structures where we might expect ears; these are external gills that "breathe" or absorb oxygen suspended in water. Some coastal giant larvae metamorphose into terrestrial adults at about 3 inches, in their second summer. Others never do metamorphose, but instead mature sexually as aquatic larvae and may grow as long as 12 inches. This latter life cycle (neoteny) is common in both the mole salamanders and this family. Dicamptodontids, found only in the Northwest, hole up in crevices between streambed rocks; they are decimated where post-logging erosion fills streams with mud.

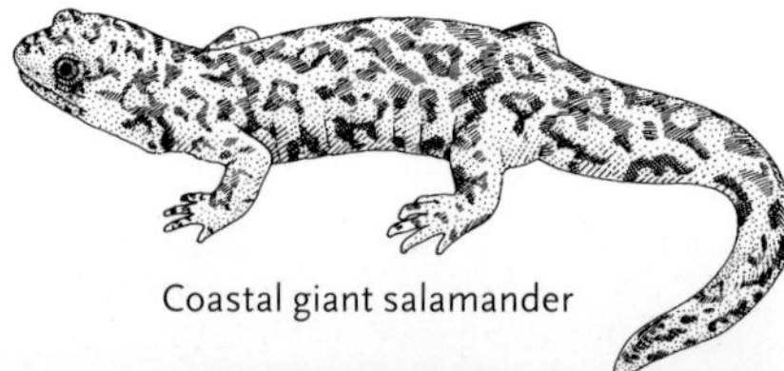
Coastal giant salamander

Northwestern Salamander

Ambystoma gracile (am-BIS-ta-ma: blunt mouth; GRASS-il-ee: plain). 6–9 in. long; large blunt head with a bulging parotoid gland behind eye; tall, narrow tail; dark brown, gray, black, or dark olive, sometimes cream-flecked. W-side. Ambystomatidae (mole salamanders).

Northwestern salamanders lay their eggs suspended in grapefruit-sized globs of clear or algae-green gelatin, which you may see attached to plants below the surface in marshy pond margins. The species ranges up to high lakes, but those higher populations commonly stay in the lake throughout life, retaining their external gills. These neotenic adults grow just as big as terrestrial adults.

Long-Toed Salamander

Ambystoma macrodactylum (macro-DAC-til-um: big toes). 5–7 in. long; wide, blunt head; dark gray-brown with a thin, irregular, full-length back stripe bright yellow to greenish or tan; one rear toe—the 2nd from outside—is longer than the others. Widespread near water.

Our widest-ranging salamander inhabits both alpine meadows and sagebrush country. In the high country it breeds even before

Coastal giant salamander

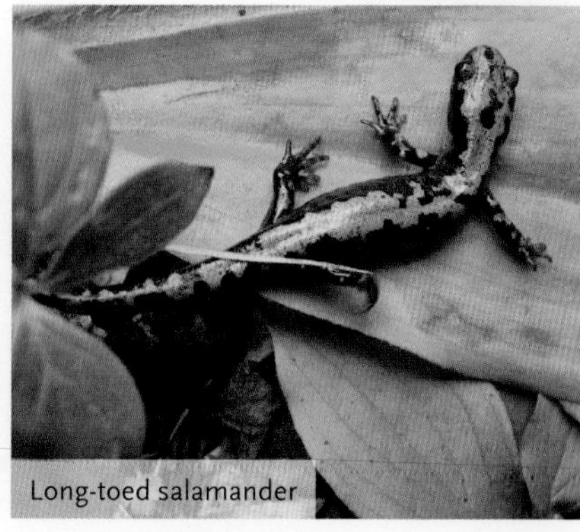
Long-toed salamander

the ice is gone, to make the most of its brief, frigid active season, and still the larvae need two summers before metamorphosing. Laying eggs in shallow water makes it vulnerable to ultraviolet radiation.

When trout were stocked in high lakes, they displaced long-toed salamanders from the top of the food chain. Finding themselves prey for the first time in untold generations, the salamanders became scarce and secretive, but generally survived. Fish have now been removed from most national park high lakes, and salamanders are multiplying.

Lungless and mole salamanders have elaborate mating rituals ending, in many species, with a procession: he walks along dropping gelatinous sperm cases and she follows, picking them up with her cloacal lips for internal fertilization. A long-toed male may interlope: he slips in between the romantic duo, mimics a female walk to escape notice, and places his sperm cases on top of the other guy's.

Western Red-Backed Salamander

Plethodon vehiculum (PLETH-o-don: many teeth; ve-HIC-you-lum: carrier). 3–4½ in. long, slender; brown or black with a full-length broad, even-edged back stripe that's red to orange or yellow, tan or even greenish. W-side forest. Plethodontidae (lungless salamanders).

Salamanders of this family have neither lungs nor gills, and breathe through their skins exclusively. Lungless salamanders of the West hatch into miniature terrestrial adults, having breezed through the larval stage within the egg. The mother lays her eggs on the ground and guards them. This species lives (by the millions) under moss and logs in the forest, or under stones in wet talus. It is easily the most abundant of the seven *Plethodon* species in our area, and the only one in western British Columbia. The seven species are hard to tell apart, with a lot of variability in each. They are among the least mobile amphibians, rarely traveling farther than a hundred yards in a lifetime. That makes the name *vehiculum* seem ironic; it probably refers to the males hauling the females around during courtship.

Western red-backed salamander

Ensatina

Ensatina eschscholtzii (en-sa-TIE-na: small sword; es-SHOLT-zee-eye: for Johann Friedrich von Eschscholtz, p. 230). 3–4½ in. long; typically mottled dark brown over orange; variable in color but always mottled and rather translucent; 5 toes on rear feet; tail has a conspicuous constriction near its base. W-side forest, usually under litter, in rotten logs, burrows, etc. Plethodontidae.

Ensatinas are the most numerous amphibians in most west-side forest regions. One study finds an enhancement of soil carbon sinks in ensatinas' consumption of tiny critters that eat leaf litter: thanks to ensatinas lowering those populations, more leaf litter ends up as humus, sequestering carbon for a time. They choose drier habitats than our other salamanders. Reportedly, they can hiss like snakes. A threatened ensatina stands as high as it can on its legs and raises

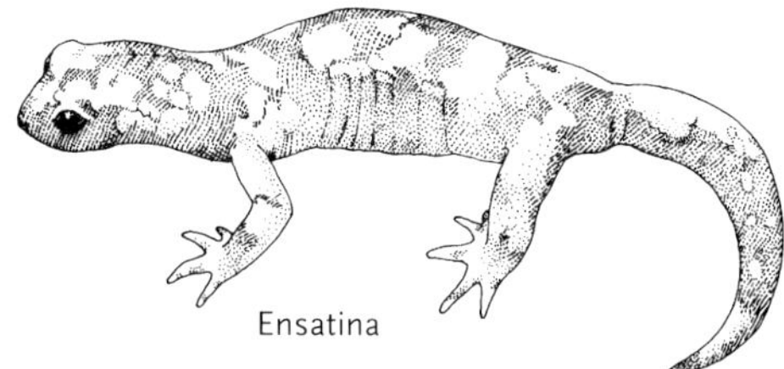
Ensatina

Clouded salamander

Oregon slender salamander

or thrashes its tail, exuding (or even throwing) a mildly toxic, sticky white mucus from glands on the tail. If the threat escalates or the tail is bitten, the tail snaps off right at its constricted base, giving the ensatina time to escape while the predator is distracted; a jettisoned tail can thrash for several minutes. The blood vessels have tiny muscles to shut them off, and the tail regenerates over a year or two. Still, it isn't a sacrifice to take lightly.

Clouded Salamander

Aneides ferreus (an-EE-id-eez: not seen; FAIR-ius: iron-colored). 3½–5 in.; brown with rather subtle patterns of brass-colored cells, especially on snout and tail; toe tips squarish. OR. Plethondontidae.

The wandering salamander, *A. vagrans*, was recently separated from *A. ferreus*, and is too similar to distinguish from it visually, but occupies a different range: Vancouver Island and northwest California. The puzzling distance between the two parts of its range led to a study concluding that it was brought to Vancouver Island from California in the 1800s, perhaps in a shipment of tanoak bark for tanning hides. Both species live in logs and snags that are rotten enough for them to make their way through, but not so far gone that the rot dries out in summer. Some live in moss mats high in rainforest canopies, even laying eggs there. Though these habitats are much farther from water than most salamanders venture, they are still soggy all year long.

Oregon Slender Salamander

Batrachoseps wrighti (ba-TRAY-co-seps: frog lizard; RIGHT-eye: for Margaret and Albert H. Wright). 3¼–4 in. long, extremely slender; dark brown above, with a vague reddish to greenish back stripe; white-blotched black beneath. OR only, w-side below 4500 ft. Plethodontidae.

Salamanders of wormlike slenderness crawl around in termite or beetle tunnels in rotten wood, preying on springtails, mites, beetle larvae, and worms. They depend on big, old logs for refuge from summer heat. They can use either the tail-breaking defense or the coiling defense—coiling and uncoiling their bodies so rapidly as to fling themselves about, perhaps in mimicry of poisonous millipedes.

Western Toad

Anaxyrus boreas (annex-EYE-rus: king—; BOR-ius: northern). Also boreal toad; *Bufo boreas*. 2–5 in. long; thick; sluggish; skin has large bumps, the largest being two oval glands behind the eyes; olive to grayish, with a narrow pale stripe down the back, and blotches on belly. Widespread. Bufonidae.

Tell toads from frogs by their warty-looking skin, toothless upper jaw, sluggish

Western toad

Pacific treefrog

movement (generally walking rather than hopping), and parotoid glands behind the eyes. These bulbous protrusions exude a thick, white, nauseating, burning poison related to digitalin, to deter predators. Ravens manage to prey on them by separating the flesh from the skin, which they leave behind.

Toads' slow pace limits them to slow, creeping invertebrate prey. Toads resist drying better than most frogs and salamanders. Our only toad, the western, inhabits animal burrows and rock crevices, and is often seen in mountain meadows and woodlands well away from watercourses. It is less strictly nocturnal than most toads, especially higher up, where nights are too cold for much toad activity. Lacking the inflatable vocal sac many of its relatives boast, it has a weak, peeping voice.

Newly metamorphosed western toads are about half an inch long. At times thousands of them can be seen in a mass dispersal, literally piling up to bask in the sun.

Western toads are declining rapidly. A 1995 study investigated their disappearance from pristine Cascade lakes. It found most eggs in some high ponds succumbing to a fungal disease common among hatchery trout. If the eggs were shielded with mylar to block ultraviolet-B rays, a healthy number survived and hatched. This was the first study to find ozone depletion threatening a species, though the ozone might not have been deadly without the hatchery trout. While an international treaty has alleviated the ozone problem, a drying climate trend could make frog pools shallower, which would increase the eggs' ultraviolet exposure.

Western toad

Pacific Treefrog

Pseudacris regilla (sue-DAY-cris: false cricket-frog; ra-JIL-a: queenlet). Also Pacific chorus frog; *Hyla regilla*. 1–2¾ in. long; skin bumpy; toes bulbous-tipped; color extremely variable—green, brown, red; in Cascades often gray-brown with long black splotches; dark eye-stripe extends to shoulder. Aquatic, but climbs shrubs or trees to sing; ubiquitous. Hylidae.

Voiced frogs employ a variety of calls, including alarm, warning, territorial, and male and female release calls. The familiar frog choruses are likely (at least around here in spring) to be mating-call duets and trios of male treefrogs. Active and vocal day and night, the male amplifies his voice with a resonating throat sac he blows up to three times the size of his head. Tree frogs

Northern red-legged frog

Cascades frog

are distinguished by bulbous toe pads that offer excellent grip on vertical surfaces. Our species has a sticky tongue for catching insects. It carries the introduced fungal disease called Bd, but seems more resistant to it than many other frogs. Overall, it seems to be thriving during the current amphibian decline. After 1980 at Mt. St. Helens it was able to disperse a distance of perhaps ten miles into the crater, considerably farther than other amphibians. Hot dry spells might have made this recolonization impossible if gophers had not recolonized first, digging burrow systems for amphibians to take shelter in.

Northern Red-Legged Frog

Rana aurora (RAY-na: the Roman name; aurora: dawn, referring to sunrise coloring). 2–4 in. long; grayish to reddish brown with small dark blotches; yellow underneath, variably rosy-tinged on rear legs and lower belly; croak is feeble, rough, and prolonged. Lower w-side forest. Ranidae.

These diurnal frogs venture pretty far from the ponds and backwaters they breed in. Though the data are inconclusive, they are thought to be declining in British Columbia and Oregon, negatively affected by non-native warm-water fish and introduced bullfrogs, along with the other usual suspects (habitat, pollution, climate).

Cascades Frog

Rana cascadae (cas-CAY-dee). 1¾–2¼ in. long; brown to yellow-olive with black spots above, yellow underneath; yellow jawline. In Cascades, mid-elev to timberline, always near water. Ranidae.

The diurnal Cascades frog basks along high-country shores and in marshy meadows. It croaks in a rapid, raspy chuckling style, several blips per second. Escaping into water, it swims off across the surface rather than diving as its relatives do. Countless tadpoles (larvae) of this species inhabit shallow seasonal ponds. Both the shallowness of the water and the high elevations expose the eggs to more intense ultraviolet radiation than other frogs' eggs, and in this time of damaged stratospheric ozone there is reason to fear this could threaten the species. Cascades frogs have disappeared from much of the southern end of their range, in California, and have declined somewhat in Oregon.

Tailed Frog

Ascaphus truei (ASK-a-fus: not digging; TRUE-eye: for F. W. True). 1–2 in. long; skin has sparse small warts; olive to dark brown with large irregular black splotches and black eye-stripe. Undisturbed mtn streams. Ascaphidae or Leiopelmatidae.

Tailed frogs spend most of their time in fast, cold creeks, coexisting abundantly (up to five per square yard) with predatory fish, but not with logging and mud. They attach their eggs like strings of beads to the downstream side of rocks. The tadpoles suck firmly onto rocks, or perhaps to your leg or boot when you wade a creek, but don't worry, they aren't bloodsuckers. The silent, nocturnal adults are less easily encountered. They don't have real tails; those little soft protuberances are male cloacas, and they fertilize the females internally. You might think a penis prototype would be an advanced item on an amphibian, but sorry, guys, it's a primitive trait that other amphibians abandoned long ago. Tailed frogs may have kept it to prevent semen from washing away in fast streams.

Tailed frog

FISH

Fish have not fully returned to our mountains since the last Ice Age. Where glaciers advanced, aquatic life necessarily retreated before them; when the glaciers retreated, fish were able to return only so far as they could swim, so each stream is generally fishless above a certain impassable waterfall. Only strong-swimming, cold-loving species—mostly salmon and trout—make it into our mountains at all, and many of these fight their way to their upper distributional limit just once in their lives, when at their peak, and at a cost of total and terminal exhaustion. They may be phenomenal waterfall leapers, but still, there are limits. Above the critical waterfall live healthy aquatic communities whose animal members—invertebrates, amphibians, and small mammals—all got there on foot or on the wing.

Higher still, mountain lake communities have been joined (and altered) by trout who rode up the trail in saddlebags or flew there in airplanes. Fish populations of our high lakes are a product of human management—again favoring trout. Sometimes trout competitors have been introduced accidentally (as bait) and lakes have then been poisoned with rotenone and restocked with trout. High lakes with and without finny predators support different species of amphibians, with effects that ripple down through the food chain. North Cascades National Park has been clearing its high lakes of fish and turning them back over to their native amphibians.

Many popular fishing lakes are stocked with catchable-size trout before and during the fishing season, and get nearly fished out each season. Remote high lakes may be stocked only occasionally and have near-natural, self-sustaining populations. Or they may support healthy trout for years at a time but lack reproducing populations for want of a proper spawning bed. The bed must be clean gravel of the right size, at the right depth, with a moderate current to keep it aerated and silt-free.

Check a lakeshore near an inlet or outlet stream and follow the stream to its first waterfall. If you find a shallow gravelly spot in early summer, you may see a trout swimming back and forth over it. A logjam at the outlet stream, or slabby shallows nearby, tend to be good places to spot fish at any time of year. Polarizing sunglasses can help you see them. Trout don't feed all day—only when the insects are most active. When the lake is first ice-free, feeding may go on from midmorning to midday. In October they may feed all afternoon. If luck brings you a calm feeding period after an extended blow, look for frenzied feeding where floating insects collected near the downwind shore.

High country trout spend a long, leisurely winter under the ice. In the smallest and highest bodies of water that support trout, they mature and spawn at 3–6 years of age while only 3–5 inches long and still displaying the parr marks typical of juvenile trout elsewhere. Fish are as cold as the water they're in, and if it's especially cold it slows down their metabolisms and their growth rates, but it doesn't threaten their health. In contrast, water that's prone to warming up in the sun (shallow and with insufficient flow in and out) can exclude trout.

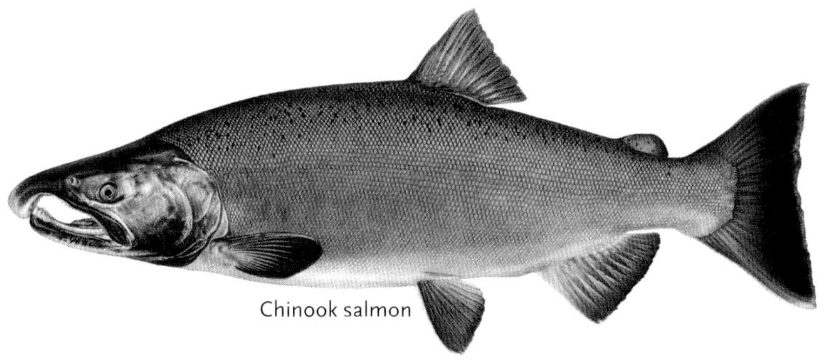
Chinook salmon

Some lakes are too clean. The aquatic food pyramid rests on algae, which depend on minerals not present in rain or snow; water has to pick these up while passing over or through the earth. Small drainage basins, high snowfall, barren or impermeable terrain, and rapid turnover of lake water often combine, in our region, to severely limit nutrients. Stocked trout may fail to thrive, or to reproduce.

The fish in this chapter are carnivores. When small they eat zooplankton, then move up to larger crustaceans and insects of all life stages. If they outgrow that phase they add snails, worms, isopods, freshwater shrimp, amphibian larvae, and fish eggs and fry to their diets. Any fish species may be fair game, even their own at younger stages.

Pacific Salmon

***Oncorhynchus* spp.** (onk-o-RINK-us: swollen snout). These three species have more than twelve rays in the anal fin. Salmonidae. Illustrations are of spawning ♂.

Chinook salmon, *O. tshawytscha* (cha-WITCH-a: a Kamchatkan native name). Also tyee, king salmon. Black spots on back and both lobes of tail fin; black gums on lower jaw; spawning adults dark, rarely very red; juveniles at 4 in. have tall parr marks bisected by the lateral line, and a dark-margined but clear-centered adipose fin. Rivers.

Sockeye salmon

Sockeye salmon and Kokanee salmon, *O. nerka* (NER-ka: the Russian name). No dark spots on back or tailfin; 28–40 long thin rough gill-rakers in first gill arch; spawning adult has greenish dark head, crimson body; ♂ is slightly humpbacked; 4-in. juveniles have small, oval parr marks almost entirely above lateral line. BC and WA rivers and lakes; hatchery population in Deschutes River system in OR.

Coho salmon

Coho salmon, *O. kisutch* (KISS-utch: Kamchatkan native name). Also silver salmon. Black spots on back and upper half of tail fin; white lower gums; spawning ♂ have brilliant red sides; 4-in. juveniles have tall parr marks bisected by lateral line, all-dark adipose fin and dark leading edge of anal fin. Mostly smaller streams.

Pacific salmon range the Pacific Rim from California to Korea; some range the Arctic from the Mackenzie to the Lena. First described to science by Georg Steller (p. 422) in Siberia, they were given species names from Russian and Kamchatkan languages. They are called salmon after the Atlantic salmon, a different genus (*Salmo*).

Salmon are anadromous, meaning that they migrate upstream from the sea to spawn. They require clear, cold, well-aerated gravelly creeks to nurse their spawn in infancy, and larger bodies of water richer in animal life to rear them to maturity. Big lakes can suffice for some species if they become landlocked by new dams or natural topographic changes, but all grow much larger if they spend time in the ocean. Salmon are among the very few few animals that have adapted to handle the chemical shock of moving between breathing salt water and breathing fresh.

Even more remarkable is their ability to navigate back to their natal stream from thousands of miles away. Once they get close to the right river, they zero in on the mineral recipe of the precise tributary of their birth by means of smell, a sense located in two shallow nostrils unconnected to their mouths. Some go only a few miles upriver, but chinook navigate the Yukon River for more than 2000 miles.

Once back at the spawning grounds where she was born, the female chooses a gravelly spot, usually in a riffle, and begins digging a trough, or redd, by turning on her side and beating with her tail. A dominant male moves in to guard her, attacking other salmon who come too close. He may nudge her repeatedly. When she signals her readiness by lowering a fin into the redd, he swims up alongside her, they open their jaws, arch their backs, quiver, and simultaneously drop her eggs and his milt. Other males now dash in and try to eject some of their own milt onto the eggs. Orange-red eggs by the thousands come out tiny, then quickly swell, absorbing water along with the fertilizing milt. The female's last maternal act is to bury them in gravel. She extends her redd, digging the next trench immediately upstream from the last, with intermittent resting spells. Different males may attend her subsequent efforts. Both parents die soon after spawning.

The eggs take a few months to hatch. The newly hatched alevin remains in the gravel several weeks, sustained by a yolk-sac attached to its belly. As the yolk is depleted, the fish adapts to a diet of zooplankton and emerges from the gravel as a fry. In a year or two fry grow to parr size, displaying the parr marks that make them easier to identify. They are smolts at whatever age they go to sea—from month-old, ¾-inch pink salmon fry to ten-year-old, 12-inch cutthroat trout in severe Alaskan habitats.

Salmon were incalculably important to all the Northwest Coast and Columbia River nations. The Indians expressed their gratitude in ceremonies and in stories of dreadful times before someone (Coyote or Raven) gave salmon to the people. Archaeologists confirm that people were in the Northwest for millennia before developing a region-wide economy based on storing salmon through winter. At around that time, about 3500 years ago, Northwest culture blossomed.

The people sure did learn how to catch salmon: with hook and line, with spears, from platforms over waterfalls, with one- or two-man dip nets of spruce-root twine, with larger basketry nets or long seine nets or wicker traps or wooden weirs. Most fishing was during spawning runs. Smoking and drying kept the bounty in season as long as possible, long past what we might consider palatable. Many tribes are thought to have consumed well over a pound of salmon per person per day. But the runs couldn't be completely counted on. Elaborate taboos were observed to prevent any offense to the Salmon and to assure his return. These practices, and manipulation of stream beds, probably significantly enhanced and sustained the salmon crop, and anthropologists

Fish vs. Civilization

Why have salmonids declined? It's easy to find answers. Start with overfishing, of course; but almost everything people have done that makes the Northwest less natural makes life harder for fish.

Silt from logging, construction, and livestock operations ruins the clean stream gravel salmonids need for spawning.

Loss of shade makes small streams too warm.

Clearing of logs that slow streams down and create pools and meanders, essential fish habitat. Many Cascadia rivers had semi-permanent logjams the size of small towns. White settlers expended huge quantities of dynamite and more than a few human lives getting rid of logjams and snags to improve navigation or even (mistakenly) to help fish get upstream. Loggers cleared countless logs from streams. Today they have wised up, and commonly place some logs in streams instead.

Splash dams were an egregious 19th-century technique for moving logs to the mill, wrecking every stream they touched.

Seasonal fluctuation is aggravated by logging, because rain and snowmelt run off much faster, leading to floods in winter and reduced, warmer streamflow in summer.

Pollution comes from mines, factories, farms, sewage, and lawn and pavement runoff.

Draining of marshes and beaver ponds eliminates habitat.

Irrigation of farms can draw off enough water to reduce creeks to warm, muddy trickles in summer.

Dams may be too high to have fish ladders: Grand Coulee Dam shut the door on an Idaho-sized patch of habitat. Electric turbines cut up smolts on the way down. Smolts die of bubbles that form in their blood due to pressure changes during the drop. Big reservoirs warm up in the sun, harbor nonnative warm-water predators, and lack enough current to move smolts downstream on schedule.

Hatchery programs began with high hopes of mitigating harm from overfishing and dams, but turned out to be problematic. Hatchery fish interbred with wild fish and diluted their finely tuned local genetic adaptations.

Aquaculture of salmon, now a big industry in British Columbia's inland waterways, can spread diseases and parasites to wild populations. And last but not least,

Warming.

have taken to calling them "cultivation" of salmon. Fishing-and-trading camp was Fat City—particularly at Celilo Falls on the Columbia, which, for one month a year for thousands of years, became the biggest city west of the Mississippi. (Today it lies drowned under a reservoir.)

Nineteenth-century white men promoted a worldwide market for canned Pacific salmon, reassuring each other that they were developing an inexhaustible resource and sparing scarcer resources on land. By the end of that century, salmon were badly overfished. Salmon populations of Washington, Oregon, and California rivers today are a fraction of what they once were—less than a tenth. Even a total halt to fishing could not restore them, as the loss of spawning habitat, and now climate change, are intractable problems. (That said, 2015 was a good year for Columbia and Snake River runs—the best since the Columbia was dammed.) Alaska and British Columbia built very few dams on salmon streams, and their runs are fairly healthy. But the run on British Columbia's Kitlope River, an entire watershed that's pristine and protected, is dwindling; the causes must lie out at sea.

For the future, the chief determinant of salmon numbers seems to be ocean conditions, including ocean temperature and its effects on all kinds of sea life. Unlike productivity on land, ocean productivity is higher toward the poles, because colder water holds more dissolved oxygen. Salmon like their water cold—both their streams and their ocean. In recent decades, they seem to do well when the Pacific Decadal Oscillation (p. 40) is in its cold phase; over the very long term they did best in the Little Ice Age. Curiously, though, populations in Alaskan lakes over the past 500 years underwent huge century-scale ups and downs that did not match up from one drainage to the next. There must be complex systems of variables at play. It looks safe to say that the more southernly salmon runs are the ones least likely to survive the next century. But northerly and southerly runs of our larger species (chinook, sockeye, and steelhead) all share the same pond, the Gulf of Alaska, during their sea years.

Chinook, the largest salmon, spawn in the largest streams and swim the greatest distances upriver. Though Chinook runs are called "spring," "summer," or "fall," actual arrival dates in Cascadia freshwater occur sporadically from April through December, and even in the other months. Two dams on the Elwha River in the Olympics wiped out a run that frequently produced individuals over 100 pounds. Between 2011 and 2014, those two dams were removed—easily the largest of more than 800 US dams demolished in recent years. Plant succession and riverbank development on the former lake bed will be fun to watch over our lifetimes, but the fish aren't waiting: chinook, coho, and steelhead have already spawned above the dam sites.

Spawning sockeye typically turn deep red both inside and out. ("Sockeye" is a crude imitation of Coast Salish words meaning "red fish.") Whereas other salmon prey on fish as adults, sockeye are filter feeders on plankton. They get their deeper color from their staple food, tiny crustaceans. They swim nearly as far upstream as chinook, and climb much higher—to 6500 feet at Redfish Lake, Idaho. That's part of the Snake River run, which has to fight its way past eight large dams, and is endangered. In contrast, the famous Fraser River run has few dams to deal with, and returned 30 million sockeye in the best recent year. Sockeye are by far the most abundant salmon in British Columbia. They seek a lake twice during their life cycle—one or two juvenile years, and then a final summer before spawning. In our mountains, branches of the Fraser run go to Chilliwack, Harrison, and Lillooet Lakes. Kokanee salmon are a smaller, landlocked form of sockeye esteemed as a sport fish in lakes east of our range.

Coho spawn in slow, low-gradient lowland streams—even urban ones. Beaver ponds make ideal rearing pools for the fry. Coho historically made up in numbers what they lacked in size, enough to rank them high in both sport and commercial catches, at least for Oregon. But today the upper-Columbia runs are extinct, the mid-Columbia runs are in danger, and the coastal and Willamette runs are down to less than 5 percent of historical numbers. Coho declines are blamed partly on warming of offshore waters with consequent loss of overall fertility and increase in warm-water predators, especially mackerel. Coho don't swim very far north during their ocean phase, leaving them the salmon most vulnerable to global warming.

Two other species, chum (*O. keta*) and pink salmon (*O. gorbuscha*), forgo the upstream heroics, limiting their efforts to a few weeks. The fry float back to sea immediately upon emerging. So they are found only in our lowest coastal streams. Chum were called "dog salmon" by Alaskan tribes who fed them to their dogs, favoring the richer chinook for themselves. (Never let your dog eat salmon or trout raw. Many dogs are lethally susceptible to a bacterium in some salmon; wild canids and bears acquire immunity from a sublethal infection in youth.) Pinks spawn and die as they approach their second birthday, so they remain the smallest anadromous salmon. On any given river they run mainly in odd- or mainly in even-numbered years. Washington and Oregon runs are in odd years.

Salmon and trout that reach large size in freshwater even eat waterfowl chicks, adult amphibians, and water shrews. In salt water they become voracious predators on fish. On their return to freshwater for spawning, most eat little or nothing, but metabolize stored fat and muscle. (There are exceptions. Sockeyes will feed during a last summer in a lake.) Spawning, they may look like they're at death's door, and they are.

The rapid decomposition of spawners is not a creepy detail, it's a central glory of salmon, one whose loss, with their decline, is an ecocatastophe in progress. It evolved because the parents' dead bodies become the major food source for their offspring.

Salmon used to move 8 million tons per year of high-nitrogen fertilizer (their bodies) from the sea up coastal valleys and far into the interior. Bears, wolves, mink, and birds that ate them spread the nutrients around, dropping them in urine and feces. The resulting fertilization of plants has been confirmed in dozens of studies: the isotopic signature of marine-based nitrogen is in plants a mile from salmon streams, but not in similar leaves in watersheds that lack salmon. Since nitrogen is a main limiting factor on plant growth here, the decline of salmon literally stunts tree growth in much of the region—as well as the populations of bears, wolves, mink, and bald eagles.

We always knew fish are good fertilizer; we knew the rivers used to shimmer crimson with spawners; the people who lived here told us in many ways. It was staring us in the face, but no one got it, no one saw the huge role of salmon in the forest nitrogen cycle, until some scientists ran the numbers in 1999.

Rainbow Trout and Steelhead

Oncorhynchus mykiss (ME-kiss: a Kamchatkan tribal name) Coloring extremely variable; spawning adults usually have a red to pink streak (the "rainbow") full length on each side, much deeper on ♂; returning sea-run fish (steelhead) are silvery all over with guanine (a protein coating on all salmonids fresh from the sea) which obscures

A spawning steelhead male redband trout of the east side, 25 or more inches.

any coloring; dorsal fin rays typically 11–12, pelvic fin rays 10, anal fin rays 10 (range 8–12); juveniles have a distinct row of 5–10 small dark spots along the back straight in front of the dorsal fin, plus 8–13 oval parr marks along the lateral line. Rainbows common in high lakes and streams; steelhead in rivers and streams. Salmonidae.

The sea-run form of this species is revered among anglers who, with good reason, think of it as an altogether different fish—steelhead. (Russians call them both *mykizha.*) At sea the trout grow faster, and grow many times larger than those who stay in freshwater. Big and strong, steelheads are hard to land, and harder still to locate. A favorite riffle for steelhead is a fiercely guarded secret.

The freshwater form is rainbow trout, the world's best-known sport fish. It is native up and down the Pacific Slope from Mexico to the Alaska Peninsula, inland throughout the Columbia River system, and in Siberia. (It is also the trout of dinner tables, both farm-raised and naturalized in streams all around the globe.)

Rainbows and steelhead are not firmly separated genetically: their progeny can go either way, though there's at least a statistical likelihood of their following in their parents', um, finsteps. Researchers found they could identify the two types of small fry within hours of hatching, with the more territorial, fast-metabolism ones becoming steelhead. Overall, more females go to sea, because females have more reproductive potential to gain by growing large. Thus rainbow males mate with steelhead females more often than the reverse. These fairly recent findings support efforts to conserve native rainbows because that can help conserve steelhead, which are threatened.

Wild steelhead usually swim to sea when two years old, and feed in the Gulf of Alaska for one to four "salt years" before their first spawning run. They take their time running upstream, and continue to eat, so they're in better condition than spawning salmon and also more inclined to bite. Ours spawn in early spring. They enter freshwater in various months, divided into "summer" and "winter" steelhead, with summer ones more often heading the longer distance to the east-side.

Cutthroat Trout

Oncorhynchus clarki (CLARK-ee: for William Clark, p. 362). Jaw lines streaked red or orange underneath; jaw longer than other trout, opening to well behind the eye; base of tongue has tiny teeth, usually palpable; dorsal fin has 9–11 rays, pelvic rays usually 9, anal rays 9 (range 8–12); adults dark-speckled; juveniles develop the throat streaks quite early. W-side; and e-side of n CasR. Salmonidae.

The reddish "cuts" on a cutthroat's throat serve to emphasize gestures and displays. As an ID character, they are less than reliable, especially when the fish is young, newly returned to freshwater, or dead. Coloring is notoriously variable in salmon and trout. Like chameleons only much slower, trout alter their camouflage in response to colors they see; experimentally blinded trout eventually contrasted sharply with their associates.

Cutthroats include a range of migratory patterns. Some populations are nonmigrating residents of small streams, maturing at just 6–8 inches; that can happen above a

Nonanadromous coastal rainbow.

A 5- to 8-inch nonanadromous coastal cutthroat.

The Lateral Line

Fish hear with their skins. Sensory neuromast cells are scattered over their bodies near the surface. These are so sensitive that rushing water overwhelms them with noise. Slow-water fish have lots of these, whereas fast-water fish like trout and sculpins have just a few distributed across their skin, and use them instead to detect current, to orient the fish to it.

For hearing, fast-water fish have a highly developed lateral line on each flank, a visible full-body-length set of neuromasts buried in a sort of canal. These screen out the white noise, yet remain sensitive to nonconstant splashes and ripples, such as an insect—or an angler's dry fly—hitting the riffled water.

waterfall barrier. (How can there be trout above barriers? Hatchery stock, of course, but also trout may have predated barriers, especially in Oregon where glaciers never extended far down the rivers.) Sea-run cutthroats don't go far out to sea; many stay in an estuary. They merely "summer" in nearshore waters for a few months annually, and some of them spawn in two or more years. With less time at sea, they don't grow as large as steelhead. Our coastal subspecies coevolved with rainbow trout and steelhead; even though they are interfertile, they maintained reproductive isolation by spawning at separate times and places. Hatchery rainbows have broken that separation down, such that hybridization of the two may be the greatest threat to cutthroats. Cutthroats were as abundant here as rainbows before hatcheries favored the rainbows and hybrids. Many cutthroat sea runs are extinct or endangered. The freshwater populations, though diminished, are now stable in virtually all rivers of the Coast Range and Vancouver Island.

Char

***Salvelinus* spp.** (sal-vel-EYE-nus: the German term Latinized). Salmonidae.

Bull trout, *S. confluentus* (con-flu-EN-tus: of rivers). Adults broadly built, the head and midsection typically as high as they are wide. Olive-greenish back and sides regularly pink- to yellow-dotted; juvenile parr marks wider than the light spaces between; dorsal fin unmarked, with 10 or 11 rays, anal fin usually with 9. Widely scattered; more common e of CasCr.

Dolly Varden trout, *S. malma* (MAL-ma: Kamchatkan term). Like bull trout but slenderer: head height greater than width. Rivers in BC and nw WA.

Brook trout, *S. fontinalis* (fon-tin-AY-lis: of springs). Dark green back and sides with "wormy" patterns and red spots surrounded by blue haloes; dorsal fin dark-spotted, with 8–10 rays, anal fin with 7–9; juveniles' broad parr marks overlaid with lighter red and yellow dots. Native to eastern NA, scattered here due to stocking.

Char are distinguished from true trout (at least when mature) by having light spots

Freshwater bull trout, 8–10 inches, not at spawning time.

Brook trout

against a darker background, rather than vice versa.

The bull trout, once an abundant western trout with huge catch limits and even bounties (because it eats salmon fry), is now in dicey condition, extinct in many watersheds and endangered in others. It requires even colder, cleaner gravelly streams for spawning than our other salmonids. After logging high in a watershed muddies the gravel and warms the water by reducing shade, it may take decades before the stream is again good enough for a bull. In an effort to preserve spawning habitat, the standard for unlogged streamside buffers is now 300 feet. But further global warming could make even a pristine stream too warm. Another threat to the species comes from introduced brook trout, which breed with bull trout to produce sterile hybrids. Brookies were, after rainbows, the second most commonly stocked trout; they are no longer stocked in watersheds with bull trout.

While our native char all spawn in mountain-stream headwaters, populations vary in how far they migrate: they may live the bulk of their lives in small streams (nonmigrating) or bigger ones, or in lakes or the ocean (anadromous). They migrate far for trout, over 115 miles on the Skagit and in the Rockies, where they reached a record 32 pounds. The Cascades record is 22½ pounds.

Dolly Varden and bull trout are hard to tell apart, and were formerly treated as a single species. Dollies were named—allegedly by the first pioneer woman to see them—for their resemblance to a polkadot print fabric of the day, which was named after a gaudy character in Dickens' *Barnaby Rudge*. It was probably a bull trout that she first called Dolly V., but when the species was split, the polkadot name went, along with the Latin name, to the coastal species on which the Dolly dots are obscured by a silvery coating. Dollies are almost always anadromous; coastal bulls sometimes, inland bulls rarely. Information on the distribution of the two species is murky, because past records are rarely identifiable to species, and even now, catches and sightings are rarely identified.

Mountain Whitefish

Prosopium williamsoni (pro-SOAP-ium: mask). Trout-shaped pale silver fish without spots; average 12 in. fully grown; mouth small, without teeth; scales large, bumpy; 10–13 rays in anal fin. US, mainly e-side, and Fraser R system. Salmonidae.

Mountain whitefish

Whitefish use their small mouths to grub around on the bottom for insect larvae; occasionally they will rise to a surface hatch. Some individuals, called pinocchio whitefish, have a distinctly longer but puggish snout, perhaps an adaptation for overturning some types of streambed material. Whitefish spawn in late fall and winter, in water as cold as 35°F. The eggs stick to rocks, so no redd needs to be dug.

Eulachon

Thaleichthys pacificus (thay-lee-IC-thiss: plentiful fish). Also candlefish. 5- to 8-in. fish, blue-gray above, silvery below; distinguished from salmon and trout by pelvic fin attached forward of dorsal fin and lacking an axillary process, a small flap or

After the Blast

Fish came back fast after the 1980 eruption of Mt. St. Helens. In a majority of the affected area's lakes and streams they peaked between 1985 and 1987 at levels somewhat higher than normal, and then settled into the normal range. Sculpins survived in streams subjected to ashfall, and soon thrived in locations where algae and midges flourished. The food web as a whole benefited from a sharp increase in sunlight on the water.

Many salmonids trying to find the stream they were born in failed in the first year or two, straying into other rivers because their own river's chemistry was overwhelmed with volcanic sediment. Some succeeded, though. Wild steelhead (but not hatchery steelhead) were exceptional, plowing through miles of ash-thick rivers to reach clear tributaries just months after the eruption. A lot of the 1980s rebound did consist of stocked trout; apparently game managers felt that "helping" the fish was more important than seeing exactly how fast nature would take care of recovery. In some cases (including Spirit Lake—the most badly damaged lake and the slowest to recover) they chose to let nature take its course, but unknown individuals came in and illegally stocked trout, which grew large enough to prey on northwestern salamander larvae when those experienced a brief population explosion. So it's likely that one cause of the rebound effect was that salmonids were given an artificial head start over their competitors, crayfish and salamanders. Clearly, ecosystems can be very good at recovering, at least from natural disturbances like volcanic eruptions.

scale just above the base of each pelvic fin. Rare; low w-side rivers in brief February or March spawning runs. Osmeridae.

Our once-common smelt, the eulachon or candlefish, may be the fattiest of all fish, so oily that it can be burned like a candle, once dried and threaded with wick. Its oil was the universal condiment in the cuisine of coastal peoples; inland people also went to the coast to trade for it. Its name ("YOU-la-kon"), is from the Chinook trading jargon. Some groups called it "salvation fish" because it returns to rivers in the hungry months of late winter. It fetched a handsome price in British Columbia well into the last century. The bitter froth of whipped soapberries suffused with eulachon oil was so popular it was nicknamed "Indian ice cream." In later times it came a teeny bit closer to ice cream with the addition of plenty of sugar.

Eulachon eggs have an outer membrane that bursts and sticks to the bottom, leaving the egg in its inner membrane attached by a thread. The larvae drift to sea immediately on hatching, so the species is seen in rivers only briefly, as spawning adults.

Dipnetting for these smelts was a quintessential regional tradition on lower Columbia tributaries during the 20th century, requiring so little skill or patience during heavier runs that bucketfuls of smelt were wasted by people more enthusiastic about hauling them in than about cooking them.

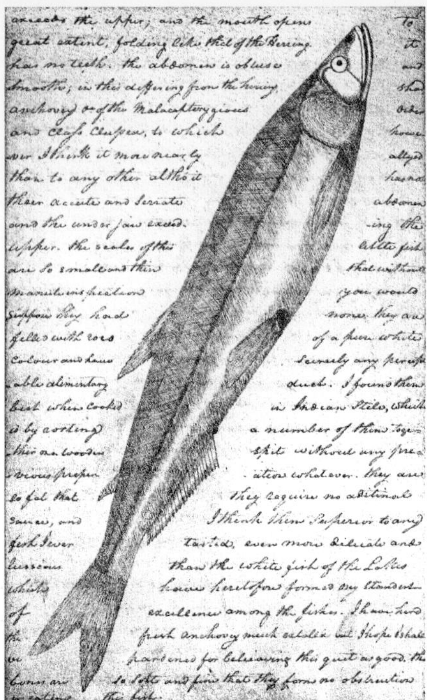

William Clark's first scientific description of the eulachon.

Those days are over, the eulachon a threatened species in the United States, an endangered species in southern British Columbia, where the ten-year decline is estimated to be at least 98 percent. The cause has not received the scrutiny that salmon decline has. Climate tops the list of suspects.

Sculpin

***Cottus* spp.** (COT-us: Greek name for some river fish). Also muddler minnows, bullheads. Scaleless, sometimes prickly, minnow-sized fishes with wide mouths, thick lips, depressed foreheads, very large pectoral fin on each side just behind the head, a 3/4-length dorsal fin in 2 parts, and unforked tail fin. Widespread in streams. Cottidae.

Torrent sculpin, *C. rhotheus* (ROWTH-ius: of noisy waters).

Slimy sculpin, *C. cognatus* (cog-NAY-tus: related).

Shorthead sculpin, *C. confusus* (con-FEW-sus: clouded).

> We are all in the gutter, but some of us are looking at the stars.
>
> — Oscar Wilde

These funny-looking little fish are adapted for life on the bottom: wide, depressed mouths for bottom-feeding; motley drab colors for camouflage against the bottom; eyes directed upward, the only direction there is to look; and huge pectoral fins to anchor them with little effort in strong current. The eggs, laid in spring, adhere to the underside of stones, and are guarded by the father.

Big fish eat little fish, true, but in the case of sculpins vs. salmonids the little fish get even by eating the eggs of the big fish. Some anglers view sculpins as a threat, but in all likelihood, nearly all the salmon eggs ending up in sculpin bellies were those not adequately buried in gravel by their mothers, and would have perished one way or another. Trout are so fond of them that they inspired a trout fly pattern, the "muddler minnow." In the balance, sculpins are not a threat to game fish.

Sculpins are found above impassable waterfalls on some of our rivers. They probably got there via waterways that crossed present-day drainage divides during unique geologic moments as the ice sheet retreated.

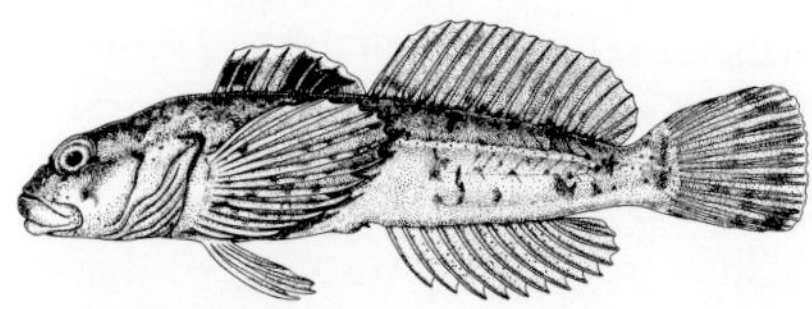

Shorthead sculpin

INSECTS

Insects—six-legged animals with jointed external skeletons made of chitin—are far and away the most diverse and successful kind of animals on earth. Over half a million species have been named, and at least as many remain to be discovered. Only a tiny sample of our insects can be discussed in this space: some of the ever-charming butterflies and dragonflies, the invaluable pollinators—bumble bees and hover flies—and a rogues' gallery of biters and bloodsuckers.

A majority of insect life cycles entail metamorphosis from a wingless larva, which does most or all of the eating and growing, to an enclosed and stationary pupa, and finally to a winged, sexual adult. Butterfly and moth larvae are called caterpillars. The larva typically molts several times while growing. Each stage, between one molt and the next, is an instar (kind of like an instance of the larva). The pupa is hardly the "resting stage" it is often called. As James and Nunnallee put it, "the pupa hosts the greatest magical trick in the natural world: construction of a butterfly from caterpillar soup . . . taking as little as 5–7 days."

Metamorphosis in the Odonata (dragonflies, p. 478) lacks a pupal stage. The larvae go through 10 to 15 aquatic instars of incrementally increasing complexity and mobility before molting into a winged adult. Later instars have proper legs, and the final larval one shows the (nonfunctional) beginnings of wings. Aphids, page 471, and ice crawlers, page 477, demonstrate other versions of incomplete metamorphosis.

INSECTS: DIPTERA (FLIES AND MOSQUITOES)

Mosquito

Family Culicidae

A female mosquito has an elaborate mouth. What we see as a mere proboscis is a tiny set of surgical tools—six stylets wrapped in the groove of a heavier labium flanked by two palps. The operation begins with the palps exploring your skin for a weakness or pore. There the labium sets down. Delicately and precisely, two pairs of stylets—one piercing, one slicing—set to work locating and entering a capillary, then bending to travel within it. The remaining two stylets are tubes. One sucks blood out while the other pumps saliva in, stimulating blood flow to the vicinity and inhibiting coagulation. Until the saliva hits, you probably feel nothing. (Mosquito detection is the chief "usefulness of hair on the legs," mused Gary Snyder in his 1951 journal from a North Cascades fire lookout.)

Unlike bee stings, which have to hurt to do their job, the bump and itch of a mosquito bite are an accident, an allergy to mosquito saliva. The first few times a species of mosquito bites you, there's no pain or welt. As you develop sensitivity to that species, your response speeds up from a day or so to one or two minutes. Eventually you may become again desensitized to that species. We rarely notice this cycle because we fail to distinguish among the species.

The females need at least one blood meal greater than their own weight in order to lay eggs. It takes human-feeding species about two minutes to draw enough. Aside from that meal, they eat pollen and nectar; some plants may depend on them as pollinators. Male mosquitoes eat nectar only, but contribute to our discomfort all the same: they hover around warm bodies in the reasonable expectation that that's where the girls are. If we wanted to, we could get males to fly down our throats by singing the pitch hummed by female wings. Male antennae have evolved into plumes that vibrate sympathetically with conspecific female wing beats, and the males home in toward any steady source of this pitch.

Each mosquito species has its own wing-beat frequencies, one for males and a slightly lower one for females; young adults speed up their wing beats as they mature. Wing beats range up to 600 per second in mosquitoes, and peak at over 1000 in their relatives, the midges. Anything over 50 beats per second is too fast to be triggered by individual nerve impulses. Instead, the

Aedes female mosquito engorged with blood.

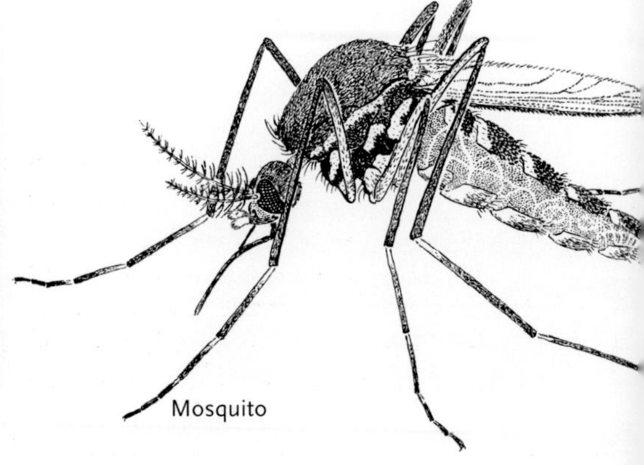

Mosquito

How To Not Get Bitten

Clothing yourself from crown to toe may be safest.

Clothes and gear impregnated with permethrin offer good protection. Permethrin is toxic, but your exposure to it is minimal with factory impregnation, and modest even with do-it-yourself spraying—if you're careful.

DEET repellents are effective and turn out to be pretty innocuous. (The health risks of bites are worse than those of DEET.) Skip products with concentrations higher than 30 percent, or 10 percent for children, 0 percent for babies. DEET stinks, and dissolves some plastics.

Alternatives to DEET—both synthetic and botanical—can also irritate skin or eyes. Botanical oils are often allergens, and a few appear to be carcinogens.

Picaridin-based repellents don't stink or damage plastics. This synthetic analog of a compound in black pepper is effective against mosquitoes, ticks, and biting flies. That said, we all know the biters are sometimes fierce enough to thumb their little noses at lab-tested "efficacy."

Repellents employing iR3535 don't stink, but may damage plastics.

PMD (related to and often combined with lemon eucalyptus) is the most lastingly effective repellent that's often described as a botanical compound, though that's a bit of a stretch.

Citronella, lemon eucalyptus, and some other pure plant oils are fairly effective (if you like the smell and aren't allergic) but have to be reapplied so often that they become impractical. "Encapsulated citronella oil nanoemulsion" may address that problem in the future.

Catnip oil lasts longer but doesn't work against ticks.

Nootkatone and other compounds from Alaska cedar (p. 92) will take a few years to reach the market, if they ever do.

It's best to apply your sunblocks and repellents separately, because sunblocks need to be reapplied much more often.

Forget wrist bands, dermal patches, vitamin B_1, and especially sound-emitting devices, which actually increased the number of bites in one scientific study.

That study liked clip-on diffusers of botanical aromatic oils, but the Environmental Working Group warns of possible health dangers from inhaling those aerosols.

There are some humans whom mosquitos avoid. Scientists analyzed their skin secretions and identified the natural repellents as ketones that are said to smell like nail-polish remover and very ripe fruit; they hope to sell those compounds some day to those of us who are not so blessed.

thoracic muscles are in two groups, each stretched by the contraction of the other, and contracting in a twitch-like reflex. The thorax shell snaps back and forth between two stable shapes, like a shoe polish tin lid, one shape holding the wings up and the other down. The nervous system need supply only a slow, unsteady pulse of signals to keep this snapping vibration going. (Many insects beat their wings in this fashion.)

Most mosquitoes are active only a short period each day. For many species, that's just before and after sunset and just before dawn. Too small to retain body heat, they need an air temperature of at least 40°F. Host choice is species-specific. Some varieties of the familiar mosquito *Culex pipiens* (PIP-ee-enz: piping) never bite people, but others rank among the peskiest. Most of our mountain mosquitoes are of genus *Aedes* (ay-EE-deez: repugnant). Unlike other genera that set their eggs afloat on still water, most *Aedes* species lay eggs in the fall on spots of bare ground likely to be briefly submerged in the spring, when the larvae take off swimming. These "wigglers" feed by filtering algae and bacteria out of water.

Females zero in on the carbon dioxide we exhale, together with lactic acid and other skin and sweat aromas. Gruesome concentrations of mosquitoes typify the Far North, where musk-oxen and nesting ducks make ideal hosts. One stoic researcher counted 189 bites on a forearm exposed for one minute. From that he extrapolated 9000 bites per minute for one entire naked person, enough to suck one-fourth of his blood in an hour.

Mosquitoes may be the best studied of all insect families because they are the deadliest to humans. Malaria, introduced here in 1830, within four years killed a majority of the Indians on the lower Columbia, shattering tribal culture and leaving the Willamette Valley open to unimpeded white settlement. Its carriers, mosquitos of genus *Anopheles* (an-AH-fel-eez: worthless), still live here, but the disease does not, possibly because mosquito numbers were sufficiently reduced by draining sloughs and lakes. In 1803, yellow fever touched our history from a safe distance: it killed nine-tenths of a French army sent to conquer Haiti and the Mississippi Valley, leaving Napoleon in a mood to sell "Louisiana" to Thomas Jefferson at a price Congress couldn't refuse. That led directly to Lewis and Clark, and ultimately to the Oregon Territory being part of the United States rather than of Mexico, Canada, or Russia.

As of 2016, the mosquito-borne disease in the region is West Nile virus. Since its 2004 arrival it has infected only a handful of people in our mountains, with no increase over the last decade. Malaria is an increasing threat in the tropics, because both the pathogen and the mosquito excel at evolving resistance to cures, repellents, and insecticides. Between that and the warming climate, we may see malaria again. Or Zika. In the meantime armies of researchers are working full time testing hundreds of compounds that repel or kill mosquitoes.

No-see-um

***Culicoides* spp.** (cue-lic-OY-deez: gnat-like). Also punkies, biting midges.

The common name suffices to identify these pests. At up to ⅛ inch long, they are just big enough to see, but small enough to invade screened cabins. They are hard to make out in the waning light of dusk, when they do most of their biting. Their stealth and our defenselessness irritate us more than the bites really hurt. No-see-ums are so localized that we can usually escape by walking 50 feet. Breeding grounds include puddles,

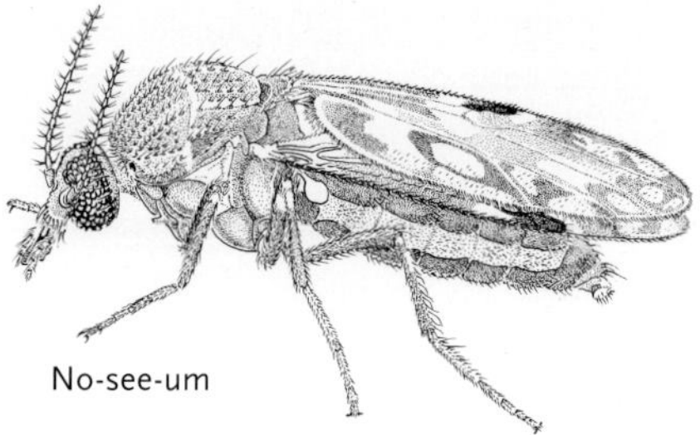

No-see-um

intertidal sands, and humus. The chief victims of this bloodsucking family are other insects, ranging from their own size on up to dragonflies. In some species the females prey on the males, and one pirate species sucks mammal blood from mosquito abdomens.

Deer Fly

***Chrysops* spp.** (CRY-sops: appearing golden).

The size of smallish house flies but much slower and softer, and ranging from dull gray-brown to nearly black, deer flies are just too easy to kill—it's an irresistible exercise in utter futility. Where there's one deer fly, there are a thousand. On a hot July day in a North Cascades basin, the only respites may be nightfall, tent netting, your fastest stride, or rain, none of which are what you had in mind for this otherwise lovely afternoon. Travel sometimes helps, since most deer flies stay within half a mile of the marsh or pond where they overwintered as larvae.

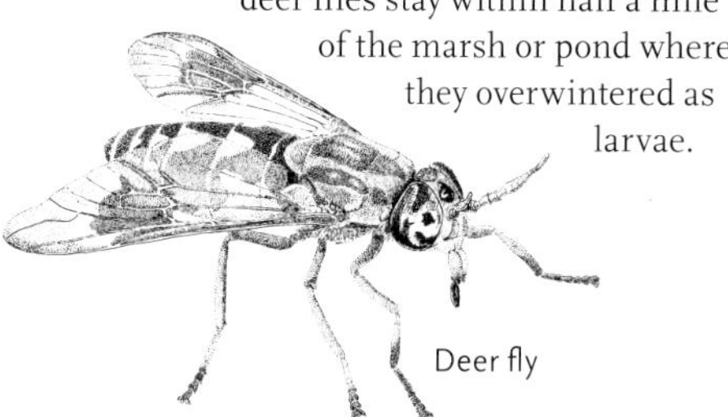
Deer fly

Horse Fly

***Tabanus* spp.** (ta-BAY-nus: the Roman term).

Horse flies resemble very large house flies. Some are black, some gray-brown, and

Horse fly

many have iridescent stripes across their big eyes. They are our biggest, fastest, strongest biting flies, so we're lucky they're sparse enough to view as individuals: when you manage to swat one, you may actually be ahead of the game for awhile. Their obsession with the tops of our heads often diverts them from our more vulnerable parts. Even so, they're hard to catch up with.

Horse flies are commonest near large-mammal habitat. The nectar- and pollen-eating males are seen less often than the bloodsucking females. With larvae going through two winters before metamorphosing into adults, horse flies are long-lived.

Horse and deer flies are also known as gad flies. Dictionaries may spell them "horsefly" and "gadfly," but entomologists prefer to keep "fly" separate in the names of true flies (order Diptera) to distinguish them from nonflies such as dragonflies and butterflies.

Black Fly

***Simulium* spp.** (sim-YOU-lium: simulator). Also buffalo gnat.

These vicious biters raise a welt out of proportion to their size, sometimes drawing

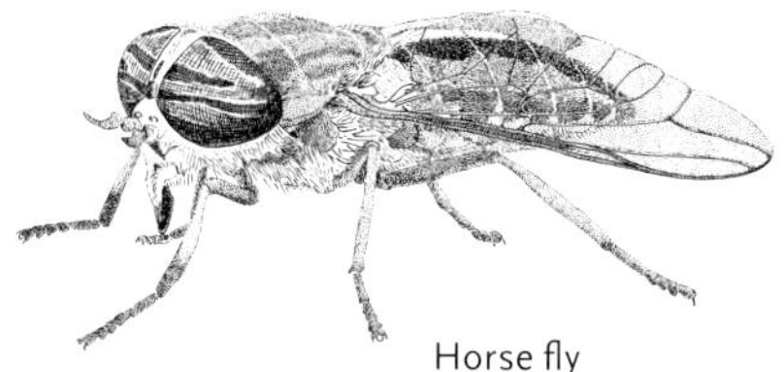
Horse fly

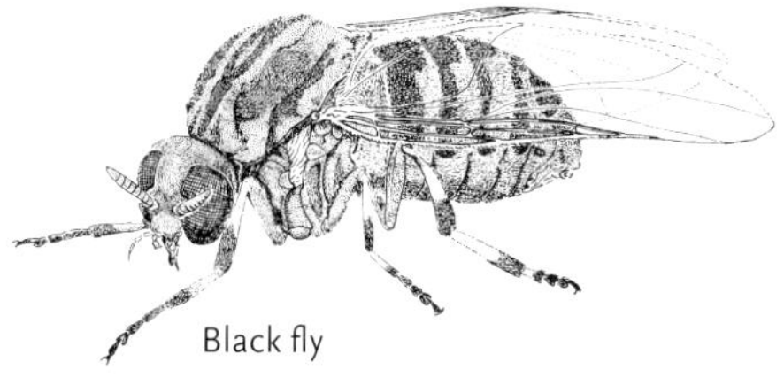
Black fly

blood, and reportedly causing bovine and human deaths when biting en masse. They render many of North America's boreal vacationlands uninhabitable for the month of June. Fortunately they tend to dissipate by midsummer. Here, they are less of a nuisance than the ubiquitous deer flies and mosquitoes.

"Black" flies are medium to dark gray, and stocky for their length (about 1/8 inch). They look humpbacked, and tilt forward while biting. Only the females bite; once fed, they dive in and out of cold, fast streams attaching eggs singly to submerged stones. The larvae stay underwater, straining plankton, moving around and then reanchoring themselves with a suction disk. Emerging from submerged pupation, the adults burst up into the air in a bubble.

Hover Fly

Family Syrphidae Also flower fly.

You feel an insect on your arm. You look down, see a yellowjacket—hold that swat! Don't let a case of mistaken identity turn deadly.

Yellowjackets—a kind of wasp—crave your salami or your protein bar, but rarely land on your skin except to sting you. If this one hasn't stung, trust it. Chances are it is a hover fly, a stingless insect that mimics bees or wasps in order to ward off predators.

Hover fly

Look closer: are the two antennae stubby and short, much smaller than the eyes? Hover fly. Or are they long, slender, and turned down? Bee or wasp. Is there a short, foot-like dark proboscis stepping around on your skin? Hover fly tongue, lapping up the salty sweat that attracted it to you. Flies also have two wings (the meaning of Diptera), and bees and wasps four, but that is less helpful; the narrow hindwings of bees and wasps (Hymenoptera: "membrane wings") are translucent and hard to see in a live situation. As for those long, downturned yellowjacket antennae, some hover flies heighten their mimicry with a "dance" behavior, waving front legs that are darker than the other four to make them look like wasp antennae.

Do hover flies do more to earn our friendship than just slurp on us, look pretty, and decline to pack heat? Absolutely. They rank high among insects beneficial to plants, and hence to farmers. The larvae of many hover flies are the leading predators of aphids. In adulthood, hover flies are second only to bees as pollinators, globally; in our high mountain meadows, flies may do more pollinating than bees. Their pollinating style has one advantage over that of bees—carrying pollen farther—and one disadvantage—being less faithful to a plant species on any given day. Whereas bees use their long tongues to draw nectar out of deep flowers, flies have short tongues, visit shallower flowers, and eat more pollen than nectar. Both males and females visit flowers,

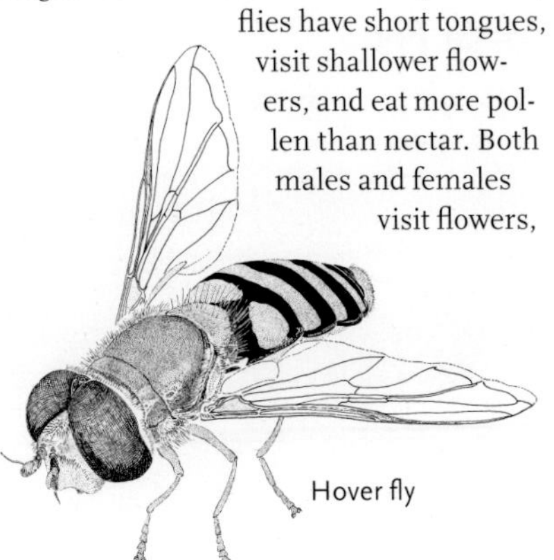
Hover fly

the females gorging on pollen proteins they require to develop their eggs, the males snacking while patrolling territory in hopes of a chance at a receptive female.

Since they seek sweat and resemble bees, hover flies are sometimes conflated with "sweat bees," a family of actual bees that earn that tag. Sweat bees are typically black or green all over and just 1/4–3/8 inch long. Our hover flies tend to measure 3/8–5/8 inch. A few thousand syrphid species have black-and-yellow-banded abdomens to mimic this or that well-armed bee or wasp. On some of our commonest ones, the thorax shines like polished brass and the huge eyes are maroon. Male eyes are plastered to each other on the top of the head; a narrow but distinct forehead separates female eyes.

Some entomologists campaign for the name "flower flies" as opposed to "hover flies," wishing to raise the family's favorables in the public eye. But hovering is more distinctive of this family: many insects pollinate, but few can compete with a hover fly at hovering. Bumble bees sashay from side to side as they descend upon a blossom, whereas male hover flies spend minutes at a time hovering perfectly. They are the insects you see maintaining a fixed position in a beam of light above a forest trail. Watch for the fly to zoom abruptly off to the side, then retake the same spot it held before. This is a male hover fly defending aerial territory where a female may show up. When he darted off, he was bouncing a rival. (Or was that the rival that won the confrontation and usurped the midair post? If you can tell which one of them came back, you've got quicker eyes than I do.)

A position in a beam of light can be maintained longer than one in the shade because the fly absorbs solar heat, supplanting calories he would otherwise burn to maintain optimum body heat for efficient hovering. This allows him more minutes hovering before he has to go find the next snack. Cost-benefit analysis confirms that the sunlit fly comes out ahead.

Bumble Bee

Bombus **spp.** (BOM-bus: "buzz"). Large, rotund, furry, yellow-and-black bees; queens in most species are 1/4–3/4 in. long, and fly in the spring; workers 1/4–3/4 in. long, appearing late spring to fall. Ubiquitous.

Much "common knowledge" about bees is actually about honey bees, which aren't even native to the Americas. The European honey bee, *Apis mellifera*, invaded America along with European culture, but is not abundant in our wilderness. A honey bee worker can sting only once, but other bees have repeat-use stingers. Honey bees have an elaborate social order and communication rituals, but most native bees are "solitary bees"—they may live gregariously, but they don't organize societies with a division of labor.

Bumble bees, our commonest bees, are in the honey bee family, and do have a strong social order though their colonies are relatively small and short-lived. Each colony begins with a queen who hibernates (among dead leaves, say) after mating with a chosen male in the fall. Typically taking a mouse or vole burrow for her nest, she secretes beeswax to make "pots." In some she lays eggs on a liner of pollen and nectar, sealing them over with more wax. Others she fills with

Bumble bee

honey (nectar concentrated within her body, by evaporation), which she sips for energy while working her muscles and pressing her abdomen onto her eggs, incubating them with body heat. The first brood is workers—small, nonmating females. Maturing in three or four weeks, they take over the nectar and pollen-gathering chores while the queen retires to the nest to incubate eggs and feed larvae.

Protein-rich pollen nourishes the growing larvae, while pure carbohydrate nectar and honey are all that the energetic adults require. Bumble bee honey is as delicious as honey bee honey but can't be exploited by large omnivores like people and bears because bumble bees don't store much for the future; the queen keeps producing just as many broods of larvae as the growing population of workers can feed. As the food supply allows, late broods will include increasing numbers of sexuals—male drones from unfertilized eggs, and new queens produced simply by more generous and prolonged feeding of female larvae. Only the queens eat well enough to survive the onset of winter. The others die in the fall, after the drones and queens have mated. By feeding only a few individuals for hibernation, bumble bees conserve nectar and pollen resources, which are scarce in cool climates.

Other key adaptations include the use of ready-made insulated nests; the relatively large, furry bodies; and the skill of raising a near-constant body temperature for flight in a wide range of weather conditions. Bernd Heinrich has cataloged such varied, extensive, and sophisticated forms of thermoregulation in insects, especially bumble bees, that he completely rejects the description of insects as cold-blooded. Arctic bumble bees have been seen in flight in a snowstorm at 6 degrees below freezing. Generally, bumble bees are the most valuable plant pollinators at high latitudes and altitudes.

Each bumble bee species has multiple color patterns; several species in a given area tend to converge on similar color patterns. (This Müllerian mimicry reinforces the effectiveness of color patterns in training predators to avoid species with defenses, such as bee stingers.) As a result, identifying them to species requires capture, expertise, and a magnifying glass. *Bombus vosnesenskii* is relatively recognizable: mostly black, some yellow on head, shoulder, and near tail, but no red-orange fur, common from cities to subalpine meadows. A more strictly montane species, *B. mixtus*, is smaller and duller in color, combining all three colors. *Bombus sitkensis* is again small and dull, but without red-orange (except of course that any bee's pollen sacs can fill up with orange pollen). *Bombus huntii*, common on east-side steppe and lower mountains, has a rich red abdomen section framed by both yellow and black at both ends.

Some bumble bee species are brood parasites (called "cuckoo" bumble bees after the best-known brood parasites.) Their queens murder queens of other bumble bee species and usurp their colonies. They produce no workers, and their legs have no pollen sacs. Worker bees on guard duty sometimes get enough stingers through an invader's armor to kill her, but a false queen can pacify workers with pheromones. Then they bring home the bacon to the mixed family. Queens of "normal" species also sometimes usurp other queens' colonies. It is not unusual to find several dead queens in a nest, or to find colonies of mixed species.

Both honey bee and bumble bee populations are threatened by a host of modern problems. Some formerly abundant bumble bee species are now hard to find, while a few have expanded their ranges. For bumble bees, two of the biggest problems are habitat loss and neonicotinoids, a new class of insecticide. Please minimize or eliminate any use of neonicotinoids in your garden. Currently, these are made by Bayer and sold as "systemic," meaning that you put them on the soil and they go into every part of every plant in that soil, persisting for weeks. That may sound like an ideal way to prevent infestations, but only if you think that all insects are bad. It's toxic to insects that eat pollen and nectar—the very insects our plants need the most.

INSECTS: HOMOPTERA (LACEWINGS AND APHIDS)

Cooley Spruce Gall Adelgid

Adelges cooleyi (a-DEL-jeez: unseen; coo-lee-eye: for Robert A. Cooley). Soft pinhead-sized bodies covered at most stages with waxy, cottony white fluff, on Douglas-fir needles and twigs (related species also on true firs or pines); wings (if present) folded roof-like over body; more conspicuous are their cone-like galls on branch tips of spruces.

Many spruces seem to have an odd, spiky sort of cone in addition to their larger papery-scaled ones. Looking closer, we can see these aren't really cones because they are at branch tips rather than several inches back, and because they are fused wholes, not a set of wiggleable scales. The spikes turn out to be simply spruce needles with a hard brownish or greenish skin drawn tight like shrinkwrap that shrunk. This is a gall, material secreted by the tree in response to chemical stimulation by an insect. Other galls include bright red marginal swellings on shrub leaves, or lightweight tan orbs on oak limbs.

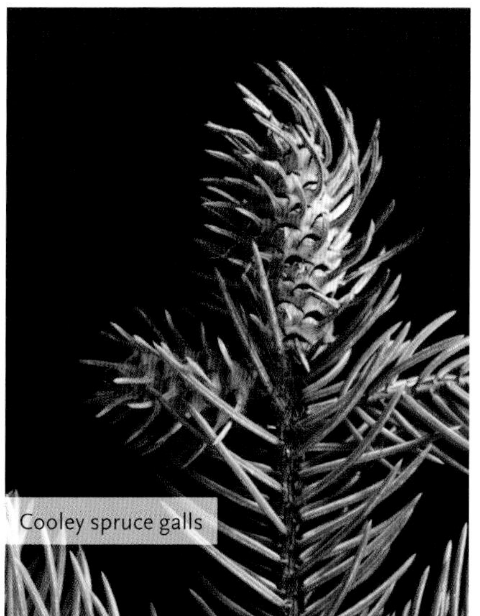
Cooley spruce galls

Though each spruce gall ends one branchlet's growth, galls in themselves are rarely a serious drain on host plants. Living adelgids (aphids) sometimes are. They suck plant juices through minute piercing tubes nearly as long as their own bodies. They seem to suck in far more plant sugar than they can consume, since they pass copious sticky honeydew excretions. Some aphids are "herded" by ants or other insects that feed on aphid honeydew, but on our fir trees honeydew is more likely to end up consumed by a dreadful-looking black smut fungus. Overall, neither the feeding nor the housing of this aphid places it among our major forest pests.

Spruce gall adelgids actually feed mostly on Douglas-firs. Their life cycle includes no larvae, pupae, or males as those terms are normally defined. Instead it is divided into five forms or castes, each egg-laying. One wingless form overwinters on spruce, then lays the eggs of the gall-making form, which emerges from the gall in late summer and flies to a fir to lay eggs. These eggs produce a fir-overwintering form, which in turn engenders two forms, one wingless and fir-bound, the other flying to spruce to beget either the spruce-overwintering form or a short-lived sexual generation. But in the Northwest sexuals are unknown, or at least very rare, and the various female forms perpetuate their clone parthenogenetically (without fertilization).

Balsam Woolly Adelgid

Adelges piceae (PIS-ee-ee: of spruces). Also balsam woolly aphid. Pinhead-sized bodies on bark or twigs of true firs, covered at some stages with waxy white "wool"; winged stage rare.

The balsam woolly adelgid coevolved in an unthreatening relationship with the fir species of Europe, but when accidentally introduced into North America it proved deadly to several American firs, including our subalpine and silver firs. Grand firs, oddly, are significantly reduced by it on the west-side below 1000 feet, but seem resistant higher up. The tree's leader may droop and break off early in an attack, then all the foliage may turn red-brown from the top downward, and the trunk hemorrhage with resin. This serious pest waxes and wanes from year to year. Several known predator species were introduced decades ago, with inconclusive results, and there is little talk of anything else to be done for our firs.

This aphid resembles the relatively innocuous Cooley spruce gall adelgid (p. 471) but feeds on true fir stems or twigs, which swell up in gouty knobs. Dispersing mainly on wind currents, it rarely grows wings. Males and galls are unknown.

With their complex (and in this case asexual) life cycle, adelgids are poorly understood. Hemlock woolly adelgids, *A. tsugae*, are an existential threat to eastern hemlocks, which they first encountered in 1951, but they are unthreateningly present on the other seven hemlock species, including our two. Apparently *A. tsugae* is native here and coevolved with our hemlocks; the Japanese strain attacking the East should get its own species name in due time.

INSECTS: COLEOPTERA (BEETLES)

Coleoptera means "sheath wings" in Greek. A beetle's forewings are modified into a hard sheath that encloses and protects the two hindwings when they are folded up, enabling it to bore into hard materials without jeopardizing its wings. This ability to both fly and bore may be a key to beetles' success. They comprise easily the largest and most diverse animal order. One of every four animal species is a beetle.

Ten-lined June Beetle

Polyphylla decemlineata (poly-FIL-a: many leaves; des-em-lin-ee-AY-ta: ten lined). ¾–1¼ in. long, brown, with broad white stripes lengthwise on back; hairy underneath; ♂ have large, thick, twisting antennae; adults found feeding on conifer foliage, or flying into lights at night.

The white, usually C-curved larvae (typical of the Scarab family) feed on plant roots, and are pests in fruit orchards. The handsome adults huff and puff audibly through their breathing holes when disturbed.

Golden Buprestid

Buprestis aurulenta (bew-PRES-tiss: Greek term, meaning "cow-swelling," for some beetle; or-you-LEN-ta: golden). Also *Cypriacis aurulenta*. ½- to ¾-in. beetle; metallic emerald green, wings have coppery-iridescent margins and conspicuous lengthwise ridges. Widespread but shy, adults may be found feeding on foliage, especially Douglas-fir.

This beetle beauty rivals our most glamorous butterflies. Foresters count it among our pests. Because it attacks trees in relatively small numbers it rarely does more than cosmetic damage, but that can add up to a lot of

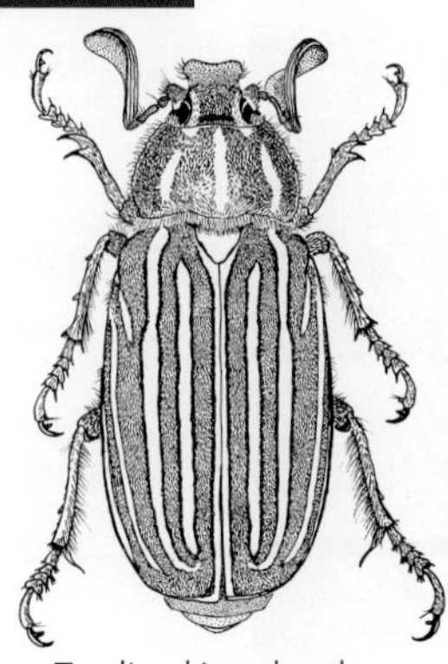

Ten-lined june beetle

Golden buprestid

dollars. The larvae bore deep into seasoned heartwood, and may continue to do so as long as 50 years after the wood is milled and built into houses. Such records make the buprestid a contender for the title of longest-lived insect, though in natural habitats the larvae mature in less than a decade.

Similar *B. langi* lacks the coppery margins, and may have pale blotches.

Black Fire Beetle

Melanophila acuminata (melon-OFF-il-a: loves black; a-cue-min-AY-ta: point-tipped). Also firebug. ½-in. pitch-black beetle with minutely jointed antennae. (Patterns of 6 to 10 pale blotches on the back identify two very similar fire beetle spp.) Around burns.

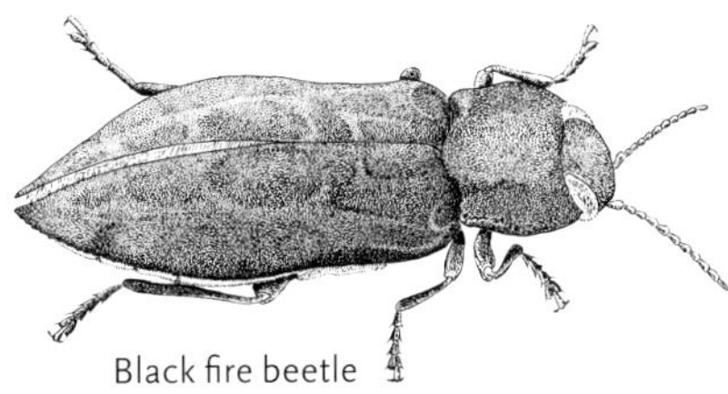

Black fire beetle

Evolution gave fire beetles no way to deal with pitch or other tree defenses against boring insects. What they got instead was a phenomenal way to get there first when a lot of trees die. Tiny infrared sensors in pits on the thorax can detect heat from as far as 70 miles away; that's far greater infrared sensitivity than any human-made device. They chase fires so efficiently that they get there in time to nip the firefighters. Laying eggs under the bark of dying pines, still smoldering, they facilitate recycling by providing entry points for decomposers.

Ponderous Borer

Trichocnemis spiculatus (trick-uc-NEE-mis hairy leg; spic-you-LAY-tus: with little spikes). Also pine sawyer, spined wood borer; *Ergates spiculatus*. Large beetles 1¾–2½ in. long; back minutely pebbled, dark reddish brown to black; thorax ("neck" area) may bear many small spines; antennae long, jointed, curved outward.

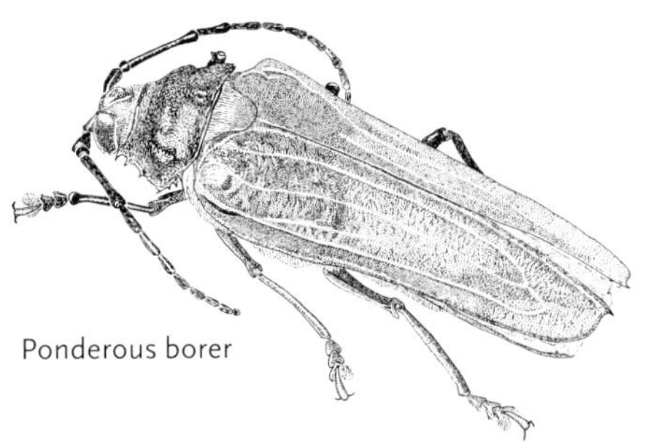

Ponderous borer

Attracted to light, these clumsy nocturnal giants startle us when they come crashing into camp. The equally ponderous larvae take several years to grow to a mature size of up to 3 inches, chewing 1- to 2-inch-diameter holes through pine or Douglas-fir heartwood. Loggers call the larvae "timber worms." One logger was inspired by their mandibles in inventing the saw chain design.

Pine Beetle

***Dendroctonus* spp.** (den-DROC-ton-us: tree murder). Small (⅛–¼ in.) black to pale brown or red beetles with tiny, elbowed, club-tipped antennae; adults and larvae both live in inner bark and are rarely seen, but their excavation patterns in the bark and cortex are distinctive.

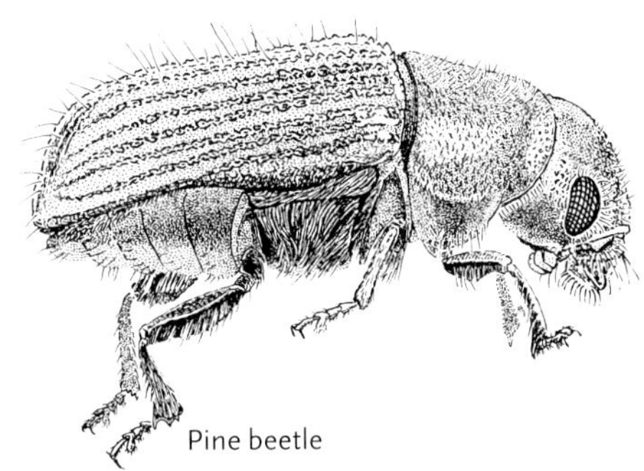

Pine beetle

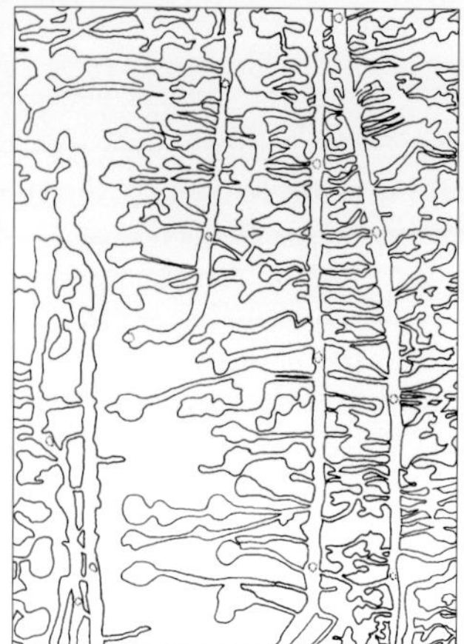

Mountain pine beetle larval galleries

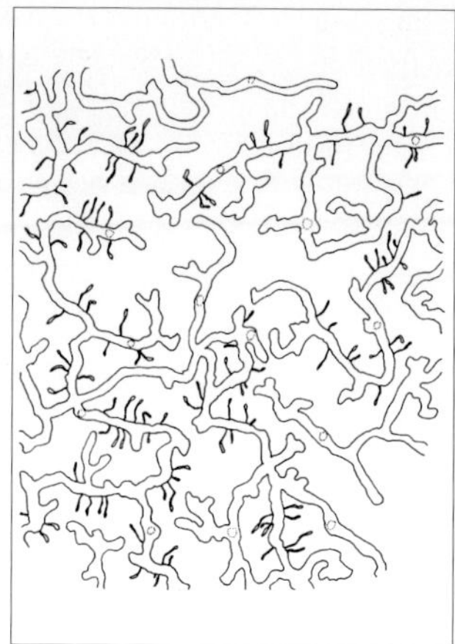

Western pine beetle larval galleries

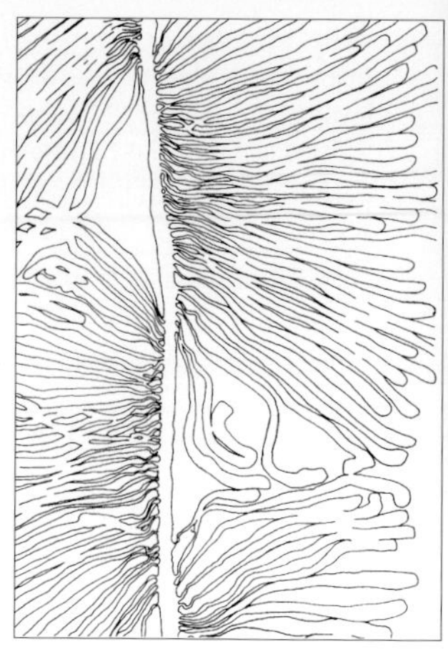

Douglas-fir beetle larval galleries

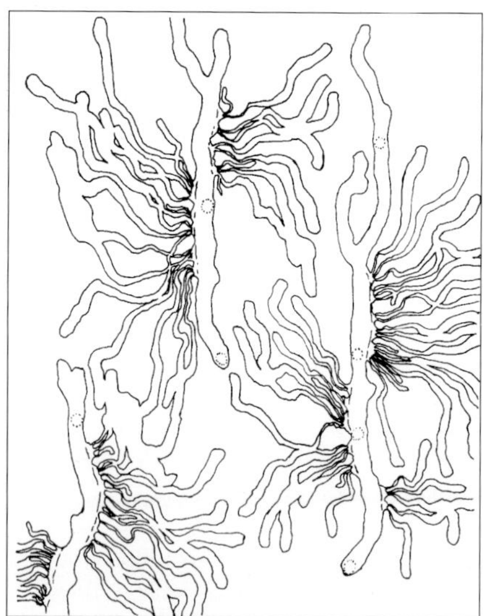

Spruce beetle larval galleries

Mountain pine beetle, *D. ponderosae* (pon-der-OH-see: of ponderosa pine, a somewhat misleading name). On lodgepole, whitebark, and ponderosa pines.

Western pine beetle, *D. brevicomis* (brev-ic-OH-mis: short hair). On ponderosa pine.

Douglas-fir beetle, *D. pseudotsugae* (soo-doe-TSOO-ghee). On e-side Douglas-fir.

Spruce beetle, *D. rufipennis* (roo-fip-EN-iss: red wing). On Engelmann spruce.

Pine beetles are among the most devastating insect killers of western trees, especially lodgepole and ponderosa pines. The first signs of their attack are small round entrance holes exuding pitch or boring-dust—the tree's counterattack, engulfing and drowning beetles. The many exit holes, a generation later, look as if they were made by a blast of buckshot.

After the bark falls away you can see branched engravings underneath. The beetles, though less than 1/8 inch wide, chew much wider egg galleries through the tender inner bark layer, just barely cutting into the sapwood. The larvae set off at right angles to the gallery, widening as they grow, and then pupating at the ends of their tunnels. From there they bore straight out through the bark upon emerging as adults. The tunnels are left packed with excreted wood dust, called frass. In most species, the egg gallery runs 6–40 inches straight up and down the wood grain, and larval tunnels run straight sideways or fan out slightly. Galleries of the western pine beetle curl and crisscross like spaghetti, and their larvae leave little impression on the inner bark, preferring the outer bark. Engraver beetles identify themselves with further variations on the theme.

These beetles are all native here. In typical years they benefit the forest by culling the damaged, diseased, or slower-growing trees. Vigorously growing trees are less palatable and better able to mount a rapid defense using pitch; the beetles must overpower the tree's health or it will overpower them. They do so by attacking en masse and by bringing wood-eating fungi along. Single females scout, then release scented pheromones to attract others to a vulnerable tree. Each female is followed into her entrance hole by a male, and they work as a pair.

Mountain and western pine beetles have occasional population outbreaks. Then their economic equation shifts, offering advantages to them if they go for big, healthy trees. The quarter-century starting in 1990 produced a sweeping epidemic of multiple beetle species, notably spruce beetle in Alaska, Yukon, and now Utah and Colorado; pine engravers (*Ips* spp.) in the Southwest; and mountain pine beetle throughout the northern Rockies and interior British Columbia.

At least three known mechanisms connect the beetle epidemics to climate change.

Bark beetles are periodically beaten back from the coldest parts of their range when severe cold snaps kill all their larvae. They expanded their range into central British Columbia and into higher elevations in Montana and Wyoming after several decades without any snaps that cold.

Warmer summers enable mountain pine beetles to produce two generations in one year, helping their populations erupt faster.

Warming has a drying effect on vegetation. Beetle epidemics tend to follow droughts, when most of a region's trees are stressed to some degree, weakening their defenses. That may go a long way toward explaining the shift from benign to destructive beetle ecology. Compared to past normals, drought may be the condition of most of western North America for the foreseeable future.

Thinning pine forests apparently helps somewhat to keep them vigorous in a drier climate, and can put trees out of range of beetle pheromonal communication—about 20 feet from the next tree. The forest management goal should be greater forest heterogeneity across the landscape—in species, in age and size, and in density.

Here, the beetles haven't been so bad; the chief recent victims are lodgepole pines in the Okanogan edge of the North Cascades and the Chilcotin edge of the Coast Mountains. In central Oregon this outbreak was mild compared to one in the 1980s. The Cascades east slope overall has more trees attacked by western spruce budworm. We have few pines and few beetles west of the Cascades, and we don't know whether climate change could some day turn the Douglas-fir beetle into a scourge of the west-side.

Looking at a lodgepole forest devastated by beetles, many people intuitively call it a "tinderbox." Whether beetle kill actually leads to more or worse fires is an interesting question that has received intense study. The answer is, it depends; but on balance, no. Lodgepole forests in late summer are pretty damn flammable even when healthy. For the newly killed red stage, lasting a year or two, the trees are full of red-brown needles and are slightly more flammable than when green. But soon, in the gray stage, with needles fallen, the dead trees are too far apart to carry a crown fire easily, and fuels on the ground may be no worse than in a green forest.

Engraver Beetle

***Scolytus* spp.** (sco-LIE-tus: truncated)
Small, 1⁄8-in. shiny blackish beetles; abdomen appearing "sawed off" a bit shorter than the end of the wing covers; known mainly by their egg galleries in the inner bark of dead and dying trees. Ubiquitous.

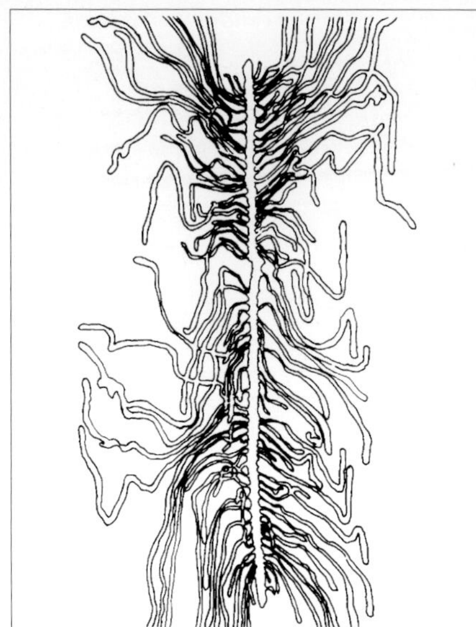

Douglas-fir pole beetle larval galleries

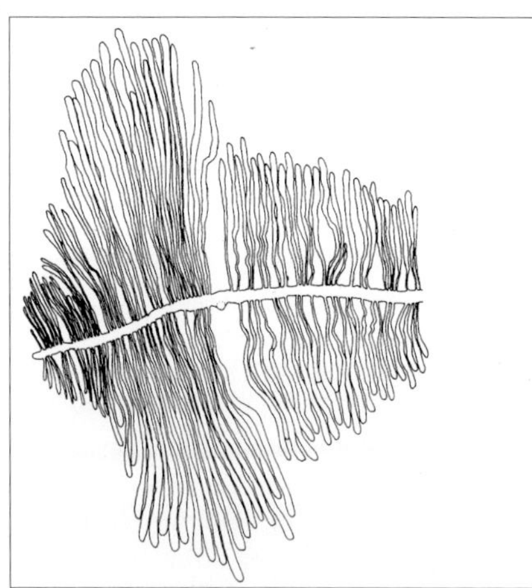

Fir engraver larval galleries

Douglas-fir engraver, *S. unispinosus* (you-ni-spy-NO-sus: one-spined).

Fir engraver, *S. ventralis* (ven-TRAY-lis: on the belly).

The Douglas-fir engraver leaves its signature on a high proportion of fallen Doug-firs in full or partial sunlight—a deep 4- to 6-inch egg gallery carved along the grain of the inner bark and sapwood, generating shallower larval tunnels that start out perpendicular but curve up or down, finally running with the grain. (The Douglas-fir pole beetle, *Pseudohylesinus nebulosus*, cuts nearly identical marks in shaded Doug-firs.)

The fir engraver carves true firs, and its signature is 90 degrees different: the main gallery runs straight across the grain, the larval tunnels with the grain.

In the Northwest alone, dozens of species in the subfamily Scolytinae take on specialized roles in recycling woody waste, a process crucial to the forest's vitality. Many of them have mycangia for holding and disseminating spores of fungi that, along with bacteria, are partners in this great symbiosis. A majority of them, like the Douglas-fir engraver, rarely attack healthy branches. Others are killers. The fir engraver, like the western pine beetle, kills a lot of trees during occasional outbreaks; it's hard to say whether these are departures from the natural order. Where *Scolytus* species aren't native, they can be disastrous, like the one that brought the Dutch elm disease fungus to America.

If not for its attackers, a tree would be virtually immortal—just as long as it could keep growing—since trees do not get old in the sense that animals do. Without beetles and fungi, would the forest stop growing short of impenetrability? It's hard to imagine such a world.

Striped Ambrosia Beetle

Trypodendron lineatum (try-po-DEN-dron: bore tree; lin-ee-AY-tum: lined). ⅛-in.-long,

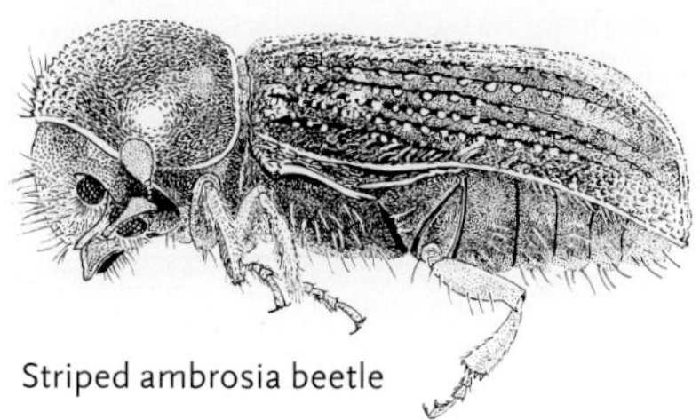

Striped ambrosia beetle

shiny black to brown beetles with faint paler stripes lengthwise on wing covers; head hidden from above by thorax, so body appears to have only two sections; antennae shaped like very fat clubs; known mainly by their heavily black-stained pinholes deep in wood. In all major w-side conifers; common in BC.

Ambrosia beetles are named for their cultivation of "ambrosia" fungi for food. They carry the fungus with them and inoculate it into holes they bore in downed or dying trees. If moisture and other conditions are perfect, the fungus will grow just fast enough to feed the beetles and their larval brood without smothering them.

Though bark beetles also bring fungal allies to their attacks on trees, their food is still the tree cambium itself. Only ambrosia beetles get their nourishment directly from the fungus, which in turn gets it from the tree; since the fungus can break down even the hardest wood, ambrosia beetles are not confined to the tender layers under the bark, but burrow straight into the sapwood and sometimes the heartwood. The fungus stains the wood around each bore hole black, wreaking economic havoc on logs that are cut in the autumn and left out through winter.

Large fallen trees take several centuries to decompose, and would take longer still if the decomposers (fungi and bacteria) didn't have borers to make a rapid initial penetration of the protective bark. The forest ecosystem needs the logs to decompose in order to make both space and nutrients available for new plants.

INSECTS: MINOR ORDERS

Snakefly

Agulla adnixa (ag-YOU-la: big neck; ad-NIX-a: attached). Reddish ½-in. fly with striking long, flexible neck; dark head; veiny clear wings folded rooflike over back; ♀ has a long upcurved taillike ovipositor.

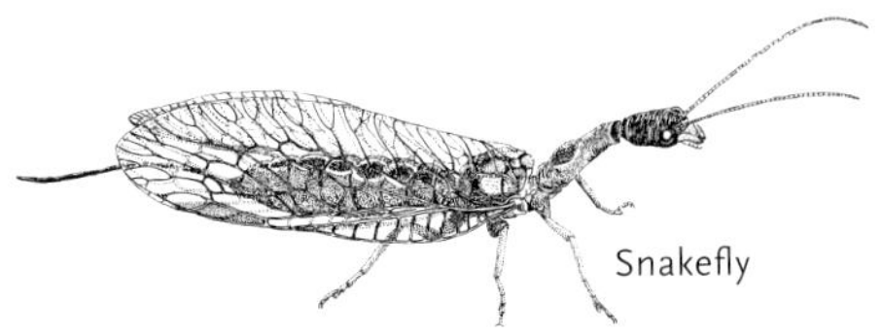
Snakefly

Orchardists value snakeflies as fierce predators of aphids. Their larvae are also beneficial, preying on wood-boring insects.

Ice Crawler

Grylloblatta chirurgica (grill-o-BLAT-a: cricket-cockroach; kye-RUR-ji-ca: surgical). Also rock crawler. Wingless; ⅜–1¼ in. long; amber to caramel color, cricket-like, with long arcing antennae and two tails. Nocturnal on snow or ice or on nearby rocks, or in caves.

This remarkable, primitive creature prefers temperatures near freezing, down to a few degrees below. Don't try holding one in your hand, as the warmth would soon kill it. You're less likely anyway to pick up the living beast than a hollow replica of one; that would be a molted exoskeleton left by one of the seven rather adultlike larval instars.

Ice crawlers scavenge on snow at night, subsisting on dead invertebrates dropped by the wind. Presumably that food resource held up pretty well in Mt. St. Helens's blast zone; within four years of the 1980 eruption, *G. chirurgica* had reinvaded.

By day they hole up in rock crevices near the snow. They've only been known to science since 1913, and were long thought to be strictly alpine and subalpine. It turns out forest populations (and species) exist, in areas with months of snow cover, active mainly in winter, in darkness. Some even

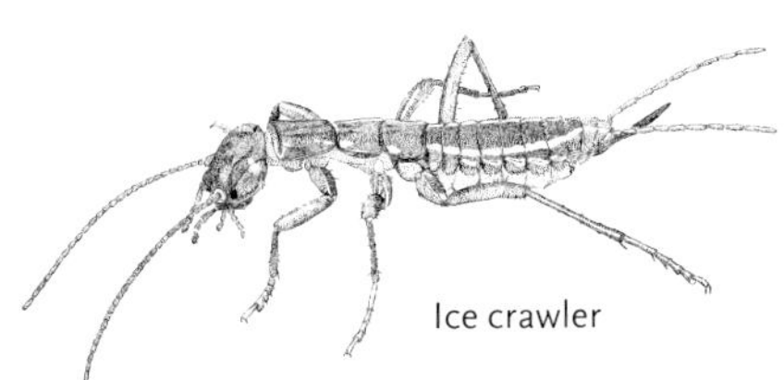
Ice crawler

live in deserts, in icy caves. At last count there were 6 named species in the Northwest, out of a total of 15, all in Asia and North America. They're all very similar, and *G. chirurgica* is no more common than the others. The number of species has risen steadily thanks to closer study, but several may prove to live on the brink, as their small ranges cease to enjoy prolonged snowpack.

Paddle-tailed darner

Sedge darner

Blue-eyed darner female placing eggs.

INSECTS: ODONATA (DRAGONFLIES AND DAMSELFLIES)

Darner

***Aeshna* and *Rhionaeschna* spp.** (EESH-na: misspelling of *aechma*, Greek for "spear"; rye-on: stream?). 2½ in. long; background color is dark brown; each flank of thorax has 2 diagonal pale stripes; face and abdominal dots also colorful. Ponds, lakes, bogs, fens.

Paddle-tailed darner, *A. palmata* (pal-MAY-ta: fanned out). Thorax stripes and face greenish yellow; dots on abdomen blue or (on some ♀) yellow. Widespread.

Sedge darner, *A. juncea* (JUN-sia: rush). Colored stripes and dots often grade from yellow-green to pale blue; thorax stripes wide. Mid- to high elevs; not in CoastR.

Blue-eyed darner, *R. multicolor* Also *Aeshna multicolor*. Eyes and entire face are bright blue, especially on ♂. Near ponds, often with pond-lilies; sometimes seen well away from water, including in cities. Low to mid-elevs.

Darners, some of the biggest, fastest dragonflies, reach 33 miles per hour intercepting prey. Dragonflies live in the fast lane, ceaselessly on the wing, feeding their high metabolisms with large numbers of unsuspecting mosquitoes and flies, quickly crushed and consumed. They may "hide" their approach by remaining in the same spot in the prey's peripheral vision, reacting instantly to prey's flight paths. In any case their predation success rates, flight speed, maneuverability, and brain executive function are all anomalously high, especially for their small brain size.

Both large size and icy waters tend to prolong development; our darners spend between two and five years as naiads.

Though they seek water for habitat,

darners also climb slopes to seek mates, in the same hilltopping behavior common in butterflies. Before seeking a mate, a male curls his abdomen down and attaches a sperm packet just behind his waist. To mate, he uses his tail-tip claspers to grasp a female by the head; she then curls her abdomen way down, forward, and up, to retrieve the packet. It's called the wheel position. Female darners often lay their eggs surreptitiously to escape the harassment of repeated attempts to mate, since most species' males don't guard their mates as some dragonflies do. In the wheel position both can fly perfectly well, facing forward. That's one advantage of long skinny abdomens.

Another is the long counterweight, for flight stability, and a third is thermoregulation: the abdomen's high surface-to-volume ratio makes it a good radiator for excess flying-muscle heat pumped out of the thorax. Giant dragonflies with 28-inch wingspans, back in the Carboniferous period, may have been among the first thermoregulators. (Insect gigantism was rife 300 million years ago, possibly thanks to a richer atmosphere. Plants had recently evolved to large sizes, but with dinosaurs still 50 million years off, a lot of oxygen was being produced and not as much consumed.) The abdomen also absorbs radiant heat: either basking or in flight, it gets positioned—east–west, north–south, up–down—to maximize or minimize heat absorption, as needed. Perching with the abdomen pointed toward the sun, to keep cool, is called the obelisk position.

Saffron-Winged Meadowhawk

Sympetrum costiferum (sim-PEE-trum: on rock, presumably to bask; cost-IF-er-um: veined). 1½ in. long; ♂ almost entirely dark red; ♀ reddish to greenish-tan; veins near front of wings tinged red to yellow; clear wing area amber-tinted in some ♀.

Our common smallish red dragonflies are the meadowhawks, of several species. Couples fly in tandem for several hours, sometimes over meadows. They drop the eggs while still in tandem, usually tapping them onto water, but sometimes on dry ground; to hatch they have to be inundated. This species may still be flying in November, outlasted only by the slightly brighter and smaller autumn meadowhawk, *S. vicinum*.

Mountain Emerald

Somatochlora semicircularis (so-mat-o-CLOR-a: body green). 2 in. long; eyes and thorax metallic green; 2 pale yellow spots beneath eyes; abdomen dull black. Sedge marshes and pond edges.

Dragonfly and damselfly larvae, as fiercely predacious as the adults, rank among the chief predators of mosquito larvae. The largest, at 2 inches, are big enough to take small tadpoles and fish. Dragonflies do without a pupal stage; instead, they metamorphose gradually through 10–15 larval instars called naiads. Some swim; more either burrow and wait for prey or crawl sluggishly on their six sturdy legs. Some use a kind of rectal jet propulsion for a burst of swimming speed.

Saffron-winged meadowhawk

Mountain emerald

They crawl up out of the water on an emergent stem when ready to molt and release their inner adult. It takes the new adult about one very vulnerable hour to straighten and stiffen its wings (by pumping blood in through the veins) for flight. The larval skin, split down the back, is left behind grasping the sedge stem.

Both larvae and adults hunt by eyesight, as they lack much in the way of hearing or smell. Adults' huge round compound eyes, comprising as many as 30,000 simple eyes, see in all directions at once. Adults use their legs to grasp prey, not to walk. They have four similar wings that gyrate in independent loops, enabling hovering and turning on a dime as well as straight-line speed. Males hover territorially while watching for females, or while guarding a mate until she lays eggs.

Hudsonian Whiteface

Leucorhinia hudsonica (loo-co-RYE-nia: white nose; hud-so-nic-a: of the Hudsonian Zone, i.e., subalpine). 1⅜ in. long; black with many deep red patches on thorax and all along abdomen (patches yellow on some ♀); white face below eyes; black dot near tip of clear wings; perches with wings below horizontal. Mid- to high-elev ponds and wet meadows.

Some of the females look like males; others substitute duller colors. (This is also true among our darners, dancers, and bluets.) This is puzzling. Different scientists hypothesize advantages in attracting either more or fewer males by looking just like one; but to most observers the males appear eager to mate with anything that moves on four long clear wings, regardless of either gender or species.

Hudsonian whiteface

Spreadwing

***Lestes* spp.** (LES-tease: robber). 1½ in. long; eyes blue on ♂, blue or brown on ♀; perch with wings angled outward.

Emerald spreadwing, *L. dryas* (DRY-us: wood nymph). ♂ metallic green with bluish iridescence; ♀ either similar or metallic copper. Marshes, fens, shallow vernal pool with sedges.

Spotted spreadwing, *L. congener* (CON-jener: of the same kind). Dull gray-brown with 2 or 4 darker spots on pale underside of thorax. Lakes, usually with cattails or bulrushes.

The wings-angled-upward attitude distinguishes this genus both from dragonflies

Emerald spreadwing

Spotted spreadwing

proper (suborder Anisoptera) who rest their wings out flat, and from its fellow damselflies (suborder Zygoptera) who fold their wings over the body. Damselfly eyes bulge out left and right like giant ear muffs, without meeting in the middle. Dancers and bluets are other damsels; darners, emeralds, and whitefaces fly with the dragons.

Many damselflies and some dragonflies become dull and dark when they cool off, helping them absorb heat more efficiently if the sun comes out again. They recover their brilliant colors when body temperature exceeds 68°F. Color also shifts with maturation.

Dancer

***Argia* spp.** (AR-gia: leisure). 1⅜ in. long; wings folded when at rest; bobs and weaves ("dances") in low flight; naiads live in streams, not ponds or bogs.

Vivid dancer, *A. vivida* ♂ brilliant blue (to blue-purple) with black bands. ♀ range from blue through purple-brown to brown.

Vivid dancers in tandem, or "wheel position."

Emma's dancer

US (and se BC); springs, small streams, irrigation ditches.

Emma's dancer, *A. emma* ♂ mostly lavender, except last two segments bluer; ♀ tan or pale blue-green. Rocky river banks.

Males of many damselflies have developed an organ that, as they commence mating, can pluck out and discard a sperm packet left by a previous male, and replace it with this male's own sperm packet. (See darners, p. 478, for dragonfly sex basics.) To reduce that risk, pairs fly around attached in tandem for several hours beginning with morning mating and ending with midday egg-laying. Using a pair of claspers at his abdomen tip to grasp her neck, he lifts her out of the water when she's done dipping her ovipositor to insert eggs onto a submerged leaf.

The vivid dancer probably spread into Canada during the 5000-year warm period that followed the last Ice Age, and then retreated south when things cooled. Geothermal warmth enabled a few to hang on near springs in British Columbia, including a couple in the northeast Coast Mountains.

NoBo Bluet

Northern bluet, *Enallagma annexum*, and boreal bluet, *E. boreale* (en-a-LAG-ma: crosswise; AN-ex-um: bound together).

NoBo bluet

1¼ in. long; ♂ abdomen brilliant to chalky blue with black bands; thorax has blue-and-black bands running its full length; blue eyes have a black dumbbell across the top; ♀ tan. Marshes and sedgey lake edges; also seen in tandem away from water.

Even experts can't tell these two species apart without putting them under a microscope, so in the field they revert to calling them "nobo" or "borthern" bluets. In the Columbia Basin these damselflies are sometimes numerous enough to cast a blue haze over a lake. A boreal bluet typically enjoys just four days of life as a reproductive adult.

INSECTS: LEPIDOPTERA (BUTTERFLIES AND MOTHS)

Aspen Leaf Miner

Phyllocnistis populiella (fill-oc-NIS-tiss: leaf rasp; pop-you-lee-EL-a: poplar—). Larva inside an aspen leaf, carving a pale, maze-like, gradually enlarging path, consuming a green epidermal layer one cell thick; adult a small drab moth. Gracillariidae.

Larvae that mine leaves evolved separately in moths, beetles, flies, and wasps; moths are most common. In each case the larva is flattened to fit between the leaf's two cuticles. This one infests and weakens aspens, occasionally reaching pest levels. From an egg laid near a leaf tip in May, a new larva makes a beeline for the leaf base, right alongside the midvein, but is so small that this part of its path is hard to see. Growing, it mows back and forth on one side of the midvein—an obstacle it will cross only where small, near the leaf tip. It may consume much of the second half of the leaf before spinning its silken cocoon and rolling the leaf edge around itself. If two mothers lay eggs on the same leaf, each larva typically settles for one side of the midvein; it sounds like nice resource partitioning, but they won't grow as big on half a leaf. More than two eggs per leaf often lead to cannibalism: a caterpillar overtaken from behind gets eaten.

Western Tent Caterpillar Moth

Malacosoma californicum (ma-la-co-SO-ma: soft body). Ws ¼–1½ in.; variably brown, forewing (the one in view when wings are folded) divided in thirds by two parallel fine lines; larvae (caterpillars) 2 in. when fully grown, bristling with tufted long hairs, generally dark brown with blue, orange, and reddish markings; egg masses plastered against twigs, especially at crotches, covered with a gray to dark brown foam that hardens to a nearly waterproof coating. Widespread on broadleaf trees and

Aspen leaf miner

Western tent caterpillars in a tent

Moths vs. Butterflies

Moths and butterflies together comprise the order Lepidoptera ("scaly wings"). The fine scales that cover them rub off easily, enabling them to escape sticky spider webs, and also play the lead role in their coloration. Some generalizations can be made about differences between the two, though there are exceptions to all except antenna shape:

Moths:

are mostly nocturnal;

have slender-tipped, or else fernlike, antennae;

have bigger bodies for their wing size;

may pupate in a chrysalis with an outer cocoon of silk;

raise their body temperatures before flying by vibrating their wings;

perch with wings spread to the sides, either flat or angled rooflike, forewings covering hindwings;

in some genera do all their eating in the larval stages.

Butterflies:

are diurnal;

have club-tipped antennae;

have smaller bodies relative to wings;

pupate in a naked, more or less rigid shell, or chrysalis;

warm their muscles before flying by basking in sunlight;

perch with left and right wings pressed together vertically, except (some families) when basking;

must eat as adults, not just as larvae.

shrubs; occasionally on conifers. Lasiocampidae.

Our region has an outbreak of tent caterpillars on red alder every ten years or so. Few alders die, but many are defoliated and achieve little growth for a year or two. Outbreaks are more often lethal to aspens, bitterbrush, or some of the other hosts.

The "tent" is a big erratic web of silk that affords caterpillar groups protection and insulation during resting periods between feeding sprees. Like their silkworm

Western tent caterpillar

relatives, tent caterpillars pupate within silken cocoons coated with a skin-irritating dust, under curled leaves. Adult tent caterpillar moths have no working mouthparts; they survive purely on what they ate as caterpillars, living just a few days to mate and lay eggs. (You can think of adult insects generally as ephemeral bridges from one larval generation to the next.) Tiny larvae are already formed within the egg cases by winter, ready to chew their way out when the leaf buds burst in spring. Larvae do most of the traveling as well as all the eating and growing; they have long bristles to help the wind carry them. Lacking wind, they crawl en masse. Tent-building, mass migration, group basking, and other social life rank them among the most social of caterpillars.

Trees are far from defenseless against foliage grazers. They need only slow the caterpillars' growth by a few percent to multiply the number taken by predators and parasites. They can do this by loading their leaves with tannin and other hard-to-assimilate chemicals. However, that requires an investment of energy that the trees do well to avoid, so they may load only some of their leaves with tannin, forcing the caterpillars to expose themselves to predatory birds while searching for palatable leaves. Or they may wait until attacked, and only then step up tannin production. Remarkably, trees may increase their tannin in response to an insect attack on a nearby tree of the same species, sensing chemicals (alarm pheromones?) cast upon the breeze by the attacked tree. This is among the clearest evidence to date of communication among plants. In the words of one enthusiastic scientist, "plants, after all, are really just very slow animals."

One-Eyed Sphinx Moth

Smerinthus cerisyi (smer-INTH-us: cord—; sair-ISS-ee-eye: for Alexandre de Cérisy). Also *S. ophthalmica*. Ws 2½–3½ in.; large heavy-bodied moth; bark-like camouflage pattern in gray to sepia; when threatened, exposes a dramatic black-blue-black eyespot within a pink smear on each of the small hindwings. Adult is nocturnal, attracted to lights, and does not feed; green larva eats willows and poplars, has a posterior horn. May–August. Sphingidae.

One recent study finds northwestern populations to be a distinct species, *S. ophthalmica*.

Black-Veined Forester

Androloma maccullochii (an-dro-LOW-ma: males fringed?) Ws 1⅝ in.; distinctive hairy yellowish shoulder pads on thorax; wide black margins surround cream patches divided by black veins; white fringe on trailing edge of wings; orange fur on upper legs; antennae threadlike, black-and-white-ringed on lower half; greenish-yellow larvae eat fireweed, sometimes stripping large patches. May–August. Noctuidae.

A few day-flying moths rival butterflies in beauty. This one and the police car moth (opposite) look rather similar except for their antennae, which show they are not closely related.

One-eyed sphinx moth

Black-veined forester

Police Car Moth

Gnophaela vermiculata (noff-EE-la: darkness—; ver-mic-you-LAY-ta: wormy-patterned). Also bluebell tiger moth. Ws 2 in.; wide black margins surround white patches divided by black veins; yellow-orange fur on cheeks; antennae plume-like; flight erratic. Bristly black-yellow larvae eat bluebells; adults often near goldenrod; mainly in WA. June–July. Erebidae or Arctiidae.

Police car moth

Swallowtail

***Papilio* spp.** (pa-PIL-ee-o: butterfly). Also *Pterourus* spp. Large butterflies with a "tail" lobe trailing each hindwing, dramatically black-patterned, often with blue or orange spots near tail. Papilionidae.

Anise swallowtail, *P. zelicaon* (zel-ic-AY-on: a name from *The Iliad*). Ws 2½–3½ in., yellow with black-lined veins, no tiger stripes crossing veins. Larvae eat desert-parsley, cow-parsnip, angelica, and other Apiaceae. April–September.

Police car moth caterpillar

Western tiger swallowtail, *P. rutulus* (ROOT-you-lus: a people known to Romans). Ws 3½–5 in., yellow with relatively narrow black tiger stripes across veins back from leading edge of wing, and along body. Abundant, often near water; larvae eat deciduous trees including willow and cottonwood. May–August.

Canadian tiger swallowtail, *P. canadensis* Also *P. glaucus*. Ws 2¼–3¼ in., smaller than western, but very similar; hindwing may be flushed with orange in its yellow area, or have one orange crescent above the yellow ones on margin. BC; Ferry County, WA. May–August.

Pale tiger swallowtail, *P. eurymedon* (you-RIM-e-don: broad guardian, i.e., the black margin). Ws 3½–4½ in., cream (♀) to whitish (♂) with broader black "tiger" stripes. Larvae eat red alder, snowbrush, not willow. May–August.

Anise Swallowtail

A Guy Worth His Salt

Butterflies congregating on moist earth are "puddling"—sipping water, and nutrients that come with it. This is very common behavior in blues and swallowtails, and also seen in a wider variety of insects. The vast majority of butterflies you see puddling are males, which offers a clue that this isn't primarily driven by thirst. Close observation finds some puddlers "pumping"—siphoning many times their body weight per hour in one end and out the other, extracting sodium from the water and adding potassium salts to the water they excrete. Plant leaves evolved potassium-sodium imbalance as a defense, and all kinds of herbivores suffer the effects and are driven to seek out sodium salt sources such as your urine or your pack straps (see porcupine, pp. 354–355). Puddlers love the mud around mineral spring seeps, or where a horse urinated on a trail.

Males gather nutrients and water to transfer them to a female when they mate. One spermatophore, or shot of ejaculate, commonly equals 15 percent of male body weight, and takes an hour to deliver. Zoologists call this a nuptial gift—something nutritious conveyed to a mate, which will nourish the progeny. For a bird, the appropriate wedding ring might be a berry, or a bug, but for a butterfly it's a big salty spermatophore. Both parents benefit when the female doesn't waste time puddling, and has more time to spend searching for the perfect spot to lay eggs.

Puddling is done by so many different animals that it's no surprise to find a variety of key ingredients in the spermatophore, not just sodium. In some species, the water itself, conveyed in gel form, is a meaningful gift. For others it's proteins, or nitrogen, the building block of proteins. That's why butterflies sip from protein-rich stuff like carrion and carnivore scats. To make sure the eggs are getting enough protein, a female will break down her own flight muscles if she's undernourished in nitrogen. By saving her from doing that, the nuptial gift lengthens her life and raises her number of egg clutches; some studies show it may not improve the health of individual larvae from that first clutch. That would be an example of a gift that increases her fitness but not necessarily the donor's.

Males of some whites accomplish the reverse, donating methyl salicylate, whose odor repels other males. For a few days that will benefit the female, protecting her from male harassment while she lays eggs; but after a point she is ready to mate again and would be better off not reeking of antiaphrodisiac. More broadly, females are unready to mate again until they have consumed the spermatophore, so bigger is always better from the male point of view.

Anise and pale swallowtails are often seen "hilltopping" on Hurricane Ridge and elsewhere; certain butterfly species use tall landmarks (trees, buildings, and even TV towers where hills are lacking) to help locate mates. The males arrive first, staking out sections of ridgeline and defending them against conspecific males while waiting for the females. Similarly, western tiger swallowtails use riverbanks, canyons, or other lineations of trees as their singles bars.

The larvae (caterpillars) flourish by late summer, and pupate over winter. The final instar of the anise swallowtail has striking black-and-yellow back bands against green, and is found on parsley-family plants such as garden fennel or anise. Late instars of the tigers have eyespots; these mock eyes function defensively, as do the antler-like scent glands that they stick out when disturbed. Early instars are camouflaged as bird droppings.

Western tiger swallowtail

Pale tiger swallowtail

Parnassian

***Parnassius* spp.** (par-NAS-ius: of Mt. Parnassus, home of the gods). Ws 2–3 in.; white with black and translucent gray markings and small red, often black-rimmed eyespots. Pupa in cocoon on or near soil. Papilionidae.

Mountain parnassian, *P. smintheus* (SMINTH-ius: a name of Apollo). Also *P. phoebus*. Fore- and hindwings usually with several red spots; antennae ringed black and white. BC and WA, above timberline, larvae black with gold dots, eat stonecrop. June–August.

Mountain parnassian

Clodius parnassian, *P. clodius* (CLOH-dius: a Roman emperor). Eyespots (usually 4) on hindwings only, antennae black. Widespread near forest edges; larvae feed on bleeding-heart; adults nectar on buckwheats. May–August.

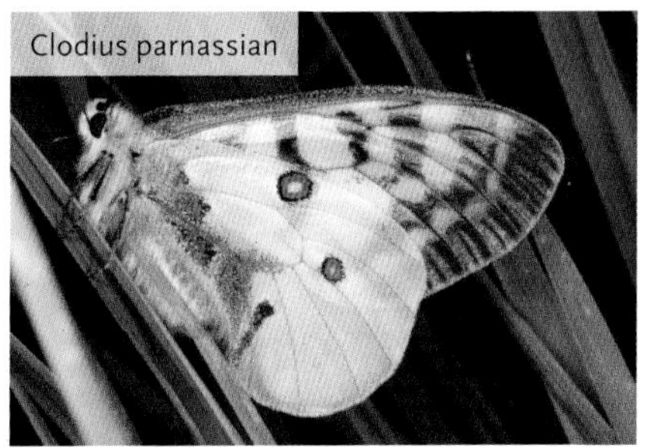
Clodius parnassian

The gray patches on parnassian wings actually just lack the minute scales that otherwise cover butterfly wings, leaving them translucent like the wings of bees or flies. Scales give butterfly and moth wings their opacity, color, and softness. Hundreds of scales dust your fingertips if you attempt to grasp a butterfly.

Female parnassians are usually seen with a waxy object on the rear end, which hardens from a liquid extruded by the male during mating, and blocks any subsequent mating. It is largest on *clodius,* whose mating style some scientists describe as rape.

Guppy and Shepard find that early snowmelt can be deadly for mountain parnassians, forcing them to begin feeding at a time of year when stonecrops are toxic to larvae. While ecologists have written papers assuming that many species will disappear from an area when it no longer has the climate they live in now, few studies have identified mechanisms that can actually cause that. This could be one such mechanism.

Western White

Pontia occidentalis (PON-sha: a name of Aphrodite; ox-i-den-TAY-lis: western). Also *Pieris occidentalis.* Ws 1¼–2 in.; white with variable degrees of gray checking, especially on top of forewing, and pastel gray-green to yellow-brown vein linings, especially under hindwing. Widespread in sun, especially on mountaintops; black-and-yellow larvae eat rockcress and other Brassicaceae. March–September. Pieridae.

Pairs of butterflies, especially whites and sulphurs, are often seen following each other upward in tall spirals. It is pleasing to think of these spiral flights as prenuptial stairways to heaven, but some observers see them as countererotic—an already-mated female's effort to escape an unwanted suitor by wearing him out in flight, or agonistic behavior between two males.

Margined White

Pieris marginalis (PIE-er-iss: a Greek Muse). Also veined white, mustard white; *P. napi, Artogeia napi.* Ws 1½–1¾ in., white, dark-stained near body; sometimes yellowish; early spring individuals have darkened veins. Widespread on moist cool sites; bright green larvae feed on mustard family. March–September (has two broods each year). Pieridae.

The introduced cabbage white, *P. rapae,* with forewing usually dark-spotted and -tipped, is a pest in vegetable gardens. This native feeds on native plants and is rarely seen in cities.

Pine White

Neophasia menapia (neo-FAY-zia: refers to another genus; men-AH-pia: Belgian?). Ws 1¾–2 in.; white with darker veins that are very fine on the ♂ and broad on ♀; forewing has blackish blotch pattern near tip and a short blackish bar extending inward from front edge; a bit of orange around margins, mainly on ♀. Green larvae eat pine and other conifer needles. June–October. Pieridae.

This is one of only three northwest butterflies that feed on conifers. Its populations

Western white

Margined white

erupt occasionally (1922, 1953, 2011) mainly east of the Cascades. They no longer seem to rank among the major pests. The eggs overwinter attached in very neat angled chains along pine needles. The larvae may respond to threats by regurgitating and waving their heads in unison.

Pine white

Western Sulphur

Colias occidentalis (COH-lius: a name of Aphrodite). Ws 1¼–2 in., yellow above, yellow or pale burnt orange below; usually with a dark dot on forewing and a white, dark-ringed dot on hindwing; ♂ has a blackish marginal band border. Larvae eat lupine, pea, and other legumes. May–September. Pieridae.

Western sulphur

Sulphurs bask with wings folded, often tipping to catch more sun on them. Two sulphur species with somewhat heavier dark margins are hyperabundant in croplands and other lowlands. The western sulphur gets up into our mountains more, though in gappy fashion, skipping most of the North Cascades, Coast Mountains, Coast Range, and central Oregon Cascades. A sulphur in those areas is likely *C. eurytheme*, or *C. philodice* on the east-side.

The Old English origins of the word "butter fly" most likely trace to a sulphur. (Sorry, it didn't originate as "flutter by.") The spelling "sulphur" started out spurious, an effort to make a Latin (or possibly Arabic) word look Greek. Spellings with *ph* and with *f* then contended in European languages for millennia. By 1900, the British had sided with sulphur, Americans with sulfur, and Canadians straddled the phence. By 2000, chemists of all three countries agreed that element 16 shall henceforth be sulfur. But lepidopterists, along with botanists and some geologists, thumb their noses at them.

Sara's Orange-Tip

Anthocharis sara (an-THOC-a-ris: flower grace). Ws 1¼–1¾ in., deep orange forewing tips above; gray-green marbling under

Sara's orange-tip

Spots and Tails

The dots framed in concentric rings that decorate many butterfly wings offer valuable protection from predators. Birds are fooled into pecking at the fake eyes, thinking them vital targets, but butterflies have little trouble flying with tattered wings. "Tails" on hindwings are similar diversionary ornaments.

We think that very large eyespots can do more, actually startling and repelling predators. The butterfly responds to an exploratory first peck by abruptly opening its folded wings; between the two "eyes" suddenly revealed, the bird imagines a larger face than it had meant to take on. Moths more often rest with wings spread. One-eyed sphinx moths (p. 484) keep the eyed part of the hindwing hidden under the forewing while they bask, well camouflaged against bark; they can quickly shift the forewings aside to reveal the eyespots.

Newly emerged butterflies go through a few hours when their wings are soft and useless. Wings first take form all wadded up in the pupa; as soon as the adult emerges it pumps fluids in through the veins to extend the wings to their proper shape. Then they need several hours to achieve rigidity. During those vulnerable hours, eyespots may save lives.

Ochre ringlet

Large wood nymph

hindwing; ground color white to (on ♀ only) yellow. Widespread in sunny habitats; bright green larvae feed on rockcress and perhaps relatives. An early flyer: late March (lowlands) to August (high). Pieridae.

Ochre Ringlet

Coenonympha tullia (see-no-NIM-fa: common nymph; TOO-lia: a daughter of Cicero). Also common ringlet; *C. ampelos*, *C. california*. Ws 1¼–1¾ in., rich ochre to straw all over except under hindwing, where gray-green divided by a pale zigzag bar; sometimes has one or more small eyespots beneath. CasR e-side, volcanic CasR, CoastR, VI; grass-green larvae eat grasses. April–October. Nymphalidae.

Wood Nymph

***Cercyonis* spp.** (ser-SIGH-o-nis: a son of the Sea God). Drab black-brown above, bark-like gray-brown beneath; two bullseye eyespots (sometimes indistinct) on each forewing, often yellow-rimmed; may have one or more much smaller eyespots on hindwings; flight erratic and dodgy. Green larvae eat grasses, adults various flowers as well as sap, dung, or carrion. Nymphalidae.

Large wood nymph, *C. pegala* (PEG-a-la: of springs). Ws 1¾–2¾ in.; second eyespot equal in size or slightly larger than the first; ♀ may be somewhat paler beneath than above. Nearly absent from nw WA. May–September, but aestivate in hottest summer.

Dark wood nymph, *C. oetus* (EE-tus: doom, i.e., blackness). Also least wood nymph. Ws 1½ in., second eyespot much smaller, sometimes inconspicuous. E-side. June–September.

Dark wood nymph

Common alpine

Alpine

***Erebia* spp.** (er-EE-bia: underworld, i.e., darkness). Ws 1½–2 in., both sides dark brown with black eyespots within orange marginal bands, at least on forewings. Stripy brown larvae eat grasses. WA and mainland BC. Nymphalidae.

Common alpine, *E. epipsodea* (ep-ip-SO-dia: like *E. psodea*). Also Butler's alpine. Nearly black, sometimes iridescent; hindwing has 3–4 roughly equal eyespots. E-side, all elevs, but prefers higher. May–August.

Vidler's alpine, *E. vidleri* (VID-ler-eye: for Captain Vidler). Short yellow-orange band on hindwing holds only one major eyespot; ashy band crosses hindwing underside. Alp/subalpine, from Mt. Rainier n. Late June–August.

Vidler's alpine

The adults bask in preparation for flight, augmenting their metabolic energy with solar energy collected in their wings.

Great arctic

Mourning cloak

Arctic

***Oeneis* spp.** (ee-NEE-iss: a mythic king). Orange-brown, except hindwing silvery gray-brown beneath; 1–3 smallish black eyespots on forewing, sometimes some on hindwing. Nymphalidae.

Great arctic, *O. nevadensis* (nev-a-DEN-sis: of the Sierra Nevada). Also Sierra Nevada arctic. Ws 2¼ in.; CasR e-side, VI, and disjunct at Saddle Mtn, OR. May–September.

Chryxus arctic, *O. chryxus* (CRIX-us: gold). Ws 1¾ in. Common here only in Okanogan NF and n-most OlyM. June–August.

Arctics, like anise swallowtails, feel a powerful drive to fly upslope. Ridgelines acquire dense, evenly spaced populations of hilltopping males, with scattered cameo appearances by eligible maidens foraying up from the more benign meadow environment. The male (lacking sharp eyesight) will rush out from his perch to greet any lepidopteran. If it's a conspecific he engages it in a spiral duet flight. While spiraling upward he sniffs out the visitor's gender, and the spiral ritual becomes either a courtship flight or a duel to defend his territory. A male's forewing bears a dark stain-like patch of pheromone-emitting scent scales.

Great arctics require more than a year of feeding to reach adulthood. They hibernate as an early-instar larva, then grow and molt a few times the following year before hibernating again in a late instar. On our mainland, nearly all great arctics fly in even-numbered years; Vancouver Island has both odd- and even-year populations.

Mourning Cloak

Nymphalis antiopa (nim-FAY-lis: nymph, a minor nature-deity; an-TIE-o-pa: a leader of Amazons). Ws 2–3¼ in.; dark red-brown above with cream yellow border lined with blue spots; drab beneath, a bark-like gray-brown with dirty white border; margins ragged. February–October. Nymphalidae.

The mourning cloak is familiar throughout the Northern Hemisphere. The adults hibernate—occasionally coming out to fly on sunny winter days—and sometimes aestivate through late summer. The caterpillars—black with black spines, white speckles, and a chain of red spots—feed on broadleaf trees and shrubs. Colonies of them may be tied together with silk threads, or may choreograph unison dances to scare off predators.

Brush-footed butterflies—the large and colorful family Nymphalidae—perch on four legs. The brush-like forelegs alongside their faces are too short to walk on, and instead have sense organs for taste-testing food.

California Tortoiseshell

Nymphalis californica Ws 1¾–2¼ in.; yellow-orange above with large black blotches on leading edge and a continuous black margin; mottled bark-like gray-brown beneath—like commas but with smoother wing outline. Widespread, occasionally abundant; larvae eat snowbrush and related plants. February–November. Nymphalidae.

Emerging from hibernation, California tortoiseshells are pale and ragged compared to the nonhibernating broods later in the year—two or even three generations a year in total. Their populations undergo wild boom-and-bust cycles for unclear reasons. During boom years, thousands of them swarm climbers, or smash against windshields as they stream through mountain passes, while the larvae defoliate snowbrush far and wide.

California tortoiseshell

Milbert's Tortoiseshell

Aglais milberti (a-GLAY-iss: Brilliance, one of the Graces; mil-BEAR-tee: for Jacques-Gérard Milbert). Also *Nymphalis milberti*. Ws 1¾ in.; dark brown above with two orange blotches on leading edge and a broad orange and yellow (to white) band just inside the narrow dark brown margins (not really a tortoiseshell pattern); brown beneath, the outer half paler. Common in high meadows, but also anywhere with nettles, the larval food; adults visit daisies. January (venturing out from hibernation) to October. Nymphalidae.

Milbert's tortoiseshell

Clusters of 20 to 900 pale green eggs—or bristly small black web-spinning caterpillars—on nettles are likely those of Milbert's tortoiseshell.

Green Comma

Polygonia faunus (poly-GO-nia: many angles; FAW-nus: a faun such as Pan). Also faun anglewing. Ws 1⅞ in., wing margins lobed erratically, as if tattered; burnt orange above with dark margins and scattered black blotches; gray-brown beneath, with a row of blue-green blotches (sometimes indistinct) near wing margins, and with inconspicuous tiny boomerang-shaped silver-white mark (the comma). Forest openings; bristly larvae eat willow, alder, rhododendron, etc. March–September. Nymphalidae.

Green comma

Green comma underside

Commas (or anglewings) flit about almost too fast to follow, then alight on a tree and disappear. (They are amazingly camouflaged against bark as soon as they fold their wings.) They overwinter as adults, tolerate cold, have been seen flying in every month of the year, and are conspicuous in September when they must gorge before hibernating. Late-blooming asters and berry-rich mammal scats are a food sources in fall, the sap around sapsucker holes in spring. Similar hoary comma, *P. gracilis*, is especially limited to higher elevations, where its larvae feed on currant leaves. Its marginal blotches are dull yellow-green.

West Coast Lady

Vanessa annabella Ws 1⅞ in., orange above with black tortoiseshell mottling and white dots near forewing tip, row of 4–5 tiny eyespots near hindwing margin; the bar near leading edge of forewing, surrounded by black, is orange on *V. annabella*, white on painted lady, *V. cardui*; underside mostly marbled dark brown with some cream, orange on forewing only. Larvae eat mallows and nettles. Occasionally ubiquitous. March–November. Nymphalidae.

The painted lady, possibly the world's most widely known butterfly, has close relatives named West Coast and American ladies. All three find our winters chilly, and populate the Northwest mainly by migrating northward in spring, breeding another two or three generations as they go. *Annabella* is the one you are likely to see in the most years. The painted lady proper, *V. cardui*, is hyperabundant here in occasional outbreak years (averaging nine years apart) but is scarce or absent in between—unless you happen across survivors from a farm-bred flock released at a wedding. (Lepidopterists are not happy about these commercial releases.)

Feminine first names are rife among butterfly scientific names. In most cases, like Vanessa, we have no record that a particular girl or woman was the honoree, but in this case Annabella is the namer's daughter.

Lorquin's Admiral

Limenitis lorquini (lim-en-EYE-tiss: harbor goddess; lor-CAN-ee: for Pierre J. M. Lorquin). Also *Basilarchia lorquini*. Ws 2½ in.; black above except red-orange forewing tips and a heavy white band (broken by black veins) across both wings parallel to margin; underside striped russet and white; flies with twitch-like beats alternating with gliding. Diverse habitats; larvae eat willow and other deciduous leaves; late instars have "antlers" on their tail ends. May–October. Nymphalidae.

The handsome admiral male is a scavenger of dung and dead things, as well as a nectar-feeder.

Greater Fritillary

***Speyeria* spp.** (spy-ER-ia: for Adolph Speyer). Also *Argynnis* spp. ♂ tawny orange with checker-like black markings above;

West coast lady

Lorquin's admiral

hindwing gray to golden tan beneath, with many round silvery-white to cream spots in both sexes; forewing golden brown beneath, with dark brown checks. Black larvae (sometimes showing orange spots or spine bases) eat violets. May–September. Nymphalidae.

Hydaspe fritillary, *S. hydaspe* (hi-DAS-pee: a river or a king). Ws 2 in.; sexes similar; underside has marginal white spots, hindwing redder rusty brown, pale mid-wing spots cream, rarely silvery. Moist montane forest.

Great spangled fritillary, *S. cybele* (SIB-el-ee: Sibyl, an earth-mother deity). Also *S. leto*. Ws 2¾ in.; ♀ blackish to chestnut brown with broad pale yellow patterned margin; pale spots on hindwing underside are silvery. Often near streams, lowland.

The greater fritillaries are easy on the eyes, hard to tell apart. Hydaspe is most often seen here; great spangled is largest, and the most sexually dimorphic—that is, the black or brown females look utterly different from the colorful males. The female aestivates (like hibernating but in summer) for a few July weeks after mating, then reawakens in August to lay the eggs. The larvae hatch in fall but don't eat or grow much until spring.

Hydaspe fritillary

Great spangled fritillary

Lesser Fritillary

***Boloria* spp.** (bo-LOR-ia: net—). Also *Clossiana* spp. Ws 1½ in.; both sexes tawny yellow-orange above with broad, fine patterns in brown (compared to checkerspots, the orange is paler, yellower, and there's much more of it than of brown). Larvae dark and bristly. Nymphalidae.

Pacific fritillary, *B. epithore* (ep-ITH-or-ee: like *B. thore*, named for Thor). Also western meadow fritillary. Bright yellow-orange above, lacking a continuous dark margin; biggest yellow cell on hindwing underside is "anvil-shaped." Sunny openings throughout our range; larvae eat violets. May–September.

Pacific fritillary

Arctic fritillary

Arctic fritillary, *B. chariclea* (car-ic-LEAH: see below). Also purplish fritillary; *B. montinus*, *B. titania*. Hindwing rust and cream beneath, with a central row of spots that may show as lavender. BC and WA, above 3000 ft.; larvae eat diverse subalpine plants. June–September.

Boloria is a montane and boreal genus. The name fritillary (in both lilies and butterflies) refers to a Roman dice-box with checkered markings.

In the *Aethiopica* (one of the five ancient Greek romantic novels) Heliodorus tells the story of Chariclea, daughter of King Hydaspes and Queen Persina. They are black, and she fair, landing her in a world of trouble from birth. She triumphs. I think naming this butterfly for her was meant to imply a smaller, paler close relative of the hydaspe fritillary.

Hoffmann's Checkerspot

Chlosyne hoffmanni (clo-SIGH-nee). Ws 1½ in.; upperside mostly blackish to halfway out, then a yellow band giving way to orange with dark brown checkering; orange and cream bands on underside. Only in CasR; larvae (black with cream side lines) and adults both feed on asters. May–August. Nymphalidae.

Edith's Checkerspot

Euphydryas editha (you-FID-rius: shapely nymph). Ws 2 in.; ♂ upperside has rows of blackish, red-orange and pale yellow cells in roughly equal measure; undersides and ♀ upperside paler because blackish scales occurs only as fine lines; under hindwing, a fine dark line separating two rows of red confirms *editha*. Meadows and rocky sites at all elevations; larvae eat paintbrush, lousewort, and relatives. April–August. Nymphalidae.

The larvae hibernate communally, nesting amid skeletonized leaves, after their third instar. The handsome pupae are cream with black and yellow markings. Identifying the notoriously variable checkerspots often requires studying their genitalia under a microscope. If it's mostly black above, with red-orange traces near the tips and front edge, and it's near snowberry, it's likely a snowberry checkerspot, *E. colon*.

Field Crescent

Phyciodes pulchella (fis-EYE-o-deez: painted?; pool-KEL-a: beautiful). Also *P. campestris*, *P. pratensis*. Ws 1¼ in., largely black-brown above with rows of red-orange and yellow-orange spots, the outermost spots crescent-shaped; low-contrast pale orange-yellow-brown patterns beneath, forewing usually black-edged. E-sides in

Hoffmann's checkerspot

Edith's checkerspot

WA, more widespread in OR; larvae eat asters. May–September. Nymphalidae.

Field crescents extend their season, as a species, by staggering their emergences from pupation. Mylitta crescent, *P. mylitta*, is 1½ inches across, with somewhat more orange than dark colors above. Feeding on thistles, it is ubiquitous, with a lowland emphasis.

Field crescent

Copper

***Lycaena* spp.** (lie-SEE-na: of a Greek mountain). Also *Epidemia* spp. Ws 1 in.; ♂ dark brown above with purplish iridescence; ♀ cocoa brown with dull orange highlights. Lycaenidae.

Purplish copper, *L. helloides* (hel-OY-deez: like species *helle*). Ws 1 in.; ♂ strongly iridescent; orange zigzag along hindwing margin, both sides, both sexes; underside pale yellow-orange with dark spots mainly on forewing. Very widespread; bright green larvae eat knotweed and sorrel. May–September.

Purplish copper

Mariposa copper, *L. mariposa* (mair-ip-OH-sa: butterfly). Ws 1 in.; ♂ slightly iridescent; orange zigzag mainly on ♀ hindwing, but often negligible; hindwings ashy gray beneath with dark chevrons, forewings yellow-orange beneath with speckles. Mid- to high-elev meadows, bogs; not in CoastR; larvae eat huckleberry foliage. June–September.

Iridescence is common among tropical butterflies. Here we find it in coppers—small brown butterflies going, in Bob Pyle's words, "from penny-brown to neon purple in the flash of a sunbeam." Iridescent butterfly scales may have microscopic ridges that reflect light prismatically, or they may be of two types on one butterfly, regularly interspersed on the wing surface and held at different angles—not unlike the way fabric designers combine contrasting warp and weft threads to weave an iridescent satin.

The purplish copper hedges its overwintering strategy: some eggs overwinter before

Mariposa copper

Hedgerow hairstreak

Boisduval's blue: An unusually fresh and bright male.

Female Boisduval's blue.

Anna's blue

hatching, others hatch into larvae that will face winter.

Hedgerow Hairstreak

Satyrium saepium (sa-TEE-rium: satyr—; SEE-pee-um: of hedges). Ws 1⅛ in.; coppery above with one oval spot on ♂ forewing, tan-brown beneath with a small bluish patch at hind corner; hindwing has 1 or 2 small thin tails. Brushy canyons, OR CasR, and e-side in WA and BC; larvae eat *Ceanothus*. May–September. Lycaenidae.

Blue

***Plebejus* spp.** (pleb-EE-us: ordinary). Ws 1–1⅜ in.; ♂ blue above, ♀ brown; white marginal fringes; gray to dirty white beneath, with rows of spots much darker on forewing than hindwing. Lycaenidae.

Boisduval's blue, *P. icarioides* (ic-airy-OY-deez: like species *icarus*) Also common blue; *Icaricia icarioides*. No orange anywhere—crescents near margin are at most just a touch rusty; underside spots are pronounced black with white rims on forewing, just white on hindwing. Anywhere with lupines, the larval (and sometimes adult) food. April–September.

Anna's blue, *P. anna*. Also *Lycaeides anna*, *L. idas*. Often has a row of orange crescents parallel to margin, on underside of blue ♂, and on both sides of brown ♀; underside may lack dark spots. Common mainly above 3000 ft.; larvae eat lupine and other Fabaceae. June–October.

Arctic blue, *P. glandon* (GLAN-don: a pass in the Alps). Also *Agriades glandon*, *A. franklinii*. Ws 1 in.; ♂ gray-blue above with black border; underside spots are black with white rims on forewing, mostly just white on hindwing. BC and WA above 5000 ft.; dark red larvae overwinter on the dark red stems of their host plant, spotted saxifrage. June–August.

Arctic blue

Summit blue

Scarce and drab, the arctic blue is nonetheless conspicuous from time to time as the only butterfly flying in gray weather on high windswept ridges. It ranges around the Arctic Circle in the lowlands, and ventures southward along the Cordilleran summits.

Summit Blue

Euphilotes glaucon (you-fill-OH-teez: after genus *Philotes*; GLAW-con: gray-blue). Also *E. battoides*. Ws 7/8 in.; ♂ blue above, ♀ brown; marginal fringes checkered black or white; grayish beneath with black spots all over; an orange arc parallel to the hindwing margin of hindwing only, often very dim on ♂. OR and WA; the larvae eat sulphurflower. July–August. Lycaenidae.

Caterpillars of these blues are attended by ants who eat "honeydew" secreted by the caterpillars. In this mutualistic symbiosis, the "stock-herding" ants sometimes attack and repulse beetles that parasitize caterpillars.

Among the "dotted blues," genus *Euphilotes*, the trend is to recognize a distinct species for each species of *Eriogonum* buckwheat as larval host. With some 250 species of *Eriogonum*, this could keep lepidopterists busy for a while. Visible differences among the new segregates have been discerned, but may overlap.

Elfin

***Callophrys* spp.** (ca-LOFF-ris: beautiful eyebrow). Also *Incisalia* spp. Lycaenidae.

Western pine elfin, *C. eryphon* Ws 1 in.; fast flyer; brown, richly patterned above and even more so beneath; hindwing purplish beneath; a very fine white zigzag line divides inner from outer portion of each wing, on both sides; older larvae pine-needle green, with paired whitish lengthwise stripes. Often abundant near pines, the larval food plant. April–July.

Moss's elfin, *C. mossii* Ws 7/8 in.; brown, with brown- or white-dashed fringe, especially on hindwing; two-toned beneath, the paler outer sections divided from darker

Western pine elfin

Richardson and Franklin

Scottish naturalist John Richardson went on John Franklin's first and second expeditions into Arctic Canada. The first was beset by starvation and cannibalism. Cartographer Robert Hood wrote the first explanation of the Aurora Borealis as an electrical and magnetic phenomenon, and then was murdered. Richardson shot Hood's murderer and rescued Franklin, and they escaped with their lives, but without Richardson's specimens. It was game of them to try again three years later; but the second expedition went relatively well. Soon, both were knighted. Richardson wrote a fauna of boreal North America, and stayed home from Franklin's tragic third expedition, which ended with all members starving, freezing, or getting eaten. He then commanded a ship in one of the many futile Franklin Party rescue attempts. One of Franklin's ships was finally found 167 years later, in 2014. Thanks to climate change, tourists will soon cruise the Northwest Passage that Franklin found so lethally impenetrable.

inner sections by a slight white line. Rocky, sunny sites with stonecrop, the larval food. March–early May.

Brown elfin

Brown elfin, *C. augustinus* (august-EYE-nus: for a helpful Inuit man nicknamed Augustus by Sir John Richardson, above). Also *Incisalia iroides*. Ws 7/8 in.; brown above, without white fringe; warm orange or even purplish brown beneath with faint dark patterning. Widespread; larvae eat salal buds and flowers, many other shrubs. March–July.

Moss's elfin is the first butterfly to emerge from a pupa in spring, sometimes while snow still covers much of the ground. Any other butterflies flying then (commas or tortoiseshells, most likely) hibernated as adults.

OTHER CREATURES

Western Black-Legged Tick

Ixodes pacificus (ick-so-deez: like birdlime, i.e., sticky). Small tick: adults about the size of this symbol: *ϕ* (distinctly smaller than the more common dog tick). With a 12× magnifying glass, you should be able to see eight legs from near the head end, and a flat oval abdomen with a dark central oval and paler red perimeter. Phylum Arthropoda, Arachnida.

Ticks are related to mites, and more distantly to spiders. This group has eight legs and two main body sections, as opposed to insects with six legs and three sections. The pale outer portion of the tick abdomen expands several-fold when engorged with blood. Ticks live by sucking blood. They climb to the tips of grasses or shrubs and wait for a chance to brush off onto a host. Western black-legged ticks typically parasitize deer, deer mice, lizards, and birds.

This is the tick that carries Lyme disease in the West. Fortunately, we don't see it very often in our mountains. (We see the much larger dog tick more often, mainly in grassy east-side areas.) But Lyme disease does occur here, and can be a severe and long-lasting illness, so it's worth knowing what to look for.

If you find a tick on you and can brush it off easily, you haven't been bitten yet, so don't worry. If it has taken hold, pluck it carefully. Use tweezers if available, grab the tick firmly by the head, not the abdomen, and tug gently, straight out. Then swab the area with antiseptic or antibiotic.

Deer ticks (the group including *Ixodes*) have a two-year, three-stage life cycle—larva, nymph, and adult. Each stage needs one blood meal from a vertebrate host. For nymphs, lizards are the preferred host, but small rodents also serve. The rodents are usually where a western black-legged tick picks up the Lyme disease spirochete. Lizard blood, in contrast, kills spirochetes; even a nymph that already picked up spirochetes during its larval meal will be disease-free after feeding on a fence lizard or an alligator lizard. That is the likely reason why Lyme disease is persistently uncommon in West Coast ticks—less than 3 percent in *Ixodes pacificus.*

Even ticks that have the germ rarely transmit it in the first day of sucking your blood, so antibiotics are not recommended unless an antibody test confirms the disease. Watch the area where the tick bit for a rash over the next 3 to 30 days—not just an ordinary immediate red bump, but a red rash that heats up and continues to spread for days. The rash may or may not show the telltale "bull's-eye" pattern. If you get the rash, see a doctor, who should prescribe a test after antibodies have had time to build up. If you test positive, antibiotics will usually stop Lyme disease.

Unfortunately, some victims go straight to the disease without ever getting the rash,

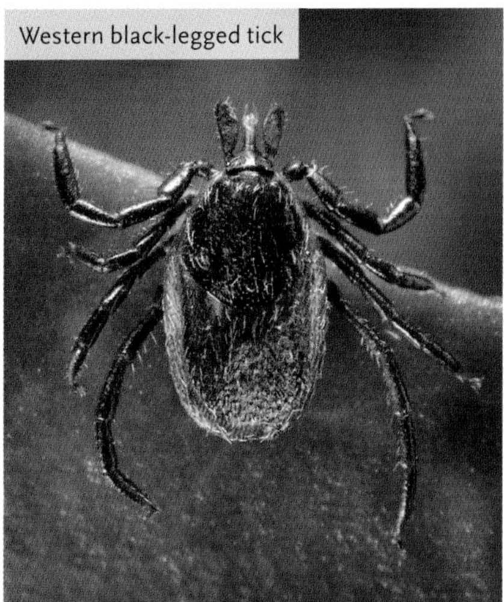
Western black-legged tick

and some are never aware of their tick bite. You can get the disease from nymph-stage ticks; half as big as adults, and paler, nymphs rarely get noticed and removed promptly. So get tested for Lyme if you develop these symptoms within a month after any rural outing: flu-like neck stiffness, fever and chills, jaw discomfort, painful muscle or joint stiffness, swollen glands, red eyes. Even at this stage, antibiotics usually work. If untreated for a few years, Lyme disease can cause irreversible neurological problems, heart problems, or a type of arthritis.

Confusion and controversy have embroiled Lyme disease, at least partly because there turn out to be many species of the genus *Borrelia* involved, producing overlapping but different symptoms, possibly interacting with each other in combination, and responding to different tests.

Banana slugs mating

Banana Slug

Ariolimax columbianus (airy-o-LIE-max: compound of slug genera *Arion* and *Limax*; co-lum-be-AY-nus: of the Columbia River). Large slugs (commonly 4–6 in., up to 10 in. when crawling); back netted with fine, dark, mostly lengthwise grooves; smooth mantle caps about 1/4 of its length, at front; large breathing hole near right-hand edge of mantle; color variable, typically olive; blackish blotches vary from covering most of the slug to a single spot on the mantle, or no spots at all. W-side forest floor. Phylum Mollusca, Gastropoda.

Slugs are snails that lost their shells during evolution. (Banana slugs actually retain a small vestigial shell, buried in their mantle.) Slugs live almost exclusively in moist, shady regions, often with calcium-poor volcanic soils—in other words, regions short on the chief raw material (calcium) and the chief need (drought) for shells, whose primary function is to conserve moisture. Slugs, when they need to conserve water, retreat under vegetation or earth and shrink to a fraction of their crawling length. They are active by night and in dim, humid daytime conditions, when humidity can be absorbed to replenish water expended in slime. They lose more water by exuding slime than via evaporation from the skin. Slime has a remarkable ability to shift instantaneously from tacky to slippery when the muscle on top of it contracts, and back to tacky when it relaxes. Crawling consists of small contractions rippling rearward, with each little section of the slug's sole alternately gripping and sliding forward.

Many slugs load their slime with bitter or caustic chemicals, to make up for lacking a protective shell. Salamanders have been seen consuming slugs, but overall the rate of predation is low. (Northwesterners of French and German extraction who fry and eat banana slugs bathe them first in vinegar to remove the slime. They say slugs aren't all that different from escargots.) A few use bright color to advertise the nasty taste; "banana slug" refers to the chrome yellow color of the southernmost races (if that word can be used for slugs) of this species and some congeners. Slugs of another Northwest genus, *Prophysaon,* decoy predators by shedding their tails, like lizards.

Slugs identify potential mates by touch, their only well-developed sense. To identify conspecifics they have various palpable structures—tiny sharp darts, delicately branched sperm packets, and overdeveloped penises—peculiar to each species. Slugs are hermaphrodites. In some, individuals produce sperm and eggs asynchronously, making self-mating impossible. In our banana slug, fertility is synchronous; two slugs may fertilize each other in one multi-hour entwining. Notoriously, banana slugs occasionally conclude mating by chewing off each other's penises. In one hypothesis, this happens when the long penises get stuck; alternatively, they might be nutritious. Banana slug penises are large, but nothing like those of one race in the Alps—32½-inch tumescences dangling from 6-inch slugs.

A slug eats many kinds of fungi and plants, rasping away at them with a tongue covered with several thousand minute teeth.

Ice Worm

Mesenchytraeus solifugus (mez-en-kit-REE-us: after genus *Enchytraeus*; so-lif-YOU-gus: fleeing the sun). Also snow worm, glacier worm. Slender body, 3/8–1 in. long, black, segmented or ringed by fine constricted bands. Evening, night, and early morning on glaciers, in spring and summer. Phylum Annelida.

Snow worms are segmented worms (oligochaete annelids) related to the enchytrae cultured and sold as aquarium food, and not too distant from leeches and earthworms. They eat snow algae (p. 504), and may get eaten by birds like dippers and rosy finches. Some kinds of spiders, insects, and nematodes (more primitive worms) are also adapted for life in snow. All are active at temperatures around 32°F, and able to survive temperatures a bit colder than that either by dehydrating to prevent tissue freezing, or by restricting freezing to their intercellular spaces. Both strategies require synthesis of special proteins to lower the freezing point of cell protoplasm to well below 32°F.

The North Cascades Glacier Climate Project calculated that the Suiattle Glacier alone held 7 billion ice worms in 2002.

Giardia

Giardia intestinalis (JAR-dia: for Alfred Giard). Also *G. duodenalis, G. lamblia.* Classification moot.

In a paper titled "My Favorite Cell: *Giardia*," two Australian parasitologists rhapsodized over giardia—"the only microorganism we know to smile." Their affection is inspired less by the smile than by *Giardia*'s unusual traits bridging the realm of protozoa with that of bacteria. (The Tree of Life project places them in a group called Fornicata, meaning arched. No sexual processes have been seen in *Giardia*.)

More to the point for hikers, it is a leading culprit worldwide in persistent diarrheal infections. Giardiasis is unquestionably an unpleasant experience; the drugs prescribed for it have unpleasant side effects, and don't always work on the first try; and for some people symptoms can linger long after the parasite is eliminated.

That said, the specter of giardia lurking in mountain streams has kicked around decade after decade without ever being scientifically demonstrated. Scientists who looked for it in streams in a popular part of the Sierra Nevada didn't find enough to worry about. A meta-study concluded that "education efforts aimed at outdoor recreationists should place more emphasis on handwashing than on water purification." In other words, the (rather weak) association between giardiasis and camping isn't about the water up there, it's about the hot water and soap that *aren't* up there next to the latrines.

So, decide for yourself. To avoid all risk of giardiasis, follow all the rules about

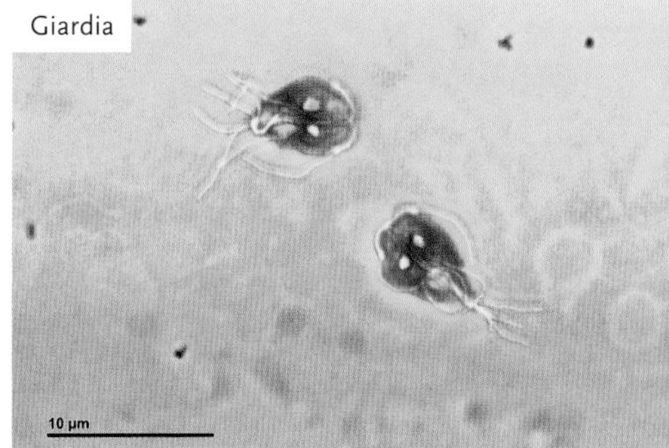

Giardia

Sun Cups

Snowfield surface low spots of a certain size amplify themselves by reflecting light to their centers, enhancing melting there. Infrared radiation bounces off of the white ridges between cups, but is absorbed by thin dirt (or algae) that gravitates into the low spot. This process eventually creates a pattern of sun cups. Dirty boot prints incorporate themselves into the pattern. But thick debris, like a conifer branch, insulates the snow, prevents melting, and ends up as a cap on a ridge. With just the right dirt and weather, the little peaks between cups can grow into slender towers, called *penitentes* in the Andes, where some reach 20 feet high.

purifying water. As for me, I'm going to continue prostrating myself to the mountain stream goddess and drinking deeply—at least at selected streams descending from trail-free drainages. I'll purify water in drainages that are heavily trodden. By humans.

What about beavers, water voles, and other giardia carriers? Yes, a great many vertebrate animals carry giardia, but many of those *Giardia* species don't infect humans. The often-heard claim that beavers are responsible for outbreaks in humans has, again, never been proven, and the scientific literature is increasingly skeptical. The clearest correlations with giardiasis are things like community swimming pools, living around farm animals, sharing a household with a person or pet with giardia, and other old standbys of what epidemiologists call the "fecal-oral route."

For every person reporting the symptoms, there are somewhere between ten and a thousand people carrying giardia but never getting symptoms. From that we can infer, first, that there are a lot of people out there to get it from; second, even if you get it, you probably won't get it; third, many of us are carriers and may not know it. That's why it behooves us to be totally scrupulous about burying our solid wastes or packing them out, and disinfecting our hands—gel hand sanitizers apparently work well.

If you go trekking in the developing world, where the water is riskier than in our mountains, take purification very seriously. You may face viruses or bacteria that require more stringent purification than giardia does.

Watermelon Snow

Chlamydomonas nivalis (clam-id-o-MO-nus: mantled unit; ni-VAY-lis: of snow). Classification moot.

Pinkness in late-lying snowfields consists of pigments in living algae. These algae are the producers in an entire food cycle in snow. Ice worms, protozoans, spiders, and insects graze on the algae, and are eaten in turn by predators like the rosy finch. Droppings

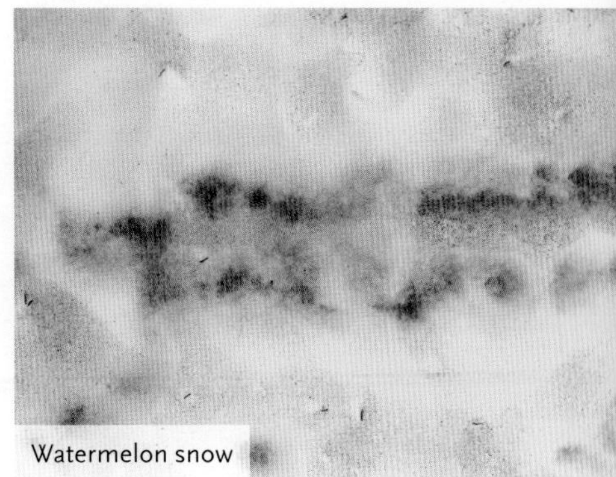
Watermelon snow

from the predators, bodies of producers and grazers, and pollen and spiders blown from downslope provide food for decomposers (bacteria and fungi) that complete the cycle. The algae live on decomposition products and on minerals that blow in as dust.

Most of the pinkness is in energy-storing oils within resting spores that sit out the winter wherever they happen to end up in the fall. In spring, under many feet of new snow, they respond to increasing light and moisture by releasing four daughter cells that swim up to the surface and turn from green to red. The red pigments protect the alga against ultraviolet damage, as they do many other plants—and now humans? Pink snow is harvested for use in cosmetics that claim to protect human skin against UV damage, moisture loss, collagen loss, and aging.

Some say watermelon snow smells or tastes like watermelon; others warn of diarrhea.

Chlamydomonas nivalis is our most abundant among the 100 or more named species of snow algae. Most are red, but some are yellow, green, or purple. With plants they share chlorophyll and a cellulose-like cell wall, but their swimming ability and well-developed eyespot are animal-like. The Whittaker five-kingdom system took green algae out of the plant kingdom and into a kingdom Protista, but some systematists now put them back in with the plants.

GEOLOGY

Have you ever thought that the Pacific Northwest is not really part of North America? There's a geologic basis for that. The continental crust under us is a mosaic of terranes, pieces that originated as Pacific island chains and were carried (by tectonic plates) to the shores of a pre-existing North America less than 250 million years ago. Geologists often speak of that older block, assembled for well over half a billion years, as North America, and of our terranes as exotic.

By 40 million years ago the terranes were all docked against North America, and the Cascadia Subduction Zone was in operation just offshore, where it remains today, producing the Cascade arc of volcanoes. Magma (molten rock) of the arc rose up through terrane rocks, covering them completely in the Cascades from northern California to around Mt. Rainier, and incompletely north of there.

Thus, most rocks you see in our mountains are either exotic terrane rocks more than 45 million years old, or igneous rocks produced by volcanism. In the United States part, those igneous rocks are nearly all younger than 45 million years. Subsequently, some of those rocks were recycled through erosion and compaction into young sedimentary rocks, which constitute the core of the Olympic Mountains but only minor elements of the Cascades and British Columbia mountains.

Cascade arc volcanism produced most, but not all, of the younger, igneous category. Exceptions include youngish basalts in the Coast Range, and Columbia River Basalt (p. 512) locally in southern Washington and northern Oregon. The latter underlies vast parts of eastern Washington and Oregon. Overall, Oregon has a higher proportion of volcanic rocks at the surface than any state or province other than Hawaii.

The terranes contribute a splendid variety of rock types and ages, as well as profound mysteries about their back stories. A broad-strokes picture of mountain-building will be helpful before I summarize those terrane stories on pages 514–516.

Plate Tectonics

The earth's surface is divided into large plates, which move. They grind along at speeds of a few inches per year. Convergence between them produces mountains. There are seven huge plates and many small ones.

New plate material is generated out of fresh basalt lava at mid-ocean ridges, where two plates move apart; material plunges back into the depths at subduction zones, where plates converge head-on and one overrides the other. The new plate material is oceanic crust, a sheet of basalt rock averaging four miles thick. Under an ocean for millions of years, the sheet may accumulate thick beds of marine sediments on top, which gradually become sedimentary rocks. All seven big plates carry some oceanic crust, and many also carry continental crust—thicker but less dense crust of many kinds of rock, but predominantly granitic.

You can think of crust as floating. Due to its thickness and low density, continental crust rides high upon its semifluid underpinnings; very little of it is covered with seawater. Conversely, most oceanic crust floats lower and does lie under seawater.

What the crust "floats" on is the mantle layer. (Complicating things, the plate layer or lithosphere is not quite the same as the crust layer: it includes all of the crust *plus* a top layer of the mantle. The plate is still a thin skin relative to the thickness of the entire mantle, which goes more than halfway to the center of the earth, ending at the core-mantle boundary. Plate motion separates lithosphere from the rest of the mantle, whereas chemistry and density distinguish crust from mantle.)

Since no one can ever see below the crust, geologists' speculations regarding the force that drives the plates are a bit like the proverbial descriptions of an elephant by several seeing-impaired persons. We're pretty sure it involves hotter stuff rising and cooler stuff sinking. This mantle convection happens because the earth heats up internally, due to radioactive decay of some elements.

Lithosphere cools as it ages—moving away from the mid-ocean ridge—and gets denser or less buoyant as it cools. Though the crust remains buoyant, the mantle lithosphere it's riding on becomes dense enough to drag it under at a subduction zone.

There, the oceanic plate descends as a slab at a 20- to 60-degree steepening slope under the overriding plate's edge. The textbook cartoon of a subduction zone in cross-section has an arrow at the same angle, suggesting that the slab slides into a slot. While the 15- to 60-degree slope was confirmed decades ago by plotting deep earthquakes, it does not follow that slabs slide at that angle. Warren Hamilton, a senior figure in plate tectonic theory, argues that there is no slot. Why would there be a slot? Gravity would pull the slab straight downward. The subduction hinge would continuously roll back, sucking the overriding plate forward. Among geophysicists today, hinge rollback and its resulting plate-driving force, slab pull, are pretty widely accepted as happening at least in some subduction trenches.

When a patch of *thickened* crust, such as an island chain, rides on oceanic crust and meets an overriding continental edge at a subduction zone, its greater buoyancy and rigidity may cause it to "jam the subduction trench," attaching to the continent and forcing the subduction zone to jump from its inboard to its outboard side. The island chain is now a new terrane accreted to the edge of the continent.

In this fashion the continents have grown for billions of years. Some scientific papers break most of North America down into terranes all with different accretion ages. Most have been together for a very long time as the proto-continent Laurentia, which at various stages was part of the supercontinents Laurasia, Pangaea, Rodinia, and Columbia. In contrast, our Northwest terranes accreted within the last 2 percent of the earth's history, and were never part of Laurentia.

I sometimes picture accretion as a roiling pot of thick soup with bits of foam appearing out of the rising part, floating off to the side, coalescing with other bits of foam, and accreting to a mass of foam along one edge. The mantle is not actually a liquid like that soup. It is mainly solid, but semifluid, flowing very, very slowly, as many solids do. (Solid glaciers flow at a glacial pace, hundred-year-old window glass gets wavy from flowing a little bit.)

Rock can of course get hot enough to melt into a true liquid—lava or magma—and the earth is generally hotter the deeper you go, but with depth comes higher

GEOLOGIC MAP OF THE PACIFIC NORTHWEST
Silverthrone Mtn.
Chilko Lake
FRASER FAULT
BRITISH COLUMBIA
Mt. Meager
Lillooet
Pemberton
Mt. Cayley
Mt. Garibaldi
N
W
E
S
Campbell River
VANCOUVER ISLAND
Harrison Lake
Hope
Princeton
Vancouver
Strait of Georgia
Fraser River
CANADA
UNITED STATES
Tofino
Barkley Sound
Bellingham
Mt. Baker
Ross Lake
Winthrop
Skagit River
Cape Flattery
Victoria
Strait of Juan de Fuca
Port Angeles
Glacier Peak
Lake Chelan
Columbia River
Pacific Ocean
Puget Sound
Seattle

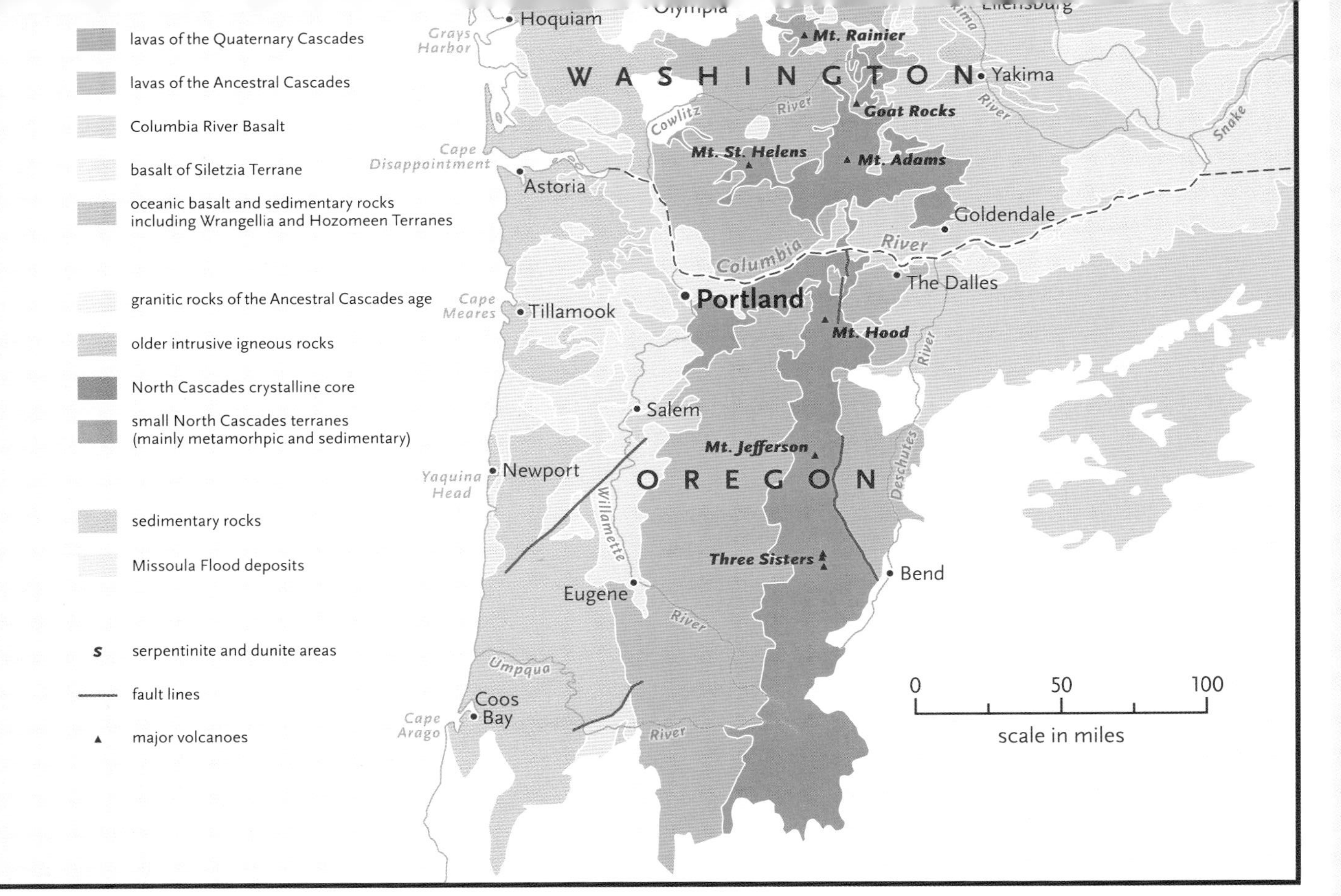
lavas of the Quaternary Cascades
lavas of the Ancestral Cascades
Columbia River Basalt
basalt of Siletzia Terrane
oceanic basalt and sedimentary rocks including Wrangellia and Hozomeen Terranes
granitic rocks of the Ancestral Cascades age
older intrusive igneous rocks
North Cascades crystalline core
small North Cascades terranes (mainly metamorhpic and sedimentary)
sedimentary rocks
Missoula Flood deposits
s serpentinite and dunite areas
fault lines
major volcanoes
W A S H I N G T O N
O R E G O N
Hoquiam
Grays Harbor
Mt. Rainier
Yakima
River
Cowlitz
River
Goat Rocks
Snake
Mt. St. Helens
Mt. Adams
Cape Disappointment
Astoria
Goldendale
Columbia
River
The Dalles
Portland
Cape Meares
Tillamook
Mt. Hood
River
Salem
Mt. Jefferson
Yaquina Head
Newport
Willamette
Deschutes
Three Sisters
Bend
Eugene
River
Umpqua
Coos Bay
Cape Arago
River
0
50
100
scale in miles

pressure that raises the melting point of the rock. The mantle is hot enough to melt if it weren't under pressure. The layer below the mantle, the outer core, is thought be on the liquid side of the heat and pressure gradients, but from there on up, most of the mantle is solid rock, which can only flow at an extremely slow pace.

Parallel to a subduction zone there typically lies a line of volcanoes called an arc. (A few arcs are truly arc-shaped, and several others become so in map projections. But not our Cascade arc.) Surprisingly, what melts rock at a subduction arc is thought to be the addition not of heat but of water—seawater carried into the depths in the oceanic slab and squeezed out into adjacent mantle minerals (chemicals rocks are made of), combining with them into new minerals, some of which have lower melting points. In a mid-ocean trench setting, on the other hand, mantle material melts because as it rises the pressure on it drops.

The melting under the volcanic arc is partial, selecting minerals with lower melting points. The current term of art, "crystal mush," describes magma as crystals mixed with melt in a wide range of ratios. As pulses of magma rise, gravity differentiates them further, selecting less-dense minerals to rise. At the same time, the primitive mantle magma evolves on its way up by melting and incorporating crustal minerals. The resulting chemical proportions determine what kind of rocks, and volcanoes, the magma will produce.

Andesite and basalt magmas in a volcanic arc reach the surface to erupt as stratovolcanoes, shield volcanoes, or cinder cones. Any remnants of that magma left behind down in the plumbing slowly crystallize as dioritic, gabbroic, or other dark intrusions.

Magma with more silica becomes dacite or rhyolite—lighter in both color and weight, and extremely viscous, like frozen peanut butter. These stiff, pale magmas reach the surface relatively rarely. They can produce lava domes, and they can also explode and leave a crater, as Mt. St. Helens did in 1980, producing copious ash and tuff.

Much more often, pale magmas solidify without reaching the surface, becoming "batholiths" or smaller "plutons" of granitic or other pale intrusive rock. Batholiths and plutons grow over millions of years by the incremental addition of thin layers. The Mt. Stuart batholith, for example, is 6 million years older near one edge than near the far edge. A mountain range may result eventually, due to the thickening or deepening of continental crust along the line of magma formation. The thickened line floats higher than the other areas of continental crust. Overlying volcanoes and surrounding materials erode off the top, exposing the intrusions, which persist for millions of years as a granitic mountain range.

This flotation principle, called isostasy, was a great breakthrough in geologic thinking, and works well for ranges—Himalayas, Alps, Appalachians—that thickened where two continents collided and crumpled together, extinguishing a subduction zone. The range as a whole can be buoyant either because its crust is thicker than adjacent crust or because it contains more of these light rocks, or both. It turns out, though, that some high regions are not held up by either crustal thickness or low density; they are raised by underlying mantle that is rising or is hotter than adjacent mantle, thereby lifting the crust above it.

Cascade Volcanoes

The volcanic Cascades fit the volcanic arc model quite well. Cascade volcanism has

Erosion Raises Mountains

We're used to thinking that erosion levels mountains. That's true; it does. But thanks to isostasy, it can also raise them a bit. Think of the mountain range as an iceberg. Famously, only the tip of the iceberg—10 percent of its mass—floats above the water line. Imagine a cylindrical iceberg 100 feet tall and at least that wide; 10 feet (10 percent) show above the water. If you melt off those top 10 feet, the berg, now 90 feet tall, rises 9 feet in order to keep 10 percent of itself above the waterline. Now suppose instead you carve those top 10 feet into a perfect cone, like sharpening the tip of a new pencil. This time the tip is still 100 feet above the base. You've removed two-thirds as much mass as in the preceding case, so the pencil-shaped berg rises two-thirds as far, 6 feet instead of 9 feet—and its point stands 16 feet above the water, 6 feet higher than before!

Similarly, when an ice age inflicts alpine glaciers on a plateau-like mountain range, they can carve deep U-shaped valleys fairly close together without much reducing the highest ridges. They have removed significant mass from the range as a whole, so it floats higher isostatically. The *average* elevation across the range is lower than before (erosion is working to level the range) but the *peak* elevations are higher. And local relief is much greater.

This effect is seen in our mountains. Mt. Olympus is made of softer, less erosion-resistant rock than some other parts of the Olympic Mountains, and it's located west of where you would expect the high point of the range to be, based on plate tectonic forces alone. Nevertheless, it is the highest peak because it lies in between the biggest U-shaped valleys—which are located where they are because heavier snows fall on the windward side of the range. You could say that, indirectly, the prevailing wind is lifting mountains!

The same mechanism tilts the North Cascades. Rock uplift is considerably faster toward their northern and especially their western sides, thanks to more snow. This has been going on for as long as the mountains have existed; the western and northern rocks have been brought up faster, from greater depths, and have higher metamorphic grade in consequence.

been active for more than 40 million years. That period is divided into High Cascades volcanism (the past 4 million years) and Ancestral Cascades volcanism (everything before that, but with production falling off considerably after 17 million years ago).

Strangely, 20th-century Northwesterners thought of our volcanoes as inactive. The Encyclopedia Britannica told us that they were "considered extinct, but must have been active within historical time." (No, that doesn't make sense.) Settlers in the 19th century left many reports of eruptions, some factual and others fanciful, but most sounding curiously blasé. That attitude passed, over the generations, into inexplicable obliviousness, even among some geologists and engineers. Rivers were dammed close to Mt. Baker and Mt. St. Helens—known to have erupted 120 years ago—and papers were published asserting that Mt. Hood, Mt. Rainier, and Glacier Peak show no sign of activity for thousands of years past.

If there was one Cascade volcano that looked particularly innocent, it was the smooth one, the one said to be a bride in Indian legends, the Fuji look-alike: Mt. St. Helens. Then, in 1980, she schooled us. Both geologists and biologists have learned a tremendous amount from Mt. St. Helens, ever since.

If all eruptions were like the 18 May one, then volcanoes would be more like holes than mountains. And yet, a close look at the fresh mess of St. Helens helped geologists to recognize similar sector collapse eruptions on other volcanoes. Our cones are prone to collapse because they get dissolved from the inside out by sulfuric acid that forms when upward-percolating volcanic gases meet groundwater. Mt. Rainier's Osceola Mudflow event in 3600 BCE left an amphitheater-shaped crater after removing a St. Helens–size quantity of rock from near the top of a Rainier taller than the one we know and love.

Columbia River Basalt

The most dramatic geologic events ever, in Washington and Oregon, were staggeringly large floods—some of icy water (p. 30), some of hot lava. The latter, the Columbia River Basalts (CRBs), erupted mainly between 16.7 and 15 million years ago—long before humanity evolved (lucky for us!) but still not very far back in geologic time. They are the youngest of the world's flood basalts, or large igneous provinces (LIPs).

Enormous volumes of lava poured out from linear fissures in eastern Oregon and Washington, spreading out flat across an area of land larger than Washington. Many of the individual flows exceed a hundred feet thick and a hundred times the volume of the largest lava flows of historic times. Some traveled more than 350 miles, and were probably in motion for several years, with a thick crust congealing on top, insulating the lava under it well enough for flow to continue. The insulated lower layer took much longer to solidify, and crystalized differently, becoming vertical polygonal columns. Between flows, hundreds or thousands of years passed, sometimes long enough for vegetation to return and soil to form.

In our mountains, CRBs turn up mainly in the walls of the Columbia Gorge, the canyons of the Klickitat, Clackamas, Naches, and Sandy Rivers—and Saddle Mountain, the sore thumb of the northern Coast Range.

LIPs are thought to arise over "hot spots" such as the Yellowstone Hot Spot. The CRB may have been an earlier production of the Yellowstone Hot Spot. Though 90 percent of the CRB erupted within the first million years, diminished eruptions continued for another 9 million. Some time after that, the Wallowa Mountains arose, an anomalous round area at the heart of the CRB vents—probably not a coincidence, but still a mystery.

("Hot spot" is a rather vague term used both by geologists who believe mantle plumes exist and by geologists who do not. Mantle plumes, if they exist, originate at the very bottom of the mantle, have hot spots at their top ends, and are independent of plate tectonics. If hot spots are not plumes, they are hot zones in the upper mantle, and may be attributable to plate tectonics.)

Mudflows

Mudflows may be the worst hazard we face from our volcanoes, because they are more common, hard to predict, and fast-moving than eruptions proper. A St. Helens mudflow on the upper reaches of the Toutle River on 18 May traveled at least 16 miles per hour; you could not have outrun it on rough terrain.

A mudflow can be described as a cross between a flash flood and a landslide of volcanic ash mud, typically having a mortar-like consistency. The mud is so dense that boulders float on it rather than tumbling along. Our volcanoes are susceptible to mudflows because their slopes often consist of loose (or merely frozen solid) ash and glacial rubble covered with snow or ice. A classic cause of large mudflows is an eruption of very hot ash melting a glacier; the mud is then a mix of new ash, glacier ice and water, and underlying old ash and rocks.

An outburst flood deposit on Glacier Peak.

Similar flows can originate without eruptive activity. Mudflows are usually considered distinct from ordinary (unheated) floods and avalanches, but it can be hard to determine whether fluctuating volcanic heat is a factor in glacial outburst floods on volcanoes. Unheated flash floods in the presence of copious loose ash act much like a typical mudflow, though they rarely get quite as big. Mudflow-type deposits from recent outburst floods can be seen on Dusty and Kennedy Creeks of Glacier Peak; on Kautz and South Tahoma Creeks and the Nisqually River of Mt. Rainier; and on the White and Sandy Rivers of Mt. Hood.

Mudflows are slow to revegetate because of their great depth and chemical uniformity. Alders are valuable pioneers on mudflows here; their nitrogen-fixing ability is crucial in the pure mineral mud.

In the grand picture of earth history there is a strong correlation between mass extinctions and LIP eruptions. LIPs may have caused extinctions by pumping sulfur dioxide and greenhouse gases into the atmosphere, triggering acid rain and rapid climate change. The Chicxulub meteor impact came while a LIP was active in India, and both probably helped eliminate the wingless dinosaurs. Efforts to correlate other extinctions with impacts have not panned out. While most or perhaps all major extinctions came during LIP events, many additional LIPs including the CRB and Siletzia did not cause major extinctions. The much older Karmutsen LIP, now partly on Vancouver Island, is suspected of at least a modest mass extinction.

Wrangellia Terrane

Most of Vancouver Island belongs to Wrangellia, a terrane that's well established among geologists, though little is known of where it was in the first half of its 400 million years. It started as an island arc far across the ocean. Ancient sedimentary and metamorphic rocks abound, along with basalt. It erupted flood basalts 220 million years ago that supply most of today's surface basalt. Prior to that it permanently joined an older terrane, which now separates northern Wrangellia (in Alaska's Wrangell Mountains) from southern Wrangellia (Vancouver Island, Haida Gwaii, and slices of nearby mainland). This enlarged island chain eventually joined a still-larger block of inland British Columbia, and the entirety slid north along the mainland for some distance before finally settling into place. The question of how far it slid and when, and how many terranes were included, is called the "Baja BC" controversy because the farther version places it off the coast of Mexico 80 million years ago.

North Cascades and Coast Mountains Terranes

The North Cascades are a beautiful mess of more than a dozen small terranes ranging to almost 500 million years old. Geologists may eventually combine them into fewer, but it's a hyper-difficult jigsaw puzzle due to extensive metamorphism and to crazy faulting that places younger terranes on top of older ones, some of them right-side up and others upside down. The terranes clearly participated in multiple episodes of intense mountain-building. Many originated as island arcs. Don't picture Hawaii, picture New Guinea, a big island with rugged mountains. Marine sedimentary rocks are relatively minor but widespread. Westward, this terrane cluster includes the San Juan Islands and small pieces along Vancouver Island's outer coast as far as Tofino. Northward, related terranes form the eastern edge of the southern Coast Mountains. Some of the major faults they moved on show up as heavy straight lines on the geologic maps. The rock west of each fault moved north (the same direction, not coincidentally, as on the San Andreas Fault and other major faults parallel to the Pacific Coast). The greatest of them is called the Fraser Fault in British Columbia (where it determines the course of the Fraser River) and the Straight Creek Fault in Washington.

The North Cascades crystalline core underwent intense metamorphism deep in the earth between 90 and 46 million years ago, requiring that it descended and rose again—25 vertical miles—very fast. During the same period, arc magmas were emplaced and many were soon metamorphosed. So it seems to have been in a volcanic arc while also colliding with other terranes. Soon after 46 million years ago it was pierced by Ancestral Cascades volcanoes, so we know it was in place here by then. Those volcanoes largely eroded off the top (as uplift continued) so their granitic batholiths are more abundant at the surface today than their volcanic rocks. Uplift slowed for a time, then resumed greater speed from 10 million years ago on.

Arc volcanism concurrent with uplift, metamorphism, and northward movement also characterize the Coast Mountains.

Geologists increasingly refer to the North Cascades as the southern end of the Coast Mountains complex, but in that range the granitic rocks, rather than metamorphic, utterly dominate at the surface. (A metamorphic core is exposed for a stretch in the center of the range farther north, but within our range it remains largely buried.) These arc magmas mostly formed between 170 million and 46 million years ago. Stretching more than 1000 miles to the northwest, they were called the world's biggest batholith. Their current name, Coast Plutonic Complex, reflects the multiplicity of intrusions over a long period of time. The complex is not a terrane—it presumably straddled, stitched together, and buried a major terrane boundary between Wrangellia on the west and the Intermountain Superterrane on the east. The volcanism took place along the continental margin, but geologists disagree about the timing of when the terranes sutured to North America.

Siletz Terrane

A simpler, larger, much younger terrane comprises the Coast Ranges, Olympics, and a slender slice of southernmost Vancouver Island. Its eastern edge lies buried under Cascade volcanoes and Columbia River basalts—possibly all the way east to Walla Walla, or perhaps just to the Cascades.

This basaltic terrane, Siletzia, was an oceanic plateau bearing islands, which erupted close to North America shortly before accreting to it. (Similar basalts of the Oregon Coast Range erupted for some time after accretion as well.) Oceanic plateaus are large igneous provinces (LIPs) along with their on-land counterparts, the flood basalts. With eight times the volume of the Columbia River Basalts, Siletzia's basalt is definitely large. Some geologists believe the Siletzia LIP was the first incarnation, before the CRB, of the Yellowstone Hot Spot.

A Rotating Block

Siletzia rotates. For at least 10 million years, a block of the continental plate has been rotating clockwise relative to the continent and relative to the line of the Cascade arc. Rotation shifted High Cascades volcanism east of the Ancestral Cascades in Oregon, west of them in British Columbia, and left it smack in the middle of them in Washington.

The hypothesis of block rotation was initially based on paleomagnetism—magnetic mineral slivers in the basalt that pointed to magnetic north when the lava first crystalized. Later it was corroborated by a great grid of GPS stations that can detect mere millimeters of movement. The GPS data show that Siletzia does rotate today at close to the speed indicated by the paleomagnetic data. But it turns out that the rotating block is much larger, embracing all of Oregon and much of southern Idaho and northern Nevada. Rotation seems to be driven jointly by California's northward movement along the San Andreas and Walker Lane faults, by spreading of the Great Basin area, and by the oblique northeastward shove of the subducting plate at the Cascadia Subduction Zone.

How can a vast region rotate while sutured on three sides to a continent that does not? It requires squeezing crust near its leading edge, and stretching crust near its trailing edge. Handily, the squeeze and the stretch were both already well known. Squeezing is seen at the Yakima Fold Belt, which includes the giant ridges under Interstate 82 between Yakima and Ellensburg and also extends northwest to include first the Seattle Fault and then the great thrust faults under the Olympic basaltic horseshoe. The stretching is taken care of by fault block mountain ranges all over the Great Basin. The Wasatch and Teton ranges mark the border with the stable continent.

There's an interesting fit between the rotation and hypotheses that arise from plotting present-day exposures of Columbia River Basalts. Several basalt flows reached far to the west, even to the Pacific along divergent paths, indicating that neither Cascades nor Coast Range stood as barriers at that time, at least not in the Rainier-to-Hood section of the range. Some Cascade volcanoes were active then, but they must have stood isolated upon a low plain. Originally flat and close to sea level, flows were subsequently raised to 2800 feet in the Gorge, 300 feet in the Oregon Coast range, 5500 feet near Mt. Adams, and 7000 feet near Mt. Rainier—but dropped to below sea level under Mt. Hood. Oregon's High Cascades stand in a trough; erupted lava is entirely responsible for elevating the range. In Washington's volcanic Cascades, the elevation of the platform under the salient volcanoes is attributable to broad uplift. The northward increase in uplift could be caused by rotation pushing this end of the block up against the obstacle posed by the North Cascades and Coast Mountains.

Similarly, the Olympic Mountains got shoved into a corner between that same obstacle and Wrangellia. The shoving force was long thought to be simply Cascadia subduction. Being the tip of the rotating block brings additional forces into play. In any case, the sedimentary rocks that dominate the Olympics all formed near where they stand today. That was underwater at the time, just off the coast soon after Siletzia docked. Thrust faults and arching then raised them up into mountains, underthrusting them against the underside of the Siletzia-related Crescent Basalts that they had been deposited on.

Earthquakes

Geology has been an exciting science for the last fifty years thanks to plate tectonics. Meanwhile, Cascadia in particular provides increased geologic excitement: first Mt. St. Helens erupted, and then we began learning about The Big One.

In an eerie parallel to the old complacency about allegedly extinct Cascade volcanoes, the belief that the Northwest lacks big earthquakes survived the first several decades of plate tectonics theory (while new buildings continued for decades to lack the appropriate seismic upgrades). After learning that we are in a subduction zone, and that other subduction zones make big earthquakes, geologists tried to figure out what makes Cascadia different. It turns out we aren't so different, we just lack a written history before 1790. The last Big One came in the night: 9:00 PM, 26 January 1700.

The tale is told in Indian legends, and it is written down in records of tsunamis in Japan. Kenji Satake's team of geologic sleuths compared the timing and size of those tsunamis with recent tsunamis whose causative earthquakes along North and South America are known, to come up with the date, hour, and magnitude. They knew what decade to look at thanks to years of dogged sleuthing by Brian Atwater and other Northwest geologists who were increasingly certain that the Cascadia Subduction Zone has a regular history of major quakes, with the most recent around 300 years ago. All up and down the coast, they had found tsunami-deposited sediments way above any historic surf level.

The tsunami reports from 1700 pencil out as a moment-magnitude 9 quake—very near the high end as quakes go—but other kinds of evidence suggest a somewhat weaker 1700 quake. Subduction earthquakes result from strain building up over time, so you might expect fairly regular periodicity. That has not been the case. Intervals between great subduction quakes here have varied widely, with something of a clustered pattern, at least in the British Columbia–Washington section of the subduction zone: clusters of three to five quakes at intervals averaging 420 years were separated by gaps averaging more than 900 years. During those gaps, however, moderate-sized great quakes often hit either the northern California section or a longer California–Oregon section.

Earthquakes on local faults are also a serious threat. A thousand years ago, Seattle had a magnitude 7.5 quake on its very own Seattle Fault. The Bainbridge Island shore next to the fault rose 21 feet. Major rockslides came down in Seattle and in the southeastern Olympics, where rock avalanches dammed several new lakes. Cascadia's biggest quake within historic times—around a 6.8—hit near Chelan in 1872. Vancouver's faults are less evident, buried as they are under thick glacial and Fraser River sediments, but those same sediments are likely to worsen the shaking. Portland is bisected by the Portland Fault, which raises the city's West Hills.

Geologic Time

4.7 billion years ago	Earth formed.
4 billion	Oldest rocks yet dated solidified from magma.
3.85 billion	Possible earliest life, primitive bacteria.
3 billion	Photosynthesis first evolves in cyanobacteria, creating free oxygen.
1.9 billion	Oldest rock crystals in our region formed from magma.
1.2 billion	First complex (eukaryotic) single-celled life.
600 million	Oxygen reached near-modern levels, leading to first animals.
600–400 million	Fungi and algae moved onto land.
430 million	Oldest North Cascades rocks formed.
252 million	Largest LIP eruption (Siberian) and largest mass extinction (Permian).
225 million	Dinosaurs became dominant land animal.
200 million	Coast Mountains, Vancouver Island, and North Cascades terranes entered a long period of mountain-building and terrane amalgamations.
100 million	Flowering plants came to dominate over spore plants.
65 million	Dinosaurs went extinct, except for birds. Mammals survived.
60 million	Peak of Laramide (main) uplift of the Rocky Mountains.
55 million	Siletzia/Crescent basalts began erupting.
46 million	Last Northwest terranes docked to continent, some still sliding north.
46 million	Ancestral Cascade arc volcanism began.
16.8 million	Columbia River Basalt floods began erupting. Cascade lavas waned.
7 million	Cascades volcanism resurgent.
4 million	Arbitrary date for shift from Ancestral to High Cascades.
2.5 million	Pleistocene Ice Ages began. Goat Rocks volcano began to grow.
1.8 million	Ancestral hominids shaped stone tools.
1.5 million	Ice-age floods on Columbia River have probably begun.
130,000	Earliest anatomically modern humans.
115,000	Most recent Ice Age began.

Recent Time

19,000 BCE Latest series of giant Missoula Floods began.

12,300 Humans occupy Paisley Caves, Oregon—earliest firm date for humans here.

12,000 Mastodon killed with spears in coastal Washington. Last Ice Age glacial maximum in Pacific Northwest.

11,400 Two explosive eruptions of Glacier Peak shot pumice far and wide.

11,000 Last of the Missoula Floods.

11,000 Clovis-style spear points used near Wenatchee. Many large mammals going extinct.

10,800 A 1300-year cold snap in the Northern Hemisphere; alpine glaciers readvanced.

9000 Puget and Okanogan Ice Sheet lobes gone from Washington.

8000 Salmon fishing common in the Columbia Gorge.

7000 4000-year warm "climatic optimum" began.

6200 Big Lava Beds poured out, south of Mt. Adams.

5700 Mt. Mazama erupted pumice far and wide, collapsed, formed Crater Lake Caldera.

4000 Possible first human effects on greenhouse gases, via grain farming.

3600 Osceola Mudflow from Mt. Rainier buried Puyallup area.

2000 Northwest Coast people began relying on stored salmon as a food, and cedar as a material.

0 Mt. Rainier built its present summit. Mt. St. Helens built its present flanks.

160 CE An Alaska cedar, logged in the 1990s, germinated in the Coast Mountains.

500 Mt. Hood erupted, producing Crater Rock and the large debris fan below it.

1500 Landslide dammed Columbia River, forming the Cascades of the Columbia.

1700 Most recent major earthquake on Cascadia Subduction Zone.

1785 Fur trade began between coastal peoples and Europeans.

1777–93 Mt. Hood eruption produced Old Maid Flat mudflow.

1820 Greatest post–Ice Age extent of glaciers in the "Little Ice Age."

1830–50 Minor eruptions on Mts. Baker, Rainier, St. Helens.

1914–17 Major eruption of Mt. Lassen, a Cascade volcano in California.

1980 Major eruption of Mt. St. Helens.

today Earth warming, glaciers retreating, species extinctions accelerating, mountains rising.

Pillow basalt metamorphosed to greenstone. Scale about 12 feet.

Columbia River Basalt in eastern part of gorge.

A basalt cinder, 3 inches.

GEOLOGY: ROCKS

Classification of the earth's materials begins with the three ways that rock material can be transformed into another kind of rock:

- **Igneous rocks** solidified from magma, which is any kind of rock melted.
- **Sedimentary rocks** were fragmentary material (such as mud) which was then compacted or chemically cemented.
- **Metamorphic rocks** recrystallized from other rocks under intense heat and pressure, without melting.

GEOLOGY: VOLCANIC IGNEOUS ROCKS

Igneous rocks are subcategorized by crystal size—fine-grained or coarse-grained—and also by chemical (or mineral) composition. High-silica rocks are considered light, low-silica rocks dark. Each darkness grade can occur with either a fine or a coarse texture. Fine and coarse textures tend to reflect origin:

- **Volcanic**, from magma that erupted upon the continental surface or the ocean floor, congealing quickly to produce fine crystals or a noncrystalline glassy texture. (Magma after it reaches the surface is called lava, both before and after it solidifies.)
- **Intrusive**, from magma that solidified into rock somewhere beneath the surface, and cooled slowly, producing large crystals—that is, coarse texture.

Basalt

The most abundant rock in Oregon and Washington and, though less visibly, in the earth's crust as a whole, basalt is the darkest of our common lava mixes. We think of it as normally black, but it ranges down to light gray and is often altered to greenish or reddish. Its surface is drab and massive, usually without conspicuous crystals or other features except, frequently, bubbles (vesicles).

These show that the lava came up from the depths full of dissolved gases. Just as uncapping a bottle of soda releases bubbles of carbon dioxide which, under pressure, had been dissolved invisibly in the liquid, so lavas often foam up as they near the surface. Abundant vesicles indicate that the rock congealed near the surface of a particular lava flow. In older basalts (for example, those of the Olympics) vesicles may appear as solid polka dots, the holes having filled with water-soluble minerals.

Basalt columns with six, five, or four sides, often neatly vertical at one level and splayed-out at another, are a familiar basalt feature. They result from shrinkage during the slow cooling of large flows. (Columns and vesicles can also occur in andesite.)

Basalt lava erupts in several styles. Cascade stratovolcanoes, often generalized as andesitic, actually range all the way from rhyolite to basalt. Middle Sister is largely basalt. Two lower-relief kinds of mountains usually made of basalt are shield volcanoes and cinder cones. Both are plentiful in the Cascades. Shield volcanoes are made of lava too fluid to create dramatic vertical relief, but the entire High Cascades Plateau, on which the prominent volcanoes stand, is made largely of basaltic shields.

Basalt can erupt as a lava fountain whose frothy lava blobs harden in the air and pile up into a cinder cone. These volcanoes stay small because they have only one eruptive episode; it may also include phases of lava flowing without spattering, leaving a lava flow.

Basalt floods are a type of volcano that doesn't produce a mountain: lava flows out flat and solidifies flat (p. 512).

Another type of basaltic effluence, that of the sea floor, is the most extensive of all. Most sea floor basalt erupts at mid-ocean ridges and remains under the ocean forever. A bit of oceanic basalt crops up in the North Cascades, mostly metamorphosed into greenstone (p. 534).

The entire east and north flanks of the Olympics consist of a huge slab of basalt bent into a horseshoe shape and wedged up 90 degrees from underneath. Some of the flows show the glassy-rinded, blob-shaped pillow structures that basalt forms when it erupts underwater. The Crescent basalts erupted first undersea and later above water because they had built up to where they emerged as islands. While being thrust up to form today's mountains, they underwent varying degrees of metamorphism and came out as the hardest, most erosion-resistant rocks in the Olympics, and the most popular with rock climbers. They underlie Mt. Deception and Mt. Constance (second- and third-highest peaks in the range) and the rest of the skyline seen from across Puget Sound.

Crescent basalts are around 55 million years old. The Oregon Coast range has a lot of what's probably the same (Siletz) basalt but without the metamorphic toughening.

Basalt about 225 million years old is widespread on Vancouver Island, and praised by climbers there, notably on Mts. Colonel Foster and Elkhorn. Like Siletzia, this Karmutsen basalt seems to be a flood basalt that erupted largely underwater (creating an oceanic plateau) but also partly above the waterline.

Experiments are underway injecting carbon dioxide into deep CRB layers, to alleviate climate change. Some minerals common in basalt combine remarkably quickly with the carbon and oxygen atoms to form new minerals, thus sequestering the CO_2 permanently and safely. That much is well established, and basalt is blessedly abundant; the question is whether the process can become cheap enough to use in mass quantities.

Andesite

Named after the world's highest volcanoes, the Andes, andesite is generalized to be the typical rock of stratovolcanoes. In the Cascades, it is abundant, notably on Mt. Rainier and Mt. Hood, but overall it is not far more abundant than other lavas.

Andesite lavas make rough gray, greenish, or sometimes reddish-brown rocks.

Andesite

Dacite

Rhyolite

Often they are speckled with crystals up to ¾ inch across, scattered throughout a fine matrix otherwise lacking crystals of visible size. These were already crystallized in the molten magma when it erupted. With close examination and a little practice, you can easily tell them from the shards of noncrystalline whole rock jumbled up in tuff.

The different lava rocks can be hard to tell apart. Color descriptions are unavoidably vague; andesite is "medium-dark," between dark basalt and light dacite and rhyolite, but actual tints overlap, and green and reddish hues are unpredictable. The technical definitions are ranges on a graph of bulk chemistry, so positive identifications may require specimens to be pulverized and analyzed by a lab. Light color correlates with silica (SiO_2) content—around 50 percent in basalt, 60 percent in andesite, 70 percent or more in rhyolite. Most magmatic SiO_2 combines with other elements to form such minerals as the feldspars; only the SiO_2 excess over about 55 percent crystallizes as the SiO_2 mineral quartz. Therefore basalt has no quartz crystals, and andesite generally has a few.

Dacite

Dacite lavas are intermediate in silica content, viscosity and color—more or less medium-gray, sometimes pinkish, brownish or buff. They include light and dark scattered crystals often, flow-streaking occasionally, and bubbles or holes rarely. They are common in Romania, known to the ancient Romans as Dacia, hence the word dacite. Here, they comprise around 75 percent of the lavas in the northern section of the High Cascades, from Glacier Peak north through British Columbia, and also Mt. St. Helens. Crater Rock on Mt. Hood is a dacite dome. Its eruptions melted enough iced-up ash and pumice to create a big debris fan which underlies the Palmer Glacier, Timberline Lodge, and the entire smooth south slope seen from Portland.

Rhyolite

Rhyolite lavas are pale, typically pinkish-tan rocks. They can be confused with tuff, which is often made of rhyolite magma that exploded rather than flowing as lava. Rhyolite is named for the Greek word for flow. Streaky or swirling flow patterns may help to distinguish it, especially from tuff or basalt. But it is actually one of the least fluid of lavas. Lava viscosity increases dramatically with silica

Types of Volcanoes

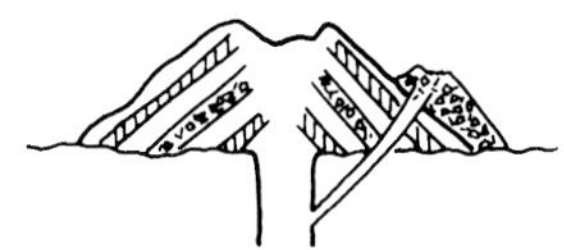

Stratovolcanoes include all the prominent Cascade volcanoes. They build up over periods of one or two million years by alternating lava flows (andesite, dacite, and basalt) with copious tuff flows and ashfall. Mt. Rainier—207 cubic miles of it, rising more than 10,000 feet—is a big one.

Cinder cones typically erupt just once, from a single vent, and rarely achieve 1000 feet of relief. They erupt as fountains of small, foamy basalt or andesite "cinders," and often extrude tonguelike basalt flows from their bases. Stratovolcanoes often produce them from satellite vents. Examples abound in central Oregon.

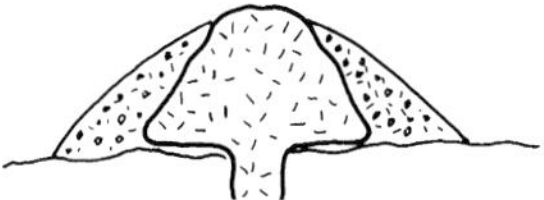

Lava domes superficially resemble cinder cones, but are massive extrusions of pasty, viscous rhyolite or dacite. The surface cracks into blocks that tumble down the sides, forming a rubbly cone, typically with less than 1000 feet of relief. Mt. Lassen is an outlier with 2700 feet of relief.

Shield volcanoes made of multiple basalt flows produce only gentle relief. A few build for millions of years: "the world's biggest mountain," Mauna Loa, is 10,000 cubic miles rising 29,000 feet above the sea floor. Cascade shield volcanoes like Larch Mountain and the Simcoes are 3000–5000 feet high.

Flood basalts are not mountains; they are so fluid when molten that they pour out flat, and reduce vertical relief by filling valleys. They have the greatest volumes of any terrestrial volcanoes. The Columbia River Basalt Group, a 10-million-year sequence of flows, contains 60,000 cubic miles of lava.

Pumice

Ashfall tuff at Mt. St. Helens, 5 inches.

content, and flowing rhyolite may be up to a thousand times more viscous than flowing basalt. "Flowing" almost seems like the wrong word—it squeezes out of the ground more like dried-up peanut butter, commonly producing a lava dome. It so resists flowing that it may plug up a given vent forever, marking the final phase of activity for some volcanoes. The southernmost major Cascade volcano, California's Mt. Lassen, is about as big a dome as rhyolite can produce.

The constipating viscosity of rhyolite may help to explain the abundance of granite—rhyolite magma that never managed to erupt. When gas-rich rhyolite magma does erupt it may explode, showering the area with pumice, ash, and larger fragments; rhyolite tuff and pumice abound in Nevada. Gas-poor rhyolite may erupt as the glassy form called obsidian.

Pumice

Magmas often reach the surface bearing a gas component that expands, sometimes explosively, as it is released from subterranean pressure, blasting globs of glassy froth sky-high—a little like a well-shaken bottle of warm Guinness. In midair, the froth freezes into rock. The rhyolite version, pumice, is so full of tiny bubbles that it's light enough to travel on the wind and to float on water. Breaking or grinding a piece of pumice may release the sulfurous smell of the original volcanic sulfur dioxide, still trapped in the bubbles. (The basalt version, cinders, or more properly scoria, has bigger bubbles and is heavier.)

Pumice fragments mantle a lot of terrain downwind of our volcanoes, including Pomas Pass (we'll call that frontier spelling) and other ridgelines for a good 20 miles east of Glacier Peak. Like St. Helens' more modest ash plume of 18 May 1980, that big Glacier Peak plume of 13,400 years ago extends in only one direction; it was a single, intense eruption so brief that the wind direction did not shift. Dust-sized ash (much of it pumice) from that blast is recognized in soil profiles all across Montana—a ways below the layer from the Crater Lake eruption of 7700 years ago.

Pumice is used for grinding away at toes or kitchen grills, and for mixing into concrete to dampen sound and reduce weight. Decorative stone stores sell big chunks as "feather rock."

Tuff

Much of the volcanic rock produced by our volcanoes was never flowing lava, but instead

Obsidian

blasted violently into the air as pyroclastic ("fire-broken") fragments. These range from bombs bigger than basketballs to dustlike ash. (Named for a weak resemblance to wood ashes, volcanic ash is no more "burnt" than any other volcanic material.) When they settle, the fragments may or may not cohere strongly enough to make tuff.

Tuff has two distinct ways of consolidating. Ashfall is material that shot up into the air and settled back to earth at modest temperatures; decades have to pass before sufficient groundwater full of dissolved silica percolates through to cement it into an ashfall tuff. Ashfall beds are typically graded: each bed from a single ash eruption has coarse fragments at its base (they fall to earth fastest) and finer fragments toward its top. Ashflow, on the other hand, comes barreling down the slopes in hot whirling volcanic gas that is exsolving out of the fragments as they fly. Such flows move so fast they are "glowing avalanches," or *nuees ardentes*. Ash is laid down fast and hard, without grading, and is quickly cemented by its own heat into a welded tuff. Where ashfall tuff is often crumbly and vulnerable to erosion, resembling a weak sandstone (and sometimes classed as a sedimentary rock), welded tuff is harder, resembling lava. Telling tuff from lava is easiest when there are inclusions; in lava these are crystals, often of a contrasting color. In tuff, they are irregular fragments about the same color and composition as the rest of the tuff.

Under Table Mountain by Mt. Baker lies a very deep formation of tuff and other lava flows. A volcano erupted there, blasting a huge vent through an ice sheet. If any mountain at all was created, the glacier soon swept it away. Wes Hildreth identified this tuff-filled caldera and named it Kulshan Caldera.

Cascade stratovolcanoes are constructed of lava flows interlayered with pyroclastic deposits both loose and tuffaceous. Lava is the stronger part, but without tuff, lava flows cannot build volcanoes combining the height, steepness, and graceful conical form of ours. Particles dumped in a heap settle at their angle of repose. (Watch sand settle in an hourglass for an elegant demonstration of this.) Angle of repose varies with particle roughness, angularity, and moisture—cling, in a word. It ranges between 33 and 37 degrees for most scree, may reach 39 degrees for cinder cones, and even higher for welded tuffs, which cheat. Flowing lava cannot come to rest at such steep angles. Pyroclastics also fill in the gaps and gouges of erosion, until the mountain approximates a 35-degree cone steepening a bit toward the top. Mt. St. Helens used to look like Mt. Fuji, more perfect than our other cones because it had erupted enough since the Ice Age to repair the disfigurements of glaciation. Then it blew perfection away.

Obsidian

Obsidian is commonly called "volcanic glass," and that's exactly what it is. Fracturing as glass does, in a pattern of concentric arcs, it is ideal for chipping into arrowheads and blades, making it a crucial trade commodity. Obsidian from Yellowstone was traded all the way to the Atlantic. The main source near here was Newberry Crater, in central Oregon. Mt. Garibaldi and the Three Sisters also produced some obsidian.

Glass is noncrystalline. Obsidian is lava that cooled without organizing its ions into crystalline minerals, which apparently can happen when magma contains no water or gases, and erupts quietly. Though obsidian is usually black or dark red-brown, it comes from a "pale" rhyolite or dacite magma.

GEOLOGY: INTRUSIVE IGNEOUS ROCKS

Granitic Rocks

Thanks to rock climbers and kitchen designers, granite has a high profile. Polished granite surfaces beautifully display granitic texture—tightly interlocked coarse crystals of varicolored minerals. Quartz is the white to buff, translucent component; feldspars are salmon to pale gray; glittering black flakes are biotite, or "black mica"; hornblende and pyroxene are dark grays.

The word "granitic" derives from these granular crystals, and the word "intrusive" describes their typical origin. While some magma (molten rock) rises and extrudes onto the earth's surface through a volcano, other magma merely intrudes among subsurface rocks and solidifies there, at depth.

Granite, 3 inches.

This may be a magmatic pulse that failed to ever reach the surface, or it may be a remnant left behind in the "roots" or "plumbing" of a volcano. In either case, if it cools in a large mass, it changes from liquid to solid state slowly, over hundreds of thousands of years, allowing its chemical compounds plenty of time to form large mineral crystals, which define the granitic subclass of igneous rocks.

Large intrusions are plutons. The very largest—those over 38 square miles at the surface—are batholiths ("deep rocks" in Greek). Near plutons you may find crack-filling intrusions where magma under pressure forced its way. These are sills if they force a crack between one preexisting rock bed and another, or dikes if they cut through beds or if there are no beds. You can think of that as horizontal sills versus vertical dikes. Either one can be an inch wide, or much, much wider. Narrow ones cool as fast as lava, producing a fine-grained rock, such as andesite. Wide dikes cool slowly, becoming coarse-grained.

Rock climbers and kitchen designers may speak of any sort of coarse-grained igneous rock as granite, but geologists do not. "Granitic rocks" is a good hedge, as it includes a broad group of light intrusive rocks. Our commonest granitics, particularly in the Coast Mountains, are granodiorite and tonalite. Granite proper appears in the photogenic Liberty Bell and Early Winters Spires, by Highway 20. Within that same Golden Horn Batholith, you can walk on naturally crumbled granite on the Crest Trail below Cutthroat Pass. Landscapers call that decomposed granite; geologists call it grus. Intrusive rocks are uncommon in our Oregon and coastal Washington mountains.

Granite is typically pinkish or yellowish white with darker speckles. Diorite is a salt-and-pepper rock, technically too dark, with less than 20 percent quartz, to be called granitic. Granodiorite, naturally, is in between, "lighter" than diorite. As you see in the photos, it isn't much lighter; the difference is not the proportion of dark crystals, but the tint of the light ones—pale feldspar versus paler quartz. In the granite photo, they are a mixture of pale gray feldspar with a greater portion of pinkish translucent quartz. In the granodiorite they look uniformly pale gray and are almost all feldspar. By "dark," geologists really mean "quartz-poor."

Intrusive and volcanic rocks types are two faces of the same chart of quartz-feldspar ratios. Each coarse (intrusive) type has a chemically equivalent fine (volcanic) type. Granodiorite is equivalent to dacite, and diorite to andesite. Sure enough, those types of lava erupted from volcanoes of the same eras and terranes as our intrusions. Granite's equivalent is rhyolite, and Golden Horn magma could conceivably have fed a rhyolitic volcano; however, failure to erupt at the surface is common among pale magmas.

Grandodiorite, 2 inches.

Diorite, 2 inches.

Gabbro, 3 inches.

Gabbro

Gabbro is the intrusive counterpart of basalt: it contains the same mix of minerals, but in coarser crystals that are inconspicuous because they lack color contrast. While basalt is the most abundant volcanic rock, gabbro is rather rare. Apparently basalt magma doesn't tend to plug up plumbing (in contrast to granite, a highly viscous magma). Marys Peak and a few nearby summits in the Coast Range owe their prominence to erosion-resistant gabbro sills. Gabbro can form bands, usually well over 4 inches wide, wider than typical bands in schist or gneiss. Bands of dark gray gabbro alternate dramatically with pale granitic bands in Fourth-of-July Basin. Early Ancestral Cascades magma produced gabbro on Copper Ridge and much of Mt. Sefrit. Gabbro outcrops are also familiar right in Victoria.

GEOLOGY: SEDIMENTARY ROCKS

Shale

Abundant throughout the Olympics, shale consists of clayey river mud carried out to sea and piled up in ocean basins to such depths that through thousands or millions of years under the weight of subsequent layers it was compacted into more or less solid rock. Most kinds of sediments have to be cemented together with water-soluble minerals to become sedimentary rocks, but

Argillite (mudstone), 3 inches.

Graywacke, 2 inches.

clay particles are so minute and flaky that they can become shale through compaction alone, or with minor amounts of cement. Shale is still close enough to simple clay that you can breathe on it and smell clay, or break a piece in your hands, or scrape it with your knife and spit on the scrapings to mix up a batch of fresh clay mud.

Shale is generally gray, and has a strong tendency to break into flattish leaves along its bedding planes. A similar rock that doesn't break in flat leaves (due to different mineral content) is mudstone. Where we find shales and mudstones, we may also find less- and more-processed beds nearby—dense clays that lay on the ocean floor too briefly and shallowly to get compacted into rock, and others that got buried long and deeply, and metamorphosed into slate or phyllite.

Sandstone

Sandstone embraces sedimentary rocks made up of compacted sand-size (0.06–2 mm) particles cemented together with water-soluble minerals like silica or calcite. In the classic blond sandstone the sand grains are almost all quartz. How do beds or beaches of nearly pure quartz sand ever collect in the first place, given that the waters erode all the diverse rocks of a watershed? Quartz is both hard and chemically stable, tending to break down to sand-size particles and then stop breaking down. In contrast, feldspars and other abundant minerals tend to end up as silt and clay mud through a process of chemical weathering with water. Eventually, the sand-size particles remaining in a beach are almost all quartz, after the finer silt washes away. This takes a long time, preferably in pounding surf, and it helps to have a quartz-rich source.

Most sandstones in our mountains had neither the quartz-rich source nor the time. Arkose sandstone rich in feldspars, common in the North Cascades, looks coarse, motley, and sometimes pinkish, resembling granite and diorite, from which it derives. It forms in lakes, riverbeds, and shallow seas near active mountain ranges where granitic rocks are rapidly uplifting and eroding. Transport and deposition are too swift to allow chemical weathering to remove the abundant feldspars.

North Cascades arkoses formed in basins nestled among the ancestral mountains. Just as fast as these basins dropped, they filled up with freshly eroded sediments. Sands in arkose around Leavenworth derive from erosion, 50–60 million years ago, of the same Mt. Stuart Batholith that stands above them today. Extensive east-side exposures are in the Wenatchee-Chiwawa River trough, the Methow Valley, and the Fraser Valley above Hope. The scarce west-side outcrops include peaks such as Gothic and Hagan.

The Olympics have a lot of "muddy" sandstone called graywacke ("gray-wacky").

A belt of graywacke together with some arkose and quartz sandstones runs across the top of the range from the Sol Duc to the Quinault. Graywacke resembles shale in its dark color and clayey odor when damp, and in being held together by clay. It differs by mixing in sand-size, angular fragments, often of andesite. It may resemble volcanic tuff, but that's as rare in the Olympics as graywacke is in the volcanic Cascades.

Graywackes like these form as turbidites in ocean subduction trenches, offshore from volcanic arcs. Avalanche-like bursts of mud-and-sand slurry course down the trench slopes at intervals of several hundred years, dumping inches or feet of sediment at a time. Unlike typical ocean sediment beds, which slowly accumulate sorted sediments, all equally fine, these turbidity currents lay down a range of particle sizes in each bed. Each turbidity avalanche bed is graded, starting at its bottom with coarse sediments, which settle quickly, and grading upward to fine sediments, which settle over days or weeks. The fine sediments of an older bed adjoin the coarse sediments of the next younger bed. If they seem to grade finer downward, subsequent faulting must have flipped them.

Limestone

Many marine sediments, such as those that become sandstone or shale, are ground-up rocks derived by erosion of the land surface. Others are ground-up or dissolved seashells. Hard-shelled marine organisms make shells out of various compounds, most abundant being calcite ($CaCO_3$). Don't just picture shellfish: the majority are one-celled, and many practice photosynthesis and have sometimes been called algae. Sedimentary rock characterized by over 50 percent calcite content is limestone. You can test for limestone with a drop of hydrochloric acid or vinegar, which will effervesce in reaction with the alkaline calcite. Some limestones are virtually pure crystalline calcite precipitated upon the ocean floor from completely dissolved shells of dead organisms. Others, such as chalk, form from plankton that secrete calcite without making a substantial shell. A median limestone might be pulverized shell material cemented together with calcite precipitated calcite.

Limestone and its magnesium-bearing cousin, dolomite, are very special rocks in important ways:

Soils derived from them are alkaline and calcium-rich, favoring certain plants and excluding others.

They dissolve—very slowly, of course, but with dramatic results including underground rivers, the world's long cave systems, and tower-shaped hills in southern China. Pure water cannot dissolve them, but groundwater easily picks up enough CO_2 to make a weak carbonic acid, which can.

They were created by living organisms (a trait shared with coal and some chert).

They (even more than coal) provide the world's major long-term carbon sink. If it hadn't been for their sequestration of carbon, the greenhouse climate would long ago have become and remained so hot that large animals probably never would have evolved. This is one of the chief self-regulating cycles described by the Gaia hypothesis: when CO_2 levels rise, calcite critters thrive, sucking up carbon faster and sequestering it in limestone, reducing CO_2 levels. Unfortunately, this

Limestone

works at a geologic pace; it can't speed up enough to save us from our carbon emissions.

Limestone and dolomite abound globally, but not here. Our mountains have only a few sizable limestone areas, all on Vancouver Island. The limestone tends to draw drainage underground, turning many creeks into empty (or intermittent) creek beds for much of the summer. Elsewhere, Mt. Baker's flanks include Chowder Ridge, a 150-million-year-old limestone bouillabaisse cropping out amid young volcanic rocks. High in the eastern Olympics, limestone fills small interstices between undersea basalt flows; minerals from the hot lava altered much of it to deep red. The Napeequa Valley and Park Butte have belts of marble, which is metamorphosed limestone.

Quartz and Chert

Quartz is the most familiar "rock crystal"—transparent (though sometimes tinted) with six generally unequal sides and a six-faceted point. It's the only stone in this chapter that forms single crystals—because it's a mineral, rather than a rock. (In geologists' terms, a rock is a mixture of minerals whose proportions to each other vary only within limits that define that kind of rock; constituent minerals may take the form of visible crystals, or not. A mineral, on the other hand, is a single chemical compound, or continuum of compounds, with one characteristic crystal shape.)

Quartz is silicon dioxide (SiO_2, also called silica) with too few impurities to disrupt its proper crystal form. It is harder than steel (ergo, too hard to scratch with a knife) lightweight and light-colored, and abundant as a rock ingredient; it is in nearly every light- to medium-colored rock you see, except limestone and marble. Its abundance at the earth's surface probably results from its light weight—it has risen among heavier materials while powerful forces stirred the earth around it for some four billion years. The heavy metals nickel and iron gravitated to the earth's core; they are the most abundant elements in the earth as a whole, whereas silica is abundant only at the surface.

Large, free-sided quartz crystals are infrequent, but they do catch the eye. Some have been found in crevices in greenstone in the Olympics. They form in rock cavities that spent a long time carrying groundwater rich in dissolved silica. The silica crystals precipitated out on the cavity lining, like sugar crystallizing on a string as rock candy. (That's backwards of course: rock candy is named after quartz crystals). Veins of quartz reflected as gleams in a prospector's eye, since lucrative metals often occur in or near them; the same subterranean streams carry both silica and metals. We aren't talking about drinking water now, but superheated brine or even brine vapor—"fluids," a

Chert, 3 inches.

Quartz veins. Scale 10 inches.

geologist would say—full of dissolved minerals that would not be water-soluble at surface temperatures.

Nearly pure quartz may also occur in an opaque cryptocrystalline form, meaning the crystals are too small to see even with a microscope. This rock, chert, resembles porcelain, whereas crystalline quartz is transparent like glass. That's no coincidence: ground-up silica rock is the main ingredient in both glass and porcelain. Both porcelain and a hard chert called Arkansas novaculite can whet a fine edge on a knife. Like glass and obsidian, chert chips with an even, shallowly concave fracture. Its dark form, flint, was second to obsidian as arrowhead material.

Cherts form in several very different ways. The commonest is similar to limestone—crumbled marine shell material settling to the ocean floor or precipitating there from solution in seawater. Whereas most seashells are made of calcite, the main mineral in limestone, there is also a large group of one-celled organisms that make a sort of shell of silica. They are the main source of chert.

Conglomerate

Typical conglomerates are petrified pebble beaches and river bars; by definition they're sedimentary rocks composed of at least 50 percent erosion-rounded stones. They require soluble minerals as glue, as well as fine rock particles to fill in the spaces. Well-cemented conglomerates will break straight through pebbles and interstices alike—a fine sight. Weaker ones break through the cementing matrix only, leaving the pebbles sticking out just like from any old gravel bank. Look for good conglomerates around Devil's Dome and Holman Peak, east of Ross Lake, and in the related terranes north along the Fraser. Ludden Peak in the Olympics and Johannesberg in the North Cascades are hardened metaconglomerate, compressed so hard during metamorphism that the pebbles were all flattened in one direction.

Conglomerate

Volcanic breccia. Scale 16 inches.

Breccia

Breccia consists of unrounded rock pieces bound up in a fine-grained matrix other than volcanic tuff. The distinction from conglomerate's erosion-rounded pieces may seem trifling, but on further thought it is puzzling, since only eroded rocks are normally deposited as sediments. There turn out to be several brecciating processes, each involving breakage, from which the Italian word *breccia* ("bretch-ia") derives.

Sedimentary breccia is often a turbidite, sort of a coarse graywacke containing shaley shards ripped from the surface of deep-sea sediments by a turbidity current. Alternatively, ordinary landslides in shaley, slaty, or limestone terrain can end up compacted into breccia.

Tectonic breccia is a mix of coarse and fine rock fragments broken by shearing forces within a fault, and then compacted. Sometimes you can visually match up the broken edges of adjacent fragments.

Volcanic breccia is the common type here. It can be simply the skin of a basalt flow that shattered and then slipped back into the lava. In this case, matrix and inclusions are of the exact same rock. Alternatively, as a body of magma rises, pieces of the surrounding rock break off and fall into it. Sometimes these pieces happen to be rocks whose melting point is much hotter than the magma, and they keep their sharp edges while swimming in melt. High-grade metamorphic rocks, for example, have a higher melting point than granitic magma.

There is a lot of breccia out there, but much of it looks like an obscure mess and fails to catch anyone's eye. It usually takes rock saws and polishers to reveal the splendid breccia sections that appear in books and as architectural facings.

GEOLOGY: METAMORPHIC ROCKS

Metamorphic rocks are those remineralized by heat and pressure, while buried. They are described below in order of their metamorphic grade, from less heat and pressure (metamorphosed at shallower depths) to more. High-grade metamorphic rocks characterize the North Cascades, and are seen, but less prevalent, in our British Columbia mountains. Olympic metamorphics, being much younger, range from low-grade slate to schist and greenstone of medium and locally high grades. The geologic process is called metamorphism; metamorphosis is for insects.

Slate and Phyllite

Slate looks like what it is: metamorphosed shale. Even the word looks like the other word altered. They share dark gray colors (varying through reds and greens in slates) and platy textures that tend to break into flat pieces. Surprisingly, the flat cleavage of slate was never the flat bedding plane of its parent rock. Bedding planes start out horizontal,

Slate, 5 inches.

as layers of sediment settling out from the water. Slaty cleavage planes, in contrast, are perpendicular to the direction of pressure during metamorphism. There may have been two or more such directions at different times, producing slate that fractures into slender "pencils." Some slates metamorphosed from mudstone, and never had distinct bedding planes; in others the bedding has faded. Sometimes the parent shale's bedding planes can be seen as streaks in slate, either happening to align with the cleavage planes or not, but no longer causing a plane of weakness.

Slate gets a slight satiny luster from microscopic crystals of mica and other minerals. Metamorphism aligned these all parallel, creating the cleavage plane and the shine. Somewhat higher-pressure metamorphism of the same rock produces larger crystals (just barely visible without a lens), a stronger, glittery but often wavy gloss, and a weaker tendency to split. That rock is phyllite, properly, though it is sold as "roofing slate." Slate is shatter-prone and weak in landforms, and phyllite just slightly less so. Both abound, often together, in the Olympics.

Serpentinite

Serpentinites are characteristically soft rocks, green, often flecked with black crystals, with a greasy luster. They got their name (and one of their minerals was named lizardite) because this look was considered reptilian. They weather into red soils difficult for most plants to grow in, with too much nickel and chromium and too little of the nutrient elements. An abrupt transition to reddish soil with sparse or stunted plant cover may be a clue to serpentine soils. They are found in a long arc around Mt. Stuart that includes a big part of the Wenatchee Mountains; all over the Twin Sisters near Mt. Baker; and in smaller outcrops scattered in the North Cascades and British Columbia. (Oregon has big serpentine areas in the Klamaths, outside of our range.)

Serpentinites form by watery low-grade metamorphism of peridotite—mantle rock brought to the surface most often in subduction zone mountain belts. Peridotite is defined by a high proportion (40 percent or more) of the yellow-green mineral olivine, which predominates in the mantle. Olivine-rich material is too heavy to reach the surface without exceptionally deep and rapid rock movement, and most of what does reach the surface is serpentinized along the way; so peridotites are uncommon at the surface even though their mantle abundance puts them among the most abundant rocks in the earth as a whole. (Also in the solar system, judging by their abundance in meteorites.) The purest mantle specimens, with over 90 percent olivine, are dunite. Geologists interested in dunite mostly have to content themselves with little bits and pieces, but at the Twin Sisters they have the world's largest outcrop of it, attesting to the violent crustal upheaval that produced the North Cascades.

Peridotite is a coarse-grained igneous rock with no fine-grained (volcanic) counterpart because lava isn't hot enough to melt it. Solid peridotite rocks occasionally shoot out of volcanoes along with molten lava, and end up as inclusions in the solidified lava. They must have crystallized long before (and below) the melting of the magma. Gem-quality olivine crystals are peridot, the August birthstone.

Schist

Metamorphic rocks differ according to exactly how much heat and pressure they underwent. As the heat and pressure increase beyond slate grade, the parallel layers may get tightly crimped, crumpled or curved, while the rock's strength increases. At the same time, the flaky crystals (mainly mica) first grow larger as slaty cleavage converts to schistose foliation; then they might be replaced altogether by coarse crystals that may show gneissose banding. Though schist derives from the Greek for "split" (as in schizophrenia), schists aren't nearly as easy to split as slates. Schistose texture, which defines schists, may be dulled and obscured by weathering or rust, but in unweathered specimens, parallel mica flakes glimmer in the sun.

In garnet-biotite schist, common just east of Glacier Peak, the garnet appears as scattered, reddish, smeared crystals ¼ inch or larger, with schistose foliation making

Serpentinite, 6 inches.

Schist

almond shapes around them. Black mica gives the rock an overall blackish hue. Garnet did not exist in these rocks until they reached the exact degree of heat and pressure that produces garnet schist. Metamorphism makes new minerals by recombining atoms into new molecules. Migration of atoms between molecules is extremely slow unless water is present—and it usually is. The mineral products are determined by heat and pressure, and by what elements are available. Mica and garnet need aluminum, which they typically get from clay minerals in shale.

Greenstone, Greenschist, Blueschist

Increasing metamorphic intensities turn basalt into these three rocks. Greenstone looks like basalt with a greenish cast, and sometimes retains pillow basalt shapes, as shown on page 520. Green pillows can be seen in the Olympics (where most basalt is at least somewhat metamorphosed) and high on Crater Mountain. Crater and Jack Mountains are part of a belt of old metamorphosed sea-floor basalt that continues north of Hope, then after a gap reappears west of Lillooet. (The Fraser River Fault sheared this terrane into two parts.) Few Oregon basalts have been buried deeply enough to metamorphose.

Mt. Shuksan and Whitechuck Mountain contain much greenschist and a little blueschist, high-grade metabasalts differing from greenstone in their schistose texture, with smeared-out lustrous crystals. Their formation requires high pressure without high temperature, that is, deep but brief burial, with rapid uplift—a combination that can happen in tempestuous subduction zones. Greenschists of Wrangellia are scattered across the southern Coast Mountains, including the Britannia Mine's ore deposits. True to its name, the extra-high-pressure version is often bluish.

Hornfels

If you ever notice that you have just left an area of granitic rocks, you may be in the vicinity of hornfels. It is a contact metamorphic rock, baked by close contact with hot intrusive magma—in other words, high-temperature, low-pressure metamorphism. (Volatiles from the magma often contribute their chemistry to the new minerals as well.) Where hornfels occurs in shale, it may grade into spotted slate and then shale as you walk a few yards farther from

Greenschist

Hornfels

the granitic intrusion. Hornfels is a fine-grained, often dark gray to black crystalline rock resembling basalt; the easiest way to tell it from basalt is by its location near granitics. The word means "horn rock" in German, referring either to animal horns or to Alpine horn mountains like the Matterhorn. The idea is that this is one tough rock. The spires we know as Hozomeen, Shuksan, and Slesse occurred where metamorphic rocks were further cooked by contact metamorphism.

Skagit gneiss, 6 inches.

Migmatite, 16 inches.

Gneiss

Gneiss ("nice") excels as mountain material: not only is it hard, but it has few microfractures to admit water and consequent frost splitting. North Cascades climbers know the Skagit Gneiss and its kin intimately; they uphold the backbone of the range—Redoubt, Triumph, Fury and Terror, Snowfield and Eldorado, Forbidden and Formidable, Boston, Buckner, Magic and Mixup, Logan, Goode, and Bonanza.

Being coarsely crystalline, gneiss resembles granitic rocks except that its grains are at least slightly flattened and aligned. The plane of flattening may show lighter and darker bands, often folded or wrinkled. Gneiss fragments may break along planes of glittery mica flakes. For the rock to be gneiss rather than schist (which also has minerals aligned and segregated in bands), fat grains must outweigh flake-sized crystals overall.

Some gneiss started out as shale or arkose and was metamorphosed by heat and pressure past the phyllite and schist stages. Other gneiss is granitic rock metamorphosed.

Migmatite

For help in visualizing mountain-building tectonics, look at the gorgeous migmatites in road cuts in the Skagit Gorge, near Ross Lake Overlook, at Chelan Falls, and scattered through the Skagit gneiss complex. It's one thing to say that when terranes scrunch together, deep rocks can flow. It's another to look at a chunk of too, too solid rock that clearly flowed like swirly cake batter full of nuts, marshmallow, and fudge. This is what goes on deep in the heart of mountains, under extreme heat and pressure, like 1330°F, at a depth of 19 miles. Even before our eyes it retains its mystery.

Formation of migmatite (from the Greek for "mix") is thought to involve partial melting. Ribbons of melt recrystallize into granitic rock. In between granitic stripes and swirls are darker, older gneiss or schist. Edges between the two are sharp, so we know that the mass as a whole didn't melt. Granitic rocks occur both as swirls and linear dikes; were these injected from nearby magma bodies, or did a crack fill with magma that oozed out of the solid rock like fat from a steak in a pan? Crumples were superimposed on earlier folds, while other cross-cutting cracks filled with silica, making quartz veins, and so on.

At least that's what we think happened. We'll never get to see it in action.

Keeping Track

All mountains walk with their toes on all waters and splash there.
—Dōgen

Once I slept on a spot of earth so steep I thought if I turned in my sleep I would fall in the river.
Nine years on I am here but that earth fell in the river it steeps in salt by now,
the run I dunked in and yelped from its cold now hot bare cobbles growing alder poles.

Valley not a fixed place but an active kerf of upwarping rock and downcutting snowmelt.
Mountains in geotimelapse ripple and melt while river writhes and flops
like a pinioned snake like thick long braid riding undulating spine.

Once I took a floppy pup along his river all the way to snow and back he laughed.
Nine years on old dog tires and lags but knows to hush while deer graze
up to us or while we circle held at forty feet in bear's black gaze.

Morels pierce umber silk where fire swept last fall all the forest's needles fell at once.
Iron donkey sinews rust to dirt where a man once worked this valley.
So deer would keep the meadow when he moved in he fenced his mules two miles down
where I camp. My knife lops nettles mule piss fed my fire wilts their acid teeth and I fatten
on their prickly succulence making flesh new from green shoots exhuming him.

As the river is never the same water twice the sloughing valley is not the same rock
nor the man the same muscle nor mind the same music. All that goes down is a line
of incremental torrent a widening froth. Still *I am this place and I have*
always
been here.

ABBREVIATIONS AND SYMBOLS

°	degrees Fahrenheit
×	by (as in length by width); also: lens magnification power
♀	female(s)
♂	male(s)
BC	British Columbia
c	central
CasR	Cascade Range
CasCr	Cascade Crest as a climatic divide between west side and east side
CoastM	Coast Mountains of British Columbia
CoastR	Coast Range of Oregon and southwest Washington
CGorge	Columbia Gorge
CO_2	Carbon dioxide
dbh	tree diameter at 4½ feet above the ground ("breast height")
e	east(ern)
elev(s)	elevation(s)
e-side	the area east of the climatic divide of the CasR and CoastM
mtn(s)	mountain(s)
n	north(ern)
NA	North America
NABCI	North American Bird Conservation Initiative
NP	National Park
OlyM	Olympic Mountains
OR	Oregon
USDA	the US Department of Agriculture and its plant species database
PNW	Pacific Northwest
s	south(ern)
spp.	species plural: any and all of the species of a genus
subsp.	subspecies
w	west(ern)
WA	Washington
ws	wingspread: the measurement across outspread wings
VI	Vancouver Island
w-side	the area west of the climatic divide of the CasR and CoastM

GLOSSARY

adipose fin A soft, fleshy bump on the back of some fish, immediately in front of the tail fin.

alevin A hatchling fish, especially a salmon or trout in the stage when it is still attached to and nourished by an egg yolk sac.

allelopathy Deposition in the soil, by plants, of chemicals that discourage growth of other plant or fungal species and thus improve the competitive fitness of the allelopathic species.

alpine The elevation zone too high for tree species to be growing numerously in upright tree form.

alternate Arranged with only one leaf at any given distance along a stem. Contrast with **opposite** or **whorled**.

anadromous Participating in a life cycle of birth and breeding in streams or lakes separated by a period of growth at sea.

anal fin A vertical fin on a fish's underside, forward from the tail fin.

angle of repose The steepest slope angle that a given loose sediment is able to hold.

anther The pollen-bearing head portion of a **stamen**.

ascending Held well above perpendicular to the stem or axis, but not nearly parallel or aligned with it; intermediate between **spreading** and **erect**.

ash Fine particles of volcanic rock (usually glassy in structure) formed when magma is blasted out of a volcano.

aspect The compass direction a slope faces.

awn A stiff, hairlike extension of the tip of a **bract** in the **floret** of a grass.

axil The crotch between a stem and a leaf.

basal (Leaves) Attached to a plant at its root crown; contrast with stem leaves.

batholith An intrusion of igneous rock exposed at the surface over a large area—technically with at least 100 square km exposed.

biomass Total living matter, usually expressed as a measure of dry weight per unit area.

bisexual With functioning stamens and pistils in the same flower.

bloom A pale, powdery coating on a surface.

boreal Of the Northern Hemisphere–wide belt dominated by coniferous forests and transitional between Arctic and **temperate** climate.

bract A modified (usually smaller) leaf, often attached just below a flower or **inflorescence**.

broadleaf Common term for all trees and shrubs other than **conifers**; very few have leaves narrow enough to be confused with conifer needles.

buttress A wide flaring out at the base of a tree.

call Any vocal communication common to birds of a given species. Compare **song**.

calyx The outermost whorl or circle of parts of most flowers—the **sepals** spoken of collectively (or a whorl of sepal-like lobes that would be sepals if they were separate all the way to their bases). Compare **corolla**.

cambium A soft layer under the bark; it lies between the new wood and new bark tissue, and turns into both as it develops.

canopy In a forest, the collective mass of branches and foliage of the taller trees; can also include the associated community of canopy-dwellers.

cap The spreading top portion of a typical mushroom, supported by a stem and supporting **gills**, tubes, or spines on its lower surface.

capsule A seedpod, technically a nonfleshy **fruit** that splits to release seeds; in mosses, the spore-containing organ.

catkin A form of **inflorescence** on certain trees and shrubs, consisting of a dense spike of minute, dry, petal-less flowers. Our species with catkins make two kinds—staminate (male) and pistillate (female).

cirque A head of a mountain valley having a characteristic amphitheater shape due to erosion by the upper end of a glacier.

class A taxonomic group broader than an **order** or **family** and narrower than a **phylum**. Examples: mammals, fishes, birds, spiders, insects, and traditionally dicots.

clastic Formed out of fragments of rock (a description of most sedimentary rocks except those formed by chemical precipitation).

climax A hypothetical condition of stability in which all **successional** changes resulting from plant community growth have taken place, so that further changes can only follow destructive disturbances.

cloaca An orifice (on birds, reptiles, fishes, and so on) through which the urinary, reproductive, and gastrointestinal tracts all discharge.

clone A group of genetically identical progeny produced by vegetative or other asexual reproduction from a single progenitor. (Only in nonscientific use is the seeming individual a clone.)

clone To reproduce asexually.

composite A member of the plant family Asteraceae (formerly Compositae), characterized by composite flower heads that resemble single flowers but are actually inflorescences of tiny flowers. Examples: daisies, thistles, dandelions.

compound leaf A structure of three or more **leaflets** resembling separate leaves on a stem except that the compound leaf terminates in a leaflet whereas a stem terminates in a flower, a bud, or a growing shoot; as with any leaf, a compound leaf has a node or swelling where it meets the stem it grows from, whereas its leaflets do not each grow from nodes of their own.

congener A member of a species in the same genus.

conifer A common name for a broad taxonomic group of trees and shrubs, many of which bear needlelike or scalelike leaves and woody "cones."

conspecific (An individual) Of the same species.

convect To move upward and downward due to temperature contrasting with that of other fluids in the same system; hot air rises, cold air sinks.

cordillera The entire mountain system of the western portions of the Americas; "mountain range" in Spanish, derived from "string."

corolla The whorl or circle of a typical flower's parts lying second from the outside; that is, the **petals** spoken of collectively. Compare **calyx**.

cosymbiont A partner in a symbiotic relationship with a given organism.

crevasse A crack in a glacier, expressing flow stresses.

crown The leafy (top) part of a tree.

crust The surface layer of the earth, averaging about 6 miles thick under the oceans and 20 miles thick in the continents, defined primarily by lower-density (lighter) rock than the **mantle** underneath.

crystal The specific structure of many chemical compounds (including all **minerals**) in which the atoms position themselves in a geometry that repeats indefinitely; often visible in broken rock surfaces.

deciduous Shedding its leaves annually; that is, not **evergreen**. (Technically, deciduous can describe any shedding part, such as petals that fall off before the pistil matures, or sepals that fall off as the fruit matures.)

dicot A member of a traditional grouping of flowering plants including all of our broadleaf trees and shrubs and virtually all of our terrestrial herbs except lilies, orchids, and grasslike plants (the monocots). Short for dicotyledon. The traditional dicots turn out to have arisen as several branches of the plant family tree, so they have been split; but all the "dicots" in this book except

Nuphar and *Asarum* are eudicots ("true dicots"), which are a single branch.

dike An igneous intrusion that is much longer and deeper than it is thick, and that cuts through the structure of the surrounding rocks.

disjunct Growing in a location distant from others of the same species.

disk flower A small, radially symmetrical flower densely clustered within a **composite** flower head, often dry and drab-colored; the disk of these flowers is the "eye" of a daisy, or the entire flower head of a thistle or a pussytoes. Only in the family Compositae.

disturbance An event that causes abrupt changes in a plant community—for example, logging, windstorms, floods, or fires.

dominant One of the trees in a stand whose **crown** is part of the highest **canopy** layer; or more generally, a plant species covering more ground than others within a given layer (herb, low shrub, tall shrub, tree) of a plant community.

dorsal fin A vertical fin in the center of a fish's back.

duff Matted, partly decayed litter on the forest floor.

elliptic A leaf shape widest at the middle and pointed at both ends, broader than **lanceolate** but less broad than **oval**.

endophyte An organism that lives symbiotically within a plant—most often, a fungus living inside plant leaves. Many of these very common and widespread symbioses appear to be **mutualistic**, but they have received little study.

entire (A leaf or leaflet margin) Smooth, lacking teeth, scallops, or lobes.

epiphyte An organism that lives attached to and supported by a host organism without directly exchanging any substances with the host and typically without causing it major harm. Lichens, mosses, ferns, and even flowering plants can be epiphytes on trees in the Pacific Northwest.

erect Positioned nearly vertically.

evergreen Bearing relatively heavy leaves that normally keep their form, color, and function on the plant for at least twelve months and often a few years. Opposite of **deciduous**; compare **persistent**.

family A taxonomic group broader than a genus or species, and narrower than an **order** or **class**. Latin names for families end in *-aceae* if they are plants and *-idae* if they are animals.

fascicle A bundle, especially the characteristic cluster of one to five pine needles sheathed at their base in tiny dry, membranous **bracts**.

fault A fracture in rock or earth where relative movement of the two sides has taken place; may be of any size.

filament The slender stalk of a **stamen**, bearing an **anther**.

flora (Literally "flowers") All of a region's plant species, collectively; a reference work cataloguing those species.

floret A small flower within a compact inflorescence such as the **head** of a **composite** or the **spikelet** of a grass.

fruit Among the seed plants, an **ovary** wall matured into a seed-bearing structure; also, more broadly, any seed-bearing or **spore**-bearing structure.

fry Young fish (both singular and plural). Among salmon and trout, the fry stage follows the **alevin** stage and precedes the **parr** stage.

fused Not separated all the way to the base; fused **petals** (or **sepals**) form a single **corolla** (**calyx**) ring or tube, usually with lobes at the front edge that can be counted for identification purposes.

gall A tumorlike growth induced on a tree or shrub by insects, fungi, or bacteria; for insects, it usually serves larvae as a protective "house."

genus Taxonomic group broader than a **species** and narrower than a **family**; the first of the two words in the scientific name (binomial) of an organism. Plural: genera.

gills (1) In aquatic animals, the respiratory organs where oxygen suspended in the water passes into the animal. (2) On some mushrooms, **spore**-bearing organs consisting of paper-thin radii on the underside of the **cap**.

gland An organ that secretes a fluid. Glands are common on plant surfaces in the form of dots or microscopic bulbs on the ends of short hairs, leading to description of the leaf or sepal as "sticky-hairy."

granitic rocks Medium to light-colored coarse-grained **igneous** rocks; see **intrusive rocks**.

head A tight, compact **inflorescence**.

herbaceous Not **woody**; with all aboveground parts normally dying or withering at the end of the growing season. Some low, soft-stemmed plants classed as herbs may persist through milder winters.

herb layer All the **herbaceous** plants and low shrubs of comparable size, as a group comprising a structural element of a plant community. Typical forest communities here have a **canopy** layer, one or two shrub or small tree layers, an herb layer, and a moss layer.

here Within our range, defined on page 17.

high-grade (Metamorphic rocks) Altered by relatively high degrees of heat and pressure.

hybrid (An individual) directly descended from, and bearing genes of, multiple species.

hyphae Minute tubular filaments that make up the body (mycelium) of a fungus. Singular: hypha.

igneous rocks Rocks that reached their present mineral composition and texture by cooling from a melt (**magma**); may be either **volcanic** or **intrusive**.

inflorescence A cluster of flowers from one stem; the cluster's pattern.

instar A pre-adult stage in insect growth separated from the next instar by molting.

intergrade To vary along a continuum between one well-defined type (such as a species or a rock type) and another.

introduced Not thought to have lived in a given area (our range) before the arrival of Euro-Americans; not **native**.

intrusive rocks **Igneous rocks** that did not surface as fluid lava in a volcanic eruption, but solidified underground. Intrusives are typically coarser-grained than volcanic rocks; geologists prefer the term "phaneritic" for any particular rock, because grain size, not mode of origin, is what you can know by examining it.

invasive **Introduced** and spreading relatively quickly.

involucral bracts Small leaves circling a stem immediately beneath an **inflorescence** such as the **composite** flower head.

irregular flower Flower whose **petals** (or **sepals**) are not all alike in size or shape; often they make a bilateral symmetry.

isostasy Tendency of the earth's crust to even out gravitational anomalies by raising ("floating") surfaces underlain by material less dense than surrounding materials.

juvenile plumage Feathers (and their color pattern) of birds old enough to fly, but not yet entering their first breeding season; the two sexes typically resemble each other at this stage.

krummholz Dwarfed, horizontally inclined shrubby growth, near **alpine** timberline, of conifer species that grow as upright trees elsewhere under more moderate conditions; from the German for "crooked wood." (This meaning is well established in English usage, though a few writers object that in German scientific usage krummholz is genetically stunted growth, and the word for environmentally stunted growth is "kruppelholz").

lanceolate (A leaf shape) Tapered to a point at each end, and broadest somewhat below the midpoint; narrower than **elliptic** or **oval**, broader than **linear**.

landlocked (Fish) Completing their life cycle in freshwater, where some barrier (usually a dam, but sometimes natural) prevents an **anadromous** (seagoing) life cycle.
larva An insect, amphibian, or other animal when in a youthful form that differs strongly from the adult form. Caterpillars are the larvae of moths and butterflies; maggots of flies; tadpoles of frogs.
lava Rock that is flowing, or once flowed, in a melted state at the earth surface in a volcanic eruption; compare **magma**.
layering Vegetative or clonal reproduction in which new new roots and stems grow from branches in contact with earth.
leader The topmost central shoot of a plant.
leaflet An apparent leaf that's actually a member of a **compound leaf**.
leafstalk A narrowed stalk portion (petiole) of a leaf, distinguished from the leaf blade.
linear (A leaf shape) Very narrow, almost uniform in width over its whole length.
lip On an orchid, the lowest, largest **petal**, specialized as a landing platform for an insect pollinator.
lobe A convexity in a leaf, calyx, or corolla outline.
low-grade (Metamorphic rocks) Altered by relatively mild degrees of heat and pressure.
lumpers Scientists inclined to reduce the numbers of species, genera, and so on, by recognizing any given distinction at a lower taxonomic rank. Opposed to **splitters**.

magma Subsurface rock in a melted, fluid state. If and when it reaches the surface, it erupts either as **lava** or into the air as **pyroclastic** fragments.
mantle The major portion of the Earth's interior, below the **crust** and above the core.
margin Edge.
matrix In rocks, the finer-grained material in which grains, crystals, or contrasting pieces of rock are embedded.
metamorphic rocks Rocks whose **mineral** composition and texture resulted from remineralization by heat or pressure below the earth surface.
metamorphism The heat-and-pressure remineralization that makes **metamorphic rocks**.
metamorphosis The process in which larval animals transform into adults.
midden A heap of organic material made by an animal. Both zoologists and anthropologists have adopted this old English word, originally a dung heap. Animal middens may include dung, but commonly include stored food items.
milt Fish semen.
mineral Any natural nonliving earth substance having a well-defined chemical formula and a characteristic crystalline structure. Rocks and soils are largely mixtures of minerals.
monocot A member of a large taxonomic group of flowering plants most of which have parallel-veined leaves and flower parts in threes. No monocots here are **woody**, and most are lilies, orchids, or aquatic or grasslike plants. Short for "monocotyledon."
moraine A usually elongate heap or hill of rock debris lying where it was deposited by a glacier when the glacier retreated from that margin.
mutualism A **symbiosis** in which both partners benefit.
mycology The branch of biology dealing with fungi.
mycophagy The eating of fungi; the collecting of wild fungi for food.
mycorrhiza A tiny organ formed jointly by plant roots and fungi that passes nutritive substances between plant and fungus. Plurals: mycorrhizae (US), mycorrhizas (UK).

naiad An aquatic **larva**, in insects that undergo several larval **instars** and no pupa.
native Thought to have lived in a given area (**our** range) before the arrival of Euro-Americans. (Scientists prefer more complex definitions of "introduced" and "native," but this definition serves our purposes.)

nature The universe as it was preceding or is outside of human civilization.

nectar A sugary liquid secreted in some kinds of flowers, attractive to pollinators.

niche The place of a species within an ecological community, in terms especially of how it exploits the habitat and other community members to meet its life requirements.

nitrogen fixation Splitting of the N_2 molecule found in air, and synthesis of the N atoms into a form usable by living organisms. Though only certain bacteria can actually do this, we loosely call plant and lichen species "nitrogen-fixing" if they host these bacteria symbiotically.

nurse log A rotting tree serving (and in many situations virtually required) as a seedbed for tree reproduction.

oblanceolate (A leaf shape) More or less tapered to each end, like **lanceolate** except broadest somewhat past the midpoint (closer to the tip); narrower than **obovate**.

obovate (A leaf shape) Roughly **oval**, rounded at both ends, like ovate except broadest somewhat past the midpoint (closer to the tip).

offset A short propagative shoot from the base of a plant, or a small bulb from the side of a plant's bulb.

old-growth Late-successional natural forest; often defined simply by the age of the oldest cohort of trees, for example 200 years for Northwest forests. However, significant "older-growth" forest characteristics continue to develop to at least 500 years of age.

opposite (Leaves) Arranged in pairs along a stem. The stem terminates in a bud, flower(s), or growing shoot; if it appears to terminate in a leaf or tendril, these are not opposite leaves, but leaflets of compound leaves. Contrast with **alternate** and **whorled**.

order A taxonomic group broader than a **family**, **genus**, or **species**, and narrower than a **class**.

ovary The egg-producing organ; in flowers, this is generally the enlarged basal portion of the **pistil**, at the base of the flower.

oval (A leaf shape) Rounded at both ends and broadest at or below the midpoint.

our Those species or other features within our range, defined on page 17.

palmate (A leaf) **compound**, with five or more **leaflets** all branching from one point.

palmately lobed Shaped (like a maple leaf) with three or more main veins branching from one point at the leaf base, and the leaf outline indented between these veins.

panicle An **inflorescence** around a main stem or axis with at least some of the side branches again branched to bear several flowers. Compare **raceme**, **spike**.

parasite An organism that draws sustenance for at least part of its life cycle out of an organism of another kind, detrimentally to that host (but without eating it).

parr marks Vertical blotches that appear on the sides of **anadromous** salmon and trout of "parr" age, which comes when feeding in freshwater, before migrating to sea.

pelvic fin One in a pair of fins midway along a fish's belly.

pendent Hanging or drooping from a point of attachment.

persistent (Leaves) Tending to stay attached even when no longer functioning, either green or not, but lacking the heavy weight and gloss typical of **evergreen** leaves.

petal A flower part, typically tender-textured and showy, in the inner of two or more concentric whorls. If there is only one whorl, its members are **sepals**, no matter how showy.

pheromone A chemical produced by an animal (or a plant, according to some) that stimulates some behavior in others of the same species.

photosynthesis The synthesis of carbohydrates out of simpler molecules as a means of converting or storing sunlight energy—the basic function of chlorophyllous or green parts of plants and algae.

phylum A very broad taxonomic group,

ranking just below the kingdom. Animal phyla include Chordata (which is a bit broader than "vertebrates") and mollusks; the traditional plant phyla (called divisions) seem to be falling out of favor.

pinna A leaf segment of a fern, branching directly off of the main fern stalk or leaf axis; the pinna may be additionally branched before reaching the ultimate leaflet or fern pinnule. Plural: pinnae. (Synonym of **leaflet**, but in current usage pinnae are on ferns and leaflets are on seed plants.)

pinnate (A leaf) **Compound**, with an odd number of at least five **leaflets** attached to a central leaf axis. If they are attached to subaxes attached in turn to a central axis, the leaf is twice-pinnate; three- and four-times pinnate leaves also exist.

pioneer A species among the first to appear on freshly disturbed (for example, burned, clearcut, deglaciated or volcanically deposited) terrain.

pistil The female organ of a flower, including the **ovary** and ovules and any **styles** or **stigmas** that catch **pollen**.

plate tectonics The dynamics of the earth's crust in terms of the relative motion of plates "floating" on an effectively fluid layer underneath; the model that has dominated geophysical thought since the 1960s (known initially as "continental drift").

pollen Dust-sized male reproductive cells (pollen grains) borne on the **anthers** of a flower, each capable, if carried by wind, animal pollinators, or other agents to the **pistil** of a **conspecific** flower, of fertilizing a female reproductive cell.

pore A minute hole; especially one allowing passage of substances between an organism and its environment.

propagate To reproduce, either sexually or not.

propagule (In lichens and mosses) Any multicelled structure more or less specialized to break off and grow into an organism independent of (but genetically identical to) the one it originated on; a means of asexual reproduction or cloning.

prostrate Growing more or less flat upon the substrate.

pupa An insect in a stationary life stage transitional from a **larva** to an adult. Plural: pupae. Verb: pupate.

pyroclastic Composed of rock fragments formed by midair solidification of **lava** during a more or less explosive volcanic eruption. Volcanic **ash** is loose fine pyroclastic material; tuff is consolidated fine pyroclastic material.

raceme A slender **inflorescence** with each flower borne on an unbranched stalk from the central axis. Compare **panicle**, **spike**.

ray flower A small, asymmetrical flower arranged radially in a **composite** flower head, typically petallike and strap-shaped for most of its length but tubular at its base, often enclosing a **pistil**; rays are the outer part of a daisy flower head, surrounding the **disk flowers**. Only in the family Compositae.

regular (A flower) With all of its **petals** approximately alike in size, shape, and spacing.

relief The vertical component of distance between high and low points on the earth surface.

resin blisters Horizontally elongate blisters, initially full of liquid pitch, conspicuous on the bark of younger fir trees.

rhizine A tough, threadlike appendage on some lichens, serving as a holdfast, not a vessel.

rhizome A rootstalk, or horizontal stem just beneath the soil surface connecting several aboveground stems, sometimes thickened for storage of starches.

rosette A **whorl** of **basal** leaves radiating from a point at or near the ground surface.

runner A stem that trails along the ground, producing several upright stems and thus enabling the plant to spread vegetatively; properly "stolon."

rut An annual period of sexual excitement and activity in mammals.

Salish Sea A place name combining the Strait of Georgia, the Strait of Juan de Fuca, Puget Sound, Hood Canal, Desolation Sound, and the smaller bodies of salt water connected connected to them.

saprobe A fungus or bacterium that absorbs its carbohydrate nutrition from dead organisms. (Because no plants do this, and phyte means "plant," the earlier term "saprophyte" is disfavored. Nongreen plants, p. 184, that get their carbohydrates indirectly from other plants via **mycorrhizae** were once mistakenly thought to be saprophytes.)

scats Feces. (Wildlife biologists' slang derived by back-formation from "scatology.")

schistosity A **metamorphic rock** texture with **minerals** in layers of visible-sized **crystal** grains.

scree Loose rock debris lying at or near its **angle of repose** upon or at the foot of a steeper rock face from which it broke off. Usually implies smaller rocks than **talus**, and can be in gullies high on a rock face.

sedimentary rocks Rocks formed by slow compaction and cementation of particles previously deposited by wind or water currents or by chemical precipitation in water.

sepal A modified leaf within the outermost whorl (the **calyx**) of a flower's parts. Typically, sepals are green and leaflike and surround a concentric whorl of **petals**, but in many cases they are quite showy and petallike. (Sepal-like parts surrounding a **composite** flower **head** are **involucral bracts**.)

serotinous Remaining closed indefinitely. Serotinous pine cones stay closed on the tree for years, then open and release their seeds in response to the heat of a fire.

shrub A **woody**-stemmed plant differentiated from a tree by lacking a single main trunk or by being shorter than some arbitrary height at maturity, such as 26 feet.

simple Not **compound**. Simple leaves range from **entire** (lacking teeth or lobes) to very deeply lobed; if lobes are divided all the way to the leaf's central rib, the leaf is compound rather than simple.

smolt A young salmon or sea trout when first migrating to sea, typically losing its **parr marks** and becoming silvery. (Derived from the same Old English word as "smelt.")

softwood Any **conifer**, in industry jargon; most, but not all, conifers have softer wood than most hardwoods.

song A relatively long and variegated bird vocalization, distinctive of a species, practiced mostly by males in the huge order Passeriformes, commonly called songbirds or perching birds.

sorus A small clump of **spore**-bearing organs visible as a raised dot, line, or crescent (and so on) on a fern or other leaf. Plural: sori.

spathe A single specialized leaf forming a hood or wrapper around an **inflorescence**.

spawn To breed (said of fish and other aquatic animals).

species The smallest or lowest important taxonomic unit; the second (lowercase) word in a **binomial** (two-word scientific name) such as *Homo sapiens*. Precise definitions or concepts of the species are in flux, the subject of centuries of debate; see page 12.

spike An **inflorescence** of flowers attached directly (without stems of their own) to a central stalk. Compare **raceme**, **panicle**.

spikelet In the **inflorescence** of a grasslike plant, a compact group of from one to several **florets** and scalelike **bracts**, on a single axis branching off of the central stem.

splitters Scientists inclined to increase the numbers of species, genera, and so on, by recognizing any given distinction at a higher taxonomic level. Opposed to **lumpers**.

spore A single cell specialized for differentiating into a new multicelled individual; corresponds functionally to a seed, since it travels; but fern and moss **spores** are genetically comparable to a **pollen** grain, since they are not the sexually produced stage in the life cycle.

spreading (Leaves, branches, and so on) Tending to grow in a horizontal to slightly raised position. Compare **erect**, **ascending**, **pendent**.

spur A hollow, closed-ended extension from a **corolla** or **calyx**, often bearing **nectar**.

steppe Arid plant communities dominated by sparse bunchgrasses or shrubs. The Northwest's "high deserts" are steppe, properly, as ecologists reserve "desert" for sites so barren that no real plant community exists.

stamen A male organ of a flower, consisting of a **pollen**-bearing **anther** at the tip of a slender **filament**; often several **stamens** surround a **pistil**.

stigma The **pollen**-receptive tip of a flower **pistil**.

stomata Minute **pores** in leaf surfaces for the **transpiration** of gases. Singular: stoma. Plural sometimes anglicized to "stomates."

style The stalk-like part of a flower's **pistil**, supporting the **stigma** and conveying male sexual cells from it to the **ovary**.

subalpine Of or in the highest elevational zone in which tree species grow in upright tree form; includes meadows, tree islands, and also forests of characteristic species such as subalpine fir and mountain hemlock.

subduction The process in which the edge of a **plate** of the earth's **crust** bends and sinks underneath the edge of an adjacent plate, and returns to the underlying **mantle**. Our mountains parallel, and are indirect products of, the Cascadia Subduction Zone where the Juan de Fuca Plate subducts under the North American Plate, immediately off our coast.

subshrub A low perennial plant with a persistent, somewhat **woody** base, thus intermediate between clearly an herb and clearly a shrub.

subspecies A taxonomic group or rank narrower than a **species**. Some taxonomists (though fewer than in the past) also like to name varieties—taxa somewhat narrower or less distinct than subspecies

substrate The base on which an organism lives, such as soil, rock, or bark.

succession Gradual change in the species composition of a plant community that results from soil and biotic interactions internal to the community.

symbiosis Intimate association of unlike organisms for the benefit of at least one of them. Symbioses can be **mutualistic**, where both or all partners benefit; **parasitic** (one benefits, one suffers); commensal (no material transferred, neither partner suffers much), or other permutations of benefit, harm, and indifference.

talus Rock debris lying at the foot of a rock face from which it broke off. Usually implies cobble- to boulder-sized fragments at the foot of a slope, in contrast to finer **scree**.

taxon Any particular **species**, **genus**, or other unit of classification. Plural: taxa.

taxonomy The scientific naming and classifying of organisms, or their organization into lines of evolutionary descent.

tectonic Related to large-scale geologic deformation such as folding, **faulting**, volcanism, and regional **metamorphism**.

temperate Of the climatically moderate parts of the world, between the Tropics and the Arctic.

tendril A slender organ that supports a climbing plant by coiling or twining around something.

tepal A **petal** or **sepal** on a flower (such as some lilies) whose petals and sepals are identical to each other.

terminal At an end, such as a growing tip of a plant or the lower end of a glacier.

terrane A geologically mapped area whose rock formations originated without a known relation to those of adjacent terranes, suggesting that at some time they may not have been near each other.

tolerance The relative ability of various plant species to thrive under a given limiting condition, such as shade, aridity, or flooding.

transpiration Emission of water vapor into the air through plant surfaces.

turf Upper soil layer permeated by a dense mat of grass or sedge roots.

veil A membrane extending from the edge of the **cap** to the stem, in certain mushrooms when immature, soon rupturing and often persisting as a ring around the stem. Also (the universal veil) in most *Amanita* mushrooms when they are very young buttons, an additional, outer membrane extending from the edge of the cap to the underground base of the mushroom, soon rupturing and often visibly persisting as a more or less cup-shaped growth at the mushroom's base.

vesicle A small hole in a volcanic rock, which originated as a gas bubble in **lava** and may now contain either contrasting minerals or air; vesicles characterize all pumice and many basalt and andesite specimens.

volcanic rocks **Igneous rocks** that solidified from fluid lava in a volcanic eruption; typically finer-grained than **intrusive rocks**.

whorled (Leaves) Arranged with three or more leaves (or other parts) around the same point along a stem or axis.

woody Reinforced with fibrous tissue so as to remain firm and functional from one year to the next. Woody plants are trees or shrubs. Opposed to **herbaceous**.

zooplankton Nonplant aquatic organisms that drift with the currents, lacking powers of either locomotion or attachment. A loose term including anything from one-celled organisms up to jellyfish and some insect **larvae**. Pronounced "zo-uh-PLANK-ton." Singular: zooplankter.

RESOURCES

Authorities for Common and Scientific Names

American Ornithologists Union Checklist of North and Middle American Birds. checklist.aou.org/taxa/.

Bradley, Robert D., et al. 2014. "Revised Checklist of North American Mammals North of Mexico, 2014." Museum of Texas Tech University Occasional Papers, No. 327.

Brodo, Irwin M., and Sylvia and Stephen Sharnoff. 2001. *Lichens of North America.* New Haven, CT: Yale University Press.

Crother, B. I. (ed.). 2012. "Scientific and Standard English Names of Amphibians and Reptiles of North America North of Mexico, With Comments Regarding Confidence In Our Understanding." *SSAR Herpetological Circular* 39:1–92.

Flora of North America Editorial Committee. 1993—. *Flora of North America North of Mexico.* 19 volumes to date, of 30 planned. New York: Oxford University Press. efloras.org/browse.aspx?flora_id=1.

Jaster, Thea, Stephen C. Meyers, and Scott Sundberg (eds.). 2016. *Oregon Vascular Plant Checklist.* oregonflora.org/checklist.php. Version 1.6. Site also includes *Oregon Plant Atlas* and *Photo Gallery.*

Klinkenberg, Brian (ed.). 2013. E-Flora BC: Electronic Atlas of the Flora of British Columbia. eflora.bc.ca. Lab for Advanced Spatial Analysis, Department of Geography, University of British Columbia, Vancouver.

Lotts, Kelly, and Thomas Naberhaus, coordinators. 2015. *Butterflies and Moths of North America.* butterfliesandmoths.org/.

McCune, Bruce, and Linda Geiser. 2009. *Macrolichens of the Pacific Northwest.* 2nd ed. Corvallis, OR: Oregon State University Press.

Weinmann, F., et al. 2002—. *Checklist of the Vascular Plants of Washington State.* Seattle: University of Washington Herbarium. biology.burke.washington.edu/herbarium/waflora/checklist.php.

Additional Recommended Websites

A bibliography of scientific papers reflected in this book is posted at www.raveneditions.com. The following list starts with landscape subjects and goes through plants and animals to geology, and then trail report forums and a few good organizations.

John Scurlock's Mountain Aerial Photography. pbase.com/nolock/root

MODIS Today: images from the latest satellite pass over the Pacific Northwest. ge.ssec.wisc.edu/modis-today/

Inciweb: current fire information. inciweb.nwcg.gov

Metzler, David, and Edward Earl. ORS (Spire Measure). peaklist.org/spire/index.html

Cliff Mass Weather Blog. cliffmass.blogspot.com

RealClimate Climate science from Climate Scientists. realclimate.org

Climate Change in Mountain Ecosystems. nrmsc.usgs.gov/centers/norock/science.

Chris Earle's Gymnosperm Database. conifers.org

Flickr.com. Searching by scientific name within flickr.com usually gets results. Some photos are misidentified, though.

Oregon Flora Project Photo Gallery. oregonflora.org/gallery.php

University of Washington Herbarium Image Collection. biology.burke.washington.edu/herbarium/imagecollection.php

Tanya Harvey's Mountain Plants of the Western Cascades. westerncascades.com

Paul Slichter's Flora and Fauna Northwest. science.halleyhosting.com

Daniel Moerman's Native American Ethnobotany database. naeb.brit.org

Turner Photographics. pnwflowers.com/browse

Stevens, P. F. (2001—). Angiosperm Phylogeny Website. Version 13 (and updated since). mobot.org/MOBOT/research/APweb/

Pacific Northwest Key Council: Keys to Mushrooms of the Pacific Northwest. svims.ca/council/

Michael Kuo's *MushroomExpert.com*. mushroomexpert.com

Mushrooms, Fungi, Mycology (CA-centric). mykoweb.com

Michael Beug's Poisonous and Hallucinogenic Mushrooms. academic.evergreen.edu/projects/mushrooms/phm/index.htm

Trevor Goward's "Enlichenment." waysofenlichenment.net/ways/home

Stephen Sharnoff's Lichens Home Page. sharnoffphotos.com/lichens/lichens_home_index.html

USDA, NRCS. 2011. *The PLANTS Database*. National Plant Data Center, Baton Rouge, LA 70874-4490 USA. plants.usda.gov

E-Fauna BC Electronic Atlas of the Wildlife of BC. ibis.geog.ubc.ca/biodiversity/efauna/

The North American Breeding Bird Survey, Results and Analysis 1966 - 2013. mbr-pwrc.usgs.gov/bbs.html

Washington Herp Atlas. www1.dnr.wa.gov/nhp/refdesk/herp/index.html

BugGuide. bugguide.net/node/view/15740

Butterflies of Canada. cbif.gc.ca/eng/species-bank/butterflies-of-canada/?id=1370403265518

Pacific Northwest Moths. pnwmoths.biol.wwu.edu

North American Bumblebees (identification). bumblebee.org/NorthAmerica2.htm

North Cascades National Park Geology. geomaps.wr.usgs.gov/parks/noca/index.html

Cascades Volcano Observatory (US Geological Survey) volcanoes.usgs.gov/observatories/cvo/cascade_volcanoes.html

ClubTread (BC-centered trail reports). forums.clubtread.com/6-trip-reports/

NWHikers (WA-centered trail reports). nwhikers.net/

OregonHikers (OR-centered trail reports). oregonhikers.org

North Cascades Institute. ncascades.org/

Olympic Park Institute. naturebridge.org/olympic

Mt. Rainier Institute. packforest.org/mtrainierinstitute/

Washington Trails Association. wta.org

The Mazamas. mazamas.org

Apps for iPhone (by Daniel Mathews)

Northwest Mountain Wildflowers

Northwest and Rocky Mountain Trees and Shrubs

Recommended Reading

Allen, John Eliot, M. Burns, and S. Burns. 2009. *Cataclysms on the Columbia: The Great Missoula Floods*. Rev. ed. Portland, OR: Ooligan.

Arno, Stephen F., and Ramona P. Hammerly. 2007. *Northwest Trees*. Rev. ed. Seattle, WA: Mountaineers.

Arno, Stephen F., and Steven Allison-Bunnell. 2002. *Flames in Our Forests: Disaster or Renewal?* Washington, DC: Island.

Arora, David. 1986. *Mushrooms Demystified*. Berkeley, CA: Ten Speed. Top-notch 960-page field guide.

Aubry, Keith B., et al. (eds.). 2012. *Biology and Conservation of Martens, Sables, and Fishers*. Ithaca, NY: Comstock.

Behnke, Robert J. 2002. *Trout and Salmon of North America*. Illus. Joseph R. Tomelleri. New York: Free Press.

Beug, M. W., A. E. Bessette, and A. R. Bessette. 2014. *Ascomycete Fungi of North America*. Austin: University of Texas Press.

Borror, Donald J. 1960. *Dictionary of Word Roots and Combining Forms*. Mountain View, CA: Mayfield.

Brayshaw, T. C. 1996. *Trees and Shrubs of British Columbia*. Victoria: Royal British Columbia Museum.

Brodo, Irwin M., and Sylvia and Stephen Sharnoff. 2001. *Lichens of North America*. New Haven, CT: Yale University Press.

Cannings, Richard and Sydney. 1996. *British Columbia: a Natural History*. Vancouver, BC: Greystone.

Chadwick, Douglas H. 2010. *The Wolverine Way*. Ventura, CA: Patagonia.

Corkran, Charlotte C., and Chris Thoms. 2006. *Amphibians of Oregon, Washington, and British Columbia*. 2nd ed. Edmonton, AB: Lone Pine.

Dalton, David A. 2008. *The Natural World of Lewis and Clark*. Columbia: University of Missouri Press.

Dalton, Meghan M., Philip W. Mote, and Amy K. Snover (eds.). 2013. *Climate Change in the Northwest: Implications for Our Landscapes, Waters, and Communities*. Washington, DC: Island Press.

Eaton, Eric R., and Kenn Kaufman. 2007. *Kaufman Field Guide to Insects of North America*. New York: Houghton Mifflin Harcourt.

Elbroch, Mark, and Kurt Rinehart. 2011. *Behavior of North American Mammals*. New York: Houghton Mifflin Harcourt.

Eyles, Nick, and Andrew Miall. 2007. *Canada Rocks*. Markham, ON: Fitzhenry and Whiteside.

Farjon, Aljos. 2008. *A Natural History of Conifers*. Portland, OR: Timber Press.

Furniss, R. L., and V. M. Carolin. 1977. *Western Forest Insects*. USDA Forest Service Misc. Publ. 1339. Source of the drawings of bark beetle galleries.

Geiger, Rudolf, et al. 2009. *The Climate Near the Ground*. 7th ed. Lanham, MD: Rowman & Littlefield.

Gillett, J. D. 1971. *Mosquitoes*. London: Weidenfeld and Nicolson.

Goward, Trevor, and Cathie Hickson. 1995. *Nature Wells Gray*. Edmonton, AB: Lone Pine.

Guppy, Crispin S., and Jon H. Shepard. 2001. *Butterflies of British Columbia*. Vancouver, BC: University of British Columbia Press.

Gunther, Erna. 1973. *Ethnobotany of Western Washington*. Seattle: University of Washington Press.

Haggard, Peter and Judy. 2006. *Insects of the Pacific Northwest*. Portland, OR: Timber Press.

Hayes, Doris W., and George A. Garrison. 1960. *Key to Important Woody Plants of Eastern Oregon and Washington*. USDA Agr. Handbook No. 148. Source of many drawings in this book.

Henson, Robert. 2014. *The Thinking Person's Guide to Climate Change*. Boston, MA: American Meteorological Society.

Heinrich, Bernd. 2003. *Winter World*. New York: HarperCollins.

Hitchcock, C. Leo, et al. 1955–69. *Vascular Plants of the Pacific Northwest*. 5 volumes. Seattle: University of Washington Press. Source of the Jeanne R. Janish drawings in this book.

James, David G., and David Nunnallee. 2011. *Life Histories of Cascadia Butterflies*. Corvallis: Oregon State University Press.

Jones, Lawrence C., Wm. P. Leonard, and D. H. Olson (eds.). 2005. *Amphibians of the Pacific Northwest*. Seattle: Seattle Audubon Society.

Kerst, Cary, and Steve Gordon. 2011. *Dragonflies and Damselflies of Oregon*. Corvallis: Oregon State University Press.

Kruckeberg, Arthur R. 1991. *Natural History of Puget Sound Country*. Seattle: University of Washington Press.

Lewis, Meriwether, and William Clark. 1953. *The Journals of Lewis and Clark*. Edited by Bernard DeVoto. Boston, MA: Houghton Mifflin.

Marshall, David B., M. G. Hunter, and A. L. Contreras (eds.). 2006. *Birds of Oregon: A General Reference*. Corvallis: Oregon State University Press.

Maser, Chris. 1998. *Mammals of the Pacific Northwest*. Corvallis: Oregon State University Press.

Mass, Cliff. 2008. *The Weather of the Pacific Northwest.* Seattle: University of Washington Press.

Mathews, Bill, and Jim Monger. 2005. *Roadside Geology of Southern British Columbia.* Missoula, MT: Mountain Press.

McCune, Bruce, and Linda Geiser. 2009. *Macrolichens of the Pacific Northwest.* 2nd ed. Corvallis: Oregon State University Press.

McKelvey, Susan Delano. 1991. *Botanical Exploration of the Trans-Mississippi West, 1790–1850.* Corvallis: Oregon State University Press.

Miller, Marli B. 2014. *Roadside Geology of Oregon.* 2nd ed. Missoula, MT: Mountain Press.

Moerman, Daniel E. 1998. *Native American Ethnobotany.* Portland, OR: Timber Press. (Also see websites.)

Moore, M. 1993. *Medicinal Plants of the Pacific West.* Santa Fe, CA: Red Crane.

Moskowitz, David. 2010. *Wildlife of the Pacific Northwest.* Portland, OR: Timber Press.

———. 2013. *Wolves in the Land of Salmon.* Portland, OR: Timber Press.

Naughton, Donna. 2012. *The Natural History of Canadian Mammals.* Toronto: Canadian Museum of Nature and University of Toronto Press.

Nisbet, Jack. 2009. *The Collector: David Douglas and the Natural History of the Northwest.* Seattle, WA: Sasquatch.

Paulson, Dennis. 2009. *Dragonflies and Damselflies of the West.* Princeton, NJ: Princeton University Press.

Perry, David A., Ram Oren, and Stephen C. Hart. 2008. *Forest Ecosystems.* 2nd ed. Baltimore, MD: Johns Hopkins University Press.

Pyle, Robert Michael. 2002. *The Butterflies of Cascadia.* Seattle, WA: Seattle Audubon Society.

Robbins, Chandler S., et al. 2001. *Birds of North America: Golden Field Guide.* 2nd ed. New York: St. Martins.

Russo, Ron. 2006. *Field Guide to Plant Galls of California and Other Western States.* Berkeley: University of California Press.

Schofield, W. B. 1992. *Some Common Mosses of British Columbia.* Victoria: Royal British Columbia Museum. Source of some moss drawings in this book.

———. 2002. *Field Guide to Liverwort Genera of Pacific North America.* Seattle: University of Washington Press. Source of the liverwort drawings in this book.

Sibley, David Allen. 2009. *The Sibley Guide to Bird Life and Behavior.* New York: Knopf.

Snyder, Gary. 1999. *The Gary Snyder Reader.* New York: Counterpoint.

St. John, Alan. 2002. *Reptiles of the Northwest.* Edmonton, AB: Lone Pine.

Sudworth, George B. 1908. *Forest Trees of the Pacific Slope.* USDA Forest Service. Source of many conifer drawings in this book.

Sumner, Judith. 2000. *Natural History of Medicinal Plants.* Portland, OR: Timber Press.

Spies, Thomas A., and Sally L. Duncan. 2009. *Old Growth in a New World: A Pacific Northwest Icon Reexamined.* Washington, DC: Island.

Tabor, Rowland, and Ralph Haugerud. 1999. *Geology of the North Cascades.* Seattle, WA: Mountaineers.

Tilford, G. L. 1997. *Edible and Medicinal Plants of the West.* Missoula, MT: Mountain Press.

Tomback, Diana F., Stephen F. Arno, and Robert E. Keane. 2001. *Whitebark Pine Communities: Ecology and Restoration.* Washington, DC: Island.

Trappe, Matt, Frank Evans, and James Trappe. 2007. *Field Guide to North America Truffles.* Berkeley, CA: Ten Speed.

Trudell, Steve, and Joe Ammirati. 2009. *Mushrooms of the Pacific Northwest.* Portland, OR: Timber Press.

Turner, Mark, and Phyllis Gustafson. 2006. *Wildflowers of the Pacific Northwest.* Portland, OR: Timber Press.

Turner, Mark, and Ellen Kuhlmann. 2014. *Trees and Shrubs of the Pacific Northwest.* Portland, OR: Timber Press.

Turner, Nancy J. 1995. *Food Plants of Coastal First Peoples.* Vancouver: University of British Columbia Press.

———. 1997. *Food Plants of Interior First Peoples*. Vancouver: University of British Columbia Press.

———. 1998. *Plant Technology of First Peoples of British Columbia*. Vancouver: University of British Columbia Press.

Turner, Nancy J., and Patrick von Aderkas. 2009. *North American Guide to Common Poisonous Plants and Mushrooms*. Portland, OR: Timber Press.

Van Pelt, Robert. 2001. *Forest Giants of the Pacific Coast*. Seattle: University of Washington Press.

———. 2007. *Identifying Mature and Old Forests in Western Washington*. Olympia: Washington State Department of Natural Resources.

———. 2008. *Identifying Old Trees and Forests in Eastern Washington*. Olympia: Washington State Department of Natural Resources.

Waitt, Richard. 2014. *In the Path of Destruction: Eyewitness Chronicles of Mt. St. Helens*. Pullman: Washington State University Press.

Welch, Lew. 2012. *Ring of Bone: Collected Poems*. Expanded edition. San Francisco, CA: City Lights.

Williams, Paul, et al. 2014. *Bumble Bees of North America*. Princeton, NJ: Princeton University Press.

SOURCES OF DIRECT QUOTATIONS

Quotations from David Douglas are from *Journal Kept by David Douglas 1823–1827.* Reprinted 1959. New York: Antiquarian Press.

Quotations from Meriwether Lewis are from *The Journals of Lewis and Clark*. Bernard DeVoto, ed. 1953. Boston: Houghton Mifflin.

p. 13 "This is a necessary . . ." Dorn, Robert D. 2001. *Vascular Plants of Wyoming*. 3rd Ed. Cheyenne: Mountain West Publishing.

"folk taxonomy . . ." Cotterill, F. P. D., et al. 2014. "Why One Century of Phenetics is Enough: Response to 'Are There Really Twice As Many Bovid Species As We Thought?'" *Systematic Biology* 63(5): 819–832.

p. 15 "It may be more fruitful . . ." Money, Nicholas P. 2013. "Against the Naming of Fungi." *Fungal Biology* 117: 463–465.

p. 52 "this bombshell study" Van Mantgem, P. J., et al. 2009. "Widespread Increase of Tree Mortality Rates in the Western United States." *Science* 323: 521–524

p. 57 McCarthy, Steve. 2009. "The Pursuit and Pleasures of the Pure Spirit." *New York Times*, 13 March 2009.

p. 80 H. K. Hines and R. Ketcham quoted in Peters, Harold J. 2008. *Seven Months to Oregon: 1853*. Tooele, Utah: Patrice Press.

p. 86 Muir, John. 1894. *The Mountains of California*. Many editions available.

p. 102 "When the boat touches . . ." Henry Marie Brackenridge, *Views of Louisiana*. Quoted in McKelvey, Susan Delano. 1991. *Botanical Exploration of the Trans-Mississippi West, 1790–1850*. Corvallis, OR: Oregon State University Press.

p. 103 Maximilian, Prince of Wied and Neuwied, quoted in McKelvey, op cit.

p. 156 Karl A. Geyer quoted in McKelvey, op cit.

p. 180 Guenther, Erna. 1973. *Ethnobotany of Western Washington*. Seattle: University of Washington Press.

p. 205 Gorham, John, and Liz Crain. 2013. *Toro Bravo*. San Francisco: McSweeney's.

p. 257 Thanks to Steve Dupey for sleuthing the false ID.

p. 297 "Occasionally a semiporous . . ." Campbell, Alsie, and Jerry F. Franklin. 1979. "Riparian Vegetation in Oregon's West Cascade Mountains." Bulletin 14, Coniferous Biome. Seattle: University of Washington Press.

p. 305 "the crunch of collapsing . . ." Shaw, C. G., and G. A. Kile, eds. *Armillaria Root Disease*. USDA FS Agr. Handbook No. 691.

p. 316 "odor like dirty gym socks . . ." Bessette, Alan. 1997. *Mushrooms of Northeast North America*. Syracuse, NY: Syracuse University Press.

p. 319 "It was as shocking . . ." Wang, L. 2001. "Fungi Slay Insects and Feed Host Plants." *Science News*, April 7, 2001. The study was Klironomos, John N., and Miranda M. Hart. 2001. "Animal Nitrogen Swap for Plant Carbon." *Nature* 410: 651–52.

p. 341 Verts, B. J., and Leslie Carraway. 1998. *Land Mammals of Oregon*. Berkeley: University of California Press.

p. 350 Townsend, John Kirk. 1839. *Narrative of a Journey across the Rocky Mountains to the Columbia River.* (Reprinted 1999. Corvallis: Oregon State University Press.)

p. 402 Welch, Lew. 2012. *Ring of Bone: Collected Poems*. Expanded Edition. San Francisco: City Lights.

p. 413 Snyder, Gary. 1999. Lookout's Journal (1952) in *The Gary Snyder Reader.* New York: Counterpoint.

p. 429 "A recording is available . . ." Kroodsma, Donald E. 2005. *The Singing Life of Birds*. Boston: Houghton Mifflin.

p. 434: "Birds don't do it . . ." Sly and Robbie with Bootsy Collins. 1987. *Rhythm Killers* (music LP).

p. 457 "no one got it until some scientists . . ." Gresh, T., J. Lichatowich, and P. Schoonmaker. 2000. "An Estimation of Historic and Current Levels of Salmon Production in the Northeast Pacific Ecosystem." *Fisheries* 25(1): 15–21.

p. 463 James and Nunnallee, in Recommended Books, p. 551.

p. 503 "the only microorganism . . ." Upcroft, Jacqui, and Peter Upcroft. 1998. "My Favorite Cell: Giardia." *BioEssays* 20(3): 256–263.

"education efforts . . ." Welch, Timothy E. 2000. "Risk of giardiasis from consumption of wilderness water in North America: A systematic review of epidemiologic data." *International Journal of Infectious Diseases* 4(2): 100–103.

p. 536 "All mountains walk . . ." Dōgen (1240). *Mountains and Waters Sutra*, trans. Arnold Kotler and Kazuaki Tanahashi, in *Moon In a Dewdrop: writings of Zen master Dōgen*. 1985. San Francisco: North Point.

p. 536 *Keeping Track* was published in a somewhat different form in *Convolvulus* (Victoria, BC).

PHOTOGRAPHY CREDITS

Reeve M. Bailey: page 462 bottom

Darlisa Black: page 38 top

Ellen Blonder, US Forest Service: pages 342, 343 right, 348, 349 top right, 351 bottom, 353 middle, 372, 379 left, 399 top, 413 right, 414, 416 top, 425 bottom, 428 middle, 446 top, 447 right, 449 bottom

Bozeman, Montana, National Park Service: page 496 left

Gary Braasch: pages 2, 44–45

Kelvin Chau: page 351 top

Dennis Chesters, NASA GOES Project: page 33 top

Christopher L. Christie: pages 192 left, 407 middle, 413 bottom, 415 left, 432 left, 433 top and middle, 441 left, 472 right, 479 right, 480 bottom left, 492 left, 498 top, 499 top right

Captain William Clark: page 462 left

Charlie Crisafulli: pages 350, 355, 445 right, 446 left, 447 left, 451

Nick Dean: pages 116 left, 122 left, 338 top, 357 left, 362 right, 394, 395 bottom, 396 top, 400 top, 402, 404 top, 407 top, 409, 417 middle, 419, 422 right, 425 top, 426 bottom, 427 upper middle and bottom, 432 right, 433 bottom, 435 upper middle, 436, 438 right, 439, 449 right, 464 left, 467 top right, 478, 480 bottom right, 483, 484 left, 485 bottom, 487 top, 488 right, 491 bottom, 492 right, 493 lower middle and bottom, 497 bottom

Richard Droker: pages 89 top, 100 lower left, 156 left, 184, 186 left and middle, 187 right, 276 top, 277 bottom, 278 bottom, 288 middle, 296 bottom left, 298 top left, 305, 324, 325 middle, 327 right, 329 top–middle left, 330 middle, 333 right, 335 middle, 398 top, 445 left

Patricia Drukker-Brammall, courtesy of Pam Schofield: pages 287 left and middle, 288 right, 289 bottom right, 290 bottom left–right, 292 top left and top left–right middle, 293 left, 295 right, 296 right, 298 bottom left–right and top right

Eric Eaton: pages 464 right, 466, 467 left middle and bottom left–right, 468 right, 469, 472 left, 473, 476 bottom right, 477

Kris Elkin: pages 198 middle, 199 top, 202 right, 523

Five Acre Geographic: pages 443 bottom, 487 upper middle, 489 top and bottom, 490, 494 right, 495 top and upper middle, 497 middle, 498 upper and lower middle, 499 bottom, 500

James Gathany, Centers for Disease Control and Prevention: page 501

Tim Hagan: pages 147 top, 196 top right, 199 bottom left, 215 left, 220 bottom left, 223 right, 243 left middle, 255 bottom, 268 top left

John and Karen Hollingsworth, US Forest Service: page 411 top middle

Jeanne R. Janish, courtesy of University of Washington Press; from *Vascular Plants of the Pacific Northwest. Parts 1–4*. By C. Leo Hitchcock et al. 1959, 1961, 1964, 1969: pages 90, 91 bottom, 93 bottom, 94 right, 95 middle and bottom, 109 middle left, 122 top, 124 bottom, 129 bottom left, 132 bottom, 143 top middle, 142 right, 144 top, 152 right, 154 top–bottom right, 155 middle left–right and bottom, 156 right, 158 bottom, 159 left and right middle, 160, 161 top left middle and top–bottom right, 164 bottom left–right, 167 right, 176 top, 179 right, 181 bottom, 183 top left–right, 193 bottom, 203 middle, 204 right, 206 bottom, 207 top left–right, 208 middle left–right, 209 top left, 216 right, 218 top, 220 right, 229 left, 233 bottom left–right, 235 middle, 236 top right, 237 bottom left, 240 top, 242 top middle, 246 bottom, 252 right, 253, 256 top, 257 top left, 261 bottom, 263 left, 267 middle,

268 right, 270 top middle and bottom right, 271 bottom, 276 right, 277 top, 278 middle, 279 top left, 280, 281 top left–right and bottom left–middle, 282 top left and top–middle right, 283 upper middle and bottom, 284 top and middle left, 285

Willis Lynn Jepson: pages 78, 80 left, 104 top left–right, 157 middle left, 196 bottom, 259 bottom left–right

Thomas Kitchin and Victoria Hurst, LeesonPhoto: page 411 bottom middle

Thomas Lawler: pages 417 bottom, 418 top, 420 left, 428 left, 437 top, 438 left, 489 middle

Tom and Pat Leeson: pages 345, 346, 366, 379 right, 387, 430 left

Gerald Lisi: pages 135 top right, 395 top, 418 bottom left, 435 top

Roy W. Lowe, US Fish and Wildlife Service: page 401

Justin Miles, Oregon Department of Fish and Wildlife: page 448 left

David Moskowitz: pages 349 bottom, 353 bottom, 361 right, 364, 368, 390

National Park Service / Crow Vecchio, page 255 bottom

Jon David Nelson: pages 363, 365, 371, 373 left, 375, 378 right, 385, 400 bottom, 404 bottom, 406, 442 bottom

Oregon Caves, National Park Service: page 487 bottom

Jo Robinson: page 38 bottom

Dennis and Esther Schmidt: pages 340, 347, 361 left, 369, 370, 374 left, 376, 377, 378 left, 381, 396 bottom, 411 bottom right, 420 right, 423

Adam Schneider Photography, page 537

Walter Siegmund: pages 67 right, 81, 117 top, 118 top, 126 top, 141, 145 top, 189 right, 212 top left, 236 bottom left, 239 bottom right, 258 bottom right, 264 bottom, 422 bottom left, 426 middle, 427 top, 449 top left, 450, 493 top, 495 lower middle and bottom, 496 right

Doug Skilton: page 270 bottom middle

Virginia Skilton: pages 88 left, 111 top, 114 left, 126 middle, 134 left middle, 147 bottom, 148 top right and bottom, 149 middle, 150 top and bottom, 167 left, 181 top middle, 187 left, 190 top middle and bottom, 191 bottom left–middle, 198 top, 203 bottom, 206 top right, 207 bottom right, 208 top middle, 210 top left, 234 top left, 236 bottom right, 237 top left, 239 bottom left, 249 middle, 257 top right, 260 middle, 270 top right, 276 bottom left, 278 top, 353 top, 362 left

Barbara Stafford: pages 287 top right, 289 bottom left, 292 bottom left, 292 bottom right, 294

Alan St. John: page 448 right

Joseph R. Tomelleri: pages 453, 457, 458, 459, 460

Sharon Torvik, Oregon Department of Fish and Wildlife: page 424

Steve Trudell: pages 301, 303, 310 bottom, 317 top, 320

Mark Turner: page 150 middle

US Bureau of Reclamation: page 411 bottom left

US Forest Service: pages 59 top, 68, 69 bottom, 70, 74 bottom, 75 bottom, 82 right, 86 left, 87 left, 89 bottom, 96 bottom, 97 right, 98, 100 top and bottom right, 101 bottom left, 106 middle, 107, 108 middle, 110, 113 bottom, 114 right, 117 middle, 125 bottom right, 130 right, 131 left, 134 right, 136 top, 142 bottom left, 149 bottom, 474, 476 top and middle

Doug Waylett: pages 125 bottom middle, 128 bottom, 132 top right, 136 bottom, 180 bottom, 222 left, 232 top middle, 254 top right, 307 middle and bottom, 325 top, 326, 330 left and right, 331 top, 332 top and bottom, 334 left and right, 335 right, 336 right, 417 top, 468 left, 479 left, 481 right, 485 top and middle, 488 left, 491 middle, 493 upper middle

Flickr

Alan Schmierer: pages 491 top, 499 left

Paul Wilson: pages 288 bottom left, 292 top right

Used under a Creative Commons Attribution 2.0 Generic license
Ruth Hartnup: page 227 right
Jason Hollinger: page 336 left
Rocky Houghtby: page 302 top
Jerry Kirkhart: pages 343 left, 357 right
Ron Knight: pages 418 left middle, 421 top, 427 lower middle
Brendan Lally: pages 374 right, 430 right
Tim Lenz / Seabamirum: page 397
Don Loarie: pages 481 bottom left, 494 bottom left
David A. Mitchell: page 415 right
Katja Schulz: page 497 top
Nigel Tate / nigel: pages 411 top left and right, 421 bottom, 426 top, 428 right, 431, 435 lower middle and bottom, 437 bottom

Used under a Creative Commons Attribution-ShareAlike 2.0 Generic license
John Brew / brewbooks: pages 146 middle, 238 bottom
Bob Danley: page 480 top
Matt Lavin: page 159 top right
photogrammal: page 182 right
Gregory "Slobirdr" Smith: page 399 bottom

Used under a Creative Commons Attribution-NoDerivs 2.0 Generic license
Steve Cyr: page 239 top left
Andy Morffew: pages 403, 407 bottom, 408, 416 bottom
Paul Sullivan: page 481 top left

Wikimedia:
Mark Thompson: page 446 bottom right

Used under a GFDL and Creative Commons Attribution–Share Alike 3.0 license
Dr. Josef Reischig, CSc.: page 503

All other photographs by the author.

INDEX

Daniel Mathews comes from a line of botanically knowledgeable forebears, who began teaching him the names of trailside plants at an early age. His love of backpacking in the Northwest drew him to a career writing field guides, beginning with *Cascade-Olympic Natural History* (the precursor of this Timber Press Field Guide) and eventually ranging to *America From the Air* (a guide to things we can see from jetliner windows). Along the way he volunteered as a fire lookout at Desolation L.O., which has one of the best views of all lookouts and certainly has the greatest literary renown, thanks to Jack Kerouac. His writing is informed by literally thousands of scientific papers as well as five decades on and off hiking trails in the Pacific Northwest.

© Stacey Mattraw